T0184035

Lecture Notes in Computer Science 11612

Commenced Publication in 1973
Founding and Former Series Editors:
Gerhard Goos, Juris Hartmanis, and Jan van Leeuwen

More information about this series at http://www.springer.com/series/7407

Michal Hospodár · Galina Jirásková ·
Stavros Konstantinidis (Eds.)

Descriptional Complexity of Formal Systems

21st IFIP WG 1.02 International Conference, DCFS 2019
Košice, Slovakia, July 17–19, 2019
Proceedings

Editors
Michal Hospodár
Slovak Academy of Sciences
Košice, Slovakia

Galina Jirásková
Slovak Academy of Sciences
Košice, Slovakia

Stavros Konstantinidis
Saint Mary's University
Halifax, NS, Canada

ISSN 0302-9743 ISSN 1611-3349 (electronic)
Lecture Notes in Computer Science
ISBN 978-3-030-23246-7 ISBN 978-3-030-23247-4 (eBook)
https://doi.org/10.1007/978-3-030-23247-4

LNCS Sublibrary: SL1 – Theoretical Computer Science and General Issues

This Springer imprint is published by the registered company Springer Nature Switzerland AG
The registered company address is: Gewerbestrasse 11, 6330 Cham, Switzerland

Preface

This volume contains the papers presented at the 21st International Conference on Descriptional Complexity of Formal Systems (DCFS 2019) held in Košice, Slovakia, during July 17–19, 2019. It was jointly organized by the Working Group 1.02 on Descriptional Complexity of the International Federation for Information Processing (IFIP), by the Košice branch of the Mathematical Institute of the Slovak Academy of Sciences, and by the Slovak Artificial Intelligence Society.

The DCFS conference series is an international venue for the dissemination of new results related to all aspects of descriptional complexity, which is a field in computer science that deals with the costs of description of objects in various computational models, such as Turing machines, pushdown automata, finite automata, grammars, and others.

DCFS became an IFIP working conference in 2016, continuing the former Workshop on Descriptional Complexity of Formal Systems, which was a result of merging together two workshop series: Descriptional Complexity of Automata, Grammars and Related Structures (DCAGRS) and Formal Descriptions and Software Reliability (FDSR). DCAGRS was previously held in Magdeburg, Germany (1999), London, Ontario, Canada (2000), and Vienna, Austria (2001). FDSR was previously held in Paderborn, Germany (1998), Boca Raton, Florida, USA (1999), and San Jose, California, USA (2000). These workshops were merged in DCFS 2002 in London, Ontario, Canada, which is regarded as the 4th DCFS. Since 2003, DCFS has been successively held in Budapest, Hungary (2003), London, Ontario, Canada (2004), Como, Italy (2005), Las Cruces, New Mexico, USA (2006), Nový Smokovec, High Tatras, Slovakia (2007), Charlottetown, Prince Edward Island, Canada (2008), Magdeburg, Germany (2009), Saskatoon, Canada (2010), Giessen, Germany (2011), Braga, Portugal (2012), London, Ontario, Canada (2013), Turku, Finland (2014), Waterloo, Ontario, Canada (2015), Bucharest, Romania (2016), Milan, Italy (2017), and Halifax, Nova Scotia, Canada (2018).

The topics of this volume include: finite state transducers, quantum automata theory, state complexity, syntactic complexity, subword complexity, quasi-Polish spaces, tree automata, jumping automata, pushdown automata with constant height, input-driven pushdown automata, simple semi-conditional grammars, and monotone WQOs.

There were 25 submissions from 15 different countries: Algeria, Canada, Chile, Czech Republic, France, Germany, Hungary, India, Italy, Japan, Latvia, Russia, Slovakia, South Korea, and the USA. The submission, single-blind refereeing process, and the collating of the proceedings were supported by the EasyChair conference system. Each submission was reviewed by at least three, and on average 3.1, Program Committee members.

The committee selected 18 papers for presentation at the conference, and publication in this volume. The program also included four invited talks by Rudolf Freund, Jarkko Kari, Benedek Nagy, and Giovanni Pighizzini.

We would like to thank the Program Committee members and the external reviewers for their help in selecting the papers. We are also very grateful to all invited speakers, contributing authors, session chairs, and all the participants for their valuable contributions that helped DCFS 2019 to be a scientifically successful event in a collaborative and friendly atmosphere.

We are also grateful to the editorial staff at Springer, in particular Alfred Hofmann and Anna Kramer, for their guidance and help during the process of publishing this volume, and for supporting the event through publication in the LNCS series.

Last but not least, we would like to thank the conference sponsors for their financial support, and the local Organizing Committee: Peter Mlynárčik and Matúš Palmovský (social program), Ivana Krajňáková and Peter Gurský (financial issues), Viktor Olejár (IT support), Juraj Šebej (conference materials). Everything was always carefully checked and slightly criticized by Jozef Jirásek to whom our sincere gratitude goes as well.

We all are looking forward to the next DCFS in Vienna, Austria.

July 2019

Michal Hospodár
Galina Jirásková
Stavros Konstantinidis

Organization

Steering Committee

Cezar Câmpeanu — University of Prince Edward Island, Charlottetown, Canada

Erzsébet Csuhaj-Varjú — Eötvös Loránd University, Budapest, Hungary

Helmut Jürgensen — Western University, London, Canada

Stavros Konstantinidis — Saint Mary's University, Halifax, Canada

Martin Kutrib (Chair) — Justus Liebig University, Giessen, Germany

Giovanni Pighizzini — University of Milan, Italy

Rogério Reis — University of Porto, Portugal

Program Committee

Suna Bensch — University of Umeå, Sweden

Erszébet Csuhaj-Varjú — Eötvös Loránd University, Budapest, Hungary

Szilárd Zsolt Fazekas — Akita University, Japan

Viliam Geffert — P.J. Šafárik University, Košice, Slovakia

Yo-Sub Han — Yonsei University, Seoul, South Korea

Kazuo Iwama — Kyoto University, Japan

Galina Jirásková — Slovak Academy of Sciences, Košice, Slovakia

Christos Kapoutsis — Carnegie Mellon University in Qatar, Doha, Qatar

Ondřej Klíma — Masaryk University, Brno, Czech Republic

Stavros Konstantinidis — Saint Mary's University, Halifax, Canada

Martin Kutrib — Justus Liebig University, Giessen, Germany

Hing Leung — New Mexico State University, Las Cruces, USA

Christof Löding — RWTH Aachen University, Germany

Tomáš Masopust — Czech Academy of Sciences, Brno, Czech Republic

Ian McQuillan — University of Saskatchewan, Saskatoon, Canada

Carlo Merghetti — University of Milan, Italy

Nelma Moreira — University of Porto, Portugal

Alexander Okhotin — St. Petersburg State University, Russia

Luca Prigioniero — University of Milan, Italy

Narad Rampersad — University of Winnipeg, Canada

Kai Salomaa — Queen's University, Kingston, Canada

Juraj Šebej — P.J. Šafárik University, Košice, Slovakia

Jeffrey Shallit — University of Waterloo, Canada

Marek Szykuła — University of Wrocław, Poland

Matthias Wendlandt — Justus Liebig University, Giessen, Germany

Lynette van Zijl — Stellenbosch University, South Africa

Additional Reviewers

Bednárová, Zuzana
Beier, Simon
Berglund, Martin
Björklund, Johanna
Brecht de, Matthew
Davies, Sylvie
Gazdag, Zsolt
Guillon, Bruno
Holzer, Markus
Keeler, Chris
Khadiev, Kamil
Křivka, Zbyněk
Loff, Bruno

Malcher, Andreas
Mika, Maksymilian
Pauly, Arno
Pighizzini, Giovanni
Sin'Ya, Ryoma
Szabari, Alexander
Villagra, Marcos
Vyalyi, Mikhail N.
Weihrauch, Klaus
Winter, Sarah
Yamakami, Tomoyuki
Young, Joshua

Invited Speakers

Rudolf Freund   TU Wien, Austria
Jarkko Kari   University of Turku, Finland
Benedek Nagy   Eastern Mediterranean University, Famagusta, Cyprus
Giovanni Pighizzini   University of Milan, Italy

Sponsors

City of Košice
Slovak Society for Computer Science

Contents

A General Framework for Sequential Grammars
with Control Mechanisms. 1
   Rudolf Freund

Low-Complexity Tilings of the Plane 35
   Jarkko Kari

Union-Freeness, Deterministic Union-Freeness and Union-Complexity. 46
   Benedek Nagy

Limited Automata: Properties, Complexity and Variants. 57
   Giovanni Pighizzini

Nondeterministic Right One-Way Jumping Finite
Automata (Extended Abstract) 74
   Simon Beier and Markus Holzer

State Complexity of Single-Word Pattern Matching in Regular Languages . . . 86
   Janusz A. Brzozowski, Sylvie Davies, and Abhishek Madan

Square, Power, Positive Closure, and Complementation
on Star-Free Languages 98
   Sylvie Davies and Michal Hospodár

Descriptional Complexity of Matrix Simple Semi-conditional Grammars 111
   Henning Fernau, Lakshmanan Kuppusamy, and Indhumathi Raman

Regulated Tree Automata. 124
   Henning Fernau and Martin Vu

Generalized de Bruijn Words and the State Complexity of Conjugate Sets . . . 137
   Daniel Gabric, Štěpán Holub, and Jeffrey Shallit

The Syntactic Complexity of Semi-flower Languages 147
   Kitti Gelle and Szabolcs Iván

Limited Nondeterminism of Input-Driven Pushdown Automata:
Decidability and Complexity 158
   Yo-Sub Han, Sang-Ki Ko, and Kai Salomaa

Computability on Quasi-Polish Spaces. 171
   Mathieu Hoyrup, Cristóbal Rojas, Victor Selivanov, and Donald M. Stull

NFA-to-DFA Trade-Off for Regular Operations   184
   Galina Jirásková and Ivana Krajňáková

State Complexity of Simple Splicing   197
   Lila Kari and Timothy Ng

Nondeterminism Growth and State Complexity   210
   Chris Keeler and Kai Salomaa

Descriptional Complexity of Iterated Uniform Finite-State Transducers   223
   Martin Kutrib, Andreas Malcher, Carlo Mereghetti,
   and Beatrice Palano

On Classes of Regular Languages Related to Monotone WQOs   235
   Mizuhito Ogawa and Victor Selivanov

State Complexity of GF(2)-Concatenation and GF(2)-Inverse
on Unary Languages   248
   Alexander Okhotin and Elizaveta Sazhneva

Pushdown Automata and Constant Height: Decidability and Bounds   260
   Giovanni Pighizzini and Luca Prigioniero

On the Decidability of Finding a Positive ILP-Instance in a Regular Set
of ILP-Instances   272
   Petra Wolf

How Does Adiabatic Quantum Computation Fit into Quantum
Automata Theory?   285
   Tomoyuki Yamakami

Author Index   299

A General Framework for Sequential Grammars with Control Mechanisms

Rudolf Freund$^{(\boxtimes)}$

Faculty of Informatics, TU Wien, Favoritenstraße 9-11, 1040 Vienna, Austria
rudi@emcc.at

Abstract. Since more than five decades, many control mechanisms have been introduced for sequential string grammars, including control graphs, matrices, permitting and forbidden contexts, and order relations. These control mechanisms then have been extended to sequential grammars working on objects different from strings, for example, to array, graph, and multiset grammars. Many relations between the languages generated by sequential grammars working on these objects with different control mechanisms were shown to be similar to the relations already proved for the string case. Within a general framework for regulated rewriting based on the applicability of rules in sequential grammars, many relations between various control mechanisms can be established in a very general setting without any reference to the underlying objects the rules are working on. Besides the well-known control mechanisms as control graphs, matrices, permitting and forbidden rules, partial order on rules, and priority relations on rules, the new variants of activation of rules as well as activation and blocking of rules are considered. Special results for strings and multisets as well as for arrays in the general variant defined on Cayley grids of finitely presented groups are exhibited based on the general results. Finally, some general results for cooperating distributed grammar systems are established.

Keywords: General framework · Regulating rewriting · Sequential grammars

1 Introduction

Already thirty years ago, a first comprehensive overview on many concepts of regulated rewriting, especially for the string case, was given the monograph on regulated rewriting by Dassow and Păun [7]. Yet as it turned out later, many of the mechanisms considered there for guiding the application of productions/rules can also be applied to other objects than strings, e.g., to n-dimensional arrays [10]. Even in the field of P systems [22] where mostly multisets are considered, such regulating mechanisms were used [4]. Using a general model for graph-controlled, programmed, random-context, and ordered grammars of arbitrary type based on

© IFIP International Federation for Information Processing 2019
Published by Springer Nature Switzerland AG 2019
M. Hospodár et al. (Eds.): DCFS 2019, LNCS 11612, pp. 1–34, 2019.
https://doi.org/10.1007/978-3-030-23247-4_1

the applicability of rules, many relations between various regulating mechanisms for sequential grammars can be established in a very general setting without any reference to the underlying objects the rules are working on, as first exhibited in [13] in a comprehensive way. In this overview paper, the results elaborated in [13] are combined with the results obtained in the general framework for sequential grammars using activation and blocking of rules as introduced in [2,3,11]. We recall special results for strings and multisets from [3] as well as results obtained in [11] for array grammars defined on Cayley grids of finitely presented groups. Finally, we establish some even new general results for cooperating distributed grammar systems.

In the following section, we recall some notions from formal language and group theory, especially for Cayley grids of finitely presented groups. In Sect. 3 we recall the main definitions of the general framework for sequential grammars of arbitrary type and the control mechanisms based on the applicability of rules as initiated in [13] and then continued in [3,11], i.e., for graph-controlled, programmed, random-context, and ordered grammars, for grammars with a priority relation on the rules, as well as for sequential grammars with activation and blocking of rules.

In Sect. 5 we summarize all the general results obtained within the framework for sequential grammars using the control mechanisms considered in this paper.

Specific results on computational completeness as well as some interesting complexity results for strings and multisets as underlying objects then are shown in Sect. 6.

In Sect. 7 we first define arrays and array grammars on Cayley grids of finitely presented groups. By proving that ordered array grammars using #-context-free array productions can generate the same language class as array grammars using arbitrary array productions, we then show that such a result not only holds for ordered array grammars but also for array grammars on Cayley grids of finitely presented groups equipped with many other control mechanisms, these results directly following from the general results summarized in Sect. 5 without needing any further proofs.

Finally, some general even new results for cooperating distributed grammar systems are elaborated in Sect. 8.

A summary of the results described in this paper and some future research topics conclude this overview paper.

2   Preliminaries

The set of integers is denoted by $\mathbb{Z}$, the set of positive integers by $\mathbb{N}$, the set of non-negative integers by $\mathbb{N}_0$. An *alphabet* V is a non-empty set of abstract *symbols*. Given V, the free monoid generated by V under the operation of concatenation is denoted by V^*; the elements of V^* are called strings, and the *empty string* is denoted by λ; $V^* \setminus \{\lambda\}$ is denoted by V^+. The cardinality of a set M is denoted by $|M|$.

Let $\{a_1, ..., a_n\}$ be an arbitrary alphabet; the number of occurrences of a symbol a_i in x is denoted by $|x|_{a_i}$; the *Parikh vector* associated with x with respect to $a_1, ..., a_n$ is $(|x|_{a_1}, ..., |x|_{a_n})$. The *Parikh image* of a language L over $\{a_1, ..., a_n\}$ is the set of all Parikh vectors of strings in L, and we denote it by $Ps(L)$. For a family of languages FL, the family of Parikh images of languages in FL is denoted by $PsFL$.

A finite multiset over the finite alphabet V, $V = \{a_1, ..., a_n\}$, is a mapping $f : V \longrightarrow \mathbb{N}_0$ and represented by $\langle f(a_1), a_1 \rangle ... \langle f(a_n), a_n \rangle$ or by any string x the Parikh vector of which with respect to $a_1, ..., a_n$ is $(f(a_1), ..., f(a_n))$. In the following we will not distinguish between a vector $(m_1, ..., m_n)$, its representation by a multiset $\langle m_1, a_1 \rangle ... \langle m_n, a_n \rangle$ or its representation by a string x having the Parikh vector $(|x|_{a_1}, ..., |x|_{a_n}) = (m_1, ..., m_n)$. Fixing the sequence of symbols $a_1, ..., a_n$ in the alphabet V in advance, the representation of the multiset $\langle m_1, a_1 \rangle ... \langle m_n, a_n \rangle$ by the string $a_1^{m_1}...a_n^{m_n}$ is unique. The set of all finite multisets over an alphabet V is denoted by V°.

For the basic notions and results of formal language theory the reader is referred to the monographs and handbooks in this area as [7,25,26], and for the basics of group theory and group presentations to [16]. The definitions and examples given in the following subsection are the basis for developing the theory of array grammars defined on Cayley grids of finitely presented groups in Sect. 7 (see [11]).

2.1 Groups and Group Presentations

Let $G = (G', \circ)$ be a group with group operation $\circ$. As is well-known, the group axioms are

- *closure*: for any $a, b \in G'$, $a \circ b \in G'$,
- *associativity*: for any $a, b, c \in G'$, $(a \circ b) \circ c = a \circ (b \circ c)$,
- *identity*: there exists a (unique) element $e \in G'$, called the *identity*, such that $e \circ a = a \circ e$ for all $a \in G'$, and
- *invertibility*: for any $a \in G'$, there exists a (unique) element a^{-1}, called the *inverse* of a, such that $a \circ a^{-1} = a^{-1} \circ a = e$.

In the following, we will not distinguish between G' and G if the group operation is obvious from the context. A group is called *commutative* (*Abelian*), if for any $a, b \in G'$, $a \circ b = b \circ a$. For any element $b \in G'$, the order of b is the smallest number $n \in \mathbb{N}$ such that $b^n = e$ provided such an n exists, and then we write $ord(b) = n$; if no such n exists, $\{b^n \mid n \geq 1\}$ is an infinite subset of G' and we write $ord(b) = \infty$.

For any set B, B^{-1} is defined as the set of symbols representing the inverses of the elements of B, i.e., $B^{-1} = \{b^{-1} \mid b \in B\}$. We now consider the strings in $(B \cup B^{-1})^*$ and two strings as different unless their equality follows from the group axioms, i.e., for any $a, b, c \in (B \cup B^{-1})^*$, $abb^{-1}c = ac$; using these reductions, we obtain a set of irreducible strings from those in $(B \cup B^{-1})^*$, the set of which we denote by $I(B)$. Then the *free group* generated by B is $F(B) = (I(B), \circ)$ with the elements being the irreducible strings over $B \cup B^{-1}$ and the group operation to be interpreted as the usual string concatenation, yet, obviously, if we concatenate two elements from $I(B)$, the resulting string eventually has to be reduced again. The identity in $F(B)$ is the empty string.

In general, B (not containing the identity) is called a *generator* of the group G if every element a from G can be written as a finite product/sum of elements from B and its inverses from B^{-1}, i.e., $a = b_1 \circ \cdots \circ b_m$ for $b_1, \ldots, b_m \in B \cup B^{-1}$. In this paper, we restrict ourselves to finitely presented groups, i.e., having a finite presentation $\langle B \mid R \rangle$ with B being a finite generator set and moreover, R being a finite set of relations among the elements of $B \cup B^{-1}$. In a similar way as in the definition of the free group generated by B, we here consider the strings in $(B \cup B^{-1})^*$ reduced according to the group axioms and the relations given in R. Informally, the group $G = \langle B \mid R \rangle$ is the largest one generated by B subject only to the group axioms and the relations in R. Formally, we will restrict ourselves to relations of the form $b_1 \circ \cdots \circ b_m = c^{-1}$ with $b_1, \ldots, b_m, c \in B \cup B^{-1}$, which equivalently may be written as $b_1 \circ \cdots \circ b_m \circ c = e$; hence, instead of such relations we may specify R by strings over $B \cup B^{-1}$ yielding the group identity, i.e., instead of $b_1 \circ \cdots \circ b_m = c^{-1}$ we take $b_1 \circ \cdots \circ b_m \circ c$ (these strings then are called *relators*).

Example 1. The free group $F(B) = (I(B), \circ)$ can be written as $\langle B \mid \emptyset \rangle$ (or even simpler as $\langle B \rangle$) because it has no restricting relations.

Example 2. The *cyclic group* of order n has the presentation $\langle \{a\} \mid \{a^n\} \rangle$ (or, omitting the set brackets, written as $\langle a \mid a^n \rangle$); it is also known as $\mathbb{Z}_n$ or as the quotient group $\mathbb{Z}/n\mathbb{Z}$.

Example 3. $\mathbb{Z}$ is a special case of an Abelian group generated by (1) and its inverse (-1), i.e., $\mathbb{Z}$ is the free group generated by (1). $\mathbb{Z}^d$ is an Abelian group generated by the unit vectors $(0, \ldots, 1, \ldots, 0)$ and their inverses $(0, \ldots, -1, \ldots, 0)$. It is well known that every finitely generated Abelian group is a direct sum of a torsion group and a free Abelian group where the torsion group may be written as a direct sum of finitely many groups of the form $\mathbb{Z}/p^k\mathbb{Z}$ for p being a prime, and the free Abelian group is a direct sum of finitely many copies of $\mathbb{Z}$.

Remark 4. Given a finite presentation of a group $\langle B \mid R \rangle$, in general it is not even decidable whether the group presented in that way is finite or infinite. If we consider (infinite) groups where the word equivalence problem $u = v$ is decidable, or equivalently, there is a decision procedure telling us whether, given two strings u and v, $uv^{-1} = e$, then we call $\langle B \mid R \rangle$ a *recursive* or *computable* finite group presentation.

2.2   Cayley Graphs

Let $G = \langle B \mid R \rangle$ be a finitely presented group with G' denoting the set of group elements. Then we define the corresponding *Cayley graph* (*Cayley grid*) of G with respect to the generating set B as the directed graph $C(G, B) = (G', E)$ with the set of nodes G' and the set E of directed edges labeled by elements of B by $E = \{(x, a, y) \mid x, y \in G', a \in B, xa = y\}$, i.e., from an element x an edge labeled by the generator a leads to y if and only if $xa = y$.

Example 5. The hexagonal grid is the Cayley graph assigned to the presentation of the group $\langle a, b, c \mid a^2, b^2, c^2, (abc)^2 \rangle$. As all three generators a, b, c are self-inverse and the direction of these elements indicates which generator is meant, we obtain a simpler picture for the hexagonal grid by replacing $a \; \diagup\!\!\diagup \; a$, $\overset{b}{\underset{b}{\rightleftarrows}}$, and $c \diagdown\!\!\diagdown c$ by $\diagup$, $-$, and $\diagdown$, respectively. Both representations are depicted in the following:

2.3 Register Machines

As a computationally complete model able to generate/accept all sets in $PsRE = Ps\left(\mathcal{L}\left(ARB\right)\right)$ we use register machines/deterministic register machines:

A *register machine* is a construct $M = (n, L_M, R_M, p_0, h)$ where n, $n \geq 1$, is the number of registers, L_M is the set of instruction labels, p_0 is the start label, h is the halting label (only used for the HALT instruction), and R_M is a set of (labeled) instructions being of one of the following forms:

- $p : (\text{ADD}\,(r)\,, q, s)$ increments the value in register r and continues with the instruction labeled by q or s,
- $p : (\text{SUB}\,(r)\,, q, s)$ decrements the value in register r and continues the computation with the instruction labeled by q if the register was non-empty, otherwise it continues with the instruction labeled by s;
- $h : \text{HALT}$ halts the machine.

M is called deterministic if in all ADD-instructions $p : (\text{ADD}\,(r)\,, q, s)$ $q = s$; in this case we write $p : (\text{ADD}\,(r)\,, q)$. Deterministic register machines can accept all recursively enumerable sets of vectors of natural numbers with k components using exactly $k + 2$ registers, for instance, see [18].

3   A General Model for Sequential Grammars and Regulated Rewriting Based on the Applicability of Rules

In this section we recall the notions for the general model of sequential grammars equipped with specific control mechanisms based on the applicability of rules as elaborated in [13] and in [3].

We first recall the main definitions of the general model for sequential grammars as established in [13], grammars generating a set of terminal objects by derivations where in each derivation step exactly one rule is applied to exactly one object.

A *(sequential) grammar* G_s is a construct $(O, O_T, w, P, \Longrightarrow_{G_s})$ where

- O is a set of *objects*;
- $O_T \subseteq O$ is a set of *terminal objects*;
- $w \in O$ is the *axiom (start object)*;
- P is a finite set of *rules*;
- $\Longrightarrow_{G_s} \subseteq O \times O$ is the *derivation relation* of G_s.

Each of the rules $p \in P$ induces a relation $\Longrightarrow_p \subseteq O \times O$ with respect to $\Longrightarrow_{G_s}$. A rule $p \in P$ is called *applicable* to an object $x \in O$ if and only if there exists at least one object $y \in O$ such that $(x, y) \in \Longrightarrow_p$; we also write $x \Longrightarrow_p y$. The derivation relation $\Longrightarrow_{G_s}$ is the union of all $\Longrightarrow_p$, i.e., $\Longrightarrow_{G_s} = \cup_{p \in P} \Longrightarrow_p$. The reflexive and transitive closure of $\Longrightarrow_{G_s}$ is denoted by $\overset{*}{\Longrightarrow}_{G_s}$.

Specific conditions on the rules in P define a special type X of grammars which then will be called *grammars of type X*.

The *language generated by* G is the set of all terminal objects that can be derived from the axiom, i.e.,

$$L(G_s) = \left\{ v \in O_T \mid w \overset{*}{\Longrightarrow}_{G_s} v \right\}.$$

The family of languages generated by grammars of type X is denoted by $\mathcal{L}(X)$.

Let $G_s = (O, O_T, w, P, \Longrightarrow_{G_s})$ be a (sequential) grammar of type X. If for every G_s of type X we have $O_T = O$, then X is called a *pure* type, otherwise it is called *extended*; X is called *strictly extended* if for any grammar G_s of type X, $w \notin O_T$ and for all $x \in O_T$, no rule from P can be applied to x.

In many cases, the type X of the grammar allows for one or even both of the following features:

A type X of grammars is called a *type with unit rules* if for every grammar $G_s = (O, O_T, w, P, \Longrightarrow_G)$ of type X there exists a grammar $G'_s = (O, O_T, w, P \cup P^{(+)}, \Longrightarrow_{G'_s})$ of type X such that $\Longrightarrow_{G_s} \subseteq \Longrightarrow_{G'_s}$ and

- $P^{(+)} = \{p^{(+)} \mid p \in P\}$,
- for all $x \in O$, $p^{(+)}$ is applicable to x if and only if p is applicable to x, and
- for all $x \in O$, if $p^{(+)}$ is applicable to x, the application of $p^{(+)}$ to x yields x back again.

A type X of grammars is called a *type with trap rules* if for every grammar $G_s = (O, O_T, w, P, \Longrightarrow_G)$ of type X there exists a grammar $G'_s = (O, O_T, w, P \cup P^{(-)}, \Longrightarrow_{G'_s})$ of type X such that $\Longrightarrow_{G_s} \subseteq \Longrightarrow_{G'_s}$ and

- $P^{(-)} = \{p^{(-)} \mid p \in P\}$, $P^{(-)} \cap P = \emptyset$;
- for all $x \in O$, $p^{(-)}$ is applicable to x if and only if p is applicable to x, and
- for all $x \in O$, if $p^{(-)}$ is applicable to x, the application of $p^{(-)}$ to x yields an object y from which no terminal object can be derived anymore.

3.1   Graph-Controlled and Programmed Grammars

A *graph-controlled grammar* (with applicability checking) of type X is a construct

$$G_{GC} = (G_s, g, H_i, H_f, \Longrightarrow_{GC})$$

where $G_s = (O, O_T, w, P, \Longrightarrow_G)$ is a grammar of type X; $g = (H, E, K)$ is a labeled graph where H is the set of node labels identifying the nodes of the graph in a one-to-one manner, $E \subseteq H \times \{Y, N\} \times H$ is the set of edges labeled by Y or N, $K : H \to 2^P$ is a function assigning a subset of P to each node of g; $H_i \subseteq H$ is the set of initial labels, and $H_f \subseteq H$ is the set of final labels. The derivation relation $\Longrightarrow_{GC}$ is defined based on $\Longrightarrow_{G_s}$ and the control graph g as follows: For any $i, j \in H$ and any $u, v \in O$, $(u, i) \Longrightarrow_{GC} (v, j)$ if and only if

- $u \Longrightarrow_p v$ by some rule $p \in K(i)$ and $(i, Y, j) \in E$ *(success case)*, **or**
- $u = v$, no $p \in K(i)$ is applicable to u, and $(i, N, j) \in E$ *(failure case)*.

The language generated by G_{GC} is defined by

$$L(G_{GC}) = \left\{ v \in O_T \mid (w, i) \Longrightarrow^*_{G_{GC}} (v, j), \ i \in H_i, j \in H_f \right\}.$$

If $H_i = H_f = H$, then G_{GC} is called a *programmed grammar*. The families of languages generated by graph-controlled and programmed grammars of type X are denoted by $\mathcal{L}(X\text{-}GC_{ac})$ and $\mathcal{L}(X\text{-}P_{ac})$, respectively. If the set E contains no edges of the form (i, N, j), then the graph-controlled grammar is said to be *without applicability checking*; the corresponding families of languages are denoted by $\mathcal{L}(X\text{-}GC)$ and $\mathcal{L}(X\text{-}P)$, respectively.

As a special variant of graph-controlled grammars we consider those where all labels are final; the corresponding family of languages generated by graph-controlled grammars of type X is abbreviated by $\mathcal{L}\left(X\text{-}GC_{ac}^{all final}\right)$. By definition, programmed grammars are just a subvariant where in addition all labels are also initial.

The notions *with/without applicability checking* in the original definition for string grammars were introduced as *with/without appearance checking* because the appearance of the non-terminal symbol on the left-hand side of a context-free rule was checked, which coincides with checking for the applicability of this rule in our general model; in both cases – applicability checking and appearance checking – we can use the abbreviation *ac*.

3.2   Matrix Grammars

A *matrix grammar* (with applicability checking) of type X is a construct $G_M = (G_s, M, F, \Longrightarrow_{G_M})$ where $G_s = (O, O_T, w, P, \Longrightarrow_G)$ is a grammar of type X, M is a finite set of sequences of the form $(p_1, \ldots, p_n)$, $n \geq 1$, of rules in P, and $F \subseteq P$. For $w, z \in O$ we write $w \Longrightarrow_{G_M} z$ if there are a matrix $(p_1, \ldots, p_n)$ in M and objects $w_i \in O$, $1 \leq i \leq n+1$, such that $w = w_1$, $z = w_{n+1}$, and, for all $1 \leq i \leq n$, either

- $w_i \Longrightarrow_{p_i} w_{i+1}$ or
- $w_i = w_{i+1}$, p_i is not applicable to w_i, and $p_i \in F$.

$L(G_M) = \{v \in O_T \mid w \Longrightarrow^*_{G_M} v\}$ is the language generated by G_M. The family of languages generated by matrix grammars of type X is denoted by $\mathcal{L}(X\text{-}MAT_{ac})$. If the set F is empty, then the grammar is said to be *without applicability checking* (*without ac* for short); the corresponding family of languages is denoted by $\mathcal{L}(X\text{-}MAT)$. We mention that in this paper we choose the definition where the sequential application of the rules in the final matrix may stop at any moment.

3.3   Random-Context Grammars

A *random-context grammar* G_{RC} of type X is a construct $(G_s, P', \Longrightarrow_{G_{RC}})$ where

- $G_s = (O, O_T, w, P, \Longrightarrow_G)$ is a grammar of type X;
- P' is a set of rules of the form (p, R, Q) where $p \in P$, $R \cup Q \subseteq P$;
- $\Longrightarrow_{G_{RC}}$ is the derivation relation assigned to G_{RC} such that for any $x, y \in O$, $x \Longrightarrow_{G_{RC}} y$ if and only if for some rule $(p, R, Q) \in P'$, $x \Longrightarrow_p y$ and, moreover, all rules from R are applicable to x as well as no rule from Q is applicable to x.

A random-context grammar $G_{RC} = (G_s, P', \Longrightarrow_{G_{RC}})$ of type X is called a *grammar with permitting contexts of type X* if for all rules (p, R, Q) in P' we have $Q = \emptyset$, i.e., we only check for the applicability of the rules in R.

A random-context grammar $G_{RC} = (G_s, P', \Longrightarrow_{G_{RC}})$ of type X is called a *grammar with forbidden contexts of type X* if for all rules (p, R, Q) in P' we have $R = \emptyset$, i.e., we only check for the non-applicability of the rules in Q. We write $X\text{-}fC_1$ if for every $p \in P$ there is only one rule of the form $(p, \emptyset, Q)$ in P'.

$L(G_{RC}) = \{v \in O_T \mid w \Longrightarrow^*_{G_{RC}} v\}$ is the language generated by G_{RC}. The families of languages generated by random context grammars, grammars with permitting contexts, and grammars with forbidden contexts of type X are denoted by $\mathcal{L}(X\text{-}RC)$, $\mathcal{L}(X\text{-}pC)$, and $\mathcal{L}(X\text{-}fC)$ or $\mathcal{L}(X\text{-}fC_1)$, respectively.

3.4   Grammars with Priority Relations on the Rules

A *grammar with a priority relation on the rules* G_{Pri} of type X is a construct $(G_s, \prec, \Longrightarrow_{G_{Pri}})$ where

- $G_s = (O, O_T, w, P, \Longrightarrow_G)$ is a grammar of type X;
- $\prec$ is a priority relation on the rules in P;
- $\Longrightarrow_{G_{Pri}}$ is the derivation relation assigned to G_{Pri} such that for any $x, y \in O$, $x \Longrightarrow_{G_{Pri}} y$ if and only if for some rule $q \in P$ $x \Longrightarrow_q y$ and, moreover, no rule p from P with $q \prec p$ is applicable to x.

$L(G_{Pri}) = \{v \in O_T \mid w \Longrightarrow^*_{G_{Pri}} v\}$ is the language generated by G_{Pri}. The family of languages generated by grammars with priority relations on the rules of type X is denoted by $\mathcal{L}(X\text{-}Pri)$.

3.5 Ordered Grammars

An *ordered grammar* G_O *of type* X is a grammar $(G_s, \prec, \Longrightarrow_{G_O})$ with the priority relation $\prec$ on the rules which is a partial order, i.e., $\prec$ fulfills the condition that for any $p, q, r \in P$, $p \prec q$ and $q \prec r$ implies $p \prec q$.

The family of languages generated by ordered grammars of type X is denoted by $\mathcal{L}(X\text{-}O)$.

3.6 Grammars with Activation and Blocking of Rules

We now recall the definition of sequential grammars with activation and blocking of rules in a similar way as introduced in [2,3,11].

A *grammar with activation and blocking of rules* (an *AB-grammar*) of type X is a construct

$$G_{AB} = (G_s, L, f_L, A, B, L_0, \Longrightarrow_{G_{AB}})$$

where $G_s = (O, O_T, w, P, \Longrightarrow_G)$ is a grammar of type X, L is a finite set of labels with each label having assigned one rule from P by the function f_L, A, B are finite subsets of $L \times L \times \mathbb{N}$, and L_0 is a finite set of tuples of the form $(q, Q, \bar{Q})$, $q \in L$, with the elements of $Q, \bar{Q}$ being of the form (l, t), where $l \in L$ and $t \in \mathbb{N}$, $t > 1$.

A derivation in G_{AB} starts with one element $(q, Q, \bar{Q})$ from L_0 which means that the rule labeled by q has to be applied to the initial object w in the first step and for the following derivation steps the conditions given by Q as activations of rules and $\bar{Q}$ as blockings of rules have to be taken into account in addition to the activations and blockings coming along with the application of the rule labeled by q. The role of L_0 is to get a derivation started by activating some rule for the first step(s) although no rule has been applied so far, but probably also providing additional activations and blockings for further derivation steps.

A configuration of G_{AB} in general can be described by the object derived so far and the activations Q and blockings $\bar{Q}$ for the next steps. In that sense, the starting tuple $(q, Q, \bar{Q})$ can be interpreted as $(\{(q, 1)\} \cup Q, \bar{Q})$, and we may also simply write $(Q', \bar{Q})$ with $Q' = \{(q, 1)\} \cup Q$. We mostly will assume Q and $\bar{Q}$ to be non-conflicting, i.e., $Q \cap \bar{Q} = \emptyset$; otherwise, we interpret $(Q', \bar{Q})$ as $(Q' \setminus \bar{Q}, \bar{Q})$.

Given a configuration $(u, Q, \bar{Q})$, in one step we can derive $(v, R, \bar{R})$ – we also write $(u, Q, \bar{Q}) \Longrightarrow_{G_{AB}} (v, R, \bar{R})$ – if and only if

- $u \Longrightarrow_G v$ using the rule r such that $(q, 1) \in Q$ and $(q, r) \in f_L$, i.e., we apply the rule labeled by q activated for this next derivation step to u; the new sets of activations and blockings are defined by

$$\bar{R} = \{(x, i) \mid (x, i+1) \in \bar{Q}, \ i > 0\} \cup \{(x, i) \mid (q, x, i) \in B\},$$
$$R = (\{(x, i) \mid (x, i+1) \in Q, \ i > 0\} \cup \{(x, i) \mid (q, x, i) \in A\})$$
$$\setminus \{(x, i) \mid (x, i) \in \bar{R}\}$$

(observe that R and $\bar{R}$ are made non-conflicting by eliminating rule labels which are activated and blocked at the same time);
or

– no rule r is activated to be applied in the next derivation step; in this case we take $v = u$ and continue with $(v, R, \bar{R})$ constructed as before provided R is not empty, i.e., there are rules activated in some further derivation steps; otherwise the derivation stops with yielding object u.

The language generated by G_{AB} is defined by

$$L(G_{AB}) = \{v \in O_T \mid (w, Q, \bar{Q}) \Longrightarrow^*_{G_{AB}} (v, R, \bar{R}) \text{ for some } (Q, \bar{Q}) \in L_0\}.$$

The family of languages generated by AB-grammars of type X is denoted by $\mathcal{L}(X\text{-}AB)$. If the set B of blocking relations is empty, then the grammar is said to be a *grammar with activation of rules* (an *A-grammar* for short) of type X; the corresponding family of languages is denoted by $\mathcal{L}(X\text{-}A)$.

4   General Results

We now recall the main results and proofs already established in [13] as well as recently exhibited in [11] and [3] for the control mechanisms defined in the preceding section.

Theorem 6. *For any arbitrary type X,*

$$\mathcal{L}(X\text{-}MAT_{ac}) \subseteq \mathcal{L}\left(X\text{-}GC^{allfinal}_{ac}\right) \subseteq \mathcal{L}(X\text{-}GC_{ac}) \text{ and}$$
$$\mathcal{L}(X\text{-}MAT) \subseteq \mathcal{L}\left(X\text{-}GC^{allfinal}\right) \subseteq \mathcal{L}(X\text{-}GC).$$

Proof. Let $G_M = (G_s, M, F, \Longrightarrow_{G_M})$ be a matrix grammar where

– $G_s = (O, O_T, w, P, \Longrightarrow_{G_s})$ is a grammar of type X and
– $M = \{(p_{i,1}, \ldots, p_{i,n_i}) \mid 1 \leq i \leq n\}$ with $p_{i,j} \in P$, $1 \leq j \leq n_i$, $1 \leq i \leq n$.

Then we construct the graph-controlled grammar $G_{GC} = (G_s, g, H_i, H_f, \Longrightarrow_{GC})$ with $g = (H, E, K)$, $H = \{(i, j) \mid 1 \leq j \leq n_i, 1 \leq i \leq n\}$, $K((i,j)) = \{p_{i,j}\}$, $1 \leq j \leq n_i$, $1 \leq i \leq n$,

$$\begin{aligned}
E = &\{((i,j), Y, (i, j+1)) \mid 1 \leq j < n_i, 1 \leq i \leq n\}\\
&\cup \{((i,j), N, (i, j+1)) \mid 1 \leq j < n_i, 1 \leq i \leq n, p_{i,j} \in F\}\\
&\cup \{((i, n_i), Y, (j, 1)) \mid 1 \leq j \leq n, 1 \leq i \leq n\}\\
&\cup \{((i, n_i), N, (j, 1)) \mid 1 \leq j \leq n, 1 \leq i \leq n, p_{i,j} \in F\}
\end{aligned}$$

and $H_i = \{(i, 1) \mid 1 \leq i \leq n\}$. As we have assumed that the sequential application of the rules of the chosen matrix may stop at any moment, we have to take $H_f = H$. By this construction it is guaranteed that G_{GC} simulates a derivation in G_M correctly by choosing a matrix to be simulated in a non-deterministic way and then applying the rules from this matrix in the desired sequence; the application of a rule $p_{i,j}$ may be skipped if and only if $p_{i,j} \in F$. G_{GC} is without applicability checking if and only if G_M is without applicability checking, which observation completes the proof.   □

By definition, we have:

Lemma 7. $\mathcal{L}(X\text{-}O) \subseteq \mathcal{L}(X\text{-}Pri)$.

The following theorem shows that forbidden contexts with only one set of forbidden rules for each rule can simulate any priority relation on the rules:

Theorem 8. *For any arbitrary type* X, $\mathcal{L}(X\text{-}Pri) \subseteq \mathcal{L}(X\text{-}fC_1)$.

Proof. Let $G_s = (O, O_T, w, P, \Longrightarrow_G)$ be a grammar of type X. Consider the grammar with a priority relation on the rules $G_{Pri} = (G_s, \prec, \Longrightarrow_{G_{Pri}})$ of type X and the corresponding grammar with forbidden contexts $G_{fC_1} = (G_s, P_{fC_1}, \Longrightarrow_{G_{fC_1}})$ of type X where

$$P_{fC_1} = \{(p, \emptyset, Q(p)) \mid p \in P\} \quad \text{with} \quad Q(p) = \{q \mid q \in P, p \prec q\}.$$

As a rule $p \in P$ can be applied in G_{fC_1} if and only if no rule from $Q(p)$ is applicable which is the same condition as for the applicability of p in G_{Pri}, we infer $L(G_{fC_1}) = L(G_{Pri})$.   □

Yet also the reverse inclusion holds, even for partial order relations, provided the type X allows for trap rules:

Theorem 9. *For any type* X *with trap rules,* $\mathcal{L}(X\text{-}fC_1) \subseteq \mathcal{L}(X\text{-}O)$.

Proof. Let $G_s = (O, O_T, w, P, \Longrightarrow_G)$ be a grammar of type X and consider the grammar with forbidden contexts $G_{fC_1} = (G_s, P_{fC_1}, \Longrightarrow_{G_{fC_1}})$ of type X with $P_{fC_1} = \{(p, \emptyset, Q(p)) \mid p \in P\}$. We now extend the underlying grammar G_s by the trap rules p^- for all rules p in P, thus obtaining the grammar $G'_s = (O, O_T, w, P \cup P^{(-)}, \Longrightarrow_{G'_s})$ where, according to the definition of grammars with trap rules,

- $P^{(-)} = \{p^{(-)} \mid p \in P\}$, $P^{(-)} \cap P = \emptyset$,
- for all $x \in O$, $p^{(-)}$ is applicable to x if and only if p is applicable to x, and
- for all $x \in O$, if $p^{(-)}$ is applicable to x, the application of $p^{(-)}$ to x yields an object y from which no terminal object can be derived anymore.

As X is a type with trap rules, G'_s again is of type X. We now define the ordered grammar $G_O = (G'_s, \prec, \Longrightarrow_{G_O})$ which by definition again is of type X, with the partial order $\prec$ on the rules in $P \cup P^{(-)}$ as follows:

$$\text{for any } p \in P, p \prec q^- \text{ for all } q \in Q(p).$$

This guarantees that $L(G_{fC_1}) = L(G_O)$, as a rule $p \in P$ can be applied in G_O if and only if no rule from $Q(p)$ is applicable which is the same condition as for the applicability of p in G_{fC_1}. On the other hand, the application of a rule in $P^{(-)}$ can never lead to a terminal result. Moreover, it is obvious to see that $\prec$ is a partial order, because $\prec \subseteq P \times P^{(-)}$ and, by definition, $P^{(-)} \cap P = \emptyset$.   □

As an immediate consequence of Lemma 7 and Theorems 8 and 9 we infer:

Corollary 10. *For any type X with trap rules,*

$$\mathcal{L}(X\text{-}O) = \mathcal{L}(X\text{-}Pri) = \mathcal{L}(X\text{-}fC_1) \subseteq \mathcal{L}(X\text{-}fC).$$

Matrix grammars (with applicability checking) can simulate random context grammars for any arbitrary type X with unit rules and trap rules:

Theorem 11. *For any arbitrary type X with unit rules and trap rules,*

$$\mathcal{L}(X\text{-}RC) \subseteq \mathcal{L}(X\text{-}MAT_{ac}).$$

Proof. Consider a *random-context grammar* $G_{RC} = (G_s, P_{RC}, \Longrightarrow_{G_{RC}})$ where $G_s = (O, O_T, w, P, \Longrightarrow_G)$ is a grammar of a type X with unit rules and trap rules; then we define the *matrix grammar* with appearance checking $G_M = (G'_s, M, F, \Longrightarrow_M)$ of type X as follows: for each rule $(p, R, Q) \in P_{RC}$, $R = \{r_i \mid 1 \le i \le m\}$, $Q = \{q_j \mid 1 \le j \le n\}$, $m, n \ge 0$, we take the matrix $\left(r_1^{(+)}, \ldots, r_m^{(+)}, q_1^{(-)}, \ldots, q_n^{(-)}, p\right)$ into M.

In that way we obtain $G'_s = (O, O_T, w, P', \Longrightarrow_{G'_s})$ where

$$P' = P \cup \left\{r^{(+)}, q^{(-)} \mid r \in R, q \in Q \text{ for some } (p, R, Q) \in P_{RC}\right\}$$

and $F = \{q^{(-)} \mid q \in Q \text{ for some } (p, R, Q) \in P_{RC}\}$. As X is a type with unit rules and trap rules, all the elements of G_M are well defined. Obviously, for all $x, y \in O$ we have $x \Longrightarrow_{(p,R,Q)} y$ if and only if $x \Longrightarrow_{\left(r_i^{(+)}, \ldots, r_m^{(+)}, q_1^{(-)}, \ldots, q_n^{(-)}, p\right)} y$ without trapping y, which implies $L(G_M) = L(G_{RC})$.

As a technical detail we mention that when the application of rules in the sequence of the matrix $\left(r_i^{(+)}, \ldots, r_m^{(+)}, q_1^{(-)}, \ldots, q_n^{(-)}, p\right)$ stops before having reached the end with applying p, either the underlying object has not yet changed as long as only the unit rules have been applied or else has already been trapped by the application of one of the trap rules, hence, no additional terminal results can arise from such situations.   □

Omitting the forbidden rules and applicability checking, respectively, from the (proof of the) preceding theorem we immediately obtain the following result:

Corollary 12. *For any arbitrary type X with unit rules,*

$$\mathcal{L}(X\text{-}pC) \subseteq \mathcal{L}(X\text{-}MAT).$$

Already in [13] graph-controlled grammars have been shown to be the most powerful control mechanism, and they can also simulate AB-grammars with the underlying grammar being of any arbitrary type X, see [3].

Theorem 13. *For any type X, $\mathcal{L}(X\text{-}AB) \subseteq \mathcal{L}(X\text{-}GC_{ac})$.*

Proof. Let $G_{AB} = (G, L, f_L, A, B, L_0, \Longrightarrow_{G_A})$ be an AB-grammar with the underlying grammar $G = (O, O_T, w, P, \Longrightarrow_G)$ being of any type X. Then we construct a graph-controlled grammar $G_{GC} = (G, g, H_i, H_f, \Longrightarrow_{GC})$ with the same underlying grammar G. The simulation power is captured by the structure of the control graph $g = (H, E, K)$. The node labels in H, identifying the nodes of the graph in a one-to-one manner, are obtained from G_{AB} as all possible triples of the forms $(q, Q, \bar{Q})$ or $(\bar{q}, Q, \bar{Q})$ with $q \in L$ and the elements of $Q, \bar{Q}$ being of the form (r, t), $r \in L$ and $t \in \mathbb{N}$ such that t does not exceed the maximum time occurring in the relations in A and B, hence, this in total is a bounded number. We also need a special node labeled $\emptyset$, where a computation in G_{GC} ends in any case when this node is reached. All nodes can be chosen to be final, i.e., $H_f = H$. $H_i = L_0$ is the set of initial labels, i.e., we start with one of the initial conditions as in the AB-grammar.

The idea behind the node $(q, Q, \bar{Q})$ is to describe the situation of a configuration derived in the AB-grammar where q is the label of the rule to be applied and $Q, \bar{Q}$ describe the activated and blocked rules for the further derivation steps in the AB-grammar. Hence, as already in the definition of an AB-grammar, we therefore assume $Q \cap \bar{Q} = \emptyset$.

Now let $g(l)$ denote the rule r assigned to label l, i.e., $(l, r) \in f_L$. Then, the set of rules assigned to $(q, Q, \bar{Q})$ is taken to be $\{g(q)\}$. The set of rules assigned to $\emptyset$ is taken to be $\emptyset$.

As it will become clear later in the proof why, the nodes $(\bar{q}, Q, \bar{Q})$ are assigned the set of rules $\{g(l) \mid (l, 1) \in Q, \ l \neq q\}$; we only take those nodes where this set is not empty.

When being in node $(q, Q, \bar{Q})$, we have to distinguish between two possibilities:

- If $g(q)$ is applicable to the object derived so far, a Y-edge has to go to every node which describes a situation corresponding to what would have been the next configuration in the AB-grammar. We then compute

$$
\begin{aligned}
\bar{R} &= \{(x, i) \mid (x, i+1) \in \bar{Q}, \ i > 0\} \cup \{(x, i) \mid (q, x, i) \in B\}, \\
R &= (\{(x, i) \mid (x, i+1) \in Q, \ i > 0\} \cup \{(x, i) \mid (q, x, i) \in A\}) \\
&\quad \setminus \{(x, i) \mid (x, i) \in \bar{R}\}
\end{aligned}
$$

(observe that R and $\bar{R}$ are made non-conflicting) as well as – if it exists – $t_0 := min\{t \mid (x, t) \in R\}$, i.e., the next time step when the derivation in the AB-grammar could continue. Hence, we take a Y-edge to every node $(p, P, \bar{P})$ where $p \in \{x \mid (x, t_0) \in R\}$ and

$$
\begin{aligned}
\bar{P} &= \{(x, i) \mid (x, i + t_0 - 1) \in \bar{R}, \ i > 0\}, \\
P &= \{(x, i) \mid (x, i + t_0 - 1) \in R\}.
\end{aligned}
$$

If $t_0 := min\{t \mid (x, t) \in R\}$ does not exist, this means that R is empty and we have to make a Y-edge to the node $\emptyset$.
- If $g(q)$ is not applicable to the object derived so far, we first have to check that none of the other rules activated at this step could have been applied,

i.e., we check for the applicability of the rules in the set of rules

$$\bar{U} := \{g(l) \mid (l,1) \in Q, \; l \neq q\}$$

by going to the node $\left(\bar{q}, Q, \bar{Q}\right)$ with a N-edge; from there no Y-edge leaves, as this would indicate the unwanted case of the applicability of one of the rules in $\bar{U}$, but with a N-edge we continue the computation in any node $\left(p, P, \bar{P}\right)$ with p, P, $\bar{P}$ computed as above in the first case. We observe that in case $\bar{R}$ is empty, we can omit the path through the node $\left(\bar{q}, Q, \bar{Q}\right)$ and directly go to the nodes $\left(p, P, \bar{P}\right)$ which are obtained as follows: we first check whether $t_0 := min\{t \mid (x,t) \in Q, \; t > 1\}$ exists or not; if not, then the computation has to end with a N-edge to node $\emptyset$. Otherwise, a N-edge goes to every node $\left(p, P, \bar{P}\right)$ with $p \in \{x \mid (x,t_0) \in Q\}$ and

$$\bar{P} = \left\{(x,i) \mid (x, i + t_0 - 1) \in \bar{Q}, \; i > 0\right\},$$
$$P = \left\{(x,i) \mid (x, i + t_0 - 1) \in Q\right\}.$$

where the simulation may continue.

In this way, every computation in the AB-grammar can be simulated by the graph-controlled grammar with taking a correct path through the control graph and finally ending in node $\emptyset$; due to this fact, we could also choose the node $\emptyset$ to be the only final node, i.e., $H_f = \{\emptyset\}$. On the other hand, if we have made a wrong choice and wanted to apply a rule which is not applicable, although another rule activated at the same moment would have been applicable, we get stuck, but the derivation simulated in this way still is a valid one in the AB-grammar, although in most standard types X, which usually are strictly extended ones, such a derivation does not yield a terminal object. Having taken $H_f = \{\emptyset\}$, such paths would not even lead to successful computations in G_{GC}.

In any case, we conclude that the graph-controlled grammar G_{GC} generates the same language as the AB-grammar G_{AB}, which observation concludes the proof. $\qquad\square$

We remark that in the construction of the graph-controlled grammar given in the preceding proof, all labels could be chosen to be final.

In the case of graph-controlled grammars with all labels being final, for any strictly extended type X with trap rules we can show that the power of rule activation is already sufficient and that the additional power of blocking is not needed.

Theorem 14. *For any strictly extended type X with trap rules,*

$$\mathcal{L}\left(X\text{-}GC_{ac}^{allfinal}\right) \subseteq \mathcal{L}\left(X\text{-}A\right).$$

Proof. Let $G_{GC} = (G_s, g, H_i, H_f, \Longrightarrow_{GC})$ be a graph-controlled grammar where $G_s = (O, O_T, w, P, \Longrightarrow_G)$ is a strictly extended grammar of type X with trap rules; $g = (H, E, K)$, $E \subseteq H \times \{Y, N\} \times H$ is the set of edges labeled by Y or N, $K : H \to 2^P$ is a function assigning a subset of P to each node of g; $H_i \subseteq H$

is the set of initial labels, and H_f is the set of final labels coinciding with the whole set H, i.e., $H_f = H$.

Then we construct an equivalent A-grammar $G_A = (G'_s, L, f_L, A, L_0, \Longrightarrow_{G_A})$ as follows: the underlying grammar G'_s is obtained from G_s by adding all trap rules, i.e., $G'_s = (O, O_T, w, P', \Longrightarrow_{G'_s})$ with $P' = P \cup P^{(-)}$, $P^{(-)} = \{p^- \mid p \in P\}$, $P^{(-)} \cap P = \emptyset$. G'_s again is strictly extended and $w \notin O_T$, hence, also in G_A rules have to be applied before terminal objects are obtained. For any node in g labeled by l with the assigned set of rules P_l we assume it to be described by $P_l = \{p_{l,i} \mid 1 \le i \le n_l\}$. For all $q \in P$ we take the labels l_{q^-} into L as well as (l_{q^-}, q^-) into f_L.

We now sketch how the transitions from a node in g labeled by l with the assigned set of rules P_l can be simulated. The assumption that all nodes are final is crucial for this construction. Arriving in some node, one of the following situations is given:

1. the underlying object is terminal and therefore no rule from P is applicable any more, as X is a strictly extended type; hence, we may stop in this node and extract the underlying object as a terminal result of the derivation, as all nodes are final;
2. the underlying object is not terminal, but no rule from $\bigcup_{i \in H} P_i$ is applicable any more; hence, even when continuing the derivation following a path through the control graph only using N-edges, the derivation cannot yield a terminal object any more; therefore, in such a case, we need not continue the derivation;
3. the underlying object is not terminal, no rule $p_{l,i}$ in P_l, $1 \le i \le n_l$, is applicable, but there is still some node k reachable from node l following a path through the control graph only using N-edges that contains an applicable rule;
4. the underlying object is not terminal, but there is some rule $p_{l,i}$ in P_l, $1 \le i \le n_l$, which is applicable.

For the simulation of these situations by the A-grammar, we therefore can restrict ourselves to the cases where when applying a rule we follow a path starting with a Y-edge and continuing with only N-edges until we reach a node containing a probably applicable rule; observe that such a path can only consist of the Y-edge, too.

In order to simulate a rule $p_{l,i}$ in P_l, $1 \le i \le n_l$, we take all activations into A which allow us to simulate the application of $p_{l,i}$ and to guess with which $p_{k,j}$ probably to continue afterwards. Hence, we consider all paths without loops $h_0 = l - h_1 - \cdots - h_n = k$ in the control graph g which start with a Y-edge and continue with only N-edges. For any such path we introduce labels $((l,i), h_1, \ldots, (k,j))$ in L and $((l,i), h_1, \ldots, (k,j)) : p_{l,i}$ in f_L; the set of all labels describing such paths from node l to any node k is denoted by $L_{l,i}$. Moreover, we use the following activations in A:

- $((l,i), h_1, \ldots, (k,j)), \{l_{q^-} \mid q \in \bigcup_{1 \le i \le n-1} P_{h_i}\}, 1)$ is used to check in the next step that no rule along the path from node l to node k is applicable; observe that for $n = 1$ the set $\bigcup_{1 \leq i \leq n-1} P_{h_i}$ is empty and the whole activation can be omitted;

– in the second next step only the designated rule $p_{k,j}$ can be applied, i.e., we take $((l,i), h_1, \ldots, (k,j)), L_{k,j}, 2)$ into A; as with every label in $L_{k,j}$ the rule $p_{k,j}$ is assigned, the intended continuation is prepared.

How can a derivation in the A-grammar be started? As $w \notin O_T$, at least one rule must be applied to obtain a terminal object; hence, we check all possibilities that a rule in an initial node in H_i or along a path in g following only N-edges from such an initial node can be applied (observe that there are only finitely many paths without loops of that kind through the control graph); for each such rule $p_{l,i}$ in node l we take all labels from $L_{l,i}$ into L_0. As by construction $p_{l,i}$ is applicable it is guaranteed that any continuation of the computation will follow a Y-edge in g and thus the simulation in G_A will follow the simulation of an applicable rule as described above.

In total, the construction given above guarantees that the simulation of a computation in G_{GC} by a computation in G_A starts correctly and continues until no rule can be applied any more. As we have assumed all nodes in g to be final and X to be a strictly extended type, i.e., no rules can be applied to a terminal object any more, the only condition to get a result is to obtain a terminal object at the end of a computation. This observation completes our proof. □

As programmed grammars are just a special case of graph-controlled grammars with all labels being final, we immediately infer the following result:

Corollary 15. *For any strictly extended type X with trap rules,*

$$\mathcal{L}(X\text{-}P_{ac}) \subseteq \mathcal{L}(X\text{-}A).$$

Combining (the proofs of) Theorems 13 and 14, we infer the following equality:

Corollary 16. *For any strictly extended type X with trap rules,*

$$\mathcal{L}\left(X\text{-}GC_{ac}^{allfinal}\right) = \mathcal{L}(X\text{-}A).$$

5 Summary of General Results

The main results elaborated for the relations between the specific regulating mechanisms in [13] and in [3] are depicted in the following diagram.

Theorem 17. *The inclusions indicated by vectors as depicted in Fig. 1 hold. Most of the relations indicated by vectors even hold for arbitrary types X; additionally needed features of being a strictly extended type or being a type with unit and/or trap rules are indicated by se, u, and t, respectively, aside the vector:*

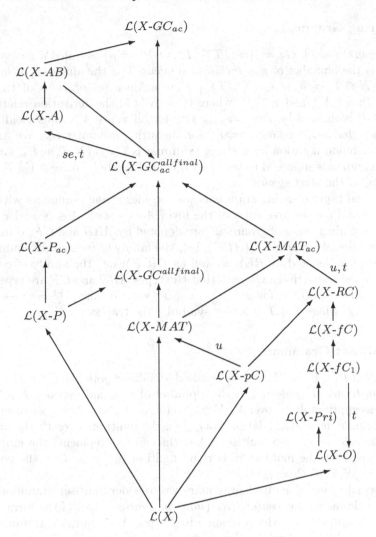

Fig. 1. Hierarchy of control mechanisms for grammars of type X.

6   Results for Strings and Multisets

As specific types of objects for the general model of a sequential grammar as introduced in Sect. 3 we now consider strings and multisets. We refer to [13] where some examples for string and multiset grammars of specific types illustrating the expressive power of this general framework are given.

6.1   String Grammars

In the general model, $G_S = ((N \cup T)^*, T^*, w, P, \Longrightarrow_P)$ is called a *string grammar*; N is the alphabet of *non-terminal symbols*, T is the alphabet of *terminal symbols*, $N \cap T = \emptyset$, $w \in (N \cup T)^+$, P is a finite set of *rules* of the form $u \to v$ with $u \in V^+$ and $v \in V^*$, where $V := N \cup T$; the derivation relation for $u \to v \in P$ is defined by $xuy \Longrightarrow_{u \to v} xvy$ for all $x, y \in V^*$, thus yielding the well-known derivation relation $\Longrightarrow_{G_S}$ for the string grammar G_S. We mention that the common notation for a string grammar is $G_S - (N, T, w, P)$, and usually the axiom w is supposed to be a non-terminal symbol, i.e., $w \in V \setminus T$, which then is called the *start symbol*.

As special types of string grammars we consider string grammars with arbitrary rules and context-free rules of the form $A \to v$ with $A \in N$ and $v \in V^*$. The corresponding types of grammars are denoted by ARB and CF, thus yielding the families of languages $\mathcal{L}(ARB)$, i.e., the family of recursively enumerable languages (also denoted by RE), as well as $\mathcal{L}(CF)$, i.e., the family of context-free languages, respectively. Observe that the types ARB and CF are types with unit rules and trap rules (for $p = w \to v \in P$, we can take $p^{(+)} = w \to w$ and $p^{(-)} = w \to F$ where $F \notin T$ is a new symbol – the trap symbol).

6.2   Multiset Grammars

$G_m = ((N \cup T)^\circ, T^\circ, w, P, \Longrightarrow_{G_m})$ is called a *multiset grammar*; N is the alphabet of *non-terminal symbols*, T is the alphabet of *terminal symbols*, $N \cap T = \emptyset$, w is a non-empty multiset over V, $V := N \cup T$, and P is a finite set of multiset rules yielding a derivation relation $\Longrightarrow_{G_m}$ on the multisets over V; the application of the rule $u \to v$ to a multiset x has the effect of replacing the multiset u contained in x by the multiset v. For the multiset grammar G_m, the common notation is $(N, T, w, P, \Longrightarrow_{G_m})$.

As special types of multiset grammars we consider multiset grammars with *arbitrary* rules as well as *context-free (non-cooperative)* rules of the form $A \to v$ with $A \in N$ and $v \in V^\circ$; the corresponding types X of multiset grammars are denoted by $mARB$ and mCF, thus yielding the families of multiset languages $\mathcal{L}(X)$. Observe that $mARB$ and mCF are types with unit rules and trap rules (for $p = w \to v \in P$, we can take $p^{(+)} = w \to w$ and $p^{(-)} = w \to F$ where F is a new symbol – the trap symbol). Even with arbitrary multiset rules, it is not possible to get $Ps(\mathcal{L}(ARB))$ [17]:

$$\mathcal{L}(mCF) = Ps(\mathcal{L}(CF)) \subsetneqq \mathcal{L}(mARB) \subsetneqq Ps(\mathcal{L}(ARB)).$$

6.3   Results for String and Multiset Grammars

It is well-known, for example see [7], that

$$\mathcal{L}(CF\text{-}RC) = \mathcal{L}(CF\text{-}P_{ac}) = \mathcal{L}(ARB) = RE.$$

Based on Theorem 17, we immediately infer the following results:

Theorem 18. *For any* $Y \in \{RC, MAT_{ac}, GC_{ac}^{allfinal}, GC_{ac}, P_{ac}, A, AB\}$,

$$\mathcal{L}(CF\text{-}Y) = \mathcal{L}(ARB) = RE.$$

As in the case of multisets the structural information contained in the sequence of symbols cannot be used, arbitrary multiset rules are not sufficient for obtaining all sets in $Ps(\mathcal{L}(ARB))$. Yet we can easily show the following:

Theorem 19. *For any* $Y \in \{O, Pri, fC_1, fC, RC, MAT_{ac}, GC_{ac}^{allfinal}, GC_{ac}, A, AB\}$,

$$PsRE = Ps(\mathcal{L}(ARB)) = \mathcal{L}(mARB\text{-}Y).$$

Proof. $PsRE = Ps(\mathcal{L}(ARB)) = \mathcal{L}(mARB\text{-}O)$ was shown in [13], hence, the statement immediately follows from Theorem 17.   □

But also non-cooperative multiset rules are sufficient with many control mechanisms:

Theorem 20. *For any* $Y \in \{MAT_{ac}, GC_{ac}^{allfinal}, GC_{ac}, A, AB\}$,

$$PsRE = Ps(\mathcal{L}(ARB)) = \mathcal{L}(mCF\text{-}Y).$$

Proof. $PsRE = Ps(\mathcal{L}(ARB)) = \mathcal{L}(mCF\text{-}MAT_{ac})$ was shown in [17], hence, the statement immediately follows from Theorem 17.   □

6.4 Computational Completeness for Context-Free AB-Grammars with Two Non-terminal Symbols

In this subsection, we recall complexity results for context-free string and multiset grammars as shown in [3], showing that computational completeness can already be obtained with two non-terminal symbols, which result is optimal with respect to the number of non-terminal symbols.

Theorem 21. *Any recursively enumerable set of strings can be generated by a context-free AB-grammar using only two non-terminal symbols.*

Proof (Sketch). The main technical details of how to use only two non-terminal symbols A and B for generating a given recursively enumerable language follow the construction given in [13] for graph-controlled grammars. The most important to be shown here is how to simulate the ADD- and SUB-instructions of a deterministic register machine with the contents of the two working registers being given by the number of symbols A and B; only at the end, both numbers are zero, whereas in between, during the whole computation, at least one symbol A or B is present. The initial string is A, and one A is also the last symbol to be erased at the end in order to obtain a terminal string.

In the following, we use X to specify one of the two non-terminal symbols A and B, and Y then stands for the other one. For any label p of the register machine we use two labels p and p'. To simplify notations, we write $(p, q, t)_U$ instead of $(p, q, t) \in U$ for $U \in \{A, B\}$.

The simulations in the AB-grammar then work as follows:

- $p : (ADD(X), q)$ is simulated by $p : X \to XX$ and $p' : Y \to YX$ with
  $(p, p', 1)_B$ as well as $(p, q, 2)_A$, $(p, q', 3)_A$, and $(p', q, 1)_A$, $(p', q', 2)_A$;
- $p : (SUB(X), q, s)$ is simulated by $p : X \to \lambda$ and $p' : Y \to Y$ with
  $(p, p', 1)_B$ as well as $(p, q, 2)_A$, $(p, q', 3)_A$, and $(p', s, 1)_A$, $(p', s', 2)_A$;

in both cases, the application of the rule labeled by p blocks the rule labeled
by p'; in any case, for the next rule labeled r to be simulated, both r and r' are
activated, again r' following r one step later.

For the halting label h, only the labeled rule $h : \Lambda \to \lambda$ is to be activated. □

This result is optimal with respect to the number of non-terminal symbols:
as it has been shown in [9], even for graph-controlled context-free grammars one
non-terminal symbol is not enough, hence, the statement immediately follows
from Theorem 13. A similar optimal result holds for multiset grammars.

Theorem 22. *Any recursively enumerable set of multisets can be generated by
an AB-grammar using context-free multiset rules and only two non-terminal
symbols.*

Proof. Given a recursively enumerable set of multisets L over the terminal alphabet $T = \{a_1, \ldots, a_k\}$, we can construct a register machine M_L generating L in
the following way: instead of speaking of a number n in register r we use the notation a_r^n, i.e., a configuration of M_L is represented as a string over the alphabet
$V = T \cup \{a_{k+1}, a_{k+2}\}$ with the two non-terminal symbols a_{k+1}, a_{k+2}.

We start with one a_{k+1} and first generate an arbitrary multiset over T step
by step adding one element a_m from T and at the same time multiply the number
of symbols a_{k+1} by p_m, where p_m is the m-th prime number. At the end of this
procedure, for the multiset $a_1^{n_1} \ldots a_k^{n_k}$ we have obtained $a_m^{n_m}$ in each register
m, $1 \leq m \leq k$, and $a_{k+1}^{p_1^{n_1} \ldots p_k^{n_k}}$ in register $k+1$. As for example, already shown
in [18], only using registers $k+1$ and $k+2$, a deterministic register machine M_L'
simulating any number of registers by this prime number encoding can compute
starting with $a_{k+1}^{p_1^{n_1} \ldots p_k^{n_k}}$ and halt if and only if $a_1^{n_1} \ldots a_k^{n_k} \in L$. Only with
halting, all registers of M_L' are cleared to zero, i.e., we end up with only one a_{k+1}
in M_L when this deterministic register machine M_L' has reached its halting label
h. So the last step of M_L before halting is just to eliminate this last a_{k+1}. During
the whole computation of M_L, the sum of symbols a_{k+1} and a_{k+2} is greater than
zero. Hence, it only remains to show how to simulate the instructions of a register
machine, which is done in a similar way as in the preceding proof; we use X to
specify one of the two non-terminal symbols a_{k+1} and a_{k+2}, and Y then stands
for the other one, i.e., $X, Y \in \{a_{k+1}, a_{k+2}\}$. For any label p of the register
machine we use two labels p and p'. The simulations in the AB-grammar work
as follows:

- a non-deterministic ADD-instruction $p : (ADD(X), q, s)$ is simulated by
  branching into two deterministic ADD-instructions even twice:
  $p : X \to X$ and $p' : Y \to Y$ with $(p, p', 1)_B$ as well as $(p, (p, X, q), 2)_A$,
  $(p, (p, X, s), 2)_A$, and $(p', (p, Y, q), 1)_A$, $(p', (p, Y, s), 1)_A$; in the third step of

the simulation, we already know whether X is present or else we have to use Y; this now allows us to simulate the four deterministic ADD-instructions $(p, \alpha, \beta) : (ADD(X), \beta)$, $\alpha \in \{X, Y\}$, $\beta \in \{q, s\}$, in a simpler way by using the rules

$(p, \alpha, \beta) : \alpha \to \alpha X$

and the activations

$((p, \alpha, \beta), \beta, 1)_A$, $((p, \alpha, \beta), \beta', 2)_A$;

- $p : (ADD(X), q)$ is simulated by $p : X \to XX$ and $p' : Y \to YX$ with $(p, p', 1)_B$ as well as $(p, q, 2)_A$, $(p, q', 3)_A$, and $(p', q, 1)_A$, $(p', q', 2)_A$;
- $p : (SUB(X), q, s)$ is simulated by $p : X \to \lambda$ and $p' : Y \to Y$ with $(p, p', 1)_B$ as well as $(p, q, 2)_A$, $(p, q', 3)_A$, and $(p', s, 1)_A$, $(p', s', 2)_A$; in both cases, the application of the rule labeled by p blocks the rule labeled by p'; in any case, for the next rule labeled r to be simulated, both r and r' are activated, again r' following r one step later;
- for the halting label h, only the labeled rule $h : a_{r+1} \to \lambda$ is to be activated.

When the final rule $h : a_{r+1} \to \lambda$ is applied, no further rule is activated, thus the derivation ends yielding the multiset $a_1^{n_1} \ldots a_k^{n_k} \in L$ as terminal result. $\square$

7 Arrays and Array Grammars on Cayley Grids

As a natural extension of string languages (e.g., see [25, 26]), arrays on the d-dimensional grid $\mathbb{Z}^d$ have been introduced and investigated since more than four decades, for example, see [5]. Applications of array grammars and array automata especially can be found in the area of pattern and picture recognition, for instance, see [23, 24, 27].

Following some ideas of Erzsébet Csuhaj-Varjú and Victor Mitrana, the investigation of array grammars and array automata on Cayley grids of finitely presented groups was started in [14] and then continued in more detail in [15]. As a first example of arrays on a Cayley grid of a non-Abelian group we refer to [1], where arrays on the hexagonal grid were considered.

In this section, first the notions and definitions for arrays defined on Cayley grids of finitely presented groups as well as for array grammars generating sets of such arrays are recalled from [15]. Following the general results collected in Sect. 5, we immediately obtain many results for array grammars defined on Cayley grids of finitely presented groups equipped with these control mechanisms. When using #-context-free array productions in the underlying array grammars, together with most of these control mechanisms considered previously in this paper, the same computational power as with arbitrary array productions can be obtained, see [11].

7.1 Arrays on Cayley Grids

In this subsection we generalize the concept of d-dimensional arrays to arrays defined on Cayley grids. Let $G = \langle B \mid R \rangle$ be a finitely presented group with

$B = \{e_1, \ldots, e_m\}$ and G' denoting the set of group elements; moreover, let $C(G)$ be the Cayley graph of G with respect to B. Throughout the rest of the paper we will assume that $B^{-1} \subseteq B$, i.e., B contains all inverses of its elements. For paths in the Cayley graph this means that for each path $v = w_1 \to \ldots \to w_n = w$ in $C(G)$ from v to w also its inverse $w = w_n \to \ldots \to w_1 = v$ is a path in $C(G)$.

A finite *array* $\mathcal{A}$ over an alphabet V on G' is a function $\mathcal{A} : G' \to V \cup \{\#\}$, where $shape(\mathcal{A}) = \{v \in G' \mid \mathcal{A}(v) \neq \#\}$ is finite and $\# \notin V$ is called the *background* or *blank symbol*, i.e., the nodes of $C(G)$ get assigned elements of $V \cup \{\#\}$. We usually will write $\mathcal{A} = \{(v, \mathcal{A}(v)) \mid v \in shape(\mathcal{A})\}$.

By V^G we denote the set of arrays over V on G'; any subset of V^G is called an array language over V on G. With respect to the finite presentation of G by $C(G)$, instead of V^G we also write $V^{C(G)}$ to emphasize that.

The *empty array* in V^G has empty shape and is denoted by Λ_G. Ordering the generators in B in a specific way as $e_1 < \cdots < e_m$, for each array $\mathcal{A} = \{(v, \mathcal{A}(v)) \mid v \in shape(\mathcal{A})\}$ in $V^G \setminus \{\Lambda_G\}$ we get a canonical representation as a list $\langle (v_1, \mathcal{A}(v_1)), \ldots, (v_n, \mathcal{A}(v_n)) \rangle$ such that $\{v_i \mid 1 \leq i \leq n\} = shape(\mathcal{A})$ and $v_i < v_{i+1}$, $1 \leq i < n$, with respect to the length-plus-lexicographic ordering of strings with the elements of G written as sums of the elements in B (the length-plus-lexicographic ordering $\prec$ is a well-ordering, where for two strings u and v, $u \prec v$ if either $|u| < |v|$ or $|u| = |v|$, $u = xay$, $v = xby$, and $a < b$). In terms of $C(G)$ this means that the elements of the array are listed in the length-plus-lexicographic ordering of the paths in $C(G)$ seen from the origin (the identity).

Example 23. Consider the hexagonal grid from Example 5. Then the "position" abc can also be reached by taking the path cba from the "origin" (the identity e). Hence, with taking the ordering $a < b < c$, the canonical representation of the array $\mathcal{A} = \{(ab, X), (abc, Y) \mid v \in shape(\mathcal{A})\} \in \{X, Y\}^{C(\langle a,b,c \mid a^2, b^2, c^2, (abc)^2 \rangle)}$ is $\langle (ab, X), (abc, Y) \rangle$.

Example 24. A *d-dimensional array* is an array over the free group $\mathbb{Z}^d$. If we take the unit vectors $e_k = (0, \ldots, 1, \ldots, 0)$ and their inverses $(0, \ldots, -1, \ldots, 0)$, the resulting Cayley graph is the well-known d-dimensional grid.

For any $v \in G'$, the *translation* $\tau_v : G' \to G'$ is defined by $\tau_v(w) = w \circ v$ for all $w \in G'$, and for any array $\mathcal{A} \in V^{C(G)}$ we define $\tau_v(\mathcal{A})$, the corresponding array translated by v, by $(\tau_v(\mathcal{A}))(w) = \mathcal{A}(w \circ v^{-1})$ for all $w \in G'$.

An array $\mathcal{A} \in V^{C(G)}$ is called *k-connected* if for any two elements v and w in $shape(\mathcal{A})$ there is a path $v = w_1 \to \cdots \to w_n = w$ in $C(G)$ with $\{w_1, \ldots, w_n\} \subseteq shape(\mathcal{A})$ such that for the distance in $C(G)$ between w_i and w_{i-1}, $d(w_i, w_{i-1})$, we have $d(w_i, w_{i-1}) \leq k$ for all $1 < i \leq n$; the distance $d(x, y)$ between two nodes x and y in $C(G)$ is defined as the length of the shortest path between x and y in $C(G)$. The subset of k-connected arrays in $V^{C(G)}$ is denoted by $V^{C(G)_k}$.

Example 25. Consider the set of one-dimensional arrays over the alphabet $\{a\}$, i.e., $\{a\}^{C(\langle (1), (-1) \rangle)}$, which in a simpler way we will also write as $\{a\}^{\mathbb{Z}^1}$. Then the

1-dimensional array $\{((0),a),((k),a)\} \in \{a\}^{\mathbb{Z}^1}$ is m-connected, i.e., in $\{a\}^{\mathbb{Z}^1_m}$, if and only if $m \geq k$.

7.2   Array Grammars on Cayley Grids

For a finitely presented group $G = \langle B \mid R \rangle$ with the set of elements G', we define an *array production* p over V and G as a triple $(W, \mathcal{A}_1, \mathcal{A}_2)$, where $W \subseteq G'$ is a finite set and $\mathcal{A}_1$ and $\mathcal{A}_2$ are mappings from W to $V \cup \{\#\}$ such that $shape(\mathcal{A}_1) \neq \emptyset$, where again the shape is defined to exactly contain the non-blank positions, i.e., $shape(\mathcal{A}_1) = \{v \in W \mid \mathcal{A}(v) \neq \#\}$. We say that the array $\mathcal{C}_2 \in V^{C(G)}$ is *directly derivable* from the array $\mathcal{C}_1 \in V^{C(G)}$ by the array production $(W, \mathcal{A}_1, \mathcal{A}_2)$ if and only if there exists a $v \in G'$ such that, for all $w \in G' \setminus \tau_v(W)$, $\mathcal{C}_1(w) = \mathcal{C}_2(w)$, as well as, for all $w \in \tau_v(W)$, $\mathcal{C}_1(w) = \mathcal{A}_1(\tau_{-v}(w))$ and $\mathcal{C}_2(w) = \mathcal{A}_2(\tau_{-v}(w))$, i.e., the sub-array of $\mathcal{C}_1$ corresponding to $\mathcal{A}_1$ is replaced by $\mathcal{A}_2$, thus yielding $\mathcal{C}_2$; we also write $\mathcal{C}_1 \Longrightarrow_p \mathcal{C}_2$.

As we already see from the definitions of an array production, the conditions for an application to an array $\mathcal{B}$ and the result of an application to $\mathcal{B}$, an array production $(W, \mathcal{A}_1, \mathcal{A}_2)$ is a representative for the infinite set of equivalent array productions of the form $(\tau_v(W), \tau_v(\mathcal{A}_1), \tau_v(\mathcal{A}_2))$ with $v \in G'$. Hence, without loss of generality, we can assume $e \in W$ (e is the identity in G) as well as $\mathcal{A}_1(e) \neq \#$. Moreover, we often will omit the set W, because it is uniquely reconstructible from the description of the two mappings $\mathcal{A}_1$ and $\mathcal{A}_2$ by $\mathcal{A}_i = \{(v, \mathcal{A}_i(v)) \mid v \in W\}$, for $1 \leq i \leq 2$. Thus, in the following, we represent the array production $(W, \mathcal{A}_1, \mathcal{A}_2)$ also by writing $\mathcal{A}_1 \to \mathcal{A}_2$, i.e., $\{(v, \mathcal{A}_1(v)) \mid v \in W\} \to \{(v, \mathcal{A}_2(v)) \mid v \in W\}$. If $|W| = 2$, i.e., $W = \{e, v\}$ for some $v \in G'$, then, for $\{(e, \mathcal{A}_1(e)), (v, \mathcal{A}_1(v))\} \to \{(e, \mathcal{A}_2(e)), (v, \mathcal{A}_2(v))\}$ we will only write $\mathcal{A}_1(e) v \mathcal{A}_1(v) \to \mathcal{A}_2(e) \mathcal{A}_2(v)$. If $|W| = 1$, i.e., $W = \{e\}$, we simply write $\mathcal{A}_1(e) \to \mathcal{A}_2(e)$.

$G_A = \left((N \cup T)^{C(G)}, T^{C(G)}, \mathcal{A}_0, P, \Longrightarrow_{G_A} \right)$ is called an array grammar over $C(G)$, where N is the alphabet of *non-terminal symbols*, T is the alphabet of *terminal symbols*, $N \cap T = \emptyset$; P is a finite non-empty set of array productions over V, where $V = N \cup T$; $\mathcal{A}_0 \in V^{C(G)}$ is the *initial array* (axiom), and $\Longrightarrow_{G_A}$ denotes the derivation relation induced by the array productions in P. In the following, we may omit $\Longrightarrow_{G_A}$ in the description of the array grammars.

In a more common notation, we also write an *array grammar* (over $C(G)$) as a septuple
$$G_A = (C(G), N, T, \#, P, \mathcal{A}_0, \Longrightarrow_{G_A}),$$
also specifying the background symbol $\# \notin N \cup T$, and, as usually done in the literature, we shall assume $\mathcal{A}_0 = \{(v_0, S)\}$, where $v_0 \in G'$ is the *start node*, and $S \in N$ is the *start symbol*.

We say that the array $\mathcal{B}_2 \in V^{C(G)}$ is *directly derivable* from the array $\mathcal{B}_1 \in V^{C(G)}$ in G_A, denoted $\mathcal{B}_1 \Longrightarrow_{G_A} \mathcal{B}_2$, if and only if there exists an array production $p = (W, \mathcal{A}_1, \mathcal{A}_2)$ in P such that $\mathcal{B}_1 \Longrightarrow_p \mathcal{B}_2$. Let $\Longrightarrow^*_{G_A}$ be the reflexive transitive closure of $\Longrightarrow_{G_A}$. The *array language generated* by the array grammar G_A, $L(G_A)$, is defined by $L(G_A) = \{\mathcal{A} \mid \mathcal{A} \in T^{C(G)}, \mathcal{A}_0 \Longrightarrow^*_{G_A} \mathcal{A}\}$.

An array production $p = (W, \mathcal{A}_1, \mathcal{A}_2)$ in P is called #-*context-free* (*of type* #-*CFA*), if $|shape\,(\mathcal{A}_1)| = 1$, i.e., $shape\,(\mathcal{A}_1) = \{e\}$, and $\mathcal{A}_1\,(e) \in N$.

For $X \in \{ARBA, \#\text{-}CFA\}$, an array grammar G is called to be of type X, if every array production in P is of the corresponding type, where $ARBA$ means that there are no restrictions on the form of the array productions. The family of k-connected array languages generated by array grammars on $C\,(G)$ of type X is denoted by $\mathcal{L}_k\,(C\,(G)\text{-}X)$; the family of arbitrary array languages generated by array grammars on $C\,(G)$ of type X is denoted by $\mathcal{L}\,(C\,(G)\text{-}X)$.

For arbitrary and #-context-free array grammars the condition to only consider languages of k-connected arrays corresponds to intersecting the generated array language with $V^{C(G)_k}$, which can be carried out by arbitrary array grammars by themselves (as, for example, proved in [11]), but is a condition imposed from "outside" when dealing with #-context-free array grammars. Yet as later we are going to show that some #-context-free array grammars equipped with specific control mechanisms can simulate any arbitrary array grammar this makes no difference any more in these cases.

Example 26. Let $G = \langle B \mid R \rangle$ be a finitely presented group and $x \in G$ with $ord\,(x) = \infty$. Let $b_1 \circ \ldots \circ b_k$ be the canonical representation of x in $\langle B \mid R \rangle$; then $(\{x^n \mid n \in \mathbb{Z}\}, \circ)$ is an infinite subgroup of G, and $x^n \neq x^m$ for $n \neq m$. Hence, along this "infinite line" we can argue many results obtained for $\mathbb{Z}^1$, e.g., how to embed simulations of Turing machine computations.

Remark 27. The possibility to compute along such infinite lines is also important if we want to (describe how to) simulate computations of a Turing machine – or similar computationally complete mechanisms (for strings) – using specific variants of (controlled) array grammars on Cayley graphs. For instance, for any computable finite group presentation of a group $\langle B \mid R \rangle$, we can effectively construct an encoding of any array language in $\mathcal{L}\,(C\,(G)\text{-}ARBA)$ given by an (arbitrary) array grammar and vice versa. The finite group presentation of the group $\langle B \mid R \rangle$ being computable is crucial for this result.

For simulating array grammars of type $C\,(G)\text{-}ARBA$, a special normal form we call *marked normal form* is very helpful; it has already been described for 1-dimensional array grammars in [12] as a special variant of the Chomsky normal form for array grammars, shown, for example, in [10], and exhibited for the general case of array grammars on Cayley grids in [11].

Lemma 28 (marked normal form). *For every array grammar of type* $C\,(G)$ - $ARBA$

$$G_A = (C\,(G), N, T, \#, P, \{(v_0, S)\}, \Longrightarrow_{G_A}),$$

we can effectively construct an equivalent array grammar of type $C\,(G)\text{-}ARBA$

$$\bar{G}_A = (C\,(G), N', T, \#, P', \{(v_0, \bar{S})\}, \Longrightarrow_{\bar{G}_A}),$$

where $N \subseteq N'$ *and all array productions in* P' *are of one of the following forms:*

1. $\bar{A}B \to C\bar{D}$, *where* $A, B, C, D \in N' \cup T$, *or*

2. $\bar{\#} \to \#$.

Before the final array production $\bar{\#} \to \#$ is applied, any intermediate array derived from the initial array $\{(v_0, \bar{S})\}$ contains exactly one barred symbol.

For applying the general results on the relations between different control mechanisms as elaborated in the rest of this section to array grammars of the types $C(G)$-$ARBA$ and $C(G)$-$\#$-CFA, the following feature of these types is essential in some cases:

Lemma 29. *The types $C(G)$-$ARBA$ and $C(G)$-$\#$-CFA – for a Cayley grid $C(G)$ – are strictly extended types with unit rules and trap rules.*

Proof. We first remark that, without loss of generality (e.g., see [11]), we may always assume that any array production contains at least one non-terminal symbol in the array on its left-hand side, i.e., in any array production $\{(v, \mathcal{A}_1(v)) \mid v \in W\} \to \{(v, \mathcal{A}_2(v)) \mid v \in W\}$ we find at least one $v_1 \in W$ such that $\mathcal{A}_1(v_1) \in N$; hence, $C(G)$-$ARBA$ can be assumed to be a strictly extended type for the succeeding proofs; $C(G)$-$\#$-CFA is a strictly extended type already by definition. Now let

$$G_A = (C(G), N, T, \#, P, \{(v_0, S)\}, \Longrightarrow_{G_A})$$

be an array grammar of type $C(G)$-$ARBA$ or $C(G)$-$\#$-CFA.

Then for every array production $p = (W, \mathcal{A}_1, \mathcal{A}_2)$ the corresponding *unit rule* is $p^+ = (W, \mathcal{A}_1, \mathcal{A}_1)$, which, when being applied, obviously does not change the underlying array.

Moreover, for the trap rules, take a new non-terminal symbol F, the *trap symbol*, which never can be erased any more, and for every array production $p = (W, \mathcal{A}_1, \mathcal{A}_2)$ we then define the corresponding *trap rule* $p^- = (W, \mathcal{A}_1, \mathcal{F}_W)$ with $\mathcal{F}_W(v) = F$ for all $v \in W$, which, when being applied, prohibits the derived array to become terminal no matter how the derivation proceeds.

In sum, we conclude that both $C(G)$-$ARBA$ and $C(G)$-$\#$-CFA are strictly extended types with unit rules and trap rules. □

7.3   Results for Array Grammars on Cayley Grids

In many papers on control mechanisms for string grammars, the proof for showing that when using arbitrary productions any new control mechanism can be simulated is omitted, often simply citing the Church-Turing thesis, which usually is a legitimate claim as any formal proof would be tedious although bringing no new insights. In case of array grammars on Cayley graphs the situation is more delicate: as long as the underlying group presentation is computable, one might still easily argue with the Church-Turing thesis as long as – for infinite groups – there is also an infinite path in the Cayley graph, which is obvious if there is a group element of infinite order – see Example 26 as well as Remark 27. Yet even if there is no such element (for examples of such group presentations we refer to [15]), in a nondeterministic way, we can find lines of arbitrary length for the necessary computations, as by definition the out-degree of every node is bounded, hence, by König's infinity lemma such a path must exist; it is important to observe that these paths need not always be computable. Therefore, in the general case of Cayley grids we need an algorithm that works directly with the power inherent to arbitrary array productions. As, according to Theorem 17, GC_{ac} is the "strongest" control mechanism, only the following result is needed (for a proof, we refer to [11]):

Lemma 30. $\mathcal{L}\left(C\left(G\right)\text{-}ARBA\text{-}GC_{ac}\right) \subseteq \mathcal{L}\left(C\left(G\right)\text{-}ARBA\right).$

In connection with the results depicted in Theorem 17, from Lemma 30 we immediately infer the following:

Theorem 31. $\mathcal{L}\left(C\left(G\right)\text{-}ARBA\text{-}Y\right) = \mathcal{L}\left(C\left(G\right)\text{-}ARBA\right)$ *for any control mechanism* Y *in* $\{O, Pri, fC_1, fC, RC, MAT_{ac}, GC_{ac}^{allfinal}, GC_{ac}, GC^{allfinal}, GC, A, AB, pC, MAT, P, P_{ac}\}.$

Already an order relation on the rules is sufficient as a control mechanism to obtain $\mathcal{L}\left(C\left(G\right)\text{-}ARBA\right)$ with #-free array productions (see [11]):

Theorem 32. $\mathcal{L}\left(C\left(G\right)\text{-}ARBA\right) \subseteq \mathcal{L}\left(C\left(G\right)\text{-}\#\text{-}CFA\text{-}O\right).$

Proof. Let $G = \langle B \mid R \rangle$ be a finitely presented group and L be an array language on $C\left(G\right)$ given by an array grammar G_A in marked normal form, see Lemma 28. Moreover, let $G'_A = \left(C\left(G\right), N, T', \#, P, \{(v_0, S')\}, \Longrightarrow_{G'_A}\right)$ be the array grammar on $C\left(G\right)$ with $T' = \{X_a \mid a \in T\}$, i.e., we replace every terminal symbol $a \in T$ from G_A by a corresponding non-terminal symbol X_a in all the array productions of G_A. We now construct an equivalent ordered array grammar $G_O = (G_s, \prec, \Longrightarrow_{G_O})$ first simulating the derivations in G'_A corresponding to derivations in G_A with the only difference that instead of the terminal symbols $a \in T$ we have the corresponding non-terminal symbols X_a, and at the end these symbols X_a are transformed into the terminal symbols $a \in T$.

The main idea is to first generate a workspace of non-terminal symbols $X_\#$ representing the blank symbol surrounded with a border of symbols $\tilde{X}_\#$ also representing #; symbols $X_\#, \tilde{X}_\#$ still occurring in the derived array at the end of a simulation of a derivation in G'_A finally will be erased as to be described later in the proof. Moreover, at the very beginning, we generate a control symbol at some place, chosen in a non-deterministic way, not interfering with the workspace, but needed for the simulations of the application of rules in G'_A. The main task then is to show how a marked array production $\bar{A}vB \rightarrow C\bar{D}$, where $A, B, C, D \in N$, can be simulated by using a suitable order relation on the rules in G_O.

We first sketch how to obtain the control symbol and the workspace: Instead of starting with $\{(v_0, S)\}$ in G_A we start with the initial array $\{(v_0, S')\}$ in G'_A. Using any of the rules $S'v\# \rightarrow S''H_A$ for any $v \in B$ and then rules of the form $H_Au\# \rightarrow \#H_A$ for any $u \in B$, the initial control symbol H_A can move to any position (node) in the Cayley graph. Using the rule $H_A \rightarrow H_0$ ends this procedure and then allows the rule $S'' \rightarrow \tilde{S}$ to be applied, which is "dominated" by the rules in $H^- \setminus \{H_0 \to F\}$, i.e., $S'' \to \tilde{S} \prec p$ for all $p \in H^- \setminus \{H_0 \to F\}$, where $H^- = \{X \to F \mid X \in V_H\}$ and V_H denotes the set of all variants of the control variable H like H_A at the beginning.

Notation: In the following, the set of all trap rules "dominating" a rule p will be written as $P(p \prec)$, i.e., $P(p \prec) = \{q \mid p \prec q\}$.

In general, the idea with the variants of the control variable H is to guide the application of another rule p by, instead of checking for the presence of the specific variant H_α of H, ensuring the absence of all other variants of H, using the rule relations $p \prec q$ for all $q \in \{X \to F \mid X \in V_H \setminus \{H_\alpha\}\}$; hence, we also write $P(p \prec) = \{X \to F \mid X \in V_H \setminus \{H_\alpha\}\}$.

The next task is to generate sufficient workspace of symbols $X_\#$ surrounded by a layer of symbols $\tilde{X}_\#$ on the border to the remaining environment of blank symbols: We start with

$$p_0 = \{(e, \tilde{S}\} \cup \{(v, \# \mid v \in B\} \to \{(e, \bar{S}\} \cup \{(v, \tilde{X}_\# \mid v \in B\},$$
$$P(p_0 \prec) = \{X \to F \mid X \in V_H \setminus \{H_0\}\}.$$

Iteratively, now a new "layer" of symbols $X_\#$ is added by first generating symbols $\hat{X}_\#$ from the symbols $\tilde{X}_\#$, then renaming the symbols $\tilde{X}_\#$ to $X_\#$ and finally renaming the symbols $\hat{X}_\#$ to $\tilde{X}_\#$, which is accomplished by the following rules p and the corresponding "dominating" set of rules $P(p \prec)$:

1. $H_0 \to H_1$, $P(H_0 \to H_1 \prec) = \{\tilde{S} \to F\}$;
2. for all $v \in B$,
   $p_v^1 = \{(e, \tilde{X}_\#), (v, \#)\} \to \{(e, \tilde{X}_\#), (v, \hat{X}_\#)\}$, $P(p_v^1 \prec) = \{X \to F \mid X \in V_H \setminus \{H_1\}\}$, $H_1 \to H_2$, $P(H_1 \to H_2 \prec) = \{p_v^{1^-} \mid v \in B\}$, where $p_v^{1^-}$ is the trap rule corresponding to the rule p_v^1, i.e., $p_v^{1^-} = \{(e, \tilde{X}_\#), (v, \#)\} \to \{(e, F), (v, F)\}$;
3. for all $v \in B$,
   $p_v^2 = \tilde{X}_\# \to X_\#$, $P(p_v^2 \prec) = \{X \to F \mid X \in V_H \setminus \{H_2\}\}$, $H_2 \to H_3$, $P(H_2 \to H_3 \prec) = \{p_v^{2^-} \mid v \in B\}$;
4. for all $v \in B$,
   $p_v^3 = \hat{X}_\# \to \tilde{X}_\#$, $P(p_v^3 \prec) = \{X \to F \mid X \in V_H \setminus \{H_3\}\}$, $H_3 \to H_1$, $P(H_3 \to H_1 \prec) = \{p_v^{3^-} \mid v \in B\}$; the iteration can start again with 2.
5. In order to stop the iteration, instead of $H_3 \to H_1$ we use the rule $H_3 \to H$, $P(H_3 \to H \prec) = \{p_v^{3^-} \mid v \in B\}$.

For the simulation in G_O we assume the marked array productions in G_A to be labeled, i.e., we write $p : \bar{A}_p v_p B_p \to C_p \bar{D}_p$.

1. We start the simulation of the application of $p : \bar{A}_p v_p B_p \to C_p \bar{D}_p$ with indicating the intention to do that by the rule $H \to H_p^1$ for the control symbol;
2. we continue with marking exactly one symbol B_p as B_p' by
   $p_1 = B_p \to B_p'$, $P(p_1 \prec) = \{X \to F \mid X \in (V_H \setminus \{H_p^1\}) \cup \{B_p'\}\}$, $H_p^1 \to H_p^2$, $P(H_p^1 \to H_p^2 \prec) = P_F$, $P_F = \{Xv\# \to FF \mid X \in N \cup \{X_\#\}, v \in B\}$,
   i.e., no blank symbol inside the workspace is allowed yet;

3. we now make a "#-hole" inside the workspace in such a way that the only non-terminal symbol having "access" to this blank position should be $\bar{A}_p$ by
$$p_2 = B'_p \to \#, \; P(p_2 \prec) = \{X \to F \mid X \in (V_H \setminus \{H_p^2\})\},$$
$$H_p^2 \to H_p^3, \; P(H_p^2 \to H_p^3 \prec) = P_F \setminus \{\bar{A}_p v_p \# \to FF\};$$
4. the "#-hole" made in the previous step now is filled correctly by
$$p_3 = \bar{A}_p v_p \# \to C_p \bar{D}_p, \; P(p_3 \prec) = \{X \to F \mid X \in (V_H \setminus \{H_p^3\})\},$$
$$H_p^3 \to H, \; P(H_p^3 \to H \prec) = P_F.$$

Using the sequence of rules as described above, we finally have simulated the application of the rule $p : \bar{A}_p v_p B_p \to C_p \bar{D}_p$ and reached the control symbol H again, which allows us to continue with simulating the next rule. At some moment we have to check whether we can switch to the terminal procedure eliminating all non-terminal symbols from $X_\#, \tilde{X}_\#, \bar{X}_\#$ and transforming every non-terminal symbol X_a, $a \in T$, into the corresponding terminal symbol a:

1. We start with $H \to H_t$,
$$P(H \to H_t \prec) = \{X \to F \mid X \in (V \setminus (\{X_a \mid a \in T\} \cup \{X_\#, \tilde{X}_\#, \bar{X}_\#\}))\};$$
2. for all $X \in \{X_\#, \tilde{X}_\#, \bar{X}_\#\}$, we take
$$p_X = X \to \#, \; P(p_X \prec) = \{X \to F \mid X \in (V_H \setminus \{H_t\})\};$$
3. for all $a \in T$, we take
$$p_a = X_a \to a, \; P(p_X \prec) = \{X \to F \mid X \in (V_H \setminus \{H_t\})\};$$
4. finally the control symbol H_t can be erased with
$$H_t \to \#, \; P(H_t \to \# \prec) = \{X \to F \mid X \in (V \setminus \{H_t\})\}.$$

Based on the construction of G_O and the explanations given above we conclude $L(G_O) = L$.   □

Looking at the general results collected in Theorem 17 we immediately infer the following results:

Corollary 33. *For any* $Y \in \{O, Pri, fC_1, fC, RC, MAT_{ac}, GC_{ac}^{allfinal}, GC_{ac}, A, AB\}$,
$$\mathcal{L}\left(C\left(G\right)\text{-}ARBA\right) \subseteq \mathcal{L}\left(C\left(G\right)\text{-}\#\text{-}CFA\text{-}Y\right).$$

A similar result can be shown for programmed array grammars by proving the following equality (for a proof, see [11]):

Lemma 34. $\mathcal{L}\left(C\left(G\right)\text{-}\#\text{-}CFA\text{-}PC_{ac}\right) = \mathcal{L}\left(C\left(G\right)\text{-}\#\text{-}CFA\text{-}GC_{ac}^{allfinal}\right).$

Combining all the general results depicted in this section, we obtain the main theorem for sequential array grammars on Cayley graphs of finitely presented groups with control mechanisms:

Theorem 35. *For any* $Y \in \{O, Pri, fC_1, fC, RC, MAT_{ac}, GC_{ac}^{allfinal}, GC_{ac}, A, AB, P_{ac}\}$,
$$\mathcal{L}\left(C\left(G\right)\text{-}\#\text{-}CFA\text{-}Y\right) = \mathcal{L}\left(C\left(G\right)\text{-}ARBA\right).$$

Similar results hold for languages of k-connected arrays:

Theorem 36. *For any* $Y \in \{O, Pri, fC_1, fC, RC, MAT_{ac}, GC_{ac}^{allfinal}, GC_{ac}, A, AB, P_{ac}\}$,
$$\mathcal{L}_k\left(C\left(G\right)\text{-}\#\text{-}CFA\text{-}Y\right) = \mathcal{L}_k\left(C\left(G\right)\text{-}ARBA\right).$$

8   Cooperating Distributed Grammar Systems

Basic results on the generating power of hybrid cooperating distributed grammar systems were established by Mitrana [19] and by Păun [21]; a general overview on this area of formal language theory is given in the monograph by Csuhj-Varjú, Dassow, Kelemen, and Păun [6].

Let $G = (O, O_T, w, P, \Longrightarrow_G)$ be a grammar of type X; for the basic derivation modes from

$$B = \{*, t\} \cup \{\leq k, = k, \geq k \mid k \geq 1\}$$

and any objects $u, v \in O$ we define

- $u \Longrightarrow_G^* v$ to denote the usual reflexive and transitive closure of $\Longrightarrow_G$;
- $u \Longrightarrow_G^t v$ if and only if $u \Longrightarrow_G^* v$ and no rule from P is applicable to v;
- $u \Longrightarrow_G^{\leq k} v$, $u \Longrightarrow_G^{=k} v$, $u \Longrightarrow_G^{\geq k} v$ if and only if $u \Longrightarrow_G^* v$ in at most k, exactly k, at least k derivation steps.

A *hybrid cooperating distributed grammar system* (*HCDG system* for short) G_{HCDG} of degree n and type X working in the derivation modes from $B' \subseteq B$ is a construct

$$G_{HCDG} = (G, P_1, \ldots, P_n, f_1, \ldots, f_n, \Longrightarrow_{G_{HCDG}})$$

where $P_i \subseteq P$ and $f_i \in B'$ for $1 \leq i \leq n$, $\cup_{i=1}^n P_i = P$, and the grammars G and $G_i = (O, O_T, w, P_i, \Longrightarrow_{G_i})$, $1 \leq i \leq n$, are grammars of type X, the derivation relations $\Longrightarrow_{G_i}$ being the restrictions of $\Longrightarrow_G$ only induced by the corresponding rule sets P_i. For any $u, v \in O$, we define $u \Longrightarrow_{G_{HCDG}} v$ if and only if $u \Longrightarrow_{G_i}^{f_i} v$ for some i, $1 \leq i \leq n$. We remark that the component P_i, i.e., the grammar G_i, in each step of the derivation in G_{HCDG} is chosen in a non-deterministic way, which also means that even the same component may be taken several times in a row.

A *cooperating distributed grammar system* (*CDG system* for short) G_{CDG} of degree n and type X working in the derivation mode f with $f \in B$ is a special case of a hybrid cooperating distributed grammar system where all derivation modes f_i equal f, i.e., a construct $G_{CDG} = (G, P_1, \ldots, P_n, f, \Longrightarrow_{G_{CDG}})$ where $P_i \subseteq P$ for $1 \leq i \leq n$, $\cup_{i=1}^n P_i = P$, and the grammars G and $G_i = (O, O_T, w, P_i, \Longrightarrow_{G_i})$, $1 \leq i \leq n$, are grammars of type X. For any $u, v \in O$, we define $u \Longrightarrow_{G_{CDG}} v$ if and only if $u \Longrightarrow_{G_i}^f v$ for some i, $1 \leq i \leq n$.

The language generated by the HCDG system G_{HCDG} is defined by $L(G_{HCDG}) = \{v \in O_T \mid w \Longrightarrow_{G_{HCDG}}^* v\}$. The family of languages generated by hybrid grammar systems of degree n and of type X working in derivation modes from B' is denoted by $\mathcal{L}(X\text{-}HCDG_n(B'))$, the family of languages generated by grammar systems of degree n and of type X working in the derivation mode f is denoted by $\mathcal{L}(X\text{-}CDG_n(f))$; in both cases we replace n by $*$ if we consider arbitrary degrees.

As a special subset of derivation modes, we consider $B_0 = \{*, = 1, \geq 1\} \cup \{\leq k \mid k \geq 1\}$, for which the following result holds:

Theorem 37. *For any type X, any $B' \subseteq B_0$, and any $n \geq 1$,*

$$\mathcal{L}(X) = \mathcal{L}(X\text{-}HCDG_n(B')).$$

Proof. Consider any HCDG system

$$G_{HCDG} = (G, P_1, \ldots, P_n, f_1, \ldots, f_n, \Longrightarrow_{G_{HCDG}})$$

where the underlying grammar is $G = (O, O_T, w, P, \Longrightarrow_G)$, $P_i \subseteq P$ and $f_i \in B'$ for $1 \leq i \leq n$, $\cup_{i=1}^n P_i = P$, and the grammars G and $G_i = (O, O_T, w, P_i, \Longrightarrow_{G_i})$, $1 \leq i \leq n$, are grammars of type X. Now any derivation $u \Longrightarrow_{G_i}^{f_i} v$ for some i, $1 \leq i \leq n$, using n steps can also be obtained by using n times the derivation mode $= 1$ with grammar G_i, which holds for every derivation mode f_i from B_0. On the other hand, every derivation mode f_i from B_0 allows for making only one derivation step before changing to any grammar G_j, $1 \leq j \leq n$.

As $\cup_{i=1}^n P_i = P$, we obtain $L(G) = L(G_{HCDG})$ for any such hybrid cooperating distributed grammar system G_{HCDG} over the set of derivation modes B_0, which observation concludes the proof. $\qquad\Box$

Theorem 38. *For any strictly extended type X, $\mathcal{L}(X) = \mathcal{L}(X\text{-}CDG_1(t))$.*

Proof. Consider a CDG system $G_{CDG} = (G, P, t, \Longrightarrow_{G_{CDG}})$ with $G = (O, O_T, w, P, \Longrightarrow_G)$ being the underlying grammar of type X. As X is a strictly extended type, any derivation in G leading to a terminal object w is maximal, i.e., $w \in L(G_{CDG})$, hence, $L(G) \subseteq L(G_{CDG})$. On the other hand, as in G_{CDG} we only have one component using exactly the same rules as in G, we also have $L(G_{CDG}) \subseteq L(G)$, hence, we conclude $L(G) = L(G_{CDG})$, and therefore $\mathcal{L}(X) = \mathcal{L}(X\text{-}CDG_1(t))$. $\qquad\Box$

The equality relation established in the preceding theorem between $\mathcal{L}(X)$ and $\mathcal{L}(X\text{-}CDG_1(t))$ need not be true for pure types, as the following simple example shows:

Example 39. Consider the grammar $G = \left(\{a\}^+, \{a\}^+, a, P, \Longrightarrow_G\right)$ with the set of rules $P = \{a \to a^2, a \to \lambda\}$ to constitute the simple pure type X_1.

Obviously, $L(G) = \{a\}^*$, hence, we get $\mathcal{L}(X_1) = \{\{a\}^*\}$.

The only $CDG_1(t)$ system of type X_1 is $G_{CDG} = (G, P, t, \Longrightarrow_{G_{CDG}})$, but $L(G_{CDG}) = \{\lambda\}$, because every terminating derivation in G_{CDG} must end in λ. Hence, $\mathcal{L}(X_1\text{-}CDG_1(t)) = \{\{\lambda\}\}$.

Thus, we obtain $\mathcal{L}(X_1) = \{\{a\}^*\} \neq \{\{\lambda\}\} = \mathcal{L}(X_1\text{-}CDG_1(t))$.

Again, the computational power of HCDG systems can be captured by GC_{ac} as control mechanism, which according to Theorem 17 is the "strongest" one.

Lemma 40. *Let X be any strictly extended type X, $B' \subseteq B$, $n \geq 1$, and*

$$G_{HCDG} = (G, P_1, \ldots, P_n, f_1, \ldots, f_n, \Longrightarrow_{G_{HCDG}})$$

be an arbitrary HCDG system, where $G = (O, O_T, w, P, \Longrightarrow_G)$ is the underlying grammar of type X, $P_i \subseteq P$, $f_i \in B'$ for $1 \leq i \leq n$, $\cup_{i=1}^{n} P_i = P$, and the grammars $G_i = (O, O_T, w, P_i, \Longrightarrow_{G_i})$, $1 \leq i \leq n$, are grammars of type X. Then we can construct an equivalent graph-controlled grammar (with applicability checking) of type X $G_{GC} = (G, g, H_i, H_f, \Longrightarrow_{GC})$ such that $L(G_{HCDG}) = L(G_{GC})$. Moreover, if $t \notin B'$, then applicability checking is not needed in G_{GC}.

Proof. Given the HCDG system G_{HCDG} and its underlying grammar G, which is the underlying grammar of the graph-controlled grammar G_{GC}, too, for G_{GC} we only have to specify the control graph $g = (H, E, K)$ as well as the sets $H_i \subseteq H$ and $H_f \subseteq H$ of initial and final labels, respectively. This can be achieved by defining subgraphs of g, which are constructed using different graphs for each derivation mode $f \in B$; for every $1 \leq i \leq n$, the nodes in the subgraphs described in the following then have assigned the set of rules P_i by K, whatever the corresponding $f_i \in B$ may be. The nodes in the graphs are of one of the following types:

normal node node label $n \in H$: n $\bigcirc$

initial node node label $n \in H_i$: n $\bullet$

In the whole control graph, there is only one *final node* which has no rules assigned to, and its label is the only one in H_f. The simulation of derivation modes in B now can be described as follows (for the derivation modes $*$ and ≤ 1 we assume that at least one derivation step is made):

derivation mode $= 1$ **or** ≤ 1: $\bullet \xrightarrow{\ Y\ } E$

derivation mode $*$ **or** ≥ 1: $Y \circlearrowleft \bullet \xrightarrow{\ Y\ } E$

derivation mode $\leq k$, $k \geq 2$:

$$\overset{1}{\bullet} \xrightarrow{\ Y\ } \cdots \overset{k}{\bigcirc}$$
$$\quad\downarrow Y \qquad\qquad \downarrow Y$$
$$\quad E \qquad\qquad\;\; E$$

derivation mode $= k$, $k \geq 2$: $\overset{1}{\bullet} \xrightarrow{\ Y\ } \cdots \overset{k}{\bigcirc} \xrightarrow{\ Y\ } E$

derivation mode $\geq k$, $k \geq 2$: $Y \circlearrowleft \overset{1}{\bullet} \xrightarrow{\ Y\ } \cdots \overset{k}{\bigcirc} \xrightarrow{\ Y\ } E$

derivation mode t: $Y \circlearrowleft \bullet \xrightarrow{\ N\ } E$

Putting together the subgraphs for the components

$$G_i = (O, O_T, w, P_i, \Longrightarrow_{G_i}), 1 \leq i \leq n,$$

we obtain the complete control graph $g = (H, E, K)$ by letting every edge pointing to E leading to the initial nodes of all the subgraphs as well as to the *final* node.

'We finally observe that only in the construction of the subgraph for the derivation mode t an edge labeled by N is needed, i.e., only in this case applicability checking is needed, which observation completes the proof.   □

As an immediate consequence of the preceding result, we obtain the following:

Theorem 41. *For any strictly extended type X, any $B' \subseteq B$, and any $n \geq 1$,*

$$\mathcal{L}\left(X\text{-}HCDG_n\left(B'\right)\right) \subseteq \mathcal{L}\left(X\text{-}GC_{ac}\right).$$

If $t \notin B'$, then we even have $\mathcal{L}\left(X\text{-}HCDG_n\left(B'\right)\right) \subseteq \mathcal{L}\left(X\text{-}GC\right)$.

9   Summary and Future Research

The formal framework for sequential grammars with regulated rewriting based on the applicability of rules has first been presented in a comprehensive way in [13] and recently extended in several papers, especially with the new concept of activation and blocking of rules, see [3,11].

Based on the general results obtained within this framework, many computational completeness results for sequential grammars working on strings or multisets, but also for sequential array grammars on Cayley grids can be shown.

There are still many other control mechanisms which might perfectly fit to be considered within this framework, for example, regular control or other derivation modes known from the area of grammar systems. Investigations how to include further control mechanisms as well as to prove relations between them and the control mechanisms considered so far thus remain as a challenge for future research.

Acknowledgements. I am very grateful to my colleagues and co-authors for many fruitful discussions as well as for their contributions to the topics described in this overview paper: First parts for the concept of the general framework were already discussed and elaborated during my stay in Magdeburg with Jürgen Dassow nearly thirty years ago. Afterwards, partial results were used in several papers, for example, with Henning Fernau, Markus Holzer, and Gheorghe Păun. The first comprehensive collection of results in [13] then was elaborated with my colleagues in Vienna, Marion Oswald and Marian Kogler. Recent results, especially for sequential grammars with activation and blocking of rules (see [2,3]), were elaborated together with Artiom Alhazov and Sergiu Ivanov.

References

1. Aizawa, K., Nakamura, A.: Grammars on the hexagonal array. In: Wang, P.S.P. (ed.) Array Grammars, Patterns and Recognizers, Series in Computer Science, vol. 18, pp. 144–152. World Scientific, Singapore (1989). https://doi.org/10.1142/S0218001489000358
2. Alhazov, A., Freund, R., Ivanov, S.: P systems with activation and blocking of rules. In: Stepney, S., Verlan, S. (eds.) UCNC 2018. LNCS, vol. 10867, pp. 1–15. Springer, Cham (2018). https://doi.org/10.1007/978-3-319-92435-9_1

3. Alhazov, A., Freund, R., Ivanov, S.: Sequential grammars with activation and blocking of rules. In: Durand-Lose and Verlan [8], pp. 51–68. https://doi.org/10.1007/978-3-319-92402-1_3

4. Cavaliere, M., Freund, R., Oswald, M., Sburlan, D.: Multiset random context grammars, checkers, and transducers. Theor. Comput. Sci. **372**(2–3), 136–151 (2007). https://doi.org/10.1016/j.tcs.2006.11.022

5. Cook, C.R., Wang, P.S.P.: A Chomsky hierarchy of isotonic array grammars and languages. Comput. Graphics Image Process. **8**, 144–152 (1978). https://doi.org/10.1016/S0146-664X(78)80022-7

6. Csuhaj-Varjú, E., Dassow, J., Kelemen, J., Păun, Gh,: Grammar Systems: A Grammatical Approach to Distribution and Cooperation. Gordon and Breach Science Publishers (1994)

7. Dassow, J., Păun, Gh.: Regulated Rewriting in Formal Language Theory. EATCS Monographs in Theoretical Computer Science, vol. 18. Springer, Heidelberg (1989)

8. Durand-Lose, J., Verlan, S. (eds.): MCU 2018. LNCS, vol. 10881. Springer, Cham (2018). https://doi.org/10.1007/978-3-319-92402-1

9. Fernau, H., Freund, R., Oswald, M., Reinhardt, K.: Refining the nonterminal complexity of graph-controlled, programmed, and matrix grammars. J. Autom. Lang. Comb. **12**(1–2), 117–138 (2007). https://doi.org/10.25596/jalc-2007-117

10. Freund, R.: Control mechanisms on #-context-free array grammars. In: Păun, Gh. (ed.) Mathematical Aspects of Natural and Formal Languages, pp. 97–137. World Scientific, Singapore (1994). https://doi.org/10.1142/9789814447133_0006

11. Freund, R.: Control mechanisms for array grammars on Cayley grids. In: Durand-Lose and Verlan [8], pp. 1–33. https://doi.org/10.1007/978-3-319-92402-1_1

12. Freund, R., Ivanov, S., Oswald, M., Subramanian, K.G.: One-dimensional array grammars and P systems with array insertion and deletion rules. In: Neary and Cook [20], pp. 62–75. https://doi.org/10.4204/EPTCS.128

13. Freund, R., Kogler, M., Oswald, M.: A general framework for regulated rewriting based on the applicability of rules. In: Kelemen, J., Kelemenová, A. (eds.) Computation, Cooperation, and Life. LNCS, vol. 6610, pp. 35–53. Springer, Heidelberg (2011). https://doi.org/10.1007/978-3-642-20000-7_5

14. Freund, R., Oswald, M.: Array automata on Cayley grids. In: Neary and Cook [20], pp. 27–28. https://doi.org/10.4204/EPTCS.128

15. Freund, R., Oswald, M.: Array grammars and automata on Cayley grids. J. Autom. Lang. Comb. **19**(1–4), 67–80 (2014). https://doi.org/10.25596/jalc-2014-067

16. Holt, D.F., Eick, B., O'Brien, E.A.: Handbook of Computational Group Theory. CRC Press, Boca Raton (2005)

17. Kudlek, M., Martín-Vide, C., Păun, Gh.: Toward a formal macroset theory. In: Calude, C.S., PĂun, G., Rozenberg, G., Salomaa, A. (eds.) WMC 2000. LNCS, vol. 2235, pp. 123–133. Springer, Heidelberg (2001). https://doi.org/10.1007/3-540-45523-X_7

18. Minsky, M.L.: Computation: Finite and Infinite Machines. Prentice Hall, Englewood Cliffs (1967)

19. Mitrana, V.: On the generative capacity of hybrid CD grammar systems. Comput. Artif. Intell. **12**(1), 231–244 (1993)

20. Neary, T., Cook, M. (eds.): MCU 2018. LNCS, vol. 128. Springer, Cham (2013). https://doi.org/10.4204/EPTCS.128

21. Păun, Gh.: Hybrid cooperating/distributed grammar systems. J. Inform. Process. Cybernet. EIK **30**(4), 231–244 (1994)

22. Păun, Gh., Rozenberg, G., Salomaa, A.: The Oxford Handbook of Membrane Computing. Oxford University Press, New York (2010)

23. Rosenfeld, A.: Picture Languages. Academic Press, Reading (1979)
24. Rosenfeld, A., Siromoney, R.: Picture languages - a survey. Lang. Des. **1**(3), 229–245 (1993). http://dl.acm.org/citation.cfm?id=198440.198442
25. Rozenberg, G., Salomaa, A. (eds.): Handbook of Formal Languages, 3 volumes. Springer, Heidelberg (1997)
26. Salomaa, A.: Formal Languages. Academic Press, New York (1973)
27. Wang, P.S.P.: An application of array grammars to clustering analysis for syntactic patterns. Pattern Recogn. **17**, 441–451 (1984). https://doi.org/10.1016/0031-3203(84)90073-6

Low-Complexity Tilings of the Plane

Jarkko Kari[(⊠)]

Department of Mathematics and Statistics, University of Turku, Turku, Finland
jkari@utu.fi

Abstract. A two-dimensional configuration is a coloring of the infinite grid $\mathbb{Z}^2$ with finitely many colors. For a finite subset D of $\mathbb{Z}^2$, the D-patterns of a configuration are the colored patterns of shape D that appear in the configuration. The number of distinct D-patterns of a configuration is a natural measure of its complexity. A configuration is considered having low complexity with respect to shape D if the number of distinct D-patterns is at most $|D|$, the size of the shape. This extended abstract is a short review of an algebraic method to study periodicity of such low complexity configurations.

Keywords: Pattern complexity · Periodicity · Nivat's conjecture ·
Low complexity configurations · Low complexity subshifts ·
Commutative algebra · Algebraic subshifts · Domino problem

1 Introduction

Commutative algebra provides powerful tools to analyze low complexity configurations, that is, colorings of the two-dimensional grid that have sufficiently low number of different local patterns. If the colors are represented as numbers, the low complexity assumption implies that the configuration is a linear combination of its translated copies. This condition can be expressed as an annihilation property under the multiplication of a power series representation of the configuration by a non-zero two-variate polynomial, leading to the study of the ideal of all annihilating polynomials. It turns out that the ideal of annihilators is essentially a principal ideal generated by a product of so-called line polynomials, i.e., univariate polynomials of two-variate monomials. This opens up the possibility to obtain results on global structures of the configuration, such as its periodicity. We first proposed this approach in [9,10] to study Nivat's conjecture. It led to a number of subsequent results [6–8,14]. In this presentation we review the main results without proofs – the given references can be consulted for more details. We start by briefly recalling the notations and basic concepts.

J. Kari—Research supported by the Academy of Finland grant 296018.

© IFIP International Federation for Information Processing 2019
Published by Springer Nature Switzerland AG 2019
M. Hospodár et al. (Eds.): DCFS 2019, LNCS 11612, pp. 35–45, 2019.
https://doi.org/10.1007/978-3-030-23247-4_2

1.1 Configurations and Periodicity

A d-dimensional *configuration* over a finite alphabet A is an assignment of symbols of A on the infinite grid $\mathbb{Z}^d$. For any configuration $c \in A^{\mathbb{Z}^d}$ and any cell $\mathbf{u} \in \mathbb{Z}^d$, we denote by $c_{\mathbf{u}}$ the symbol that c has in cell $\mathbf{u}$. For any vector $\mathbf{t} \in \mathbb{Z}^d$, the *translation* $\tau^{\mathbf{t}}$ by $\mathbf{t}$ shifts a configuration c so that $\tau^{\mathbf{t}}(c)_{\mathbf{u}} = c_{\mathbf{u}-\mathbf{t}}$ for all $\mathbf{u} \in \mathbb{Z}^d$. We say that c is *periodic* if $\tau^{\mathbf{t}}(c) = c$ for some non-zero $\mathbf{t} \in \mathbb{Z}^d$. In this case $\mathbf{t}$ is a *vector of periodicity* and c is also termed $\mathbf{t}$-*periodic*. We mostly consider the two-dimensional setting $d = 2$. In this case, if there are two linearly independent vectors of periodicity then c is called *two-periodic*. A two-periodic $c \in A^{\mathbb{Z}^2}$ has automatically horizontal and vertical vectors of periodicity $(k, 0)$ and $(0, k)$ for some $k > 0$, and consequently a vector of periodicity in every rational direction. A two-dimensional periodic configuration that is not two-periodic is called *one-periodic*.

1.2 Pattern Complexity

Let $D \subseteq \mathbb{Z}^d$ be a finite set of cells, a *shape*. A D-*pattern* is an assignment $p \in A^D$ of symbols in shape D. A *(finite) pattern* is a D-pattern for some finite D. Let us denote by A^* the set of all finite patterns over alphabet A, where the dimension d is assumed to be known from the context. We say that a finite pattern p of shape D *appears* in configuration c if for some $\mathbf{t} \in \mathbb{Z}^d$ we have $\tau^{\mathbf{t}}(c)|_D = p$. We also say that c *contains* pattern p. For a fixed D, the set of D-patterns that appear in a configuration c is denoted by $\mathcal{L}_D(c)$. We denote by $\mathcal{L}(c)$ the set of all finite patterns that appear in c, i.e., the union of $\mathcal{L}_D(c)$ over all finite $D \subseteq \mathbb{Z}^d$.

The *pattern complexity* of a configuration c with respect to a shape D is the number of D-patterns that c contains. A sufficiently low pattern complexity forces global regularities in a configuration. A relevant threshold happens when the pattern complexity is at most $|D|$, the number of cells in shape D. Hence we say that c has *low complexity* with respect to shape D if

$$|\mathcal{L}_D(c)| \leq |D|.$$

We call c a *low complexity configuration* if it has low complexity with respect to some finite shape D.

1.3 Nivat's Conjecture

The original motivation to this work is the famous conjecture presented by Maurice Nivat in his keynote address for the 25th anniversary of the European Association for Theoretical Computer Science at ICALP 1997. It concerns two-dimensional configurations that have low complexity with respect to a rectangular shape.

Conjecture 1 ([12]). Let $c \in A^{\mathbb{Z}^2}$ be a two-dimensional configuration. If c has low complexity with respect to some rectangle $D = \{1, \ldots, n\} \times \{1, \ldots, m\}$ then c is periodic.

The conjecture is still open but several partial and related results have been established. The best general bound was proved in [5] where it was shown that for any rectangle D the condition $|\mathcal{L}_D(c)| \leq |D|/2$ is enough to guarantee that c is periodic. This fact can also be proved using the algebraic approach [14].

The analogous conjecture in dimensions higher than two fails, as does a similar claim in two dimensions for many other shapes than rectangles [4]. We return to Nivat's conjecture and our results on this problem in Sect. 2.

1.4   Basic Concepts of Symbolic Dynamics

Let $p \in A^D$ be a finite pattern of shape D. The set $[p] = \{c \in A^{\mathbb{Z}^d} \mid c|_D = p\}$ of configurations that have p in domain D is called the *cylinder* determined by p. The collection of cylinders $[p]$ is a base of a compact topology on $A^{\mathbb{Z}^d}$, the *prodiscrete* topology. The topology is equivalently defined by a metric on $A^{\mathbb{Z}^d}$ where two configurations are close to each other if they agree with each other on a large region around cell $\mathbf{0}$ – the larger the region the closer they are. Cylinders are clopen in the topology: they are both open and closed.

A subset X of $A^{\mathbb{Z}^2}$ is called a *subshift* if it is closed in the topology and closed under translations. By a compactness argument, every configuration c that is not in X contains a finite pattern p that prevents it from being in X: no configuration that contains p is in X. We can then as well define subshifts using forbidden patterns: given a set $P \subseteq A^*$ of finite patterns we define

$$X_P = \{c \in A^{\mathbb{Z}^d} \mid \mathcal{L}(c) \cap P = \emptyset\},$$

the set of configurations that do not contain any of the patterns in P. Set X_P is a subshift, and every subshift is X_P for some P. If $X = X_P$ for some finite P then X is a *subshift of finite type* (SFT).

In this work we are interested in subshifts that have low pattern complexity. For a subshift $X \subseteq A^{\mathbb{Z}^d}$ (or actually for any set X of configurations) we define its language $\mathcal{L}(X) \subseteq A^*$ to be the set of all finite patterns that appear in some element of X, that is, the union of sets $\mathcal{L}(c)$ over all $c \in X$. For a fixed shape D, we analogously define $\mathcal{L}_D(X) = \mathcal{L}(X) \cap A^D$, the union of all $\mathcal{L}_D(c)$ over $c \in X$. We say that X has low complexity with respect to shape D if $|\mathcal{L}_D(X)| \leq |D|$. For example, in Theorem 8 we fix shape D and a small set $P \subseteq A^D$ of at most $|D|$ allowed patterns of shape D. Then $X = X_{A^D \setminus P} = \{c \in A^{\mathbb{Z}^d} \mid \mathcal{L}_D(c) \subseteq P\}$ is a low complexity SFT since $\mathcal{L}_D(X) \subseteq P$ and $|P| \leq |D|$.

The *orbit* of a configuration c is the set $\mathcal{O}(c) = \{\tau^{\mathbf{t}}(c) \mid \mathbf{t} \in \mathbb{Z}^2\}$ of all its translates, and the *orbit closure* $\overline{\mathcal{O}(c)}$ of c is the topological closure of its orbit. The orbit closure is a subshift, and in fact it is the intersection of all subshifts that contain c. In terms of finite patters, $c' \in \overline{\mathcal{O}(c)}$ if and only if every finite pattern that appears in c' appears also in c. Of course, the orbit closure of a low complexity configuration is a low complexity subshift.

A configuration c is called *uniformly recurrent* if for every $c' \in \overline{\mathcal{O}(c)}$ we have $\overline{\mathcal{O}(c')} = \overline{\mathcal{O}(c)}$. This is equivalent to $\overline{\mathcal{O}(c)}$ being a *minimal subshift* in the sense that it has no proper non-empty subshifts inside it. A classical result by Birkhoff on dynamical systems implies that every non-empty subshift contains a minimal subshift, so there is a uniformly recurrent configuration in every non-empty subshift [3].

1.5 Algebraic Concepts

To use commutative algebra we assume that $A \subseteq \mathbb{Z}$, i.e., the symbols in the configurations are integers. We also maintain the assumption that A is finite. We express a d-dimensional configuration $c \in A^{\mathbb{Z}^d}$ as a formal power series over d variables $x_1, \ldots x_d$ where the monomials address cells in a natural manner $x_1^{u_1} \cdots x_d^{u_d} \longleftrightarrow (u_1, \ldots, u_d) \in \mathbb{Z}^d$, and the coefficients of the monomials in the power series are the symbols at the corresponding cells. Using the convenient vector notation $\mathbf{x} = (x_1, \ldots x_d)$ we write $\mathbf{x}^{\mathbf{u}} = x_1^{u_1} \cdots x_d^{u_d}$ for the monomial that represents cell $\mathbf{u} = (u_1, \ldots u_d) \in \mathbb{Z}^d$. Note that all our power series and polynomials are *Laurent* as we allow negative as well as positive powers of variables. Now the configuration $c \in A^{\mathbb{Z}^d}$ can be coded as the formal power series

$$c(\mathbf{x}) = \sum_{\mathbf{u} \in \mathbb{Z}^d} c_{\mathbf{u}} \mathbf{x}^{\mathbf{u}}.$$

Because $A \subseteq \mathbb{Z}$ is finite, the power series $c(\mathbf{x})$ is *integral* (the coefficients are integers) and *finitary* (there are only finitely many different coefficients). Henceforth we treat configurations as integral, finitary power series.

Note that the power series are indeed formal: the role of the variables is only to provide the position information on the grid. We may sum up two power series, or multiply a power series with a polynomial, but we never plug in any values in the variables. Multiplying a power series $c(\mathbf{x})$ by a monomial $\mathbf{x}^{\mathbf{t}}$ simply adds $\mathbf{t}$ to the exponents of all monomials, thus producing the power series of the translated configuration $\tau^{\mathbf{t}}(c)$. Hence the configuration $c(\mathbf{x})$ is $\mathbf{t}$-periodic if and only if $\mathbf{x}^{\mathbf{t}} c(\mathbf{x}) = c(\mathbf{x})$, that is, if and only if $(\mathbf{x}^{\mathbf{t}} - 1)c(\mathbf{x}) = 0$, the zero power series. Thus we can express the periodicity of a configuration in terms of its *annihilation* under the multiplication with a *difference binomial* $\mathbf{x}^{\mathbf{t}} - 1$. Very naturally then we introduce the *annihilator ideal*

$$\mathrm{Ann}(c) = \{f(\mathbf{x}) \in \mathbb{C}[\mathbf{x}^{\pm 1}] \mid f(\mathbf{x})c(\mathbf{x}) = 0\}$$

containing all the polynomials that annihilate c. Here we use the notation $\mathbb{C}[\mathbf{x}^{\pm 1}]$ for the set of Laurent polynomials with complex coefficients. Note that $\mathrm{Ann}(c)$ is indeed an ideal of the Laurent polynomial ring $\mathbb{C}[\mathbf{x}^{\pm 1}]$.

Our first observation relates the low complexity assumption to annihilators. Namely, it is easy to see using elementary linear algebra that any low complexity configuration has at least some non-trivial annihilators:

Lemma 2 ([9]). *Let c be a low complexity configuration. Then $\mathrm{Ann}(c)$ contains a non-zero polynomial.*

One of the main results of [9] states that if a configuration c is annihilated by a non-zero polynomial (e.g., due to low complexity) then it is automatically annihilated by a product of difference binomials.

Theorem 3 ([9]). *Let c be a configuration annihilated by some non-zero polynomial. Then there exist pairwise linearly independent $\mathbf{t}_1, \ldots, \mathbf{t}_m \in \mathbb{Z}^d$ such that*

$$(\mathbf{x}^{\mathbf{t}_1} - 1) \cdots (\mathbf{x}^{\mathbf{t}_m} - 1) \in \mathrm{Ann}(c).$$

Note that if $m = 1$ then the configuration is $\mathbf{t}_1$-periodic. Otherwise, for $m \geq 2$, annihilation by $(\mathbf{x}^{\mathbf{t}_1} - 1) \cdots (\mathbf{x}^{\mathbf{t}_m} - 1)$ can be considered a form of generalized periodicity.

In the two-dimensional setting $d = 2$ we find it sometimes more convenient to work with the *periodizer ideal*

$$\mathrm{Per}(c) = \{f(\mathbf{x}) \in \mathbb{C}[\mathbf{x}^{\pm 1}] \mid f(\mathbf{x})c(\mathbf{x}) \text{ is two-periodic}\}$$

that contains those two-variate Laurent polynomials whose product with configuration c is two-periodic. Clearly also $\mathrm{Per}(c)$ is an ideal of the Laurent polynomial ring $\mathbb{C}[\mathbf{x}^{\pm 1}]$, and we have $\mathrm{Ann}(c) \subseteq \mathrm{Per}(c)$. In the two-dimensional case we have a very good understanding of the structure of the ideals $\mathrm{Ann}(c)$ and $\mathrm{Per}(c)$, see Theorems 9 and 10 in Sect. 3.

2   Contributions to Nivat's Conjecture

In [9] we reported an asymptotic result on Nivat's conjecture. The complete proof appeared in [10]. Recall that the Nivat's conjecture claims – taking the contrapositive of the original statement – that every non-periodic configuration has high complexity with respect to every rectangle. Our result states that this indeed holds for all sufficiently large rectangles:

Theorem 4 ([9,10]). *Let c be a two-dimensional configuration that is not periodic. Then $\mathcal{L}_D(c) > |D|$ holds for all but finitely many rectangles D.*

Recall that Theorem 3 gives for a low complexity configuration an annihilator of the form $(\mathbf{x}^{\mathbf{t}_1} - 1) \cdots (\mathbf{x}^{\mathbf{t}_m} - 1)$. If $m = 1$ then c is periodic, so it is interesting to consider the cases of $m \geq 2$. Szabados proved in [14] that Nivat's conjecture holds in the case $m = 2$. Note that this case is equivalent to c being the sum of two periodic configurations [9].

Theorem 5 ([14]). *Let c be a two-dimensional configuration that has low complexity with respect to some rectangle. If c is the sum of two periodic configurations then c itself is periodic.*

We have also considered other types of configurations. Particularly interesting are uniformly recurrent configurations since they occur in all non-empty subshifts. Recently we proved that they satisfy Nivat's conjecture, even when rectangles are generalized to other *discrete convex shapes*. We call shape $D \subseteq \mathbb{Z}^2$ convex if $D = S \cap \mathbb{Z}^2$ for some convex set $S \subseteq \mathbb{R}^2$. In particular, every rectangle is convex.

Theorem 6 ([6]). *Two-dimensional uniformly recurrent configuration that has low complexity with respect to a finite discrete convex shape D is periodic.*

The presence of uniformly recurrent configurations in subshifts then directly yields the following corollary.

Theorem 7 ([6]). *Let X be a non-empty two-dimensional subshift that has low complexity with respect to a finite discrete convex shape D. Then X contains a periodic configuration. In particular, the orbit closure of a configuration that has low complexity with respect to D contains a periodic configuration.*

Note that the periodic element in the orbit closure of c means that c contains arbitrarily large periodic regions.

The existence of periodic elements provides us with an algorithm to determine if a given low complexity SFT is empty. This is a classical argument by Hao Wang [16]: There is a semi-algorithm for non-emptyness of arbitrary SFTs, and there is a semi-algorithm for the existence of a periodic configuration in a two-dimensional SFT. The latter semi-algorithm is based on the fact that if a two-dimensional SFT contains a periodic configuration then it also contains a two-periodic configuration, and these can be effectively enumerated and tested. Now, since we know that a two-dimensional SFT that has low complexity with respect to a convex shape is either empty or contains a periodic configuration, the two semi-algorithms together yield an algorithm to test emptyness.

Theorem 8 ([6]). *There is an algorithm that – given a set of at most $|D|$ patterns $P \subseteq A^D$ over a two-dimensional convex shape D – determines whether there exists a configuration $c \in A^{\mathbb{Z}^2}$ such that $\mathcal{L}_D(c) \subseteq P$.*

3   Line Polynomials and the Structure of the Annihilator Ideal

For a polynomial $f(\mathbf{x}) = \sum f_{\mathbf{u}} \mathbf{x}^{\mathbf{u}}$, we call $\mathrm{Supp}(f) = \{\mathbf{u} \in \mathbb{Z}^d \mid f_{\mathbf{u}} \neq 0\}$ its *support*. A *line polynomial* is a polynomial with all its terms aligned on the same line: f is a line polynomial in direction $\mathbf{u} \in \mathbb{Z}^d$ if and only if $\mathrm{supp}(f)$ contains at least two elements and $\mathrm{supp}(f) \subseteq \mathbb{Z}\mathbf{u}$. (Note that this definition differs slightly from the one in [9,10] where the line containing the non-zero terms was not required to go through the origin. The definitions are the same up to multiplication by a monomial, i.e. a translation.) Multiplying a configuration by a line polynomial is a one-dimensional process: different discrete lines $\mathbf{v} + \mathbb{Z}\mathbf{u}$ in the direction $\mathbf{u}$ of the line polynomial get multiplied independently of each other.

Difference binomials $\mathbf{x}^{\mathbf{t}} - 1$ are line polynomials so the special annihilator provided by Theorem 3 is a product of line polynomials. Annihilation by a difference binomial means periodicity – and this fact generalizes to any line polynomial: a configuration that is annihilated by a line polynomial in direction $\mathbf{u}$ is $n\mathbf{u}$-periodic for some $n \in \mathbb{Z}$. This is due to the fact that the line polynomial annihilator specifies a linear recurrence along the discrete lines in direction $\mathbf{u}$.

The annihilator and the periodizer ideals of a configuration have particularly nice forms in the two-dimensional setting. Recall that $\langle f \rangle = \{gf \mid g \in \mathbb{C}[\mathbf{x}^{\pm 1}]\}$ is the *principal ideal* generated by Laurent polynomial f. It turns out that a two-dimensional periodizer ideal is a principal ideal generated by a product of line polynomials.

Theorem 9 (adapted from [10]). *Let c be a two-dimensional configuration with a non-trivial annihilator. Then $\mathrm{Per}(c) = \langle f \rangle$ for a product $f = f_1 \cdots f_m$ of some line polynomials $f_1, \ldots, f_m$.*

By merging line polynomials in the same directions we can choose f_i in the theorem above so that they are in pairwise linearly independent directions. In this case m, the number of line polynomial factors, only depends on c. We denote $m = \mathrm{Ord}(c)$ and call it the *order* of c. If $\mathrm{Ord}(c) = 1$ then c is periodic, and Theorem 5 states that the Nivat's conjecture is true among configurations of order two.

Theorem 9 directly implies a simple structure on the annihilator ideal: any annihilation of c factors through the two-periodic configuration $f_1 \cdots f_m c$.

Theorem 10 ([10]). *Let c be a two-dimensional configuration with a non-trivial annihilator. Then $\mathrm{Ann}(c) = f_1 \cdots f_m H$ where $f_1, \ldots, f_m$ are line polynomials and H is the annihilator ideal of the two-periodic configuration $f_1 \cdots f_m c$.*

As pointed out above, if c is annihilated by a line polynomial then c is periodic. The structure of $\mathrm{Per}(c)$ and $\mathrm{Ann}(c)$ allows us to generalize this to other annihilators. If a two-dimensional configuration c is annihilated (or even periodized) by a polynomial without any line polynomial factors then it follows from Theorem 9 that $\mathrm{Per}(c)$ is generated by polynomial 1, that is, c itself is already two-periodic. Similarly, if $\mathrm{Per}(c)$ contains a polynomial whose line polynomial factors are all in a common direction then $\mathrm{Per}(c) = \langle f \rangle$ is generated by a line polynomial f in this direction, implying that c has a line polynomial annihilator and is therefore periodic. Such situations have come up in the literature under the theme of covering codes on the grid [1].

Example 11. Consider the problem of placing identical broadcasting antennas on the grid $\mathbb{Z}^2$ in such a way that each cell that does not contain an antenna receives broadcast from exactly a antennas and every cell containing an antenna receives exactly b broadcasts. Assume that $D \subseteq \mathbb{Z}^2$ is the shape of coverage by an antenna at the origin. Let us represent this broadcast range as the Laurent polynomial $f(\mathbf{x}) = \sum_{\mathbf{u} \in D} \mathbf{x}^{\mathbf{u}}$. Let c be a configuration over $A = \{0, 1\}$ where we interpret $c_{\mathbf{u}} = 1$ as the presence of an antenna in cell $\mathbf{u}$. Now, c is a solution to the antenna placement problem if and only if $f(\mathbf{x})c(\mathbf{x})$ is the power series $(b-a)c(\mathbf{x}) + a\mathbb{1}(\mathbf{x})$ where $\mathbb{1}(\mathbf{x})$ is the constant one power series $\mathbb{1}(\mathbf{x}) = \sum_{\mathbf{u} \in \mathbb{Z}^2} \mathbf{x}^{\mathbf{u}}$. Indeed, $(b - a)c(\mathbf{x}) + a\mathbb{1}(\mathbf{x})$ has values b and a in cells containing and not containing an antenna, respectively. In other words, c is a valid placement of antennas if and only if multiplying $c(\mathbf{x})$ with polynomial $f(\mathbf{x}) - (b - a)$ results in the two-periodic configuration $a\mathbb{1}(\mathbf{x})$. If $f(\mathbf{x}) - (b - a)$ has no line polynomial factors then we know that this condition forces c to be two-periodic. For example, if $D = \{(x, y) \mid |x| + |y| \le 1\}$ so that each antenna only broadcasts to its own cell and the four neighboring cells, then $b - a \ne 1$ implies two-periodicity of any solution.   □

4   Low Complexity Configurations in Algebraic Subshifts

In [7] we considered low complexity configurations in algebraic subshifts where the alphabet A is a finite field $\mathbb{F}_p$. As Lemma 2 works as well in this setup, we have that every low complexity configuration c is annihilated by a non-zero polynomial $f \in \mathbb{F}_p[\mathbf{x}^{\pm 1}]$. We then have that c is an element of the *algeraic subshift* $S_f = \{c \in A^{\mathbb{Z}^d} \mid fc = 0\}$ of all configurations over $A = \mathbb{F}_p$ that are annihilated by f. So, to prove Nivat's conjecture it is enough to prove it for elements of algebraic subshifts. Clearly S_f is of finite type, defined by forbidden patterns of shape $D = -\mathrm{Supp}(f)$. We remark that the theory of this type of algebraically defined subshifts is well developed, see for example [13].

Example 12. Let $A = \mathbb{F}_2$. The Ledrappier subshift (also known as the 3-dot system) is S_f for $f = 1 + x_1 + x_2$. Elements of S_f are the space-time diagrams of the binary state XOR cellular automaton that adds to the state of each cell modulo 2 the state of its left neighbor.   □

While Lemma 2 works just fine over finite fields $\mathbb{F}_p$, Theorem 3 does not: it is not true that every element of every algebraic subshift would be annihilated by a product of difference polynomials. However, configurations over $\mathbb{F}_p$ can be also considered as configurations over $\mathbb{Z}$, without making calculations modulo p. If a configuration c over $\mathbb{F}_p$ has low complexity then it also has low complexity as a configuration over $\mathbb{Z}$, and thus in $\mathbb{Z}$ it has a special annihilator $(\mathbf{x}^{t_1} - 1) \cdots (\mathbf{x}^{t_m} - 1)$ provided by Theorem 3. Now, considering all calculations modulo p we see that this special annihilator is also an annihilator over $\mathbb{F}_p$. We conclude that even over $\mathbb{F}_p$, every low complexity configuration has an annihilator that is a product of difference binomials.

Example 13. Let c be a low complexity configuration in the Ledrappier subshift of Example 12. It is then annihilated by $f = 1 + x_1 + x_2$ and by some $g = (\mathbf{x}^{t_1} - 1) \cdots (\mathbf{x}^{t_m} - 1)$ that is a product of difference binomials. Because f does not have line polynomial factors while all irreducible factors of g are line polynomials, we have that f and g do not have any common factors. Replacing x_2 by $f - 1 - x_1$ in g, we can entirely eliminate variable x_2 from g, obtaining a new annihilator $g' = g - f'f$ of c having no occurrence of variable x_2. This annihilator $g'(x_1)$ is non-zero because f and g do not have common factors, which implies that c is horizontally periodic. We can repeat the same reasoning in the vertical direction, obtaining that c is two periodic.   □

The reasoning in the example above can be generalized to other algebraic subshifts.

Theorem 14. ([7]). *Let c be a low complexity configuration of an algebraic subshift S_f.*

- *If f has no line polynomial factors then c is two-periodic.*
- *If all line polynomial factors of f are in a common direction then c is periodic.*

Note that in the theorem there is no assumption about the low complexity shape D, so the applicability of the theorem is not restricted to rectangles or convex shapes.

5 Conclusions and Perspectives

There remains many open questions for future study. Obviously, the full version of Nivat's conjecture is still unsolved. Our Theorem 6 suggests that perhaps periodicity is forced by the low complexity condition not only on rectangles but on other convex shapes as well, as conjectured by Julien Cassaigne in [4]. In his examples of non-periodic low complexity configurations, the low complexity shape D is always non-convex. Moreover, all two-dimensional low complexity configurations that we know consist of periodic sublattices [4, 7]. For example, even lattice cells may form a configuration that is horizontally but not vertically periodic while the odd cells may have a vertical but no horizontal period. The interleaved non-periodic configuration may have low complexity with respect to a scatted shape D that only sees cells of equal parity. We wonder if there exist any low complexity configurations without a periodic sublattice structure.

Theorem 5 proves Nivat's conjecture for configurations of order two. However, $\mathrm{Ord}(c) = 2$ case is special in the sense that c is then a sum of periodic configurations, that is, finitary power series. In general, any configuration with a non-trivial annihilator is a sum of periodic power series [9], but already when $\mathrm{Ord}(c) = 3$ these power series may be necessarily non-finitary [8]. It seems then that proving Nivat's conjecture for configurations of order three would reflect the general case better than the order two case. We also remark that proving Nivat's conjecture (for all convex shapes) would render the results of Sect. 2 obsolete.

There are also very interesting questions concerning general low complexity SFTs. By Theorem 7, a two-dimensional SFT that is low complexity with respect to a convex shape contains periodic configurations. Might this be true for non-convex shapes as well? If so, analogously to Theorem 8, this would yield and algorithm to decide emptyness of general low complexity SFTs. What about higher dimensions? We do not know of any aperiodic low complexity SFT in any dimension d of the space. The following example recalls a family of particularly interesting low complexity SFTs.

Example 15. A d-dimensional cluster tile is a finite subset $D \subseteq \mathbb{Z}^d$, and a co-tiler is a subset $C \subseteq \mathbb{Z}^d$ such that $C \oplus D = \mathbb{Z}^d$. Visually, C gives positions where copies of tiles D can be placed so that every cell gets covered by exactly one tile. Looking at the situation from an arbitrary covered cell $\mathbf{u}$, we see that C is a co-tiler of D if and only if the set $\mathbf{u} - D$ contains precisely one element of C, for every $\mathbf{u} \in \mathbb{Z}^d$. Representing a co-tiler C as the indicator configuration $c_{\mathbf{u}} = 1$ if $\mathbf{u} \in C$ and $c_{\mathbf{u}} = 0$ if $\mathbf{u} \notin C$, we have that the set of valid co-tilers for tile D is a low complexity SFT: The only allowed patterns of shape $-D$ are those that contain single 1, and there are $|D|$ such patterns.

The periodic cluster tiling problem asks whether every tile that has a co-tiler also has a periodic co-tiler [11,15]. This is a special case of the more general question on arbitrary low complexity SFTs discussed above. The periodic cluster tiling problem was recently answered affirmatively in the two-dimensional case [2]. In [9] we gave a simple algebraic proof in any number of dimensions for the case – originally handled in [15] – where $|D|$ is a prime number.   □

Finally, the structure of the annihilator ideal is not known in dimension higher than two. We wonder how Theorem 10 might generalize to the three-dimensional setting.

References

1. Axenovich, M.A.: On multiple coverings of the infinite rectangular grid with balls of constant radius. Discrete Math. **268**(1), 31–48 (2003). https://doi.org/10.1016/S0012-365X(02)00744-6
2. Bhattacharya, S.: Periodicity and decidability of tilings of $\mathbb{Z}^2$. CoRR abs/1602.05738 (2016). https://arxiv.org/abs/1602.05738
3. Birkhoff, G.D.: Quelques théorèmes sur le mouvement des systèmes dynamiques. Bull. Soc. Math. France **40**, 305–323 (1912). https://doi.org/10.24033/bsmf.909
4. Cassaigne, J.: Subword complexity and periodicity in two or more dimensions. In: Rozenberg, G., Thomas, W. (eds.) Developments in Language Theory. Foundations, Applications, and Perspectives, pp. 14–21. World Scientific (1999)
5. Cyr, V., Kra, B.: Nonexpansive $\mathbb{Z}^2$-subdynamics and Nivat's Conjecture. Trans. Amer. Math. Soc. **367**(9), 6487–6537 (2015). https://doi.org/10.1090/S0002-9947-2015-06391-0
6. Kari, J., Moutot, E.: Decidability and periodicity of low complexity tilings. CoRR abs/1904.01267 (2019). http://arxiv.org/abs/1904.01267
7. Kari, J., Moutot, E.: Nivat's conjecture and pattern complexity in algebraic subshifts. Theoret. Comput. Sci. (2019, to appear). https://doi.org/10.1016/j.tcs.2018.12.029
8. Kari, J., Szabados, M.: An algebraic geometric approach to multidimensional words. In: Maletti, A. (ed.) CAI 2015. LNCS, vol. 9270, pp. 29–42. Springer, Cham (2015). https://doi.org/10.1007/978-3-319-23021-4_3
9. Kari, J., Szabados, M.: An algebraic geometric approach to Nivat's conjecture. In: Halldórsson, M.M., Iwama, K., Kobayashi, N., Speckmann, B. (eds.) ICALP 2015. LNCS, vol. 9135, pp. 273–285. Springer, Heidelberg (2015). https://doi.org/10.1007/978-3-662-47666-6_22
10. Kari, J., Szabados, M.: An algebraic geometric approach to Nivat's conjecture. CoRR abs/1605.05929 (2016). http://arxiv.org/abs/1605.05929
11. Lagarias, J.C., Wang, Y.: Tiling the line with translates of one tile. Invent. Math. **124**, 341–365 (1996). https://doi.org/10.1007/s002220050056
12. Nivat, M.: Keynote address at the 25th anniversary of EATCS, during ICALP (1997)

13. Schmidt, K.: Dynamical systems of algebraic origin. Progress in mathematics. Birkhäuser, Basel (1995). https://doi.org/10.1007/978-3-0348-0277-2
14. Szabados, M.: Nivat's conjecture holds for sums of two periodic configurations. In: Tjoa, A.M., Bellatreche, L., Biffl, S., van Leeuwen, J., Wiedermann, J. (eds.) SOFSEM 2018. LNCS, vol. 10706, pp. 539–551. Springer, Cham (2018). https://doi.org/10.1007/978-3-319-73117-9_38
15. Szegedy, M.: Algorithms to tile the infinite grid with finite clusters. In: Proceedings 39th Annual Symposium on Foundations of Computer Science, FOCS 1998, pp. 137–147. IEEE Computer Society (1998). https://doi.org/10.1109/SFCS.1998.743437
16. Wang, H.: Proving theorems by pattern recognition - II. Bell Syst. Tech. J. **40**(1), 1–41 (1961). https://doi.org/10.1002/j.1538-7305.1961.tb03975.x

Union-Freeness, Deterministic Union-Freeness and Union-Complexity

Benedek Nagy[✉]

Department of Mathematics, Faculty of Arts and Sciences,
Eastern Mediterranean University, Famagusta, North Cyprus, Mersin-10, Turkey
nbenedek.inf@gmail.com

Abstract. Union-free expressions are regular expressions without using the union operation. Consequently, union-free languages are described by regular expressions using only concatenation and Kleene star. The language class is also characterised by a special class of finite automata: 1CFPAs have exactly one cycle-free accepting path from each of their states. Obviously such an automaton has exactly one accepting state. The deterministic counterpart of such class of automata defines the deterministic union-free languages. A regular expression is in union (disjunctive) normal form if it is a finite union of union-free expressions. By manipulating regular expressions, each of them has equivalent expression in union normal form. By the minimum number of union-free expressions needed to describe a regular language, its union-complexity is defined. For any natural number n there are languages such that their union complexity is n. However, there is not known any simple algorithm to determine the union-complexity of any language. Regarding the deterministic union-free languages, there are regular languages such that they cannot be written as a union of finitely many deterministic union-free languages.

1 Introduction

The family of regular languages is one of the most known, most common and most applied class of languages. It is the smallest, the simplest class of the Chomsky hierarchy. The descriptions of the regular languages by regular expressions are widely used. They are generated by regular, by left-linear and by right-linear grammars. They are accepted by finite state automata: both nondeterministic and deterministic variants characterize this class of languages. Recently various classes of subregular languages play also importance [5,9].

In this paper we will consider special subclasses of the regular languages. The main topic is the class of union-free languages, they are defined by regular expressions without the union. They were first mentioned as star-dot regular languages in [2]. Later on, in [4], their description by equations were examined, and it was shown that this class cannot be axiomatized by a finite set of equations.

© IFIP International Federation for Information Processing 2019
Published by Springer Nature Switzerland AG 2019
M. Hospodár et al. (Eds.): DCFS 2019, LNCS 11612, pp. 46–56, 2019.
https://doi.org/10.1007/978-3-030-23247-4_3

Automata theoretical characterisation was given in [11] allowing to define the deterministic counterpart of the class, the family of deterministic union-free languages [3,7,8].

It is also known [2,10] that every regular language is a finite union of union-free languages. The union-complexity of the regular languages is defined subsequently based on minimal decompositions [1,10,12]. However, there are regular languages that cannot be obtained as a finite union of deterministic union-free languages [8]. On the other hand allowing infinite unions one is able to describe every recursively enumerable language. Therefore infinite unions are usually not allowed when languages are described.

The structure of the paper is as follows. In the next section we define the union-free languages based on regular expressions, we show their characterisation by 1-cycle-free path automata, and we define deterministic union-free regular languages and a new class between the union-free and deterministic union-free class. In Sect. 3 some properties of the mentioned three language classes, e.g., closure properties are summarised. Section 4 is about the union decomposition of regular languages and the union-complexity.

2 The Union-Free Language Classes and Their Corresponding Automata Classes

In this section first we define the union-free languages and then we recall the corresponding class of finite automata. We assume that the reader is familiar with the basic concepts of formal languages and automata, thus for each unexplained concepts she/he is referred to any standard textbook on the topic, e.g., to [6] or the Handbook chapter [13]. Here we show only specific notions closely related to the topic of this paper. The empty word is denoted by λ, V is a finite alphabet, while $+, \cdot, *$ are the regular operations on languages, i.e., the union, the concatenation and the Kleene star.

Definition 1 (Union-free expression, union-free language). *A regular expression is union-free expression if only the operators concatenation and Kleene star are used in its description. A language is union-free if there is a union-free description that defines it.*

A kind of related idea is to define and use star-free expressions, where only union and concatenation are allowed in regular expressions. They define exactly the class of finite languages. Since the class of finite languages has already their well-known name, in the literature, the terms of star-free expressions and languages usually refer to expressions which are defined by operations union, concatenation and complement, and the corresponding language family [13]. Similarly, in the literature sometimes a wider class of languages are called union-free, those which have a description by operations concatenation, Kleene star and complement [9]. However, in this paper, the above stricter concept is used.

The empty language is described as regular expression $\emptyset$. Each other regular expression can be written in a tree form, in which the leaves are representing elements of $V \cup \{\lambda\}$ and the other nodes are representing the regular operations. The language $\emptyset$ is very special, in the rest of the paper we assume that the language we consider is not the empty one.

Definition 2. *A 5-tuple* $\mathbf{A} = (Q, S, V, \delta, F)$ *is a non-deterministic finite automaton, with the finite set of states* Q. *Further,* $S \in Q$ *is the initial state,* V *is the (input) alphabet and* $F \subset Q$ *is the set of final (or accepting) states. The function* $\delta : Q \times (V \cup \{\lambda\}) \to 2^Q$ *is the transition function. A path is called accepting path of the word* w *if it is written as* $(S = Q_0)a_1Q_1a_2Q_2...a_{n-1}Q_{n-1}a_nQ_n$ *where* $Q_{i+1} \in \delta(Q_i, a_{i+1})$ *for every* $0 \le i < n$ *with* $Q_n \in F$ *and* $w = a_1a_2...a_n$ *($a_i \in V \cup \{\lambda\}$). A word is accepted by the finite automata if it has an accepting path.*

A path $Q_0a_1Q_1a_2Q_2 \ldots a_{n-1}Q_{n-1}a_nQ_n$ is called a cycle if $Q_0 = Q_n$ (where $n > 0$). A path without any repeated state is called cycle-free path. Two cycle-free paths $Q_0a_1 \ldots a_nQ_n$ and $P_0b_1 \ldots b_mP_m$ are called alternative paths, if they are not identical, but $Q_0 = P_0$ and $Q_n = P_m$.

In this paper we use only automata with the following property: for each state Q_i of the automaton there is an accepting path that contains Q_i. Consequently, there is no useless and sink states and the automaton may not be fully determined, i.e., it may happen that for a state Q_i and an input letter a the transition function assigns the empty set.

Definition 3 (1CFPA, d-1CFPA and n-1CFPA). *A nondeterministic finite automaton* $\mathbf{A}$ *is a 1 cycle-free path automaton, a 1CFPA, for short, if there is a unique cycle-free accepting path from each of its states. Moreover, if the automaton* $\mathbf{A}$ *has no* λ-*transition, then it is an n-1CFPA, and if it is a deterministic, then it d-1CFPA.*

Figure 1 shows an example. As a consequence of the definition above, a 1CFPA has exactly one final state. From now on F will refer not only for the set of final states, but for its unique element as well. The following result is proven in [11].

Theorem 4. *The family of languages which are described by union-free expressions and the family of languages recognized by 1CFPAs are exactly the same.*

Proposition 5. *Since from every state* R *there is exactly one transition is going to the direction of* F *(without cycle), the word which transfers the state* R *to* F *in cycle-free path is unique for each state.*

Definition 6. (backbone). *The backbone of the automaton is the cycle-free path from the initial state* (S) *to the final state* (F). *The other parts of the automaton are the loops, sub-loops etc. The word accepted by the backbone is called the backbone word.*

In a directed graph there are two different concepts that are somewhat analogous to cycles in the undirected graphs. Cycles in undirected graph allow to

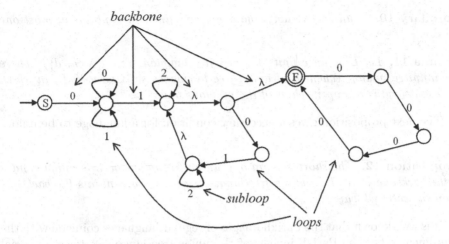

Fig. 1. An example for a 1-cycle-free-path-automaton.

visit a node more than once in a path, while they also allow to connect nodes in alternative paths. The directed cycles allow to return to an already visited node in a path (in a directed graph). Two alternative paths (as two halves of an undirected cycle) give the chance to reach the same target node from a start node in two different cycle-free way. Based on that we can compare the graphs of the classes of automata accepting the union-free and the finite languages.

Proposition 7. *Every union-free language is accepted by automata with graphs having no alternative paths. Every automaton with one final state and without alternative paths is accepting a union-free language. Every finite language is accepted by automata with no cycles. Cycle-free automata accept finite languages.*

As we have already mentioned the class of finite languages is an important subclass of the class of regular languages. Both the classes of nondeterministic and deterministic variants of cycle-free finite state automata correspond to the class of finite languages. The classes of the union-free languages form a hierarchy as we describe here. The result of Theorem 4 allows us to call the language classes accepted by n-1CFPAs and d-1CFPAs as λ-*free nondeterministic union-free* and *deterministic union-free*, respectively. We also use the abbreviated names *n-union-free* and *d-union-free* for these classes of languages.

3   Properties of Union-Free Language Classes

Now we detail some properties of the languages defined above.

Lemma 8. *There are infinitely many non-comparable x-union-free languages with $x \in \{\lambda, n, d\}$.*

Lemma 9. *A union-free language is infinite if and only if every regular expression contain Kleene star that describes it.*

Corollary 10. *A union-free language is either infinite or contains at most one word.*

Lemma 11. *Let L be an infinite x-union-free language ($x \in \{\lambda, n, d\}$). There are infinitely many sequences of union-free languages starting with L, in which each language is a proper subset of the previous one.*

The next proposition gives a necessary condition for a language to be union-free.

Proposition 12. *The shortest word of a union-free language L is unique and it is the backbone word. In a union-free language each word contains the backbone word in scattered way.*

It is well-known that the Parikh images of regular languages coincide with the semi-linear sets. The Parikh images of the union-free languages form a special subset of the semi-linear sets, and at the same time, they form a special superset of the linear sets.

Definition 13 (Conditional-linear sets). *A set of vectors W is conditional-linear if the following condition holds. Every vector α is in W if and only if it can be written in the form*

$$\alpha = \alpha_0 + \delta_1 n_1 \alpha_1 + \delta_2 n_2 \alpha_i + \cdots + \delta_m n_m \alpha_m,$$

where n_j are non-negative integers and α_j are fixed vectors of non-negative integers, and δ_i are conditional coefficients defined in the following way: $\delta_1 = 1$, and if $i > 1$, then δ_i is either without any condition and equals to 1, or depends on the coefficient of some α_j with $j < i$, and in such a case it equals to 1 if $\delta_j n_j > 0$ and to 0 if $\delta_j n_j = 0$:

$$\delta_i = 1, \qquad\qquad\qquad \text{if there is no condition for } \alpha_i;$$

$$\delta_i = \begin{cases} 1, & \text{if } \delta_j n_j > 0; \\ 0, & \text{if } \delta_j n_j = 0; \end{cases} \qquad \text{if } \alpha_i \text{ depends on the coefficient of } \alpha_j.$$

Having $\delta_i = 1$ for all i without any conditions, the linear sets can be obtained. Thus conditional-linear sets are a kind of generalisations of linear sets. Moreover, all conditional linear sets are semilinear, i.e., they are finite unions of linear sets. However, there are semilinear sets that are not conditional linear.

Theorem 14. *Conditional-linear sets coincide with the Parikh images of union-free languages.*

Let L be a union-free language. Note that $\lambda \in L$ if and only if the backbone word is the empty word. This implies that every terminal is under a Kleene star in the tree of the regular expression. Under these circumstances the language can be accepted by a 1CFPA with backbone word λ. If L is n-union-free and $\lambda \in L$, then $S = F$ in the corresponding n-1CFPA. Since every 1CFPA (and thus d-1CFPA) has exactly one accepting state, languages which cannot be accepted by deterministic finite automata with only one final state are not d-union-free languages.

Now, we are in the position to claim the theorem about the closure properties of union-free languages.

Theorem 15 (Closure properties of union-free languages). *The family of union-free languages is closed under the operations concatenation and Kleene star. Further, it is closed under the following operations: reversal, homeomorphism, substitution by union-free expression, Kleene plus, and for any fixed natural number n it is closed under the n-th power.*

The family of union-free languages is not closed under the following operations: union (of course), intersection, intersection with regular languages, complement, difference, symmetric difference, cyclic permutation, permutation, shuffle, inverse morphism and substitution by regular expression.

Corollary 16. *The family of union-free languages is not a cone, not an AFL and not an anti-AFL.*

On the other hand we have only anti-closure properties for the deterministic counterpart:

Theorem 17 (Closure properties of d-union-free languages). *The class of deterministic union-free languages is not closed under union, complement, difference, intersection, intersection by regular languages, concatenation, square, Kleene star, reversal, cyclic shift, permutation, homomorphism, and inverse morphism.*

We are turning to hierarchy results. On one hand it is clear by definition that all d-union-free languages are n-union-free languages and all n-union-free languages are union-free. The language a^*b^* is union-free. However, it is not n-union-free. The language $(aa + ab + ba + bb)^*$ is n-union-free, but not d-union-free. Thus, we can state the following:

Corollary 18. *There is a proper hierarchy among the union-free classes:*

$$d\text{-union free} \subsetneq n\text{-union-free} \subsetneq union\text{-free}.$$

4   Union-Complexity of Regular Languages

We start this section by a decomposition result [2,10].

Definition 19. *A regular expression is in union normal form if it is a finite union of union-free expressions.*

Theorem 20. *For each regular language there is a regular expression in union normal form that describes it.*

Moreover, based on the following equivalences among regular expressions,

1. $(x + y)^*$ can be written in the form $(x^*y^*)^*$,
2. $(x + y)z$ can be written in the form $(xz + yz)$,
3. $x(z + v)$ can be written in the form $(xz + xv)$,
4. $(x + y)(z + v)$ can be written in the form $(xz + xv) + (yz + yv)$,

where x, y, z and v are arbitrary regular expressions, one can efficiently find an equivalent expression in union normal form for any regular expression.

And now we have some notes about the regular expressions containing the union operation, but describing union-free regular languages.

Let r be a regular expression. For the sake of simplicity assume that its tree is a binary tree, which means that all unions and concatenations have exactly two components, while the Kleene stars have exactly one.

Theorem 21. *Let r be a regular expression. If every union operation is under a Kleene star operation in the tree form of r, then r defines a union-free regular language.*

The class of union-free languages is an interesting class including several languages since we have:

Corollary 22. *For each regular language L the language L^* is union-free regular.*

Now, based on [10, 12] we are going to define the union-complexity of languages by specific decompositions.

A decomposition $L = \bigcup_{i=1}^{n} L_i$ is called proper, if there is no language L_j such that $L_j \subseteq \bigcup_{i=1}^{j-1} L_i \cup \bigcup_{i=j+1}^{n} L_i$. (One needs all the languages L_i to describe L, i.e., there is no useless member of the union.) A normal form is called proper normal form if it gives a proper decomposition.

Definition 23 (Union-complexity). $L = \bigcup_{i=1}^{n} L_i$ *is a minimal decomposition of the language L if each L_i is a union-free language and there is no $m < n$ such that $L = \bigcup_{i=1}^{m} L_i$, where each L_i is union-free. Then, n is called the union-complexity of language L.*

Every minimal decomposition is a proper decomposition, but the converse does not hold, there are proper decompositions which are not minimal.

Now we are showing special minimal decompositions: a minimal decomposition of L is given by maximal union-free languages, if there is no L_i' such that $L_i' \supset L_i$ and replacing L_i with L_i' in the union, the resulted language L is the same as before.

Proposition 24. *The minimal decomposition by maximal union-free languages of a regular language may not be unique.*

Consider the language over $V = \{a, b\}$ containing all words that do not contain bb as a consecutive substring. Its union-complexity is 2, but there are two minimal decompositions using maximal union-free languages:

$$((ba)^*a^*)^* + ((ba)^*a^*)^*b((ab)^*a^*)^*,$$

and

$$((ab)^*a^*)^* + ((ba)^*a^*)^*b((ab)^*a^*)^*.$$

Let $\mathbf{L}_n$ be the family of languages which can be written as union of n union-free languages.

Theorem 25. *The families $\mathbf{L}_n$ and $\mathbf{L}_m$ are in the following relation:*

$$\mathbf{L}_n \supsetneq \mathbf{L}_m \text{ iff } n > m.$$

The previous theorem presents an infinite hierarchy of regular languages, in which the union-free ones are the simplest ones. The planet of regular languages is shown in Fig. 2, where the "west pole" is the empty language, the west region contains the union-free languages, the south region contains the finite languages. The intersection of the classes of union-free and finite languages includes the empty language and all the singleton languages. A singleton contains exactly one word. The union-complexity grows to the east direction.

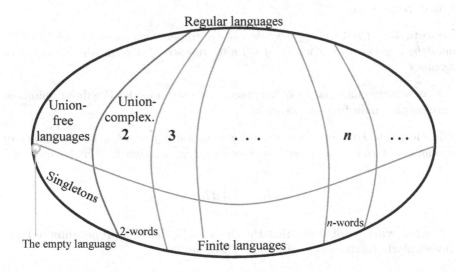

Fig. 2. The "planet" of regular languages.

We can summarise the known results about the union-complexity in the following theorem.

Theorem 26. *The union-complexity of union-free languages is at most 1: it is 0 for the empty language and 1 for every nonempty union-free language.*

For every finite language, its union-complexity is exactly the cardinality of the language.

A language is regular if and only if its union-complexity is finite.

For each regular language L the union-complexity of L^* is 1.

In [1] it has been proven that the union-complexity of regular languages is computable. However, the method is very complex and cannot be used in practical applications. Some lower and upper bound may be computed much faster, e.g., a union normal form of a regular language defines an upper bound for its union-complexity. On the other hand one can also obtain lower bounds by analysing the short words of the language:

Proposition 27. *Let L be a regular language. Fix a natural number n and let $Z_n = \{w \in L \mid |w| \le n\}$. Consider any subset Z of Z_n with maximal cardinality such that any of the elements of Z does not contain any other elements of Z in a scattered way. Then $|Z|$ is a lower bound for the union-complexity of L.*

While every regular language can be expressed as a union of a finite number of union-free languages, this is not true if we replace union-free languages by d-union-free languages.

Theorem 28. *The language described by the regular expression $((a+b)(a+b))^*$ cannot be expressed as a union of a finite number of deterministic union-free languages.*

As new subregular classes of languages, we may consider the finite unions of deterministic union-free languages [8].

Definition 29. *For every positive integer m, we define dL_m as the family of languages that can be expressed as a union of m d-union-free languages. Furthermore, let*

$$dL_* = \bigcup_{i=1}^{\infty} dL_i.$$

The following result shows that the classes dL_n define a proper infinite hierarchy similarly to the classes shown in Theorem 25.

Theorem 30. *Let n and m be positive integers. The families dL_n and dL_m are in the following relation:*

$$dL_n \supsetneq dL_m \text{iff } n > m.$$

Moreover,

$$dL_* \supsetneq dL_m.$$

5   Conclusions

We examined in detail the classes of union-free and deterministic union-free languages, moreover we have defined a new class between them, namely the class of n-union-free languages. Various properties of these classes were shown. Since every regular language is a finite union of union-free languages, the union-complexity as a complexity measure of the regular languages was considered. Although it is known that the union-complexity of the regular languages can be computed, there is not known any efficient algorithm to do it. It was also recalled that there is a union-free language which cannot be written as a finite union of d-union-free languages.

References

1. Afonin, S., Golomazov, D.: Minimal union-free decompositions of regular languages. In: Dediu, A.H., Ionescu, A.M., Martín-Vide, C. (eds.) LATA 2009. LNCS, vol. 5457, pp. 83–92. Springer, Heidelberg (2009). https://doi.org/10.1007/978-3-642-00982-2_7

2. Brzozowski, J.A.: Regular expression techniques for sequential circuits. Ph.D. Dissertation, Department of Electrical Engineering, Princeton University, Princeton, June 1962

3. Brzozowski, J.A., Davies, S.: Most complex deterministic union-free regular languages. In: Konstantinidis, S., Pighizzini, G. (eds.) DCFS 2018. LNCS, vol. 10952, pp. 37–48. Springer, Cham (2018). https://doi.org/10.1007/978-3-319-94631-3_4

4. Crvenković, S., Dolinka, I., Ésik, Z.: On equations for union-free regular languages. Inf. Comput. **164**(1), 152–172 (2001). https://doi.org/10.1006/inco.2000.2889

5. Holzer, M., Kutrib, M.: Structure and complexity of some subregular language families. In: Konstantinidis, S., Moreira, N., Reis, R., Shallit, J. (eds.) The Role of Theory in Computer Science - Essays Dedicated to Janusz Brzozowski, pp. 59–82. World Scientific (2017). https://doi.org/10.1142/9789813148208_0003

6. Hopcroft, J.E., Ullman, J.D.: Introduction to Automata Theory, Languages and Computation. Addison-Wesley, Reading (1979)

7. Jirásková, G., Masopust, T.: Complexity in union-free regular languages. Int. J. Found. Comput. Sci. **22**, 1639–1653 (2011). https://doi.org/10.1142/S0129054111008933

8. Jirásková, G., Nagy, B.: On union-free and deterministic union-free languages. In: Baeten, J.C.M., Ball, T., de Boer, F.S. (eds.) TCS 2012. LNCS, vol. 7604, pp. 179–192. Springer, Heidelberg (2012). https://doi.org/10.1007/978-3-642-33475-7_13

9. Kutrib, M., Wendlandt, M.: Expressive capacity of subregular expressions. RAIRO ITA Theor. Inform. Appl. **52**(2–3–4), 201–218 (2018). https://doi.org/10.1051/ita/2018014

10. Nagy, B.: A normal form for regular expressions. In: Calude, C., Calude, E., Dinnen, M.J. (eds.) Supplemental Papers for DLT 2004, pp. 51–60. CDMTCS Report 252, Auckland (2004)

11. Nagy, B.: Union-free regular languages and 1-cycle-free-path-automata. Publ. Math. Debrecen **68**, 183–197 (2006)

12. Nagy, B.: On union-complexity of regular languages. In: Proceedings of the 11th IEEE International Symposium on Computational Intelligence and Informatics, pp. 177–182 (2010)
13. Yu, S.: Regular languages. In: Rozenberg, G., Salomaa, A. (eds.) Handbook of Formal Languages, pp. 41–100. Springer, Heidelberg (1997). https://doi.org/10.1007/978-3-642-59136-5_2

Limited Automata: Properties, Complexity and Variants

Giovanni Pighizzini[✉]

Dipartimento di Informatica, Università degli Studi di Milano, Milan, Italy
pighizzini@di.unimi.it

Abstract. Limited automata are single-tape Turing machines with severe rewriting restrictions. They have been introduced in 1967 by Thomas Hibbard, who proved that they have the same computational power as pushdown automata. Hence, they provide an alternative characterization of the class of context-free languages in terms of recognizing devices. After that paper, these models have been almost forgotten for many years. Only recently limited automata were reconsidered in a series of papers, where several properties of them and of their variants have been investigated. In this work we present an overview of the most important results obtained in these researches. We also discuss some related models and possible lines for future investigations.

1 A Short Introduction with a Classical Example

This paper is devoted to *limited automata*. These devices have been introduced, with the aim of generalizing the notion of determinism in context-free languages, by Thomas N. Hibbard in 1967, who originally called them *scan limited automata*. We present an overview of the most important results on limited automata: we discuss their computational power, their descriptional complexity, the relationships between deterministic and nondeterministic versions. Finally, we shortly discuss some variants of these devices and some related models. In the paper we will also address some problems related to these devices which, in our opinion, deserve investigation.

In order illustrate the model, we start by presenting a classical example which will turn out to be useful in the paper.

Suppose we need to verify that a sequence of brackets is correctly balanced. A quite natural way to proceed is to start from the first opening bracket and search for the corresponding closing bracket. To locate it, a counter which is incremented for each opening bracket and decremented for each closing bracket can be helpful. When during this process the counter reaches the initial value, the closing bracket is reached. These operations can be iterated for each opening bracket in order to verify the matching of all the pairs of brackets and the correct nesting in the sequence.

© IFIP International Federation for Information Processing 2019
Published by Springer Nature Switzerland AG 2019
M. Hospodár et al. (Eds.): DCFS 2019, LNCS 11612, pp. 57–73, 2019.
https://doi.org/10.1007/978-3-030-23247-4_4

We could use a different and perhaps more simple strategy. Instead of locating the first opening bracket, we start by locating the first closing one: the corresponding opening bracket is necessarily the last bracket before it, that must be of the same type. If these two brackets are removed or rewritten by a different symbol, the same procedure can be repeated on the sequence so modified: locate the first closing bracket, check if the last bracket before it is of the same type, and overwrite these two brackets. When no more closing brackets are left in the sequence, even none opening bracket can be left. In this case the original sequence was balanced. Otherwise, in the following cases the sequence is not balanced:

- At the end, the sequence left on the tape contains some opening bracket.
- After locating a closing bracket, no opening bracket before it is found.
- After locating a closing bracket, the last opening bracket found before it is of a different type.

Suppose now that the sequence of brackets is written on a Turing machine tape, one bracket per cell, and suppose that the computation of the machine starts, as usual, with the head scanning the cell containing the first input symbol. In this way, each input cell is reached for the first time while moving the head from left to right. We can observe that, applying the above described strategy, the following facts hold:

- A cell containing a closing bracket is overwritten only when the head visits it for the first time. After that operation the head is moved back to the left to search an opening bracket.
- A cell containing an opening bracket is overwritten only when the head visits it for the second time. In this case the cell is entered by the head from the right.
- After one of these two *active visits*, a cell can be visited further many times, but it cannot be overwritten, so it is "frozen".

As we will discuss in the paper, each context-free language can be recognized by a strategy similar to the one we just described. In particular, each context-free language can be recognized by a single-tape machine which is able to overwrite the contents of each tape cell *only in the first two visits*. This is the basic idea under the computational model of *limited automata* that we discuss in this work. The device we have outlined for this specific case is called 2-*limited automaton*, since each cell can be overwritten only in the first two visits and, after that, it is never modified.

2   Limited Automata

Given an integer $d \geq 0$, a *d-limited automaton* is a Turing machine with a single tape, which initially contains the input, one symbol for each tape cell. At the left and at the right of the input there are cells containing the two special symbols $\triangleright$

and ◁ called, respectively, the *left* and the *right end-markers*. The machine head cannot leave the tape segment delimited by the two end-markers, i.e., it cannot move to the left of the cell containing ▷ and to the right of cell containing ◁.

In d-limited automata, each tape cell can be overwritten only in the first d visits. After that the cell is "frozen", so it cannot be further modified. The cells containing the two end-markers cannot be never overwritten.

Acceptance is defined in a standard way, as for Turing machines. More technical details can be found in [28,29].[1]

We will now discuss the computational power of these models, in the nondeterministic and deterministic cases. Then, we will present descriptional complexity aspects and several open problems. We will conclude the section by shortly discussing time complexity.

2.1 Computational Power, Determinism and Nondeterminism

In Sect. 1 we described how a 2-limited automaton can accept the language of balanced sequences of brackets. We remind the reader that such a language is called *Dyck language*. More precisely, given an alphabet Ω_k containing k types of brackets (hence $2k$ symbols) we denote by D_k the *Dyck language* over it.

Dyck languages are important in the investigation of context-free languages, because they capture the recursive structure of any context-free language. This fact is formalized in the following famous result:

Theorem 1 (Chomsky-Schützenberger Theorem [2]). *Each context-free language L over an alphabet Σ can be represented as a homomorphic image $L = h(D_k \cap R)$, for some integer $k > 0$, where $R \subseteq \Omega_k^*$ is a regular language and $h : \Omega_k \to \Sigma^*$ is a homomorphism.*

Theorem 1 suggests a way to build, for any context-free language L, a recognizer which is the combination of the following devices, as depicted in Fig. 1:

- A one-way nondeterministic machine T that on each input $w \in \Sigma^*$ produces a string $z \in h^{-1}(w)$.
- A machine A_D recognizing the Dyck language D_k.
- A one-way finite automaton A_R accepting the regular language R.

As machine A_D we can use the 2-limited automaton for the recognition of D_k outlined in Sect. 1. Using the fact that the homomorphism h can be supposed to be non-erasing [20], it is possible to combine these machines in such a way that also the resulting machine accepting the given context-free language L is a 2-limited automaton. (Details can be found in [26,28]). This allows to conclude that each context-free language is accepted by a 2-limited automaton.

The converse also holds. Furthermore, by allowing a larger, but still constant number of initial visits in which rewritings are possibles, the computational power does not increase. By summarizing:

---

[1] Actually, the original definition of d-limited automata was given by Hibbard by considering some kinds of rewriting systems [9]. It is not difficult to reformulate it, as we did, in terms of Turing machines.

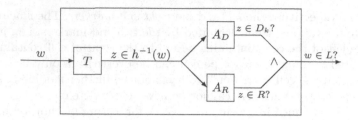

Fig. 1. A machine accepting $L = h(D_k \cap R)$.

Theorem 2 ([9]). *For each $d \geq 2$, the class of languages accepted by d-limited automata coincides with the class of context-free languages.*

The just outlined conversion from context-free languages to 2-limited automata is intrinsically nondeterministic. Actually, the conversion presented by Hibbard is different and preserves the determinism. Hence, each deterministic context-free language is accepted by a deterministic 2-limited automaton. However, determinism is not preserved by the converse transformation in the form presented in [9]. Indeed, the problem of the equivalence between the class of deterministic context-free language and the class of languages accepted by deterministic 2-limited automata was left open in that paper. This problem was recently solved in [29], by giving a transformation from 2-limited automata to pushdown automata which preserves the determinism. The transformation is based on an extension of *transition tables*, originally introduced by Shepherdson [32] to obtain a simulation of two-way finite automata by equivalent one-way ones.

Theorem 3 ([29]). *The class of languages accepted by deterministic 2-limited automata coincides with the class of deterministic context-free languages.*

It is an easy observation that Theorem 3 cannot be extended to $d > 2$. For instance, the following language, which is not deterministic, can be accepted by a deterministic 3-limited automaton A:

$$L = \{a^n b^n c \mid n \geq 0\} \cup \{a^n b^{2n} d \mid n \geq 0\}.$$

To recognize L, A can scan the tape from left to right, to locate the right end-marker and, moving back, it can read the last input symbol. If the symbol is a c, then A has to verify whether or not the number of the a's in the input coincides with the number of the b's. To this aim, A continues to move to the left, to find a cell containing an a, which is rewritten by the symbol X. Then it moves to the right to search a cell containing a b, which is also rewritten by the symbol X. This process is repeated up to reach the left end-marker while searching an a. When the last symbol of the input is a d, the only difference in the procedure is that for each a the automaton A has to overwrite two occurrences of the letter b.

We point out that the main motivation of the original work of Hibbard was to extend the notion of determinism for context-free languages (indeed, the title of [9] is *"A Generalization of Context-Free Determinism"*). With respect to the number d of initial visits in which rewriting are allowed, by extending the last example he proved the existence of an infinite hierarchy of deterministic languages:

Theorem 4 ([9]). *For each $d > 2$ there exists a language which is recognized by a deterministic d-limited automaton, but which cannot be accepted by any deterministic $(d-1)$-limited automaton.*

In [9] it is claimed (without proof) that the set of palindromes cannot be accepted by deterministic d-limited automata, for any integer d. As a consequence, the above hierarchy of deterministic languages does not cover all the class of context-free languages. It would be interesting to have a formal proof of this fact.

Results comparing the degrees of nondeterminism that can be defined according to the above hierarchy and measures of nondeterminism for pushdown automata are presented in [18].

By allowing to overwrite tape cells only in the first visit, the computational power of limited automata reduces to the class of regular languages.

Theorem 5 ([34, Thm. 12.1]). *The class of languages accepted by 1-limited automata coincides with the class of regular languages.*

Concerning the computational power of limited automata, we finally mention the case where the number of initial visits to each cell in which rewritings are possible is not constant, but it is bounded by a function $f(n)$ of the input length n. This case was studied by Wechsung and Brandstädt which gave a characterization in terms of languages accepted by space bounded *one-way auxiliary pushdown automata*, namely pushdown automata with a one-way input tape, extended with a two-way work tape. The space is measured by taking into account *only the work tape.*

Theorem 6 ([36]). *For any recursive function $f(n)$, the class of languages accepted by $f(n)$-limited automata coincides with the class of languages accepted by auxiliary pushdown automata in space $O(f(n))$.*

2.2 Descriptional Complexity

To study the descriptional complexity of a formal system, we have to consider the *size* of its description, namely the number of symbols which are used to write down its description. In the case of limited automata over a given input alphabet Σ, the size is a polynomial in the cardinalities of the state set and of the working alphabet. For pushdown automata we also have to take into account how many symbols can be written on the pushdown store in one single move. However, if each move is allowed to increase the height of the pushdown by adding at most one symbol, then the size is polynomial in the number of states and in the cardinality of the pushdown alphabet. In a similar way, to define the size of context-free grammars, we have to take into account the maximal length of the right-hand sides of productions. For grammars in Chomsky normal form or, more in general, grammars in which the production right-hand sides have length at most 2, the size is polynomial in the number of variables. Finally, for finite automata, the size is polynomial with respect to the number of states.

We introduce a family of languages which will be useful to discuss descriptional complexity results.

For each integer $n > 0$, let K_n be the set of all strings over the alphabet $\{a, b\}$ consisting of the concatenation of blocks of length n, where the last block is equal to one of the previous blocks. Formally:

$$K_n = \{x_1 \cdots x_k x \mid k > 0,\ x_1, \ldots, x_k, x \in \{a, b\}^n, \exists j, 1 \le j \le k,\ x_j = x\}.$$

A deterministic 2-limited automaton for K_n

To accept K_n, a deterministic 2-limited automaton M_n can first make a scan from left to right of the input to locate the right end-marker (this "consumes" the first visit to each tape cell). Then M_n inspects each block x_j of length n starting from $j = k$ up to $j = 1$, and compares it, symbol by symbol, with the last block x. This can be done by moving the head back and forth between the block under consideration and the last block, using a counter modulo n to identify the corresponding positions that need to be compared in the two blocks, while marking the symbols of x_j. In this phase or in the first scan, M_n also checks if the length of the input is a multiple of n. The implementation of M_n can be done by using $O(n)$ states and a working alphabet of $O(1)$ symbols.

A nondeterministic 1-limited automaton for K_n

In a first complete scan of the tape, the automaton nondeterministically marks two cells. No more rewriting operations are possible after this phase. The first marked cell is guessed to be the leftmost position of the required block x_j, while the other one is guessed to be the leftmost position of the last block x. In a second phase, using a counter modulo n, the machine can verify that the input length is a multiple of n, the last marked position corresponds to the leftmost symbol of the last block of length n, and the other marked position is the leftmost symbol of another block of length n. Finally, the automaton makes n scans of the part of the tape which contains the two selected blocks: in the ith scan it checks if the ith symbols in the marked blocks are equal. The implementation produces a nondeterministic 1-limited automaton with $O(n)$ states.

Lower bounds for K_n

The following lower bounds for the recognition of K_n by pushdown and finite automata can be proved:

- To accept and to generate K_n, pushdown automata and context-free grammars require exponential size in n.
  The proof can be done by using the *interchange lemma* for context-free languages [19]. The argument is similar to that used in [29] for a slightly different language.
- Any one-way deterministic automaton accepting K_n requires a number of states double exponential in n.

The proof uses distinguishability arguments. Let $x_1, x_2, \ldots, x_{2^n}$ be a list of all strings in $\{a, b\}^n$, in some fixed order, and F be the set of all functions from $\{1, 2, \ldots, 2^n\}$ to $\{0, 1\}$. For each $f \in F$, consider the string $w_f = x_1^{f(1)} x_2^{f(2)} \cdots x_{2^n}^{f(2^n)}$. Given $f, g \in F$, with $f \neq g$, it can be verified that any string x_i with $f(i) \neq g(i)$ distinguishes w_f and w_g. Since $\#F = 2^{2^n}$, the lower bound follows.

The size cost of the simulation of 2-limited automata by pushdown automata has been investigated in [29] by proving an exponential upper bound. The result has been recently improved, by showing that the upper bound remains exponential if we simulate a d-limited automaton, with $d > 2$, by a pushdown automaton [14]. Considering the lower bound given for the size of pushdown automata accepting K_n, we obtain:

Theorem 7 ([14,29]). *For each $d > 1$, the size cost of the transformation of d-limited automata into equivalent pushdown automata is exponential.*

Concerning the transformation of *deterministic* 2-limited automata into equivalent deterministic pushdown automata, it has been proved a double exponential upper bound, which reduces to a simple exponential if the input is given to the pushdown automaton with an extra special symbol marking the right end. The optimality of the exponential bounds can be proved using K_n. We conjecture that the double exponential upper bound cannot be reduced.

For the converse transformations, we have the following result:

Theorem 8 ([29]). *The size cost of the transformation of pushdown automata into 2-limited automata is polynomial. Furthermore, the polynomial transformation preserves determinism.*

By Theorem 5, 1-limited automata have the same power of finite state automata. The proof of this result was obtained by Wagner and Wechung by adapting the Shepherdson's technique for the transformation of two-way finite automata into equivalent one-way ones [32]: given a 1-limited automaton, a nondeterministic one-way automaton is created which keeps in its state a transition table corresponding to the portion of the tape at the left of the head. The table is used to replace parts of computations that from the current head position finally reach for the first time the position to the right of it, by making a sequence of moves which visit some of the already scanned tape cells.

By analyzing the cost of such a simulation and by considering the family of languages K_n, the following costs can be obtained:

Theorem 9 ([28]). *The size costs of the transformation of 1-limited automata into equivalent one-way nondeterministic and deterministic finite automata are exponential and double exponential, respectively.*

We point out that the double exponential cost in Theorem 9 is related to a double role of the nondeterminism in 1-limited automata. When the head of a 1-limited automaton reaches for the first time a tape cell, it overwrites the contents according to a nondeterministic choice.[2] Furthermore, the set of nondeterministic choices that are allowed during the next visits to the same cell depends on the symbol that has been chosen to rewrite it in the first visit and that cannot be further changed, namely it depends on the nondeterministic choice which was made during the first visit.

When the given 1-limited automaton is *deterministic*, the same simulation produces a *one-way deterministic* finite automaton of exponential size. The optimality can be easily proved by considering the reversal of the language K_n.

We briefly discuss the *unary case*, namely, the case of languages defined over a one-letter alphabet. It is well known that, under this restriction, the classes of context-free and of regular languages coincide [4]. Hence, for each $d \geq 0$, unary d-limited automata recognize only regular languages. Since the family K_n of witness languages used in Theorem 9 is defined over a binary alphabet, it is quite natural to ask if there is any difference in the unary case.

A first result comparing the sizes of unary 1-limited automata and those of equivalent two-way nondeterministic finite automata was presented in [28]. Kutrib and Wendlandt proved state lower bounds for the simulation of unary d-limited automata by different variants of finite automata [14,15]. More recently, the following result has been proved:

Theorem 10 ([30]). *For each integer $n > 0$, the singleton language $\{a^{2^n}\}$ is accepted by a deterministic 1-limited automaton of size $O(n)$, while each one-way nondeterministic finite automaton accepting it needs $2^n + 1$ states.*

The upper bound in Theorem 10 was obtained by making use of the construction and of the properties of the *binary carry sequence*, an infinite sequence of integers related base 2 representation [33].

With a small modification, it can be shown that for each $n > 0$ even the language $\{a^{2^n}\}^*$ can be accepted by a deterministic 1-limited automaton of size $O(n)$, while each *two-way nondeterministic finite automaton* accepting it requires 2^n states [30].

The results comparing the sizes of finite automata and 1-limited automata are summarized in Fig. 2. The upper bounds in the diagram follow from the simulations of 1-limited automata by finite automata (see Theorem 9 and the discussion after it). All the lower bounds, with the exception of those from 1-limited automata to one-way deterministic finite automata (arrow (a) in Fig. 2) and to deterministic 1-limited automata (b), are witnessed by the unary language $\{a^{2^n}\}^*$. For the double exponential lower bound from 1-limited automata to one-way deterministic automata (a), the binary witness K_n can be used. It is an open problem if the same gap can be achieved in the unary case. From our experience on unary languages we conjecture a negative answer. The exponential lower bound from 1-limited automata to deterministic 1-limited automata (b)

---

[2] We could have moves that do not change the contents of a cell even in the first visit, as we seen in the above example of 1-limited automaton accepting K_n. For a such a move, we can imagine that the cell is rewritten by the same symbol which is already in it.

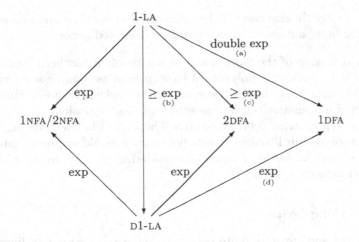

Fig. 2. State costs of conversions of 1-limited automata (1-LA) and deterministic 1-limited automata (D1-LA) into equivalent one-way and two-way deterministic and non-deterministic finite automata (1DFA, 1NFA, 2DFA, 2NFA).

is a consequence of the double exponential lower bound to one-way deterministic automata (a) and of the cost of the simulation of deterministic 1-limited automata by one-way deterministic automata (d).

At the moment we do not know direct simulations of 1-limited automata by *deterministic* 1-limited automata (b) and by *two-way deterministic* automata (c). For instance, it should be interesting to know if simulating 1-limited automata by *two-way* (instead of *one-way*) deterministic automata the cost reduces from a double exponential to a simple exponential.

By summarizing, we can propose the following problems:

Problem 1. Study the size cost of the simulation of *unary* 1-limited automata by one-way deterministic finite automata (unary version of (a)).

Problem 2. Study the size cost of the simulation of 1-limited automata by *deterministic* 1-limited automata, in the general and in the unary case (b).

Problem 3. Study the size cost of the simulation of 1-limited automata by *two-way deterministic* finite automata, in the general and in the unary case (c).

We point out that the last two problems are variants of the question of the cost of the elimination of nondeterminism from two-way automata, proposed by Sakoda and Sipser in 1978 [31], which is still open (for a recent survey, see [25]). In particular, concerning Problem 2, we observe that for the elimination of the nondeterminism from 1-limited automata an exponential lower bound is known, while for the corresponding problem in two-way finite automata the best known lower bound is polynomial [3].

It could be also interesting to study a "relaxed" version of the problem of Sakoda and Sipser, in which the simulating machine could overwrite the contents of tape cells during the first visit:

Problem 4. Study the size costs of the simulations of one-way and two-way non-deterministic finite automata by *deterministic* 1-limited automata.

A relaxed version of the Sakoda and Sipser problem has been recently considered in [5], by proving a polynomial blowup from two-way nondeterministic automata to single-tape deterministic machines working in linear time. Since each 1-limited automaton can be converted into an equivalent one working in linear time also preserving determinism (see Theorem 11 below), proving that the simulation proposed in Problem 4 costs polynomial would improve that result.

Problem 4 can be further relaxed by considering simulations by deterministic d-limited automata, for $d > 1$.

2.3 Time Complexity

While one-way and two-way finite automata can always accept in linear time, with respect to the input length, there are 1-limited automata that use quadratic time [6].

The Shepherdson's technique, used by Wagner and Wechsung to prove Theorem 5, has been recently refined to prove that, with only a polynomial increase in the size, 1-limited automata can be forced to work in linear time. Roughly, the main idea is that the running time of 1-limited automata can be reduced by avoiding computation paths which move back to the left and visit too many tape cells before reaching again the current position. This is done with a tricky simulation which stores transition tables on a tape track.

Theorem 11 ([6])**.** *With a polynomial size increase, each 1-limited automaton can be transformed into an equivalent 1-limited automaton which works in linear time. Furthermore, determinism can be preserved in such a conversion.*

We point out that the machine obtained in Theorem 11 is also a *Hennie machines*, namely, a single-tape Turing machine working in linear time. It is known that these devices can recognize only regular languages.[3]

In our knowledge, at the moment there are no other results concerning the time complexity of limited automata.

3 Strongly Limited Automata

In Sect. 2, using the Chomsky-Schützenberger representation theorem (Theorem 1), we discussed how to construct for any context-free language a 2-limited automaton accepting it. We remind the reader that such a 2-limited automaton is obtained by combining three machines T, A_R and A_D, as summarized in Fig. 1. While T and A_R are finite state machines, A_D is the only "context-free component" in the construction. In fact, its purpose is that of recognizing a Dyck

---

[3] The proof of this result has been given by Hennie, for the deterministic case [8]. Several improvements have been presented in the literature. See [24] for a survey.

language D_k. A_D can be implemented as the 2-limited automaton described in Sect. 1. However, we can notice that in order to recognize D_k, A_D does not use all the capabilities of 2-limited automata. For instance, it moves from left to right only to search closing brackets: in this phase, A_D does not need neither to change the state nor to make any rewriting, except when it finally reaches the cell containing a closing bracket, where it starts to move to the left to search a symbol not yet overwritten, which is expected to be the corresponding opening bracket. While moving to the left, A_D ignores the contents of cells that have been already overwritten.

Since, as we wrote, A_D is the only "context-free component" in the construction and it can be implemented without using all the capabilities of 2-limited automata, we can ask if it is possible to restrict the moves of 2-limited automata, without reducing the computational power.

In [27] we gave a positive answer to this question, by introducing *strongly limited automata*, a restriction of 2-limited automata which closely imitates the moves that are used by limited automata to accept Dyck languages. In particular, strongly limited automata satisfy the following restrictions:

- While moving to the right, a strongly limited automaton always uses the initial state q_0 until a cell (which has not been yet overwritten) is modified. Then, it enters a different state and starts to move to the left.
- While moving to the left, the automaton ignores the cells that have been already overwritten and, without changing its internal state, overwrites the other ones it meets, up to some position where it enters q_0 and starts again to move to the right.
- In the final phase of the computation, which starts when the right end-marker is reached, the automaton inspects all tape cells, to check whether or not the string which is finally on the tape belongs to a given 2-strictly locally testable language. Roughly, this means that all the factors of two letters of this string (including the end-markers) belong to a given set.

We shortly discuss some examples (for more examples see [26, 27]).

Example 1. The language $L = \{a^n b^n \mid n \geq 0\}$ can be accepted by a strongly limited automaton which in the initial state q_0 moves the head to the right to search the first cell containing a b. When it finds such a cell, it rewrites the contents by the symbol X and moves the head to the left, until it finds the first not overwritten symbol, which is expected to be an a. If so, the symbol is overwritten, the automaton re-enters the state q_0 to search another b. When no more b's are left on the tape, the head reaches the right end-marker. At this point the automaton verifies if the string on the tape is of the form $\triangleright X^* \triangleleft$.

Example 2. A more interesting example is the recognition of the deterministic context-free language $\{a^n b^{2n} \mid n \geq 0\}$, which can be done by a strongly limited automaton that guesses the position of each second b, using the following strategy:

- Moving the head *from left to right*, when the automaton reads an a it continues to move to the right, while when it reads a b it makes a nondeterministic choice between further moving to the right (so leaving the b in the cell) or rewriting the cell by X and turning the head to the left.
- Moving the head *from right to left*, when the automaton reads a b it rewrites it by Y and continues to move to the left (notice that such a b was left unchanged in the previous visit, when moving from left to right), while when it reads an a, it replaces the contents by Z, turning the head to the right.
- In the final scan, which starts when the right end-marker is reached, the machine accepts if and only if the string on the tape belongs to $\rhd Z^*(YX)^* \lhd$.

We can modify the above algorithm in order to recognize the language $\{a^n b^n \mid n \geq 0\} \cup \{a^n b^{2n} \mid n \geq 0\}$. While moving from left to right, when the head reaches a cell containing b three actions are possible: either the automaton continues to move to the right, without any rewriting, or it rewrites the cell by X, turning to the left, or it rewrites the cell by W, also turning the head to the left. While moving from right to left, the automaton behaves as the one above described for $\{a^n b^{2n} \mid n \geq 0\}$. The input is accepted if and only if the string which is finally on the tape belongs to $\rhd Z^* W^* \lhd + \rhd Z^*(YX)^* \lhd$.   □

In spite of the restrictions on moves, strongly limited automata have the same computational power as limited automata, namely they characterize context-free languages. Furthermore they are polynomially related in size to pushdown automata:

Theorem 12 ([27]).

(i) *Each context-free language L is accepted by a strongly limited automaton whose description has a size which is polynomial with respect to the size of a given context-free grammar generating L or of a given pushdown automaton accepting L.*

(ii) *Each strongly limited automaton $\mathcal{M}$ can be simulated by a pushdown automaton of size polynomial with respect the size of $\mathcal{M}$.*

The proof of (i) was obtained using a variant of the representation theorem of Chomsky-Schützenberger, proved by Okhotin [20], where Dyck languages extended with neutral symbols and letter-to-letter homomorphisms are used. (ii) was proven by providing a direct simulation.

In Example 2 we described a strongly limited automaton accepting the deterministic context-free language $\{a^n b^{2n} \mid n \geq 0\}$. The automaton makes use of nondeterministic choices. It is not difficult to prove that this cannot be avoided (see [27]). Hence:

Theorem 13 ([27]). *The class of languages accepted by deterministic strongly limited automata is properly included in the class of deterministic context-free languages.*

Strongly limited automata are allowed to change state only when they reverse the head direction. If we remove this restriction, the language $\{a^n b^{2n} \mid n \geq 0\}$ (and other deterministic context-free languages which are not accepted by deterministic strongly limited automata) can be easily recognized in a deterministic way. In order to have a model polynomially related in size to pushdown automata and whose deterministic version is equivalent to deterministic pushdown automata, in [27] *almost strongly limited automata* have been proposed. They are obtained from strongly limited automata by relaxing some of the restrictions on state changes. In almost strongly limited automata there is a set of states Q_R, including the initial state q_0, which can be used while moving to the right, and a set of states Q_L which can be used while moving to the left. State changes are possible while moving to the left or to the right (which is not possible in strongly limited automata), except on the cells that have been already overwritten. Furthermore, almost strongly limited automata have to satisfy all the other restrictions given for strongly limited automata.

By adapting the arguments used to prove Theorem 12, it can be shown that almost strongly limited automata characterize context-free languages and are polynomially related in size to pushdown automata. Since almost strongly limited automata are restrictions of 2-limited automata, from Theorem 3 it follows that each deterministic almost strongly limited automaton recognizes a deterministic context-free language. At the moment, we do not know if the converse holds.

Problem 5. Does the class of languages accepted by deterministic almost strongly limited automata coincide with the class of deterministic context-free languages?

4   Some Related Models

In this section we shortly discuss some restricted variants of Turing machines, presented in the literature, which recognize context-free languages.

4.1   Wechsung's Model

We have seen that limited automata are single-tape Turing machines defined by limiting the *active visits* to each tape cell from the beginning of the computation: in a d-limited automaton only the first d visits to each cell can modify the contents.

We can consider a similar restriction, where for a fixed integer d, *only the last d visits* to each cell can be active.

Such a model was implicitly introduced by Wechsung, by considering a complexity measure for one-tape Turing machines called *return complexity* [35, 36]. Indeed, this measure counts the maximum number of visits to a tape cell, starting from the first visit which modifies the cell contents. Machines with return complexity 1 characterize regular languages (each cell, after the first rewriting, will be never visited again, hence rewritings are useless). Furthermore, it has been shown that for each $d \geq 2$, return complexity d characterizes context-free languages.[4] Even with respect to return complexity, there exists a hierarchy of deterministic languages (cf. Theorem 4 in the case of limited automata). However, this hierarchy is not comparable with the class of deterministic context-free languages. For instance, it can be easily seen that the set of palindromes, which is not a deterministic context-free language, can be recognized by a deterministic machine with return complexity 2. However, there are deterministic context-free languages that cannot be recognized by any deterministic machine with return complexity d, for any integer d [22,23].

It seems interesting to investigate the possibility of finding a class of machines containing both limited automata and Wechsung's machines and still characterizing context-free languages. One natural attempt can be that of considering machines such that for each tape cell the number of visits counted starting from the first active visit up to the last one is bounded by a given constant.

4.2 Forgetting, Deleting and Restarting Automata

With motivations deriving mainly from linguistics, in a series of papers Jancar, Mráz, and Plátek introduced and studied *forgetting automata* [10–12]. These devices are single-tape machines that can erase tape cells by rewriting their contents with a unique special symbol, that cannot be further overwritten. However, overwritten cells are kept on the tape and are still considered during the computation. For instance, the state can be changed while visiting an erased cell. Different variants, depending on the allowed operations, have been investigated.

In a variant of forgetting automata that characterizes context-free languages, when a cell which contains an input symbol is visited while moving to the left, it is rewritten by the unique special symbol, while it can remain unchanged while moving to the right. This way of operating has some similarities with that of strongly limited automata, which, however, can use nonunary rewriting alphabets.[5] Furthermore, in strongly limited automata overwritten cells are completely ignored (namely, the head direction and the state cannot be changed while visiting them) except in the final scan of the tape from the right to the left end-marker.

If erased cells are completely ignored in forgetting automata, the resulting computational model, called *deleting automata*, is less powerful. In fact it is not able to recognize all context-free languages [12].

A modification of forgetting automata, called *restarting automata*, was introduced in [13] and widely considered in the literature. Variants of restarting automata characterizing context-free languages have been obtained. For more details see [21].

---

[4] The maximum number of visits to a cell up to the last rewriting, namely the measure corresponding to limited automata, is sometimes called *dual return complexity* [34].

[5] A nonunary rewriting alphabet is necessary for strongly limited automata to recognize all context-free languages. For instance, to recognize the set of palindromes, a working alphabet of at least 3 symbols is required [27].

4.3 No Space Overhead Machines

With the aim of investigating computations with very restricted resources, Hemaspaandra, Mukherji, and Tantau studied *single-tape Turing machine with absolutely no space overhead* [7]. The model is very close to "realistic computations", where the space is measured without any hidden constants. To this aim, these machines use the binary alphabet $\Sigma = \{0, 1\}$ (plus two end-marker symbols) and only the portion of the tape which at the beginning of the computation contains the input. Furthermore, no other symbols are available, namely only symbols from Σ can be used to rewrite the tape. Despite these strong restrictions, these machines are able to recognize in polynomial time all context-free languages over Σ.

5 Further Remarks

In this work we presented limited automata, discussed some of their main properties, in particular concerning computational power, descriptional complexity, determinism versus nondeterminism. We shortly discussed some related models.

This overview is only partial. Much more space would be necessary to make an exhaustive and more detailed work.

We conclude by adding a couple of further remarks.

First we point out that *reversibility* in limited automata has been investigated in [16]. *Probabilistic* extensions of limited automata have been recently introduced and studied in [37].

We do not know any result relating limited automata, or their variants, with *input-driven pushdown automata*, also known as *nested word automata* [1,17]. It is known that these devices recognize a proper subclass of deterministic context-free languages, which properly contains the class of regular languages. It should be interesting to know if this class can be characterized by some restricted versions of limited automata.

Acknowledgment. I am very grateful to Luca Prigioniero for his valuable and helpful comments.

References

1. Alur, R., Madhusudan, P.: Adding nesting structure to words. J. ACM **56**(3), 16:1–16:43 (2009). https://doi.org/10.1145/1516512.1516518
2. Chomsky, N., Schützenberger, M.: The algebraic theory of context-free languages. In: Braffort, P., Hirschberg, D. (eds.) Computer Programming and Formal Systems, Studies in Logic and the Foundations of Mathematics, vol. 35, pp. 118–161. Elsevier (1963). https://doi.org/10.1016/S0049-237X(08)72023-8
3. Chrobak, M.: Finite automata and unary languages. Theoret. Comput. Sci. **47**(3), 149–158 (1986). https://doi.org/10.1016/0304-3975(86)90142-8. Errata: **302**(1–3), 497–498 (2003)

4. Ginsburg, S., Rice, H.G.: Two families of languages related to ALGOL. J. ACM **9**(3), 350–371 (1962). https://doi.org/10.1145/321127.321132
5. Guillon, B., Pighizzini, G., Prigioniero, L., Průša, D.: Two-way automata and one-tape machines. In: Hoshi, M., Seki, S. (eds.) DLT 2018. LNCS, vol. 11088, pp. 366–378. Springer, Cham (2018). https://doi.org/10.1007/978-3-319-98654-8_30
6. Guillon, B., Prigioniero, L.: Linear-time limited automata. Theoret. Comput. Sci. (2019, in press). https://doi.org/10.1016/j.tcs.2019.03.037
7. Hemaspaandra, L.A., Mukherji, P., Tantau, T.: Context-free languages can be accepted with absolutely no space overhead. Inform. Comput. **203**(2), 163–180 (2005). https://doi.org/10.1016/j.ic.2005.05.005
8. Hennie, F.C.: One-tape, off-line Turing machine computations. Inf. Control **8**(6), 553–578 (1965)
9. Hibbard, T.N.: A generalization of context-free determinism. Inf. Control **11**(1/2), 196–238 (1967)
10. Jančar, P., Mráz, F., Plátek, M.: Characterization of context-free languages by erasing automata. In: Havel, I.M., Koubek, V. (eds.) MFCS 1992. LNCS, vol. 629, pp. 307–314. Springer, Heidelberg (1992). https://doi.org/10.1007/3-540-55808-X_29
11. Jancar, P., Mráz, F., Plátek, M.: A taxonomy of forgetting automata. In: Borzyszkowski, A.M., Sokołowski, S. (eds.) MFCS 1993. LNCS, vol. 711, pp. 527–536. Springer, Heidelberg (1993). https://doi.org/10.1007/3-540-57182-5_44
12. Jančar, P., Mráz, F., Plátek, M.: Forgetting automata and context-free languages. Acta Inform. **33**(5), 409–420 (1996). https://doi.org/10.1007/s002360050050
13. Jančar, P., Mráz, F., Plátek, M., Vogel, J.: Restarting automata. In: Reichel, H. (ed.) FCT 1995. LNCS, vol. 965, pp. 283–292. Springer, Heidelberg (1995). https://doi.org/10.1007/3-540-60249-6_60
14. Kutrib, M., Pighizzini, G., Wendlandt, M.: Descriptional complexity of limited automata. Inform. Comput. **259**(2), 259–276 (2018). https://doi.org/10.1016/j.ic.2017.09.005
15. Kutrib, M., Wendlandt, M.: On simulation cost of unary limited automata. In: Shallit, J., Okhotin, A. (eds.) DCFS 2015. LNCS, vol. 9118, pp. 153–164. Springer, Cham (2015). https://doi.org/10.1007/978-3-319-19225-3_13
16. Kutrib, M., Wendlandt, M.: Reversible limited automata. Fund. Inform. **155**(1–2), 31–58 (2017). https://doi.org/10.3233/FI-2017-1575
17. Mehlhorn, K.: Pebbling mountain ranges and its application to DCFL-recognition. In: de Bakker, J., van Leeuwen, J. (eds.) ICALP 1980. LNCS, vol. 85, pp. 422–435. Springer, Heidelberg (1980). https://doi.org/10.1007/3-540-10003-2_89
18. Nasyrov, I.R.: Deterministic realization of nondeterministic computations with a low measure of nondeterminism. Cybernetics **27**(2), 170–179 (1991). https://doi.org/10.1007/BF01068368
19. Ogden, W.F., Ross, R.J., Winklmann, K.: An "interchange lemma" for context-free languages. SIAM J. Comput. **14**(2), 410–415 (1985). https://doi.org/10.1137/0214031
20. Okhotin, A.: Non-erasing variants of the Chomsky–Schützenberger theorem. In: Yen, H.-C., Ibarra, O.H. (eds.) DLT 2012. LNCS, vol. 7410, pp. 121–129. Springer, Heidelberg (2012). https://doi.org/10.1007/978-3-642-31653-1_12
21. Otto, F.: Restarting automata and their relations to the Chomsky hierarchy. In: Ésik, Z., Fülöp, Z. (eds.) DLT 2003. LNCS, vol. 2710, pp. 55–74. Springer, Heidelberg (2003). https://doi.org/10.1007/3-540-45007-6_5

22. Peckel, J.: On a deterministic subclass of context-free languages. In: Gruska, J. (ed.) MFCS 1977. LNCS, vol. 53, pp. 430–434. Springer, Heidelberg (1977). https://doi.org/10.1007/3-540-08353-7_164

23. Peckel, J.: A deterministic subclass of context-free languages. Časopis pro pěstování matematiky **103**(1), 43–52 (1978). http://eudml.org/doc/21335

24. Pighizzini, G.: Nondeterministic one-tape off-line Turing machines. J. Autom. Lang. Comb. **14**(1), 107–124 (2009). https://doi.org/10.25596/jalc-2009-107. http://arXiv.org/abs/0905.1271

25. Pighizzini, G.: Two-way finite automata: old and recent results. Fund. Inform. **126**(2–3), 225–246 (2013). https://doi.org/10.3233/FI-2013-879

26. Pighizzini, G.: Guest column: one-tape Turing machine variants and language recognition. SIGACT News **46**(3), 37–55 (2015). https://doi.org/10.1145/2818936.2818947

27. Pighizzini, G.: Strongly limited automata. Fund. Inform. **148**(3–4), 369–392 (2016). https://doi.org/10.3233/FI-2016-1439

28. Pighizzini, G., Pisoni, A.: Limited automata and regular languages. Internat. J. Found. Comput. Sci. **25**(7), 897–916 (2014). https://doi.org/10.1142/S0129054114400140

29. Pighizzini, G., Pisoni, A.: Limited automata and context-free languages. Fund. Inform. **136**(1–2), 157–176 (2015). https://doi.org/10.3233/FI-2015-1148

30. Pighizzini, G., Prigioniero, L.: Limited automata and unary languages. Inform. Comput. **266**, 60–74 (2019). https://doi.org/10.1016/j.ic.2019.01.002

31. Sakoda, W.J., Sipser, M.: Nondeterminism and the size of two way finite automata. In: Lipton, R.J., Burkhard, W.A., Savitch, W.J., Friedman, E.P., Aho, A.V. (eds.) Proceedings 10th Annual ACM Symposium on Theory of Computing (STOC 1978), pp. 275–286. ACM (1978). https://doi.org/10.1145/800133.804357

32. Shepherdson, J.C.: The reduction of two-way automata to one-way automata. IBM J. Res. Dev. **3**(2), 198–200 (1959). https://doi.org/10.1147/rd.32.0198

33. Sloane, N.J.A.: The on-line encyclopedia of integer sequences. http://oeis.org/A007814

34. Wagner, K.W., Wechsung, G.: Computational Complexity. D. Reidel Publishing Company, Dordrecht (1986)

35. Wechsung, G.: Characterization of some classes of context-free languages in terms of complexity classes. In: Bečvář, J. (ed.) MFCS 1975. LNCS, vol. 32, pp. 457–461. Springer, Heidelberg (1975). https://doi.org/10.1007/3-540-07389-2_233

36. Wechsung, G., Brandstädt, A.: A relation between space, return and dual return complexities. Theoret. Comput. Sci. **9**, 127–140 (1979). https://doi.org/10.1016/0304-3975(79)90010-0

37. Yamakami, T.: Behavioral strengths and weaknesses of various models of limited automata. In: Catania, B., Královič, R., Nawrocki, J., Pighizzini, G. (eds.) SOFSEM 2019. LNCS, vol. 11376, pp. 519–530. Springer, Cham (2019). https://doi.org/10.1007/978-3-030-10801-4_40

Nondeterministic Right One-Way Jumping Finite Automata (Extended Abstract)

Simon Beier and Markus Holzer[✉]

Institut für Informatik, Universität Giessen, Arndtstr. 2, 35392 Giessen, Germany
{simon.beier,holzer}@informatik.uni-giessen.de

Abstract. Right one-way jumping finite automata are deterministic devices that process their input in a discontinuous fashion. We generalise these devices to nondeterministic machines. More precisely we study the impact on the computational power of these machines when allowing multiple initial states and/or a nondeterministic transition function including spontaneous or λ-transitions. We show inclusion relations and incomparability results of the induced language families. Since for right-one way jumping devices the use of spontaneous transitions is subject to different natural interpretations, we also study this subject in detail, showing that most interpretations are equivalent to each other and lead to the same language families. Finally we also study inclusion and incomparability results to classical language families and to the families of languages accepted by finite automata with translucent letters.

1 Introduction

Right one-way jumping finite automata (ROWJFAs) were introduced in [4] as a deterministic variant of jumping finite automata [9], a machine model for discontinuous information processing, that is allowed to read letters from anywhere in the input string, not necessarily only from left of the remaining input. In a right one-way jumping finite automaton the device moves the input head deterministically from left-to-right starting from the leftmost letter in the input and when it reaches the end of the input word, it returns to the beginning and continues the computation. The language families induced by these two automata models are quite interesting since they have relations to semi-linear sets, see, e.g., [1–3,5,6,11]. While languages that are accepted by jumping finite automata are permutation closed and semi-linear [9], the permutation closed languages that are accepted by ROWJFAs are exactly those languages with a finite number of positive Myhill-Nerode equivalence classes [1], that is, the permutation closed language under consideration can be written as the finite union of Myhill-Nerode classes. This is a nice transfer of a classical result on finite automata that states that a language is regular or accepted by a deterministic finite automaton if and only if the number of Myhill-Nerode equivalence classes is finite, to the case

© IFIP International Federation for Information Processing 2019
Published by Springer Nature Switzerland AG 2019
M. Hospodár et al. (Eds.): DCFS 2019, LNCS 11612, pp. 74–85, 2019.
https://doi.org/10.1007/978-3-030-23247-4_5

where the index (number of equivalence classes) of the Myhill-Nerode relation is not finite any more. Since many generalizations of finite automata such as, e.g., nondeterminism, multiple initial states, etc. do note change their accepting power, the question arises whether a similar result is valid for ROWJFAs, too? We answer this question for two types of generalizations, namely nondeterministic transitions and/or multiple initial states, for jumping finite automata and ROWJFAs.

For jumping finite automata the generalizations to nondeterministic transitions functions and/or multiple initial states do not change the computational power of these devices and leads to the language family **JFA**. This is in sharp contrast to ROWJFAs, where these generalizations increase the computational power of these devices and thus induce a mesh of language families and their permutation closed variants that are strictly included within each other (due to the trivial inclusion relations), subject to one exception. For the case of nondeterministic ROWJFAs and nondeterministic ROWJFAs with multiple initial states, we find that the induced languages families **NROWJ** and **MNROWJ** coincide in case we consider permutation closed languages. Then this language family is nothing other than **JFA**, the family of all languages accepted by jumping finite automata. The corresponding deterministic language families **ROWJ** and **MROWJ** of all languages accepted by ROWJFAs and those with multiple initial states satisfy **ROWJ** $\subset$ **MROWJ** and **pROWJ** $\subset$ **pMROWJ**, resp., where the prefix **p** refers to the permutation closed language family in question. By results in [2], it was shown that the permutation closed languages over binary alphabets accepted by ROWJFAs with multiple initial states are those languages that are a finite union of permutation closed languages, where each language has a finite number of positive Myhill-Nerode equivalence classes. For arbitrary alphabets we have a characterization which is a bit more sophisticated and uses the quotient of a language by a word. Although the generalization of ROWJFAs to nondeterministic ROWJFAs with and without multiple initial states is straightforward, it is not clear how to describe the semantics of these machines in case of spontaneous or λ-transitions. This issue is discussed in detail and we give three different semantics, where it turns out that two of them are equivalent. The introduced generalizations nicely fit into the known landscape of the language families that were considered earlier. We further prove inclusion and incomparability results to classical language families such as the deterministic context-free languages, context-free languages, and context-sensitive languages. In some of our proofs a nice and tight relation between languages accepted by ROWJFAs and variants thereof to semi-linear sets and languages with finite positive Myhill-Nerode equivalence classes [1, 2] is exploited.

Because ROWJFAs share some features of finite automata with translucent letters [10] since their input letter reading mechanism looks similar, it is natural to consider the relation of the language families given by these automata to ROWJFAs and generalizations thereof. In passing we solve an open problem on deterministic finite automata with translucent letters stated in [10]. Due to space constraints all proofs are omitted and will be given in a journal version of this paper.

2 Preliminaries

We assume the reader to be familiar with the basics in automata and formal language theory as contained, for example, in [7]. Let $\mathbb{N} = \{0, 1, 2, \ldots\}$ be the set of non-negative integers. We use $\subseteq$ for inclusion and $\subset$ for proper inclusion of sets. We denote the powerset of a set S by 2^S. For a binary relation $\sim$ let $\sim^+$ and $\sim^*$ denote the transitive closure of $\sim$ and the transitive-reflexive closure of $\sim$, respectively. In the standard manner, $\sim$ is extended to $\sim^n$, where $n \geq 0$. Let Σ be an alphabet. Then Σ^* is the set of all words over Σ, including the empty word λ. For a language $L \subseteq \Sigma^*$ define the set $\mathsf{perm}(L) = \cup_{w \in L} \mathsf{perm}(w)$, where $\mathsf{perm}(w) = \{ v \in \Sigma^* \mid v \text{ is a permutation of } w \}$. A language L is called *permutation closed* if $L = \mathsf{perm}(L)$. The length of a word $w \in \Sigma^*$ is denoted by $|w|$. For the number of occurrences of a symbol a in w we use the notation $|w|_a$. If Σ is the ordered alphabet $\Sigma = \{a_1, a_2, \ldots, a_k\}$, the function $\psi : \Sigma^* \to \mathbb{N}^k$ with $w \mapsto (|w|_{a_1}, |w|_{a_2}, \ldots, |w|_{a_k})$ is called the *Parikh-mapping*. The set $\psi(L)$ is called the *Parikh-image* of L. Two languages over the same ordered alphabet are said to be *Parikh-equivalent* if and only if they have the same Parikh-image. The language L is called *letter-bounded* if and only if $L \subseteq a_1^* a_2^* \cdots a_k^*$.

For a vector $c \in \mathbb{N}^k$ and a finite set $P \subset \mathbb{N}^k$ let $L(c, P)$ denote the subset $L(c, P) = \{ c + \sum_{x_i \in P} \lambda_i \cdot x_i \mid \lambda_i \in \mathbb{N} \}$ of $\mathbb{N}^k$. Sets of the form $L(c, P)$, for a $c \in \mathbb{N}^k$ and a finite $P \subset \mathbb{N}^k$, are called *linear* subsets of $\mathbb{N}^k$. A subset of $\mathbb{N}^k$ is said to be *semi-linear* if it is a finite union of linear subsets. Moreover, a language $L \subseteq \Sigma^*$ is called *semi-linear* if its Parikh-image $\psi(L)$ is semi-linear.

For an alphabet Σ and a language $L \subseteq \Sigma^*$, let $\sim_L$ be the *Myhill-Nerode equivalence relation* on Σ^*. So, for $v, w \in \Sigma^*$, we have $v \sim_L w$ if and only if, for all $u \in \Sigma^*$, the equivalence $vu \in L \Leftrightarrow wu \in L$ holds. For $w \in \Sigma^*$, we call the equivalence class $[w]_{\sim_L}$ *positive* if and only if $w \in L$.

We define a *nondeterministic finite automaton with multiple start states and spontaneous or λ - transitions*, a λ-MNFA for short, as a tuple $A = (Q, \Sigma, R, S, F)$, where Q is the finite *set of states*, Σ is the finite *input alphabet*, R is a function from $Q \times (\Sigma \cup \{\lambda\})$ to 2^Q, $S \subseteq Q$ is the set of *start states*, and $F \subseteq Q$ is the set of *final states*. The elements of R are referred to as *rules* of A and we simply write $pa \to q \in R$ instead of $q \in R(p, a)$, for $p, q \in Q$ and $a \in \Sigma \cup \{\lambda\}$.

A *configuration* of A is a string in $Q\Sigma^*$. The automaton A makes a *transition* from configuration paw to configuration qw if $pa \to q \in R$, where $p, q \in Q$, $a \in \Sigma \cup \{\lambda\}$, and $w \in \Sigma^*$. We denote this by $paw \vdash_A qw$ or just $paw \vdash qw$ if it is clear which automaton we are referring to. The *language accepted by* A is

$$L(A) = \{ w \in \Sigma^* \mid \exists s \in S, f \in F : sw \vdash^* f \}.$$

We say that A *accepts* $w \in \Sigma^*$ if $w \in L(A)$ and that A *rejects* w otherwise.

The automaton A is called a *nondeterministic finite automaton with multiple start states*, an MNFA, if $R(p, \lambda) = \emptyset$ for all $p \in Q$. We call A a *nondeterministic finite automaton with λ-transitions*, a λ-NFA, if $|S| = 1$. If A is an MNFA and a λ-NFA, we say that A is a *nondeterministic finite automaton*, an NFA.

The automaton A is said to be a *deterministic finite automaton with multiple start states*, an MDFA, if A is an MNFA and $|R(p,a)| \leq 1$ for all $p \in Q$ and $a \in \Sigma$. Finally, we call A a *deterministic finite automaton*, a DFA, if it is an MDFA and an NFA. It is well known that for all the aforementioned types of automata are computational equivalent and the family of languages accepted by any of these devices is referred to as the family of regular languages **REG**. Observe that these automata read the input in a symbol by symbol manner from left to right.

Besides the family of regular languages **REG**, we also use the following language families: let **DCF**, **CF**, and **CS** be the families of deterministic context-free, context-free, and context-sensitive languages. Moreover, we are interested in families of permutation closed languages. These language families are referred to by a prefix **p**. For instance, **pREG** denotes the language family of all permutation closed regular languages.

3 Variants of Nondeterministic Jumping Finite Automata

We start our investigation with the generalization of jumping automata to variants of jumping automata with multiple initial states. Originally, jumping finite automata were introduced in [9] as deterministic or nondeterministic devices with a sole initial state. The idea behind a jumping finite automaton is that the device no longer reads the input from left to right, but is allowed to read letters from anywhere in the input string. For a λ-MNFA $A = (Q, \Sigma, R, S, F)$ this behaviour can be modelled by a binary relation, the *jumping relation*, which is symbolically denoted by $\curvearrowright_A$, over *configurations* from $Q\Sigma^*$ and is defined as follows: consider an $a \in \Sigma \cup \{\lambda\}$, words $x, y \in \Sigma^*$, states $p, q \in Q$, and $pa \to q \in R$. Then, we write $pxay \curvearrowright_A qxy$ or just $pxay \curvearrowright qxy$ if it is clear which automaton we are referring to. The *language accepted by A interpreted as a jumping finite automaton* is

$$L_J(A) = \{\, w \in \Sigma^* \mid \exists s \in S, f \in F : sw \curvearrowright^* f \,\}.$$

We say that A interpreted as a jumping finite automaton *accepts* $w \in \Sigma^*$ if $w \in L_J(A)$, otherwise A interpreted as a jumping finite automaton *rejects* the word w.

Example 1. Let A be the DFA $A = (\{q_0, q_1, q_2, q_3\}, \{a, b\}, R, q_0, \{q_3\})$, where R consists of the rules $q_0b \to q_1$, $q_0a \to q_2$, $q_2b \to q_3$, and $q_3a \to q_2$. The automaton A is depicted in Fig. 1. It holds

$$L(A) = (ab)^+ \quad \text{and} \quad L_J(A) = \mathsf{perm}\left((ab)^+\right) = \{\, w \in \{a, b\}^+ \mid |w|_a = |w|_b \,\}.$$

Observe, that $L_J(A)$ is a permutation closed language that is non-regular but context-free.   □

It can easily be seen that $L_J(A) = \mathsf{perm}(L(A))$ holds in general. That is why, for $X, Y \in \{\mathrm{DFA}, \mathrm{MDFA}, \mathrm{NFA}, \mathrm{MNFA}, \lambda\text{-NFA}, \lambda\text{-MNFA}\}$, the family of languages accepted by automata of type X interpreted as jumping finite automata

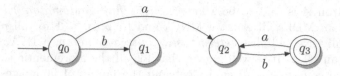

Fig. 1. The DFA A with $L(A) = (ab)^+$ interpreted as a jumping finite automaton accepts the language $L_J(A) = \{ w \in \{a,b\}^+ \mid |w|_a = |w|_b \}$.

equals the family of languages accepted by automata of type Y interpreted as jumping finite automata. This language family is referred to as **JFA**. Clearly, we have **JFA = pJFA** and it obeys a nice characterization.

Theorem 2. *A language L is in* **JFA** *if and only if L is permutation closed and semi-linear.* $\square$

Moreover **pCF** $\subset$ **JFA** $\subset$ **pCS** and **JFA** strictly contains **pROWJ**; here **ROWJ** refers to the family of languages that are accepted by right one-way finite jumping automata, an automaton model introduced in the next subsection—in addition **JFA** is incomparable to the families **REG**, **DCF**, **CF**, **ROWJ**; for these results see, e.g., [1,4,5,9].

Let us take a look at the descriptional complexity of these devices. It is obvious that the standard automata construction from the theory of finite state devices also applies to our setting whenever the underlying machine is interpreted as a jumping finite automaton. Hence, the conversion of a type X automaton, for $X \in \{\text{MDFA}, \text{MNFA}, \lambda\text{-NFA}, \lambda\text{-MNFA}\}$, to an equivalent NFA device (both machines interpreted as jumping automata) results in state complexity increase of at most one state, which is used to simulate the union of languages for automata of types from $\{\text{MDFA}, \text{MNFA}, \lambda\text{-MNFA}\}$. Removing spontaneous transitions does not increase the number of states at all. The remaining conversion from an NFA to a DFA is at most 2^n, where n is the number of states of the NFA, due to the powerset construction that can be successfully applied in our setting, too. Since the equivalence needs to be w.r.t. the Parikh image of the languages one can prove a better conversion bound. Namely, in [8] it was shown that for each NFA with n states a Parikh equivalent DFA with $e^{O(\sqrt{n \log n})}$ states can be constructed and that this bound is asymptotically tight. Thus, in our setting this result reads as follows:

Theorem 3. *Let A be an n-state NFA. Then $e^{O(\sqrt{n \log n})}$ states are sufficient and necessary in the worst for a DFA B to accept the language $L_J(A)$ if B is interpreted as a jumping finite automaton, that is, $L_J(B) = L_J(A)$.* $\square$

3.1 Right One-Way Jumping Finite Automata

We deal with a variant of jumping finite automata, namely so called right one-way jumping finite automata, which were introduced in [4] in the deterministic case. We now generalize the definition of these devices to nondeterministic machines without λ-transitions. Their behaviour can be described as follows. The read head starts the computation at the leftmost symbol of the input and moves to the right. If $R(p,a) \neq \emptyset$ for the current state p and the next input symbol a, one of the possible transitions is executed, the symbol a is consumed, and the read head moves on to the next symbol. If, however, $R(p,a) = \emptyset$, the read head jumps over a, does not consume it, and moves on to the next symbol. When the head reaches the end of the input, it jumps back to the beginning and continues the computation, which goes on until no input symbol is left.

A formal definition is given in the following: let $A = (Q, \Sigma, R, S, F)$ be an MNFA. The *right one-way jumping relation*, symbolically denoted by $\circlearrowright_A$, over $Q\Sigma^*$ is defined as follows. Let $p, q \in Q$, $a \in \Sigma$, $w \in \Sigma^*$, and $q \in R(p,a)$. Then, we have $paw \circlearrowright_A qw$. Now, let $p \in Q$, $a \in \Sigma$, and $w \in \Sigma^*$ with $R(p,a) = \emptyset$. In this case we get $paw \circlearrowright_A pwa$. We also write $\circlearrowright$ instead of $\circlearrowright_A$ if it is clear which automaton we are referring to. The *language accepted by A interpreted as a right one-way jumping finite automaton* is

$$L_R(A) = \{\, w \in \Sigma^* \mid \exists s \in S, f \in F : sw \circlearrowright^* f \,\}.$$

In order to keep the presentation simple, we speak of a ROWJFA MROWJFA, NROWJFA, and MNROWJFA, respectively, if we interpret a DFA, MDFA, NFA, and a MNFA as a right one-way device, respectively. The corresponding language families are referred to as **ROWJ, MROWJ, NROWJ**, and **MNROWJ**, resp. Clearly, for unary alphabets all these families correspond with **REG**.

Example 4. We continue our previous example. To show how ROWJFAs work, we give an example computation of A, interpreted as an ROWJFA on the input word $aabbba$:

$$q_0aabbba \circlearrowright q_2abbba \circlearrowright^2 q_3bbaa \circlearrowright^3 q_2abb \circlearrowright^2 q_3ba \circlearrowright^2 q_2b \circlearrowright q_3$$

That shows $aabbba \in L_R(A)$. Analogously, one can see that every word that contains the same number of a's and b's and that begins with an a is in $L_R(A)$. On the other hand, no other word can be accepted by A, interpreted as an ROWJFA So, we get $L_R(A) = \{\, w \in a\{a,b\}^* \mid |w|_a = |w|_b \,\}$. Notice that this language is non-regular and not closed under permutation.   □

Now the question arises how the right one-way jumping relation can be generalized to work on automata with λ-transitions? Sometimes we call these transitions also *spontaneous* transitions. To cope with spontaneous transitions we have three different interpretation possibilities for the right one-way jumping relation—as above we speak of λ-NROWJFAs (λ-MNROWJFAs, respectively), if λ-NFAs (λ-MNFAs, respectively) are interpreted as right one-way jumping devices:

Type 1. The *first type of right one-way jumping finite automata* is only allowed to jump over an input symbol, if A cannot perform a λ-transition in the current state. So, the *right one-way jumping relation of type 1*, symbolically denoted by $\circlearrowright_{A,1}$, over $Q\Sigma^*$ is defined as follows. Let $p, q \in Q$, $a \in \Sigma \cup \{\lambda\}$, $w \in \Sigma^*$, and $q \in R(p, a)$. Then, we have $paw \circlearrowright_{A,1} qw$. Now, let $p \in Q$, $a \in \Sigma$, and $w \in \Sigma^*$ with $R(p, a) = \emptyset = R(p, \lambda)$. In this case it holds $paw \circlearrowright_{A,1} pwa$.

Type 2. If the *second type of right one-way jumping finite automata* has no transition for the current state and the next input symbol, but can perform a λ-transition in the current state, the automaton is allowed to choose if it performs a jump or if it uses a λ-transition. However, if the automaton decides to jump, it has to jump over all the following input symbols that cannot be read in the current state and must read the next input symbol that can be read in the current state. Not until now, the automaton is allowed to perform a λ-transition again. So, we set

$$\Sigma_{R,p} = \{\, a \in \Sigma \mid R(p, a) \neq \emptyset \,\}$$

for $p \in Q$. Therefore the *right one-way jumping relation of type 2*, symbolically denoted by $\circlearrowright_{A,2}$, over $Q\Sigma^*$ is defined as follows. For $p, q \in Q$, $w \in \Sigma^*$, and $q \in R(p, \lambda)$ it holds $pw \circlearrowright_{A,2} qw$. Now, let $p, q \in Q$, $a \in \Sigma$, $v \in (\Sigma \setminus \Sigma_{R,p})^*$, and $w \in \Sigma^*$ with $q \in R(p, a)$. Then, we get $pvaw \circlearrowright_{A,2} qwv$.

Type 3. If the *third type of right one-way jumping finite automata* has no transition for the current state and the next input symbol, but can perform a λ-transition in the current state, the automaton is allowed to choose if it jumps over the next input symbol or if it uses a λ-transition. Thus, the *right one-way jumping relation of type 3*, symbolically denoted by $\circlearrowright_{A,3}$, over $Q\Sigma^*$ is defined as follows. Let $p, q \in Q$, $a \in \Sigma \cup \{\lambda\}$, $w \in \Sigma^*$, and $q \in R(p, a)$. In this case we have $paw \circlearrowright_{A,3} qw$. For $p \in Q$, $a \in \Sigma$, and $w \in \Sigma^*$ with $R(p, a) = \emptyset$ it holds $paw \circlearrowright_{A,3} pwa$.

Let $i \in \{1, 2, 3\}$. We also write $\circlearrowright_i$ instead of $\circlearrowright_{A,i}$ if it is clear which automaton we are referring to. The *language accepted by A interpreted as a right one-way jumping finite automaton of type i* is defined to be

$$L_{Ri}(A) = \{\, w \in \Sigma^* \mid \exists s \in S, f \in F : sw \circlearrowright_i^* f \,\}.$$

This give rise to the language families λ_i**NROWJ** (λ_i**MNROWJ**, respectively) of all languages accepted by λ-NROWJFAs (λ-MNROWJFAs, respectively) of type i, for $1 \leq i \leq 3$. Again, all these families correspond with **REG** for unary alphabets.

Example 5. Let $A = (\{q_0, q_1, \ldots, q_5\}, \{a, b, c\}, R, \{q_0\}, \{q_5\})$ be the λ-NROW JFA with

$$R = \{q_0\lambda \rightarrow q_1, q_0a \rightarrow q_4, q_1a \rightarrow q_2, q_1b \rightarrow q_2,$$

$$q_1c \rightarrow q_3, q_3a \rightarrow q_4, q_4b \rightarrow q_5, q_5a \rightarrow q_4\}.$$

The automaton A is depicted in Fig. 2.

It is easy to see that that $L(A) = \{\lambda, c\}(ab)^+$. Let L refer to the language $\{\, w \in \{a, b\}^+ \mid |w|_a = |w|_b \,\}$. For the three interpretations on how to cope with spontaneous transitions we get the following languages—let letter $x \in \{a, b\}$, words $u, v \in \{b, c\}^*$, and $w \in \{a, b, c\}^*$:

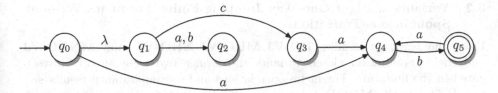

Fig. 2. The λ-NROWJFA A with $L(A) \subset L_{R1}(A) \subset L_{R2}(A) \subset L_{R3}(A) \subset L_J(A)$.

- In type 1 we have the computations $q_0aw \circlearrowright_1 q_4w$, $q_0xw \circlearrowright_1^2 q_2w$, and $q_0cvaw \circlearrowright_1^2 q_3vaw \circlearrowright_1^{|v|+1} q_4wv$. This implies

$$L_{R1}(A) = \{\, w \in a\{a, b\}^* \mid |w|_a = |w|_b \,\} \cup cL.$$

- For type 2 we get the behaviour $q_0vaw \circlearrowright_2 q_4wv$, $q_0xw \circlearrowright_2^2 q_2w$, and finally $q_0cvaw \circlearrowright_2^2 q_3vaw \circlearrowright_2 q_4wv$. That gives us

$$L_{R2}(A) = \{\lambda, c\}L.$$

- In type 3 it holds $q_0vaw \circlearrowright_3^{|v|+1} q_4wv$, $q_0vxw \circlearrowright_3^{|v|+2} q_2wv$, and moreover $q_0vcuaw \circlearrowright_3^{|v|+2} q_3uawv \circlearrowright_3^{|u|+1} q_4wvu$. Hence, we have

$$L_{R3}(A) = L \cup \{\, b^n cw \mid n \geq 0, w \in \{a, b\}^+, |b^n cw|_a = |b^n cw|_b \,\}.$$

Furthermore, we get

$$L_J(A) = \mathsf{perm}(L(A)) = \{\, w \in \{a, b, c\}^* \mid |w|_a = |w|_b > 0, |w|_c \in \{0, 1\} \,\}.$$

It follows

$$L(A) \subseteq L_{R1}(A) \subseteq L_{R2}(A) \subseteq L_{R3}(A) \subseteq L_J(A)$$

where the inclusions are strict. This inclusion chain is not a coincidence, as we will see next.   □

From our definitions, we can deduce:

Lemma 6. *Let $A = (Q, \Sigma, R, S, F)$ be a λ-MNROWJFA. Then, the following holds:*

1. *We have $L(A) \subseteq L_{R1}(A) \subseteq L_{R2}(A) \subseteq L_{R3}(A) \subseteq L_J(A)$ and these languages are semi-linear.*
2. *If A is an MNROWJFA, then $L_R(A) = L_{Ri}(A)$, for $1 \leq i \leq 3$. Hence the inclusion chain $L(A) \subseteq L_R(A) \subseteq L_J(A)$ applies.*
3. *If $R(p, a) \neq \emptyset$, for every state $p \in Q$ and letter $a \in \Sigma$, then $L(A) = L_{Ri}(A)$, for $1 \leq i \leq 3$.*   □

Lemma 6 implies that every regular language is accepted by a ROWJFA, because every regular language is accepted by a DFA with total transition function. On the other hand, we have seen in our example that ROWJFAs can accept non-regular languages. Indeed, it was already shown in [4] that **REG $\subset$ ROWJ**.

3.2   Variants of Right One-Way Jumping Finite Automata Without Spontaneous Transitions

From the language families **ROWJ**, **MROWJ**, **NROWJ**, and **MNROWJ** and their permutation closed variants the former two were already investigated in the literature. For inclusion relations and incomparability results see, e.g., [1,2]. Clearly, **MROWJ** consists exactly of the finite unions of languages from **ROWJ**. However, it is not clear that every language from **pMROWJ** is a finite union of languages from **pROWJ**. Nice characterizations for both language families were obtained. More precisely, a permutation closed language L is in **ROWJ** if and only if the Myhill-Nerode relation $\sim_L$ has only a finite number of positive equivalence classes [1]. In [2], concerning the language family **MROWJ** it was shown that for a permutation closed language L the following statements are equivalent: (1) For all $w \in \Sigma^*$, the language $L/^d w$ is in **pMROWJ**, where

$$L/^d w = \{\, v \in \Sigma^* \mid vw \in L \text{ and } (|v|_a = 0 \vee |w|_a = 0), \text{ for every } a \in \Sigma \,\}$$

is the *disjoint quotient* of a language $L \subseteq \Sigma^*$ by a word $w \in \Sigma^*$, and (2) there is an $n \geq 0$ and permutation closed languages $L_1, L_2, \ldots, L_n \subseteq \Sigma^*$ such that $L = \bigcup_{i=1}^n L_i$ and for all $i \in \{1, 2, \ldots, n\}$ the language L_i has only a finite number of positive Myhill-Nerode equivalence classes. Both characterization results are based on a relation between languages accepted by ROWJFAs and MROWJFAs and semi-linear sets. For our language families we find the following situation.

Theorem 7. *The following strict inclusions of language families hold:*

1. **ROWJ** $\subset$ **MROWJ** *and* **ROWJ** $\subset$ **NROWJ**.
2. **MROWJ** $\subset$ **MNROWJ** *and* **NROWJ** $\subset$ **MNROWJ**. $\square$

The languages used in the proof of the previous theorem show that the language families **MROWJ** and **NROWJ** are incomparable.

Corollary 8. *The language families* **MROWJ** *and* **NROWJ** *are incomparable.* $\square$

Before we investigate the hierarchy of permutation closed language families we first state a result that shows that whenever the underlying device is nondeterministic and accepts a permutation closed language it does not matter whether the automaton has multiple initial states or not. Moreover, we show that the induced language family coincides with **JFA**, the family of languages accepted by jumping finite automata.

Theorem 9. *We have* **pNROWJ** = **pMNROWJ** = **JFA**. $\square$

From [2], we know **pROWJ** $\subset$ **pMROWJ**. Furthermore, the permutation closed language $\{\, w \in \{a, b\}^* \mid |w|_a \neq |w|_b \,\}$ is clearly in **JFA**, but was shown to be not in **pMROWJ** in [2]. Hence, together with the previous theorem we get:

Theorem 10. *It holds* **pROWJ** $\subset$ **pMROWJ** $\subset$ **pNROWJ** = **pMNROWJ**. $\square$

3.3 Variants of Right One-Way Jumping Finite Automata with Spontaneous Transitions

In this subsection we study λ-NROWJFAs and λ-MNROWJFAs under the three semantics introduced earlier. Observe that by definition we have the inclusions **MNROWJ** $\subseteq$ λ_i**MNROWJ** and **NROWJ** $\subseteq$ λ_i**NROWJ** $\subseteq$ λ_i**MNROWJ**, for every $i \in \{1, 2, 3\}$. First we show that λ-NROWJFAs and λ-MNROWJFAs have the same computational power, if we fix the semantics.

Lemma 11. *For $i \in \{1, 2, 3\}$, we have* λ_i**NROWJ** $=$ λ_i**MNROWJ**. $\qquad\square$

Next we consider the case when the semantics on λ-MNROWJFAs varies. We show that λ-MNROWJFAs of type 1 are at most as powerful as those of type 2 and those of type 3:

Lemma 12. *We have* λ_1**MNROWJ** $\subseteq$ λ_2**MNROWJ** *and* λ_1**MNROWJ** $\subseteq$ λ_3**MNROWJ**. $\qquad\square$

Our next result shows that MNROWJFAs have indeed the same power as λ-MNROWJFAs of type 2.

Lemma 13. *We have* **MNROWJ** $=$ λ_2**MNROWJ**. $\qquad\square$

By definition, it holds **MNROWJ** $\subseteq$ λ_1**MNROWJ**. Thus, the previous three Lemmas 11, 12 and 13 give us the following equalities of language families.

Corollary 14. *We have* **MNROWJ** $=$ λ_i**NROWJ** $=$ λ_i**MNROWJ**, *for i with $i \in \{1, 2\}$.* $\qquad\square$

In contrast to the last result, λ-NROWJFAs of type 3 are more powerful than MNROWJFAs.

Theorem 15. *It holds* **MNROWJ** $\subset$ λ_3**NROWJ**. $\qquad\square$

Our language families are all included in the complexity classes **NTIME**(n^2) and in **NSPACE**(n):

Theorem 16. *For $i \in \{1, 2, 3\}$, the family λ_i**MNROWJ** is properly included in* **NTIME**(n^2) *and in* **NSPACE**(n). $\qquad\square$

For a λ-MNROWJFA A and $i \in \{1, 2, 3\}$ the language $L_{Ri}(A)$ contains a Parikh-equivalent regular sublanguage, because of Lemma 6. The only Parikh-equivalent sublanguage of a letter-bounded language is the language itself, so we get the following.

Corollary 17. *The letter-bounded languages contained in λ_3**MNROWJ** are exactly the regular letter-bounded languages.* $\qquad\square$

As a consequence, the language $\{\, a^n b^n \mid n \geq 0 \,\}$ is not in λ_3**MNROWJ**. On the other hand, it was shown in [4] that **ROWJ** contains non-context-free languages. It follows:

Corollary 18. *Let $F \in \{\mathbf{ROWJ}, \lambda_3\mathbf{MNROWJ}\}$ and $G \in \{\mathbf{DCF}, \mathbf{CF}\}$. Then, the language families F and G are incomparable.* $\qquad\square$

4   Relations to Finite-State Acceptors with Translucent Letters

Finite-state acceptors with translucent letters were defined in [10]. For these devices, depending on the current internal state, some letters of the input alphabet are translucent, which means that the automaton does not see them and reads the first letter which is not translucent. So, their behaviour is similar to ROWJFAs, which jump over some letters of the input alphabet, also depending on the current state of the automaton. We will investigate the inclusion relations between the language families induced by finite-state acceptors with translucent letters and those families which come from ROWJFAs and their nondeterministic variants.

A *finite-state acceptor with translucent letters*, a NFAwtl for short, is a tuple $A = (Q, \Sigma, \tau, S, F, \delta)$, where Q is the finite *set of states*, Σ is the finite *input alphabet*, $\tau : Q \to 2^{\Sigma}$ is the *translucency mapping*, $S \subseteq Q$ is the set of *start states*, $F \subseteq Q$ is the set of *final states*, and $\delta : Q \times \Sigma \to 2^Q$ is the *transition function*. For each state $q \in Q$ the letters from $\tau(q)$ are *translucent in state q*. The automaton A is called *deterministic*, a DFAwtl for short, if $|S| = 1$ and $|\delta(q, a)| \leq 1$, for all $(q, a) \in Q \times \Sigma$.

A *configuration* of A is a string in $Q\Sigma^*$. The automaton A makes a *transition* from configuration $pvaw$ to configuration qvw if $q \in \delta(p, a)$, where $p, q \in Q$, $v \in (\tau(p))^*$, $a \in \Sigma \setminus \tau(p)$, and $w \in \Sigma^*$. We denote this by $pvaw \vdash_A qvw$ or just $pvaw \vdash qvw$ if it is clear which automaton we are referring to. Then, the *language accepted by A* is

$$L(A) = \{\, w \in \Sigma^* \mid \exists s \in S, f \in F, v \in (\tau(f))^* : sw \vdash^* fv \,\}.$$

We say that A *accepts* $w \in \Sigma^*$ if $w \in L(A)$ and that A *rejects* w otherwise. The family of all languages accepted by a NFAwtl (DFAwtl, respectively) will be denoted by **NTRANS** (**DTRANS**, respectively). These families are incomparable to the language families induced by ROWJFAs and their nondeterministic variants:

Theorem 19. *Consider language families* $F \in \{\textbf{DTRANS}, \textbf{NTRANS}\}$ *and* $G \in \{\textbf{ROWJ}, \lambda_3\textbf{NROWJ}\}$. *Then, the families F and G are incomparable.* $\Box$

From [10] it is known that **pNTRANS** = **JFA**. The family **pDTRANS** has the following inclusion relations to **pROWJ** and **pMROWJ**.

Theorem 20. *We have* **pROWJ** $\subset$ **pDTRANS**. *The families* **pDTRANS** *and* **pMROWJ** *are incomparable.* $\Box$

In [10] it was shown that for each NFAwtl A there is an NFAwtl $B = (Q, \Sigma, \tau, S, F, \delta)$ with $L(A) = L(B)$ and for all $w \in \Sigma^*$, $s \in S$, $f \in F$, and $v \in (\tau(f))^*$ with $sw \vdash_B^* fv$ it holds $v = \lambda$. It was stated as an open problem if this property also holds for DFAswtl. We can solve this open problem:

Corollary 21. *There is a DFAwtl A such that there does not exist a DFAwtl* $B = (Q, \Sigma, \tau, \{s\}, F, \delta)$ *with* $L(A) = L(B)$ *and for all* $w \in \Sigma^*$, $f \in F$, *and* $v \in (\tau(f))^*$ *with* $sw \vdash_B^* fv$ *it holds* $v = \lambda$. $\Box$

5   Conclusions

We have investigated nondeterministic variants of ROWJFAs and showed inclusion and incomparability results of the induced language families. In order to complete the picture of these new language families, it remains to study closure properties and decision problems for these devices. Since languages accepted by variants of jumping automata are all semi-linear, it is worth to consider their relation to Petri Nets, since a wide variety of them enjoy semi-linear reachability sets—see, e.g., [12].

References

1. Beier, S., Holzer, M.: Properties of right one-way jumping finite automata. In: Konstantinidis, S., Pighizzini, G. (eds.) DCFS 2018. LNCS, vol. 10952, pp. 11–23. Springer, Cham (2018). https://doi.org/10.1007/978-3-319-94631-3_2
2. Beier, S., Holzer, M.: Semi-linear lattices and right one-way jumping finite automata (extended abstract). In: Hospodár, M., Jirásková, G. (eds.) CIAA 2019. LNCS, vol. 11601. Springer, Cham (2019, to appear)
3. Beier, S., Holzer, M., Kutrib, M.: Operational state complexity and decidability of jumping finite automata. In: Charlier, É., Leroy, J., Rigo, M. (eds.) DLT 2017. LNCS, vol. 10396, pp. 96–108. Springer, Cham (2017). https://doi.org/10.1007/978-3-319-62809-7_6
4. Chigahara, H., Fazekas, S., Yamamura, A.: One-way jumping finite automata. Int. J. Found. Comput. Sci. 27(3), 391–405 (2016). https://doi.org/10.1142/S0129054116400165
5. Fernau, H., Paramasivan, M., Schmid, M.L.: Jumping finite automata: characterizations and complexity. In: Drewes, F. (ed.) CIAA 2015. LNCS, vol. 9223, pp. 89–101. Springer, Cham (2015). https://doi.org/10.1007/978-3-319-22360-5_8
6. Fernau, H., Paramasivan, M., Schmid, M.L., Vorel, V.: Characterization and complexity results on jumping finite automata. Theoret. Comput. Sci. 679, 31–52 (2017). https://doi.org/10.1016/j.tcs.2016.07.006
7. Harrison, M.A.: Introduction to Formal Language Theory. Addison-Wesley, Boston (1978)
8. Lavado, G.J., Pighizzini, G., Seki, S.: Operational state complexity under parikh equivalence. In: Jürgensen, H., Karhumäki, J., Okhotin, A. (eds.) DCFS 2014. LNCS, vol. 8614, pp. 294–305. Springer, Cham (2014). https://doi.org/10.1007/978-3-319-09704-6_26
9. Meduna, A., Zemek, P.: Jumping finite automata. Int. J. Found. Comput. Sci. 23(7), 1555–1578 (2012). https://doi.org/10.1142/S0129054112500244
10. Nagy, B., Otto, F.: Finite-state acceptors with translucent letters. In: Bel-Enguix, G., Dahl, V., De La Puente, A.O. (eds.) Proceedings 1st Workshop on AI Methods for Interdisciplinary Research in Language and Biology (BILC 2011), pp. 3–13. SciTePress, Setúbal (2011). https://doi.org/10.5220/0003272500030013
11. Vorel, V.: On basic properties of jumping finite automata. Int. J. Found. Comput. Sci. 29(1), 1–16 (2018). https://doi.org/10.1142/S0129054118500016
12. Yen, H.-C.: Petri nets and semilinear sets (extended abstract). In: Sampaio, A., Wang, F. (eds.) ICTAC 2016. LNCS, vol. 9965, pp. 25–29. Springer, Cham (2016). https://doi.org/10.1007/978-3-319-46750-4_2

State Complexity of Single-Word Pattern Matching in Regular Languages

Janusz A. Brzozowski[1], Sylvie Davies[2]([✉]), and Abhishek Madan[1]

[1] David R. Cheriton School of Computer Science, University of Waterloo,
Waterloo, ON N2L 3G1, Canada
`brzozo@uwaterloo.ca, a7madan@edu.uwaterloo.ca`
[2] Department of Pure Mathematics, University of Waterloo,
Waterloo, ON N2L 3G1, Canada
`sldavies@uwaterloo.ca`

Abstract. The state complexity $\kappa(L)$ of a regular language L is the number of states in the minimal deterministic finite automaton recognizing L. In a general pattern-matching problem one has a set T of texts and a set P of patterns; both T and P are sets of words over a finite alphabet Σ. The matching problem is to determine whether any of the patterns appear in any of the texts, as prefixes, or suffixes, or factors, or subsequences. In previous work we examined the state complexity of these problems when both T and P are regular languages, that is, we computed the state complexity of the languages $(P\Sigma^*) \cap T$, $(\Sigma^* P) \cap T$, $(\Sigma^* P \Sigma^*) \cap T$, and $(\Sigma^* \shuffle P) \cap T$, where $\shuffle$ is the shuffle operation. It turns out that the state complexities of these languages match the naïve upper bounds derived by composing the state complexities of the basic operations used in each expression. However, when P is a single word w, and Σ has two or more letters, the bounds are drastically reduced to the following: $\kappa((w\Sigma^*) \cap T) \leqslant m+n-1$; $\kappa((\Sigma^* w) \cap T) \leqslant (m-1)n - (m-2)$; $\kappa((\Sigma^* w \Sigma^*) \cap T) \leqslant (m-1)n$; and $\kappa((\Sigma^* \shuffle w) \cap T) \leqslant (m-1)n$. The bounds for factor and subsequence matching are the same as the naïve bounds, but this is not the case for prefix and suffix matching. For unary languages, we have a tight upper bound of $m+n-2$ in all four cases.

Keywords: All-sided ideal · Combined operation · Factor · Finite automaton · Left ideal · Pattern matching · Prefix · Regular language · Right ideal · State complexity · Subsequence · Suffix · Two-sided ideal

1 Introduction

The *state complexity* of a regular language L, denoted $\kappa(L)$, is the number of states in the minimal deterministic finite automaton (DFA) recognizing L. The

---

This work was supported by the Natural Sciences and Engineering Research Council of Canada grant No. OGP0000871.

M. Hospodár et al. (Eds.): DCFS 2019, LNCS 11612, pp. 86–97, 2019.
https://doi.org/10.1007/978-3-030-23247-4_6

state complexity of an *operation* on regular languages is the worst-case state complexity of the resulting language, expressed in terms of the input languages' state complexities. A language attaining this worst-case state complexity is called a *witness* for the operation.

The state complexities of "basic" regular operations such as intersection and concatenation have been thoroughly studied [7–9]. There has also been some attention devoted towards "combined" operations such as concatenation with Σ^* to form languages called *ideals* [3]. A practical application of ideals is in *pattern matching*, or finding occurrences of a pattern in a text, commonly as either prefixes, suffixes, factors, or subsequences. (For a detailed treatment of pattern matching, see [4].) Brzozowski et al. [1] formulated several pattern matching problems as the construction of a regular language, using the intersection between a text language T and an ideal of a pattern language P. In the general case, given that $\kappa(T) \leqslant n$ and $\kappa(P) \leqslant m$, and denoting ⊔⊔ as the shuffle operation, the following state complexity bounds were shown to be tight:

1. *Prefix:* $\kappa((P\Sigma^*) \cap T) \leqslant mn$.
2. *Suffix:* $\kappa((\Sigma^*P) \cap T) \leqslant 2^{m-1}n$.
3. *Factor:* $\kappa((\Sigma^*P\Sigma^*) \cap T) \leqslant (2^{m-2}+1)n$.
4. *Subsequence:* $\kappa((P \sqcup\!\sqcup \Sigma^*) \cap T) \leqslant (2^{m-2}+1)n$.

These bounds are in fact the naïve bounds derived from composing the state complexity of the intersection between the Σ^*-concatenated pattern language and the text language. However, these bounds are exponential in m, which leads to the following question: to what degree would restricting P lower the bounds? In this paper, we focus on restricting P to be a single word; that is, $P = \{w\}$.

Single-word pattern matching has many practical applications. For example, a common use of the `grep` utility in Unix is to search for the files in a directory in which a search word appears. In bioinformatics, a DNA sequence t is often searched to locate a sequence of nucleotides w [5]. There has also been work in distributed systems to "learn" common execution patterns from log files and use them to identify anomalous executions in new logs [6].

In this paper, we show that for languages T and $\{w\}$ such that $\kappa(T) \leqslant n$ and $\kappa(\{w\}) \leqslant m$, the following upper bounds hold:

1. Prefix: $\kappa((w\Sigma^*) \cap T) \leqslant m + n - 1$.
2. Suffix: $\kappa((\Sigma^*w) \cap T) \leqslant (m-1)n - (m-2)$.
3. Factor: $\kappa((\Sigma^*w\Sigma^*) \cap T) \leqslant (m-1)n$.
4. Subsequence: $\kappa((\Sigma^* \sqcup\!\sqcup w) \cap T) \leqslant (m-1)n$.

Furthermore, in each case there exist languages T_n and $\{w\}_m$ that meet the upper bounds. All of these bounds can be achieved using a binary alphabet, but not using a unary alphabet.

2 Terminology and Notation

A *deterministic finite automaton (DFA)* is a 5-tuple $\mathcal{D} = (Q, \Sigma, \delta, q_0, F)$, where Q is a finite non-empty set of *states*, Σ is a finite non-empty *alphabet*, $\delta \colon Q \times \Sigma \rightarrow$

Q is the *transition function*, $q_0 \in Q$ is the *initial* state, and $F \subseteq Q$ is the set of *final* states. We extend δ to functions $\delta \colon Q \times \Sigma^* \to Q$ and $\delta \colon 2^Q \times \Sigma^* \to 2^Q$ as usual.

A language $L(\mathcal{D})$ is *accepted* by $\mathcal{D}$ if, for all $w \in L(\mathcal{D})$, $\delta(q_0, w) \in F$. If q is a state of $\mathcal{D}$, then the language $L_q(\mathcal{D})$ of q is the language accepted by the DFA $(Q, \Sigma, \delta, q, F)$. Let L be a language over Σ. The *quotient* of L by a word $x \in \Sigma^*$ is the set $x^{-1}L = \{y \in \Sigma^* \mid xy \in L\}$. In a DFA $\mathcal{D} = (Q, \Sigma, \delta, q_0, F)$, if $\delta(q_0, w) = q$, then $L_q(\mathcal{D}) = w^{-1}L(\mathcal{D})$.

Two states p and q of $\mathcal{D}$ are *indistinguishable* if $L_p(\mathcal{D}) = L_q(\mathcal{D})$. A state q is *reachable* if there exists $w \in \Sigma^*$ such that $\delta(q_0, w) = q$. A DFA $\mathcal{D}$ is *minimal* if it has the smallest number of states and the smallest alphabet among all DFAs accepting $L(\mathcal{D})$. It is well known that a DFA is minimal if it uses the smallest alphabet, all of its states are reachable, and no two states are indistinguishable.

We sometimes define transition functions as transformations induced by letters, written as $a \colon t$ where $t \colon Q \to Q$, for all $a \in \Sigma$. In particular, we use $\mathbb{1}$ to denote the identity transformation (i.e., $\delta(q, a) = q$ for all $q \in Q$), and $(q_0, q_1, \ldots, q_{k-1})$ to denote a *k-cycle*, where $\delta(q_i, a) = q_{i+1}$ for $0 \leqslant i \leqslant k - 2$ and $\delta(q_{k-1}, a) = q_0$. For states not in $\{q_0, q_1, \ldots, q_{k-1}\}$, the k-cycle acts as the identity transformation.

Throughout the paper, we fix $w = a_1 \cdots a_{m-2}$, where $a_i \in \Sigma$ for $1 \leqslant i \leqslant m - 2$. Let $w_0 = \varepsilon$ (where ε denotes the empty word) and for $1 \leqslant i \leqslant m - 2$, let $w_i = a_1 \cdots a_i$. We write $W = \{w_0, w_1, \ldots, w_{m-2}\}$ for the set of all prefixes of w. Note that if the state complexity of $\{w\}$ is m, then w is of length $m - 2$.

3   Matching a Single Prefix

Theorem 1. *Suppose $m \geqslant 3$ and $n \geqslant 2$. If w is a non-empty word, $\kappa(\{w\}) \leqslant m$ and $\kappa(T) \leqslant n$ then we have*

$$\kappa((w\Sigma^*) \cap T) \leqslant \begin{cases} m + n - 1, & \text{if } |\Sigma| \geqslant 2; \\ m + n - 2, & \text{if } |\Sigma| = 1. \end{cases}$$

Furthermore, these upper bounds are tight.

Remark 1. When $|\Sigma| = 1$ (that is, P and T are languages over a unary alphabet), the tight upper bound $m + n - 2$ actually holds in *all four cases* we consider in this paper. This is because if L is a language over a unary alphabet Σ, then the ideals $L\Sigma^*$, $\Sigma^* L$, $\Sigma^* L \Sigma^*$ and $\Sigma^* \sqcup\!\sqcup L$ coincide; thus the prefix, suffix, factor and subsequence matching cases coincide.

Proof. We first derive upper bounds for the two cases of $|\Sigma|$.

Upper Bounds: Let $\mathcal{D}_T = (Q, \Sigma, \delta, q_0, F_T)$, where $Q = \{q_0, \ldots, q_{n-1}\}$, be a DFA accepting T. Let $P = \{w\}$ and let the minimal DFA of P be $\mathcal{D}_P =$

$(W \cup \{\emptyset\}, \Sigma, \alpha, w_0, \{w_{m-2}\})$. Here w_{m-2} is the only final state, and $\emptyset$ is the empty state. Define α as follows: for $0 \leqslant i \leqslant m - 2$, we set

$$\alpha(w_i, a) = \begin{cases} w_{i+1}, & \text{if } a = a_i; \\ \emptyset, & \text{otherwise.} \end{cases}$$

Also define $\alpha(\emptyset, a) = \emptyset$ for all $a \in \Sigma$. Let the state reached by w in $\mathcal{D}_T$ be $q_r = \delta(q_0, w)$; we construct a DFA $\mathcal{D}_L$ that accepts $L = (w\Sigma^*) \cap T$. As shown in Fig. 1, let $\mathcal{D}_L = (Q \cup (W \setminus \{w_{m-2}\}) \cup \{\emptyset\}, \Sigma, \beta, w_0, F_T)$, where β is defined as follows: for $q \in Q \cup (W \setminus \{w_{m-2}\}) \cup \{\emptyset\}$ and $a \in \Sigma$,

$$\beta(q, a) = \begin{cases} \delta(q, a), & \text{if } q \in Q; \\ \alpha(q, a), & \text{if } q \in W \setminus \{w_{m-2}, w_{m-3}\}; \\ q_r, & \text{if } q = w_{m-3}, \text{ and } a = a_{m-2}; \\ \emptyset, & \text{otherwise.} \end{cases}$$

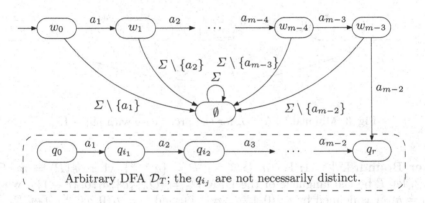

Arbitrary DFA $\mathcal{D}_T$; the q_{i_j} are not necessarily distinct.

Fig. 1. DFA $\mathcal{D}_L$ for matching a single prefix. The final state set F_T is a subset of the states from the arbitrary DFA $\mathcal{D}_T$; final states are not marked on the diagram.

Recall that in a DFA $\mathcal{D}$, if state q is reached from the initial state by a word u, then the language of q is equal to the quotient of $L(\mathcal{D})$ by u. Thus the language of state q_r is the quotient of T by w, that is, the set $w^{-1}T = \{y \in \Sigma^* \mid wy \in T\}$. The DFA $\mathcal{D}_L$ accepts a word x if and only if it has the form wy for $y \in w^{-1}T$; we need the prefix w to reach the arbitrary DFA $\mathcal{D}_T$, and w must be followed by a word that sends q_r to an accepting state, that is, a word y in the language $w^{-1}T$ of q_r. So $L = \{wy \mid y \in w^{-1}T\} = \{wy \mid y \in \Sigma^*, wy \in T\} = (w\Sigma^*) \cap T$. That is, L is the set of all words of T that begin with w, as required. It follows that the state complexity of L is less than or equal to $m + n - 1$. If $|\Sigma| = 1$, all the $\Sigma \setminus \{a_i\}$ are empty and state $\emptyset$ is not needed. Hence the state complexity of L is less than or equal to $m + n - 2$ in this case.

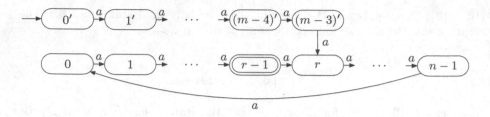

Fig. 2. Minimal DFA of L for the case $|\Sigma| = 1$.

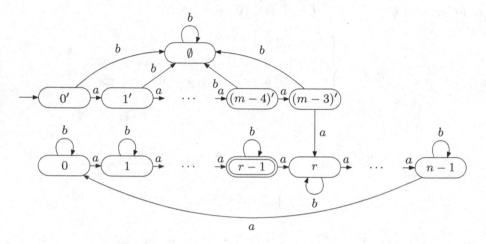

Fig. 3. Minimal DFA of L for the prefix case with $|\Sigma| > 1$.

Lower Bound, $|\Sigma| = 1$: For $m \geqslant 3$, let $P = \{a^{m-2}\}$ where $\kappa(P) = m$. For $n \geqslant 2$, let T be the language of the DFA $\mathcal{D}_n = (Q_n, \{a\}, \delta_1, 0, \{r - 1\})$, where $\kappa(T) = n$, δ_1 is defined by a: $(0, 1, \ldots, n - 1)$, and $r = \delta_1(0, a^{m-2})$. Let $\mathcal{D}_L$ be the DFA shown in Fig. 2 for the language $L = (P\Sigma^*) \cap T$. Obviously $\mathcal{D}_L$ has $m + n - 2$ states and they are all reachable. Since the shortest word accepted from any state is distinct from that of any other state, all the states are pairwise distinguishable. Hence P and T constitute witnesses that meet the required bound.

Lower Bound, $|\Sigma| \geqslant 2$: For $m \geqslant 3$, let $P = \{a^{m-2}\}$ where $\kappa(P) = m$. For $n \geqslant 2$, let T be the language of the DFA $\mathcal{D}_n = (Q_n, \{a, b\}, \delta_2, 0, \{r - 1\})$ where $\kappa(T) = n$, δ_2 is defined by a: $(0, 1, \ldots, n - 1)$ and b: $\mathbb{1}$, and $r = \delta_2(0, a^{m-2})$. Construct the DFA $\mathcal{D}_L$ for the language $L = (P\Sigma^*) \cap T$ as is shown in Fig. 3. It is clear that all states are reachable and distinguishable by their shortest accepted words. $\qquad\square$

4 Matching a Single Suffix

Let $w, x, y, z \in \Sigma^*$. We introduce some notation:

- $x \preceq_p y$ means x is a prefix of y, and $x \succeq_s y$ means x has y as a suffix.
- If $x \succeq_s y$ and $y \preceq_p z$, we say y is a *bridge* from x to z or that y *connects* x to z. We also denote this by $x \to y \to z$.
- $x \twoheadrightarrow y \twoheadrightarrow z$ means that y is the *longest* bridge from x to z. That is, $x \to y \to z$, and whenever $x \to w \to z$ we have $|w| \leq |y|$. Equivalently, y is the longest suffix of x that is also a prefix of z.

Proposition 1. *If the state complexity of $\{w\}$ is m, then the state complexity of $\Sigma^* w$ is $m - 1$.*

Proof. Let $\mathcal{A} = (W, \Sigma, \delta_{\mathcal{A}}, w_0, \{w_{m-2}\})$ be the DFA with transitions defined as follows: for all $a \in \Sigma$ and $w_i \in W$, we have $w_i a \twoheadrightarrow \delta_{\mathcal{A}}(w_i, a) \twoheadrightarrow w$. That is, $\delta_{\mathcal{A}}(w_i, a)$ is defined to be the maximal-length bridge from $w_i a$ to w, or equivalently, the longest suffix of $w_i a$ that is also a prefix of w. Note that if $a = a_{i+1}$, then $\delta_{\mathcal{A}}(w_i, a) = w_{i+1}$.

We observe that every state $w_i \in W$ is reachable from w_0 by the word w_i, and that each state w_i is distinguished from all other states by $a_{i+1} \cdots a_{m-2}$. It remains to be shown that $\Sigma^* w = L(\mathcal{A})$. In the following, for convenience, we simply write δ rather than $\delta_{\mathcal{A}}$.

We claim that for $x \in \Sigma^*$, we have $w_i x \twoheadrightarrow \delta(w_i, x) \twoheadrightarrow w$. That is, the defining property of the transition function extends nicely to words. Recall that the extension of δ to words is defined inductively in terms of the behavior of δ on letters, so it is not immediately clear that this property carries over to words.

We prove this claim by induction on $|x|$. If $x = \varepsilon$, this is clear. Now suppose $x = ya$ for some $y \in \Sigma^*$ and $a \in \Sigma$, and that $w_i y \twoheadrightarrow \delta(w_i, y) \twoheadrightarrow w$. Let $\delta(w_i, y) = w_j$ and let $\delta(w_i, x) = \delta(w_j, a) = w_k$. We want to show that $w_i x \twoheadrightarrow w_k \twoheadrightarrow w$.

First we show that $w_i x \to w_k \to w$. We know $w_k \preceq_p w$, so it remains to show that $w_i x \succeq_s w_k$. Since $w_k = \delta(w_i, x) = \delta(w_j, a)$, by definition we have $w_j a \twoheadrightarrow w_k \twoheadrightarrow w$. Since $\delta(w_i, y) = w_j$, we have $w_i y \twoheadrightarrow w_j \twoheadrightarrow w$. In particular, $w_i y \succeq_s w_j$ and thus $w_i x = w_i ya \succeq_s w_j a$. Thus $w_i x \succeq_s w_j a \succeq_s w_k$ as required.

Next, we show that whenever $w_i x \to w_\ell \to w$, we have $|w_\ell| \leq |w_k|$. If $w_\ell = \varepsilon$, this is immediate, so suppose $w_\ell \neq \varepsilon$. Since $w_i x = w_i ya \succeq_s w_\ell$, and w_ℓ is nonempty, it follow that w_ℓ ends with a. Thus $w_\ell = w_{\ell-1} a$. Since $w_i ya \succeq_s w_{\ell-1} a$, we have $w_i y \succeq_s w_{\ell-1}$. Additionally, $w_{\ell-1} \preceq_p w$, so $w_i y \to w_{\ell-1} \to w$. Since $w_i y \twoheadrightarrow w_j \twoheadrightarrow w$, we have $|w_{\ell-1}| \leq |w_j|$. Since $w_i y \succeq_s w_j$ and $w_i y \succeq_s w_{\ell-1}$ and $|w_j| \geq |w_{\ell-1}|$, we have $w_j \succeq_s w_{\ell-1}$. Thus $w_j a \succeq_s w_{\ell-1} a = w_\ell$. It follows that $w_j a \to w_\ell \to w$. But recall that $\delta(w_i, x) = \delta(w_j, a) = w_k$, so $w_j a \twoheadrightarrow w_k \twoheadrightarrow w$, and $|w_\ell| \leq |w_k|$ as required.

Now, we show that $\mathcal{A}$ accepts the language $\Sigma^* w$. Suppose $x \in \Sigma^* w$ and write $x = yw$. The initial state of $\mathcal{A}$ is $w_0 = \varepsilon$. We have $yw \twoheadrightarrow \delta(\varepsilon, yw) \twoheadrightarrow w$, that is, $\delta(\varepsilon, yw)$ is the longest suffix of yw that is also a prefix of w. But this longest suffix is simply w itself, which is the final state. So x is accepted. Conversely, suppose $x \in \Sigma^*$ is accepted by $\mathcal{A}$. Then $\delta(\varepsilon, x) = w$, and thus $x \twoheadrightarrow w \twoheadrightarrow w$ by definition. In particular, this means $x \succeq_s w$, and so $x \in \Sigma^* w$. $\square$

Next we establish an upper bound on the state complexity of $(\Sigma^* w) \cap T$. The upper bound in this case is quite complicated to derive. Suppose w has state complexity m and T has state complexity at most n, for $m \geqslant 3$ and $n \geqslant 2$. Let $\mathcal{A}$ be the $(m-1)$-state DFA for $\Sigma^* w$ defined in Proposition 1, and let $\mathcal{D}$ be an n-state DFA for T with state set Q_n, transition function α, and final state set F. The direct product $\mathcal{A} \times \mathcal{D}$ with final state set $\{w\} \times F$ recognizes $(\Sigma^* w) \cap T$. We claim that this direct product has at most $(m-1)n - (m-2)$ reachable and pairwise distinguishable states, and thus the state complexity of $(\Sigma^* w) \cap T$ is at most $(m-1)n - (m-2)$.

Since $\mathcal{A}$ has $m-1$ states and $\mathcal{D}$ has n states, there are at most $(m-1)n$ reachable states. It will suffice to show that for each word w_i with $1 \leqslant i \leqslant m-2$, there exists a word $w_{f(i)} \neq w_i$ and a state $p_i \in Q_n$ such that (w_i, p_i) is indistinguishable from $(w_{f(i)}, p_i)$. This gives $m-2$ states that are each indistinguishable from another state, establishing the upper bound.

We choose $f(i)$ so that $w_i \twoheadrightarrow w_{f(i)} \twoheadrightarrow w_{i-1}$. In other words, $w_{f(i)}$ is the longest suffix of w_i that is also a *proper* prefix of w_i. To find p_i, first observe that there exists a non-final state $q \in Q_n$ and a state $r \in Q_n$ such that $\alpha(r, w) = q$. Indeed, if no such states existed, then for all states r, the state $\alpha(r, w)$ would be final. Thus we would have $\Sigma^* w \subseteq T$, and the state complexity of $(\Sigma^* w) \cap T = \Sigma^* w$ would be $m-1$, which is lower than our upper bound since $n \geqslant 2$. Now, set $p_i = \alpha(r, w_i)$, and note that $\alpha(p_i, a_{i+1}) = p_{i+1}$, and $\alpha(p_i, a_{i+1} \cdots a_{m-2}) = q$.

To establish the upper bound, we will need two technical lemmas. Their proofs can be found in [2].

Lemma 1. *If $i < m-2$ and $a \neq a_{i+1}$, or if $i = m-2$, then $\delta_{\mathcal{A}}(w_i, a) = \delta_{\mathcal{A}}(w_{f(i)}, a)$.*

Lemma 2. *If $i < m-2$, then $\delta_{\mathcal{A}}(w_{f(i)}, a_{i+1}) = w_{f(i+1)}$.*

Proposition 2. *Suppose $m \geqslant 3$ and $n \geqslant 2$. If w is non-empty, $\kappa(\{w\}) \leqslant m$, and $\kappa(T) \leqslant n$, then we have $\kappa((\Sigma^* w) \cap T) \leqslant (m-1)n - (m-2)$.*

Proof. It suffices to prove that states (w_i, p_i) and $(w_{f(i)}, p_i)$ are indistinguishable for $1 \leqslant i \leqslant m-2$. We proceed by induction on the value $m-2-i$.

The base case is $m-2-i = 0$, that is, $i = m-2$. Our states are (w_{m-2}, p_{m-2}) and $(w_{f(m-2)}, p_{m-2})$. By Lemma 1, we have $\delta_{\mathcal{A}}(w_{m-2}, a) = \delta_{\mathcal{A}}(w_{f(m-2)}, a)$ for all $a \in \Sigma$. Thus non-empty words cannot distinguish the states. But recall that $p_{m-2} = q$ is a non-final state, so the states we are trying to distinguish are both non-final, and thus the empty word does not distinguish the states either. So these states are indistinguishable.

Now, suppose $m-2-i > 0$, that is, $i < m-2$. Assume that states (w_{i+1}, p_{i+1}) and $(w_{f(i+1)}, p_{i+1})$ are indistinguishable. We want to show that (w_i, p_i) and $(w_{f(i)}, p_i)$ are indistinguishable. Since $f(i) < i < m-2$, both states are non-final, and thus the empty word cannot distinguish them. By Lemma 1, if $a \neq a_{i+1}$, then $\delta_{\mathcal{A}}(w_i, a) = \delta_{\mathcal{A}}(w_{f(i)}, a)$ for all $a \in \Sigma$. So only words that start with a_{i+1} can possibly distinguish the states. But by Lemma 2, letter a_{i+1} sends the states to (w_{i+1}, p_{i+1}) and $(w_{f(i+1)}, p_{i+1})$, which are indistinguishable by the induction hypothesis. Thus the states cannot be distinguished. $\square$

Next we show that the upper bound of Proposition 2 is tight.

Definition 1. *Let T be the language accepted by the DFA $\mathcal{D}$ with state set Q_n, alphabet Σ, initial state 0, final state set $\{0, \ldots, n-2\}$, and transformations $a: (0, \ldots, n-1)$ and $b: \mathbb{1}$. See Fig. 4.*

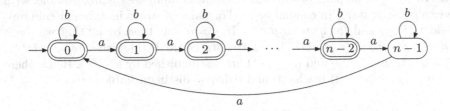

Fig. 4. Witness language T of Definition 1.

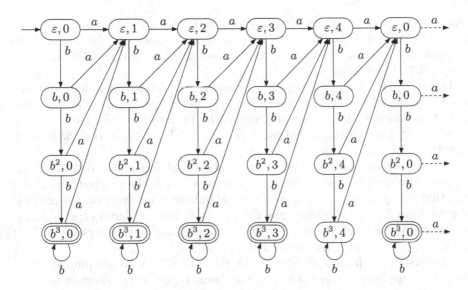

Fig. 5. DFA $\mathcal{A} \times \mathcal{D}$ for matching a single suffix, with $m = 5$ and $n = 5$. Column 0 is duplicated for a cleaner diagram; the DFA contains only one copy of this column.

Theorem 2. *Suppose $m \geqslant 3$ and $n \geqslant 2$. There exists a word w and a language T, with $\kappa(\{w\}) = m$ and $\kappa(T) = n$, such that $\kappa((\Sigma^* w) \cap T) = (m-1)n - (m-2)$.*

Proof. Let $\Sigma = \{a, b\}$ and let $w = b^{m-2}$. Let $\mathcal{A}$ be the DFA for $\Sigma^* w$. Let T be the language of Definition 1. The DFA $\mathcal{A} \times \mathcal{D}$ is illustrated in Fig. 5.

We show that $\mathcal{A} \times \mathcal{D}$ has $(m - 1)n - (m - 2)$ reachable and pairwise distinguishable states. For reachability, for $0 \leqslant i \leqslant m - 2$ and $0 \leqslant q \leqslant n - 1$, we can reach (b^i, q) from the initial state $(\varepsilon, 0)$ by the word $a^q b^i$. For distinguishability, note that all $m - 1$ states in column $n - 1$ are indistinguishable, and so collapse to one state under the indistinguishability relation. Indeed, given states $(b^i, n-1)$ and $(b^j, n-1)$, if we apply a both states are sent to $(\varepsilon, 0)$, and if we apply b we simply reach another pair of non-final states in column $n-1$. Hence at most $(m-1)n - (m-2)$ of the reachable states are pairwise distinguishable. Next consider (b^i, q) and (b^j, q) with $i < j$ and $q \neq n-1$. We can distinguish these states by b^{m-2-j}. So pairs of states in the same column are distinguishable, with the exception of states in column $n-1$. For pairs of states in different columns, consider (b^i, p) and (b^j, q) with $p < q$. If $q \neq n-1$, then by a^{n-1-q} we reach $(\varepsilon, n-1+p-q)$ and $(\varepsilon, n-1)$. These latter states are distinguished by $w = b^{m-2}$. If $q = n-1$, then (b^i, p) and $(b^j, n-1)$ are distinguished by b^{m-2-i}. Hence there are $(m-1)n - (m-2)$ reachable and pairwise distinguishable states.   □

5   Matching a Single Factor

Proposition 3. *If the state complexity of $\{w\}$ is m, then the state complexity of $\Sigma^* w \Sigma^*$ is $m-1$.*

Proof. Let $\mathcal{A} = (W, \Sigma, \delta_{\mathcal{A}}, w_0, \{w_{m-2}\})$ be the DFA with transitions defined as follows: for all $a \in \Sigma$ and $w_i \in W$, we have $w_i a \twoheadrightarrow \delta_{\mathcal{A}}(w_i, a) \twoheadrightarrow w$. Recall from Proposition 1 that $\mathcal{A}$ recognizes $\Sigma^* w$. We modify $\mathcal{A}$ to obtain a DFA $\mathcal{A}'$ that accepts $\Sigma^* w \Sigma^*$ as follows.

Let $\mathcal{A}' = (W, \Sigma, \delta_{\mathcal{A}'}, w_0, \{w_{m-2}\})$, where $\delta_{\mathcal{A}'}$ is defined as follows for each $a \in \Sigma$: $\delta_{\mathcal{A}'}(w_i, a) = \delta_{\mathcal{A}}(w_i, a)$ for $i < m-2$, and $\delta_{\mathcal{A}'}(w_{m-2}, a) = w_{m-2}$. Note that $\mathcal{A}'$ is minimal: state w_i can be reached by the word w_i, and states w_i and w_j with $i < j$ are distinguished by $a_{j+1} \cdots a_{m-2}$. It remains to show that $\mathcal{A}'$ accepts $\Sigma^* w \Sigma^*$.

To simplify the notation, we write δ' instead of $\delta_{\mathcal{A}'}$ and δ instead of $\delta_{\mathcal{A}}$. Suppose x is accepted by $\mathcal{A}'$. Write $x = yz$, where y is the shortest prefix of x such that $\delta'(\varepsilon, y) = w_{m-2}$. Since y is minimal in length, for every proper prefix y' of y, we have $\delta'(\varepsilon, y') = w_i$ for some $i < m-2$. It follows that $\delta'(\varepsilon, y) = \delta(\varepsilon, y)$ by the definition of δ'. So $\delta(\varepsilon, y) = w_{m-2}$, and hence y is accepted by $\mathcal{A}$. It follows that $y \in \Sigma^* w$. This implies $x = yz \in \Sigma^* w \Sigma^*$.

Conversely, suppose $x \in \Sigma^* w \Sigma^*$. Write $x = ywz$ with y minimal. Since $yw \in \Sigma^* w$, we have $\delta(\varepsilon, yw) = w_{m-2}$. Furthermore, yw is the shortest prefix of x such that $\delta(\varepsilon, yw) = w_{m-2}$, since if there was a shorter prefix then y would not be minimal. This means that $\delta(\varepsilon, yw) = \delta'(\varepsilon, yw)$ by the definition of δ'. So $\delta'(\varepsilon, ywz) = w_{m-2}$ and hence $x = ywz$ is accepted by $\mathcal{A}'$.   □

Fix w with state complexity m, and let $\mathcal{A}$ and $\mathcal{A}'$ be the DFAs for $\Sigma^* w$ and $\Sigma^* w \Sigma^*$, respectively, as described in the proof of Proposition 3. Fix T with state complexity at most n, and let $\mathcal{D}$ be an n-state DFA for T with state set Q_n and final state set F. The direct product DFA $\mathcal{A}' \times \mathcal{D}$ with final state set $\{w\} \times F$ recognizes $(\Sigma^* w \Sigma^*) \cap T$. Since $\mathcal{A}' \times \mathcal{D}$ has $(m-1)n$ states, this gives an upper bound of $(m-1)n$ on the state complexity of $(\Sigma^* w \Sigma^*) \cap T$.

Theorem 3. *Suppose $m \geqslant 3$ and $n \geqslant 2$. There exists a word w and a language T, with $\kappa(\{w\}) = m$ and $\kappa(T) = n$, such that $\kappa((\Sigma^* w \Sigma^*) \cap T) = (m-1)n$.*

Proof. Let $\Sigma = \{a, b\}$ and let $w = b^{m-2}$. Let $\mathcal{A}'$ be the DFA for $\Sigma^* w \Sigma^*$. Let T be the language of Definition 1. The DFA $\mathcal{A}' \times \mathcal{D}$ is illustrated in Fig. 6.

We show that $\mathcal{A}' \times \mathcal{D}$ has $(m-1)n$ reachable and pairwise distinguishable states. For reachability, for $0 \leqslant i \leqslant m-2$ and $0 \leqslant q \leqslant n-1$, we can reach (b^i, q) from the initial state $(\varepsilon, 0)$ by the word $a^q b^i$. For distinguishability, suppose we have states (b^i, q) and (b^j, q) in the same column q, with $i < j$. By b^{m-2-j} we reach $(b^{m-2+i-j}, q)$ and (w, q), with $b^{m-2+i-j} \neq w$. Then by a we reach (ε, qa) and (w, qa), which are distinguishable by a word in a^*. For states in different columns, suppose we have (b^i, p) and (b^j, q) with $p < q$. By a sufficiently long word in b^*, we reach (w, p) and (w, q). These states are distinguishable by a^{n-1-q}. So all reachable states are pairwise distinguishable. $\qquad\square$

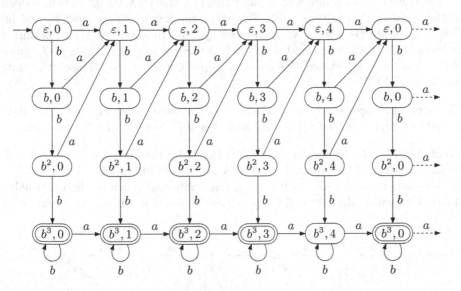

Fig. 6. DFA $\mathcal{A}' \times \mathcal{D}$ for matching a single factor, with $m = 5$ and $n = 5$. Column 0 is duplicated for a cleaner diagram; the DFA contains only one copy of this column.

6 Matching a Single Subsequence

Proposition 4. *If the state complexity of $\{w\}$ is m, then the state complexity of $\Sigma^* \sqcup\!\sqcup w$ is $m - 1$.*

Proof. Define a DFA $\mathcal{A} = (W, \Sigma, \delta_{\mathcal{A}}, \varepsilon, \{w\})$ where $\delta_{\mathcal{A}}(w_i, a_{i+1}) = w_{i+1}$, and $\delta_{\mathcal{A}}(w_i, a) = w_i$ for $a \neq a_{i+1}$. Note that $\mathcal{A}$ is minimal: state w_i is reached by word w_i and states w_i, w_j with $i < j$ are distinguished by $a_{j+1} \cdots a_{m-2}$. We claim that $\mathcal{A}$ recognizes $\Sigma^* \sqcup\!\sqcup w$.

Write δ rather than $\delta_{\mathcal{A}}$ to simplify the notation. Suppose $x \in \Sigma^* \sqcup\!\sqcup w$. Then we can write $x = x_0 a_1 x_1 a_2 x_2 \cdots a_{m-2} x_{m-2}$, where $x_0, \ldots, x_{m-2} \in \Sigma^*$. We claim that $\delta(\varepsilon, x_0 a_1 x_1 \cdots a_i x_i) = w_j$ for some $j \geqslant i$. We proceed by induction on i. The base case $i = 0$ is trivial.

Now, suppose that $i > 0$ and $\delta(\varepsilon, x_0 a_1 x_1 \cdots a_{i-1} x_{i-1}) = w_j$ for some $j \geqslant i-1$. Then $\delta(\varepsilon, x_0 a_1 x_1 \cdots a_i x_i) = \delta(w_j, a_i x_i)$. We consider two cases:

- If $j = i - 1$, we have $\delta(w_{i-1}, a_i x_i) = \delta(w_i, x_i) = w_k$ for some k with $k \geqslant i$, as required.
- If $j > i - 1$, we have $\delta(w_j, a_i x_i) = w_k$ for some k with $k \geqslant i$, as required.

This completes the inductive proof. It follows then that $\delta(\varepsilon, x) = w_{m-2} = w$, and so x is accepted by $\mathcal{A}$. Conversely, if x is accepted by $\mathcal{A}$, then it is clear from the definition of the transition function that the letters $a_1, a_2, \ldots, a_{m-2}$ must occur within x in order, and so $x \in \Sigma^* \sqcup\!\!\sqcup w$. $\qquad\square$

Fix w with state complexity m, and let $\mathcal{A}$ be the DFA for $\Sigma^* \sqcup\!\!\sqcup w$ described in the proof of Proposition 4. Fix T with state complexity at most n, and let $\mathcal{D}$ be an n-state DFA for T with state set Q_n and final state set F. The direct product DFA $\mathcal{A} \times \mathcal{D}$ with final state set $\{w\} \times F$ recognizes $(\Sigma^* \sqcup\!\!\sqcup w) \cap T$. Since $\mathcal{A} \times \mathcal{D}$ has $(m-1)n$ states, this gives an upper bound of $(m-1)n$ on the state complexity of $(\Sigma^* \sqcup\!\!\sqcup w) \cap T$.

Theorem 4. *Suppose $m \geqslant 3$ and $n \geqslant 2$. There exists a word w and a language T, with $\kappa(\{w\}) = m$ and $\kappa(T) = n$, such that $\kappa((\Sigma^* \sqcup\!\!\sqcup w) \cap T) = (m-1)n$.*

Proof. Let $\Sigma = \{a, b\}$ and let $w = b^{m-2}$. Let $\mathcal{A}$ be the DFA for $\Sigma^* \sqcup\!\!\sqcup w$. Let T be the language of Definition 1. The DFA $\mathcal{A} \times \mathcal{D}$ is illustrated in Fig. 7.

We show that $\mathcal{A} \times \mathcal{D}$ has $(m-1)n$ reachable and pairwise distinguishable states. For reachability, for $0 \leqslant i \leqslant m-2$ and $0 \leqslant q \leqslant n-1$, we can reach (b^i, q)

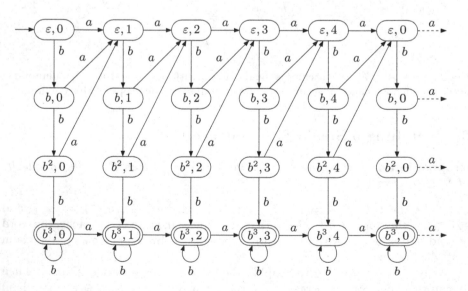

Fig. 7. DFA $\mathcal{A} \times \mathcal{D}$ for matching a single subsequence, with $m = 5$ and $n = 5$. Column 0 is duplicated for a cleaner diagram; the DFA contains only one copy of this column.

from the initial state $(\varepsilon, 0)$ by the word $a^q b^i$. For distinguishability, suppose we have states (b^i, q) and (b^j, q) in the same column q, with $i < j$. By b^{m-2-j} we reach $(b^{m-2+i-j}, q)$ and (w, q), with $b^{m-2+i-j} \neq w$. These states are distinguishable by a word in a^*. For states in different columns, suppose we have (b^i, p) and (b^j, q) with $p < q$. By a sufficiently long word in b^*, we reach (w, p) and (w, q). These states are distinguishable by a^{n-1-q}. So all reachable states are pairwise distinguishable. □

7   Conclusions

Building on previous work, we investigated the state complexity of "pattern matching" operations on regular languages, based on finding all words in a text language T which contain the single word w as either a prefix, suffix, factor, or subsequence. In all cases, the bounds were significantly lower than the general case, where w is replaced by a regular language P. Prefix matching is now linear in the input languages' state complexities, and the remaining cases are polynomial in the input state complexities. The general bounds were polynomial for prefix matching and exponential in the other cases. It is also worth noting that a binary alphabet is sufficient to reach all these bounds, including subsequence matching, whose bound was defined in terms of a growing alphabet in the general case. For languages with a unary alphabet, the state complexity was linear in all four cases.

References

1. Brzozowski, J.A., Davies, S., Madan, A.: State complexity of pattern matching in regular languages. Theoret. Comput. Sci. (2018). https://doi.org/10.1016/j.tcs.2018.12.014
2. Brzozowski, J.A., Davies, S., Madan, A.: State complexity of pattern matching in regular languages. CoRR abs/1806.04645 (2018). http://arxiv.org/abs/1806.04645
3. Brzozowski, J.A., Jirásková, G., Li, B.: Quotient complexity of ideal languages. Theoret. Comput. Sci. **470**, 36–52 (2013). https://doi.org/10.1016/j.tcs.2012.10.055
4. Crochemore, M., Hancart, C.: Automata for matching patterns. In: Rozenberg, G., Salomaa, A. (eds.) Handbook of Formal Languages, pp. 399–462. Springer, Heidelberg (1997). https://doi.org/10.1007/978-3-662-07675-0_9
5. Elloumi, M., Iliopoulos, C., Wang, J.T., Zomaya, A.Y.: Pattern Recognition in Computational Molecular Biology: Techniques and Approaches. Wiley, Hoboken (2015)
6. Fu, Q., Lou, J.G., Wang, Y., Li, J.: Execution anomaly detection in distributed systems through unstructured log analysis. In: Wang, W., Kargupta, H., Ranka, S., Yu, P.S., Wu, X. (eds.) Proceedings 9th IEEE International Conference on Data Mining, ICDM 2009, pp. 149–158. IEEE Computer Society (2009). https://doi.org/10.1109/ICDM.2009.60
7. Gao, Y., Moreira, N., Reis, R., Yu, S.: A survey on operational state complexity. J. Autom. Lang. Comb. **21**(4), 251–310 (2016)
8. Maslov, A.N.: Estimates of the number of states of finite automata. Soviet Math. Doklady **11**, 1373–1375 (1970)
9. Yu, S., Zhuang, Q., Salomaa, K.: The state complexities of some basic operations on regular languages. Theoret. Comput. Sci. **125**, 315–328 (1994). https://doi.org/10.1016/0304-3975(92)00011-F

Square, Power, Positive Closure, and Complementation on Star-Free Languages

Sylvie Davies[1] and Michal Hospodár[2(✉)]

[1] David R. Cheriton School of Computer Science,
University of Waterloo, Waterloo, ON N2L 3G1, Canada
sylvie.davies@uwaterloo.ca
[2] Mathematical Institute, Slovak Academy of Sciences,
Grešákova 6, 040 01 Košice, Slovakia
hosmich@gmail.com

Abstract. We examine the deterministic and nondeterministic state complexity of square, power, positive closure, and complementation on star-free languages. For the state complexity of square, we get a non-trivial upper bound $(n-1)2^n - 2(n-2)$ and a lower bound of order $\Theta(2^n)$. For the state complexity of the k-th power in the unary case, we get the tight upper bound $k(n-1) + 1$. Next, we show that the upper bound kn on the nondeterministic state complexity of the k-th power is met by a binary star-free language, while in the unary case, we have a lower bound $k(n-1) + 1$. For the positive closure, we show that the deterministic upper bound $2^{n-1} + 2^{n-2} - 1$, as well as the nondeterministic upper bound n, can be met by star-free languages. We also show that in the unary case, the state complexity of positive closure is $n^2 - 7n + 13$, and the nondeterministic state complexity of complementation is between $(n-1)^2 + 1$ and $n^2 - 2$.

1 Introduction

The state complexity of a regular language L, $\mathrm{sc}(L)$, is the smallest number of states in any deterministic finite automaton (DFA) recognizing the language L. The state complexity of a unary regular operation $\circ$ is the function from $\mathbb{N}$ to $\mathbb{N}$ given by $n \mapsto \max\{\mathrm{sc}(L^\circ) \mid \mathrm{sc}(L) \leq n\}$. The nondeterministic state complexity of a regular language or a unary regular operation is defined analogously using the representation of languages by nondeterministic finite automata (NFAs).

The (nondeterministic) state complexity of star, reversal, square, power, and complementation was examined in [4,6,10–12,14,18]. Researchers also investigated the complexity of operations on some subregular classes. For example,

S. Davies—Research supported by the Natural Sciences and Engineering Research Council of Canada under grant No. OGP0000871.
M. Hospodár—Research supported by VEGA grant 2/0132/19 and grant APVV-15-0091.

M. Hospodár et al. (Eds.): DCFS 2019, LNCS 11612, pp. 98–110, 2019.
https://doi.org/10.1007/978-3-030-23247-4_7

Câmpeanu et al. [3] considered finite languages, and Pighizzini and Shallit [13] studied operational state complexity on unary regular languages.

The class of *star-free languages* is the smallest class containing finite languages and closed under complementation, union, and concatenation. In 1965, Marcel-Paul Schützenberger [15] proved that a language is star-free if and only if its syntactic monoid is group-free, that is, it has only trivial subgroups. An equivalent condition is that the minimal DFA of a star-free language is permutation-free, that is, there is no string that induces a non-trivial permutation on any subset of the set of states.

The operational state complexity of basic regular operations on star-free languages represented by DFAs was examined by Brzozowski and Liu [1], while Holzer, Kutrib, and Meckel [7] considered basic operations on star-free languages represented by NFAs. Except for reversal on DFAs, all regular upper bounds have been shown to be met by star-free languages.

In this paper, we continue this research and study the state complexity and nondeterministic state complexity of square, power, positive closure, and complementation on star-free languages. As the main result of this paper, we get nontrivial upper and lower bounds for square on DFAs in Sect. 3. In Sect. 4, we obtain tight upper bounds for positive closure on DFAs and NFAs, and for power on unary DFAs and binary NFAs. Moreover, we present lower and upper bounds for complementation on unary NFAs that are better than in [7].

2 Preliminaries

Let Σ be a finite non-empty alphabet of symbols. Then Σ^* denotes the set of strings over Σ including the empty string ε. A language is any subset of Σ^*.

A *nondeterministic finite automaton* (NFA) is a 5-tuple $A = (Q, \Sigma, \cdot, s, F)$ where Q is a finite set of states, Σ is a finite alphabet, $\cdot \colon Q \times \Sigma \to 2^Q$ is the transition function which is naturally extended to the domain $2^Q \times \Sigma^*$, $s \in Q$ is the initial state, and $F \subseteq Q$ is the set of final states. We say that (p, a, q) is a *transition* in NFA A if $q \in p \cdot a$. The *language accepted* by the NFA A is the set $L(A) = \{w \in \Sigma^* \mid s \cdot w \cap F \neq \emptyset\}$.

An NFA A is a *deterministic finite automaton* (DFA) if $|q \cdot a| = 1$ for each q in Q and each a in Σ. In a DFA, each symbol a in Σ induces a *transformation* on the set Q, given by $q \mapsto q \cdot a$. We frequently describe the transitions of DFAs by just describing their induced transformations.

The state complexity of L, $\mathrm{sc}(L)$, is the smallest number of states in any DFA for L. The nondeterministic state complexity of L, $\mathrm{nsc}(L)$, is defined analogously. It is well known that if a language L is finite with the longest string of length ℓ, then $\mathrm{sc}(L) \leq \ell + 2$ and $\mathrm{nsc}(L) \leq \ell + 1$.

The reader may refer to [2,8,16,17] for details and all unexplained notions.

3   Square

In this section, we investigate the square operation on the class of star-free languages represented by DFAs. Let $A = (Q, \Sigma, \cdot, s, F)$ be an arbitrary DFA. As is well known, we may construct a DFA B recognizing $L(A)^2$ as follows:

- The state set of B is $Q \times 2^Q$, where 2^Q is the set of all subsets of Q.
- The initial state of B is $(s, \emptyset)$ if $s \notin F$, or $(s, \{s\})$ if $s \in F$.
- The final state set is $F_B = \{(q, S) \mid S \cap F \neq \emptyset\}$.
- The transition function $\odot$ is defined as follows for each $a \in \Sigma$:

$$(q, S) \odot a = \begin{cases} (q \cdot a, S \cdot a), & \text{if } q \cdot a \notin F; \\ (q \cdot a, S \cdot a \cup \{s\}), & \text{if } q \cdot a \in F. \end{cases}$$

To simplify the notation, we write $(q, S)a$ instead of $(q, S) \odot a$, and we write qa and Sa instead of $q \cdot a$ and $S \cdot a$ for each q in Q and each subset S of Q.

We will use the following lemma.

Lemma 1. *Let $q \in F$ and $T \subseteq Q$. Suppose (q, T) is reachable via w in B. For each $p \in T$, there is a suffix x of w such that $sx = p$ and $fx = q$ for some $f \in F$.*

Proof. Write $w = w_1 \cdots w_k y$ where $w_1 \cdots w_i$ is the i-th shortest prefix of w contained in $L(A)$. Let $z_i = w_{i+1} \cdots w_k$ and $z_k = \varepsilon$. Then $(s, \emptyset)w = (q, T) = (q, \{sz_1 y, sz_2 y, sz_3 y, \ldots, sz_k y\})$. Let x be $z_i y$ with $sz_i y = p$ and let $f = sw_1 \cdots w_i$.   □

Upper Bound. For each q in Q, define the following set of states:

$$\mathrm{SCC}(q) = \{p \in Q \mid \exists x, y \in \Sigma^* \text{ such that } qx = p \text{ and } py = q\}.$$

The set $\mathrm{SCC}(q)$ is called the *strongly connected component* (SCC) of A containing q; it is the maximal set of states containing q such that for each state p in the set, there are directed paths leading from q to p and from p to q. Of particular importance is the component $\mathrm{SCC}(s)$ containing the initial state s.

Proposition 2. *Let A be a DFA of a star-free language in which all states are reachable. Consider the number of reachable states in the DFA B for $L(A)^2$.*

1. *If s is the unique final state of A, then $L(A) = L(A)^2$ and at most n states are reachable.*
2. *Otherwise, if $\mathrm{SCC}(s) = \{s\}$, then at most $(n-2)2^n + 2^{n-1} + 1$ states are reachable.*
3. *Otherwise, let $i = |\mathrm{SCC}(s)|$ and $j = |\mathrm{SCC}(s) \setminus F|$. Then the number of reachable states is at most $(n-1)2^n - 2(n-2-j) - j2^{n-i+1}$.*

The maximum value of these bounds is $(n-1)2^n - 2(n-2)$, corresponding to case (3) with either $j = 0$ or $i = n$.

Proof. Statement (1) holds true since only states of the form $(q, \{q\})$ are reachable. For (2), suppose $\mathrm{SCC}(s) = \{s\}$. The initial state of B in this case is either $(s, \emptyset)$ or $(s, \{s\})$. Let a be a letter and let $sa = q$. If $q = s$ then $(s, \emptyset)a = (s, \emptyset)$ and $(s, \{s\})a = (s, \{s\})$, so no new states are reached. If $q \neq s$, we reach $(q, \emptyset)$ or $(q, \{q\})$ if q is non-final, and we reach $(q, \{s\})$ or $(q, \{q, s\})$ if q is final. If $q \neq s$, then $q \notin \mathrm{SCC}(s)$, so we can never return to a state with s in the first component. Thus all non-initial states with s in the first component are unreachable.

Now consider states (q, S) with $q \neq s$. If q is non-final, there are at most 2^n reachable states of the form (q, S). If q is final, there are at most 2^{n-1} reachable states of the form (q, S), since S must contain s. Let $|F| = k$, and note:

- If $s \in F$, there are at most $(n - k)2^n + (k - 1)2^{n-1} + 1$ reachable states.
- If $s \notin F$, there are at most $(n - k - 1)2^n + k2^{n-1} + 1$ reachable states.

Both values are maximized by taking k as small as possible:

- If $s \in F$, we cannot take $k = 1$ or else we are in case (1) (since then s is the unique final state of automaton A), so taking $k = 2$ we get the upper bound $(n - 2)2^n + 2^{n-1} + 1$.
- If $s \notin F$, taking $k = 1$ gives $(n - 2)2^n + 2^{n-1} + 1$ again.

Now, we consider (3). Let q be a *non-final* state in $\mathrm{SCC}(s)$. Let T be a set that contains $\mathrm{SCC}(s) \setminus \{q\}$. We claim that (q, T) is unreachable.

Suppose for a contradiction that (q, T) is reachable. Then there is a state (p, U) and letter a such that $(p, U)a = (q, T)$. Since q is non-final, we have $pa = q$ and $Ua = T$. Notice that Ua contains $\mathrm{SCC}(s) \setminus \{q\}$ since T contains $\mathrm{SCC}(s) \setminus \{q\}$. Construct a subset V of U as follows: for each element $u \in \mathrm{SCC}(s) \setminus \{q\}$, choose one element $v \in U$ such that $va = u$. Then $|V| = |\mathrm{SCC}(s) \setminus \{q\}|$.

If $v \in V$, we have $va \in \mathrm{SCC}(s) \setminus \{q\}$, so there is a path from v to the initial state s. Since all states of A are reachable, there is also a path from s to v. Therefore v belongs to $\mathrm{SCC}(s)$. It follows that $V \subseteq \mathrm{SCC}(s)$. Since $|V| = |\mathrm{SCC}(s) \setminus \{q\}|$, we must have $V = \mathrm{SCC}(s) \setminus \{r\}$ for some state $r \in \mathrm{SCC}(s)$. Then $(\mathrm{SCC}(s) \setminus \{r\})a = (\mathrm{SCC}(s) \setminus \{q\})$.

We claim that $r = p$. To see this, first note that p must be in $\mathrm{SCC}(s)$. Indeed, there is a path from s to p since all states of A are reachable, and there is a path from p to s since $pa = q$ and $q \in \mathrm{SCC}(s)$. Now, if $r \neq p$, then $p \in V = \mathrm{SCC}(s) \setminus \{r\}$. But then $q \in Va$, which is impossible since $Va = \mathrm{SCC}(s) \setminus \{q\}$. It follows that $r = p$ and thus $V = \mathrm{SCC}(s) \setminus \{p\}$.

Thus we have $pa = q$ and $(\mathrm{SCC}(s) \setminus \{p\})a = \mathrm{SCC}(s) \setminus \{q\}$. But this means that a acts as a permutation on $\mathrm{SCC}(s)$. Since $L(A)$ is star-free, a must act as the identity on $\mathrm{SCC}(s)$. Therefore $p = q$ and $V = \mathrm{SCC}(s) \setminus \{q\}$.

This means that if T contains $\mathrm{SCC}(s) \setminus \{q\}$, then the state (q, T) only has immediate predecessors (that is, states from which (q, T) can be reached in one transition) of the form (q, U), where U contains a subset $V = \mathrm{SCC}(s) \setminus \{q\}$. We claim that either $\mathrm{SCC}(s) = \{s\}$, or all states (q, T) with $\mathrm{SCC}(s) \subseteq T$ are unreachable. Indeed, consider a path leading from the initial state to (q, T). If $q \neq s$, then (q, T) is unreachable since every state in the path must have q as the first component. If $q = s$, then the second component of the initial state which is either $(s, \emptyset)$ or $(s, \{s\})$ must contain $\mathrm{SCC}(s) \setminus \{s\}$, and this occurs only if $\mathrm{SCC}(s) = \{s\}$. If $\mathrm{SCC}(s) = \{s\}$, we are in case (2), which has been dealt with. Thus if $\mathrm{SCC}(s) \subsetneq T$, then (q, T) is unreachable, as required.

We can also show that if $q \notin \mathrm{SCC}(s)$ is non-final, then the states (q, Q) and $(q, Q \setminus \{q\})$ are not reachable. Indeed, suppose we have $(p, S)a = (q, Q \setminus \{q\})$. Since q is non-final, we have $pa = q$ and $Sa = Q \setminus \{q\}$. Note that S cannot contain p, since otherwise Sa would contain q. Also, we must have $|S| \geq |Q \setminus \{q\}|$. It follows that $S = Q \setminus \{p\}$. But then $pa = q$ and $(Q \setminus \{p\})a = Q \setminus \{q\}$, so a is a permutation of Q and thus the identity. Then $p = q$ and $S = Q \setminus \{q\}$, meaning $(p, S) = (q, Q \setminus \{q\})$. Thus our target state $(q, Q \setminus \{q\})$ can only be reached from itself, so it is unreachable. A similar argument shows that (q, Q) is unreachable.

Now we count the number of potentially reachable states in this case. Consider a state (q, S). If q is final, then S must contain s, and so for each final state q we get 2^{n-1} potentially reachable states. For each non-final state q, we have an upper bound of 2^n reachable states (q, S). If $|F| = k$, this gives a total upper bound of $(n - k)2^n + k2^{n-1}$. But we can get a better bound, since we know that if $q \in \mathrm{SCC}(s)$ is non-final and S contains $\mathrm{SCC}(s) \setminus \{q\}$, then (q, S) is not reachable. For each of the j non-final states $q \in \mathrm{SCC}(s)$, there are 2^{n-i+1} unreachable states (q, S) such that S contains $\mathrm{SCC}(s) \setminus \{q\}$. For each of the $n - k - j$ non-final states $q \notin \mathrm{SCC}(s)$, there are 2 unreachable states (q, Q) and $(q, Q \setminus \{q\})$. Subtracting these states gives an upper bound of $(n - k)2^n + k2^{n-1} - 2(n - k - j) - j2^{n-i+1}$.

If we plug in $k = 2$ here, we get the stated upper bound. If we plug in $k \geq 3$ we get something smaller than the stated upper bound. However, for $k = 1$ we get something larger than the stated bound, so we need to do some extra work.

Suppose $|F| = k = 1$, and set $F = \{q\}$. We can assume $q \neq s$ since otherwise we are in case (1). Since $s \notin F$, the initial state of the square DFA is $(s, \emptyset)$. We claim states (s, S) with $q \in S$ are not reachable.

To see this, suppose for a contradiction that a state (s, S) with $q \in S$ is reachable. To reach (s, S) we must first pass through some reachable state of the form (q, T). So there exists a string y such that $qy = s$ and $Ty = S$. Choose $p \in T$ such that $py = q$. Let w be a string leading from the initial state to (q, T). Then by Lemma 1, there exists a suffix x of w such that $sx = p$ and $qx = q$. Now $sxy = py = q$ and $qxy = qy = s$, so the string xy swaps s and q. This is a contradiction, since $L(A)$ is star-free.

So let us take our previous bound of $(n - k)2^n + k2^{n-1} - 2(n - k - j) - j2^{n-i+1}$, set $k = 1$, and subtract these new states we have proved to be unreachable. There are 2^{n-1} states (s, S) with $q \in S$. However, we have already counted the states (s, Q) and $(s, Q \setminus \{s\})$ as not reachable, so instead of subtracting 2^{n-1} we subtract $2^{n-1} - 2$. Thus we get $(n-1)2^n + 2^{n-1} - 2(n-1-j) - j2^{n-i+1} - 2^{n-1} + 2 = (n - 1)2^n - 2(n - 2 - j) - j2^{n-i+1}$, as required. $\square$

Lower Bound. For $n \geq 4$, we define a function $f(n)$ as follows. Let $k = \lfloor n/2 \rfloor$. For $0 \leq i \leq n-1$, define $d(i) = min\{|k-1-i|, |k+1-i|\}$. Define a function $g(n,i)$ as follows:

$$g(n,i) = \begin{cases} 2^n - 2, & \text{if } i = k; \\ 2^{n-1}, & \text{if } i \in \{k-1, k+1\}; \\ 2^n - 2^{k-d(i)} \sum_{j=1}^{d(i)} \binom{k+1+d(i)}{k+1+j}, & \text{if } n \text{ is odd}, i \notin \{k-1, k, k+1\}; \\ 2^n - 2^{k-d(i)} \sum_{j=1}^{d(i)} \binom{k+d(i)}{k+j}, & \text{if } n \text{ is even}, i < k-1; \\ 2^n - 2^{k-1-d(i)} \sum_{j=1}^{d(i)} \binom{k+1+d(i)}{k+1+j}, & \text{if } n \text{ is even}, i > k+1. \end{cases}$$

$$(1)$$

Now set $f(n) = \sum_{i=0}^{n-1} g(n,i)$. We claim that $f(n)$ is a lower bound on the state complexity of the square of a star-free language with state complexity n. Based on the results of computational random searches, we conjecture that this lower bound is tight, but we were unable to prove a matching upper bound.

Our witness for this lower bound is the DFA A defined as follows. Fix $n \geq 4$ and let $Q = \{0, 1, \ldots, n-1\}$. A transformation t of Q is *monotonic* if $p \leq q$ implies $pt \leq qt$ for all $p, q \in Q$. Let Σ be the set of all monotonic transformations of Q. By [9, Theorem 2.1], we have $|\Sigma| = \binom{2n-1}{n-1}$. Let $k = \lfloor n/2 \rfloor$ as before. Finally, let $A = (Q, \Sigma, \cdot, k, \{k-1, k+1\})$ be the DFA where $q \cdot t = qt$ for all $t \in \Sigma$.

Theorem 3. *Let $n \geq 4$, define A as above, and let B be the DFA for the square $L(A)^2$. The number of reachable and pairwise distinguishable states of B is precisely $f(n)$.*

Proof. We claim that the function $g(n,i)$ counts the number of reachable states of B with the form (i, S), for $i \in Q$ and $S \subseteq Q$. Thus the total number of reachable states is given by $f(n)$, which takes the sum of the $g(n,i)$ terms for each $i \in Q$. We must prove that the counting function $g(n,i)$ is correct, and also that all of the reachable states we count are pairwise distinguishable.

The initial state of B is $(k, \emptyset)$. First we show that the states $(k, \{k-j\})$ and $(k, \{k+j\})$ are reachable for each $j \geq 2$ such that the state in question is in Q. From the initial state, apply the transformation $(k \to k-1)$ to reach $(k-1, \{k\})$. Now apply the transformation which sends $k-1$ to k, fixes everything below $k-1$, and sends everything above $k-1$ to $k+j$. We reach $(k, \{k+j\})$. Symmetrically, from the initial state, apply $(k \to k+1)$ to reach $(k+1, \{k\})$. Then apply the transformation that sends $k+1$ to k, fixes everything above $k+1$, and sends everything below $k+1$ to $k-j$. We reach $(k, \{k-j\})$.

Next, we show that $(k, \{k-2, k-3, \ldots, 0\})$ and $(k, \{k+2, k+3, \ldots, n-1\})$ are reachable. Assume we have reached $(k, \{k-2, k-3, \ldots, k-j\})$ for some $j \geq 2$. Apply $(k \to k+1)$ to reach $(k+1, \{k, k-2, k-3, \ldots, k-j\})$. Then apply the transformation that fixes 0 and every $q \geq k+2$, sends $k+1$ to k, sends k to $k-2$, and sends q to $q-1$ if $1 \leq q \leq k-1$. We reach $(k, \{k-2, k-3, \ldots, k-j-1\})$ and by applying these two transformations repeatedly we reach $(k, \{k-2, k-3, \ldots, 0\})$. A symmetric argument works for $(k, \{k+2, k+3, \ldots, n-1\})$.

Next, we show the following states are reachable: $(k-1, Q)$, $(k-1, Q\setminus\{k-1\})$, $(k+1, Q)$, $(k+1, Q\setminus\{k+1\})$. From $(k, \{k-2, k-3, \ldots, 0\})$, apply $(k \to k-1)$ to reach $(k-1, \{k, k-2, k-3, \ldots, 0\})$. Repeatedly apply $(k \to k+1 \to \cdots \to n-2 \to n-1)$ to reach $(k-1, Q \setminus \{k-1\})$. Then apply $(k \to k-1)$ to reach $(k-1, Q)$. Symmetrically, we can reach $(k+1, Q\setminus\{k+1\})$ and then $(k+1, Q)$.

Next, we describe how to reach states of the form (q, S) where S satisfies certain properties. For each q, we define:

$$S_{<q} = \{p \in S \mid p < q\}, \quad S_{>q} = \{p \in S \mid p > q\}, \quad S_q = S \cap \{q\}.$$

Then S is the disjoint union $S_{<q} \cup S_q \cup S_{>q}$. We claim that (q, S) is reachable if one of the following conditions holds:

1. n is odd, $|S_{<q}| \leq \min\{q, k+1\}$, and $|S_{>q}| \leq \min\{n-q-1, k-1\}$.
2. n is odd, $|S_{<q}| \leq \min\{q, k-1\}$, and $|S_{>q}| \leq \min\{n-q-1, k+1\}$.
3. n is even, $|S_{<q}| \leq \min\{q, k+1\}$, and $|S_{>q}| \leq \min\{n-q-1, k-2\}$.
4. n is even, $|S_{<q}| \leq \min\{q, k-1\}$, and $|S_{>q}| \leq \min\{n-q-1, k\}$.

Additionally, if q is a final state ($k-1$ or $k+1$), then S must contain the initial state k.

To see this, first observe that $S_{<q}$ always has size at most q and $S_{>q}$ always has size at most $n-q-1$; no sets exist which do not satisfy these bounds. Now suppose condition (1) holds; then n is odd and $n = 2k+1$. Observe that $Q_{<k+1}$ has size $k+1$ and $Q_{>k+1}$ has size $n - (k+1) - 1 = 2k+1-k-1-1 = k-1$. Since $|S_{<q}| \leq k+1$ and $|S_{>q}| \leq k-1$, there is a monotonic transformation that sends $Q_{<k+1}$ to $S_{<q}$ and $Q_{>k+1}$ to $S_{>q}$; we can define the transformation as follows: For i in $Q_{<k+1}$, map i to the $(i+1)$-th smallest element of $S_{<q}$, or to the largest element of $S_{<q}$ if $i+1 > |S_{<q}|$. For $i \in Q_{>k+1}$, map i to the $(i-(k+1))$-th smallest element of $S_{>q}$, or to the largest element of $S_{>q}$ if $i-(k+1) > |S_{>q}|$. Finally, $k+1$ is mapped to q. If S contains q, reach $(k+1, Q)$ and apply this transformation to reach (q, S). Otherwise, reach $(k+1, Q\setminus\{k+1\})$ and apply this transformation to reach (q, S).

If condition (2), (3) or (4) holds, we use symmetric arguments. For condition (2), observe that $Q_{<k-1}$ has size $k-1$ and $Q_{>k-1}$ has size $k+1$. Since the condition implies $|S_{<q}| \leq k-1$ and $|S_{>q}| \leq k+1$, there is a monotonic transformation that sends $Q_{<k-1}$ to $S_{<q}$ and $Q_{>k-1}$ to $S_{>q}$, defined analogously to the transformation before. For condition (3), $Q_{<k+1}$ has size $k+1$, but since $n = 2k$ is even, the set $Q_{>k+1}$ has size $n - (k+1) - 1 = 2k - k - 1 - 1 = k-2$. For condition (4), $Q_{<k-1}$ has size $k-1$ and $Q_{>k-1}$ has size k.

This argument shows that all states (q, S) which satisfy the four conditions described above (and satisfy $k \in S$ if q is final) are reachable. Now we count the number of states satisfying these conditions.

Case 1: States of the form $(k-1, S)$. Note that $S_{<k-1}$ has size at most $k-1$. If n is odd, then $S_{>k-1}$ has size at most $k+1$. If n is even, then $S_{>k-1}$ has size at most k. So for all S, either condition (2) or condition (4) is satisfied. Also, since $k-1$ is final, S must contain the initial state k. Thus every state $(k-1, S)$ with $k \in S$ is reachable; there are 2^{n-1} such states.

Case 2: States of the form $(k+1, S)$. One may verify that for all S, either condition (1) or condition (3) is satisfied. Since $k+1$ is final, S must contain k. Thus every state $(k+1, S)$ with $k \in S$ is reachable; there are 2^{n-1} such states.

Case 3: States of the form (k, S). Note that $S_{<k}$ has size at most k. If n is odd then $S_{>k}$ has size at most k. If n is even then $S_{>k}$ has size at most $k-1$. If $|S_{<k}| \le k-1$, then condition (2) or condition (4) is satisfied. If $|S_{<k}| = k$, then condition (1) or condition (3) is satisfied unless $S_{>k}$ is too large. The only way it can be too large is if n is odd and $|S_{>k}| = k$, or n is even and $|S_{>k}| = k-1$. But in both these cases, we have $|S_{<k}| + |S_{>k}| = n-1$ and thus $S_{<k} \cup S_{>k} = Q \setminus \{k\}$. So there are only two choices for S that do not meet a reachability condition: Q and $Q \setminus \{k\}$. Thus there are $2^n - 2$ reachable states of the form (k, S).

Case 4: States of the form (q, S), $q < k-1$. Write $q = k-1-d$ with $d \ge 1$. Then $S_{<q}$ has size at most $k-1-d$. If n is odd, then $S_{>q}$ has size at most $k+1+d$. If n is even, then $S_{>q}$ has size at most $k+d$. We always have $|S_{<q}| \le k+1$. If n is odd, then condition (2) is met as long as $|S_{>q}| \le k+1$. If n is even, then condition (4) is met as long as $|S_{>q}| \le k$. Let us count the number of sets S which fail these conditions.

Write S as the disjoint union $S_{<q} \cup S_q \cup S_{>q}$. There are 2^{k-1-d} choices for $S_{<q}$ and 2 choices for S_q. If n is odd, to fail condition (2), we need $|S_{>q}| = k+1+j$ for some j with $1 \le j \le d$. For each j, there are $\binom{k+1+d}{k+1+j}$ choices for $S_{>q}$; to get the total we sum over j. So when n is odd, there are $2^{k-d}(\sum_{j=1}^{d} \binom{k+1+d}{k+1+j})$ choices for S.

If n is even, to fail condition (4), we need $|S_{>q}| = k+j$ for some j such that $1 \le j \le d$. For each j, there are $\binom{k+d}{k+j}$ choices for $S_{>q}$. Summing over j, when n is even, there are $2^{k-d}(\sum_{j=1}^{d} \binom{k+d}{k+j})$ choices for S.

Case 5: States of the form (q, S), $q > k+1$. Write $q = k+1+d$ with $d \ge 1$. Then $S_{<q}$ has size at most $k+1+d$. If n is odd, then $S_{>q}$ has size at most $k-1-d$. If n is even, then $S_{>q}$ has size at most $k-2-d$. We always have $|S_{>q}| \le k-2$. Thus condition (1) (if n is odd) or (3) (if n is even) is met as long as $|S_{<q}| \le k+1$. We count the number of sets that fail these conditions.

Write S as the disjoint union $S_{<q} \cup S_q \cup S_{>q}$. If n is odd, there are 2^{k-1-d} choices for $S_{>q}$. If n is even, there are 2^{k-2-d} choices for $S_{>q}$. There are two choices for S_q. To fail condition (1) or (3), whichever is relevant, we need $|S_{<q}| = k+j+1$ for some j with $1 \le j \le d$. For each j, there are $\binom{k+1+d}{k+1+j}$ choices. So if n is odd, there are $2^{k-d}(\sum_{j=1}^{d} \binom{k+1+d}{k+1+j})$ choices for S. If n is even, there are $2^{k-1-d}(\sum_{j=1}^{d} \binom{k+1+d}{k+1+j})$ choices for S.

This covers all cases, and taking the sum of all the above counts for each $q \in Q$ gives the lower bound $f(n)$ stated earlier.

Finally, we prove distinguishability of all the reached states. We assume that $n \ge 5$ here; the case $n = 4$ can be verified computationally. Distinguishability can be proved using just four monotonic transformations $\{a, b, c, d\}$, defined as follows for $q \in Q$:

- $qa = q + 1$ if $0 \leq q \leq n - 2$ and $(n-1)a = (n-1)$,
- $qb = q - 1$ if $1 \leq q \leq n - 1$ and $0b = 0$,
- $qc = 0$ if $0 \leq q \leq k$ and $qc = q$ otherwise,
- $qd = n - 1$ if $k \leq q \leq n - 1$ and $qd = q$ otherwise.

We claim that it suffices to prove the following statements:

- For each $q \in Q$, there is a string x_q that is accepted by q in A, not accepted by any other state of A, and not accepted by any state of B of the form $(p, \emptyset)$ for $p \in Q$.
- For each $q \in Q$, there is a string y_q that is accepted by $(q, \emptyset)$ in B, not accepted by $(p, \emptyset)$ for $p \neq q$, and not accepted by any state of A.

Indeed, let (p, S) and (q, T) be two distinct states of B. If $S \neq T$, then there exists a state r which belongs to the symmetric difference of S and T; then x_r distinguishes the states. If $S = T$, then $p \neq q$, and y_p distinguishes the states.

We define x_q as follows: If $0 \leq q \leq k - 1$, then $x_q = a^{k-1-q}d$. If $q = k$, then $x_q = ac$. If $k + 1 \leq q \leq n - 1$, then $x_q = b^{q-(k+1)}c$. We define y_q as follows: If $0 \leq q \leq k$, then $y_q = a^{k+1-q}cac$. If $k + 1 \leq q \leq n - 1$, then $y_q = b^{q-(k+1)}cac$.

Now we verify these strings have the desired properties. Since $n \geq 5$, we have $n - 1 \neq k + 1$, and thus d sends every state of A to a non-final state except for $k - 1$, which it fixes. Similarly, c sends every state of A to a non-final state except for $k + 1$, which it fixes. It follows easily that x_q is accepted by q in A, but rejected in each other state of A.

Now consider $(p, \emptyset)$ in B; observe that for all $i \geq 0$, the state $(p, \emptyset)a^i$ does not contain $k - 1$ in its second component. Therefore if $q \leq k - 1$, then $(p, \emptyset)$ does not accept x_q. A similar argument works if $q \geq k + 1$. For $q = k$, the second component of $(p, \emptyset)a$ cannot contain $k + 1$, and it follows x_q is not accepted.

Next consider whether $(p, \emptyset)$ in B accepts y_q. Observe that $(p, \emptyset)a^{k+1-q}c$ contains k in the second component if and only if $p = q$. Thus $(p, \emptyset)a^{k+1-q}ca$ contains $k + 1$ in the second component if and only if $p = q$. It follows then when $q \leq k + 1$, the state $(p, \emptyset)$ accepts y_q if and only if $p = q$. If $q \geq k + 1$, a similar argument applies. Finally, no state of A accepts y_q because k is not in the image of $a^{k+1-q}c$ or $b^{q-(k+1)}c$, but on the other hand, k is the only state of A which accepts ac. This completes the proof. $\square$

4   Power, Positive Closure, and Complementation

Here we consider the k-th power, positive closure, and complementation on star-free and unary star-free languages.

By definition, every finite and every co-finite language is star-free. In the unary case, the minimal DFA for a star-free language must have the cycle of length one, because otherwise the string $w = a$ performs a non-trivial permutation on the states of this cycle. It follows that every unary star-free language is either finite or co-finite. Notice that the binary language $\{a, b\}^*a$ is star-free since its minimal DFA is permutation-free, but it is neither finite nor co-finite.

In the following four theorems, we consider the k-th power and the positive closure on star-free languages represented by DFAs and NFAs.

Theorem 4 (Power on Unary DFAs). *Let L be a unary star-free language with $\mathrm{sc}(L) \leq n$. Then $\mathrm{sc}(L^k) \leq k(n-1)+1$ and this bound is tight.*

Proof. The upper bound is the same as in the case of unary regular languages [14, Theorem 3]. For tightness, consider the co-finite language $L = a^{n-1}a^*$. We have $L^k = a^{k(n-1)}a^*$, which is a co-finite language with desired complexity. □

Theorem 5 (Power on NFAs). *Let $n, k \geq 2$. Let L be a star-free language over an alphabet Σ with $\mathrm{nsc}(L) \leq n$. Then $\mathrm{nsc}(L^k) \leq kn$, and this bound is tight if $|\Sigma| \geq 2$. In the unary case, a lower bound is $k(n-1)+1$.* □

Theorem 6 (Positive Closure on DFAs). *Let $n \geq 6$. Let L be a star-free language over an alphabet Σ with $\mathrm{sc}(L) \leq n$. Then*
- *$\mathrm{sc}(L^+) \leq 2^{n-1} + 2^{n-2} - 1$, and this bound is tight if $|\Sigma| \geq 4$;*
- *if $|\Sigma| = 1$, then $\mathrm{sc}(L^+) \leq n^2 - 7n + 13$, and this bound is tight.* □

Theorem 7 (Positive closure on NFAs). *Let L be a star-free language with $\mathrm{nsc}(L) \leq n$. Then $\mathrm{nsc}(L^+) \leq n$, and the bound is tight already in the unary case.*

Proof. The upper bound is the same as for regular languages. For tightness, consider the co-finite language $L = a^{n-1}a^*$. Then $L^+ = L$, so $\mathrm{nsc}(L^+) = n$. □

Next we consider complementation. In [7, Theorem 11], an upper bound $O(n^2)$ and a lower bound $(n-1)(n-2)$ were obtained. We provide a more precise upper bound and a better lower bound in the following theorem.

Theorem 8 (Complementation on Unary NFAs). *Let $n \geq 3$. Let L be a unary star-free language with $\mathrm{nsc}(L) \leq n$. Then $\mathrm{nsc}(L^c) \leq n^2 - 2$. There exists a unary star-free language L with $\mathrm{nsc}(L^c) \geq (n-1)^2 + 1$.*

Proof. First, let L be finite. Then the longest string in L is of length at most $n-1$. Thus L, as well as L^c, is accepted by a DFA with $n+1$ states, so $\mathrm{nsc}(L^c) \leq n+1$. Next, let L be co-finite. Recall that if we transform a unary n-state NFA for L to the Chrobak normal form, we get a tail with at most $n^2 - 2$ states and disjoint cycles of length $x_1, x_2, \ldots, x_k$ [5, Theorem 3.5]. The DFA equivalent to this NFA has a tail with at most $n^2 - 2$ states and a single cycle of length $\mathrm{lcm}(x_1, x_2, \ldots, x_k)$. Since L is co-finite, all states in this cycle must be final, so they can be merged into one state. Thus, in the minimal DFA for L, so also for L^c, the total number of states is at most $n^2 - 1$. Since the minimal DFA for L^c includes a state from which no string is accepted, we can omit it, and we get the desired upper bound. For the

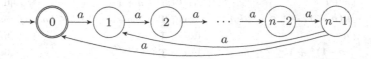

Fig. 1. A lower bound example for complementation on unary star-free languages.

Table 1. Descriptional complexity of operations on star-free and regular languages. For the state complexity of square on star-free languages, we have $\sum_{i=0}^{n-1} g(n,i) \leq \circ \leq (n-1)2^n - 2(n-2)$ where $g(n,i)$ is defined by (1).

	Star-free	$|\Sigma|$	Source	Regular	$|\Sigma|$	Source
$\mathrm{sc}(K \cup L)$	mn	2	[1, Theorem 1]	mn	2	[12, (1)]
$\mathrm{sc}(K \cap L)$	mn	2	[1, T1]	mn	2	[18, T4.3]
$\mathrm{sc}(KL)$	$m2^n - 2^{n-1}$	4	[1, T2]	$m2^n - 2^{n-1}$	2	[12, (2)]
$\mathrm{sc}(L^*)$	$(3/4)2^n$	4	[1, T4]	$(3/4)2^n$	2	[12, (3)]
$\mathrm{sc}(L^R)$	$2^n - 1$	$n-1$	[1, T5]	2^n	2	[11, Prop.1]
$\mathrm{sc}(L^2)$	$\circ$	$\binom{2n-1}{n-1}$	**here, Sect. 3**	$n2^n - 2^{n-1}$	2	[14, T1]
$\mathrm{sc}(L^+)$	$\mathbf{(3/4)2^n - 1}$	**4**	**here, T6**	$(3/4)2^n - 1$	2	[12, (3)]
$\mathrm{nsc}(K \cup L)$	$m+n+1$	2	[7, T2]	$m+n+1$	2	[6, T1]
$\mathrm{nsc}(K \cap L)$	mn	2	[7, T3]	mn	2	[6, T3]
$\mathrm{nsc}(KL)$	$m+n$	2	[7, T6]	$m+n$	2	[6, T7]
$\mathrm{nsc}(L^*)$	$n+1$	1	[7, T13]	$n+1$	1	[6, T9]
$\mathrm{nsc}(L^R)$	$n+1$	2	[7, T8]	$n+1$	2	[10, T2]
$\mathrm{nsc}(L^c)$	2^n	2	[7, T5]	2^n	2	[10, T5]
$\mathrm{nsc}(L^k)$	$\mathbf{kn}$	**2**	**here, T5**	kn	2	[4, T3]
$\mathrm{nsc}(L^+)$	$\mathbf{n}$	**1**	**here, T7**	n	1	[6, T9]

Table 2. Descriptional complexity of operations on unary star-free and unary regular languages:

	Unary star-free	Source	Unary regular	Source
$\mathrm{sc}(K \cup L)$	$\max\{m,n\}$	[1, T6(1)]	mn; $\gcd(m,n)=1$	[13, T4]
$\mathrm{sc}(K \cap L)$	$\max\{m,n\}$	[1, T6(1)]	mn; $\gcd(m,n)=1$	[13, T4]
$\mathrm{sc}(KL)$	$m+n-1$	[1, T6(2)]	mn; $\gcd(m,n)=1$	[18, T5.4]
$\mathrm{sc}(L^*)$	$n^2 - 7n + 13$	[1, T6(3)]	$(n-1)^2 + 1$	[18, T5.3]
$\mathrm{sc}(L^k)$	$\mathbf{k(n-1)+1}$	**here, T4**	$k(n-1)+1$	[14, T4]
$\mathrm{sc}(L^+)$	$\mathbf{n^2 - 7n + 13}$	**here, T6**	$(n-1)^2$	[18, T5.3]
$\mathrm{nsc}(K \cup L)$	$m+n \leq \cdot \leq m+n+1$	[7, T9]	$m+n+1$; $m \neq kn$	[6, T2]
$\mathrm{nsc}(K \cap L)$	$\Theta(m^2)$; $n = m+1$	[7, T10]	mn; $\gcd(m,n)=1$	[6, T4]
$\mathrm{nsc}(KL)$	$m+n-1 \leq \cdot \leq m+n$	[7, T12]	$m+n-1 \leq \cdot \leq m+n$	[6, T8]
$\mathrm{nsc}(L^*)$	$n+1$	[7, T13]	$n+1$	[6, T9]
$\mathrm{nsc}(L^k)$	$\mathbf{k(n-1)+1 \leq \cdot \leq kn}$	**here, T5**	$k(n-1)+1 \leq \cdot \leq kn$	[6, T8]
$\mathrm{nsc}(L^+)$	$\mathbf{n}$	**here, T7**	n	[6, T9]
$\mathrm{nsc}(L^c)$	$\mathbf{(n-1)^2 + 1 \leq \cdot \leq n^2 - 2}$	**here, T8**	$2^{\Theta(\sqrt{n \log n})}$	[6, T6]

lower bound, consider the language L accepted by the NFA shown in Fig. 1. The language L consists of strings of length $cn + d(n-1)$ with $c \geq 1$ and $d \geq 0$ and the empty string. By [18, Lemma 5.1(ii)], the longest string in L^c is of length $(n-1)^2$. It follows that $\mathrm{nsc}(L^c) = (n-1)^2 + 1$. □

5 Conclusion

We examined the deterministic and nondeterministic state complexity of square, power, positive closure, and complementation on star-free languages. Our results are summarized in Tables 1 and 2 where also the size of alphabet used to describe witnesses is displayed. The tables also show all known results concerning descriptional complexity of basic regular operations on star-free and regular languages. Notice that the deterministic state complexity of square on star-free languages and the nondeterministic state complexity of union, intersection, concatenation, power, and complementation on unary star-free languages remain open.

References

1. Brzozowski, J.A., Liu, B.: Quotient complexity of star-free languages. Internat. J. Found. Comput. Sci. **23**(6), 1261–1276 (2012). https://doi.org/10.1142/S0129054112400515

2. Brzozowski, J.A., Szykula, M.: Large aperiodic semigroups. Internat. J. Found. Comput. Sci. **26**(7), 913–932 (2015). https://doi.org/10.1142/S0129054115400067

3. Câmpeanu, C., Culik, K., Salomaa, K., Yu, S.: State complexity of basic operations on finite languages. In: Boldt, O., Jürgensen, H. (eds.) WIA 1999. LNCS, vol. 2214, pp. 60–70. Springer, Heidelberg (2001). https://doi.org/10.1007/3-540-45526-4_6

4. Domaratzki, M., Okhotin, A.: State complexity of power. Theoret. Comput. Sci. **410**(24–25), 2377–2392 (2009). https://doi.org/10.1016/j.tcs.2009.02.025

5. Geffert, V.: Magic numbers in the state hierarchy of finite automata. Inform. Comput. **205**(11), 1652–1670 (2007). https://doi.org/10.1016/j.ic.2007.07.001

6. Holzer, M., Kutrib, M.: Nondeterministic descriptional complexity of regular languages. Internat. J. Found. Comput. Sci. **14**(6), 1087–1102 (2003). https://doi.org/10.1142/S0129054103002199

7. Holzer, M., Kutrib, M., Meckel, K.: Nondeterministic state complexity of star-free languages. Theoret. Comput. Sci. **450**, 68–80 (2012). https://doi.org/10.1016/j.tcs.2012.04.028

8. Hopcroft, J.E., Ullman, J.D.: Introduction to Automata Theory, Languages and Computation. Addison-Wesley, Boston (1979)

9. Howie, J.M.: Products of idempotents in certain semigroups of transformations. Proc. Edinburgh Math. Soc. **17**(3), 223–236 (1971). https://doi.org/10.1017/S0013091500026936

10. Jirásková, G.: State complexity of some operations on binary regular languages. Theoret. Comput. Sci. **330**(2), 287–298 (2005). https://doi.org/10.1016/j.tcs.2004.04.011

11. Leiss, E.L.: Succint representation of regular languages by boolean automata. Theoret. Comput. Sci. **13**, 323–330 (1981). https://doi.org/10.1016/S0304-3975(81)80005-9

12. Maslov, A.N.: Estimates of the number of states of finite automata. Soviet Math. Doklady **11**, 1373–1375 (1970)
13. Pighizzini, G., Shallit, J.: Unary language operations, state complexity and Jacobsthal's function. Internat. J. Found. Comput. Sci. **13**(1), 145–159 (2002). https://doi.org/10.1142/S012905410200100X
14. Rampersad, N.: The state complexity of L^2 and L^k. Inform. Process. Lett. **98**(6), 231–234 (2006). https://doi.org/10.1016/j.ipl.2005.06.011
15. Schützenberger, M.P.: On finite monoids having only trivial subgroups. Inf. Control **8**(2), 190–194 (1965). https://doi.org/10.1016/S0019-9958(65)90108-7
16. Sipser, M.: Introduction to the Theory of Computation. Cengage Learning (2012)
17. Yu, S.: Regular languages. In: Rozenberg, G., Salomaa, A. (eds.) Handbook of Formal Languages, pp. 41–110. Springer, Heidelberg (1997). https://doi.org/10.1007/978-3-642-59136-5_2
18. Yu, S., Zhuang, Q., Salomaa, K.: The state complexities of some basic operations on regular languages. Theoret. Comput. Sci. **125**(2), 315–328 (1994). https://doi.org/10.1016/0304-3975(92)00011-F

Descriptional Complexity of Matrix Simple Semi-conditional Grammars

Henning Fernau[1](✉) (iD), Lakshmanan Kuppusamy[2] (iD),
and Indhumathi Raman[3] (iD)

[1] Fachbereich 4 – Abteilung Informatikwissenschaften, CIRT,
Universität Trier, 54286 Trier, Germany
`fernau@uni-trier.de`
[2] School of Computer Science and Engineering, VIT, Vellore 632 014, India
`klakshma@vit.ac.in`
[3] Department of Applied Mathematics and Computational Sciences,
PSG College of Technology, Coimbatore 641 004, India
`ind.amcs@psgtech.ac.in`

Abstract. Matrix grammars are one of the first approaches ever proposed in regulated rewriting, prescribing that rules have to be applied in a certain order. Typical descriptional complexity measures incorporate the number of nonterminals or the length, i.e., the number of rules per matrix. In simple semi-conditional (SSC) grammars, the derivations are controlled by a permitting string or by a forbidden string associated to each rule. The maximum length i of permitting strings and the maximum length j of forbidden strings are called the degree of such grammars. Matrix SSC grammars (MSSC) put matrix grammar control on SSC rules. We consider the computational completeness of MSSC grammars with degrees $(2, 1)$, $(2, 0)$ and $(3, 0)$. The results are important in the following aspects. (i) With permitting strings alone, it is unknown if SSC grammars are computational complete, while MSSC grammars describe RE even with severe further restrictions on their descriptional complexity. (ii) Matrix grammars with appearance checking with three nonterminals are computationally complete; however, the length is unbounded. With our constructions for MSSC grammars, we can even bound the length.

Keywords: Simple semi-conditional grammars · Matrix grammars · Computational completeness · Geffert normal forms · Descriptional complexity

1 Introduction

Matrix grammars (introduced by Ábrahám [1]) are regulated grammars in which rules are grouped into finite sequences called matrices. When a matrix is chosen to be applied, all rules in the sequence are applied in the given order. In semi-conditional (SC) grammars (introduced by Păun [14]), each rule is associated

© IFIP International Federation for Information Processing 2019
Published by Springer Nature Switzerland AG 2019
M. Hospodár et al. (Eds.): DCFS 2019, LNCS 11612, pp. 111–123, 2019.
https://doi.org/10.1007/978-3-030-23247-4_8

with two strings called the permitting string and the forbidden string. A rule can be applied to a sentential form w only if w contains the permitting string and does not contain the forbidden string as a subword. If both these control strings (permitting and forbidden) are absent in a rule, then the rule is called *unconditional*; otherwise, the rule is termed *conditional*. The most interesting case is when the involved rewriting rules are context-free; we will focus on this case in the following. Clearly, these are the rules which are responsible for a SC grammar to characterize the class of recursively enumerable languages, henceforth denoted RE [10,12,15]. With semi-conditional grammars, two variants are of special interest: (i) *simple semi-conditional grammars* (denoted as SSCG) in which at most either the permitting string or the forbidden string is present for each rule, see [10]; (ii) *permitting grammars* in which the forbidden string is absent for every rule, see [6]. Key observations in these domains include:

- Matrix grammars with appearance checking, having three nonterminals, are computationally complete, i.e., they characterize RE [3]. However, the lengths of the matrices are unbounded. It is not clear how to restrict the length while still bounding the number of nonterminals. It is known that matrix grammars without appearance checking are not computationally complete; see [8].
- The generative power of permitting grammars with no erasing rules is strictly included in the class of context-sensitive languages; refer to [6]. It is open if permitting grammars with erasing context-free rules describe RE.
- Results on the computational completeness of simple semi-conditional grammars are tabulated in Fig. 1(a). It is unknown, for example, if five nonterminals or five conditional rules suffice to describe RE.
- Matrix simple semi-conditional (MSSC) grammars, matrix controlled grammars with SSC rules (introduced in [11]) have been known to characterize RE while limiting several descriptional complexity measures at the same time. These devices are in the focus of our paper.

The results of the paper are tabulated in Fig. 1(b), including results from [11]. Our results clearly improve on the previously published ones. The many results we obtained can be viewed as trade-off results between different measures of descriptional complexity. We highlight the record-holders of single measures by putting them in bold-face in the table.

2   Preliminaries and Definitions

In this paper, it is assumed that the reader is familiar with the fundamentals of language theory and mathematics in general. Let Σ^* denote the free monoid generated by a finite set Σ called the alphabet under an operation termed concatenation. Any element of Σ^* is called a *word* or string (over Σ), while the *empty word* λ is the unit of Σ^*. Any subset of Σ^* is called a language. A word v is a *subword* (or substring) of $x \in \Sigma^*$ if there are words u, w such that $x = uvw$. Let $sub(x) \subseteq \Sigma^*$ denote the set of all subwords of $x \in \Sigma^*$. Clearly, $sub(x)$ is a finite language. Given a word $w \in \Sigma^*$, $|w|$ represents the length of w. Recall that

Degree	#NT	#CR	#MAT	LEN	Ref.
$(2,1)$	6	6	2	4	[11]
$(3,1)$	7	4	1	6	[11]
$(2,1)$	6	4	2	2	Thm. 6
$(2,1)$	6	3	2	3	Thm. 7
$(2,1)$	6	3	1	4	Thm. 8
$(2,1)$	5	4	1	4	Thm. 10
$(2,1)$	5	3	3	2	Thm. 12
$(2,0)$	6	2	1	5	Thm. 9
$(2,0)$	5	3	1	5	Thm. 11
$(2,0)$	5	5	3	2	Thm. 13
$(2,0)$	5	2	2	4	Thm. 14
$(2,0)$	4	6	2	7	Thm. 18
$(3,0)$	4	5	3	3	Thm. 15
$(3,0)$	4	7	4	2	Thm. 16
$(3,0)$	4	3	2	5	Thm. 17

(b) Descriptional complexity measures of MSSC grammars describing RE

Degree	#NT	#CR	Ref.
$(2,1)$	13	12	[12]
$(2,1)$	12	10	[15]
$(2,1)$	10	9	[9]
$(2,1)$	9	8	[4]
$(3,1)$	11	8	[15]
$(3,1)$	9	8	[13]
$(3,1)$	7	7	[4]
$(4,1)$	7	6	[4]
$(4,1)$	6	8	[4]

(a) Descriptional complexity measures of SSC grammars describing RE

Fig. 1. Summary of computational completeness results for SSC and MSSC grammars; #NT, #CR and #MAT denote the number of nonterminals, the number of conditional rules, and the number of conditional matrices, respectively. LEN gives an upper bound on the lengths of matrices.

a type-0 grammar can be specified by a quadruple $G = (N, T, S, P)$, where N is the *nonterminal* alphabet, T is the *terminal* alphabet, $S \in N$ is the *start symbol* and P is a finite set of re-write rules of the form $x \to y$, with $x, y \in (N \cup T)^*$. Type-0 grammars characterize the class RE of recursively enumerable languages. Rule $x \to y$ is *context-free* if $x \in N$.

2.1   Matrix (and) Semi-conditional Grammars

Matrix and Semi-conditional grammars have been introduced within the area of regulated rewriting [2,14], mostly to enhance the power of context-free grammars beyond context-free languages. Matrix control allows to express that some rules have to be applied in a certain order, while semi-conditional control attaches permitting and forbidden strings to rules that confine the applicability of these rules. In the special case of simple semi-conditional grammars [10], only either permitting or forbidden strings may be present.

A matrix simple semi-conditional grammar (MSSC grammar for short) combines simple semi-conditional grammars and matrix grammars [11].

Definition 1. *An MSSC grammar is a quadruple $G = (N, T, S, M)$, where N, T and S have the same meaning as in a type-0 grammar and M is a finite set of sequences (called matrices) of the form*

$$m = [(A_1 \to x_1, P_1, F_1), \ldots, (A_\ell \to x_\ell, P_\ell, F_\ell)], \tag{1}$$

where $\ell \geq 1$, $A_k \in N$, $x_k \in (N \cup T)^*$, $P_k, F_k \in (N \cup T)^+ \cup \{0\}$ *such that* $P_k = 0$ *or* $F_k = 0$ *for each* $1 \leq k \leq \ell$. *The strings* P_k *and* F_k *above are called the* permitting *and* forbidding *conditions, respectively;* 0 *is a special symbol,* $0 \notin N \cup T$. *If* $P_k = F_k = 0$, *then rule* $(A \rightarrow x_k, P_k, F_k)$ *is called* unconditional; *otherwise, it is called* conditional. *Let* c_m *denote the number of conditional rules in matrix* m *from* (1). *We call matrix* m conditional *if* $c_m \geq 1$ *and* unconditional *if* $c_m = 0$. *Moreover,* m *is called a* multi-production *matrix if* $\ell \geq 2$ *and is called a* single-production *matrix if* $\ell = 1$. *Number* $\ell_m := \ell$ *is termed the* length *of* m.

Reconsider m *from* (1). *Let* $\alpha_0, \alpha_\ell \in (N \cup T)^*$. *Then,* $\alpha_0 \Rightarrow_m \alpha_\ell$ *holds if there are strings* $\alpha_1, \ldots, \alpha_{\ell-1} \in (N \cup T)^*$ *such that, for all* $k = 1, \ldots, \ell$, *if* $P_k \neq 0$, *then* $P_k \in sub(\alpha_{k-1})$, *and if* $F_k \neq 0$, *then* $F_k \notin sub(\alpha_{k-1})$, *and furthermore,* $\alpha_{k-1} = \alpha'_{k-1} A_k \alpha''_{k-1}$ *and* $\alpha_k = \alpha'_{k-1} x_k \alpha''_{k-1}$. *Define* $\Rightarrow_G = \bigcup_{m \in M} \Rightarrow_m$. *Now,* $L(G) = \{w \mid S \Rightarrow_G^* w \wedge w \in T^*\}$ *is the* language *described by* G.

Observe that all conditions have to be met to successfully apply a matrix to a string; otherwise, the derivation does not succeed. More classical matrix grammars (without appearance checking) can be viewed as MSSC grammars where all matrices are unconditional. Likewise, simple semi-conditional grammars (abbreviated as SSC(G)) correspond to MSSC grammars where all matrices have length one. We now define six measures on the descriptional complexity of MSCC grammars that are crucial for our further studies.

Definition 2. *An MSSC grammar* $G = (N, T, S, M)$ *is of* size $(i, j; n; c, p, l)$, *if in every rule* $(A \rightarrow x, \alpha, \beta)$ *of a matrix* $m \in M$, *we have*

- $|\alpha| \leq i$ *and* $|\beta| \leq j$, *(the pair* (i, j) *is also called the* degree *of* G*);*[1]
- $|N| \leq n$ *(an upper bound on the number of* nonterminals*);*
- $\sum_{m \in M} c_m \leq c$ *(bounding the total number of* conditional *rules in* G*);*
- $|\{m \in M \mid \ell_m > 1\}| \leq p$ *(upper-bounding the number of* multi-production *matrices in* G*);*
- $\max\{\ell_m \mid m \in M\} \leq l$ *(bounding the matrix lengths in* G*).*

We denote by $\mathsf{MSSC}(i, j; n; c, p, l)$ the family of languages generated by MSSC grammars of size $(i, j; n; c, p, l)$. If the forbidding conditions are absent in every rule of M, then the degree of the system is $(i, 0)$ and is denoted as *matrix permitting grammar* (or *MP grammar* for short). For brevity, we simplify the notation $(A \rightarrow x, \alpha, 0)$ to $(A \rightarrow x, \alpha)$ and $(A \rightarrow x, 0, 0)$ to $(A \rightarrow x)$. For MP grammars, we abbreviate for the corresponding classes of languages $\mathsf{MP}(i; n; c, p, l) = \mathsf{MSSC}(i, 0; n; c, p, l)$. If $l = 1$, then $p = 0$, and (as noticed above), we rather face SSC grammars, so that we could write $\mathsf{MSSC}(i, j; n; c, 0, 1) = \mathsf{SSC}(i, j; n, c)$.

2.2 Geffert Normal Forms

In [7], quite a number of normal forms for type-0 grammars have been derived. They all differ by the number of nonterminals that are used and also by the

---

[1] Here, the convention $|0| = 0$ applies.

number of non-context-free rules. We will hence speak of (n, r)-GNF to refer to a Geffert normal form with n nonterminals and r non-context-free rules. However, all these normal forms characterize the class of recursively enumerable languages, or RE languages for short. The best known normal form is the $(5, 2)$-GNF with nonterminals S (start symbol) and A, B, C, D that uses context-free rules with S as its left-hand side in its first phase; after using the context-free rules, in a second phase non-context-free erasing rules $AB \to \lambda$ and $CD \to \lambda$ are applied to finally derive a string $t \in T^*$. Hence, the derivation in a grammar in $(5,2)$-GNF proceeds in two phases, where the first phase splits into two stages. In phase one, stage one, rules of the form $S \to uSa$ are used, with $u \in \{A, C\}^*$, $a \in T$. In stage two, rules of the form $S \to uSv$ are used, with $u \in \{A, C\}^*$ and $v \in \{B, D\}^*$. It is also shown in [7] that any attempt to mix the applications of rules of these two types cannot yield to a terminal string in view of the chosen encodings. Also, rules of the form $S \to uv$ are available that prepare the transition into phase two, where (i.e., in phase two) the erasing non-context-free rules are used exclusively. The normal form variations we discuss next are always derived from $(5,2)$-GNF by applying morphisms to all context-free rules, where in particular $S \mapsto S$ maintains the start symbol, so that in particular the rules involving the start symbol keep up the same form as with $(5,2)$-GNF, without further mentioning this below.

GNF with 4 Nonterminals. We now discuss another normal form of type-0 grammars due to Geffert [7]. We then list some important properties of this normal form that are discussed and proved in [4,5]. These follow from the constructions of the normal form and well-known properties of $(5,2)$-GNF.

The normal form $(4,1)$-GNF is obtained from $(5,2)$-GNF normal form (using nonterminals S, A, B, C, D) by applying the morphism $A \mapsto AB, B \mapsto C, C \mapsto A$ and $D \mapsto BC$ to all context-free rules. Moreover, we add one non-context-free erasing rule $ABC \to \lambda$. This means that the following properties hold:

Proposition 3 [5]. *The following properties hold for $(4,1)$-GNF grammars:*

1. *If $S \Rightarrow^* w$, then $w \in \{A, AB\}^*\{S, \lambda\}\{BC, C\}^*(T(\{BC, C\} \cup T)^* \cup \{\lambda\})$.*
2. *If $S \Rightarrow^* w$, then $sub(w) \cap (\{BBB\} \cup \{C\}\{B\}^*\{A\}) = \emptyset$.*
3. *If $S \Rightarrow^* w$, with $w = w't$, where $w' \in \{A, AB\}^+\{BC, C\}^+$, $t \in (T(\{BC, C\} \cup T)^* \cup \{\lambda\})$, then w' contains exactly one occurrence from $\{ABC, AC, ABBC\}$ as a substring. We refer to this substring as the* central part *of w.*
   Only with ABC as central part, possibly $w' \Rightarrow^* \lambda$ as intended in a derivation that yields a terminal string. If AC or $ABBC$ occur as a central part of the string, then it will not derive to a terminal string.
4. *If $S \Rightarrow^* w$, with $w = w't$, where $w' \in \{A, AB\}^+ \cup \{BC, C\}^+$ and $t \in (T(\{BC, C\} \cup T)^* \cup \{\lambda\})$, then w does not derive any terminal string.*
5. *Again, the derivation proceeds in two phases, the first one is split into two stages. Only in phase two (where non-context-free erasing rules are applied), a central part will appear.*

The normal form $(4,2)$-GNF is obtained from $(5,2)$-GNF (using nonterminals S, A, B, C, D) by applying the morphism $A \mapsto CAA$, $B \mapsto BBC$, $C \mapsto CA$
and $D \mapsto BC$ to all context-free rules. Moreover, the two non-context-free
erasing rules $AB \to \lambda$ and $CC \to \lambda$ are added. Then if $S \Rightarrow^* w$, then
$w \in \{CA, CAA\}^* \{S, \lambda\} \{BC, BBC\}^* (T(\{BC, BBC\} \cup T)^* \cup \{\lambda\})$.

Remark 4. Though the *central part* is either AB or CC, unwanted strings like
AC or CB can appear in the center; the derivation is stuck in these cases. Similar
properties as stated in the previous proposition can be derived for $(4,2)$-GNF.

GNF with 3 Nonterminals. In [7], it was also proved that every RE language
is generated by a type-0 grammar with three nonterminals only. The context-
free rules of this $(3,1)$-GNF normal form (where $N = \{S, A, B\}$) are obtained
from $(5,2)$-GNF by applying the morphism $A \mapsto AB$, $B \mapsto BBA$, $C \mapsto ABB$
and $D \mapsto BA$. The only non-context-free rule is $ABBBA \to \lambda$. It is sometimes
more practical to work with the two non-context-free erasing rule $BBB \to \lambda$
and $AA \to \lambda$ instead, leading to a grammar in $(3,2)$-GNF.

Remark 5. The *central part* for $(3,1)$-GNF or $(3,2)$-GNF is either BBB or AA,
but unwanted strings like $ABBA$ or $ABBBBA$ are possible in the center.

3   Computational Completeness of MSSC Grammars

In the proofs, we are making use of several variations of Geffert normal form as
discussed above, starting with $(4,1)$-GNF.

Theorem 6. $MSSC(2, 1; 6; 4, 2, 2) = RE$.

Proof. Let $L \in RE$ be generated by a grammar in $(4,1)$-GNF of the form $G =
(N, T, P \cup \{ABC \to \lambda\}, S)$ such that P contains only context-free productions
and $N = \{S, A, B, C\}$ (see Proposition 3). Next, we define the MSSC grammar
$G' = (N', T, P' \cup P'', S)$, where $N' = N \cup \{A', C'\}$ (assuming that $\{A', C'\} \cap N =
\emptyset$), P' contains (single-production) matrices of the form $[(S \to \alpha, 0, 0)]$ whenever
$S \to \alpha \in P$ and P'' contains the following two (multi-production) matrices plus
the (single-production) matrix $m3 = [(C' \to \lambda, 0, A')]$:

$$m1 = [(A \to A', 0, C'), (C \to C')],$$
$$m2 = [(B \to \lambda, A'B), (A' \to \lambda, A'C')].$$

We now show that $L(G') = L(G)$.

First, it is clear that context-free rules like $S \to \alpha \in P$ can be easily simulated
by single-production matrices of the form $[(S \to \alpha, 0, 0)]$ and vice versa. In fact,
it could be that $m1$ is applied in-between applying matrices $[(S \to \alpha, 0, 0)]$, but
then only matrices $[(S \to \alpha, 0, 0)]$ can apply until switching to Phase two, where
$m2$ might follow, which is discussed in detail next, assuming that $m1$ would have
been applied last, not changing the resulting sentential form.

According to Proposition 3, then (after Phase one of the GNF grammar), ignoring boundary cases, we face a string of the form $\alpha\xi\beta t$, where $\alpha \in \{A, AB\}^*$, $\xi \in \{ABC, AC, ABBC\}$, $\beta \in \{B, BC\}^*$ and $t \in T(\{B, BC\} \cup T)^* \cup \{\lambda\}$. Assume that $\xi = ABC$, i.e., we are still in the situation that (in case $t \in T^*$) $\alpha\xi\beta t$ might derive a terminal string in G. Applying $ABC \to \lambda$ in G, we could arrive at $\alpha\beta t$. This can be simulated by $\alpha\xi\beta t \Rightarrow_{m1} \alpha A'BC'\beta t \Rightarrow_{m2} \alpha C'\beta t \Rightarrow_{m3} \alpha\beta t$. By induction, this shows that $L(G) \subseteq L(G')$.

We are now finishing the proof of the converse direction $L(G) \supseteq L(G')$ by explaining the decisive induction step, starting out with some $\alpha\xi\beta t$ (as above) that is derivable both in G and in G'. If $\alpha\xi\beta t$ is the current sentential form in G' with $\xi = ABC$, then clearly only $m1$ applies (due to the absence of primed symbols). This means that any occurrence of A (which must be in $\alpha\xi$) and any occurrence of C (from $\xi\beta t$) is turned into the primed counterparts. Now, the presence of A' and C' prevents applying $m1$ or $m3$, forcing us into applying matrix $m2$ next. Now, the context checks become important. Both rules check for the presence of a certain symbol to the right of A'. As both checked symbols are different and there is only one occurrence of A' in the sentential form, the first rule in $m2$ must remove the occurrence of B to the right of A'. Moreover, to the right of that occurrence of B, C' must occur in the sentential form, which enforces that in fact the A occurring in ξ must have been turned into A' when applying $m1$, and likewise the C occurring in ξ must have been turned into C' before. In other words, we know that $\alpha ABC\beta t \Rightarrow_{m1} \alpha A'BC'\beta t \Rightarrow_{m2} \alpha C'\beta t$. Due to the presence of C' and the absence of A', $m3$ is the only applicable rule, leading to $\alpha\beta t$ as intended.

However, there are also situations to study where we know that within G, there will be no terminal string derivable at all, while this might happen within the simulated grammar G'.

Case 1. Consider the sentential form $\alpha AC\beta t$. Now, we could apply $m1$, turning one occurrence of A within αA into A' and one occurrence of C within $C\beta t$ into C'. Now, $m2$ is the only applicable rule. In order to apply the first rule in $m2$, B must have been sitting to the right of the A-occurrence that we have replaced when applying $m1$, but this means that now we find A' within the part of the word previously called α, where no C- or C'-occurrences are to be found, which would be necessary to apply the second rule of $m2$. In a sense, the A-occurrence in the central part AC serves as a barrier between the possible substrings AB within α and the C-ocurrences to match with. Hence, the derivation gets stuck.

Case 2. Consider the sentential form $\alpha ABBC\beta t$. Now, again $m1$ is the only applicable matrix. Turning one occurrence of A within αA into A' and one occurrence of C within $C\beta t$ into C'. With a similar argument as in the previous case, one sees that not both rules of the only applicable matrix $m2$ can be applied in sequence. Here, the second B-occurrence in the central part $ABBC$ serves as a barrier between the possible substrings AB within αAB and the C-ocurrences to match with.

Case 3. Boundary cases. This concerns situations where there is no central part available at all. In particular, this means that we are facing sentential forms like αt or βt with $\alpha \in \{A, AB\}^*$, $\beta \in \{B, BC\}^*$ and $t \in T(\{B, BC\} \cup T)^* \cup \{\lambda\}$. Now, either none of the matrices apply, or $m1$ might apply but then the derivation is stuck, because the permitting context $A'C'$ in $m2$ cannot be met.

In summary, we have shown that whenever starting with a string w that is derivable both in G' and in G, with G', we will be forced to produce a string that is also derivable in G, which proves that $L(G) \supseteq L(G')$, so that together with our previous considerations, we have shown that $L(G) = L(G')$ as claimed. $\square$

Notice that in the proof of the preceding theorem, we showed that after applying $m2$, we were forced to apply $m3$. So, the idea of simply appending $m3$ to $m2$ would work, giving a sort of trade-off result in terms of parameters. As the only purpose of the context check in the rule of $m3$ was to guarantee that $m3$ is not applied in another situation, we can furthermore omit context checks in the appended rule $C' \to \lambda$. Hence, otherwise following the same reasoning as before, the two (multi-production) matrices

$$m1 = [(A \to A', 0, A'), (C \to C')],$$
$$m2 = [(B \to \lambda, A'B), (A' \to \lambda, A'C'), (C' \to \lambda)]$$

provide the simulation of the non-context-free rule $ABC \to \lambda$ of a type-0 grammar G in $(4, 1)$-GNF. This shows the following result.

Theorem 7. $MSSC(2, 1; 6; 3, 2, 3) = RE$. $\square$

With a similar intuition, one could observe that an application of matrix $m1$ should be always followed by an application of $m2$. By tuning a bit on the roles of A' and C', we propose the multi-production matrix

$$m = [(A \to A', 0, A'), (C \to C'), (B \to \lambda, A'B), (C' \to \lambda, A'C')]$$

to work together with the one-production matrix $[(A' \to \lambda, 0, 0)]$ in order to simulate the non-context-free rule $ABC \to \lambda$. This can be worked out to prove:

Theorem 8. $MSSC(2, 1; 6; 3, 1, 4) = RE$. $\square$

Working out further the idea of merging matrices of Theorem 6, as $m1$, $m2$ and $m3$ must be applied in order, one can observe that the forbidden context checks become obsolete, leading us to use the following (multi-production) matrix

$$m = [(A \to A'), (C \to C'), (B \to \lambda, A'B), (A' \to \lambda, A'C'), (C' \to \lambda)]$$

to simulate the non-context-free rule $ABC \to \lambda$. This idea yields the following.

Theorem 9. $MSSC(2, 0; 6; 2, 1, 5) = MP(2; 6; 2, 1, 5) = RE$. $\square$

So far, we derived our results starting off from $(4, 1)$-GNF. We needed two more nonterminals in order to uniquely mark the boundaries of the central part of the sentential form. We are first trying to reduce the number of nonterminals at the expense of more conditional rules. To this end, we continue discussing our previous constructions, in particular, those based on the proof of Theorem 6. Observe that an application of matrix $m1$ should be always followed by an application of $m2$. By merging the roles of A' and C' within #, we propose the multi-production matrix

$$m = [(A \to \#, 0, \#), (B \to \lambda, \#B, 0), (C \to \#, \#C, 0), (\# \to \lambda, \#\#, 0)]$$

to work together with the one-production matrix $[(\# \to \lambda, 0, 0)]$ in order to simulate the non-context-free rule $ABC \to \lambda$. This idea can be worked out to prove the following result.

Theorem 10. $MSSC(2, 1; 5; 4, 1, 4) = RE$.   □

Combining the ideas leading to the previous two theorems, we would again combine everything within one long matrix, now having the possibility to remove all forbidden context checks. This leads us to the following result, based on

$$m = [(A \to \#), (B \to \lambda, \#B), (C \to \#, \#C), (\# \to \lambda, \#\#), (\# \to \lambda)].$$

Theorem 11. $MSSC(2, 0; 5; 3, 1, 5) = MP(2; 5; 3, 1, 5) = RE$.

In order to aim at the use of fewer nonterminals (but possibly with more small-length matrices), we turn to another GNF, namely, to $(4, 2)$-GNF, which we are going to use in the following, trading off the number of conditional rules with avoiding forbidden strings.

Theorem 12. $MSSC(2, 1; 5; 3, 3, 2) = RE$.

Proof. Let $L \in RE$ be generated by a grammar in $(4, 2)$-GNF of the form $G = (N, T, P \cup \{AB \to \lambda, CC \to \lambda\}, S)$ such that P contains only context-free productions and $N = \{S, A, B, C\}$ (see Remark 4). Next, we define the MSSC grammar $G' = (V', T, P' \cup P'', S)$, where $N' = N \cup \{\#\}$ (assuming that $\# \notin N$), P' contains (single-production) matrices of the form $[(S \to \alpha, 0, 0)]$ whenever $S \to \alpha \in P$ and P'' contains the three (multi-production) matrices:

$$m1 = [(A \to \#, 0, \#), (B \to \#)],$$
$$m2 = [(C \to \#, 0, \#), (C \to \#)],$$
$$m3 = [(\# \to \lambda, \#\#, 0), (\# \to \lambda)].$$

We can show $L(G') = L(G)$ by an inductive argument.   □

Theorem 13. $MSSC(2, 0; 5; 5, 3, 2) = MP(2; 5; 5, 3, 2) = RE$.

Proof. Let $L \in RE$ be generated by a grammar in $(4, 2)$-GNF of the form $G = (N, T, P \cup \{AB \to \lambda, CC \to \lambda\}, S)$ such that P contains only context-free productions and $N = \{S, A, B, C\}$ (see Remark 4). Next, we define the

MSSC grammar $G' = (N', T, P' \cup P'', S)$, where $N' = N \cup \{\#\}$ (assuming that $\# \notin N$), P' contains (single-production) matrices of the form $[(S \to \alpha, 0)]$ whenever $S \to \alpha \in P$ and P'' contains the three (multi-production) matrices:

$$m1 = [(A \to \#, AB), (B \to \#, \#B)]$$
$$m2 = [(C \to \#, CC), (C \to \#, \#C)]$$
$$m3 = [(\# \to \lambda, \#\#), (\# \to \lambda)].$$

We can show $L(G') = L(G)$ by an inductive argument.   □

Observe that in a correct simulation in Theorem 13, $m1$ must be followed by $m3$ and $m2$ must be followed by $m3$, as well. Hence, by appending $m3$ to $m1$ and to $m2$, we can obtain another computational completeness result with less but longer matrices, omitting the context conditions in the matrices $m1$ and $m2$ from the proof of Theorem 13.

Theorem 14. *MSSC$(2, 0; 5; 2, 2, 4) = $ MP$(2; 5; 2, 2, 4) = $ RE.*   □

In order to further lower the number of nonterminals that we have to use, we are moving on to GNFs that are more parsimonious in this respect, i.e., to $(3, 2)$-GNF or (equivalently) to $(3, 1)$-GNF.

Theorem 15. *MSSC$(3, 0; 4; 5, 3, 3) = $ MP$(3; 4; 5, 3, 3) = $ RE.*

Proof. Let $L \in$ RE be generated by a grammar in $(3, 2)$-GNF of the form $G = (N, T, P \cup \{AA \to \lambda, BBB \to \lambda\}, S)$ such that P contains only context-free productions and $N = \{S, A, B\}$. We define the MSSC grammar $G' = (N', T, P' \cup P'', S)$, where $N' = N \cup \{\#\}$ (assuming that $\# \notin N$), P' contains (single-production) matrices of the form $[(S \to \alpha, 0)]$ whenever $S \to \alpha \in P$ and P'' contains the following three matrices with five conditional rules:

$$m1 = [(B \to \#, BBB), (B \to \#, 0), (B \to \#, \#B\#)]$$
$$m2 = [(A \to \#\#, AA), (A \to \#\#, 0), (\# \to \lambda, \#\#\#)]$$
$$m3 = [(\# \to \lambda, \#\#\#), (\# \to \lambda, 0), (\# \to \lambda, 0)].$$

The intended simulation of $\alpha ABBBA\beta t \Rightarrow_G \alpha\beta t$ works as follows.

$$\alpha ABBBA\beta t \Rightarrow_{m1} \alpha A\#\#\#A\beta t \Rightarrow_{m3} \alpha AA\beta t \Rightarrow_{m2} \alpha\#\#\#\beta t \Rightarrow_{m3} \alpha\beta t.$$

Again, we have to prove that $L(G) = L(G')$ by an inductive argument based on some case analysis.   □

Can we somehow shorten the matrices involved in the previous construction? What somehow comes to mind that the matrix dealing with A are stronger than those dealing with B in the sense of being more deterministic. As the non-determinism observed with the matrix $m1$ dealing with BBB is not a crucial drawback, one could use $m2' = [(A \to \#, AA), (A \to \#\#, \#A)]$ instead. Checking cases one sees that this does not create any additional problems indeed. We can also try to use $\#\#$ instead of $\#\#\#$ for marking purposes, which would allow us to shorten the length of $m3$ as well. Still, we have to split the matrix dealing with BBB, which is done as follows (at the cost of additional context checks):

$$m0 = [(B \to \#, BBB), (B \to \#, BB\#)],$$
$$m1 = [(B \to \#, \#B\#), (\# \to \lambda, \#\#\#)],$$
$$m2 = [(A \to \#, AA), (A \to \#, \#A)],$$
$$m3 = [(\# \to \lambda, \#\#), (\# \to \lambda)].$$

We explain the necessity of these context checks by one example: If we omitted the BBB check in the first rule of $m1$, we might enter the matrix not having BBB as the central part, but without the $BB\#$ context of the second rule, it might be that we had replaced two occurrences of B's that are both not within BBB, so that we could re-apply $m0$, or possibly also directly apply $m3$. Also observe that with the proposed version, the shortcut of applying $m3$ immediately after $m0$ would lead to no continuation, because the central part would have been successfully destroyed, so that from now on no other matrix is applicable. Based on this construction, one can show (analogously to the previous case):

Theorem 16. $MSSC(3, 0; 4; 7, 4, 2) = MP(3; 4; 7, 4, 2) = RE.$ $\square$

We are now going to follow the strategy again to merge some of the matrices. Also, we could be more parsimonous with checking contexts in this case. This leads us to the following matrices simulating the non-context-free rules:

$$m1 = [(B \to \#, 0), (B \to \#, 0), (B \to \lambda, \#B\#), (\# \to \lambda, \#\#), (\# \to \lambda, 0)],$$
$$m2 = [(A \to \#, 0), (A \to \#, 0), (\# \to \lambda, \#\#), (\# \to \lambda, 0)].$$

These two matrices with three conditional rules form the basis of the following.

Theorem 17. $MSSC(3, 0; 4; 3, 2, 5) = MP(3; 4; 3, 2, 5) = RE.$ $\square$

Alternatively, we could use more conditional rules and longer matrices (but smaller degrees) with the following matrix $m1'$ replacing $m1$ above: $m1' = [(B \to \#, 0), (B \to \#, \#B), (\# \to \#, B\#), (\# \to \#, A\#), (B \to \lambda, \#A), (\# \to \lambda, \#\#), (\# \to \lambda, 0)]$. Observe that if we have a string $w \in \{A, B, \#\}^*$ with two $\#$-occurrences and moreover $\{\#A, \#B, A\#, B\#\} \subseteq sub(w)$, then either $A\#B$ and $B\#A$ or both $A\#A$ and $B\#B$ are substrings of w. Now if some B is deleted to produce w', so that afterwards $\#\#$ is a substring of w', then only $A\#B\#A \in sub(w)$ follows. This implies that $BBB \to \lambda$ is correctly simulated.

Theorem 18. $MSSC(2, 0; 4; 6, 2, 7) = MP(2; 4; 6, 2, 7) = RE.$ $\square$

4 Conclusions and Discussions

We have tried to describe the frontier of computational completeness for MSSC grammars, obtaining quite a lot of trade-off results between the six descriptional complexity measures that we studied. The natural question is if our bounds can be further improved or if there are more trade-off results than already presented. We are working on the idea of re-using the start nonterminal within matrices.

Conversely, it would be also good to know which descriptional complexity restrictions lead to language classes smaller than RE. For instance, we believe that, irrespectively of the size of the other parameters, one nonterminal is insufficient to describe all of RE. This can be seen by inspecting the proof of the corresponding result for graph-controlled grammars in [3, Theorem 15].

However, whether or not two or three nonterminals might suffice is open. Let us finally sketch the difficulties that we face when trying to use previous results on matrix languages in particular. In the proof of [3, Corollary 6], showing that three nonterminals $\{A, B, C\}$ suffice to generate any RE-language by using context-free matrix grammars with appearance checking, the appearance checks have been performed on rules $X \to C^g$ (for some large number g encoding failure). Picking some nonterminal $Y \neq X$, this check could be simulated by an SSC rule $(Y \to Y, 0, X)$. This bounds the degree to $(0, 1)$, as no permitting string checks are ever needed, and the nonterminals to three, yet, all other interesting parameters are unbounded. As the matrix length is a classical parameter in matrix grammars, this observation might revive some interest in the descriptional complexity of more classical rewriting systems (as matrix grammars): there are still open problems in that area. For instance, it is also still unknown if context-free matrix grammars with two nonterminals only describe RE.

References

1. Ábrahám, S.: Some questions of phrase-structure grammars. I. Comput. Linguist. **4**, 61–70 (1965)
2. Dassow, J., Păun, G.: Regulated Rewriting in Formal Language Theory. EATCS Monographs in Theoretical Computer Science, vol. 18. Springer, Heidelberg (1989)
3. Fernau, H., Freund, R., Oswald, M., Reinhardt, K.: Refining the nonterminal complexity of graph-controlled, programmed, and matrix grammars. J. Autom. Lang. Comb. **12**(1/2), 117–138 (2007). https://doi.org/10.25596/jalc-2007-117
4. Fernau, H., Kuppusamy, L., Oladele, R., Raman, I.: Improved descriptional complexity results for simple semi-conditional grammars (2019). Submitted to Fund. Inform
5. Fernau, H., Kuppusamy, L., Oladele, R.O.: New nonterminal complexity results for semi-conditional grammars. In: Manea, F., Miller, R.G., Nowotka, D. (eds.) CiE 2018. LNCS, vol. 10936, pp. 172–182. Springer, Cham (2018). https://doi.org/10. 1007/978-3-319-94418-0_18
6. Gazdag, Z., Tichler, K.: On the power of permitting semi-conditional grammars. In: Charlier, É., Leroy, J., Rigo, M. (eds.) DLT 2017. LNCS, vol. 10396, pp. 173–184. Springer, Cham (2017). https://doi.org/10.1007/978-3-319-62809-7_12
7. Geffert, V.: Normal forms for phrase-structure grammars. RAIRO Theor. Inform. Appl. **25**, 473–498 (1991)
8. Hauschildt, D., Jantzen, M.: Petri net algorithms in the theory of matrix grammars. Acta Inform. **31**, 719–728 (1994). https://doi.org/10.1007/BF01178731
9. Masopust, T.: Formal models: regulation and reduction. Ph.D. thesis, Faculty of Information Technology, Brno University of Technology, Brno, Czech Republic (2007)

10. Meduna, A., Gopalaratnam, M.: On semi-conditional grammars with productions having either forbidding or permitting conditions. Acta Cybern. **11**(4), 307–323 (1994). http://www.inf.u-szeged.hu/actacybernetica/edb/vol11n4/Meduna1994ActaCybernetica.xml

11. Meduna, A., Kopeček, T.: Simple semi-conditional versions of matrix grammars with a reduced regulating mechanism. Comput. Inform. **23**, 287–302 (2004). http://www.cai.sk/ojs/index.php/cai/article/view/430

12. Meduna, A., Švec, M.: Reduction of simple semi-conditional grammars with respect to the number of conditional productions. Acta Cybern. **15**(3), 353–360 (2002). http://www.inf.u-szeged.hu/actacybernetica/edb/vol15n3/Meduna2002ActaCybernetica.xml

13. Okubo, F.: A note on the descriptional complexity of semi-conditional grammars. Inform. Process. Lett. **110**(1), 36–40 (2009). https://doi.org/10.1016/j.ipl.2009.10.002

14. Păun, G.: A variant of random context grammars: semi-conditional grammars. Theoret. Comput. Sci., pp. 1–17. (1985). https://doi.org/10.1016/0304-3975(85)90056-8

15. Vaszil, G.: On the descriptional complexity of some rewriting mechanisms regulated by context conditions. Theoret. Comput. Sci. **330**, 361–373 (2005). https://doi.org/10.1016/j.tcs.2004.06.032

Regulated Tree Automata

Henning Fernau[(⊠)] [ID] and Martin Vu

Universität Trier, FB IV—Abteilung Informatikwissenschaften, CIRT,
54286 Trier, Germany
{fernau,s4vivuuu}@uni-trier.de

Abstract. Regulated rewriting is one of the classical areas in Formal Languages, as tree automata are a classical topic. Somewhat surprisingly, there have been no attempts so far to combine both areas. Here, we start this type of research, introducing regulated tree automata, proving in particular characterizations of the yields of such regulated automata.

Keywords: Regulated rewriting · Graph control · Tree automata · Yield operation

1 Introduction

The area of regulated rewriting, still well-covered by the classical monograph of Dassow and Păun [4], drew its main motivation from the idea to enrich context-free grammars with certain control mechanisms in order to be able to model linguistic features that are not expressible with traditional context-free grammars, yet keeping at least some of the beauties of these. More specifically, programmed grammars, matrix grammars, and grammars with regular control were introduced and studied around 1970. It soon became clear that control involving so-called appearance checks tends to be too powerful in the sense that all recursively enumerable languages can be characterized this way. This somewhat counter-acts the idea of keeping some of the advantages of context-free grammars over, say, Turing machines. Therefore, we are mainly focusing on models without appearance checks in the following. Applications and motivations are also underlined in the relatively recent monograph by Meduna and Zemek [15].

Conversely, finite tree automata have been invented to allow for processing (mostly ordered) trees (as opposed to strings) in a simple manner. Trees not only showed up as a kind of intermediate data structure within compilers, but they are a ubiquitous data structure when it comes to processing semi-structured documents and also for working with natural languages [2,12,13].

Recall the basic well-known link between context-free grammars and derivation trees, often established in practice via considering pushdown automata. However, it is not possible to go this way in connection with regulated rewriting, as already observed by Meduna and Kolář in [14]. The basic reason is that the work of pushdown automata rather corresponds to leftmost (or rightmost)

© IFIP International Federation for Information Processing 2019
Published by Springer Nature Switzerland AG 2019
M. Hospodár et al. (Eds.): DCFS 2019, LNCS 11612, pp. 124–136, 2019.
https://doi.org/10.1007/978-3-030-23247-4_9

derivations in a very strict sense (called leftmost-1 in [4]). Yet, this strict interpretation does not increase the descriptive power of context-free languages, which counter-acts one of the basic motivations for considering regulated rewriting.

Rather, we are going to follow here the path pioneered by Doner, Thatcher (and also to Wright) [5,16] who showed that the context-free string languages are just the languages that can be obtained by mapping the tree language accepted by some finite tree automaton to its so-called yield, which means that, given an ordered tree, we read the labels of the leaves from left to right. We will obtain similar results for regulated tree grammars in this paper. As tree automata usually come in two working modes (top-down versus bottom-up), our studies also revive the question of generating versus accepting (or analyzing) grammars [1].

We are going to present basic results concerning regulated tree automata and their yields. Due to reasons of space, (straightforward) formal induction arguments are not given here. Most of these can be found in [17].

2   Definitions

2.1   Classical Regulated Rewriting

There are several ways to introduce the basic control mechanisms of regulated rewriting. We are giving a simplified exposition now, basically following [7], adapted to the case of not allowing appearance checks.

A *graph-controlled grammar* is an 8-tuple $G = (V_N, V_T, P, S, \Gamma, \Sigma, \Phi, h)$ where

- (V_N, V_T, P, S) define, as in a phrase structure grammar, the set of nonterminals, terminals, context-free core rules, and the start symbol, respectively;
- Γ is a digraph, i.e., $\Gamma = (U, E)$, with $E \subseteq U \times U$;
- $\Sigma \subseteq U$ are the initial vertices;
- $\Phi \subseteq U$ are the final vertices;
- $h : U \to (2^P \setminus \{\emptyset\})$ relates vertices with rule sets.

We say that $(x, u) \Rightarrow (y, v)$ holds in G with $(x, u), (y, v) \in (V_N \cup V_T)^* \times U$ if, for some $x_1, x_2, \alpha, \beta \in (V_N \cup V_T)^*$,

$$x = x_1 \alpha x_2, \quad y = x_1 \beta x_2, \quad \alpha \to \beta \in h(u), \quad \text{and} \quad (u, v) \in E.$$

The reflexive transitive closure of $\Rightarrow$ is denoted by $\stackrel{*}{\Rightarrow}$. The language generated by G (where P contains only context-free (generating, non-erasing) rules from $V_N \times (V_N \cup V_T)^+$) is defined by

$$L^{gen}(G) = \{x \in V_T^* \mid \exists u \in \Sigma \, \exists v \in \Phi \, ((S, u) \stackrel{*}{\Rightarrow} (x, v))\}.$$

The corresponding language family is written $\mathcal{L}^{gen}(\mathrm{G}, \mathrm{CF} - \varepsilon)$, as we do not allow ε-rules. If P contains only context-free (accepting) rules from $(V_N \cup V_T)^+ \times V_N$, then the language accepted by G is defined by

$$L^{acc}(G) = \{x \in V_T^* \mid \exists u \in \Sigma \, \exists v \in \Phi \, ((x, u) \stackrel{*}{\Rightarrow} (S, v))\},$$

yielding the language family $\mathcal{L}^{acc}(\mathrm{G}, \mathrm{CF} - \varepsilon)$.

We consider three special cases of graph-controlled grammars in the following.

– A *grammar with regular control* is a graph-controlled grammar where every vertex contains exactly one rule. Usually, these grammars are introduced via regular control languages, but the correspondance with automata graphs is obvious. By $\mathcal{L}^{gen}(\text{rC,CF} - \varepsilon)$, the family of languages generated by context-free grammars with regular control is denoted.
– A *programmed grammar* is a grammar with regular control with no designated initial or final vertices, i.e., formally $\Sigma = \Phi = U$. This means that it is possible to start a derivation in each vertex containing a rule whose left-hand side equals the start symbol S, and it is possible to stop anywhere when a terminal string has been derived. As language families, we obtain, e.g., $\mathcal{L}^{gen}(\text{P}, \text{CF} - \varepsilon)$.
– A *matrix grammar* is a grammar with regular control obeying the additional restriction:
   • Initial and final vertices coincide. Only the initial vertices (not necessarily containing rules with left-hand side S) are allowed to have more than one in-going arc. Only predecessors of final vertices are allowed to have more than one out-going arc. Moreover, between every predecessor of a final vertex and every initial vertex, there is an arc.
As language families, we obtain, e.g., $\mathcal{L}^{gen}(\text{M}, \text{CF} - \varepsilon)$.

With literally the same restrictions, we can define, for instance, $\mathcal{L}^{acc}(\text{M}, \text{CF} - \varepsilon)$. Recall that all language families introduced in this subsection coincide [1,4].

Remark 1. The formalization of regular control is possibly most different from the one found in traditional textbooks. However, if $\Gamma = (U, E)$ together with Σ, Φ, h defines the control graph structure, then we can relate a finite automaton A with state set U as follows: We have a transition (u, r, v) if $h(u) = \{r\}$; Σ is the set of initial states, and if $u \in \Phi$ and $(u, v) \in E$, then v is a final state of A. Now, if $u_1, u_2, \ldots, u_n$ describes a directed path from $u_1 \in \Sigma$ to $u_n \in \Phi$, then via $\{r_i\} = h(u_i)$ this corresponds to a sequence of rules $r_1 r_2 \ldots r_n$, which, when fed into A, will be accepted. Also the converse construction is possible. Hence, we can in particular assume that the automaton A that describes the set of permitted rule sequences is deterministic.

2.2 Tree Automata

Let $\mathbb{N}$ be the set of nonnegative integers and let $(\mathbb{N}^*, \cdot, \varepsilon)$ (or simply $\mathbb{N}^*$) be the free monoid generated by $\mathbb{N}$. For $y, x \in \mathbb{N}^*$, we write $y \leq x$ iff there is a $z \in \mathbb{N}^*$ with $x = y \cdot z$. "$y < x$" abbreviates: $y \leq x$ and $y \neq x$. As usual, $|x|$ denotes the length of the word x.

We now give the necessary definitions for trees and tree automata. More details can be found, e.g., in [2], where also many examples can be found.

A *ranked alphabet* V is a finite set of symbols together with a finite relation called rank relation $r_V \subset V \times \mathbb{N}$. Define $V_n := \{f \in V \mid (f, n) \in r_V\}$. Since elements in V_n are often considered as *function symbols* (standing for functions of *arity* n), elements in V_0 are also called *constant symbols*. A *tree over* V is a

mapping $t : \Delta_t \to V$, where the domain Δ_t is a finite subset of $\mathbb{N}^*$ such that
(1) if $x \in \Delta_t$ and $y < x$, then $y \in \Delta_t$; (2) if $y \cdot i \in \Delta_t$, $i \in \mathbb{N}$, then $y \cdot j \in \Delta_t$
for $1 \leq j \leq i$. An element of Δ_t is also called a *node* of t, where the node ε
is the *root* of the tree. Then $t(x) \in V_n$ whenever, for $i \in \mathbb{N}$, $x \cdot i \in \Delta_t$ iff
$1 \leq i \leq n$. If $t(x) = A$, A is the *label* of x. Let V^t denote the set of all finite trees
over V. By this definition, trees are rooted, directed, acyclic graphs in which
every node except the root has one predecessor and the direct successors of any
node are linearly ordered from left to right. Interpreting V as a set of function
symbols, V^t can be identified with the well-formed terms over V. A *frontier
node* in t is a node $y \in \Delta_t$ such there is no $x \in \Delta_t$ with $y < x$. If $y \in \Delta_t$ is
not a frontier node, it is called *interior node*. The *depth* of a tree t is defined as
$\text{depth}(t) = \max\{|x| \mid x \in \Delta_t\}$, whereas the *size* of t is given by $|\Delta_t|$. Letters will
be viewed as trees of size one and depth zero.

We are now going to define a catenation on trees. Let \$ be a new symbol, i.e.,
\$ $\notin V$, of rank 0. Let $V_\$^t$ denote the set of all trees over $V \cup \{\$\}$ which contain
exactly one occurrence of label \$. By definition, only frontier nodes can carry
the label \$. For trees $u \in V_\$^t$ and $t \in (V^t \cup V_\$^t)$, we define an operation $\#$ to
replace the frontier node labelled with \$ of u by t according to

$$u\#t(x) = \begin{cases} u(x), & \text{if } x \in \Delta_u \wedge u(x) \neq \$; \\ t(y), & \text{if } x = z \cdot y \wedge u(z) = \$ \wedge y \in \Delta_t. \end{cases}$$

If $U \subseteq V_\$^t$ and $T \subseteq (V^t \cup V_\$^t)$, then $U\#T := \{u\#t \mid u \in U \wedge t \in T\}$. For $t \in V^t$
and $x \in \Delta_t$, the *subtree* of t at x, denoted by t/x, is defined by $t/x(y) = t(x \cdot y)$
for any $y \in \Delta_{t/x}$, where $\Delta_{t/x} := \{y \mid x \cdot y \in \Delta_t\}$. $\text{ST}(T) := \{t/x \mid t \in T \wedge x \in \Delta_t\}$
is the set of subtrees of trees from $T \subseteq V^t$. Furthermore, for any $t \in V^t$ and any
tree language $T \subseteq V^t$, the *quotient* of T and t is defined as:

$$U_T(t) := \begin{cases} \{u \in V_\$^t \mid u\#t \in T\}, & \text{if } t \in V^t \setminus V_0; \\ t, & \text{if } t \in V_0. \end{cases}$$

Let V be a ranked alphabet and m be the maximum rank of the symbols
in V. A *(bottom-up) (finite-state) tree automaton* over V is a quadruple $A = (Q, V, \delta, F)$ such that Q is a finite state alphabet (disjoint with V_0), $F \subseteq Q$ is
a set of final states, and $\delta = (\delta_0, \ldots, \delta_m)$ is an $m + 1$-tuple of state transition
functions, where $\delta_0(a) = \{a\}$ for $a \in V_0$ and $\delta_k : V_k \times (Q \cup V_0)^k \to 2^Q$ for
$k = 1, \ldots, m$. In this definition, the constant symbols at the frontier nodes are
taken as sort of initial states. Now, a transition relation (also denoted by δ) can
be recursively defined on V^t by letting

$$\delta(f(t_1, \ldots, t_k)) := \begin{cases} \{f\}, & \text{if } k = 0; \\ \bigcup_{q_i \in \delta(t_i), i=1,\ldots,k} \delta_k(f, q_1, \ldots, q_k), & \text{if } k > 0. \end{cases}$$

A tree t is accepted by A iff $\delta(t) \cap F \neq \emptyset$. The tree language accepted by A is
denoted by $L^t(A)$. A is *deterministic* if each of the functions δ_k maps each possible argument to a set of cardinality at most one. Deterministic tree automata
can be viewed as algorithms for labelling the nodes of a tree with states. Analogously to the case of string automata, it can be shown that nondeterministic

and deterministic bottom-up finite-state tree automata accept the same class of tree languages, namely the *regular tree languages*, at the expense of a possibly exponential state explosion.

Rules are sometimes also written like $f(q_1, \ldots, q_k) \to q$ instead of saying that $q \in \delta_k(f, q_1, \ldots, q_k)$. Sometimes, also *$\varepsilon$-moves* are allowed, written like $q' \to q$, i.e., no part of the tree is consumed, only the state is changed. As in the string case, finite tree automata with ε-moves only accept regular tree languages.

An alternative view on the work of tree automata is that of labelling a tree with states. To this end, we will formally view all symbols from Q as having rank zero, so that they may serve as labels of frontier nodes. Now, A (or more specifically, its transition function δ) defines a derivation relation $\vdash_\delta$ on $(V \cup Q)^t$ by $s \vdash_\delta t$ if $s \neq t$ and there are trees $u \in (V \cup Q)_\$^t$, $s' = f(q_1, \ldots, q_k)$, $t' = q$ with $s = u \# s'$, $t = u \# t'$, $f \in V_k$, $q \in \delta_k(f, q_1, \ldots, q_k)$. Clearly, $s \in V^t$ is accepted by a tree automaton $A = (Q, V, \delta, F)$ if $s \vdash_\delta^* q_f$ for some $q_f \in F$. If we consider δ as a set of rules, it makes also sense to define $s \vdash_{\delta'} t$ for subsets of rules $\delta' \subseteq \delta$. We will use this notation when defining regulated tree automata.

It is also possible to define tree automata $A = (Q, V, \delta, I)$ that work top-down. Rules are now of the form $q \to f(q_1, \ldots, q_k)$, and the derivation relation basically reverses the arrows. Hence, also finite top-down tree automata characterize the regular tree languages. However, deterministic finite top-down tree automata are a strictly weaker model.

We already informally recalled the Theorem of Doner, Thatcher (and also to Wright) [5,16]. To formally state it, we provide the necessary key notion: For $t \in V^t$, we define the *yield-operator* $\mathcal{Y}$ as follows:

$$\mathcal{Y}(t) = \begin{cases} t(\varepsilon), & \text{if } t(\varepsilon) \in V_0; \\ \mathcal{Y}(t/1) \cdots \mathcal{Y}(t/k), & \text{if } t(\varepsilon) \in V_k, k > 0. \end{cases}$$

In words, the recursion means that the yield of a tree with a root with k children equals the concatenation of the yields of the trees whose roots are these children. The operator naturally extends to tree languages and tree language families.

Theorem 2 (Doner, Thatcher, Wright). *A string language is context-free if and only if it is the yield of a regular tree language.*

Notice that the proof of this result makes use of the fact that for context-free languages, we can assume that they are generated by some context-free grammar without erasing productions, neglecting the possibility to describe the empty word itself. As it is still an open problem whether or not we can get rid of erasing rules with regulated grammars as introduced in the previous subsection, we restricted our attention to regulated grammars without erasing rules there, as we strive for analogues of Theorem 2 in the following.

2.3   Regulated Tree Automata

We are now defining the central new notion of this paper, combining the two classical worlds so far introduced. Hence, a *graph-controlled finite tree automaton* is an 8-tuple $A = (Q, V, \delta, F, \Gamma, \Sigma, \Phi, h)$ where

- $A' = (Q, V, \delta, F)$ define a finite tree automaton;
- Γ, Σ, Φ define the graph structure as in graph-controlled grammars;
- $h : U \rightarrow (2^\delta \setminus \{\emptyset\})$ relates vertices with rule sets; notice that we consider δ as a set of rules here.

We say that $(s, u) \models (t, v)$ holds via A with $(s, u), (t, v) \in (Q \cup V)^t \times U$ if

$$s \vdash_{h(u)} t \quad \text{and} \quad (u, v) \in E.$$

The reflexive transitive closure of $\models$ is denoted by $\models^*$. The tree language accepted by A (assuming that A' works bottom-up) is defined by

$$L^{bu}(A) = \{t \in V^t \mid \exists q \in F \, \exists u \in \Sigma \, \exists v \in \Phi((t, u) \models^* (q, v))\}.$$

Similarly, we can define acceptance for top-down automata, yielding the language $L^{td}(A)$. This gives the tree language families $\mathcal{L}^t(G, bu)$ and $\mathcal{L}^t(G, td)$, depending on whether bottom-up or top-down automata are considered. If we want to explicitly rule out ε-moves, we add $-\varepsilon$ to our notations. As the notions of regular control, matrix and programmed have been introduced in Subsect. 2.1 as simple syntactical restrictions of graph control, we can carry over them immediately to regulated finite tree automata, giving, e.g., the notion of a matrix finite tree automaton. This also gives language families such as $\mathcal{L}^t(P, td, -\varepsilon)$.

3   Basic Results for Regulated Tree Automata

By the definitions themselves, we can conclude (also confer [11], but mind the partially different definitions):

Lemma 3. *Let* $\mu \in \{bu, td\}$. *Then, we have*

$$\mathcal{L}^t(P, \mu) \subseteq \mathcal{L}^t(rC, \mu) \subseteq \mathcal{L}^t(G, \mu) \quad and \quad \mathcal{L}^t(M, \mu) \subseteq \mathcal{L}^t(rC, \mu).$$

Proposition 4. *For* $C \in \{G, P, rC, M\}$, $\mathcal{L}^t(C, bu) = \mathcal{L}^t(C, td)$.

Proof. Recall [2] that for any finite top-down tree automaton A_{td}, one can construct an equivalent finite bottom-up automaton A_{bu} by simply reversing the relation $\vdash$, plus exchanging initial and final states. Similarly, we can simulate $A = (A_{td}, \Gamma, \Sigma, \Phi, h)$ by $A' = (A_{bu}, \Gamma', \Sigma', \Phi', h')$, where $\Gamma' = (U', E')$ is obtained from $\Gamma = (U, E)$ by reversing the arcs, $\Sigma' = \Phi$, $\Phi' = \Sigma$, and h' associates the reversed rule variants of $h(u)$ to $u \in U' = U$. Clearly, if $(\Gamma, \Sigma, \Phi, h)$ satisfies the restrictions imposed by $C \in \{G, P, rC, M\}$, then $(\Gamma', \Sigma', \Phi', h')$ does so, as well. The converse inclusion is similarly seen.   □

Hence, we can from now on consider either the bottom-up or the top-down case, whatever is more convenient to us. We are going to present a sequence of technical lemmas that combine classical ideas from tree automata and from regulated rewriting. Illustrations by examples can be found in the Appendix.

Lemma 5. $\mathcal{L}^t(G, bu) \subseteq \mathcal{L}^t(rC, bu)$.

Proof. We only sketch the construction. Consider a graph-controlled finite tree automaton is an 8-tuple $A = (Q, V, \delta, F, \Gamma, \Sigma, \Phi, h)$. We derive an equivalent finite tree automaton with regular control $A_r = (Q, V, \delta, F, \Gamma_r, \Sigma_r, \Phi_r, h_r)$ as follows. Let $\Gamma = (U, E)$. Then, $\Gamma_r = (U_r, E_r)$ with $U_r = \bigcup_{u \in U}\{u\} \times h(u)$, $E_r = \{((u, x), (v, y)) \mid (u, x), (v, y) \in U_r, (u, v) \in E\}$, $\Sigma_r = \bigcup_{u \in \Sigma}\{u\} \times h(u)$, $\Phi_r = \bigcup_{u \in \Phi}\{u\} \times h(u)$, and $h_r((u, x)) = \{x\}$ for $(u, x) \in U_r$. By construction, $|h_r((u, x))| = 1$ for all $(u, x) \in U_r$. Moreover, if $(s, u) \models (t, v)$ holds via A, then $s \vdash_{h(u)} t$ and $(u, v) \in E$, so that for some $x \in h(u)$, $s \vdash_{\{x\}} t$, i.e., $(s, (u, x)) \models (t, (v, y))$ holds via A_r for all $y \in h(v)$. Induction shows the claim. $\square$

Lemma 6. $\mathcal{L}^t(rC, bu) \subseteq \mathcal{L}^t(P, bu)$.

Proof. We are modifying bottom-up tree automata with regular control step by step in order to obtain an equivalent programmed control. (i) We can assume that initial vertices (from Σ) have no in-going arcs and that there is only one final vertex (i.e., $|\Phi| = 1$) that has no out-going arcs. This can be easily seen by keeping in mind the relation to regular languages and hence to finite string automata (as control devices) as recalled in Remark 1. (ii) Moreover, by using a shadow state alphabet Q', the finite tree automaton itself can check if the derivation control had started in some $u_i \in \Sigma$ and also that the corresponding rule was used only once. Namely, the starting rules (that have to process a terminal symbol at some leaf node of the tree) will lead to a primed state q' (when it would go to q in the original automaton), and the fact that exactly one primed state was ever entered is then propagated to the root of the tree. Here, it is also necessary to split vertices of the control graph. More specifically, if vertex v contains a rule $f(q_1, \ldots, q_k) \to q$, we create k many twins of v, say, $v_1, \ldots, v_k$, and then v_i contains the rule $f(q_1, \ldots, q_{i-1}, q_i', q_{i+1}, \ldots, q_k) \to q'$ to properly propagate the prime information. This already shows that we can now let any vertex be initial in our control graph without changing the set of accepted trees. (iii) As a further step, we can introduce another shadow state alphabet $\hat{F}$ as a new set of final states and modify the rules associated to the control graph vertices so that (only and exactly) when moving to u_f, with $\{u_f\} = \Phi$, such a final state $\hat{q}$ is entered. This step might involve splitting vertices v that are predecessors of u_f into v and $\hat{v}$, where $\hat{v}$ contains the rule introducing $\hat{q}$, while v contains the rule introducing the corresponding state q. Otherwise, v and $\hat{v}$ have the same predecessors. However, u_f is the only successor of $\hat{v}$ (and not a successor of v), while all other successor vertices that previously existed for v are still successor vertices of v (and not for $\hat{v}$). Now, we can (formally) let every vertex be a final vertex without changing the accepted tree language. Again, the correctness of the construction is seen by induction. $\square$

Remark 7. For all statements made so far in this section, similar results hold when disallowing ε-moves. We refrain from making this explicit. However, this is no longer obvious for the following construction. This also gives a first **open question** in the area of regulated tree automata.

Lemma 8. $\mathcal{L}^t(P, bu) \subseteq \mathcal{L}^t(M, bu)$.

Recall that in the classical construction simulating programmed grammars by matrix grammars, the state information is maintained in a special nonterminal. We follow the same idea here, but with tree automata, this is technically more involved due to the absence of erasing rules.

Proof. Consider a programmed automaton $A = (Q, V, \delta, F, \Gamma, \Sigma, \Phi, h)$ with $\Gamma = (U, E)$ and $\Sigma = \Phi = U$. Now, we can also assume that the rules associated to start vertices are of the form $a \to q$ for some terminal $a \in V_0$ and some state q, this way (formally) specifying $\hat{\Sigma} \subseteq \Sigma$. (a) We add rules by $r = a \to [q, u]$ and introduce a new vertex $\hat{v}$, with $h(\hat{v}) = \{r\}$ and $v \in \Sigma$, for those u that are successors of v in Γ. More formally, this means that we introduce for each $v \in \hat{\Sigma}$ as many twins as there are successors of v in Γ. This also defines a new set of initial vertices Σ', with more vertices to be added. All these vertices $\hat{v}$ have outgoing arcs to all vertices from Σ'. (b) For each $q \in Q \cup V_0$ and each $u, v \in U \setminus \Sigma$ with $(u, v) \in E$, we introduce a new rule $[q, u] \to [q, v]$ and a new vertex $[q, u, v]$ into Γ' hosting this new rule. All these vertices also belong to Σ'. (c) Introduce an arc from each vertex $[q, u, v]$ to the vertex u containing the rule $h(u)$. All such vertices u have arcs to all vertices from Σ'. (d) For each $q \in Q \cup V_0$ and each $u, v \in U \setminus \Sigma$ with $(u, v) \in E$ and each $1 \leq i \leq k$ with $h(u) = \{f(p_1, \ldots, p_k) \to p\}$ such that $p_i = q$, we introduce a new rule $f(p_1, \ldots, p_{i-1}, [p_i, u], p_{i+1}, \ldots, p_k) \to [p, v]$; moreover, we create a vertex $[q, i, u, v]$ containing exactly this newly created rule, put it into Σ' and link it to all vertices from Σ'. (e) For each $q \in Q \cup V_0$ and each $u, v \in U \setminus \Sigma$ with $(u, v) \in E$, if $h(u) = \{q \to p\}$, i.e., u hosts an ε-move, then we introduce the new rule $[q, u] \to [p, v]$ and call the vertex hosting this rule $[q, 1, u, v]$ for simplicity. Again, such vertices are put into Σ' and linked to all vertices from Σ'. To summarize, we described a new graph-controlled automaton $A' = (Q', V', \delta', F', \Gamma', \Sigma', \Phi', h')$ with $\Gamma' = (U', E')$, where $Q' \supseteq Q$, $V' \supseteq V$, $\delta' \supseteq \delta$, Σ', $U' \supseteq U$ and E' as specified above. As final state set F', we take $F' = F \times U$. The final vertices (from Φ') contain U and all vertices from Σ' introduced in steps (a), (d) and (e). Clearly, A' is with matrix control. Again, the correctness of the construction is seen by induction. $\qquad\square$

We can summarize our results as follows.

Theorem 9. Let $\mu_M, \mu_P, \mu_{rC}, \mu_G \in \{bu, td\}$. Then, we have

$$\mathcal{L}^t(M, \mu_M) = \mathcal{L}^t(P, \mu_P) = \mathcal{L}^t(rC, \mu_{rC}) = \mathcal{L}^t(G, \mu_G) \quad and$$

$$\mathcal{L}^t(M, \mu_M, -\varepsilon) \subseteq \mathcal{L}^t(P, \mu_P, -\varepsilon) = \mathcal{L}^t(rC, \mu_{rC}, -\varepsilon) = \mathcal{L}^t(G, \mu_G, -\varepsilon).$$

This result gives rise to the following natural second **open question**: Is the trivial inclusion $\mathcal{L}^t(G, td, -\varepsilon) \subseteq \mathcal{L}^t(G, td)$ strict or not? Recall that for classical finite tree automata, we can dispose of ε-moves as a normal form.

4   Relation to String Languages

We already introduced the yield operator above that allows us to associate strings to trees and hence string languages to tree languages. Recall Theorem 2.

Lemma 10. $\mathcal{Y}(\mathcal{L}^t(G, bu)) \subseteq \mathcal{L}^{acc}(G, CF - \varepsilon)$.

Proof. Consider a graph-controlled finite tree automaton $A = (Q, V, \delta, F, \Gamma, \Sigma, \Phi, h)$ with $\Gamma = (U, E)$. We are going to construct a graph-controlled context-free grammar $G_A = (V_N, V_T, P, q_f, \Gamma, \Sigma, \Phi, h')$ such that $\mathcal{Y}(L^{bu}(A)) = L^{acc}(G_A)$. As it is usually the case with nondeterministic automata, we can assume (without loss of generality) that A only one final (accepting) state, i.e., $F = \{q_f\}$. We construct a simulating accepting grammar G_A as follows: $N = Q$, $T = V_0$, $w \to q \in h'(u)$ if $q \in Q$, $w = w_1 \cdots w_k$, $w_j \in V_0 \cup Q$ whenever $g(w_1, \ldots, w_k) \to q \in h(u)$ for some $g \in V_k$ (*).

Now, each derivation of A producing a certain yield can be simulated by G_A, where the correct labels of inner nodes are guessed during the derivation due to (*). Conversely, these guesses according to (*) label the inner nodes of a derivation tree in a way corresponding to a tree that can be accepted by A.

A formal reasoning would be a relatively tedious exercise, based on the ideas originating from Doner, Thatcher and Wright in the late sixties, which can be also found in any textbook on tree languages. Therefore, we only sketch the basic idea of the inductive step of the proof in the following. Recall that the definition of $\vdash$ transforms trees with leaf labels from $(V_0 \cup Q)$ into trees with leaf labels from $(V_0 \cup Q)$; extending the definition of the yield operator $\mathcal{Y}$ accordingly, this means that sentential forms of G_A are transformed. Notice that the graph control stays the same, which allows the induction to succeed.   □

Literally the same construction allows us to state:

Lemma 11. $\mathcal{Y}(\mathcal{L}^t(G, td)) \subseteq \mathcal{L}^{gen}(G, CF - \varepsilon)$.

For the converse direction, we need a normal form result for regulated context-free grammars that might be of independent interest. A graph-controlled context-free grammar $G = (V_N, V_T, P, S, \Gamma, \Sigma, \Phi, h)$ is called *arity-deterministic* if for each nonterminal $A \in N$, there exists a unique number $\alpha(A)$ (called the *arity* of A) such that any rule $A \to w \in P$ (in the generating case) or $w \to A \in P$ (in the accepting case) obeys $|w| = \alpha(A)$.

Theorem 12 (Arity-deterministic normal form). *For any* $L \in \mathcal{L}^{acc}(G, CF - \varepsilon)$, *there exists an arity-deterministic context-free ε-free graph-controlled context-free grammar G accepting L. A similar statement holds for generating grammars.*

As the induction proof given in [9, Theorem 2] can be easily adapted to our case, we omit it here. We only mention that similar results are also true for other forms of control, like matrix grammars.

Lemma 13. $\mathcal{Y}(\mathcal{L}^t(G, bu)) \supseteq \mathcal{L}^{acc}(G, \mathrm{CF} - \varepsilon)$.

Proof [Sketch]. Starting with an arity-deterministic graph-controlled context-free grammar G, we can easily interpret its rules as transitions of a controlled finite tree automaton A_G. More specifically, we can consider $V_N \cup V_T$ as a ranked alphabet V, with $V_0 = V_T$. For any rule $w \to A$, we introduce a rule $\delta_{i,k}(A, w_1, \ldots, w_k) = \{A'\}$, where $|w| = \alpha(A) = k$. Notice that we have to formally distinguish the nonterminal A of arity k from the state A' that has, in a sense, arity zero. A_G accepts derivation trees of G. Conversely, the yield of any tree that derives S' (in A_G) corresponds to a sentential form that derives S (in G). For further details, we refer to [9, Lemma 2].   □

Lemma 14. $\mathcal{Y}(\mathcal{L}^t(G, td)) \supseteq \mathcal{L}^{gen}(G, \mathrm{CF} - \varepsilon)$.

Together with the results from the previous section, we conclude a known fact:

Theorem 15. Let $\mu_M, \mu_P, \mu_{rC}, \mu_G \in \{gen, acc\}$. Then, we have

$$\mathcal{L}^{\mu_M}(\mathrm{M}, \mathrm{CF} - \varepsilon) = \mathcal{L}^{\mu_P}(\mathrm{P}, \mathrm{CF} - \varepsilon) = \mathcal{L}^{\mu_{rC}}(\mathrm{rC}, \mathrm{CF} - \varepsilon) = \mathcal{L}^{\mu_G}(\mathrm{G}, \mathrm{CF} - \varepsilon).$$

Remark 16. As the constructions presented in this section do not introduce chain rules (into context-free grammars) and as chain rules correspond to ε-moves for tree automata, the open questions formulated in the previous section easily translate into **open questions** in the more classical realm of regulated context-free grammars as follows: *Does there exist a normal form for regulated context-free grammars (without erasing productions) that allows us to avoid chain-rules?* Related to this is another **open question** in the more classical realm of regulated context-free grammars: *Does there exist a Chomsky normal form result?* Loosely speaking, this corresponds to an arity-bounded normal form for derivation trees.

5 Adding Appearance Checks

Appearance checks (or maybe better said applicability checks, see [11]) are one of the key features introduced within regulated rewriting. On the level of graph control, this corresponds to considering bicolored digraphs as control structure [7,18]. For reasons of space, we refrain from giving a formal definition in this extended abstract. Notice that there are two ways of interpreting appearance checks in connection with control by bicolored digraphs, with the choice interpretation that first selects a rule in the rule set $h(u)$ and then checks for applicability of the selected tree rewriting rule, or with the interpretation that only considers $h(u)$ to be not applicable if none of the rules in $h(u)$ is applicable. We signal the choice interpretation by adding a c as a subscript. We can prove:

Theorem 17. Let $\mu \in \{bu, td\}$. Then, we have

$$\mathcal{L}^t(\mathrm{M}, \mu, \mathrm{ac}) = \mathcal{L}^t(\mathrm{P}, \mu, \mathrm{ac}) = \mathcal{L}^t(\mathrm{rC}, \mu, \mathrm{ac}) = \mathcal{L}^t(\mathrm{G}, \mu, \mathrm{ac}) = \mathcal{L}^t(\mathrm{G}_c, \mu, \mathrm{ac}).$$

We could state similar results as in Theorem 9 for the case when disallowing ε-moves. We have to distinguish more carefully between the bottom-up and the top-down cases due to the following results.

Theorem 18. *Let* $\mu \in \{gen, acc\}$. *Then, we have* $\mathcal{L}^\mu(\mathrm{M}, \mathrm{CF} - \varepsilon, \mathrm{ac}) = \mathcal{L}^\mu(\mathrm{P}, \mathrm{CF} - \varepsilon, \mathrm{ac}) = \mathcal{L}^\mu(\mathrm{rC}, \mathrm{CF} - \varepsilon, \mathrm{ac}) = \mathcal{L}^\mu(\mathrm{G}, \mathrm{CF} - \varepsilon, \mathrm{ac}) = \mathcal{L}^\mu(\mathrm{G}_c, \mathrm{CF} - \varepsilon, \mathrm{ac})$. *Moreover,* $\mathcal{L}^{gen}(\mathrm{M}, \mathrm{CF} - \varepsilon, \mathrm{ac}) = \mathcal{Y}(\mathcal{L}^{\mathrm{t}}(\mathrm{M}, td, \mathrm{ac})) \subsetneq \mathcal{L}^{acc}(\mathrm{M}, \mathrm{CF} - \varepsilon, \mathrm{ac}) = \mathcal{Y}(\mathcal{L}^{\mathrm{t}}(\mathrm{M}, bu, \mathrm{ac}))$.

Corollary 19. $\mathcal{L}^{\mathrm{t}}(\mathrm{M}, td, \mathrm{ac}) \subsetneq \mathcal{L}^{\mathrm{t}}(\mathrm{M}, bu, \mathrm{ac})$.

Proof. The inclusion itself is seen as before; notice that we can simulate a rule $q \to f(q_1, \ldots, q_k)$ that is applied in appearance checking by some ε-move that checks for the presence of q. If the converse inclusion would hold, as well, then the yields of both tree language families would coincide, which contradicts known facts on regulated rewriting, see [1]. $\qquad\square$

6   Conclusions

We started investigations on regulated tree automata in this paper. This new way of looking at trees and regulated rewriting opens up quite an ample ground of research. Apart from the concrete open problems mentioned throughout the paper, which mostly also extend to the case admitting appearance checks, we ask the following, more concrete research questions.

- So far, we completely neglected studying closure properties or algorithmic questions of (variants of) regulated tree automata. It seems to be the case that the standard constructions for showing certain closure properties of regular tree languages (see [2]) transfer to the regulated case, but, moreover, we conjecture positive closure results for (general) tree homomorphisms, to give one concrete **open question** in this area.
- There are many relations between regulated rewriting and parallel rewriting; see [4,8]. We are not aware of a theory of parallel tree automata. We would also expect (again) relations to the question of accepting versus generating grammars [6]. Also, the area of grammar systems is barely touched [3,9, 10]. Due to the connections between regulated rewriting and cooperating distributed grammar systems (CDGS), see [3], these investigations might also stir some new interest in and even give some new proof ideas for some old open problems. For instance, it is still open whether (context-free) matrix languages can be characterized by CDGS working in $= k$-mode. Can results from tree automata be helpful here? We refer to [9] for results on cooperating distributed tree automata.
- Operations on trees have been one of the cornerstones for developing practically useful mechanisms [13] for formalizing *mild context-sensitivity*. The relations between, for instance, tree adjoining languages and variants of regulated context-free grammars have been largely unexplored until today. Apart

from this concrete question, we have the hope that combining tree processing with regulated rewriting mechanisms opens up new (practical) applications of regulated rewriting, also leading to new algorithmic questions.

Finally, we like to once more point to the various open problems in the area of classical regulated rewriting scattered throughout the paper. This should renew the interest of the Formal Language community in that area. We hope that the approach via considering tree languages might be a way to solve some of these problems. A crucial key to all these questions are normal forms. For instance, can ε-rules be removed as shown for random context grammars in [19]?

References

1. Bordihn, H., Fernau, H.: Accepting grammars with regulation. Int. J. Comput. Math. **53**(1–2), 1–18 (1994). https://doi.org/10.1080/00207169408804310
2. Comon, H., et al.: Tree Automata, Techniques and Applications (2007). http://tata.gforge.inria.fr/
3. Csuhaj-Varjú, E., Dassow, J., Kelemen, J., Păun, G.: Grammar Systems: A Grammatical Approach to Distribution and Cooperation. Gordon and Breach, Newark (1994). https://dl.acm.org/citation.cfm?id=561869
4. Dassow, J., Păun, G.: Regulated Rewriting in Formal Language Theory. EATCS Monographs in Theoretical Computer Science, vol. 18. Springer, Heidelberg (1989)
5. Doner, J.: Tree acceptors and some of their applications. J. Comput. Syst. Sci. **4**(5), 406–451 (1970). https://doi.org/10.1016/S0022-0000(70)80041-1
6. Fernau, H., Bordihn, H.: Remarks on accepting parallel systems. Int. J. Comput. Math. **56**, 51–67 (1995). https://doi.org/10.1080/00207169508804387
7. Fernau, H.: Graph-controlled grammars as language acceptors. J. Autom. Lang. Comb., pp. 79–91. (1997). https://doi.org/10.25596/jalc-1997-079
8. Fernau, H.: Parallel grammars: a phenomenology. Grammars **6**(1), 25–87 (2003). https://doi.org/10.1023/A:1024087118762
9. Fernau, H.: Cooperating distributed tree automata. In: Bordihn, H., Kutrib, M., Truthe, B. (eds.) Languages Alive; Dassow Festschrift. LNCS, vol. 7300, pp. 75–85. Springer, Heidelberg (2012). https://doi.org/10.1007/978-3-642-31644-9_5
10. Fernau, H., Holzer, M., Bordihn, H.: Accepting multi-agent systems: the case of cooperating distributed grammar systems. Comput. Artif. Intell. **15**, 123–139 (1996)
11. Freund, R., Kogler, M., Oswald, M.: A general framework for regulated rewriting based on the applicability of rules. In: Kelemen, J., Kelemenová, A. (eds.) Computation, Cooperation, and Life. LNCS, vol. 6610, pp. 35–53. Springer, Heidelberg (2011). https://doi.org/10.1007/978-3-642-20000-7_5
12. Gécseg, F., Steinby, M.: Tree Automata. Akadémiai Kiadó, Budapest (1984)
13. Kallmeyer, L.: Parsing Beyond Context-Free Grammars. Cognitive Technologies. Springer, Heidelberg (2010). https://doi.org/10.1007/978-3-642-14846-0
14. Meduna, A., Kolář, D.: Regulated pushdown automata. Acta Cybern. **14**(4), 653–664 (2000). http://www.inf.u-szeged.hu/actacybernetica/edb/vol14n4/Meduna2000ActaCybernetica.xml
15. Meduna, A., Zemek, P.: Regulated Grammars and Automata. Springer, New York (2014). https://doi.org/10.1007/978-1-4939-0369-6

16. Thatcher, J.W.: Characterizing derivation trees of context-free grammars through a generalization of finite automata theory. J. Comput. Syst. Sci. 1(4), 317–322 (1967). https://doi.org/10.1016/S0022-0000(67)80022-9
17. Vu, M.: Regulierte Grammatiken und regulierte Baumautomaten. Bachelorarbeit, Informatikwissenschaften, Universität Trier, Germany (2016)
18. Wood, D.: Bicolored digraph grammar systems. RAIRO Theor. Inform. Appl. 7(1), 45–52 (1973). http://www.numdam.org/article/M2AN_1973__7_1_45_0.pdf
19. Zetzsche, G.: On erasing productions in random context grammars. In: Abramsky, S., Gavoille, C., Kirchner, C., Meyer auf der Heide, F., Spirakis, P.G. (eds.) ICALP 2010. LNCS, vol. 6199, pp. 175–186. Springer, Heidelberg (2010). https://doi.org/10.1007/978-3-642-14162-1_15

Generalized de Bruijn Words and the State Complexity of Conjugate Sets

Daniel Gabric[1], Štěpán Holub[2], and Jeffrey Shallit[1($\boxtimes$)]

[1] School of Computer Science, University of Waterloo,
Waterloo, Ontario N2L 3G1, Canada
{dgabric,shallit}@uwaterloo.ca
[2] Department of Algebra, Faculty of Mathematics and Physics,
Charles University, Prague, Czech Republic
holub@karlin.mff.cuni.cz

Abstract. We consider a certain natural generalization of de Bruijn words, and use it to compute the exact maximum state complexity for the language consisting of the conjugates of a single word. In other words, we determine the state complexity of cyclic shift on languages consisting of a single word.

1 Introduction

Let x, y be words. We say x and y are *conjugates* if one is a cyclic shift of the other; equivalently, if there exist words u, v such that $x = uv$ and $y = vu$. For example, the English words `listen` and `enlist` are conjugates.

The set of all conjugates of a word x is denoted by $C(x)$. Thus, for example, $C(\mathtt{eat}) = \{\mathtt{eat}, \mathtt{tea}, \mathtt{ate}\}$. We also write $C(L)$ for the set of all conjugates of elements of the language L.

For a regular language L let $\mathrm{sc}(L)$ denote the *state complexity* of L: the number of states in the smallest complete DFA accepting L. State complexity is sometimes also called *quotient complexity* [5]. The state complexity of the cyclic shift operation $L \to C(L)$ for arbitrary regular languages L was studied in Maslov's pioneering 1970 paper [17]. More recently, Jirásková and Okhotin [14] improved Maslov's bound, and Jirásek and Jirásková studied the state complexity of the conjugates of prefix-free languages [13].

In this note we investigate the state complexity of the finite language $C(x)$, over all words x of length N. In other words, we determine the state complexity of cyclic shift on languages consisting of a single word. Clearly $\mathrm{sc}(C(x))$ achieves its minimum—namely, $N+2$—at words of the form a^N, where a is a single letter. By considering random words, it seems likely that $\mathrm{sc}(C(x)) = O(N^2)$.

M. Hospodár et al. (Eds.): DCFS 2019, LNCS 11612, pp. 137–146, 2019.
https://doi.org/10.1007/978-3-030-23247-4_10

Our main result makes this precise:

Theorem 1. *Let Σ_k be an alphabet of cardinality $k \geq 2$, and let $N \geq 1$ be an integer. Define $r = \lfloor \log_k N \rfloor$ and $v = (k^{r+1} - 1)/(k - 1)$. Then*

$$\max_{w \in \Sigma_k^n} \mathrm{sc}(C(w)) = 2v + N(N - 2r - 1) + 1.$$

Furthermore, we characterize those words x achieving this maximum.

Our theorem depends on a certain natural generalization of de Bruijn words, of independent interest, which is introduced in the next section.

2   Generalized de Bruijn Words

De Bruijn words (also called de Bruijn sequences) have a long history [3,4,8, 10,16], and have been extremely well studied [9,18]. Let Σ_k denote the k-letter alphabet $\{0, 1, \ldots, k - 1\}$. Traditionally, there are two distinct ways of thinking about these words: for integers $k \geq 2$, $n \geq 1$ they are

(a) the words w having each word of length n over Σ_k exactly once as a factor; or
(b) the words w having each word of length n over Σ_k exactly once as a factor, when w is considered as a "circular word", or "necklace", where the word "wraps around" at the end back to the beginning.

For example, for $k = 2$ and $n = 4$, the word

$$0000111101100101000$$

is an example of the first interpretation and

$$0000111101100101$$

is an example of the second.

In this paper, we are concerned with the second (circular) interpretation of de Bruijn words, and we write $D(k, n)$ for the set of all such words. Obviously, such words exist only for lengths of the form k^n. Is there a sensible way to generalize this class of words so that one could speak fruitfully of (generalized) de Bruijn words of every length?

One natural way to do so is to use the notion of *subword complexity* (also called *factor complexity* or just *complexity*). For $0 \leq i \leq N$ let $\gamma_i(w)$ denote the number of distinct length-i factors of the word $w \in \Sigma_k^N$ (considered circularly). For all words w, there is a natural upper bound on $\gamma_i(w)$ for $0 \leq i \leq N$, as follows:

$$\gamma_i(w) \leq \min(k^i, N). \tag{1}$$

This is immediate, since there are at most k^i words of length i over Σ_k, and there are at most N positions where a word could begin in w (considered circularly).

Ordinary de Bruijn words are then precisely those words w of length k^n for which $\gamma_n(w) = k^n$. But even more is true: $w \in D(k, n)$ also achieves the upper bound in (1) for *all* $i \leq k^n$. To see this, note that if $i \leq n$, then every word of length i occurs as a prefix of some word of length n, and every word of length n is guaranteed to appear in w. On the other hand, all k^n (circular) factors of each length $i \geq n$ are distinct, because their length-n prefixes are all distinct.

This motivates the following definition:

Definition 1. *A word x of length N over a k-letter alphabet is said to be a generalized de Bruijn word if $\gamma_i(x) = \min(k^i, N)$ for all $0 \leq i \leq N$.*

Table 1 gives the lexicographically least de Bruijn words for a two-letter alphabet, for lengths 1 to 31, and the number of such words (counted up to cyclic shift). This forms sequence A317586 in the *On-Line Encyclopedia of Integer Sequences* (OEIS) [20]. The second author has computed these numbers up to $N = 63$.

We point out an alternative characterization of our generalized de Bruijn words.

Proposition 1. *A word $w \in \Sigma_k^N$ is a generalized de Bruijn word iff both of the following hold:*

(a) $\gamma_r(w) = k^r$; and
(b) $\gamma_{r+1}(w) = N$,

where $r = \lfloor \log_k N \rfloor$.

Proof. A generalized de Bruijn word trivially has these properties. An argument similar to the discussion before Definition 1 shows that the two properties imply the bound in Eq. (1). □

The main result of this section is the following.

Theorem 2. *For all integers $k \geq 2$ and $N \geq 1$ there exists a generalized de Bruijn word of length N over a k-letter alphabet.*

Proof. For $k = 2$ the proof can be found in [19], although strangely it is not explicitly stated anywhere in the paper. (Lemma 3 implies it.)

For $k > 2$ we can derive this result from a paper by Lempel [15]. Lempel proved that for all $k \geq 2$, $n \geq 1$, $N \leq k^n$, there exists a circular word $w = w(k, n, N)$ of length N for which the factors of size n are distinct. (Also see [6,11].) However, as stated, this result is not strong enough for our purposes. For example, there are circular words, such as 000101 of length 6, having 6 distinct factors of length 4, but only 3 distinct factors of length 2. For our purposes, then, we need a stronger version of the result, which can nevertheless be obtained from a further analysis of Lempel's proof.

An *Eulerian graph* is a directed graph in which, for each vertex v, the indegree of v is equal to the outdegree of v. By a *closed chain* we mean a sequence of edges (a, v_1), (v_1, v_2), (v_2, v_3), $\ldots$, (v_{n-1}, a), where each edge is distinct, but

Table 1. Generalized de Bruijn words.

N	Lexicographically least generalized binary de Bruijn word of length N	Number of such words
1	0	2
2	01	1
3	001	2
4	0011	1
5	00011	2
6	000111	3
7	0001011	4
8	00010111	2
9	000010111	4
10	0000101111	3
11	00001011101	6
12	000010100111	13
13	0000100110111	12
14	00001001101111	20
15	000010011010111	32
16	0000100110101111	16
17	00000100110101111	32
18	000001001101011111	36
19	0000010100110101111	68
20	00000100101100111101	141
21	000001000110100101111	242
22	0000010001101001011111	407
23	00000100011001110101111	600
24	000001000110010101101111	898
25	0000010001100101011011111	1440
26	00000100011001010011101111	1812
27	000001000110010100111011111	2000
28	0000010001100101001110101111	2480
29	00000100011001010011101011111	2176
30	000001000110010110100111011111	2816
31	0000010001100101001110101101111	4096

vertices may be repeated. Each closed chain forms an Eulerian graph and each connected Eulerian graph admits a closed chain containing all its edges.

Let G_k^n be the k-ary de Bruijn graph of order n. This is a directed graph where the vertices are the words of length n, and edges join a word x to a word y if $x = at$ and $y = tb$ for some letters a, b and a word t. So every vertex of G_k^n has k incoming edges, and k outgoing edges, and therefore the underlying graph G_k^n is regular of degree $2k$. By Proposition 1, building a generalized de Bruijn word of length $N = k^n + j$, where $0 \leq j \leq (k-1)k^n$, over a k-letter alphabet then amounts to constructing a closed chain of length N in G_k^n that visits every vertex.

One of Lempel's main results [15, Theorem 1] states that such a closed chain exists, but does not mention explicitly whether it visits every vertex. In the proof, the chain is obtained by constructing a connected Eulerian graph using [15, Lemma 6]. Now, the analysis of the proof of [15, Lemma 6] shows that the constructed Eulerian graph is not only connected (which is the explicit concern of the lemma) but also spanning. The closed chain is eventually obtained as a complement of a graph G (denoted as T_p in [15]), where G is an Eulerian graph contained in G_k^n such that the degree of each vertex in G is at most $2(k-1)$. Therefore, its complement is obviously spanning.   □

Remark 1. We have not been able to find this precise notion of generalized de Bruijn word in the literature anywhere, although there are some papers that come very close. For example, Iványi [12] considered the analogue of Eq. (1) for ordinary (non-circular) words. He called a word w *supercomplex* if the analogue of the upper bound (1) is attained not only for w, but also for all prefixes of w. However, binary supercomplex words do not exist past length 9. The third author also considered the analogue of Eq. (1) for ordinary words [19]. However, Lemma 3 of that paper actually implies the existence of our generalized (circular) de Bruijn words of every length over a binary alphabet, although this was not stated explicitly. Anisiu, Blázsik, and Kása [2] discussed a related concept: namely, those length-N words w for which $\max_{1 \leq i \leq N} \rho_i(w) = \max_{x \in \Sigma_k^N} \max_{1 \leq i \leq N} \rho_i(x)$ where $\rho_i(w)$ denotes the number of distinct length-i factors of w (here considered in the ordinary sense, not circularly). Also see [7].

We now count the total number of factors of a generalized de Bruijn word. This is a generalization of Theorem 2 of [19] to all $k \geq 2$, adapted for the case of circular words.

Proposition 2. *If $w \in \Sigma_k^N$ is a generalized de Bruijn word, then*

$$\sum_{0 \leq i \leq N} \gamma_i(w) = \frac{k^{r+1} - 1}{k - 1} + N(N - r),$$

where $r = \lfloor \log_k N \rfloor$.

Proof. We have

$$\sum_{0 \leq i \leq N} \gamma_i(w) = \sum_{0 \leq i \leq N} \min(k^i, N)$$

$$= \sum_{0 \leq i \leq r} k^i + \sum_{r < i \leq N} N$$

$$= \frac{k^{r+1} - 1}{k - 1} + N(N - r).$$ □

3   State Complexity

We start with a general upper bound on state complexity.

Theorem 3. *Let Σ be an alphabet of cardinality $k \geq 2$ and let $L \subseteq \Sigma^N$. Define $m = |L|$, $r = \lfloor \log_k m \rfloor$ and $v = (k^{r+1} - 1)/(k - 1)$. If $N \geq 2r + 1$ then $\mathrm{sc}(L) \leq 2v + m(N - 2r - 1) + 1$.*

Proof. A *level* is a set of all nodes at a particular distance from the root. The complete k-ary tree of $r + 1$ levels therefore corresponds to words of length $\leq r$, and the total number of nodes in this tree is $1 + k + \cdots + k^r = \frac{k^{r+1}-1}{k-1}$.

The language L can be accepted by a DFA with the following topology: there is a complete k-ary tree of $r + 1$ levels rooted at the initial state p_ϵ. At the very next level there are at most m nodes, and these nodes form the roots of at most m chains of $N - 2r - 1$ nodes each. These chains need not be disjoint, but will be in the worst case. At the end, there is another complete k-ary tree of $r + 1$ levels culminating in a single accepting state. Finally, there is also a single non-accepting state that captures all transitions not yet defined. The total number of states is therefore $2v + m(N - 2r - 1) + 1$.

More formally, define

$$X = \Sigma^{\leq r} \cup \{x \ : \ r < |x| < N - r - 1 \text{ and } x \text{ is a prefix of an element of } L\}$$
$$Y = \{y \ : \ |y| = N - r - 1 \text{ and } y \text{ is a prefix of an element of } L\}$$

The states of our DFA are d, a "dead" state; p_x, for $x \in X$; and s_z, for all z with $|z| \leq r$. The states p_x correspond to prefixes of words of L and the states s_z correspond to suffixes of words of L.

The initial state is p_ϵ.

The transitions are given by $\delta(p_x, a) = p_{xa}$ for $x \in X$ and $a \in \Sigma$ and $\delta(p_y, a) = s_z$, if $y \in Y$ and $yaz \in L$; $\delta(s_{av}, a) = s_v$ for $v \in \Sigma^{<i}$ and $a \in \Sigma$. All other transitions go to d.

Finally, the unique final state is s_ϵ. $\square$

This construction is illustrated in Fig. 1 for $k = 2$, $N = 12$, $m = 10$, $r = 3$, $v = 15$, $N - 2r - 1 = 5$, and

$L = \{000010100000, 000101100010, 011110100001, 100110011111, 101011110111, \\ 110100100110, 110101010011, 110110101101, 111001100101, 111110110100\}.$

As a corollary, we now get an upper bound on $\mathrm{sc}(C(x))$:

Corollary 1. *If x is a word of length N over a k-letter alphabet, with $k \geq 2$, then*

$$\mathrm{sc}(C(x)) \leq 2v + N(N - 2r - 1) + 1,$$

where $r = \lfloor \log_k n \rfloor$ and $v = (k^{r+1} - 1)/(k - 1)$.

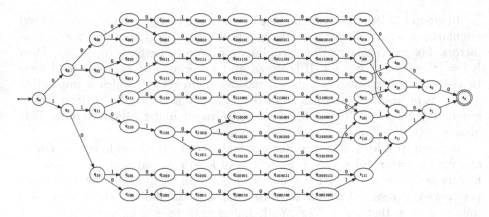

Fig. 1. Example of the construction.

Proof. Let x be a word of length N, and let $L = C(x)$. Set $m = |L| \le N$, $r = \lfloor \log_k N \rfloor$ and $v = (k^{r+1} - 1)/(k - 1)$. The inequality $N \ge 2r + 1$ holds in all cases except $k = 2$ and $n = 2$; this case can be checked separately. Theorem 3 therefore yields $\mathrm{sc}(L) \le 2v + N(N - 2r - 1) + 1$, as desired.   □

It now remains to prove that there exist words that achieve this upper bound. In fact, such words are exactly the generalized de Bruijn words defined in Sect. 2.

Theorem 4. *A length-N word x over a k-letter alphabet satisfies*

$$\mathrm{sc}(C(x)) = 2v + N(N - 2r - 1) + 1,$$

where $r = \lfloor \log_k N \rfloor$ and $v = (k^{r+1} - 1)/(k - 1)$ iff x is a generalized de Bruijn word.

Proof. Suppose x is a generalized de Bruijn word. We first show that there are $2v + N(N - 2r - 1) + 1$ inequivalent words for the Myhill-Nerode equivalence relation R associated with $C(x)$. This will show $\mathrm{sc}(C(x)) \ge 2v + N(N - 2r - 1) + 1$ and hence, by Corollary 1, that $\mathrm{sc}(C(x)) = 2v + N(N - 2r - 1) + 1$.

Representatives of the Myhill-Nerode classes can be classified as follows:

(a) all the words of length $\le r$;
(b) all the factors of conjugates of x of length ℓ, for $r < \ell < N - r$;
(c) for each word w of length $\le r$, the lexicographically least factor z of $C(x)$ of length $N - r$ for which $zw \in C(x)$;
(d) the single equivalence class corresponding to words not in $C(x)$.

There are v words in (a), and v words in (c), there are $N(N - 2r - 1)$ words in (b), and one word in (d).

We need to see that these are all inequivalent. Since all the words in $C(x)$ are of length N, no two factors of different lengths can be equivalent. It therefore suffices to examine pairs of words of identical length.

In group (a), let y, z be two distinct words of length $j \leq r$. Since x, considered circularly, contains all factors of length $r = \lfloor \log_k N \rfloor$, it contains y and z as factors. Let yy' (resp., zz') be a conjugate of x with prefix y (resp., z). Then $|y'| = |z'| = N - j \geq r + 1$. If both yz' and zz' occur in $C(x)$, we would have two separate occurrences of z' in x (considered circularly), which is impossible since x is of length N and has N distinct factors of length $N - j$ (considered circularly). So $yz' \notin C(x)$ and y, z are inequivalent under Myhill-Nerode. This gives $v = (k^{r+1} - 1)/(k - 1)$ equivalence classes.

In group (b), let y, z be two distinct factors of $C(x)$ (considered circularly) of length j with $r < j < N - r$. Since x is of length N and contains N distinct factors of length r, the first r symbols of y (resp., z) uniquely determine the position of y (resp., z) within x (considered as a circular word). So there is a unique y' such that $yy' \in C(x)$, and similarly, there is a unique z' such that $zz' \in C(x)$. Just as in case (a), since $|y'| = |z'| \geq r + 1$, we see that $y' \neq z'$. This gives $N(N - 2r)$ equivalence classes.

In group (c), for each word t of length $\leq r$, let x_t be the lexicographically least word of length $n - r$ such that $x_t t \in C(x)$. (We know such a word exists because each such t is a factor of x, considered circularly.) Let t, u be distinct words of length j. Then since $|x_t| \geq r + 1$, the word x_t occurs in exactly one location in x, considered circularly, and there it must be followed by t. So $x_t u \notin C(x)$, so x_t and x_u are inequivalent under Myhill-Nerode. This gives $v = (k^{r+1} - 1)/(k - 1)$ equivalence classes.

Now let us prove the reverse direction. Suppose x is such that $\mathrm{sc}(C(x)) = 2v + N(N - 2r - 1) + 1$. Then from the upper bound in Corollary 1 and the construction of Theorem 3 from which it is derived, we know that all the words corresponding to the states of the automaton in Theorem 3 are pairwise inequivalent under Myhill-Nerode. But there are k^r such words of length r and N such words of length $r + 1$. Hence, by Proposition 1, we have that x is a generalized de Bruijn word. $\square$

For $k = 2$ the maximum state complexity of $C(x)$ over length-N words x is given in Table 2 for $1 \leq N \leq 10$. It is sequence A316936 in the OEIS [20].

4   Final Comments

We do not currently know an accurate asymptotic expression for the number of generalized de Bruijn words of length N, except in few simple cases. If $N = k^n$, then it follows from known results [1] that this number is (counted up to cyclic shift) $(k!)^{k^{n-1}}/k^n$.

Thus far we represented generalized de Bruijn words of length $k^n + j$ as closed chains in G_k^n that visit each vertex. However, in the case of the ordinary de Bruijn word, it is well known that it is more convenient to represent such a word as an Eulerian path in the graph G_k^{n-1}. This exploits a natural correspondence between edges of G_k^{n-1} and vertices of G_k^n. This point of view helps to understand generalized de Bruijn words of length $k^n + 1$. They correspond to Eulerian paths

Table 2. Maximum state complexity of conjugates of binary words of length N.

N	$\max_{x \in \Sigma_2^N} \mathrm{sc}(C(x))$
1	3
2	5
3	7
4	11
5	15
6	21
7	29
8	39
9	49
10	61

in G_k^{n-1} where one edge is doubled. It is straightforward to see that the only edge which can be doubled so that the resulting graph remains Eulerian is a loop. Therefore, each generalized de Bruijn word of length $k^n + 1$ is obtained from an ordinary de Bruijn word of length k^n by replacing a factor a^{n-1} with a^n where a is a single letter. For $k = 2$, it follows that the number of such words is $2^{2^{n-1}}/2^{n-1}$. A similar argument yields the same number of generalized de Bruijn words of length $2^n - 1$.

Already for $k^n \pm 2$ these kinds of considerations become very complex. We leave this as a challenging open problem.

Acknowledgments. We thank the anonymous referees for helpful comments and suggestions.

References

1. van Aardenne-Ehrenfest, T., de Bruijn, N.G.: Circuits and trees in oriented linear graphs. Simon Stevin **28**, 203–217 (1951)
2. Anisiu, M., Blázsik, Z., Kása, Z.: Maximal complexity of finite words. Pure Math. Appl. **13**, 39–48 (2002)
3. de Bruijn, N.G.: A combinatorial problem. Proc. Konin. Neder. Akad. Wet. **49**, 758–764 (1946)
4. de Bruijn, N.G.: Acknowledgement of priority to C. Flye Sainte-Marie on the counting of circular arrangements of 2^n zeros and ones that show each n-letter word exactly once. Technical report 75-WSK-06, Department of Mathematics and Computing Science, Eindhoven University of Technology, The Netherlands (1975)
5. Brzozowski, J.A.: Quotient complexity of regular languages. J. Autom. Lang. Comb. **15**(1/2), 71–89 (2010). https://doi.org/10.25596/jalc-2010-071
6. Etzion, T.: An algorithm for generating shift-register cycles. Theoret. Comput. Sci. **44**, 209–224 (1986). https://doi.org/10.1016/0304-3975(86)90118-0

7. Flaxman, A., Harrow, A.W., Sorkin, G.B.: Strings with maximally many distinct subsequences and substrings. Electron. J. Combin. **11**(1), 8 (2004). http://www.combinatorics.org/Volume11/Abstracts/v11i1r8.html
8. Flye Sainte-Marie, C.: Question 48. L'Intermédiaire Math. **1**, 107–110 (1894)
9. Fredricksen, H.: A survey of full length nonlinear shift register cycle algorithms. SIAM Rev. **24**, 195–221 (1982). https://doi.org/10.1137/1024041
10. Good, I.J.: Normal recurring decimals. J. London Math. Soc. **21**, 167–169 (1946)
11. Hemmati, F., Costello Jr., D.J.: An algebraic construction for q-ary shift register sequences. IEEE Trans. Comput. **27**(12), 1192–1195 (1978). https://doi.org/10.1109/TC.1978.1675025
12. Iványi, A.: On the d-complexity of words. Ann. Univ. Sci. Budapest. Sect. Comput. **8**, 69–90 (1987)
13. Jirásek, J., Jirásková, G.: Cyclic shift on prefix-free languages. In: Bulatov, A.A., Shur, A.M. (eds.) CSR 2013. LNCS, vol. 7913, pp. 246–257. Springer, Heidelberg (2013). https://doi.org/10.1007/978-3-642-38536-0_22
14. Jirásková, G., Okhotin, A.: State complexity of cyclic shift. RAIRO Theor. Inform. Appl. **42**(2), 335–360 (2008). https://doi.org/10.1051/ita:2007038
15. Lempel, A.: m-ary closed sequences. J. Combin. Theory **10**, 253–258 (1971)
16. Martin, M.H.: A problem in arrangements. Bull. Am. Math. Soc. **40**, 859–864 (1934)
17. Maslov, A.N.: Estimates of the number of states of finite automata. Dokl. Akad. Nauk SSSR **194**(6), 1266–1268 (1970). In Russian. English translation in Soviet Math. Doklady **11**(5), 1373–1375 (1970)
18. Ralston, A.: De Bruijn sequences — a model example of the interaction of discrete mathematics and computer science. Math. Mag. **55**, 131–143 (1982). https://doi.org/10.2307/2690079
19. Shallit, J.: On the maximum number of distinct factors of a binary string. Graphs Combin. **9**(2–4), 197–200 (1993). https://doi.org/10.1007/BF02988306
20. Sloane, N.J.A. et al.: The on-line encyclopedia of integer sequences (2019). https://oeis.org

The Syntactic Complexity of Semi-flower Languages

Kitti Gelle and Szabolcs Iván[✉]

Department of Computer Science, University of Szeged, Szeged, Hungary
{kgelle,szabivan}@inf.u-szeged.hu

Abstract. Semi-flower languages are those of the form L^* for some finite maximal prefix code L, or equivalently, those recognizable by a so-called semi-flower automaton, in which all the cycles have a common state q_0, which happens to be the initial state and the only accepting state.

We show that the syntactic complexity of these languages is exactly $n^n - n! + n$ (where n stands for the state complexity as usual) and that this bound is reachable with an alphabet of size n.

1 Introduction

The state complexity of a regular language is the number of states of its minimal automaton, or equivalently, the number of classes of its syntactic right-congruence. The syntactic complexity of a language is the number of classes of its syntactic congruence, or equivalently, the size of the transition monoid of its minimal automaton.

It is clear (and already observed by Maslov [9]) that if a language has state complexity n, then it can have a syntactic complexity of at most n^n as there are only so many transformations of an n-element set. Moreover, as three functions (an elementary swap, a circular permutation and a rank-$(n-1)$ function) can generate all the transformations of a finite set, this maximal syntactic complexity can be reached by an automaton over a ternary alphabet. For the case of binary alphabets, Holzer and König [7] gave upper bounds for the maximal size of the transition monoid of an n-state minimal automaton while for the unary case and for the binary case for prime n, they determined a sharp bound.

When $\mathcal{C}$ is a class of regular languages, then its syntactic complexity is a function over the single integer variable n, namely it is the maximum possible syntactic complexity of a language belonging to $\mathcal{C}$ and having state complexity at most n. That is, for the whole class of the regular languages, this complexity is n^n. In the recent years, there is a growing interest of determining the syntactic complexity of subregular classes of languages (proper subclasses of the regular

S. Iván—Ministry of Human Capacities, Hungary grant 20391-3/2018/FEKUSTRAT is acknowledged. Szabolcs Iván was supported by the János Bolyai Scholarship of the Hungarian Academy of Sciences.

M. Hospodár et al. (Eds.): DCFS 2019, LNCS 11612, pp. 147–157, 2019.
https://doi.org/10.1007/978-3-030-23247-4_11

languages), e.g. for ideal and prefix- or factor closed languages [6], prefix-, suffix-, bifix- and factor-free languages [4], several classes of star-free languages [3], R- and J-trivial languages [2], regular ideals [5] amongst others.

It is also an interesting question to determine the alphabet size needed to reach the maximum possible syntactic complexity: for the whole class of regular languages, an alphabet of ternary size suffices, but e.g. for factor-closed languages an alphabet of size 6 is needed [4], while for bifix-free languages $(n - 2)^{n-3} + (n - 3)2^{n-3} - 1$ generators are needed if $n \geq 6$ [13].

In the recent years, Singh and Krishna initiated the investigation of semi-flower automata [10–12], which are the minimal automata of valid code words over a finite maximal prefix code. In particular, in [12] they showed that if a circular semi-flower automaton over a binary alphabet has a single "branching point in", or bpi (a state q is called a bpi if there are at least two tuples $(p, a) \in Q \times \Sigma$ with $pa = q$), then it has a linear syntactic complexity, and if it possesses exactly two bpis, then $2n(n + 1)$ is a sharp bound on its syntactic complexity. Clearly, this is a serious restriction: it essentially restricts the elementary transformations to a circular permutation and some semi-flower transformation of rank at most 2 (for the definitions, see the Notation section). They also remark that over a ternary alphabet there exists a semi-flower automaton with two bpis having larger syntactic complexity than $2n(n + 1)$.

In this paper we determine that the syntactic complexity of languages recognizable by semi-flower automata (without placing any restriction on the number of their "branch points going in") is $n^n - n! + n$ and show that this bound is reachable by an alphabet of size n.

2 Notation and Some Facts

We assume the reader has some knowledge in automata and formal language theory (a standard resource is [8]). In this paper an *automaton* is a triple $\mathcal{A} = (Q, \Sigma, \cdot)$ with Q and Σ being the finite sets of *states* and *input symbols* or *letters*, and $\cdot$ is an action $Q \times \Sigma \to Q$, written in infix notation: $q \cdot a$ for $q \in Q$ and $a \in \Sigma$. The action is extended to words acting on the states in the usual unique way as $q \cdot \varepsilon = q$ for the empty word ε and $q \cdot (ua) = (q \cdot u) \cdot a$ for each word $u \in \Sigma^*$ and $a \in \Sigma$. The transformation $q \mapsto q \cdot u$ for the word $u \in \Sigma^*$ is denoted as $u^{\mathcal{A}}$. The action is also extended to sets of states as $Q' \cdot u = \{q \cdot u : q \in Q'\}$.

When $f : Q \to Q$ is a transformation of some set Q, and $q \in Q$ is a member of its domain, then we often write $q \cdot f$ for $f(q)$, that is, writing the function application as a right action, moreover, for composing functions we define $f \circ g$ as $q \mapsto (q \cdot f) \cdot g$ (note the order). This way it holds that $(uv)^{\mathcal{A}} = u^{\mathcal{A}} \circ v^{\mathcal{A}}$.

We denote the transition monoid of an automaton $\mathcal{A} = (Q, \Sigma, \cdot)$ by $T(\mathcal{A})$, that is, $T(\mathcal{A})$ is the monoid over the set $\{u^{\mathcal{A}} : u \in \Sigma^*\} \subseteq Q^Q$, equipped by function composition where $u^{\mathcal{A}} \circ v^{\mathcal{A}} = (uv)^{\mathcal{A}}$. For a function $f : Q \to Q$, let rank(f) stand for $|Qf|$, the size of the image of f.

The automaton $\mathcal{B} = (Q, \Delta, \bullet)$ is a *renaming* of the automaton $\mathcal{A} = (Q, \Sigma, \cdot)$ if for each $b \in \Delta$ there exists some $b' \in \Sigma$ with $b^{\mathcal{B}} = (b')^{\mathcal{A}}$. Since in that case

$(b_1 \ldots b_k)^{\mathcal{B}} = (b'_1 \ldots b'_k)^{\mathcal{A}}$ for each k and $b_1, \ldots, b_k \in \Delta$, we get that $T(\mathcal{B})$ is a submonoid of $T(\mathcal{A})$. The automaton $\mathcal{B} = (Q', \Sigma, \bullet)$ is a *sub-automaton* of $\mathcal{A} = (Q, \Sigma, \cdot)$ if $Q' \subseteq Q$ and the action of $\mathcal{B}$ is the restriction of the action of $\mathcal{A}$: $q \bullet a = q \cdot a$ for each $q \in Q'$ and $a \in \Sigma$. The automaton $\mathcal{B}$ is a *homomorphic image* or *quotient* of $\mathcal{A}$ if there exists some surjective mapping $h : Q \to Q'$ such that $h(q \cdot a) = h(q) \bullet a$. If the mapping h is a bijection, then the two automata are *isomorphic*. An automaton which is a homomorphic image of a subautomaton of $\mathcal{A}$ is called a *divisor* of $\mathcal{A}$.

An automaton $\mathcal{A} = (Q, \Sigma, \cdot)$ is *minimal* with respect to some initial state $q_0 \in Q$ and a set $F \subseteq Q$ of final states if $\{q_0 \cdot u : u \in \Sigma^*\} = Q$ and for each pair $p \neq q$ of distinct states, there exists a word $u \in \Sigma^*$ with either $pu \in F$ and $qu \notin F$ or $pu \notin F$ and $qu \in F$.

The *language recognized* by $\mathcal{A} = (Q, \Sigma, \cdot)$ from $q_0 \in Q$ with $F \subseteq Q$ is the set $L(\mathcal{A}, q_0, F) = \{u \in \Sigma^* : q_0 \cdot u \in F\}$ of words. A language $L \subseteq \Sigma^*$ is *recognizable* or *regular* if $L = L(\mathcal{A}, q_0, F)$ for some finite automaton $\mathcal{A}$, initial state q_0 and set F of final states. It is well-known that for any regular language L there exists a minimal automaton $\mathcal{A}_L$ which recognizes L from some initial state with some set of final states, moreover, $\mathcal{A}_L$ divides every automaton in which L can be recognized.

$\mathcal{A}$ is called a *semi-flower automaton* [10] (in short, SFA) if all cycles in $\mathcal{A}$ have a common state. An automaton $\mathcal{A}$ is called *circular* if some letter acts as a circular permutation on the states of $\mathcal{A}$, and is a *circular semi-flower automaton*, CSFA in short [11], if it is both circular and semi-flower.

Clearly, any circular automaton $\mathcal{A} = (Q, \Sigma, \cdot)$ is minimal with respect to any initial state $q_0 \in Q$ and the set $F = \{q_0\}$ of final states: if a induces a circular permutation in $\mathcal{A}$, then we have $Q = \{q_0 \cdot a^k : 0 \leq k < n\}$ where $n = |Q|$. On the other hand, if $p = q_0 \cdot a^k$ and $q = q_0 \cdot a^t$ are distinct states, then $p \cdot a^{n-k} = q_0$ while $q \cdot a^{n-k} \neq q_0$.

Let $[n]$ stand for the set $\{1, \ldots, n\}$. We call a function $f : [n] \to [n]$ a *semi-flower transition* over $[n]$ if $i < i \cdot f$ for each $1 \leq i < n$. We denote the rotation operation by $+$: for a state $i \in [n]$ and an integer k, let $i + k$ stand for $((i + k - 1) \mod n) + 1$. In particular, $n + 1 = 1$, and the mapping $i \mapsto i + 1$ (which happens to be a circular permutation) is a semi-flower transition.

The following proposition relates circular semi-flower automata and semi-flower transitions:

Proposition 1. *An automaton $\mathcal{A}$ over some alphabet Σ is a semi-flower automaton if and only if it is isomorphic to some automaton of the form $([n], \Sigma, \cdot)$ such that each letter induces a semi-flower transition over $[n]$.*

This latter form is called a normal form *of semi-flower automata.*

Proof. If each letter induces a semi-flower transition over $[n]$ in $\mathcal{A} = ([n], \Sigma, \cdot)$ then we claim that each cycle contains the state n.

Indeed, let $p_1 \xrightarrow{a_1} p_2 \xrightarrow{a_2} \ldots \xrightarrow{a_k} p_{k+1} = p_1$ be a cycle in $\mathcal{A}$. Then $p_i \geq p_{i+1}$ for some i, which, as a_i induces a semi-flower transition, can happen only if $p_i = n$. Thus, $\mathcal{A}$ is semi-flower.

For the other direction, assume $\mathcal{A} = (Q, \Sigma, \cdot)$ is an n-state semi-flower automaton and let $q_n \in Q$ be a common state of all the cycles of $\mathcal{A}$. Then, considering the graph G with vertex set $V = Q - \{q_n\}$ and edge set $\{(p, pa) : a \in \Sigma, p, pa \in V\}$ we get that G is a directed acyclic graph, hence its vertices can be ordered as $q_1 < q_2 < \ldots < q_{n-1}$ such that for each edge (p, q) of G we have $p < q$. Then, the mapping $q_i \mapsto i$ establishes an isomorphism between $\mathcal{A}$ and a semi-flower automaton in normal form. $\qquad\square$

Clearly, if $\mathcal{A}$ is a *circular* semi-flower automaton in normal form, then the letter a inducing a circular permutation of $[n]$ has to induce the function $i \mapsto i+1$ as this is the only semi-flower permutation over $[n]$.

3   Minimal Circular Semi-flower Automata and Syntactic Complexity

A language L is a *semi-flower language* if $L = L(\mathcal{A}, q_0, \{q_0\})$ for some semi-flower automaton $\mathcal{A} = (Q, \Sigma, \cdot)$ and state $q_0 \in Q$, which is a common state of all cycles of $\mathcal{A}$.

A language $P \subseteq \Sigma^+$ is a *prefix code* if there are no words $u, v \in P$ with u being a proper prefix of v, and is a *maximal prefix code* if additionally, for any word $w \notin P$, the set $P \cup \{w\}$ is not prefix-free anymore. If P is a maximal prefix code, $u \in \Sigma^*$ is a proper prefix of some member of P and $a \in \Sigma$ is a letter, then ua is still a (not necessarily proper) prefix of some member of P. A good reference on codes is [1].

It holds that semi-flower languages are exactly languages of the form P^* for some finite maximal prefix code $P \subseteq \Sigma^+$. Indeed, given $L = L(\mathcal{A}, q_0, \{q_0\})$ for the semi-flower automaton $\mathcal{A}$, we can take the language

$$P = \{u \in \Sigma^* : q_0 u = q_0, q_0 v \neq q_0 \text{ for any proper nonempty prefix } v \text{ of } u\}$$

which is a finite language since otherwise some cycle would avoid the initial-final state q_0. For the other direction, for a finite maximal prefix-free language P one can take the state set as $Q = \{u \in \Sigma^* : u \text{ is a proper prefix of some } v \in P\}$, define the action as $u \cdot a = \varepsilon$ if $ua \in P$ and ua otherwise, and pick ε as q_0, the resulting semi-flower automaton recognizes the language P^*.

The syntactic complexity of a class $\mathcal{L}$ of regular languages is a unary function over the single variable n: for each n, its value is defined as

$$\max\left\{|T(\mathcal{A}_L)| : L \in \mathcal{L} \text{ and } \mathcal{A}_L \text{ has at most } n \text{ states}\right\}.$$

Since up to isomorphism and renaming there is only a finite number of automata having at most n states, this notion is well-defined for any class $\mathcal{L}$ of regular languages.

In this paper we show that the syntactic complexity of semi-flower languages is exactly $n^n - n! + n$ by analyzing the size of $T(\mathcal{A})$ for a particular (circular) semi-flower automaton $\mathcal{A} = \mathcal{A}_n$ for each n.

4   The Transition Monoid of Semi-flower Automata

If in an n-state automaton $\mathcal{A}$, no letter acts as a permutation on the state set, then its transition monoid does not contain any nontrivial permutation, thus in that case, $|T(\mathcal{A})| \leq n^n - n! + 1$.

Clearly, if some letter induces a permutation in a semi-flower automaton, then it has to be a circular permutation (otherwise there would be two disjoint cycles in its graph). So in the remaining part of the section we deal with the transition monoid of an n-state *circular* semi-flower automaton.

Let us begin by handling the permutations present in $T(\mathcal{A})$ when $\mathcal{A}$ is a circular semi-flower automaton.

Proposition 2. *If $f : Q \to Q$ is a permutation belonging to $T(\mathcal{A})$ for some circular semi-flower automaton $\mathcal{A}$ over the state set Q, in which a induces a circular permutation, then f is induced by some word of the form a^k where $0 \leq k < n$.*

Proof. Let us assume $\mathcal{A} = ([n], \Sigma, \cdot)$ is in the normal form specified by Proposition 1. Since the only permutation which is a semi-flower transition is the transformation $i \mapsto i + 1$, $b^{\mathcal{A}}$ has to be this function for each letter b inducing a permutation.

Also, if $f = (b_1 b_2 \ldots b_k)^{\mathcal{A}}$ is a permutation, then each $b_i^{\mathcal{A}}$ has to be a permutation, thus $f = (a^k)^{\mathcal{A}}$ in that case for some k and, as $(a^n)^{\mathcal{A}}$ is the identity map, we get $f = (a^k)^{\mathcal{A}}$ for some $0 \leq k < n$. $\square$

Note that there are n such permutations, so $T(\mathcal{A})$ contains n permutations and all its other members have rank less than n. Hence, the absolute maximum syntactic complexity an n-state (circular) semi-flower automaton can have is $n^n - n! + n$. In the rest of the paper we show that this bound is attainable.

Let us fix $n \geq 1$, the state set $Q = [n]$ and the n-state automaton $\mathcal{A} = (Q, \Sigma, \cdot)$ for the rest of the section, where

$$\Sigma = \{b_i : i \in [n]\}$$

where for each $i \in [n]$, the action of b_i is defined as

$$j \cdot b_i = \begin{cases} j + 1, & \text{if } j < n; \\ i, & \text{otherwise.} \end{cases}$$

Since all the functions $b_i^{\mathcal{A}}$ are semi-flower transitions over $[n]$, $\mathcal{A}$ is a semi-flower automaton over n letters. Observe that b_1 induces the circular permutation $i \mapsto i+1$, thus $\mathcal{A}$ is a circular semi-flower automaton. To make a visual distinction, we also refer to b_1 as a and to ease notation, we frequently identify the mapping $b^{\mathcal{A}}$ with the letter b.

In the rest of the section we aim to show that $T(\mathcal{A})$ contains all the transformations of $[n]$ with rank less than n. Since the circular permutation induced by a is also present, we also have n permutations in $T(\mathcal{A})$ by Proposition 2, so this yields $|T(\mathcal{A})| = n^n - n! + n \geq n^n - n! + 1$, proving that the syntactic complexity of semi-flower languages is $n^n - n! + n$ as well (and this bound is attainable by a circular semi-flower automaton over n letters.)

In the following, we show that several fundamental transformations, as "merging" two states, or "swapping" two states of some proper subset of the state set, each belong to $T(\mathcal{A})$.

Lemma 3. *For all $p, q \in Q$, the function $f_{p,q} : Q \to Q$, where $p \cdot f = q$ and for all $r \neq p$ we have $r \cdot f = r$, belongs to $T(\mathcal{A})$.*

Proof. Let us consider the function $f = a^{n-p} \circ b_{q+n-p+1} \circ a^{p-1}$. (Here $q+(n-p+1)$ is understood with the rotation operation from the Notation section, so this value is a member of $[n]$).

Clearly, for p we have $p \cdot a^{n-p} = n$, $n \cdot b_{q+n-p+1} = q+n-p+1$ (in the rotating sense) and $(q+n-p+1) \cdot a^{p-1} = q+n = q$, so that $p \cdot f = q$. On the other hand, for any $r \neq p$ we have $r \cdot a^{n-p} = r+n-p \neq n$ so $(r+n-p) \cdot b_{q+n-p+1} = r+n-p+1$ and $(r+n-p+1) \cdot a^{p-1} = r+n = r$. Thus indeed, $r \cdot f = r$ for each $r \neq p$.

For an example, see Fig. 1.   □

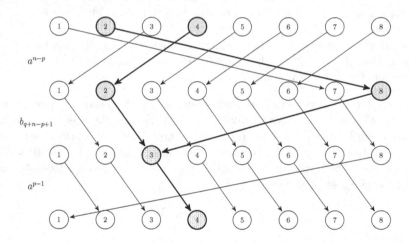

Fig. 1. The semi-flower transitions creating a function $f_{p,q}$ which merges two states (Here $p = 2, q = 4$).

As a corollary we can collapse the kernel of any transformation of Q, each kernel class to one member of the class. (Recall that the kernel of a function $f : Q_1 \to Q_2$ is the equivalence relation $\sim_f$ over Q_1 defined as $p \sim_f q \Leftrightarrow pf = qf$.)

Corollary 4. *For any transformation $f : Q \to Q$, there exists some function $g \in T(\mathcal{A})$ such that*

- *for each $p, q \in Q$, $pf = qf$ if and only if $pg = qg$;*
- *for each $p \in Q$, $pgf = pf$.*

In other words, g associates to each state $q \in Q$ a representative state of the class of q in the kernel of f.

Proof. Lemma 3 states $f_{p,q}$ is a member of $T(\mathcal{A})$ for each $p, q \in Q$.

Let $C \subseteq Q$ be a nonempty set of states. We claim that there exists some function $g_C \in T(\mathcal{A})$ and a state $p \in C$ such that $C \cdot g_C = \{p\}$ and $r \cdot g_C = r$ for each $r \notin C$. Indeed, let $C = \{q_1, \ldots, q_k\}$. If C is a singleton, then the identity function trivially satisfies the conditions, so assume $|C| > 1$.

Then the function $f_{q_1,q_k} \circ f_{q_2,q_k} \circ \ldots \circ f_{q_{k-1},q_k}$ satisfies the claim with $p = q_k$.

Hence, for any transformation $f : Q \to Q$, if $C_1, \ldots, C_k \subseteq Q$ are the classes of the kernel of f (that is, the sets C_i give a partition of Q and for each $p, q \in Q$, $p \cdot f = q \cdot f$ if and only if p and q belong to the same C_i), then the function $g = g_{C_1} \circ \ldots \circ g_{C_k}$ satisfies the conditions of the corollary. $\square$

The next lemma states that if we have some proper subset Q' of the states, then we can swap two of these states and retain the other members of Q' in their original place with some function from $T(\mathcal{A})$:

Lemma 5. *Assume $Q' \subsetneq Q$ is some subset of the states and $p, q \in Q'$. Then some function $f : Q \to Q$ satisfying $p \cdot f = q$, $q \cdot f = p$ and $r \cdot f = r$ for all $r \in Q' - \{p, q\}$ belongs to $T(\mathcal{A})$.*

Proof. If $p = q$, then the claim holds trivially as the identity belongs to $T(\mathcal{A})$ so we can assume $p \neq q$.

By $|Q'| < n$, there exists some state $\ell \notin Q'$. We claim that the function $f = f_{p,\ell} \circ f_{q,p} \circ f_{\ell,q}$ satisfies the conditions of the Lemma. Indeed, if $r \notin \{p, q, \ell\}$, then none of the functions involved moves r, so that $r \cdot f = r$ for each $r \in Q' - \{p, q\}$; and clearly, $p \cdot f_{p,\ell} = \ell$, $\ell \cdot f_{q,p} = \ell$ and $\ell \cdot f_{\ell,q} = q$ shows $p \cdot f = q$ and similarly $q \cdot f_{p,\ell} = q$, $q \cdot f_{q,p} = p$ and $p \cdot f_{\ell,q} = p$ shows $q \cdot f = p$.

So this $f \in T(\mathcal{A})$ satisfies the conditions of the lemma.

For an example, see Fig. 2. $\square$

Now in order to show an arbitrary function $f : Q \to Q$ with rank less than n, we dissect f as $f = f_1 \circ \pi \circ g$ where f_1 collapses the kernel classes of f into their representative elements (we can do that according to Corollary 4), π is an appropriate permutation on these representatives (Lemma 6 ensures the existence of such a suitable permutation in $T(\mathcal{A})$), and g is a "monotone" mapping (Lemma 7 will ensure that $g \in T(\mathcal{A})$).

Lemma 6. *For each $Q' \subsetneq Q$ and permutation $\pi : Q' \to Q'$ there exists some $f \in T(\mathcal{A})$ extending π: $q \cdot f = q \cdot \pi$ for each $q \in Q'$.*

Proof. By Lemma 5 we get that for any *transposition* t swapping two states of Q' there exists some member belonging to $T(\mathcal{A})$ which extends t. Since every permutation π can be written as a composition of transpositions, and $T(\mathcal{A})$ is closed under composition, we get that each permutation of $Q' \subsetneq Q$ can be extended to some member of $T(\mathcal{A})$. $\square$

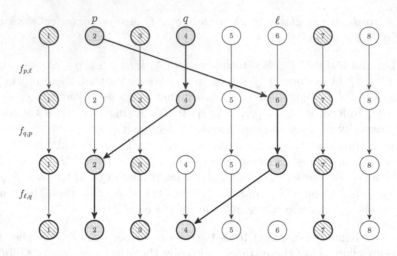

Fig. 2. Steps for building a swap function for two states (here $p = 2, q = 4$) from semi-flower transitions. The marked states belong to Q'.

For the sets $Q' \subseteq Q$, let us call a mapping $f : Q' \to Q$ *monotone* if $i < j$, $i, j \in Q'$ implies $i \cdot f < j \cdot f$. Our next lemma states that all the monotone maps belong to $T(\mathcal{A})$.

Lemma 7. *For each set $Q' \subseteq Q$ and monotone mapping $f : Q' \to Q$ there exists some $f' \in T(\mathcal{A})$ extending f.*

Proof. The statement is vacuously satisfied when $Q' = \emptyset$ so assume $Q' \neq \emptyset$.

For two functions $f, g : Q' \to Q$, let us define $d(f, g)$ as $\sum_{q \in Q'} |q \cdot f - q \cdot g|$. We show that if for two monotone functions $f, g : Q' \to Q$ we have $d(f, g) > 0$, and g has some extension $g_* \in T(\mathcal{A})$, then there also exists some monotone function $g' : Q' \to Q$ having an extension $g'_* \in T(\mathcal{A})$ with $d(f, g') < d(f, g)$. As this distance can only have nonnegative integer values, and the identity function is a monotone function belonging to $T(\mathcal{A})$ (so we can start the induction somewhere), this proves the statement.

So let us consider two monotone functions $f, g : Q' \to Q$ with $d(f, g) > 0$. This means that there exists some state $q \in Q'$ with $q \cdot f \neq q \cdot g$. Let us choose q so that $q' \cdot f = q' \cdot g$ for each $q' < q$.

There are two cases: either $q \cdot f < q \cdot g$ or $q \cdot g < q \cdot f$.

If $q \cdot f < q \cdot g$, then no state r with $q \cdot f \leq r < q \cdot g$ can be in the image of g: by monotonicity, $p \cdot g = r < q \cdot g$ would yield $p < q$ but by the choice of q, $p \cdot g = p \cdot f < q \cdot f$ holds in that case. By Lemma 3, the function $g_0 = f_{q \cdot g, q \cdot f}$ belongs to $T(\mathcal{A})$, and $q \cdot (g \circ g_0) = (q \cdot g) \cdot g_0 = q \cdot f$, and since g is injective, we have $q' \cdot g \neq q \cdot g$ if $q' \neq q$, so that $q' \cdot g \cdot g_0 = q' \cdot g$ for each $q' \in Q'$. Observe also that $g \circ g_0$ is still a monotone function. As $g \circ g_0$ belongs to $T(\mathcal{A})$ if so does g, and $d(f, g \circ g_0) < d(f, g)$, this proves the claim in this subcase.

If $q \cdot g < q \cdot f$, then consider the following sequence $q = q_0 < q_1 < \ldots$ of members of Q': first, let us set $q_0 = q$, then for each $t \geq 0$, if $(q_t \cdot g) + 1$ belongs to the image of g, say $p \cdot g = (q_t \cdot g) + 1$ for the state $p \in Q'$, then let us set $q_{t+1} = p$, otherwise let q_t be the terminating element of the sequence.

As g is a monotone function, we get that $q_t < q_{t+1}$ holds for each t where the sequence is defined for q_{t+1}. Thus, the sequence has to be finite. Moreover, by construction, the sequence $q_0 \cdot g, q_1 \cdot g, \dots$ contains consecutive states by definition for the states $q_0 < q_1 < \dots$, thus, by $q_0 \cdot g < q_0 \cdot f$, applying induction we get $q_t \cdot g < q_t \cdot f$ for each valid index t. Hence, for the last state q_t of the sequence we have by construction that $q_t \cdot g < q_t \cdot f$ and that $(q_t \cdot g) + 1$ does not belong to the image of g. (Observe that being less than $q_t \cdot f$, the state $q_t \cdot g$ cannot be n.) By Lemma 3, the function $g_0 = f_{q_t \cdot g, (q_t \cdot g)+1}$ belongs to $T(\mathcal{A})$ so again, for the monotone function $g \cdot g_0$ we get $q_t \cdot g \cdot g_0 = (q_t \cdot g) + 1$ and for any other member q of Q', $q \cdot g = q \cdot g \cdot g_0$. Again, $g \circ g_0$ belongs to $T(\mathcal{A})$ if so does g, and $d(f, g \circ g_0) < d(f, g)$, proving this subcase and the lemma as well. $\square$

Lemma 8. *For each $Q' \subsetneq Q$ and injective mapping $f : Q' \to Q$ there exists some $g \in T(\mathcal{A})$ extending f.*

Proof. Let $Q' = \{q_1, \dots, q_k\}$ with $q_1 < \dots < q_k$ and let $\pi : Q' \to Q'$ be the unique permutation with $q_i \cdot \pi \cdot f < q_{i+1} \cdot \pi \cdot f$ for each $1 \leq i < k$. (That is, $q_i \cdot \pi$ is q_j if and only if $q_i \cdot f$ is the jth least element of $Q' \cdot f$.)

Then $f = \pi \circ f'$ for the monotone map $f' : Q' \to Q$ with $q_i \cdot f' = (q_i \cdot \pi^{-1}) \cdot f$, hence by Lemmas 6 and 7 there is some function $g \in T(\mathcal{A})$ extending f (Fig. 3). $\square$

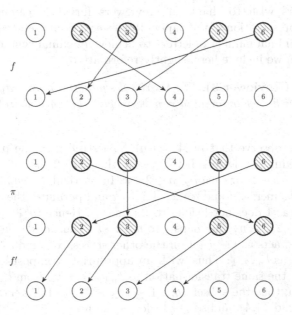

Fig. 3. Example of the decomposition $f = \pi \cdot f'$. The marked states are belonging to Q'.

Equipped with our lemmas, we can prove the main theorem of the present paper:

Theorem 9. *The monoid $T(\mathcal{A})$ contains all the transformations of $[n]$ having rank less than n, thus $|T(\mathcal{A})| = n^n - n! + n$ is the syntactic complexity of the semi-flower languages.*
This bound can be reached by an alphabet of size n for each n.

Proof. Let $f : Q \to Q$ be a function with $\mathrm{rank}(f) < n$. By Corollary 4, there exists some function $g \in T(\mathcal{A})$ mapping each state to a representative of its kernel class, that is, with some $Q' \subsetneq Q$, $|Q'| = \mathrm{rank}(f)$ such that $Q \cdot g = Q'$, satisfying $q \cdot g \cdot f = q \cdot f$ for each state $q \in Q$, moreover, with $p \cdot f = q \cdot f$ implying $p \cdot g = q \cdot g$. Then, let f' denote the restriction of f to Q'. Then, by construction, f' is an injective mapping from Q' to Q, thus it has an extension $g' \in T(\mathcal{A})$ by Lemma 8. Thus, for the mapping $h = g \circ g'$ we have $q \cdot h = q \cdot g \cdot g' = q \cdot g \cdot f' = q \cdot g \cdot f = q \cdot f$ for each state $q \in Q$, proving the theorem. $\square$

5   Conclusion

We showed that the syntactic complexity of semi-flower languages is exactly $n^n - n! + n$ and that in order to reach this complexity, an alphabet of linear size suffices. We left open the question whether n letters are needed to achieve this or maybe an even smaller alphabet suffices.

The authors wish to thank the reviewers for their careful work which improved the presentation of the paper. Reviewer 3 even sketched a proof showing that the minimal number of letters to achieve maximal syntactic complexity is $\lceil \frac{n+1}{2} \rceil$, which we include here, slightly reformatted.

Theorem 10 (Reviewer 3). *The maximal syntactic complexity $n^n - n! + n$ of an n-state semi-flower automaton can be reached by an alphabet of size $\lceil \frac{n+1}{2} \rceil$ and this bound is sharp.*

Proof. One can observe that in $\mathcal{A} = ([n], \Sigma, \cdot)$ studied in the previous section still contains redundant letters. If $1 < k < n$, then $(n+2-k) \cdot a^{k-2} \cdot b_k = k$ while $i \cdot a^{k-2} \cdot b_k = i + k - 1$ for each $i \neq n + 2 - k$. In particular, the image of $i = 1$ is also k, so $a^{k-2}b_k$ merges 1 and $n+2-k$ into k and permutes the $(n-1)$-element set $\{2, \ldots, n\}$ (as 1 does not belong to its image). Hence $(a^{k-2}b_k)^{(n-1)!}$ acts as the identity on $\{2, \ldots, n\}$ and maps 1 to $n+2-k$. Thus, $a(a^{k-2}b_k)^{(n-1)!}$ maps n to $n+2-k$ and acts as $i \mapsto i+1$ on the other states, so it induces the the same transformation as b_{n+2-k}. Thus, with an appropriate composition of b_1 and b_2 one can induce the same transformation as $b_{n+2-2} = b_n$, from b_1 and b_3 we get b_{n-1} and so on, thus the subset $\{b_i : 1 \leq i \leq \lceil \frac{n+1}{2} \rceil\}$ of Σ generates the same transition monoid $T(\mathcal{A})$, and so $\lceil \frac{n+1}{2} \rceil$ letters suffice.

On the other hand, assume $\mathcal{A} = ([n], \Delta, \cdot)$ is a semi-flower automaton in normal form. Let us define the distance of two states $p \leq q \in [n]$ as $d(p,q) = \min\{q - p, n + p - q\}$, that is, their "circular" distance and if $p > q$, then let

$d(p,q) = d(q,p)$. Clearly, $d(p,q) = d(pa, qa)$ whenever a has rank n. Assume $w = a_1 \ldots a_k$ induces a transformation of rank $n - 1$. Then there is a least index $i \in [k]$ such that a_i induces a transformation of rank $n - 1$ and each a_j, $j < i$ induces the permutation $\ell \mapsto \ell+1$. Let $p \neq q$ be the states merged by a_i and p', q' be the states with $p'a_1 \ldots a_{i-1} = p$ and $q'a_1 \ldots a_{i-1} = q$. Then, w merges the states p' and q' whose distance is $d(p', q') = d(p, q)$ depending only on a_i. Hence, if $T(\mathcal{A})$ contains all the transformations of rank $n - 1$, then for each possible distance $D > 0$, the alphabet Δ has to contain at least one letter of rank $n - 1$ merging two states of distance D. Since there are $\lfloor \frac{n}{2} \rfloor$ possible distances on the cycle of length n, along with the letter inducing the circular permutation an alphabet of size at least $\lfloor \frac{n}{2} \rfloor + 1 = \lceil \frac{n+1}{2} \rceil$ is needed in a circular semi-flower automaton to generate all the transformations of rank $(n - 1)$. $\square$

References

1. Berstel, J., Perrin, D., Reutenauer, C.: Codes and Automata (Encyclopedia of Mathematics and Its Applications). Cambridge University Press, New York (2009). https://dl.acm.org/citation.cfm?id=1708078
2. Brzozowski, J., Li, B.: Syntactic complexity of R- and J-trivial regular languages. Int. J. Found. Comput. Sci. **25**(07), 807–821 (2014). https://doi.org/10.1142/S0129054114400097
3. Brzozowski, J., Li, B., Liu, D.: Syntactic complexities of six classes of star-free languages. J. Autom. Lang. Comb. **17**(2), 83–105 (2012)
4. Brzozowski, J.A., Li, B., Ye, Y.: Syntactic complexity of prefix-, suffix-, bifix-, and factor-free regular languages. Theoret. Comput. Sci. **449**, 37–53 (2012). https://doi.org/10.1016/j.tcs.2012.04.011. Preliminary version at DCFS 2011
5. Brzozowski, J.A., Szykuła, M., Ye, Y.: Syntactic complexity of regular ideals. Theory Comput. Syst. **62**(5), 1175–1202 (2018). https://doi.org/10.1007/s00224-017-9803-8
6. Brzozowski, J.A., Ye, Y.: Syntactic complexity of ideal and closed languages. In: Mauri, G., Leporati, A. (eds.) DLT 2011. LNCS, vol. 6795, pp. 117–128. Springer, Heidelberg (2011). https://doi.org/10.1007/978-3-642-22321-1_11
7. Holzer, M., König, B.: On deterministic finite automata and syntactic monoid size. Theoret. Comput. Sci. **327**(3), 319–347 (2004). https://doi.org/10.1016/j.tcs.2004.04.010
8. Hopcroft, J.E., Ullman, J.D.: Introduction to Automata Theory, Languages and Computation. Addison-Wesley, Reading (1979)
9. Maslov, A.N.: Estimates of the number of states of finite automata. Dokl. Akad. Nauk SSSR **194**, 1266–1268 (1970). in Russian. English translation in Soviet Math. Doklady **11**(5), 1373–1375 (1970)
10. Singh, S.N.: Semi-Flower Automata. Ph.D. thesis, IIT Guwahati, India (2012)
11. Singh, S.N., Krishna, K.V.: The holonomy decomposition of some circular semi-flower automata. Acta Cybernet. **22**(4), 791–805 (2016). https://doi.org/10.14232/actacyb.22.4.2016.4
12. Singh, S.N., Krishna, K.V.: On syntactic complexity of circular semi-flower automata. In: Câmpeanu, C. (ed.) CIAA 2018. LNCS, vol. 10977, pp. 312–323. Springer, Cham (2018). https://doi.org/10.1007/978-3-319-94812-6_26
13. Szykuła, M., Wittnebel, J.: Syntactic complexity of bifix-free regular languages. Theoret. Comput. Sci. (2019, to appear). https://doi.org/10.1016/j.tcs.2018.12.025

Limited Nondeterminism of Input-Driven Pushdown Automata: Decidability and Complexity

Yo-Sub Han[1], Sang-Ki Ko[2], and Kai Salomaa[3(✉)]

[1] Department of Computer Science, Yonsei University, 50, Yonsei-Ro,
Seodaemun-Gu, Seoul 120-749, Republic of Korea
emmous@yonsei.ac.kr
[2] AI Research Center, Korea Electronics Technology Institute, Seongnam,
Gyeonggi-do, Republic of Korea
sangkiko@keti.re.kr
[3] School of Computing, Queen's University, Kingston, Ontario K7L 3N6, Canada
ksalomaa@cs.queensu.ca

Abstract. We study the decidability and computational complexity for several decision problems related to limited nondeterminism of finite-state automata equipped with a pushdown stack. Ambiguity and tree width are two measures of nondeterminism considered in the literature. As a main result, we prove that the problem of deciding whether or not the tree width of a nondeterministic pushdown automaton is finite is decidable in polynomial time. We also prove that the k-tree width problem for nondeterministic input-driven pushdown automata (respectively, nondeterministic finite automata) is complete for exponential time (respectively, for polynomial space).

Keywords: Nondeterminism · Tree width · Ambiguity ·
Input-driven pushdown automata

1 Introduction

Nondeterminism plays a fundamental role in automata and formal language theory. There have been various ways to quantify the nondeterminism of automaton models [8,9,12,17,18]. For instance, the expressive power of finite automata is the same even if we allow the use of nondeterminism since both deterministic (DFA) and nondeterministic finite automata (NFA) accept the class of regular languages. However, the descriptional complexity of minimal DFAs and NFAs accepting the same regular language differs significantly as it is well-known that the determinization of NFAs causes an exponential blow-up in size of the resulting DFAs in the worst-case.

On the other hand, for some models such as pushdown automata, the expressive power of the automata is strictly increased if we allow the use of nondeterminism. In other words, there exist (context-free) languages that can be

© IFIP International Federation for Information Processing 2019
Published by Springer Nature Switzerland AG 2019
M. Hospodár et al. (Eds.): DCFS 2019, LNCS 11612, pp. 158–170, 2019.
https://doi.org/10.1007/978-3-030-23247-4_12

described by a nondeterministic pushdown automaton (NPDA) and not by a determinististic PDA (DPDA).

The *ambiguity* of a nondeterministic machine means the number of accepting computations on an input string. An NFA is said to be an *unambiguous finite-state automaton (UFA)* if it has a unique accepting computation on every accepted string. Obviously, every DFA is an UFA. Similarly, there are *finitely ambiguous automata* where the number of accepting computations is bounded by a constant. For the remaining automata that have an unbounded number of accepting computations, we can further distinguish between *polynomially ambiguous* and *exponentially ambiguous* depending on the relationship between the length of the string and the number of accepting computations on the string [14]. Chan and Ibarra [5] proved that the problem of deciding whether or not the ambiguity of a given NFA is bounded by a given integer k is PSPACE-complete. They also showed that the problem of deciding whether or not the ambiguity of an NFA is bounded by a constant can be solved in polynomial space by applying a matrix algorithm. Later, Weber and Seidl [20] presented a polynomial time algorithm for the problem by observing a simple criterion which characterizes the infinite degree of ambiguity of an NFA.

There is another approach for quantifying the nondeterminism of automata models called *leaf size* [3,12], *path size* [16,17], or *tree width* [18]. The tree width means the total number of (complete and incomplete) computations on an input string regardless of the acceptance of the string. Palioudakis et al. [18] considered NFAs having finite tree width where the computation on any input string has a constant number of branches. They gave effective characterizations of such NFAs and a tight bound for the determinization as a function of the tree width and the size of an NFA. They also revealed that the problem of deciding whether or not a given NFA has finite tree width is decidable in polynomial time.

Okhotin and Salomaa [17] studied the descriptional complexity of determinizing an NIDPDA that has limited nondeterminism. They called an NIDPDA with at most k computations on any input a k-*path NIDPDA*. In other words, the tree width of the NIDPDA is bounded by k. It is known that the size of the smallest DIDPDA obtained from an NIDPDA of size n is $2^{\Theta(n^2)}$ [2] but in the case of a k-path NIDPDA, the determinization yields a DIDPDA of size at most $\Theta(n^k)$. They also provided an algorithm for deciding whether or not a given NIDPDA has the k-path property and showed that the problem is P-complete for a fixed k. Finally, Caralp et al. [4] studied the decision problems regarding the ambiguity of NIDPDAs by investigating an interesting extension of IDPDAs. They proposed an extension of IDPDAs by means of positive integer weights associated with transitions. Then, they define the *multiplicity* of an NIDPDA as the supremum of multiplicities over all possible input strings, which is defined as the degree of ambiguity here. They proved that the k-*boundedness problem* (the problem of deciding whether or not the ambiguity is bounded by k) is EXPTIME-complete (complete for exponential time) and the *finiteness problem* (the problem of deciding whether or not the ambiguity is bounded by a constant) is solvable in polynomial time.

We study several unsolved cases of the complexity and decidability questions related to limited nondeterminism for computational models such as NFAs, NID-PDAs, and NPDAs. For instance, the decidability of the problem of deciding whether or not a given NIDPDA has finite tree width (i.e., finite path size) has been left open in [17]. We complete the complexity and decidability landscape presented in Table 1 regarding the decision problems about the ambiguity and the tree width of NFAs, NIDPDAs, and NPDAs. In Sect. 2, we give basic definitions and notations that are used throughout the paper. Section 3 provides the results on the decision problems for the tree width and ambiguity of NPDAs. In Sect. 4, we present the new results on the decision problems for the tree width of NIDPDAs and NFAs. Lastly, Sect. 5 concludes the paper.

Table 1. The complexity landscape of decision problems regarding the nondeterminism in NFAs, NIDPDAs, and NPDAs. Our results are written in bold. We assume that the integer k is given as part of input and represented in unary notation.

Problem	For NPDAs		For NIDPDAs	For NFAs
k-ambiguity	**Undecidable (Proposition 4)**		EXPTIME-c [4]	PSPACE-c [5]
k-tree width	$k \geq 3$	Undecidable [17]	**EXPTIME-c**	**PSPACE-c**
	$k < 3$	P **(Proposition 3)**	**(Theorem 5)**	**(Theorem 6)**
Finite tree width	P **(Theorem 2)**		P **(Theorem 2)**	P [18]
Finite ambiguity	Undecidable [10,21]		P [4]	P [20]

2 Preliminaries

We briefly present definitions and notations used throughout the paper. The reader may refer to the textbooks [11,19,21] for complete knowledge of automata and formal language theory.

Let Σ be a finite alphabet and Σ^* be a set of all strings over Σ. A language over Σ is any subset of Σ^*. The symbol $\emptyset$ denotes the empty language, the symbol λ denotes the null string and Σ^+ denotes $\Sigma^* \setminus \{\lambda\}$.

A *nondeterministic finite automaton* (NFA) is specified by a quintuple $A = (\Sigma, Q, q_0, F, \delta)$ where Σ is a finite alphabet, Q is a finite set of states, q_0 is the initial state, $F \subseteq Q$ is the set of final states and δ is a multi-valued transition function from $Q \times \Sigma$ into 2^Q. The automaton A is *deterministic* (a DFA) if δ is a (single-valued) function $Q \times \Sigma \to Q$. It is well known that the NFAs and DFAs all recognize the regular languages [7,19,21].

A *nondeterministic pushdown automaton* (NPDA) is specified by a tuple $P = (Q, \Sigma, \Gamma, \delta, q_0, Z_0, F)$, where Q is a finite set of states, Σ is a finite input alphabet, Γ is a finite stack alphabet, $\delta : Q \times (\Sigma \cup \{\lambda\}) \times \Gamma \to 2^{Q \times \Gamma^{\leq 2}}$ is a transition function, $q_0 \in Q$ is the start state, Z_0 is the initial stack symbol and $F \subseteq Q$ is the set of final states. Our definition restricts that each transition of P has at most two stack symbols, that is, each transition can push or pop at most one symbol. We use $|\delta|$ to denote the number of transitions in δ.

A *configuration* of an NPDA P is a triple (q, w, v), where $q \in Q$ is the current state, $w \in \Sigma^*$ is the remaining input, and $v \in \Gamma^*$ is the contents on the stack. Denote the set of configurations of P by $C(P)$ and we define the single step computation relation as $\vdash_P \subseteq C(P) \times C(P)$. The language $L(P)$ is the set of strings accepted by P.

Consider $q, p \in Q$, $b \in (\Sigma \cup \lambda)$, $X \in \Gamma$ and $u \in \Gamma^*$. If $(p, u) \in \delta(q, b, X)$, we say that $(q, b, X) \rightarrow (p, u)$ is a transition of P, and it is called a λ-transition if $b = \lambda$ (i.e., a λ-transition does not consume an input symbol). For $q \in Q$, $b \in (\Sigma \cup \lambda)$ and $X \in \Gamma$, a transition $(q, b, X) \rightarrow (p, u)$ is *nondeterministic* if

1. for some $(p', u') \neq (p, u)$, $(p', u') \in \delta(q, b, X)$, or,
2. b is an element of Σ and $\delta(q, \lambda, X) \neq \emptyset$, or,
3. $b = \lambda$ and there exists $c \in \Sigma$ such that $\delta(q, c, X) \neq \emptyset$.

A transition $(q, b, X) \rightarrow (p, u)$ is nondeterministic if, roughly speaking, the tuple (q, b, X) allows the NPDA to make also a different transition.

The question whether a λ-transition involves a nondeterministic step may depend on what is the next input symbol and we need to be a little more precise in the definition. A λ-transition $(q, \lambda, X) \rightarrow (p, u)$ is said to be *inherently nondeterministic* if there exist $(p', u') \neq (p, u)$ such that $(p', u') \in \delta(q, \lambda, X)$ (i.e., the case 1. holds). A λ-transition $(q, \lambda, X) \rightarrow (p, u)$ which is not inherently nondeterministic, is said to be Z-*nondeterministic*, $\emptyset \neq Z \subseteq \Sigma$, if the set Z consists of all alphabet symbols $c \in \Sigma$ such that $\delta(q, c, X) \neq \emptyset$. Note that applying an inherently nondeterministic λ-transition always involves a nondeterministic step. Applying a Z-nondeterministic ($Z \subseteq \Sigma$) λ-transition involves a nondeterministic step only if the next input symbol belongs to Z.

A *nondeterministic input-driven pushdown automaton* (NIDPDA) [1,15,17] is a restricted version of an NPDA, where the input alphabet Σ consists of three disjoint classes, Σ_c, Σ_r, and Σ_l. Namely, $\Sigma = \Sigma_c \cup \Sigma_r \cup \Sigma_l$. The class where the input symbol belongs to determines the type of stack operation: The automaton always pushes a symbol onto the stack when it reads a *call symbol* in Σ_c. If the input symbol is a *return symbol* in Σ_r, the automaton pops a symbol from the stack. Finally, the automaton neither uses the stack nor even examines the content of the stack for the *local symbols* in Σ_l. Formally, the input alphabet is defined as $\widetilde{\Sigma} = (\Sigma_c, \Sigma_r, \Sigma_l)$, where three components are finite disjoint sets.

An NIDPDA is formally defined by a tuple $A = (\widetilde{\Sigma}, \Gamma, Q, q_0, F, \delta_c, \delta_r, \delta_l)$, where $\Sigma = \Sigma_c \cup \Sigma_r \cup \Sigma_l$ is the input alphabet, Γ is the finite set of stack symbols, Q is the finite set of states, $q_0 \in Q$ is the start state, $F \subseteq Q$ is the set of final states, $\delta_c : Q \times \Sigma_c \rightarrow 2^{Q \times \Gamma}$ is the transition function for the push operations, $\delta_r : Q \times (\Gamma \cup \{\bot\}) \times \Sigma_r \rightarrow 2^Q$ is the transition function for the pop operations, and $\delta_l : Q \times \Sigma_l \rightarrow 2^Q$ is the local transition function. We use $\bot \notin \Gamma$ to denote the top of an empty stack. The single step transition relation $\vdash_A$ of an NIDPDA A is described as follows:

- **Push operation:** $(q, aw, v) \vdash_A (q', w, \gamma v)$ for all $a \in \Sigma_c, (q', \gamma) \in \delta_c(q, a), \gamma \in \Gamma, w \in \Sigma^*$ and $v \in \Gamma^*$.

- **Pop operation:** $(q, aw, \gamma v) \vdash_A (q', w, v)$ for all $a \in \Sigma_r, q' \in \delta_r(q, \gamma, a), \gamma \in \Gamma, w \in \Sigma^*$ and $v \in \Gamma^*$; furthermore, $(q, aw, \lambda) \vdash_A (q', w, \lambda)$, for all $a \in \Sigma_r, q' \in \delta_r(q, \bot, a)$ and $w \in \Sigma^*$.
- **Local operation:** $(q, aw, v) \vdash_A (q', w, v)$, for all $a \in \Sigma_l, q' \in \delta_l(q, a), w \in \Sigma^*$ and $v \in \Gamma^*$.

An *initial configuration* of an NIDPDA $A = (\widetilde{\Sigma}, \Gamma, Q, s, F, \delta_c, \delta_r, \delta_l)$ is (s, w, λ), where s is the start state and w is an input word. an NIDPDA accepts a word if A arrives at a final state by reading the word from the initial configuration. Formally, we write the language recognized by A as

$$L(A) = \{w \in \Sigma^* \mid (s, w, \lambda) \vdash_A^* (q, \lambda, v) \text{ for some } q \in F, v \in \Gamma^*\}.$$

We call the languages recognized by NIDPDAs the *input-driven pushdown languages*. The class of input-driven pushdown languages is a strict subclass of deterministic context-free languages and a strict superclass of regular languages. While many closure properties such as complement and intersection do not hold for context-free languages, input-driven pushdown languages are closed under most operations including other basic operations such as concatenation, union, and Kleene-star.

Below we use NPDA to define various nondeterminism measures since the same definition holds for NIDPDA and NFA as they are special cases of NPDA.

Computation Trees and Tree Width [18] **(a.k.a. Path Size** [16]**).** Let us consider an NPDA $A = (Q, \Sigma, \Gamma, \delta, q_0, Z_0, F)$ and be $C = (q, w, y)$, where $q \in Q$ is a state, $w \in \Sigma^*$ is the remaining input, and $y \in \Gamma^*$ is the current stack contents, be a configuration of A. Then, the initial configuration of the NPDA A on a string w is $C_0 = (q_0, w, Z_0)$. If a configuration C in one computation step of A yields configurations $C_1, \ldots, C_m, m \geq 0$, we denote it by $C \vdash_A (C_1, \ldots, C_m)$. For example, the successor configurations of a configuration $C = (q, bu, Xs)$ are obtained by applying m different transitions applicable to triple (q, b, X) and also by applying λ-transitions applicable to (q, λ, X). Now the *computation tree* of A on input w is defined as follows:

1. the root node is labelled by the initial configuration C_0;
2. if a node v is labelled by a configuration C and $C \vdash_A (C_1, \ldots, C_m), m \geq 0$, then the node v has m children that are labelled, respectively, by $C_1, \ldots, C_m$ in the computation tree;
3. if a node v is labelled by configuration C and no computation step is defined in C, then the node v is a leaf node.

Intuitively, the tree width measure counts the number of partial computations on a given input and for NFAs it is normally defined in terms of the number of leaves of the computation tree. However, since an NPDA A may have infinite cycles caused by λ-transitions we define the *tree width of A* on an input w, $\mathrm{tw}_A(w)$, as the maximal number of pairwise independent nodes in the computation tree of A on w. (For automaton models that do not allow infinite cycles, such as NFAs or NIDPDAs, this value coincides with the number of leaves of the computation tree.)

The (maximum) tree width of A on strings of length m is defined as $\mathrm{tw}_A(m) = \max\{\mathrm{tw}_A(w) \mid w \in \Sigma^m\}$. The tree width of A is finite if the values $\mathrm{tw}_A(m)$, where $m \in \mathbb{N}$, are bounded and in that case we denote $\mathrm{tw}_A^{\mathrm{sup}} = \sup_{m \in \mathbb{N}} \mathrm{tw}_A(m)$.

Note that we can define the tree width of any other nondeterministic devices exactly in the same way. (For devices without a pushdown stack, we just omit the third component.) We say that an NPDA A has tree width k if the tree width of A on any string is at most k and there exists a string w where the tree width of A on w is k, that is, if $\mathrm{tw}_A^{\mathrm{sup}} = k$.

Ambiguity [5,20]. An automaton (which can be either an NFA, an NPDA, or an NIDPDA) A is *unambiguous* if any string has at most one accepting computation. The degree of ambiguity of A on a string w is the number of accepting computations of A on w and denoted by $\mathrm{da}_A(w)$. More formally, $\mathrm{da}_A(w)$ is the number of leaves of the computation tree of A on w that are labeled by accepting configurations.

The *degree of ambiguity* of A on strings of length m is defined as $\mathrm{da}_A(m) = \max\{\mathrm{da}_A(w) \mid w \in \Sigma^m\}$. The degree of ambiguity of A is finite if the values $\mathrm{da}_A(m)$, where $m \in \mathbb{N}$, are bounded as follows: $\mathrm{da}_A^{\mathrm{sup}} = \sup_{m \in \mathbb{N}} \mathrm{da}_A(m)$.

The automaton A is *unambiguous* if $\mathrm{da}_A^{\mathrm{sup}} = 1$. Clearly, every deterministic automaton is unambiguous.

3   Problems on Tree Width and Ambiguity for NPDAs

Okhotin and Salomaa [17] show that deciding whether a given NPDA has tree width (at most) k is undecidable for $k \geq 3$. Additionally, it is shown in [17] that for a given $k \in \mathbb{N}$ one can decide in polynomial time whether or not the tree width of a given NIDPDA is k. However, the question whether we can decide whether the tree width of a given NIDPDA is finite is left open in [17].

We give an algorithm that decides finiteness of tree width in polynomial time even for general NPDAs. The crucial observation is that, in fact, the algorithm does not need to rely on specific properties of input-driven computation and, instead, it is sufficient to check for an NPDA M whether some nondeterministic transition can be used an unbounded number of times, that is, the tree width of M is infinite if and only if in computations of M some nondeterministic transition can be used an unbounded number of times.

The above property is stated formally in Lemma 1 and the proof of the lemma follows directly from the definition of computation trees and tree width using the fact that the number of transitions is finite.

For λ-transitions we have to be a little more precise in defining the use of a nondeterministic transition. In the below lemma when saying that computation on input w *uses a nondeterministic transition* $(q, \lambda, X) \to (p, u)$ this means that either (i) the λ-transition is inherently nondeterministic, or (ii) the λ-transition is Z-nondeterministic and the next input character belongs to $Z \subseteq \Sigma$.

Lemma 1. *For an NPDA M, $\mathrm{tw}_M^{\mathrm{sup}}$ is infinite if and only if there exists a nondeterministic transition $(q, b, X) \to (p, u)$ of M such that for all $c \in \mathbb{N}$ there*

exists a word w such that M has a computation on w that uses the transition
$(q, b, X) \to (p, u)$ *as a nondeterministic transition*[1] *more than c times.*

Theorem 2. *We can decide whether or not the tree width of a given NPDA is finite in polynomial time.*

Proof. Let $P = (Q, \Sigma, \Gamma, \delta, q_0, Z_0, F)$ be an NPDA. By Lemma 1, the tree width of P is infinite if and only if there exist computations that use an unbounded number nondeterministic steps involving some nondeterministic transition $(q, b, X) \to (p, u)$ where $q, p \in Q$, $b \in \Sigma \cup \{\lambda\}$, $X \in \Gamma$, $u \in \Gamma^*$. Consequently we can decide whether or not the tree width of P is infinite by finding such a transition. A technical issue we need to take care of is that a Z-nondeterministic ($Z \subseteq \Sigma$) λ-transition involves a nondeterministic step only if the next input character belongs to Z.

Consider $q, p \in Q$, $b \in \Sigma \cup \{\lambda\}$, $X \in \Gamma$ and $u \in \Gamma^*$ such that the transition $t = (q, b, X) \to (p, u)$ is nondeterministic. When $b = \lambda$, this means that either $(q, \lambda, X) \to (p, u)$ is inherently nondeterministic or it is Z-nondeterministic for some $\emptyset \neq Z \subseteq \Sigma$. From the given NPDA P, for a nondeterministic transition t we construct a new NPDA P_t which, roughly speaking, reads a character only when simulating a nondeterministic step of P involving the transition t.

We have three cases to consider. In cases 1. and 2. the set of states of P_t will be the same as the set of states of the original NPDA P but in the third case P_t will need additional states.

1. When $t = (q, b, X) \to (p, u)$ is not a λ-transition, i.e., $b \in \Sigma$, we construct the NPDA P_t by replacing the input labels of all transitions except the transition t by λ and replacing the set of final states by the singleton set $\{q\}$.
2. If $b = \lambda$ and $t = (q, \lambda, X) \to (p, u)$ is inherently nondeterministic, P_t is constructed from P by replacing the input labels of all transitions other than t by λ and, furthermore, the transition t is replaced by $(q, \$, X) \to (p, u)$ where \$ is a new input symbol.
3. Suppose then that $t = (q, \lambda, X) \to (p, u)$ is Z-nondeterministic for $\emptyset \neq Z \subseteq \Sigma$, i.e., t is not inherently nondeterministic. If Q is the state set of P, the states of P_t will have a second component, i.e., state set of P_t is $Q \times \{0, 1\}$. The purpose of the second components is just to enforce that after applications of t that are "counted as a nondeterministic transition", the next real transition of P that is simulated must use an input symbol in the set Z.
   In real transitions $t' = (r, d, Y) \to (s, v)$, $d \in \Sigma$, the input symbols are again replaced by λ. More precisely, if $d \notin Z$, t' is replaced by $((r, 0), \lambda, Y) \to ((s, 0), v)$ and if $d \in Z$, t' is replaced by both $((r, 0), \lambda, Y) \to ((s, 0), v)$ and

$$((r, 1), \lambda, Y) \to ((s, 0), v). \tag{1}$$

   λ-transitions $t' = (r, \lambda, Y) \to (s, v)$ that are distinct from t are replaced by $((r, 0), \lambda, X) \to ((s, 0), v)$ and $((r, 1), \lambda, X) \to ((s, 1), v)$. Finally, the transition t itself is replaced by $((q, 0), \$, X) \to ((p, 1), u)$, $((q, 1), \$, X) \to ((p, 1), u)$, and $((q, 0), \lambda, X) \to ((p, 0), u)$.

---

[1] This is explained in the paragraph before the lemma. Whether or not a λ-transition involves a nondeterministic step may depend on the next input symbol.

In cases 1. and 2. it is clear that P_t accepts an infinite number of input strings if and only if P has computations that use the transition t an unbounded number of times. Note that in case 1. and 2. all applications of the transition t are nondeterministic.

The construction in the case 3. enforces that P_t accepts an infinite number of strings if and only if P has computations that use t *as a nondeterministic transition* an unbounded number of times. This is verified as follows. The only real (non-λ) transitions of P_t are

$$((q,0),\$,X) \to ((p,1),u) \text{ and } ((q,1),\$,X) \to ((p,1),u).$$

Thus, applying a real transition of P_t changes the second component of the state to 1 (or makes the second component remain 1 if it was 1 already). When the second component of the state is one, only transitions that simulate a λ-transition of P can be applied until we apply a transition (1) that simulates a real transition of P on $d \in Z$, that is, on an input symbol with respect to which the λ-transition t is nondeterministic.

Our algorithm constructs the NPDA P_t for each nondeterministic transition t of P. Thus, we can decide whether the tree width of P is infinite by checking whether for some nondeterministic transition t the language $L(P_t)$ is infinite. Otherwise, our algorithm answers that the tree width of P is finite. We describe the process in pseudocode in Algorithm 1.

Algorithm 1. Algorithm deciding the finiteness of the tree width of P

Input   : An NPDA $P = (Q, \Sigma, \Gamma, \delta, q_0, Z_0, F)$
Output: Finiteness of the tree width of P
foreach transition t of P **do**
   if t is nondeterministic **then**
      Construct P_t from P;
      if $|L(P_t)| = \infty$ **then**
        | **return** False
      end
   end
end
return True

Clearly, our algorithm terminates in polynomial time since testing the finiteness of a context-free language can be done in polynomial time. First we convert an NPDA into a context-free grammar using the standard triple construction [11] and again convert the grammar into the Chomsky normal form. Then, we draw a dependency graph with nodes labeled by nonterminals of the context-free grammar. For instance, if there is a rule such as $S \to AB|BC|a$, we draw edges from S to A, B and C. Now we can decide whether or not the context-free grammar generates an infinite number of strings by finding any cycle from the nonterminal dependency graph. Since we repeat the above procedure $|Q|^2 \cdot (|\Sigma|+1) \cdot |\Gamma|^3$ times in the worst case, the total procedure terminates in polynomial time. Strictly speaking, instead of all transitions, it is sufficient to enumerate the left sides of the transitions and the above estimation can obviously be improved.   □

Thus, for a given NPDA we can decide in polynomial time whether the tree width is finite and deciding whether the tree width equals $k \geq 3$ is undecidable [17]. Next we consider the remaining case of k being 1 or 2.

Proposition 3. *For a given NPDA P and an integer $k \in \{1, 2\}$, it is decidable whether or not the tree width of P is bounded by k in polynomial time.*

Proof. Consider the case when $k = 1$. Given an NPDA $P = (Q, \Sigma, \Gamma, \delta, q_0, Z_0, F)$ and a transition of P, we can check whether the transition is useful by changing the target state of the transition to the only final state of P and checking whether the modified NPDA accepts any string. Since the emptiness of an NPDA can be decided in polynomial time, we can find useful transitions in polynomial time. Then, we check whether or not there exists a nondeterministic transition which is useful in P. If there is such a transition, we can decide that the tree width of P is not bounded by 1 because we can reach the state and choose a transition between two choices.

Let us consider the case when $k = 2$. Similarly to the previous case, we first find useful transitions from P. If there exists a useful transition with at least 3 nondeterministic choices, then the tree width is at least 3. Otherwise, we need to check whether a nondeterministic transition is reachable from another nondeterministic transition.

First we choose a nondeterministic useful transition of P that corresponds to a tuple (q, a, A). We modify P by replacing the labels of all transitions by λ except the chosen transition and change the target state, say p, of the chosen transition to p' which is the created copy of p. Let us change the label of the chosen transition to a special symbol $\star$, where $\star \notin \Sigma \cup \{\lambda\}$.

So far, the only transition with a non-empty label is the chosen transition. Then, we choose a nondeterministic useful transition from the copied NPDA and change the target state of the transition to the only final state. It is easy to verify that the only string that can be accepted by the constructed NPDA is $\star$ after two nondeterministic choices. Since there are a polynomial number of pairs of nondeterministic transitions of P and the acceptance of the string $\star$ can be decided in polynomial time, we can decide whether or not the tree width of P is bounded by 2 in polynomial time.   □

Harrison [10] shows using a reduction from the Post Correspondence Problem that it is undecidable whether a context-free grammar G is ambiguous and a simple modification of the proof shows that finite ambiguity is undecidable for context-free grammars.[2] By converting the grammars to pushdown automata it follows that the same property is undecidable for NPDAs.

For the sake of completeness, we show below that for an NPDA P it is undecidable whether the ambiguity of P is bounded by a fixed $k \in \mathbb{N}$. The proof

---

[2] For original references see Wood [21].

is modified from a construction showing that deciding the exact tree width of an IDPDA is undecidable [17].

Let $\Sigma = \{a, b\}$. Recall that an instance of the Post Correspondence Problem (PCP) is a set of pairs of words $I = \{(u_1, v_1), \ldots, (u_n, v_n)\} \subseteq \Sigma^* \times \Sigma^*$, $n \geq 1$, and a solution to the instance I a sequence of indices $\ell_1, \ldots, \ell_k$ with each $1 \leq \ell_i \leq n$ such that: $u_{\ell_1} \cdots u_{\ell_k} = v_{\ell_1} \cdots v_{\ell_k}$. It is well known that for a given PCP instance I it is undecidable to determine whether or not I has a solution [10,11,19,21].

Proposition 4. *Let $k \geq 1$ be fixed. For a given NPDA P it is undecidable whether or not the degree of ambiguity of P is bounded by k.*

4   Problems on Tree Width for NIDPDAs and NFAs

It is known that we can decide whether or not the tree width of an NIDPDA is bounded by a fixed integer k in polynomial time [17]. However, for the complexity of deciding whether tree width is bounded by a variable k, only an EXP-TIME upper bound has been known.

Theorem 5. *Given an NIDPDA A and an integer $k \geq 1$, the problem of determining whether or not the tree width of A is bounded by k is EXPTIME-complete.*

Proof. Note that the EXPTIME upper bound is already proven by Okhotin and Salomaa [17]. They have shown that for an NIDPDA A with n states and an integer $k \geq 0$, we can decide whether or not $\mathrm{tw}_A^{\mathrm{sup}} \leq k$ in time $poly(k^k \cdot n^k)$.

We prove the EXPTIME-hardness by reduction from the intersection emptiness of deterministic top-down tree automata [6]. It is known that a deterministic top-down tree automaton can be translated into a DIDPDA in polynomial time [2]. Thus, we can convert k deterministic top-down tree automata into k DIDPDAs in polynomial time and then, the intersection emptiness of the k DIDPDAs is also EXPTIME-hard (in fact, EXPTIME-complete).

Now we construct a new NIDPDA A that has the initial state connected to the initial states of k DIDPDAs by transitions on a new local symbol \$. We first create a new final state f of A which will be the only final state of A. This implies that we change all final states of the k DIDPDAs into non-final states. Then, for each final state of all k DIDPDAs, we create two nondeterministic transitions labelled by a new symbol '#' that go to the sole final state f of A. It is easy to see that the tree width of A is $2k$ if and only if the k DIDPDAs have a non-empty intersection.

We can see that the problem of deciding whether or not the tree width of an NIDPDA is bounded by a given integer $2k$ decides also whether the intersection of k deterministic top-down tree automata is empty. As a result, we conclude that the k-tree width problem for NIDPDAs is EXPTIME-complete.   □

Now we consider the tree width of an NFA. It is known that there is a simple polynomial time algorithm to decide whether the tree width of an NFA is finite [18]. Here we show that the problem of deciding whether or not the tree width of an NFA is bounded by a given integer k is PSPACE-complete. The proof is inspired by the corresponding result for the degree of ambiguity by Chan and Ibarra [5].

Theorem 6. *Given an NFA A and an integer $k \geq 1$, the problem of determining whether or not the tree width of A is bounded by k is PSPACE-complete.*

Proof. Let $A = (\Sigma, Q, q_0, F, \delta)$ be an input NFA. We construct a DFA $A' = (\Sigma, Q', q_0', F', \delta')$, where $Q' = (Q \cup \#)^{k+1}$ is the set of states, $q_0' = (q_0, \#, \ldots, \#)$ is the initial state, $F' = \{(q_1, q_2, \ldots, q_{k+1}) \in Q^{k+1} \mid |\{q_1, q_2, \ldots, q_{k+1}\} \cap Q| = k+1\}$ is the set of final states, and δ' is the transition function that simulates at most $k+1$ computations of A in the $(k+1)$-tuple states in Q' simultaneously. From the initial state $q_0' = (q_0, \#, \ldots, \#)$, A' changes its first component according to the transition function δ of A. For instance, if $\delta(q_0, a) = \{p\}$, then A' moves from $(q_0, \#, \ldots, \#)$ to $(p, \#, \ldots, \#)$ by reading the character a. If A' encounters a nondeterministic computation step such as $\delta(p, a) = \{p_1, p_2\}$ from $(p, \#, \ldots, \#)$, then A' moves to $(p_1, p_2, \#, \ldots, \#) \in Q'$ by reading a. The idea is to replace the first '$\#$' entries of the $(k+1)$-tuple into the target states of the nondeterministic choices of A. In this way, we can decide whether or not the tree width of A is k since $L(A')$ is empty if and only if the tree width of A is k.

Obviously, the number of states in A' is bounded by $(n+1)^{k+1}$. The non-emptiness of $L(A')$ can be decided in nondeterministic polynomial space by guessing a candidate string w of length smaller than $(n+1)^{k+1}$.

The PSPACE-hardness can be obtained by slightly modifying the proof of Theorem 5 on the EXPTIME-hardness reduction. If we simply replace the k DIDPDAs with k DFAs, then we can see that the problem of deciding whether or not the tree width of an NFA is k is PSPACE-hard from the PSPACE-completeness of the DFA intersection emptiness [13].   □

5   Conclusion

As the main result we have shown that the question whether the tree width of an NPDA is finite can be decided in polynomial time. This question was previously open even for NIDPDAs. The main open problem is whether or not for input-driven pushdown automata with unbounded ambiguity, the degree of growth of ambiguity can be decided effectively. Similarly questions can naturally be asked also about tree width growth rates. The elegant structural characterization given by Weber and Seidl [20] for NFAs with polynomial or exponential ambiguity growth rates does not seem to work in the presence of stack operations. On the other hand, when stack operations are input-driven, showing undecidability using a reduction from the Post Correspondence Problem, analogously as done e.g. in Proposition 4, clearly is not possible either.

References

1. Alur, R., Madhusudan, P.: Visibly pushdown languages. In: Babai, L. (ed.) Proceedings 36th Annual ACM Symposium on Theory of Computing (STOC 2004), pp. 202–211. ACM, New York (2004). https://doi.org/10.1145/1007352.1007390
2. Alur, R., Madhusudan, P.: Adding nesting structure to words. J. ACM **56**(3), 16:1–16:43 (2009). https://doi.org/10.1145/1516512.1516518
3. Björklund, H., Martens, W.: The tractability frontier for NFA minimization. J. Comput. System Sci. **78**(1), 198–210 (2012)
4. Caralp, M., Reynier, P.-A., Talbot, J.-M.: Visibly pushdown automata with multiplicities: finiteness and K-boundedness. In: Yen, H.-C., Ibarra, O.H. (eds.) DLT 2012. LNCS, vol. 7410, pp. 226–238. Springer, Heidelberg (2012). https://doi.org/10.1007/978-3-642-31653-1_21
5. Chan, T., Ibarra, O.H.: On the finite-valuedness problem for sequential machines. Theoret. Comput. Sci. **23**(1), 95–101 (1983)
6. Fernau, H., Krebs, A.: Problems on finite automata and the exponential time hypothesis. Algorithms **10**(1), 24:1–24:25 (2017). https://doi.org/10.3390/a10010024
7. Gécseg, F., Steinby, M.: Tree languages. In: Rozenberg, G., Salomaa, A. (eds.) Handbook of Formal Languages, pp. 1–68. Springer, Heidelberg (1997). https://doi.org/10.1007/978-3-642-59126-6_1
8. Goldstine, J., Kappes, M., Kintala, C.M.R., Leung, H., Malcher, A., Wotschke, D.: Descriptional complexity of machines with limited resources. J. UCS **8**(2), 193–234 (2002). https://doi.org/10.3217/jucs-008-02-0193
9. Goldstine, J., Leung, H., Wotschke, D.: Measuring nondeterminism in pushdown automata. J. Comput. Syst. Sci. **71**(4), 440–466 (2005)
10. Harrison, M.: Introduction to Formal Language Theory. Addison-Wesley, Boston (1978)
11. Hopcroft, J., Ullman, J.: Introduction to Automata Theory, Languages, and Computation. Addison-Wesley, Reading (1979)
12. Hromkovic, J., Seibert, S., Karhumäki, J., Klauck, H., Schnitger, G.: Communication complexity method for measuring nondeterminism in finite automata. Inform. Comput. **172**(2), 202–217 (2002). https://doi.org/10.1006/inco.2001.3069
13. Kozen, D.: Lower bounds for natural proof systems. In: Proceedings of 18th Annual Symposium on Foundations of Computer Science (SFCS 1977), pp. 254–266. IEEE Computer Society (1977). https://doi.org/10.1109/SFCS.1977.16
14. Leung, H.: Separating exponentially ambiguous finite automata from polynomially ambiguous finite automata. SIAM J. Comput. **27**(4), 1073–1082 (1998)
15. Mehlhorn, K.: Pebbling mountain ranges and its application to DCFL-recognition. In: de Bakker, J., van Leeuwen, J. (eds.) ICALP 1980. LNCS, vol. 85, pp. 422–435. Springer, Heidelberg (1980). https://doi.org/10.1007/3-540-10003-2_89
16. Okhotin, A., Salomaa, K.: Complexity of input-driven pushdown automata. SIGACT News **45**(2), 47–67 (2014). https://doi.org/10.1145/2636805.2636821
17. Okhotin, A., Salomaa, K.: Input-driven pushdown automata with limited nondeterminism. In: Shur, A.M., Volkov, M.V. (eds.) DLT 2014. LNCS, vol. 8633, pp. 84–102. Springer, Cham (2014). https://doi.org/10.1007/978-3-319-09698-8_9
18. Palioudakis, A., Salomaa, K., Akl, S.G.: State complexity of finite tree width NFAs. J. Autom. Lang. Comb. **17**(2), 245–264 (2012)

19. Shallit, J.O.: A Second Course in Formal Languages and Automata Theory. Cambridge University Press, Cambridge (2008)
20. Weber, A., Seidl, H.: On the degree of ambiguity of finite automata. Theoret. Comput. Sci. **88**(2), 325–349 (1991)
21. Wood, D.: Theory of Computation. Harper & Row (1986)

Computability on Quasi-Polish Spaces

Mathieu Hoyrup[1]([✉]), Cristóbal Rojas[2], Victor Selivanov[3,4],
and Donald M. Stull[1]

[1] Université de Lorraine, CNRS, Inria, LORIA, 54000 Nancy, France
{mathieu.hoyrup,donald.stull}@inria.fr
[2] Universidad Andres Bello, Santiago, Chile
crojas@mat-unab.cl
[3] A.P. Ershov Institute of Informatics Systems SB RAS, Novosibirsk, Russia
vseliv@iis.nsk.su
[4] Kazan Federal University, Kazan, Russia

Abstract. We investigate the effectivizations of several equivalent
definitions of quasi-Polish spaces and study which characterizations hold
effectively. Being a computable effectively open image of the Baire space
is a robust notion that admits several characterizations. We show that
some natural effectivizations of quasi-metric spaces are strictly stronger.

1 Introduction

Classical descriptive set theory (DST) [11] deals with hierarchies of sets, functions and equivalence relations in Polish spaces. Theoretical Computer Science,
in particular Computable Analysis [21], motivated an extension of the classical DST to non-Hausdorff spaces; a noticeable progress was achieved for the
ω-continuous domains and quasi-Polish spaces [3,18]. The theory of quasi-Polish
spaces is already a well-established part of classical DST [3,5].

Theoretical Computer Science and Computable Analysis especially need an
effective DST for some effective versions of the mentioned classes of topological
spaces. A lot of useful work in this direction was done in Computability Theory
but only for the discrete space $\mathbb{N}$, the Baire space $\mathcal{N}$, and some of their relatives
[6,16]. For a systematic work to develop the effective DST for effective Polish
spaces see e.g. [7,14,15]. There was also some work on the effective DST for
effective domains and approximation spaces [2,18-20].

This project has received funding from the European Union's Horizon 2020 research
and innovation programme under the Marie Skłodowska-Curie grant agreement No
731143
C. Rojas was supported by Marie Curie RISE project CID.
V. Selivanov was supported by Inria program Invited Researcher and the Regional
Mathematical Center of Kazan Federal University (project 1.13556.2019/13.1 of the
Ministry of Education and Science of Russian Federation).
D.M. Stull was supported by Inria post-doc program.

M. Hospodár et al. (Eds.): DCFS 2019, LNCS 11612, pp. 171–183, 2019.
https://doi.org/10.1007/978-3-030-23247-4_13

In this paper we continue the search of a "correct" version of a computable quasi-Polish space initiated in [13,20]. By a correct version we mean one having properties similar to effective versions of those in the classical case: the computable quasi-Polish spaces have to subsume the well established classes of computable Polish spaces and computable ω-continuous domains and to admit a good enough effective DST.

We identify effective versions of quasi-Polish spaces satisfying these specifications. One of them is the class of computable effectively open images of the Baire space identified and studied in [20]. We provide some characterizations of this class which are effective versions of the corresponding known characterizations of quasi-Polish spaces in [3]. However we show that some natural effectivizations of complete quasi-metric spaces are strictly stronger.

The results of this paper were obtained in September 2018 during a research stay of the second and third authors in Inria, Nancy. On the final stage of preparing this paper the preprint [4] appeared where some of our results where obtained independently (using a slightly different approach and terminology), notably Definition 8 and Theorem 9.

In order to make our discussion of effective spaces closer to the corresponding classical theory, we use an approach based on the canonical embeddings of cb_0-spaces into the Scott domain $\mathcal{P}(\omega)$ and on the computability in this domain. This approach (which emphasizes the notion of effective continuity rather than the equivalent notion of computability w.r.t. admissible representations more popular in Computable Analysis) was promoted in [12,19].

We start in the next section with recalling definitions of some notions of effective spaces and of effective DST in such spaces; we also try to simplify and unify rather chaotic terminology in this field. In Sects. 2 and 3 we establish the main technical tools used in the sequel. In Sect. 4 we propose a definition of effective quasi-Polish spaces and prove characterizations of this notion. In Sect. 5 we propose two effective notions of quasi-metric space and prove that they differ from the notion of effective quasi-Polish space.

2   Preliminaries

Here we recall some known notions and facts, with a couple of new observations.

Notions similar to those considered below were introduced (sometimes independently) and studied in [9,12,19] under different names. We use a slightly different terminology, trying to simplify it and make it closer to that of classical topology. Note that the terminology in effective topology is still far from being fixed. All topological spaces considered in this paper are assumed to be countably based. Such a space satisfying the T_0-separation axiom is sometimes called a cb_0-space, for short. We recall that $(W_e)_{e\in\mathbb{N}}$ is some effective enumeration of the computably enumerable (c.e.) subsets of $\mathbb{N}$.

Definition 1. *An **effective topological space** is a countably-based T_0 topological space coming with a numbering $(B_i^X)_{i\in\mathbb{N}}$ of a basis, such that there is a computable function $f : \mathbb{N}^2 \to \mathbb{N}$ such that $B_i^X \cap B_j^X = \bigcup_{k\in W_{f(i,j)}} B_k^X$.*

Many popular spaces (e.g., the discrete space $\mathbb{N}$ of naturals, the space of reals $\mathbb{R}$, the domain $\mathcal{P}(\omega)$, the Baire space $\mathcal{N} = \mathbb{N}^{\mathbb{N}}$, the Cantor space $\mathcal{C} = 2^{\mathbb{N}}$ and the Baire domain $\mathbb{N}^{\leq \mathbb{N}} = \mathbb{N}^* \cup \mathbb{N}^{\mathbb{N}}$ of finite and infinite sequences of naturals) are effective topological spaces in an obvious way. The effective topological space $\mathbb{N}$ is trivial topologically but very interesting for Computability Theory. We use some almost standard notation related to the Baire space. In particular, $[\sigma]$ denotes the basic open set induced by $\sigma \in \mathbb{N}^*$ consisting of all $p \in \mathcal{N}$ having σ as an initial segment; we sometimes call such sets cylinders. Let ε denote the empty string in $\mathbb{N}^*$.

In [17,19] the effective Borel and effective Hausdorff hierarchies in arbitrary effective topological spaces X were introduced. Also the effective Luzin hierarchy is defined naturally [20]. Below we use the simplified notation for levels of these hierarchies like $\Pi_n^0(X)$, $\Sigma_n^1(X)$ or $\Sigma_n^{-1}(X)$ (which naturally generalizes the notation in computability theory) and some of their obvious properties. We will also use the expression *effective open set* for sets in the class $\Sigma_1^0(X)$, which are the sets $\bigcup_{i \in W} B_i^X$ for some c.e. set $W \subseteq \mathbb{N}$.

Definition 2. *If X, Y are effective topological spaces then a function $f : X \to Y$ is **computable** if the sets $f^{-1}(B_i^Y)$ are uniformly effective open sets.*

As observed in [20], for any effective topological space X, the equality relation $=_X$ on X is in $\Pi_2^0(X \times X)$. The argument in [20] shows that also the specialization partial order $\leq_X$ has the same descriptive complexity. In particular, every singleton is in the boldface class $\boldsymbol{\Pi}_2^0(X)$.

With any effective topological space X we associate the *canonical embedding* $e : X \to \mathcal{P}(\omega)$ defined by $e(x) = \{n \mid x \in B_n^X\}$ (in [19] the canonical embedding was denoted as O_ξ; we changed the notation here to make it closer to that of the paper [5] which is cited below). The canonical embedding is a computable homeomorphism between X and the subspace $e[X]$ of $\mathcal{P}(\omega)$. It can be used to study computability on cb$_0$-spaces [12,19] using the fact that the computable functions on $\mathcal{P}(\omega)$ coincide with the enumeration operators [16].

The more popular and general approach to computability on topological spaces is based on representations [21]. The relation between the two approaches is based on the so called enumeration representation $\rho : \mathcal{N} \to \mathcal{P}(\omega)$ defined by $\rho(x) = \{n \mid \exists i(x(i) = n + 1)\}$. The function ρ is a computable effectively open surjection. The canonical embedding e induces the **standard representation** $\rho_X = e^{-1} \circ \rho_A$ of X where $A = e(X)$ and ρ_A is the restriction of ρ to $\rho^{-1}(A)$. The function ρ_X is a computable effectively open surjection. We will implicitly identify any effective topological space X with its image under the canonical embedding, so that X is a subspace of $\mathcal{P}(\omega)$, and ρ_X is the restriction of ρ to $\rho^{-1}(X)$.

Note that for effective topological spaces X and Y, $f : X \to Y$ is computable iff there exists a computable function $F : \mathrm{dom}(\rho_X) \to \mathrm{dom}(\rho_Y)$ such that $\rho_Y \circ F = f \circ \rho_X$.

3   Results on Π_2^0-Sets

This section contains the technical tools that will be used to prove the characterizations of effective quasi-Polish spaces.

Definition 3. *Let X be an effective topological space. We say that $A \subseteq X$ is* **computably overt** *if the set $\{i \in \mathbb{N} : B_i^X \cap A \neq \emptyset\}$ is c.e.*

Observe that the overt information does not uniquely determine the set, but only its closure. In the literature, overt and computably overt sets are often assumed to be closed. It is important to note that in this paper, no such assumption is made.

We recall that if X is an effective topological space then a set is in $\Pi_2^0(X)$ if it is an intersection of Boolean combinations of uniformly effective open subsets of X. We prove an effective version of Theorem 68 in [3].

Lemma 4. *Let X be an effective topological space. For $A \subseteq X$,*

- *$A \in \Pi_2^0(X)$ iff $\rho_X^{-1}(A) \in \Pi_2^0(dom(\rho_X))$,*
- *A is computably overt iff $\rho_X^{-1}(A)$ is computably overt.*

Proof. If $A \in \Pi_2^0(X)$ then one easily obtains $\rho_X^{-1}(A) \in \Pi_2^0(\mathrm{dom}(\rho_X))$. We now prove that if $\rho_X^{-1}(A) \in \Sigma_2^0(\mathrm{dom}(\rho_X))$ then $A \in \Sigma_2^0(X)$, which implies the same result for the class Π_2^0. Let $\rho_X^{-1}(A) = \mathrm{dom}(\rho_X) \cap \bigcup_n U_n \setminus V_n$ where $U_n, V_n \in \Sigma_1^0(\mathcal{N})$ uniformly and $V_n \subseteq U_n$. Then the set

$$A' := \bigcup_{\sigma, n} \rho_X([\sigma] \cap U_n) \setminus \rho_X([\sigma] \cap V_n)$$

belongs to $\Sigma_2^0(X)$, because the image of a $\Sigma_1^0(\mathcal{N})$-set is a $\Sigma_1^0(X)$-set uniformly. We show that $A = A'$. The inclusion $A' \subseteq A$ is straightforward. For the other inclusion, let $x \in A$. One has $\rho_X^{-1}(x) \in \boldsymbol{\Pi}_2^0(\mathcal{N})$ so $\rho_X^{-1}(x)$ is quasi-Polish so it is a Baire space ([3]). One has $\rho_X^{-1}(x) \subseteq \bigcup_n U_n \setminus V_n$. By Baire category, there exists n such that $\rho_X^{-1}(x) \cap U_n \setminus V_n$ is somewhere dense in $\rho_X^{-1}(x)$, i.e. there exists $\sigma \in \mathbb{N}^*$ such that $\emptyset \neq \rho_X^{-1}(x) \cap [\sigma] \subseteq U_n \setminus V_n$. As a result, $x \in \rho_X([\sigma] \cap U_n) \setminus \rho_X([\sigma] \cap V_n) \subseteq A'$.

If A is computably overt then $[\sigma] \cap \rho_X^{-1}(A) \neq \emptyset$ iff $\rho_X([\sigma]) \cap A \neq \emptyset$ which is c.e. as $\rho_X([\sigma]) \in \Sigma_1^0(X)$, uniformly in σ.

If $\rho_X^{-1}(A)$ is computably overt then $[\sigma] \cap A \neq \emptyset$ iff $\rho_X^{-1}([\sigma]) \cap \rho_X^{-1}(A) \neq \emptyset$ is a c.e. relation as $\rho_X^{-1}([\sigma]) \in \Sigma_1^0(X)$, uniformly in i.

An important property of computably overt Π_2^0-sets is that they contain computable points. It is a crucial ingredient in the next results.

Proposition 5 ([10]). *In a computable Polish space, a Π_2^0-set is computably overt if and only if it contains a dense computable sequence.*

Moreover, the next result shows that in a computably overt Π_2^0-set, not only can one find an effective indexing over $\mathbb{N}$ of a dense set of elements, but one can even find an effective indexing over $\mathcal{N}$ of *all* its elements.

Lemma 6. *Let $A \subseteq \mathcal{N}$ be non-empty. The following are equivalent:*

(i) A is a computably overt Π_2^0-set,
(ii) There exists a computable effectively open surjective map $f : \mathcal{N} \to A$.

When we write that $f : \mathcal{N} \to A$ is open, we mean that for each $\sigma \in \mathbb{N}^*$, there exists an open set $U_\sigma \subseteq \mathcal{N}$ such that $f([\sigma]) = A \cap U_\sigma$. f is effectively open when U_σ is effectively open, uniformly in σ.

Proof. Assume (i). Let $A = \bigcap_n A_n$ where A_n are uniformly effective open sets. We can assume w.l.o.g. that $A_{n+1} \subseteq A_n$.

One can build a computable sequence $(u_\sigma)_{\sigma \in \mathbb{N}^*}$ such that $u_\epsilon = \epsilon$ and:

- If τ properly extends σ then u_τ properly extends u_σ,
- If $|\sigma| = n$ then $[u_\sigma] \subseteq A_n$,
- $[u_\sigma]$ intersects A,
- $[u_\sigma] \cap A$ is contained in $\bigcup_{i \in \mathbb{N}} [u_{\sigma \cdot i}]$.

We build this sequence inductively in σ. Given u_σ intersecting A with $|\sigma| = n$, one can compute a covering of $[u_\sigma] \cap A_{n+1}$ with cylinders properly extending u_σ and extract the cylinders intersecting A. Let $(u_{\sigma \cdot i})_{i \in \mathbb{N}}$ be some computable enumeration of them.

We now define f. For each $p \in \mathcal{N}$, the sequence $u_{p \restriction n}$ converges to some $q \in \mathcal{N}$. We define $f(p) = q$. One easily checks that the function $f : \mathcal{N} \to A$ is computable, onto and effectively open as $f([\sigma]) = [u_\sigma] \cap A$.

Now assume (ii). The function f has a computable right-inverse, i.e. $g : A \to \mathcal{N}$ such that $f \circ g$ is the identity on A. Indeed, given $p \in A$, one can enumerate all the cylinders intersecting $f^{-1}(p)$ as $[\sigma] \cap f^{-1}(p) \neq \emptyset$ iff $p \in f([\sigma])$ which can be recognized as $f([\sigma])$ is effectively open. Hence one can progressively build an element of the closed set $f^{-1}(p)$.

The function g is a partial computable function from $\mathcal{N} \to \mathcal{N}$. Its domain is Π_2^0 and contains A. One has $p \in A \iff p$ belongs to the domain of g and $p = f \circ g(p)$. As a result, A is Π_2^0. The image under f of a dense computable sequence in $\mathcal{N}$ is a dense computable sequence in A, so the set of cylinders intersecting A is c.e.

This result can be extended to subsets of $\mathcal{P}(\omega)$.

Lemma 7. *Let $A \subseteq \mathcal{P}(\omega)$ be non-empty. The following are equivalent:*

(i) A is a computably overt Π_2^0-set,
(i) There exists a computable effectively open surjective map $f : \mathcal{N} \to A$.

Proof. If A is a computably overt Π_2^0-set then so is $\rho^{-1}(A)$, so there exists a computable effectively open onto function $f : \mathcal{N} \to \rho^{-1}(A)$. The function $\rho \circ f$ satisfies the required conditions.

Conversely, assume that $f : \mathcal{N} \to A$ is a computable effectively open surjective function.

Claim. There exists a computable function $g : \rho^{-1}(A) \to \mathcal{N}$ such that $f \circ g = \rho$.

Proof (of the claim). Given $p \in \rho^{-1}(A)$, let $A_p = \{q \in \mathcal{N} : f(q) = \rho(p)\}$. The set A_p is a computably overt Π_2^0-set relative to p. Indeed, it is Π_2^0 relative to p because equality is Π_2^0 in $\mathcal{P}(\omega)$. It is computably overt relative to p because a cylinder $[\sigma]$ intersects A_p iff $\rho(p) \in f([\sigma])$ which is a c.e. relation in p as f is effectively open. As a result, by relativizing Proposition 5, one can compute an element in A_p. Everything is uniform in p, so there is a computable function g mapping each $p \in \rho^{-1}(A)$ to an element of A_p, hence $f \circ g(p) = \rho(p)$.

Now, one has $q \in \rho^{-1}(A)$ iff $g(q)$ is defined and $f \circ g(q) = \rho(q)$. Both relations are Π_2^0, so $\rho^{-1}(A) \in \Pi_2^0(\mathcal{N})$ hence $A \in \Pi_2^0(\mathcal{P}(\omega))$ by Lemma 4. Moreover, A is computably overt because for each basic open set B of $\mathcal{P}(\omega)$, $B \cap A \neq \emptyset$ iff $f^{-1}(B) \neq \emptyset$, which is a c.e. relation.

4   Effective Quasi-Polish Spaces

According to Theorem 23 of [3], the quasi-Polish spaces (defined originally as the countably based completely quasi-metrizable spaces) coincide with the continuous open images of the Baire space. Effectivizing this definition, we obtain the following candidate for a notion of effective quasi-Polish space.

Definition 8. *An effective topological space X is an* **effective quasi-Polish space** *if X is the image of $\mathcal{N}$ under a computable effectively open map, or X is empty.*

Of course this notion is preserved by computable homeomorphisms (bijections that are computable in both directions).

Theorem 9. *Let X be an effective topological space with its standard representation ρ_X. The following statements are equivalent:*

1. *X is effective quasi-Polish,*
2. *The image of X under its canonical embedding in $\mathcal{P}(\omega)$ is a computably overt Π_2^0-subset of $\mathcal{P}(\omega)$,*
3. *$\mathrm{dom}(\rho_X)$ is a computably overt Π_2^0-subset of $\mathcal{N}$.*

Proof. The equivalence 1. $\iff$ 2. is the content of Lemma 7. The equivalence 2. $\iff$ 3. is the content of Lemma 4 for the space $\mathcal{P}(\omega)$.

We also formulate the effective version of Theorem 21 of [3].

Theorem 10. *Let X be an effective quasi-Polish space. A subspace $Y \subseteq X$ is an effective quasi-Polish space iff Y is a computably overt Π_2^0-subset of X.*

Proof. Via the canonical embedding, we have $Y \subseteq X \subseteq \mathcal{P}(\omega)$. We start by assuming that Y is a computably overt Π_2^0-subset of X. As $Y \in \Pi_2^0(X)$ and $X \in \Pi_2^0(\mathcal{P}(\omega))$, one has $Y \in \Pi_2^0(\mathcal{P}(\omega))$. To show that Y is computably overt in $\mathcal{P}(\omega)$, simply observe that for a basic open set B of $\mathcal{P}(\omega)$, B intersects Y iff $B^X := B \cap X$ intersects Y. It is a c.e. relation as Y is computably overt in X.

If Y is effective quasi-Polish then it is a computably overt Π_2^0-subset of $\mathcal{P}(\omega)$ so it is a computably overt Π_2^0-subset of X, which is a subspace of $\mathcal{P}(\omega)$.

Sometimes it is easier to work with a computably admissible representation other than the standard representation.

Theorem 11. *Let X be an effective topological space. If X admits a computably admissible representation whose domain is a computably overt Π_2^0-subset of $\mathcal{N}$, then X is an effective Polish space.*

Proof. Let δ be a computably admissible representation of X such that $\mathrm{dom}(\delta)$ is a computably overt Π_2^0-subset of $\mathcal{N}$. By definition of computably admissible, δ is computably equivalent to ρ_X, i.e. there exist partial computable functions $F, G :\subseteq \mathcal{N} \to \mathcal{N}$ satisfying $\rho_X = \delta \circ F$ and $\delta = \rho_X \circ G$. We show that $\mathrm{dom}(\rho_X)$ is a computably overt Π_2^0-set.

We recall that ρ_X is the restriction of the representation ρ of $\mathcal{P}(\omega)$ to $\rho^{-1}(X)$. We show that $\mathrm{dom}(\rho_X) = \rho^{-1}(X)$ is a computably overt Π_2^0-set. Let $p \in \mathcal{N}$. One has $p \in \mathrm{dom}(\rho_X) = \rho^{-1}(X)$ iff $F(p)$ is defined, $F(p) \in \mathrm{dom}(\delta)$ and $\rho(G \circ F(p)) = \rho(p)$. All these conditions are Π_2^0, so $\rho^{-1}(X)$ belongs to $\Pi_2^0(\mathcal{N})$.

One has $[\sigma] \cap \mathrm{dom}(\rho_X) \neq \emptyset$ iff $\delta^{-1}(\rho([\sigma])) \neq \emptyset$ which is c.e. in σ as $\mathrm{dom}(\delta)$ is computably overt.

5   Effective Quasi-Metric Spaces

We now propose two effective versions of quasi-metric spaces and compare them with the notion of effective quasi-Polish space. A quasi-metric on a set X is a function $d : X \times X \to \mathbb{R}_{\geq 0}$ satisfying:

- $d(x, z) \leq d(x, y) + d(y, z)$,
- $x = y$ iff $d(x, y) = d(y, x) = 0$.

The quasi-metric d induces a metric $\hat{d}(x, y) = \max(d(x, y), d(y, x))$.

Definition 12. *A **computable quasi-metric space** is a triple (X, d, S) where d is a quasi-metric on X and $S = \{s_i\}_{i \in \mathbb{N}}$ is a $\hat{d}$-dense sequence such that $d(s_i, s_j)$ are uniformly computable.*

We recall that a real number x is **right-c.e.** if $x = \inf_i q_i$ for some computable sequence of rationals $(q_i)_{i \in \mathbb{N}}$.

Definition 13. *A **right-c.e. quasi-metric space** is a triple (X, d, S) where d is a quasi-metric on X and $S = \{s_i\}_{i \in \mathbb{N}}$ is a $\hat{d}$-dense sequence such that $d(s_i, s_j)$ are uniformly right-c.e.*

Every right-c.e. quasi-metric space is an effective topological space with the basis of balls $B(s, r) = \{x \in X : d(s, x) < r\}$ with $s \in S$ and r positive rational. To see this, we consider formal inclusion between balls: $B(s, q) \sqsubseteq B(t, r)$ iff $d(t, s) + q < r$. Formal inclusion is c.e. and $B_i \cap B_j = \bigcup_{k : B_k \sqsubseteq B_i \text{ and } B_k \sqsubseteq B_j} B_k$, so the axiom of effective topological spaces is satisfied. As a result, any such space has its standard representation δ_S. We define another representation.

Definition 14. *The* **Cauchy representation** δ_C *is defined in the following way: a point $x \in X$ is represented by any sequence $s_n \in S$ such that $d(s_n, s_{n+1}) < 2^{-n}$ and s_n converges to x in the metric $\hat{d}$.*

Theorem 15. *On a right-c.e. quasi-metric space, the Cauchy representation is computably equivalent to the standard representation.*

Proof. For the proof we will also consider a slightly different representation δ'_C where x is represented by any sequence s_n such that $d(s_n, x) < 2^{-n}$ and s_n converges to x in $\hat{d}$.

We prove the following computable reductions: $\delta_C \leq \delta'_C \leq \delta_S \leq \delta_C$.

Proof of $\delta_C \leq \delta'_C$. Assume we are given a δ_C-name of x, which is essentially a sequence $(s_n)_{n \in \mathbb{N}}$ such that $d(s_n, s_{n+1}) < 2^{-n}$ and $\lim_{n \to \infty} \hat{d}(s_n, x) = 0$. One easily checks that the sequence $(s_{n+1})_{n \in \mathbb{N}}$ is a δ_C-name for x.

Proof of $\delta'_C \leq \delta_S$. Assume we are given a δ'_C-name of x, which is essentially a sequence s_n such that $d(s_n, x) < 2^{-n}$ and $\lim_{n \to \infty} \hat{d}(s_n, x) = 0$. We show that we can enumerate the basic balls containing x. Indeed, we show that $x \in B(s, r)$ if and only if there exists n such that $d(s, s_n) < r - 2^{-n}$. First assume that the latter inequality holds. By the triangle inequality,

$$d(s, x) \leq d(s, s_n) + d(s_n, x) < r - 2^{-n} + 2^{-n} = r.$$

Conversely, if $d(s, x) < r$ then as $\hat{d}(s_n, x)$ converges to 0, for sufficiently large n one has $d(x, s_n) + 2^{-n} < r - d(s, x)$ so $d(s, s_n) \leq d(s, x) + d(x, s_n) < r - 2^{-n}$.

Proof of $\delta_S \leq \delta_C$. Assume we are given an enumeration of the basic balls containing x, call it $U_1, U_2, U_3, \ldots$. We build a sequence $(s_n)_{n \in \mathbb{N}}$ as follows.

We take s_0 such that $d(s_0, x) < 1$, which we can find by looking for a ball of radius 1 containing x. Once $s_0, \ldots, s_n$ have been defined, we look for s_{n+1} satisfying:

- $s_{n+1} \in U_1 \cap \ldots \cap U_{n+1}$,
- $d(s_n, s_{n+1}) < 2^{-n}$,
- $d(s_{n+1}, x) < 2^{-n-1}$.

Such a point must exist, as if x' is sufficiently $\hat{d}$-close to x, the first and third conditions are satisfied, and $d(s_n, x') \leq d(s_n, x) + d(x, x') < 2^{-n} + d(x, x')$ by induction hypothesis, so $d(s_n, x') < 2^{-n}$ if $d(x, x')$ is sufficiently small. Such a point can be effectively found, d is right-c.e. on S.

The sequence $(s_n)_{n \in \mathbb{N}}$ satisfies the conditions of being a δ_C-name of x. Indeed, $d(x, s_n)$ converge to 0, as for each rational ϵ there exists $s \in S$ such that $\hat{d}(s, x) < \epsilon$, so the ball $B(s, \epsilon)$ appears as some U_i, so for $n \geq i$, $d(x, s_n) \leq d(x, s) + d(s, s_n) < 2\epsilon$.

We recall that a quasi-metric d is (Smyth-)complete if every Cauchy sequence converges in the metric $\hat{d}$, and that a space is quasi-Polish iff it is completely quasi-metrizable [3]. One direction of this equivalence admits an effective version.

Theorem 16. *Every right-c.e. quasi-metric space that is complete is an effective quasi-Polish space.*

Proof. The domain of the Cauchy representation is a computably overt Π_2^0-set. Indeed, the relation $\forall n, d(s_n, s_{n+1}) < 2^{-n}$ is Π_2^0, and any finite sequence satisfying this condition can be extended (to an ultimately constant sequence, e.g.). As the Cauchy representation is computably equivalent to the standard representation, we can apply Theorem 11.

Proposition 17. *In a right-c.e. quasi-metric space, the following conditions are equivalent for a point x:*

- *x is computable,*
- *The numbers $d(s, x)$ are right-c.e., uniformly in $s \in \mathcal{S}$.*

Proof. One has $x \in B(s, r) \iff d(s, x) < r$. The first relation is c.e. iff x is computable. The second relation is c.e. iff $d(s, x)$ is right-c.e.

We recall that a real number x is left-c.e. if $-x$ is right-c.e.

Proposition 18. *In a computable quasi-metric space, the following conditions are uniformly equivalent for a point x:*

- *x is computable,*
- *The numbers $d(s, x)$ are right-c.e., uniformly in $s \in \mathcal{S}$,*
- *The numbers $d(s, x)$ and $d(x, s)$ are right-c.e. and left-c.e. respectively, uniformly in $s \in \mathcal{S}$.*

Proof. We only have to prove that for a computable point x, the numbers $d(x, s)$ are uniformly left-c.e. Let $(s_n)_{n \in \mathbb{N}}$ be a computable δ_C-name of x. We show that $d(x, s) = \sup_n d(s_n, s) - 2^{-n}$ which is left-c.e., uniformly in s.

Indeed, $d(x, s) \geq d(s_n, s) - d(s_n, x)$, and as $d(x, s_n) \leq \hat{d}(x, s_n)$ converges to 0, $d(x, s) \leq d(x, s_n) + d(s_n, s)$ is arbitrarily close to $d(s_n, s)$.

6   Separation

Classically, a space is quasi-Polish if and only if it is completely quasi-metrizable [3]. However the proof is not constructive. We know that each right-c.e. quasi-metric space that is complete is an effective quasi-Polish space, but that the converse fails. For this, we fully characterize the effective notions of quasi-Polish space in a restricted case.

Let $[0, 1]_<$ come with the quasi-metric $d(x, y) = \max(0, x - y)$, with the rational points as $\hat{d}$-dense sequence. It is a computable quasi-metric space that is complete. For $\alpha \in (0, 1)$, the subspace $[\alpha, 1]_<$ is an effective topological subspace of $[0, 1]_<$. We investigate when it is an effective quasi-Polish space, a computably quasi-metrizable space, and a right-c.e. quasi-metrizable space.

Proposition 19. *The space $[\alpha, 1]_<$ is an effective quasi-Polish space iff α is left-c.e. relative to the halting set.*

Proof. Observe that the set $\{q : (q, 1] \cap A \neq \emptyset\}$ is always c.e. Therefore, $[\alpha, 1]_<$ is an effective quasi-Polish space if and only if $[\alpha, 1] \in \Pi_2^0([0, 1]_<)$ by Theorem 10 (the c.e. conditions is always satisfied as observed above). This is equivalent to the existence of uniformly right-c.e. numbers r_i such that $[\alpha, 1] = \bigcap_i (r_i, 1]$, i.e. $\alpha = \sup_i r_i$. This is equivalent to α being left-c.e. relative to the halting set.

Proposition 20. *The space $[\alpha, 1]_<$ admits a computably equivalent computable quasi-metric structure if and only if α is right-c.e.*

Proof. Assume first that α is right-c.e. There is a computable enumeration $S = \{q_i\}_{i \in \mathbb{N}}$ of the rational numbers in $(\alpha, 1]$. The quasi-metric $d(x, y) = \max(0, x - y)$ is computable on S.

Conversely, assume a computable quasi-metric d with an associate set $S = \{s_i\}_{i \in \mathbb{N}}$. We now prove that the points s_i are uniformly computable real numbers, which implies that $\alpha = \inf_s s_i$ is right-c.e. The function mapping a real number $x \in [\alpha, 1]$ to $d(x, s_i)$ is left-c.e. (x is given using the standard Cauchy representation). Indeed, from x one can compute a name of x in $[0, 1]_<$, from which one can compute a name of x in $[\alpha, 1]_<$ and we can apply the uniform relative version of Proposition 18.

The left-c.e. function $x \mapsto d(x, s_i)$ is non-decreasing. Indeed, for $x \leq x'$, one has $d(x, s_i) \leq d(x, x') + d(x', s_i) = d(x', s_i)$. Therefore, it can be extended to a left-c.e. non-decreasing function f over $[0, 1]$. Indeed, if $f_0 : [0, 1] \to \mathbb{R}$ is a left-c.e. function such that $f_0(x) = d(x, s_i)$ for $x \in [\alpha, 1]$, then $f(x) := \inf\{f_0(x') : x' \in [x, 1]\}$ is left-c.e. non-decreasing and agrees with $d(x, s_i)$ on $[\alpha, 1]$.

As a result, for $q \in \mathbb{Q}$, $q > s_i$ if and only if $f(q) > 0$ which is a c.e. condition, so s_i is right-c.e. Of course, s_i is left-c.e. as it is a computable point of $[\alpha, 1]_<$.

Proposition 21. *The space $[\alpha, 1]_<$ admits a computably equivalent right-c.e. quasi-metric structure if and only if α is left-c.e. or right-c.e.*

Proof. If α is right-c.e. then there is a computable quasi-metric structure by Proposition 20. If α is left-c.e. then we can take $S = \{s_i\}_{i \in \mathbb{N}}$ with $s_i = \max(q_i, \alpha)$, where $(q_i)_{i \in \mathbb{N}}$ is a computable enumeration of the rational numbers in $[0, 1]$. We can take the restriction of the quasi-metric $d(x, y) = \max(0, x - y)$. It is right-c.e. on S. To approximate $d(s_i, s_j)$ from the right, do the following: if $q_i \leq q_j$ then output 0 (correct as $s_i \leq s_j$ in that case). If $q_i > q_j$ then start approximating $d(q_i, s_j)$ from the right (possible as s_j is left-c.e.) and switching to 0 if we eventually see that $q_i < \alpha$. Conversely, assume a right-c.e. metric structure (d', S). Given $q \in \mathbb{Q} \cap [\alpha, 1]$, $d'(s_i, q)$ is uniformly right-c.e. Indeed, each such q is a computable point of the right-c.e. quasi-metric space $([\alpha, 1]_<, d', S)$, so by Proposition 17, $d'(s_i, q)$ is right-c.e.

Claim. Given $s \in S$, $\epsilon > 0$, one can compute $\delta > 0$ such that $B'(s, \delta) \subseteq B(s, \epsilon)$.

Proof. (of the claim) The identity from the quasi-metric space $[\alpha, 1]_<$ to the quasi-metric space is computable, so $B(s, \epsilon)$ is effectively open in $[\alpha, 1]_<$, hence can be expressed as a union of d'-balls. One can find one of them, $B'(t, r)$, containing s. One has $d'(t, s) < r$ and $d'(t, s)$ is right-c.e., so one can compute $\delta > 0$ such that $d'(t, s) + \delta < r$. One has $B'(s, \delta) \subseteq B'(t, r) \subseteq B(s, \epsilon)$.

Let $\delta_{s,\epsilon}$ be obtained from the previous Claim. Consider thet set $E = \{q \in \mathbb{Q} \cap [0, 1] : \exists s \in S, \epsilon > 0, d'(s, q) < \delta_{s,\epsilon} \text{ and } d(s, q) > \epsilon\}$.It is a c.e. set. It is disjoint from $[\alpha, 1]$: if $q \in [\alpha, 1]$ and $q \in B'(s, \delta_{s,\epsilon})$ then $q \in B(s, \epsilon)$. As a result, $\sup E$ is left-c.e. and $\sup E \leq \alpha$. If α is not left-c.e. then $\sup E < \alpha$. As a result, we can fix some rational number q_0 between $\sup E$ and α, and work with rationals above q_0 only, so that they do not belong to E.

Let $F = \{(q, \epsilon) : q \in \mathbb{Q} \cap [q_0, 1], \epsilon > 0, \exists s \in S, \text{ such that } d'(s, q) < \delta_{s,\epsilon}\}$. F is c.e. so $I := \inf\{q + \epsilon : (q, \epsilon) \in F\}$ is right-c.e. If $q > \alpha$ then there must exist $s \in S$ such that $s \leq q$, i.e. $d'(s, q) = 0$, so $(q, \epsilon) \in F$ for every $\epsilon > 0$. As a result, $I \leq \alpha$. If α is not right-c.e. then $I < \alpha$.

Take $(q, \epsilon) \in F$ such that $q + \epsilon < \alpha$. Let $s \in S$ witness that $(q, \epsilon) \in F$. One has $d'(s, q) < \delta_{s,\epsilon}$ and $d(s, q) \geq d(\alpha, q) > \epsilon$ so $q \in E$, giving a contradiction.

Therefore, α is left-c.e. or right-c.e.

Corollary 22. *There exists an effective quasi-Polish space which cannot be presented as a right-c.e. quasi-metric space.*

Proof. Take α that is left-c.e. relative to the halting set but neither left-c.e. nor right-c.e., and apply Propositions 19 and 21.

7   Discussion and Open Questions

By a *computable Polish space* we mean an effective topological space X induced by a computable complete metric space (X, d, S) [8,15,21]. Most of the popular Polish spaces are computable.

By a *computable ω-continuous domain* [1] we mean a pair (X, b) where X is an ω-continuous domain and $b : \mathbb{N} \to X$ is a numbering of a domain base in X modulo which the approximation relation $\ll$ is c.e. Any computable ω-continuous domain (X, b) has the induced effective base β where $\beta_n = \{x \mid b_n \ll x\}$. Most of the popular ω-continuous domains are computable.

By Theorem 1 in [20], both the computable Polish spaces and computable ω-continuous domains are computable effective images of the Baire space, hence they are effective quasi-Polish, hence the notion of effective quasi-Polish space introduced in this paper is a reasonable candidate for capturing the computable quasi-Polish spaces. By Theorem 4 in [13] (which extends Theorem 4 in [20]), any effective quasi-Polish space satisfies the effective Suslin-Kleene theorem. By Theorem 5 in [20], any effective quasi-Polish space satisfies the effective Hausdorff theorem.

It seems that our search, as well as the independent search in [4] resulted in natural and convincing candidates for capturing the computable quasi-Polish spaces. Nevertheless, many interesting closely related questions remain open. Since the class of quasi-Polish spaces admits at least ten seemingly different characterizations [3], the status of effective analogues of these characterizations deserves additional investigation. In particular, this concerns the characterization of quasi-Polish spaces as the subspaces of non-compact elements in (ω-algebraic or ω-continuous) domains.

References

1. Abramsky, S.: Domain theory. In: Abramsky, S., Gabbay, D., Maibaum, T.S.E. (eds.) Handbook of Logic in Computer Science. Clarendon Press, Oxford (1994)
2. Becher, V., Grigorieff, S.: Borel and Hausdorff hierarchies in topological spaces of choquet games and their effectivization. Math. Struct. Comput. Sci. **25**(7), 1490–1519 (2015). https://doi.org/10.1017/S096012951300025X
3. de Brecht, M.: Quasi-polish spaces. Ann. Pure Appl. Logic **164**(3), 356–381 (2013)
4. Brecht de, M., Pauly, A., Schröder, M.: Overt choice. CoRR abs/1902.05926 (2019). http://arxiv.org/abs/1902.05926
5. Chen, R.: Notes on quasi-Polish spaces. CoRR abs/1902.05926 (2018). http://arxiv.org/abs/1809.07440
6. Gao, S.: Invariant Descriptive Set Theory. CRC Press, New York (2009)
7. Gregoriades, V.: Classes of polish spaces under effective Borel isomorphism. Mem. Amer. Math. Soc. **240**(1135) (2016). https://doi.org/10.1090/memo/1135
8. Gregoriades, V., Kispéter, T., Pauly, A.: A comparison of concepts from computable analysis and effective descriptive set theory. Math. Struct. Comput. Sci. **27**(8), 1414–1436 (2017). https://doi.org/10.1017/S0960129516000128
9. Grubba, T., Schröder, M., Weihrauch, K.: Computable metrization. MLQ Math. Log. Q. **53**(4–5), 381–395 (2007). https://doi.org/10.1002/malq.200710009
10. Hoyrup, M.: Genericity of weakly computable objects. Theory Comput. Syst.**60**(3), 396–420 (2017). https://doi.org/10.1007/s00224-016-9737-6
11. Kechris, A.S.: Classical Descriptive Set Theory, GTM, vol. 156. Springer, New York (1995). https://doi.org/10.1007/978-1-4612-4190-4
12. Korovina, M.V., Kudinov, O.V.: Towards computability over effectively enumerable topological spaces. Electron. Notes Theor. Comput. Sci. **221**, 115–125 (2008). https://doi.org/10.1016/j.entcs.2008.12.011
13. Korovina, M., Kudinov, O.: On higher effective descriptive set theory. In: Kari, J., Manea, F., Petre, I. (eds.) CiE 2017. LNCS, vol. 10307, pp. 282–291. Springer, Cham (2017). https://doi.org/10.1007/978-3-319-58741-7_27
14. Louveau, A.: Recursivity and compactness. In: Müller, G.H., Scott, D.S. (eds.) Higher Set Theory. LNM, vol. 669, pp. 303–337. Springer, Heidelberg (1978). https://doi.org/10.1007/BFb0103106
15. Moschovakis, Y.N.: Descriptive Set Theory. Mathematical Surveys and Monographs, Second edition. American Mathematical Society (2009). http://www.math.ucla.edu/~ynm/lectures/dst2009/dst2009.pdf
16. Rogers Jr., H.: Theory of Recursive Functions and Effective Computability. MIT Press, Cambridge (1987). https://mitpress.mit.edu/books/theory-recursive-functions-and-effective-computability. (Reprint from 1967)
17. Selivanov, V.: On index sets in the Kleene-Mostowski hierarchy. Trans. Inst. Math. **2**, 135–158 (1982). in Russian

18. Selivanov, V.L.: Towards a descriptive set theory for domain-like structures. Theoret. Comput. Sci. **365**(3), 258–282 (2006). https://doi.org/10.1016/j.tcs.2006.07.053

19. Selivanov, V.L.: On the difference hierarchy in countably based T_0-spaces. Electron. Notes Theor. Comput. Sci. **221**, 257–269 (2008). https://doi.org/10.1016/j.entcs.2008.12.022

20. Selivanov, V.: Towards the effective descriptive set theory. In: Beckmann, A., Mitrana, V., Soskova, M. (eds.) CiE 2015. LNCS, vol. 9136, pp. 324–333. Springer, Cham (2015). https://doi.org/10.1007/978-3-319-20028-6_33

21. Weihrauch, K.: Computable Analysis. Springer, Heidelberg (2000). https://doi.org/10.1007/978-3-642-56999-9

NFA-to-DFA Trade-Off for Regular Operations

Galina Jirásková and Ivana Krajňáková[✉]

Mathematical Institute, Slovak Academy of Sciences,
Grešákova 6, 040 01 Košice, Slovakia
{jiraskov,krajnakova}@saske.sk

Abstract. We examine the operational state complexity assuming that the operands of a regular operation are represented by nondeterministic finite automata, while the language resulting from the operation is required to be represented by a deterministic finite automaton. We get tight upper bounds 2^n for complementation, reversal, and star, 2^m for left and right quotient, 2^{m+n} for union and symmetric difference, $2^{m+n} - 2^m - 2^n + 2$ for intersection, $2^{m+n} - 2^n + 1$ for difference, $\frac{3}{4} 2^{m+n}$ for concatenation, and 2^{mn} for shuffle. We use a binary alphabet to describe witnesses for complementation, reversal, star, and left and right quotient, and a quaternary alphabet otherwise. Whenever we use a binary alphabet, it is always optimal.

1 Introduction

The state complexity of a regular language L, $\mathrm{sc}(L)$, is the smallest number of states in any deterministic finite automaton (DFA) recognising L. The state complexity of a k-ary regular operation $\circ$ is a function from $\mathbb{N}^k$ to $\mathbb{N}$ given by

$$(n_1, n_2, \ldots, n_k) \mapsto \max\{\mathrm{sc}(\circ(L_1, L_2, \ldots, L_k)) \mid \mathrm{sc}(L_i) \le n_i \text{ for } i = 1, 2, \ldots, k\}.$$

The first results on the state complexity of basic regular operations have been obtained by Maslov [11], Birget [1], and Yu et al. [15]. Holzer and Kutrib [6] considered the representation of regular languages by nondeterministic finite automata (NFAs) and defined and studied the nondeterministic state complexity of regular languages and operations in an analogous way. Jirásek Jr. et al. [8,9] investigated operational state complexity using representation of regular languages by self-verifying and unambiguous finite automata. Notice that in all of the above mentioned cases, the arguments and the results of regular operations are represented by the same computational model.

Research supported by grant VEGA 2/0132/19 and grant APVV-15-0091. This work was conducted as a part of PhD study of the second author at Comenius University in Bratislava.

M. Hospodár et al. (Eds.): DCFS 2019, LNCS 11612, pp. 184–196, 2019.
https://doi.org/10.1007/978-3-030-23247-4_14

In this paper, we consider the NFA-to-DFA trade-off for regular operations, that is, we assume that the arguments of an operation are represented by NFAs, while the resulting language is required to be represented by a DFA. Our motivation comes from the following two streams of research.

While investigating operational state complexity on self-verifying or unambiguous automata, which are nondeterministic, the NFA-to-DFA trade-off provides an upper bound on the complexity of the corresponding operation since every DFA is self-verifying as well as unambiguous. As shown in [8,9], these upper bounds are tight for several operations.

Our second motivation comes from the research on the state complexity of combined operations that began with the paper by Salomaa et al. [12]. If a combined operation does not contain complementation, we can perform all the included operations using NFAs. Then, the NFA-to-DFA trade-off for the outermost operation can be used to get an upper bound on the desired complexity of a given combined operation.

We examine the NFA-to-DFA trade-off for complementation, intersection, union, difference, symmetric difference, reversal, star, concatenation, shuffle, and left and right quotient. For each of these operations, we get tight upper bound on its NFA-to-DFA trade-off. To describe witnesses, we use either binary or quaternary alphabets. The binary alphabet is always optimal in the sense that the corresponding upper bounds cannot be met by any unary languages.

To conclude this introduction, let us mention that the trade-offs between different models of finite automata have been studied for the forever operator defined as $L \mapsto (\Sigma^* L^c)^c$ by Birget [2] and Hospodár et al. [7].

2   Preliminaries

We assume that the reader is familiar with basic notions in formal languages and automata theory. For details and all unexplained notions, the reader may refer to [14].

Let Σ be a finite non-empty alphabet. Then Σ^* denotes the set of all words over Σ including the empty word ε. If $u, v, w \in \Sigma^*$ and $w = uv$, then u is *prefix* of w. Moreover, if $u \neq w$, then u is a *proper prefix* of w. A *language* over an alphabet Σ is any subset of Σ^*.

If K and L are languages over Σ, then the *complement* of L is $L^c = \Sigma^* \setminus L$. The *intersection, union, difference, and symmetric difference* of K and L are defined as for arbitrary sets. Next, we consider the following regular operations: *concatenation* $KL = \{uv \mid u \in K \text{ and } v \in L\}$, *star* $L^* = \bigcup_{i \geq 0} L^i$ where $L^0 = \{\varepsilon\}$ and $L^{i+1} = L^i L$, *reversal* $L^R = \{w^R \mid w \in L\}$, *shuffle* $K \sqcup\!\!\sqcup L = \{u_1 v_1 u_2 v_2 \cdots u_k v_k \mid u_i, v_i \in \Sigma^*, u_1 u_2 \cdots u_k \in K, v_1 v_2 \cdots v_k \in L\}$, *right quotient* $KL^{-1} = \{x \in \Sigma^* \mid xy \in K \text{ for some } y \in L\}$, and *left quotient* $L^{-1} K = \{x \in \Sigma^* \mid yx \in K \text{ for some } y \in L\}$.

A *nondeterministic finite automaton* (NFA) is a 5-tuple $A = (Q, \Sigma, \cdot, s, F)$, where Q is a finite non-empty set of states, Σ is a finite input alphabet, $s \in Q$ is the *starting (or initial)* state, $F \subseteq Q$ is the set of *final (or accepting)* states, and $\cdot: Q \times \Sigma \to 2^Q$ is the transition function which can be extended to the domain $2^Q \times \Sigma^*$ in the natural way. The language recognised by the NFA A is the set of words $L(A) = \{w \in \Sigma^* \mid s \cdot w \cap F \neq \emptyset\}$.

An NFA A is a *deterministic finite automaton* if $|q \cdot a| = 1$ for each $q \in Q$ and $a \in \Sigma$. In such a case we write $q \cdot a = q'$ instead of $q \cdot a = \{q'\}$, and use $q \xrightarrow{a} q'$ to denote that $q \cdot a = q'$. Sometimes we permit non-deterministic automata to have more initial states; in such a case we use an abbreviation NNFA from [14].

A subset S of Q is *reachable* in an NNFA $A = (Q, \Sigma, \cdot, I, F)$ if $S = I \cdot w$ for some $w \in \Sigma^*$, and it is *co-reachable* if it is reachable in the reversed automaton A^R obtained from A by reversing all its transitions and swapping the roles of the initial and final states.

Every NNFA $A = (Q, \Sigma, \cdot, I, F)$ has an equivalent deterministic finite automaton $\mathcal{D}(A) = (2^Q, \Sigma, \cdot, I, \{T \subseteq Q \mid T \cap F \neq \emptyset\})$. The DFA $\mathcal{D}(A)$ is called the *subset automaton* of A. The following observation provides a sufficient condition that guarantees distinguishability of all states in a subset automaton. We use this lemma throughout the paper.

Lemma 1 (Distinguishability). *Let A be an NFA such that for every state q of A the singleton set $\{q\}$ is co-reachable in A. Then every two distinct states of the subset automaton $\mathcal{D}(A)$ are distinguishable.*

Proof. Let us take two distinct subsets S and T of $\mathcal{D}(A)$. Without loss of generality, let $q \in S \setminus T$. Since the set $\{q\}$ is co-reachable in A, there is a word w_q that is accepted by A from the state q and rejected from every other state. It follows that in $\mathcal{D}(A)$, the word w_q is accepted from S and rejected from T. Hence S and T are distinguishable in $\mathcal{D}(A)$. $\square$

The next lemma shows that every subset of the state set of the NFA from Fig. 1 is reachable in the corresponding subset automaton. It also shows that to reach every non-empty subset, the final state $n - 1$ may be visited only in the very last steps. This is an important property which is used later the get the results for concatenation.

Lemma 2 (Reachability). *Let $A = (\{0, 1, \ldots, n - 1\}, \{a, b\}, \cdot, 0, \{n - 1\})$ be the NFA from Fig. 1. where $i \cdot a = \{i + 1\}$ if $0 \leq i \leq n - 2$, and $i \cdot b = \{0, i\}$. Then for each subset S of $\{0, 1, \ldots, n - 1\}$, there exists a word $u_S \in \{a, b\}^*$ such that $0 \cdot u_S = S$. Moreover,*

(1) if $S \neq \emptyset$ and $n - 1 \notin S$, then $n - 1 \notin 0 \cdot u'$ for each prefix u' of u_S;
(2) if $n - 1 \in S$ and $0 \notin S$, then $n - 1 \notin 0 \cdot u'$ for each proper prefix u' of u_S,
(3) if $n - 1 \in S$ and $0 \in S$, then $u_S = u'b$ and $n - 1 \notin 0 \cdot u''$ for each proper prefix u'' of u',

Proof. In the subset automaton $\mathcal{D}(A)$, each singleton set $\{i\}$ is reached from the initial subset $\{0\}$ by a^i and the empty set is reached from $\{n - 1\}$ by a. Each set $\{i_1, i_2, \ldots, i_k\}$ of size k, where $2 \leq k \leq n$ and $0 \leq i_1 < i_2 < \cdots < i_k \leq n - 1$, is reached from the set $\{i_2 - i_1, i_3 - i_1, \ldots, i_k - i_1\}$ of size $k - 1$ by ba^{i_1}. This

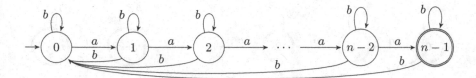

Fig. 1. A binary witness NFA for determinization and complementation.

proves the reachability of all subsets of $\{0, 1, \ldots, n-1\}$ by induction. Hence for each $S \subseteq \{0, 1, \ldots, n-1\}$, there is a word $u_S \in \{a, b\}^*$ such that $0 \cdot u_S = S$. By a careful analysis of the proof above, we get the properties (1), (2), and (3). $\square$

3 Complementation, Reversal, Star, and Concatenation

In this section we examine the NFA-to-DFA trade-off for basic unary operations and concatenation. We start with complementation. Its state complexity is n while its non-deterministic state complexity is 2^n [10]. The next theorem shows that its NFA-to-DFA trade-off is 2^n as well.

Theorem 3 (Complementation). *Let L be a language over Σ recognised by an n-state NFA. Then* $\mathrm{sc}(L^c) \leq 2^n$, *and the bound is tight if* $|\Sigma| \geq 2$.

Proof. Since $\mathrm{sc}(L^c) = \mathrm{sc}(L)$, the upper bound follows from the upper bound on determinization. For tightness, let L be the language recognised by the NFA A shown in Fig. 1. By Lemma 2, every subset of $\{0, 1, \ldots, n-1\}$ is reachable in the subset automaton $\mathcal{D}(A)$. Since every singleton set is co-reachable in A via a word in a^*, all states of $\mathcal{D}(A)$ are pairwise distinguishable by Lemma 1. $\square$

Notice that the binary alphabet used in the previous proof is optimal since every unary n-state NFA can be simulated by a DFA of $2^{O(\sqrt{n \ln n})}$ states as shown by Chrobak [5]. Let us continue with the reversal operation. Note that it is enough to take the reversal of any DFA with one final state meeting the upper bound 2^n on the state complexity of reversal. Such a binary DFA was described by Šebej [13]. Here we describe a different witness with significantly simpler proof.

Theorem 4 (Reversal). *Let L be a language over Σ recognised by an n-state NFA, where $n \geq 2$. Then* $\mathrm{sc}(L^R) \leq 2^n$, *and the bound is tight if $|\Sigma| \geq 2$.*

Proof. Let L be accepted by an n-state NFA $A = (Q, \Sigma, \cdot, s, F)$. By reversing all the transitions in A and taking F as the set of starting states and $\{s\}$ as set of final states we obtain an n-state NNFA that accepts L^R. It follows that L^R is accepted by a DFA with at most 2^n states.

To prove tightness, consider the binary language L recognised by the n-state NFA $N = (\{0, 1, \ldots, n-1\}, \{a, b\}, \cdot, 0, \{0, 1, \ldots, n-1\})$ shown in Fig. 2

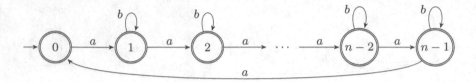

Fig. 2. A binary witness NFA for reversal meeting the upper bound 2^n.

where $i \cdot a = \{i + 1 \bmod n\}$, $i \cdot b = \{i\}$ if $i \geq 1$. By reversing NFA N we get an NNFA N^R that recognises L^R.

The set of initial state of N^R is $\{0, 1, \ldots, n-1\}$ and its unique final state is 0. Notice that each subset of the state set of N^R can be shifted cyclically by one by reading a, and the state 0 can be eliminated from every set containing 0 by reading b. It follows that every subset of $\{0, 1, \ldots, n-1\}$ can be reached from the initial subset $\{0, 1, \ldots, n-1\}$ in the subset automaton $\mathcal{D}(N^R)$. Next, every set $\{i\}$ is co-reachable in N^R via a word in a^* and using Lemma 1 we get that every two distinct states of the $\mathcal{D}(N^R)$ are distinguishable.   □

The binary alphabet used in the previous theorem is optimal for the same reason as in the case of complementation. We continue with the star operation. While its state complexity is $\frac{3}{4}2^n$ [11] and its nondeterministic state complexity is $n + 1$ [10], we show that the NFA-to-DFA trade-off for star is 2^n.

Theorem 5 (Star). *Let $n \geq 2$. Let L be a language over an alphabet Σ recognised by an n-state NFA. Then $\mathrm{sc}(L^*) \leq 2^n$, and the bound is tight if $|\Sigma| \geq 2$.*

Proof. Let L be recognised by an n-state NFA $A = (Q, \Sigma, \cdot, s, F)$. Construct an NNFA N recognising L^* from A as follows. First, for each transition (p, a, q) in A with $q \in F$, add the transition (p, a, s). Next, if $s \notin F$, then add a new initial and final state q_0 to accept the empty word. Consider the subset automaton $\mathcal{D}(N)$. The only reachable set in $\mathcal{D}(N)$ containing the state q_0 is the initial subset $\{s, q_0\}$. All the remaining reachable sets are subsets of Q. Moreover, if a reachable set contains a final state of A, then it also contains the state s. If A has a final state different from s, then at least 2^{n-2} sets are unreachable in $\mathcal{D}(N)$, so the upper bound is $1 + (3/4)2^n$ in this case. If $F = \{s\}$, then the construction above results in the same automaton, so $L^* = L$. In such a case, the upper bound is 2^n.

To prove tightness, consider the binary language L recognised by the n-state NFA $A = (\{0, 1, \ldots, n-1\}, \{a, b\}, \cdot, 0, \{0\})$ shown in Fig. 3 where for each state i, $i \cdot a = \{i + 1 \bmod n\}$, $i \cdot b = \{0, i\}$ if $i \geq 1$. Then $L^* = L$. In the subset automaton $\mathcal{D}(A)$, the empty set is reached from the initial subset $\{0\}$ by b. The reachability of all non-empty subsets is proved exactly the same way as in the proof of Lemma 2. Since every singleton set is co-reachable in A via a word in a^*, all the states of $\mathcal{D}(A)$ are pairwise distinguishable by Lemma 1.   □

The witness from the previous proof is described over a binary alphabet. It is impossible to meet the upper bound 2^n in the unary case since every unary

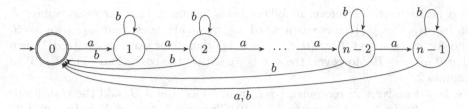

Fig. 3. A binary witness NFA for star meeting the upper bound 2^n.

n-state NFA can be simulated be a DFA with $2^{O(\sqrt{n \ln n})}$ states. The unary language recognised by the NFA from Fig. 4 provides a lower bound $(n-1)^2 + 2$; notice that this NFA is not unambiguous. We conjecture that this lower bound is tight. Our computations support this conjecture.

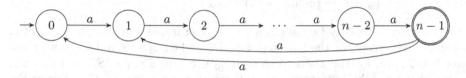

Fig. 4. A possible unary witness for star meeting the bound $(n-1)^2 + 2$.

We conclude this section with the concatenation operation the state complexity of which is $m2^n - 2^{n-1}$ [11] and nondeterministic complexity is $m+n$ [6]. The next theorem shows that NFA-to-DFA trade-off for concatenation is $\frac{3}{4}2^{m+n}$, that is, it is exponential in both m and n.

Theorem 6 (Concatenation). *Let K and L be non-empty languages over an alphabet Σ recognised by an m-state and n-state NFA, respectively, with $m, n \geq 3$. Then $sc(KL) \leq \frac{3}{4}2^{m+n}$, and the bound is tight if $|\Sigma| \geq 4$.*

Proof. Let $A = (Q_A, \Sigma, \cdot_A, s_A, F_A)$ and $B = (Q_B, \Sigma, \cdot_B, s_B, F_B)$ be NFAs recognising K and L, respectively, with $|Q_A| = m$, $|Q_B| = n$ Construct an NNFA N for KL from NFAs A and B as follows. For each transition (p, a, q) in NFA A with $q \in F_A$, add the transition (p, a, s_B). The set of initial states of N is $\{s_A\}$ if $s_A \notin F_A$, or $\{s_A, s_B\}$ if $s_A \in F_A$. The set of final states of N is F_B. The following condition holds in the subset automaton $\mathcal{D}(N)$: each reachable subset containing a state from F_A must contain the state s_B. It follows that at least 2^{m+n-2} are unreachable in $\mathcal{D}(N)$, and the upper bound follows.

For tightness, let $\Sigma = \{a, b, c, d\}$ and K and L be the languages over Σ recognised by the NFAs $A = (\{q_0, q_1, \ldots, q_{m-1}\}, \Sigma, \cdot_A, q_0, \{q_{m-1}\})$ and $B = (\{0, 1, \ldots, n-1\}, \Sigma, \cdot_B, 0, \{n-1\})$ shown in Fig. 5. Notice that transitions on a and b in A are the same as in the NFA in Fig. 1 and perform the identity function in B. The roles of the transitions on c and d in B are the same as the roles of a and b in A. Therefore, it follows from Lemma 2 that for every subset S of $\{q_0, q_1, \ldots, q_{m-1}\}$, there is a word u_S in $\{a, b\}^*$ such that $q_0 \cdot_A u_S = S$, and for every subset T of $\{0, 1, \ldots, n-1\}$, there is a word v_T in $\{c, d\}^*$ such that $0 \cdot_B v_T = T$. Moreover, the words u_S satisfy the conditions (1), (2), (3) in Lemma 2.

To get an NFA N recognising KL from NFAs A and B, add the transitions $(q_{m-2}, a, 0)$, $(q_{m-1}, b, 0)$, and $(q_{m-1}, c, 0)$. The initial state of N is $\{q_0\}$ and its unique final state is $n-1$. Let $S \subseteq \{q_0, q_1, \ldots, q_{m-1}\}$ and $T \subseteq \{0, 1, \ldots, n-1\}$ be two subsets such that if $q_{m-1} \in S$ then $0 \in T$. The following transitions use the words $u_S \in \{a, b\}^*$ and $v_T \in \{c, d\}^*$ given by Lemma 2 to show that the set $S \cup T$ is reachable in the subset automaton $\mathcal{D}(N)$:

$$\{q_0\} \xrightarrow{a^{m-1}} \{q_{m-1}, 0\} \xrightarrow{b} \{q_0, q_{m-1}, 0\} \xrightarrow{d} \{q_0, 0\};$$
$$\{q_0, 0\} \xrightarrow{v_T} \{q_0\} \cup T \xrightarrow{u_S} S \cup T \qquad \text{if } S \neq \emptyset;$$
$$\{q_0, 0\} \xrightarrow{a} \{q_1, 0\} \xrightarrow{d} \{0\} \xrightarrow{v_T} T;$$

let us emphasise that by Lemma 2, while reading u_S, the final state q_{m-1} of A is not visited, except for the last step if $q_0 \notin S$ and $q_{m-1} \in S$ and when we must have $0 \in T$, and for the last two steps if $q_0 \in S$ and $q_{m-1} \in S$ when u_S ends with b that fixes the initial state 0 of B which must be in T. This proves the reachability of $\frac{3}{4} 2^{m+n}$ states in the subset automaton $\mathcal{D}(N)$.

To prove distinguishability, notice that each singleton set $\{j\}, 0 \le j \le n-1$ is co-reachable in N via a word in c^*. Next, $\{q_{m-1}\}$ is co-reachable by c^n, and each $\{q_i\}, 0 \le i \le m-2$ is co-reachable via a word in $c^n a^*$. By Lemma 1, all states of $\mathcal{D}(N)$ are pairwise distinguishable. □

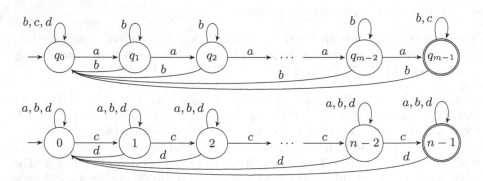

Fig. 5. Witness NFAs for concatenation meeting the upper bound $\frac{3}{4} 2^{m+n}$.

The witness in the previous proof is defined over a quaternary alphabet. Consider binary languages $K = (a + b)^* a(a + b)^{m-2}$ and $L = (a + b)^{n-1}$ recognised by an m-state and n-state NFA, respectively. Then $KL = (a + b)^* a(a + b)^{m+n-3}$, the minimal DFA for which has 2^{m+n-4} states. This gives the lower bound $(1/16) 2^{m+n}$ in the binary case which is asymptotically the same as the upper bound for quaternary case. In the unary case the upper bound is $2^{O(\sqrt{(m+n)\ln(m+n)})}$. A lower bound $1 + F(n-1)$ is given by languages $K = \{\varepsilon\}$ and L equal to the witness for determinization in the unary case; here $F(n)$ is Landau's function given by $F(n) = \max\{\mathrm{lcm}(x_1, \ldots, x_k) \mid n = x_1 + \cdots + x_k\}$, and with $F(n) \approx 2^{\sqrt{n \ln n}}$.

4   Boolean Operations

Here we consider NFA-to-DFA trade-off for four binary Boolean operations. First, we recall some notions. We call a state q of a DFA $A = (Q, \Sigma, \cdot, s, F)$ a *sink state* if $q \cdot a = q$ for every letter $a \in \Sigma$. The state q is called *dead* if reading every word from the state q results in a non-accepting state of A.

To get an automaton recognising union, intersection, difference, or symmetric difference of two languages we use the product construction as described below. Let $A = (Q_A, \Sigma, \cdot_A, s_A, F_A)$ and $B = (Q_B, \Sigma, \cdot_B, s_B, F_B)$ be two DFAs over an alphabet Σ. Let $\circ \in \{\cap, \cup, \setminus, \oplus\}$. Then the language $L(A) \circ L(B)$ is recognised by the product automaton $M_\circ = (Q_A \times Q_B, \Sigma, \cdot, (s_A, s_B), F_\circ)$ where $(p, q) \cdot a = (p \cdot_A a, q \cdot_B a)$ for all $p \in Q_A$, $q \in Q_B$, and $a \in \Sigma$, and

$$F_\circ = \begin{cases} F_A \times F_B, & \text{if } \circ = \cap; \\ (F_A \times Q_B) \cup (Q_A \times F_B), & \text{if } \circ = \cup; \\ F_A \times (Q_B \setminus F_B), & \text{if } \circ = \setminus; \\ (F_A \times (Q_B \setminus F_B)) \cup ((Q_A \setminus F_A) \times F_B), & \text{if } \circ = \oplus. \end{cases}$$

If the operation inputs are given by NFAs, we first apply the subset construction to get DFAs for those inputs. Then we construct the corresponding product automaton. Notice that every subset automaton has at least one rejecting sink state, namely, the empty set. The following lemma provides upper bounds for Boolean operations on DFAs considering the presence of the rejecting sink states.

Lemma 7. *Let K and L be languages over Σ accepted by DFAs with m and n states respectively. Assume that both DFAs have a rejecting sink state. Then $\mathrm{sc}(K \cup L) \leq mn$, $\mathrm{sc}(K \oplus L) \leq mn$, $\mathrm{sc}(K \cap L) \leq mn - m - n + 2$, and $\mathrm{sc}(K \setminus L) \leq mn - n + 1$.*

Proof. For each Boolean operation $\circ \in \{\cup, \cap, \setminus, \oplus\}$, the language $K \circ L$ is recognised by the product automaton $M_\circ$ which has mn states. This gives the upper bounds for union and symmetric difference. Let d_A and d_B be the rejecting sink states of A and B, respectively. Then in the product automaton $M_\cap$ recognizing $K \cap L$, the states (d_A, q) with $q \in Q_B$ and the states (p, d_B) with $p \in Q_A$ are dead and can be merged into one sink state. This gives the upper bound $(m-1)(n-1)+1 = mn - m - n + 2$. In the product automaton $M_\setminus$ recognising $K \setminus L$, the states (d_A, p) with $p \in Q_B$ are dead, which gives the upper bound $(m-1)n + 1 = mn - n + 1$. $\square$

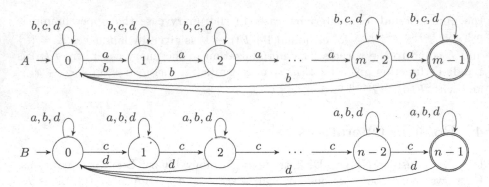

Fig. 6. Quaternary witnesses for Boolean operations.

Now we are ready to get tight upper bounds on NFA-to-DFA trade-off for Boolean operations.

Theorem 8. *Let $\dot{K}$ and L be languages over Σ recognised by an m-state and n-state NFA, respectively, where $m, n \geq 2$. Then $\mathrm{sc}(K \cup L), \mathrm{sc}(K \oplus L) \leq 2^{m+n}$, $\mathrm{sc}(K \cap L) \leq 2^{m+n} - 2^m - 2^n + 2$, and $\mathrm{sc}(K \setminus L) \leq 2^{m+n} - 2^n + 1$. All these bounds are tight if $|\Sigma| \geq 4$.*

Proof. Let A be an m-state NFA recognising K and B be an n-state NFA recognising L. Consider the corresponding subset automata $\mathcal{D}(A)$ and $\mathcal{D}(B)$ with 2^m and 2^n states, respectively. Both of them have at least one rejecting sink state, namely, the empty set. Then all upper bounds follow from Lemma 7.

For tightness, let K and L by the languages recognised by NFAs A and B from Fig. 6. Notice that transitions on a and b in A are the same as in the NFA in Fig. 1 and perform the identity function in B. The roles of the transitions on c and d in B are the same as the roles of a and b in A. Moreover c and d perform the identity function in A. It follows from Lemma 2 that for every $S \subseteq \{0, 1, \ldots, m-1\}$, there is a word $u_S \in \{a, b\}^*$ such that $0 \cdot_A u_S = S$, and for every $T \subseteq \{0, 1, \ldots, n-1\}$, there is a word $v_T \in \{c, d\}^*$ such that $0 \cdot_B v_T = T$.

Let $\circ \in \{\cup, \oplus, \cap, \setminus\}$. Construct the product automaton $M_\circ$ from DFAs $\mathcal{D}(A)$ and $\mathcal{D}(B)$. The initial state of $M_\circ$ is $(\{0\}, \{0\})$. Let $S \subseteq \{0, 1, \ldots, m-1\}$ and $T \subseteq \{0, 1, \ldots, n-1\}$. Then the state (S, T) is reachable in $M_\circ$ from the initial state by the word $u_S v_T$. Hence each state of $M_\circ$ is reachable.

To prove distinguishability first consider union. Then (S, T) is final in $M_\cup$ if $m - 1 \in S$ or $n - 1 \in T$. Let (S, T) and (S', T') be two distinct states of $M_\cup$. Then $S \neq S'$ or $T \neq T'$. In the first case, without loss of generality let $s \in S \setminus S'$. Consider the word $a^{m-1-s} c^n$. Notice that

$$(S, T) \xrightarrow{a^{m-1-s} c^n} (\{m-1\} \cup S_1, \emptyset) \text{ for some } S_1 \subseteq \{0, 1, \ldots, m-1\};$$

$$(S', T') \xrightarrow{a^{m-1-s} c^n} (S'_1, \emptyset) \text{ where } m - 1 \notin S'_1.$$

It follows that $a^{m-1-s}c^n$ is accepted by $M_\cup$ from (S,T) and rejected from (S',T'). The case of $T \neq T'$ is symmetric. We can prove distinguishability for symmetric difference in the exact same manner. We can also find the appropriate words that distinguish the desired number of states in the product automaton for intersection and difference. □

Notice that the upper bounds in the previous theorem cannot be met by unary languages. The cases of binary and ternary alphabets remain open.

5   Shuffle, Left and Right Quotient

Here we consider three more binary operations. In all three cases the upper bound constructions are similar to the case when the operation inputs are given by DFAs. Our lower bound for shuffle is the same as the upper bound on its state complexity. The lower bound for left quotient is greater by one than its state complexity. For right quotient, the NFA-to-DFA trade-off is 2^m, while its (nondeterministic) state complexity is m.

Theorem 9 (Shuffle). *Let K and L be languages over Σ recognised by an m-state and n-state NFA, respectively, where $m, n \geq 3$. Then $\mathrm{sc}(K \shuffle L) \leq 2^{mn}$, and the bound is tight if $|\Sigma| \geq 4$.*

Proof. Let $A = (Q_A, \Sigma, s_A, \cdot_A, F_A)$ and $B = (Q_B, \Sigma, s_B, \cdot_B, F_B)$ be an m-state and n-state NFAs recognising the languages K and L, respectively. Then the language $K \shuffle L$ is recognised by mn-state NFA

$$N = (Q_A \times Q_B, \Sigma, \cdot, (s_A, s_B), F_A \times F_B)$$

where for each $(p,q) \in Q_A \times Q_B$ and $a \in \Sigma$,

$$(p,q) \cdot a = \{(p,q') \mid q' \in q \cdot_B a\} \cup \{(p',q) \mid p' \in p \cdot_A a\}.$$

It follows that $\mathrm{sc}(K \shuffle L) \leq 2^{mn}$.

The m-state and n-state partial DFAs over $\{a,b,c,d,f\}$ meeting this upper bound have been described in [4, Proof of Theorem 1]. Notice in that the role of c and d in that proof is to reach the set $Q_A \times Q_B$ in the subset automaton. The same goal can be achieved if we replace c and d by the transitions on letter e defined as follows: $0 \cdot_A e = \{0,1\}$, $i \cdot_A e = \{i+1\}$, if $1 \leq i \leq m-2$, and $0 \cdot_B e = \{0,1\}$, $j \cdot_B e = \{j+1\}$, if $1 \leq j \leq n-2$. As a result we get a quaternary witness for shuffle. □

In the unary case the upper bound for shuffle is again $2^{O(\sqrt{(m+n)\ln(m+n)})}$.

Theorem 10 (Left and Right Quotient). *Let K and L be languages over an alphabet Σ recognised by an m-state and n-state NFA, respectively, where $m, n \geq 2$. Then $\mathrm{sc}(L^{-1}K), \mathrm{sc}(KL^{-1}) \leq 2^m$, and the bounds are tight if $|\Sigma| \geq 2$.*

Proof. Let $A = (Q_A, \Sigma, s_A, \cdot_A, F_A)$ be an m-state NFA recognising K. The language $L^{-1}K$ is recognised by the m-state NFA N obtained from A by changing the set of initial states to $\{s_A \cdot_A w \mid w \in L\}$. The language KL^{-1} is recognised by the m-state NFA N obtained from A by changing the set of final states to $\{q \in Q_A \mid q \cdot_A w \in F_A \text{ for some } w \in L\}$. Hence $\mathrm{sc}(L^{-1}K), \mathrm{sc}(KL^{-1}) \leq 2^m$.

For tightness, notice that $\{\varepsilon\}^{-1}K = K\{\varepsilon\}^{-1} = K$. Therefore, the upper bound 2^m is met in both cases by $L = \{\varepsilon\}$ and K equal to the binary m-state witness NFA for determinization given by Lemma 2; for distinguishability, notice that each singleton set is co-reachable in this NFA.   □

The binary alphabet used in the theorem above is optimal since determinization in the unary case is in $2^{O(\sqrt{n \ln n})}$.

6   Conclusions

We investigated the NFA-to-DFA trade-off for several regular operations. Our results are summarised in Table 1. The table also displays the size of alphabet used to describe our witnesses. Whenever we used a binary alphabet, it was is always optimal in the sense that the corresponding upper bounds cannot be met by any unary languages. The table also compares our results to the known results on the state complexity and the nondeterministic state complexity of all considered operations [3,6,10,11,15].

Table 2 shows the operational state complexity on languages represented by self-verifying and unambiguous finite automata from [8,9]. The NFA-to-DFA trade-off for concatenation, shuffle, left and right quotient is up to one state almost the same as the complexity of these operations on unambiguous automata. The same holds for left quotient on self-verifying automata.

Table 1. The NFA-to-DFA trade-off vs (nondeterministic) state complexity.

	NFA-to-DFA	$|\Sigma|$	DFA	$|\Sigma|$	NFA	$|\Sigma|$
Complementation	2^n	2	n	1	2^n	2
Reversal	2^n	2	2^n	2	$n+1$	2
Star	2^n	2	$\frac{3}{4} \cdot 2^n$	2	$n+1$	1
Concatenation	$\frac{3}{4}2^{m+n}$	4	$m2^n - 2^{n-1}$	2	$m+n$	2
Union	2^{m+n}	4	mn	2	$m+n+1$	2
Symmetric difference	2^{m+n}	4	mn	2	?	
Intersection	$2^{m+n} - 2^m - 2^n + 2$	4	mn	2	mn	2
Difference	$2^{m+n} - 2^n + 1$	4	mn	2	?	
Shuffle	2^{mn}	4	$\leq 2^{mn}$	5	mn	2
Left quotient	2^m	2	$2^m - 1$	2	$m+1$	2
Right quotient	2^m	2	m	1	m	1

Table 2. Operational complexity for self-verifying and unambiguous automata.

	SVFA	$|\Sigma|$	UFA	$|\Sigma|$
Complementation	n	1	$n^{2-\epsilon} \leq \cdot \leq$ $2^{0.79n+\log n}$	1
Reversal	$2n+1$	2	n	1
Star	$\frac{3}{4} \cdot 2^n$	$\frac{3}{4} \cdot 2^n + 1$	$\frac{3}{4} \cdot 2^n$	3
Concatenation	$\Theta(3^{\frac{m}{3}} 2^n)$	$3^{\frac{m}{3}} + 2^n + 1$	$\frac{3}{4} \cdot 2^{m+n} - 1$	7
Union	mn	2	$mn + m + n \leq \cdot \leq$ $m + n2^{0.79n+\overline{\log} n}$	4
Symmetric difference	mn	2	?	
Intersection	mn	2	mn	2
Difference	mn	2	?	
Shuffle	?		$2^{mn} - 1$	5
Left quotient	$2^m - 1$	$2^m + 1$	$2^m - 1$	2
Right quotient	$3^{\frac{m}{3}}$	$3^{\frac{m}{3}} + 2$	$2^m - 1$	2

Acknowledgement. We would like to kindly thank Michal Hospodár for his valuable notes and comments.

References

1. Birget, J.: Intersection and union of regular languages and state complexity. Inf. Process. Lett. **43**(4), 185–190 (1992). https://doi.org/10.1016/0020-0190(92)90198-5
2. Birget, J.: The state complexity of $\overline{\Sigma^* \overline{L}}$ and its connection with temporal logic. Inf. Process. Lett. **58**(4), 185–188 (1996). https://doi.org/10.1016/0020-0190(96)00044-0
3. Brzozowski, J.A.: Quotient complexity of regular languages. J. Autom. Lang. Comb. **15**(1/2), 71–89 (2010). https://doi.org/10.25596/jalc-2010-071
4. Câmpeanu, C., Salomaa, K., Yu, S.: Tight lower bound for the state complexity of shuffle of regular languages. J. Autom. Lang. Comb. **7**(3), 303–310 (2002). https://doi.org/10.25596/jalc-2002-303
5. Chrobak, M.: Finite automata and unary languages. Theor. Comput. Sci. **47**(3), 149–158 (1986). https://doi.org/10.1016/0304-3975(86)90142-8
6. Holzer, M., Kutrib, M.: Nondeterministic descriptional complexity of regular languages. Int. J. Found. Comput. Sci. **14**(6), 1087–1102 (2003). https://doi.org/10.1142/S0129054103002199
7. Hospodár, M., Jirásková, G., Mlynárčik, P.: Descriptional complexity of the forever operator. Int. J. Found. Comput. Sci. **30**(1), 115–134 (2019). https://doi.org/10.1142/S0129054119400069
8. Jirásek, J.Š., Jirásková, G., Szabari, A.: Operations on self-verifying finite automata. In: Beklemishev, L.D., Musatov, D.V. (eds.) CSR 2015. LNCS, vol. 9139, pp. 231–261. Springer, Cham (2015). https://doi.org/10.1007/978-3-319-20297-6_16

9. Jirásek Jr., J., Jirásková, G., Šebej, J.: Operations on unambiguous finite automata. Int. J. Found. Comput. Sci. **29**(5), 861–876 (2018). https://doi.org/10.1142/S012905411842008X
10. Jirásková, G.: State complexity of some operations on binary regular languages. Theor. Comput. Sci. **330**(2), 287–298 (2005). https://doi.org/10.1016/j.tcs.2004.04.011
11. Maslov, A.N.: Estimates of the number of states of finite automata. Sov. Math. Dokl. **11**(5), 1373–1375 (1970)
12. Salomaa, A., Salomaa, K., Yu, S.: State complexity of combined operations. Theor. Comput. Sci. **383**(2–3), 140–152 (2007). https://doi.org/10.1016/j.tcs.2007.04.015
13. Šebej, J.: Reversal of regular languages and state complexity. In: Pardubská, D. (ed.) Proceedings of the Conference on Theory and Practice of Information Technologies, ITAT 2010. CEUR Workshop Proceedings, vol. 683, pp. 47–54. CEUR-WS.org (2010). http://ceur-ws.org/Vol-683/paper8.pdf
14. Yu, S.: Regular languages. In: Rozenberg, G., Salomaa, A. (eds.) Handbook of Formal Languages, pp. 41–110. Springer, Heidelberg (1997). https://doi.org/10.1007/978-3-642-59136-5_2
15. Yu, S., Zhuang, Q., Salomaa, K.: The state complexities of some basic operations on regular languages. Theor. Comput. Sci. **125**(2), 315–328 (1994). https://doi.org/10.1016/0304-3975(92)00011-F

State Complexity of Simple Splicing

Lila Kari and Timothy Ng[✉]

School of Computer Science, University of Waterloo,
Waterloo, Ontario N2L 3G1, Canada
{lila.kari,tim.ng}@uwaterloo.ca

Abstract. Splicing, as a binary word/language operation, was inspired
by the DNA recombination under the action of restriction enzymes and
ligases, and was first introduced by Tom Head in 1987. Splicing systems
as generative mechanisms were defined as consisting of an initial starting
set of words called an axiom set, and a set of splicing rules—each encoding a splicing operation—, as their computational engine to iteratively
generate new strings starting from the axiom set. Since finite splicing systems (splicing systems with a finite axiom set and a finite set of splicing
rules) generate a subclass of the family of regular languages, descriptional
complexity questions about splicing systems can be answered in terms
of the size of the minimal deterministic finite automata that recognize
their languages. In this paper we focus on a particular type of splicing
systems, called simple splicing systems, where the splicing rules are of
a particular form. We prove a tight state complexity bound of $2^n - 1$
for (semi-)simple splicing systems with a regular initial language with
state complexity $n \geq 3$. We also show that the state complexity of a
(semi-)simple splicing system with a finite initial language is at most
$2^{n-2} + 1$, and that whether this bound is reachable or not depends on
the size of the alphabet and the number of splicing rules.

1 Introduction

In [10] Head described a language-theoretic operation, called *splicing*, which
models DNA recombination, a cut-and-paste operation on DNA double-stranded
molecules, under the action of restriction enzymes and ligases. A *splicing system*
is a formal language model which consists of a set of *initial words*, I (representing double-stranded DNA strings), and a set of *splicing rules* R (representing
restriction enzymes). The most commonly used definition for a splicing rule is
a quadruplet of words $r = (u_1, v_1; u_2, v_2)$. This rule splices two words $x_1 u_1 v_1 y_1$
and $x_2 u_2 v_2 y_2$: the words are cut between the factors u_1, v_1, respectively u_2, v_2,
and the prefix (the left segment) of the first word is recombined by catenation
with the suffix (the right segment) of the second word; see Fig. 1 and also [16].
The words $u_1 v_1$ and $u_2 v_2$ are the restriction sites in the rule r. A splicing system generates a language which contains every word that can be obtained by
successively applying rules to axioms and the intermediately produced words.

© IFIP International Federation for Information Processing 2019
Published by Springer Nature Switzerland AG 2019
M. Hospodár et al. (Eds.): DCFS 2019, LNCS 11612, pp. 197–209, 2019.
https://doi.org/10.1007/978-3-030-23247-4_15

The most natural variant of splicing systems, often referred to as *finite splicing systems*, is to consider a finite set of axioms and a finite set of rules.

Several different types of splicing systems have been proposed in the literature, and Bonizzoni et al. [1] showed that the classes of languages they generate are related. Shortly after the introduction of splicing in formal language theory, Culik II and Harju [4] proved that finite splicing systems can only generate regular languages; see also [11,15]. Gatterdam [7] gave $(aa)^*$ as an example of a regular language which cannot be generated by a finite splicing system; thus, the class of languages generated by finite splicing systems is strictly included in the class of regular languages.

Fig. 1. Splicing of the words $x_1u_1v_1y_1$ and $x_2u_2v_2y_2$ by the rule $r = (u_1, v_1; u_2, v_2)$.

Descriptional complexity considers the complexity of a language in terms of the size of a computational device (in this case splicing system) that generates or recognizes it. For instance, Mateescu et al. [14] consider a number of descriptional complexity measures for simple splicing systems, such as the number of rules, the number of words in the initial language, the maximum length of a word in the initial language, and the sum of the lengths of all words in the initial language. Loos et al. [13] consider the descriptional complexity of finite splicing systems by using the number of rules, the length of the rules, and the size of the initial language as complexity measures. Păun [16] proposed using the radius, the largest u_i in a rule, as a descriptional complexity measure.

As the class of languages generated by splicing systems forms a subclass of the family of regular languages, their descriptional complexity can also be considered in terms of the finite automata that recognize them. For example, Loos et al. [13] gave a bound on the number of states required for a nondeterministic finite automaton to recognize the language generated by an equivalent finite splicing system.

We focus our attention on simple splicing systems, that is, splicing systems where the rules $(u_1, v_1; u_2, v_2)$ are of a particular form: $u_1 = u_2 = a$, are singleton letters, and $v_1 = v_2 = \varepsilon$ are the empty word. The descriptional complexity of simple splicing systems was considered by Mateescu et al. [14] in terms of the size of a right linear grammar that generates a simple splicing language. Here we consider the descriptional complexity of simple splicing systems in terms of deterministic state complexity [6]. In other words, we measure the descriptional complexity of a simple splicing system in terms of the size of the minimal deterministic finite automaton that recognizes the language generated by the splicing system.

In this paper, we prove tight state complexity bounds for simple and semi-simple splicing systems with regular and finite initial languages. In Sect. 2, we fix notation and definitions for simple splicing systems. We consider the state complexity of simple splicing systems with regular and finite initial languages in Sect. 3. In Sect. 4, we give tight state complexity bounds for semi-simple splicing systems with finite initial languages. We consider the state complexity of the crossover operation related to simple splicing systems in Sect. 5.

2 Preliminaries

Let Σ be a finite alphabet. We denote by Σ^* the set of all finite words over Σ, including the empty word, which we denote by ε. We denote the length of a word w by $|w| = n$. If $w = xyz$ for $x, y, z \in \Sigma^*$, we say that x is a prefix of w, y is a factor of w, and z is a suffix of w.

A deterministic finite automaton (DFA) is a tuple $A = (Q, \Sigma, \delta, q_0, F)$ where Q is a finite set of states, Σ is an alphabet, δ is a function $\delta : Q \times \Sigma \to Q$, $s \in Q$ is the initial state, and $F \subset Q$ is a set of final states. We extend the transition function δ to a function $Q \times \Sigma^* \to Q$ in the usual way. A DFA A is complete if δ is defined for all $q \in Q$ and $a \in \Sigma$. We will make use of the notation $q \xrightarrow{w} q'$ for $\delta(q, w) = q'$, where $w \in \Sigma^*$ and $q, q' \in Q$. A state $q \in Q$ is called a sink state if $\delta(q, a) = q$ for all $a \in \Sigma$ and $q \notin F$.

Each letter $a \in \Sigma$ defines a transformation of the state set Q. Let $\delta_a : Q \to Q$ be the transformation on Q induced by a, defined by $\delta_a(q) = \delta(q, a)$. We extend this definition to words by composing the transformations $\delta_w = \delta_{a_1} \circ \delta_{a_2} \circ \cdots \circ \delta_{a_n}$ for $w = a_1 a_2 \cdots a_n$. We denote by $\operatorname{im} \delta_a$ the image of δ_a, defined $\operatorname{im} \delta_a = \{\delta(p, a) \mid p \in Q\}$.

The language recognized or accepted by A is $L(A) = \{w \in \Sigma^* \mid \delta(q_0, w) \in F\}$. A state q is called *reachable* if there exists a string $w \in \Sigma^*$ such that $\delta(q_0, w) = q$. Two states p and q of A are said to be *equivalent* if $\delta(p, w) \in F$ if and only if $\delta(q, w) \in F$ for every word $w \in \Sigma^*$. A DFA A is minimal if each state $q \in Q$ is reachable from the initial state and no two states are equivalent. The state complexity of a regular language L is the number of states of the minimal complete DFA recognizing L [6].

A nondeterministic finite automaton (NFA) is a tuple $A = (Q, \Sigma, \delta, I, F)$ where Q is a finite set of states, Σ is an alphabet, δ is a function $\delta : Q \times \Sigma \to 2^Q$, $I \subseteq Q$ is a set of initial states, and F is a set of final states. The language recognized by an NFA A is $L(A) = \{w \in \Sigma^* \mid \bigcup_{q \in I} \delta(q, w) \cap F \neq \emptyset\}$. As with DFAs, transitions of A can be viewed as transformations on the state set. Let $\delta_a : Q \to 2^Q$ be the transformation on Q induced by a, defined by $\delta_a(q) = \delta(q, a)$. The image of δ_a is defined by $\operatorname{im} \delta_a = \{\delta(p, a) \mid p \in Q\}$. We make use of the notation $P \xrightarrow{w} P'$ for $P' = \bigcup_{q \in P} \delta(q, w)$, where $w \in \Sigma^*$ and $P, P' \subseteq Q$.

2.1 Simple Splicing Systems

In this paper we will use the notation of Păun [16], even though simple splicing systems can be defined using any of the three definitions of splicing. The splicing operation is defined via sets of quadruples $r = (\alpha_1, \alpha_2; \alpha_3, \alpha_4)$

with $\alpha_1, \alpha_2, \alpha_3, \alpha_4 \in \Sigma^*$ called splicing rules. For two strings $x = x_1\alpha_1\alpha_2x_2$ and $y = y_1\alpha_3\alpha_4y_2$, applying the rule $r = (\alpha_1, \alpha_2; \alpha_3, \alpha_4)$ produces a string $z = x_1\alpha_1\alpha_4y_2$, which we denote by $(x, y) \vdash^r z$.

A *splicing scheme* is a pair $\sigma = (\Sigma, \mathcal{R})$ where Σ is an alphabet and $\mathcal{R}$ is a set of splicing rules. For a splicing scheme $\sigma = (\Sigma, \mathcal{R})$ and a language $L \subseteq \Sigma^*$, we denote by $\sigma(L)$ the language

$$\sigma(L) = L \cup \{z \in \Sigma^* \mid (x, y) \vdash^r z, \text{where } x, y \in L, r \in \mathcal{R}\}.$$

Then we define $\sigma^0(L) = L$ and $\sigma^{i+1}(L) = \sigma(\sigma^i(L))$ for $i \geq 0$ and

$$\sigma^*(L) = \lim_{i \to \infty} \sigma^i(L) = \bigcup_{i \geq 0} \sigma^i(L).$$

For a splicing scheme $\sigma = (\Sigma, \mathcal{R})$ and an initial language $L \subseteq \Sigma^*$, we say the triple $H = (\Sigma, \mathcal{R}, L)$ is a *splicing system*. The language generated by H is defined by $L(H) = \sigma^*(L)$.

Mateescu et al. [14] define a restricted class of splicing systems called simple splicing systems. A *simple splicing system* is a triple $H = (\Sigma, M, I)$, where Σ is an alphabet, $M \subseteq \Sigma$ is a set of markers, and I is a finite initial language over Σ. For $a \in M$, we have $(x, y) \vdash^a z$ if and only if $x = x_1ax_2$, $y = y_1ay_2$, and $z = x_1ay_2$ for some $x_1, x_2, y_1, y_2 \in \Sigma^*$.

In other words, a simple splicing system is a system in which the set of rules is $\mathcal{M} = \{(a, \varepsilon; a, \varepsilon) \mid a \in M\}$ and the initial language I is finite. Since the rules are determined solely by our choice of $M \subseteq \Sigma$, the set M is used in the definition of the simple splicing system rather than the set of rules $\mathcal{M}$. Based on these properties, one can deduce that the class of languages generated by simple splicing systems is subregular [4,15]. Mateescu et al. [14] show that these languages form a proper subclass of the extended star-free languages.

In this paper, we will relax the condition that the initial language of a simple splicing system must be a finite language. We will consider also simple splicing systems with regular initial languages. By [16], it is clear that such a splicing system will also produce a regular language. In the following, we will use the convention that I denotes a finite language and L denotes an infinite language.

3   State Complexity of Simple Splicing

In this section, we will give tight state complexity bounds for simple splicing systems with regular and finite initial languages. First, we will define an NFA that recognizes the language of a given simple splicing system. The construction follows a more general construction due to Loos et al. [13] for finite splicing systems. This construction is a simplification of a construction by Pixton [15], which itself is a simplification of the original proof of regularity of finite splicing due to Culik II and Harju [4].

Proposition 1. *Let $H = (\Sigma, M, L)$ be a simple splicing system with a regular initial language L and let L be recognized by a DFA with n states. Then there exists an NFA A'_H with n states such that $L(A'_H) = L(H)$.*

Proof. Let $H = (\Sigma, M, L)$ and let $A = (Q, \Sigma, \delta, q_0, F)$ be a DFA for L. We will define the NFA $A_H = (Q', \Sigma, \delta', q_0, F)$, where $Q' = Q \cup Q_M$ with $Q_M = \{p_a, p'_a \mid a \in M\}$ and the transition function δ' is defined

- $\delta'(q, a) = \{\delta(q, a)\}$ if $q \in Q$ and $a \in \Sigma$,
- $\delta'(q, \varepsilon) = \{p_a\}$ if $q \in Q$, $a \in M$, and $\delta(q, a)$ is not the sink state,
- $\delta'(p_a, a) = \{p'_a\}$ if $p_a \in Q_M$,
- $\delta'(p'_a, \varepsilon) = \operatorname{im} \delta_a$ if $p'_a \in Q_M$ and $a \in M$.

First, we describe the construction of [13]. Let $\mathcal{M} = \{(a, \varepsilon; a, \varepsilon) \mid a \in M\}$ be the set of rules for H. For each rule $(\alpha_1, \alpha_2; \alpha_3, \alpha_4) \in \mathcal{M}$, add new states and transitions corresponding to $\alpha_1 \alpha_4$ and $\alpha_3 \alpha_2$. That is, if $\alpha_1 = a_1 \cdots a_i$, $\alpha_2 = b_1 \cdots b_j$, $\alpha_3 = c_1 \cdots c_k$, and $\alpha_4 = d_1 \cdots d_\ell$, then add states and transitions corresponding to a path $r_0 \xrightarrow{a_1} r_1 \xrightarrow{a_2} \cdots \xrightarrow{d_\ell} r_{i+\ell}$ for $\alpha_1 \alpha_4$ and a path $s_0 \xrightarrow{c_1} s_1 \xrightarrow{c_2} \cdots \xrightarrow{b_j} s_{j+k}$ corresponding to $\alpha_3 \alpha_2$. Now consider each path $q \xrightarrow{\alpha_1 \alpha_2} q'$ in A such that q is reachable from the initial state q_0 and a final state of A is reachable from q'. We add an ε-transition from q to r_0 and from s_{j+k} to q'. Similarly, for each path $t \xrightarrow{\alpha_3 \alpha_4} t'$, add ε-transitions from t to s_0 and from $r_{i+\ell}$ to t'.

Now, since H is a simple splicing system, this construction can be simplified further. Since every rule of H is of the form $(a, \varepsilon; a, \varepsilon)$, we only need to add states and transitions for $p_a \xrightarrow{a} p'_a$ for each rule. Then add ε-transitions from states q of A to p_a if q has an outgoing transition on a to a non-sink state of A. From each state p'_a, add ε-transitions to each state of A with an incoming transition on a. Recall that $\operatorname{im} \delta_a$ is the image of the transformation of δ induced by a, and therefore it is the set of states of A with an incoming transition on a.

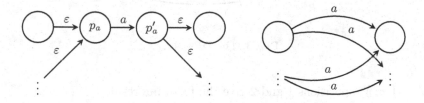

Fig. 2. New states and transitions for $a \in M$ (left), after ε-removal (right).

Finally, we can simplify this NFA by removing ε-transitions in the usual way to obtain an NFA $A'_H = (Q, \Sigma, \delta', q_0, F)$, where

$$\delta'(q, a) = \begin{cases} \{\delta(q, a)\}, & \text{if } \delta(q, a) \text{ is the sink state;} \\ \{\delta(q, a)\}, & \text{if } a \notin M; \\ \operatorname{im} \delta_a, & \text{if } a \in M. \end{cases}$$

Figure 2 illustrates the new states and transitions added for $a \in M$ before and after ε-removal. Observe that by removing the ε-transitions, we also remove the states that were initially added earlier in the construction of A_H. Thus, the state set of A'_H is exactly the state set of the DFA A recognizing L.   □

Given a splicing system $H = (\Sigma, M, L)$, one can obtain a DFA that recognizes $L(H)$ by performing the subset construction on A'_H. As shown in Proposition 1, if L is recognized by a DFA with n states, then A'_H also has n states. By applying the subset construction and observing that the empty set is not reachable from any subset of Q in A'_H, this gives an upper bound of $2^n - 1$ states for a DFA equivalent to A'_H.

We will now show that there exists a family of regular languages L_n with state complexity n such that a simple splicing system $H = (\Sigma, M, L_n)$ with one marker requires $2^n - 1$ states for an equivalent DFA to recognize it.

Proposition 2. *For $|\Sigma| \geq 3$ and $n \geq 3$, there exists a simple splicing system with a regular initial language $H = (\Sigma, M, L_n)$ with $|M| = 1$ where L_n is a regular language with state complexity n such that the minimal DFA for $L(H)$ requires at least $2^n - 1$ states.*

Proposition 2 is proved via the family of languages L_n accepted by DFAs A_n, shown in Fig. 3, with $M = \{c\}$.

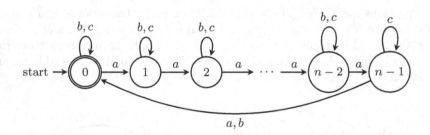

Fig. 3. The DFA A_n.

Together, Propositions 1 and 2 give the following result.

Theorem 3. *For a simple splicing system with a regular initial language $H = (\Sigma, M, L_n)$ where $M \subseteq \Sigma$ and $L_n \subseteq \Sigma^*$ has state complexity n, the state complexity of $L(H)$ is at most $2^n - 1$ and this bound can be reached in the worst case.*

We will now consider simple splicing systems with a finite initial language. We will show that the upper bound of Proposition 1 is not reachable in this case.

Proposition 4. *Let $H = (\Sigma, M, I)$ be a simple splicing system with a finite initial language, where I is a finite language recognized by a DFA A with n states. Then a DFA recognizing $L(H)$ requires at most $2^{n-2} + 1$ states.*

We will show that this bound is reachable. We note that the lower bound witness used in the following lemma is defined over an alphabet with size exponential in the number of states of the DFA recognizing the initial language.

Lemma 5. *There exists a simple splicing system with a finite initial language* $H = (\Sigma, M, I_n)$ *where* I_n *is a finite language with state complexity* n *such that a DFA recognizing* $L(H)$ *requires* $2^{n-2} + 1$ *states.*

Together, Proposition 4 and Lemma 5 give the following result.

Theorem 6. *For a simple splicing system with a finite initial language* $H = (\Sigma, M, I_n)$ *where* $M \subseteq \Sigma$ *and* $I_n \subseteq \Sigma^*$ *has state complexity* n, *the state complexity of* $L(H)$ *is at most* $2^{n-2} + 1$ *and this bound can be reached in the worst case.*

The bound of Lemma 5 is reached by a witness defined over an alphabet size of $2^{n-3} + 1$. An obvious question is whether this bound can be reached via a smaller alphabet. We will consider in the following the state complexity of simple splicing systems with a finite initial language for small, fixed alphabets. We begin with a general observation on the transition function of a DFA recognizing the language of a simple splicing system.

Lemma 7. *Let* $H = (\Sigma, M, L)$ *be a simple splicing system with a regular initial language and let* A_H *be an NFA recognizing* $L(H)$. *If* $a \in M$ *and* δ' *is the transition function of* A_H, *then* $|\operatorname{im} \delta'_a| = 2$.

First, we will consider simple splicing systems with a finite initial language defined over a unary alphabet.

Proposition 8. *Let* $H = (\{a\}, M, I)$ *be a simple splicing system where* M *is nonempty and* I *is a finite language containing a word of length at least 2. Then the minimal DFA recognizing* $L(H)$ *has exactly two states.*

Next, we consider simple splicing systems with a finite initial language defined over a binary alphabet. We will show that the small size of the alphabet restricts the number of transformations that can be performed on the state set and that the upper bound on the number of states falls far below the upper bound of Proposition 4 as a result.

Proposition 9. *Let* $H = (\{a, b\}, M, I)$ *be a simple splicing system where* I *is a finite language with state complexity* n. *Then the minimal DFA recognizing* $L(H)$ *has at most* $2n - 3$ *states and this bound is reachable in the worst case.*

We will now consider the state complexity of simple splicing systems with a finite initial language defined over a ternary alphabet. We will show that the upper bound of $2^{n-2} + 1$ from Proposition 4 cannot be reached with an alphabet of size 3.

Proposition 10. *Let* $H = (\{a, b, c\}, M, I)$ *be a simple splicing system where* I *is a finite language with state complexity* n. *Then the minimal DFA recognizing* $L(H)$ *has at most* $2^{\frac{n}{2}} + 1$ *states if* n *is even and* $3 \cdot 2^{\frac{n-3}{2}} + 1$ *states if* n *is odd.*

We note that the upper bound of the previous lemma is similar to the state complexity of the reversal operation on finite languages [2]. We will use this result as inspiration for a family of lower bound witnesses in the following lemma.

Lemma 11. *There exists a family of finite languages $I_n \subseteq \{a, b, c\}^*$, for $n \geq 4$, recognized by a DFA with n states such that the minimal DFA for a simple splicing system $H = (\{a, b, c\}, M, I_n)$ requires at least $2^{\frac{n}{2}} + 1$ states if n is even and $3 \cdot 2^{\frac{n-3}{2}} + 1$ states if n is odd.*

The family of witness languages I_n used to prove Lemma 11 is accepted by DFAs A_n, shown in Fig. 4, with $M = \{c\}$.

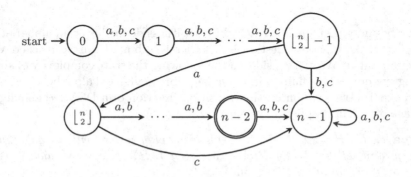

Fig. 4. The ternary witness DFA A_n.

Together, Proposition 10 and Lemma 11 give us the following theorem.

Theorem 12. *For a simple splicing system with a finite initial language $H = (\Sigma, M, I_n)$ where $|\Sigma| = 3$, $M \subseteq \Sigma$, and $I_n \subseteq \Sigma^*$ has state complexity n, the state complexity of $L(H)$ is at most $2^{\frac{n}{2}} + 1$ states if n is even and $3 \cdot 2^{\frac{n-3}{2}} + 1$ states if n is odd and this bound can be reached in the worst case.*

4   State Complexity of Semi-simple Splicing

In this section, we will give tight state complexity bounds for semi-simple splicing systems with regular and finite initial languages. In particular, we will show that the upper bound is reachable for semi-simple splicing systems with a finite initial language defined over a fixed alphabet.

Goode and Pixton [9] generalize simple splicing systems by defining semi-simple splicing systems. A splicing system is semi-simple if every rule is of the form $(a, \varepsilon; b, \varepsilon)$ for $a, b \in \Sigma$. Again, rather than explicitly define a set of rules $\mathcal{M}$, we refer instead to the set $M^{(2)} \subseteq \Sigma \times \Sigma$ of pairs of symbols, which determines the set of rules. As with simple splicing systems, one can conclude that the class of languages generated by semi-simple splicing systems is subregular [4,15].

In the following, we will give a construction for an NFA that recognizes the language generated by a semi-simple splicing system. As with the NFA for simple splicing systems from Proposition 1, the construction will follow the more general construction for finite splicing systems of Loos et al. [13].

Proposition 13. *Let $H = (\Sigma, M^{(2)}, L)$ be a semi-simple splicing system with a regular initial language. Then there exists an NFA B'_H with n states such that $L(B'_H) = L(H)$.*

It is clear from Proposition 13 that for a given regular language L, the language of a semi-simple splicing system $H = (\Sigma, M^{(2)}, L)$ can require $2^n - 1$ states in the worst case. Since a simple splicing system is also a semi-simple splicing system, the lower bound witness from Proposition 2 holds. Therefore, we can focus on the more interesting case of semi-simple splicing systems with finite initial languages. First, we observe that even with semi-simple splicing rules, the upper bound on the number of states for a DFA recognizing a semi-simple splicing system with a finite initial language remains the same.

Proposition 14. *Let $H = (\Sigma, M^{(2)}, I)$ be a semi-simple splicing system with a finite initial language where I is a finite language recognized by a DFA A with n states. Then a DFA recognizing $L(H)$ requires at most $2^{n-2} + 1$ states.*

The proof of this fact is identical to the proof of Proposition 4.

Recall from Lemma 5, that the lower bound witness for simple splicing systems with a finite initial language was defined over an alphabet with size exponential in the state complexity of the initial language. We will show in the following lemma that for semi-simple splicing systems with a finite initial language, a lower bound witness defined over an alphabet of size 3 exists.

Lemma 15. *Let $n \geq 4$. Then there exists a semi-simple splicing system with a finite initial language $H = (\Sigma, M^{(2)}, I_n)$ where $|\Sigma| = 3$ and I_n is a finite language with state complexity n such that $L(H)$ is recognized by a DFA that requires at least $2^{n-2} + 1$ states.*

The family of witness languages I_n of Lemma 15 is accepted by DFAs A_n, shown in Fig. 5, with $\Sigma = \{a, b, c\}$ and $M^{(2)} = \{(a, c)\}$.

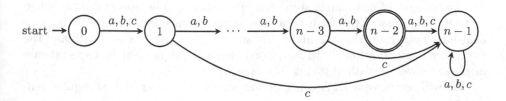

Fig. 5. The ternary witness DFA A_n.

From Proposition 14 and Lemma 15, we have the following result.

Theorem 16. *For a semi-simple splicing system with a finite initial language* $H = (\Sigma, M^{(2)}, I_n)$ *where* $M \subseteq \Sigma$ *and* $I_n \subseteq \Sigma^*$ *has state complexity* n, *the state complexity of* $L(H)$ *is at most* $2^{n-2} + 1$ *and this bound can be reached in the worst case.*

5   State Complexity of the Crossover Operation

In this section, we will give tight state complexity bounds for the crossover operation [3], which can be thought of as a single step of semi-simple splicing. Mateescu et al. [14] gave an algebraic characterization of the class of languages generated by simple splicing systems based on the crossover operation therein. A similar such characterization for the class of languages generated by semi-simple splicing systems is given by Ceterchi [3].

For $M = M_1 \times M_2 \subseteq \Sigma \times \Sigma$, define the operation $\diamond_M$ on two strings $u, v \in \Sigma^+$ by

$$u \diamond_M v = \begin{cases} u'av', & \text{if } u = u'a, v = bv' \, for (a,b) \in M, u', v' \in \Sigma^*; \\ \text{undefined}, & \text{otherwise.} \end{cases}$$

Then for two languages $L_1, L_2 \subseteq \Sigma^*$, we have

$$L_1 \diamond_M L_2 = \{x \diamond_M y \mid x \in L_1, y \in L_2\}.$$

The operation $\diamond_M$ is a variant of the Latin product defined in [8]. Based on $\diamond_M$, we define the *crossover operation* $\natural_M$ for $M \subseteq \Sigma \times \Sigma$ and two languages $L_1, L_2 \subseteq \Sigma^*$ by

$$L_1 \natural_M L_2 = \text{pref}(L_1) \diamond_M \text{suff}(L_2),$$

where $\text{pref}(L_1)$ is the set of prefixes of words in L_1 and $\text{suff}(L_2)$ is the set of suffixes of words in L_2. From this definition, the operation $\natural_M$ can be viewed as a combination of operations under each of which the regular languages are closed. Therefore, it is easy to see that the regular languages are closed under $\natural_M$.

Note that by restricting M to pairs (a, a) for $a \in \Sigma$, we get an operation that can be thought of as a single step of simple splicing. The operation $\natural_M$, when restricted to pairs of the form (a, a) has some similarities to many operations that have been studied in the literature, such as the chop operation [12] and the word blending operation [5]. In fact, word blending can be seen as a special case of the crossover operation, taking $M = \{(a, a) \mid a \in \Sigma\}$.

We will now give a DFA construction for the crossover of two regular languages.

Proposition 17. *Let A and B be two DFAs defined over Σ with m and n states, respectively. Then for any $M \subseteq \Sigma \times \Sigma$, there exists a DFA C such that $L(C) = L(A) \natural_M L(B)$ and C has at most $m \cdot 2^n$ states.*

Proof. Let $A = (Q_A, \Sigma, \delta_A, s_A, F_A)$ and $B = (Q_B, \Sigma, \delta_B, s_B, F_B)$ be two DFAs. We will construct a DFA $C = (Q_C, \Sigma, \delta_C, s_C, F_C)$ that recognizes $A\sharp_M B$ for some $M \subseteq \Sigma \times \Sigma$, defined by

- $Q_C = Q_A \times 2^{Q_B}$,
- $s_C = \langle s_A, \emptyset \rangle$,
- $F_C = \{\langle q, P \rangle \in Q_A \times 2^{Q_B} \mid P \cap F_B \neq \emptyset\}$,

and the transition function δ_C is defined for $q \in Q_A$, $P \subseteq Q_B$, and $a \in \Sigma$ by $\delta_C(\langle q, P \rangle, a) = \langle q', P' \rangle$, where $q' = \delta_A(q, a)$ and

$$P' = \begin{cases} \mathrm{im}(\delta_B)_b, & \text{if } (a,b) \in M \text{ and } q' \text{ is not a sink state;} \\ \bigcup_{p \in P} \delta_B(p, a), & \text{otherwise.} \end{cases}$$

Informally, the machine traces a computation of A and computations of B. For each pair $(a, b) \in M$, whenever a transition on a occurs in A, all states of B with incoming transitions on b are added to the computation. It is clear from the definition of C that $L(C) = L(A)\sharp_M L(B)$ and it has at most $m \cdot 2^n$ states. $\qquad\square$

We will show that the bound of Proposition 17 is reachable, even when M is restricted to pairs of the form (a, a).

Lemma 18. *There exist languages A_m and B_n over Σ with $|\Sigma| \geq 4$ recognized by DFAs with m and n states, respectively, and a subset $M \subseteq \Sigma \times \Sigma$ such that the minimal DFA for $L(A_m)\sharp_M L(B_n)$ requires at least $m \cdot 2^n$ states.*

The families of witness languages of Lemma 18 are accepted by DFAs A_m and B_n, shown in Fig. 6, with $M = \{(d, d)\}$.

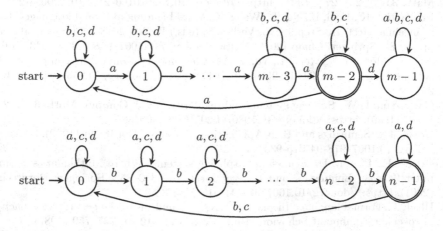

Fig. 6. The DFAs A_m (above) and B_n (below).

Together, Proposition 17 and Lemma 18 give us the following theorem.

Theorem 19. *For regular languages L_m and L_n, with $m, n \geq 3$, defined over an alphabet Σ, with $|\Sigma| \geq 4$, and a subset $M \subseteq \Sigma \times \Sigma$, if L_m has state complexity m and L_n has state complexity n, then $L_m \sharp_M L_n$ has state complexity at most $m \cdot 2^n$ and this bound can be reached in the worst case.*

6 Conclusion

We have given tight bounds for the state complexity of simple and semi-simple splicing systems and the associated crossover operation. In almost all cases, the exponential upper bound was easily reached via splicing systems defined over a fixed-size alphabet with one rule. The exception is with simple splicing systems with a finite initial language, where a natural open problem to consider is the worst-case state complexity when the initial languages are defined over alphabets of size between 3 and 2^{n-3}.

References

1. Bonizzoni, P., Ferretti, C., Mauri, G., Zizza, R.: Separating some splicing models. Inform. Process. Lett. **79**(6), 255–259 (2001)
2. Câmpeanu, C., Culik, K., Salomaa, K., Yu, S.: State Complexity of Basic Operations on Finite Languages. In: Boldt, O., Jürgensen, H. (eds.) WIA 1999. LNCS, vol. 2214, pp. 60–70. Springer, Heidelberg (2001). https://doi.org/10.1007/3-540-45526-4_6
3. Ceterchi, R.: An algebraic characterization of semi-simple splicing. Fund. Inform. **73**(1–2), 19–25 (2006)
4. Culik II, K., Harju, T.: Splicing semigroups of dominoes and DNA. Discrete Appl. Math. **31**(3), 261–277 (1991). https://doi.org/10.1016/0166-218X(91)90054-Z
5. Enaganti, S.K., Kari, L., Ng, T., Wang, Z.: Word blending in formal languages: the brangelina effect. In: Stepney, S., Verlan, S. (eds.) UCNC 2018. LNCS, vol. 10867, pp. 72–85. Springer, Cham (2018). https://doi.org/10.1007/978-3-319-92435-9_6
6. Gao, Y., Moreira, N., Reis, R., Yu, S.: A survey on operational state complexity. J. Autom. Lang. Comb. **21**(4), 251–310 (2017). https://doi.org/10.25596/jalc-2016-251
7. Gatterdam, R.W.: Splicing systems and regularity. Int. J. Comput. Math. **31**(1–2), 63–67 (1989). https://doi.org/10.1080/00207168908803788
8. Golan, J.S.: Semirings and their Applications. Springer, Dordrecht (1999). https://doi.org/10.1007/978-94-015-9333-5
9. Goode, E., Pixton, D.: Semi-simple splicing systems. Where Mathematics. Computer Science, Linguistics and Biology Meet, pp. 343–352. Springer, Dordrecht (2001). https://doi.org/10.1007/978-94-015-9634-3_30
10. Head, T.: Formal language theory and DNA: an analysis of the generative capacity of specific recombinant behaviors. Bull. Math. Biol. **49**(6), 737–759 (1987)
11. Head, T., Pixton, D.: Splicing and regularity. In: Esik, Z., Martín-Vide, C., Mitrana, V. (eds.) Recent Advances in Formal Languages and Applications. SCI, vol. 25, pp. 119–147. Springer, Heidelberg (2006). https://doi.org/10.1007/978-3-540-33461-3_5

12. Holzer, M., Jakobi, S.: Chop operations and expressions: descriptional complexity considerations. In: Mauri, G., Leporati, A. (eds.) DLT 2011. LNCS, vol. 6795, pp. 264–275. Springer, Heidelberg (2011). https://doi.org/10.1007/978-3-642-22321-1_23

13. Loos, R., Malcher, A., Wotschke, D.: Descriptional complexity of splicing systems. Internat. J. Found. Comput. Sci. **19**(4), 813–826 (2008)

14. Mateescu, A., Păun, G., Rozenberg, G., Salomaa, A.: Simple splicing systems. Discrete Appl. Math. **84**(1–3), 145–163 (1998). https://doi.org/10.1016/S0166-218X(98)00002-X

15. Pixton, D.: Regularity of splicing languages. Discrete Appl. Math. **69**(1–2), 101–124 (1996). https://doi.org/10.1016/0166-218X(95)00079-7

16. Păun, G.: On the splicing operation. Discrete Appl. Math. **70**(1), 57–79 (1996). https://doi.org/10.1016/0166-218X(96)00101-1

Nondeterminism Growth and State Complexity

Chris Keeler[✉] and Kai Salomaa

School of Computing, Queen's University, Kingston, Ontario K7L 2N8, Canada
{keeler,ksalomaa}@cs.queensu.ca

Abstract. Tree width (respectively, string path width) measures the maximal number of partial (respectively, complete) computations of a nondeterministic finite automaton (NFA) on an input of given length. We study the growth rate of the tree width and string path width measures. As the main result we show that the degree of the polynomial bounding the tree width of an NFA differs by at most one from the degree of the polynomial bounding the string path width. Also we show that for $m \geq 4$ there exists an m-state NFA with finite string path width such that any equivalent finite tree width NFA needs $2^{m-2} + 1$ states.

1 Introduction

Deterministic and nondeterministic finite automata (DFA and NFA) define the class of regular languages, and have been systematically studied for over 60 years. More recently there has been much interest in automata employing limited nondeterminism [2,5,12]. Different *measures of nondeterminism* allow us to quantify the amount and type of nondeterminism present in an NFA's computations.

Ambiguity is probably the first nondeterminism measure to be studied systematically. The *ambiguity* [9,10,12,14] of an NFA A on an input string counts the number of accepting computations of A on that string and the *tree width* [5,11] of A counts the number of all computations of A on the input string. The *string path width* [6,7] lies between tree width and ambiguity, as it does not count the partial computations counted by tree width, but it does count complete nonaccepting computations. We extend each of these measures of nondeterminism to functions on integers, and consider the growth rate of the corresponding function with respect to worst-case inputs of given length. The growth rate of ambiguity and tree width has been considered, respectively, e.g., in [9,12,14] and in [5].

State complexity is another topic in automata theory with much recent research [4,8]. The study of state complexity aspects of limited nondeterminism was initiated by Goldstine et al. [2] who showed that there exists an m-state NFA A such that any finite *branching* NFA equivalent to A needs 2^{m-1} states. More generally, Goldstine et al. [2] gave a spectrum result which establishes that there exist regular languages for which different finite amounts of nondeterminism yield incremental savings in the number of states. Hromkovič et al. [5] have

© IFIP International Federation for Information Processing 2019
Published by Springer Nature Switzerland AG 2019
M. Hospodár et al. (Eds.): DCFS 2019, LNCS 11612, pp. 210–222, 2019.
https://doi.org/10.1007/978-3-030-23247-4_16

shown that there exist m-state NFAs with linear ambiguity such that any equivalent finitely ambiguous NFA needs close to 2^m states. Palioudakis et al. [11] showed that there exists an m-state unambiguous NFA such that an equivalent NFA with finite tree width needs 2^{m-1} states. Here we establish a similar state complexity blow-up between NFAs of finite string path width and finite tree width, respectively.

The contents of this paper are as follows. Section 2 recalls definitions and fixes the notation. Section 3.1 shows that an NFA has polynomial string path width if and only if its tree width is polynomial and, furthermore, that the degrees of the polynomials differ by at most one. Also, it is shown that for NFAs without useless states the degree of the polynomial bounding the growth rate of ambiguity coincides with the polynomial bounding string path width. Section 3.2 shows that an NFA has exponential string path width if and only if it has exponential tree width. Section 4 gives polynomial-time algorithms to decide whether the growth rate of an NFA's tree width (respectively, string path width) is polynomial or exponential, and additionally, to compute the degree of the polynomial bounding the growth. These algorithms utilize existing algorithms from the literature [9,14]. Section 5 shows that for $m \geq 4$ there exists an m-state NFA A with finite string path width such that any finite tree width NFA equivalent to A needs at least $2^{m-2} + 1$ states.

2 Preliminaries

Here we recall definitions and notation needed in later sections. We assume that the reader is familiar with finite automata, and point them to resources such as [13]. The set of strings over an alphabet Σ is denoted as Σ^*, Σ^+ is the set of nonempty strings and the set of strings of length ℓ over Σ is Σ^ℓ. We use $|S|$ to mean the cardinality of a finite set S, ε to mean the empty string, and $\mathbb{N}$ to mean the set of positive integers. Consider a function $f(\ell) : \mathbb{N} \to \mathbb{N}$. If for $d \in \mathbb{N}$, $f(\ell) \in O(\ell^d)$, (respectively, $\in \Theta(\ell^d)$), then we say that f has *polynomial growth degree* d (respectively, *strict* polynomial growth degree d). If $f(\ell) \in 2^{\Theta(\ell)}$, then we say that $f(\ell)$ has *exponential growth*.

A *nondeterministic finite automaton* (NFA) is a 5-tuple $A = (Q, \Sigma, \delta, q_0, F)$ consisting of a finite set of states Q, a finite alphabet Σ, a transition function $\delta : Q \times \Sigma \to 2^Q$, an initial state $q_0 \in Q$, and a set of final states $F \subseteq Q$. The transition function is extended in the usual way as a function $\delta : Q \times \Sigma^* \to 2^Q$ and the language recognized by A is $L(A) = \{w \in \Sigma^* \mid \delta(q_0, w) \cap F \neq \emptyset \}$.

The NFA A is a *deterministic* finite automaton (DFA) if $|\delta(q, c)| \leq 1$ for all $q \in Q$ and $c \in \Sigma$. If $\delta(q, c)$ is always a singleton set, A is a complete DFA.

Without loss of generality, we assume that all states of an NFA are *reachable* from the start state. In the event that there are non-reachable states, they can simply be removed. Unless otherwise specified, we do not assume that every state can reach a final state, i.e., states need not be *co-reachable*.

A *path* of A from $p_1 \in Q$ to $p_{\ell+1} \in Q$ on a string $a_1 \cdots a_\ell \in \Sigma^*$ is an ordered sequence of the form $(p_1, a_1, p_2, a_2, \ldots, p_\ell, a_\ell, p_{\ell+1})$ such that $p_{i+1} \in \delta(p_i, a_i)$,

$1 \leq i \leq \ell$. The set of all paths from state q to state p on string $w \in \Sigma^*$ is denoted as paths (q, w, p).

A path of A from the initial state q_0 to a state p on string w is a *(complete) computation* on w and it is an *accepting computation* if $p \in F$. A path of A from the initial state q_0 to a state p on a prefix w_1 of w is a *partial computation* of A on w if either $w_1 = w$ (complete computation) or $w = w_1 b w_2$, $b \in \Sigma$, and $\delta(p, b) = \emptyset$. That is, a partial computation on w must read the string as far as it can, until it encounters an undefined transition.

For $L \subseteq \Sigma^*$, the Myhill-Nerode equivalence relation of L, $\equiv_L \subseteq \Sigma^* \times \Sigma^*$, is defined by setting for $x, y \in \Sigma^*$:

$$x \equiv_L y \quad \text{iff} \quad (\forall z \in \Sigma^*) \; xz \in L \Leftrightarrow yz \in L.$$

For a regular language L, the number of equivalence classes of $\equiv_L$ gives the number of states of the minimal complete DFA recognizing L [13].

The *ambiguity* of an NFA A on a string w, denoted $\mathrm{da}(A, w)$, is the number of accepting computations of A on w. The ambiguity of A on all strings of length ℓ is $\mathrm{da}(A, \ell) = \max\{\mathrm{da}(A, w) \mid w \in \Sigma^\ell\}$, and the ambiguity of A is $\mathrm{da}(A) = \sup_{\ell \in \mathbb{N}}\{\mathrm{da}(A, \ell)\}$. Note that $\mathrm{da}(A)$ may be infinite.

The *string path width* [3,6], roughly speaking, counts the number of complete computations and tree width [11] counts the number of partial computations. Formally this is defined as follows. For an NFA A and string w, the *string path width* of A on w, $\mathrm{spw}(A, w)$, is the number of complete computations of A on w and the *tree width* of A on w, $\mathrm{tw}(A, w)$, is the number of partial computations of A on w. Again for $\ell \in \mathbb{N}$, we define $\mathrm{spw}(A, \ell) = \max\{\mathrm{spw}(A, w) \mid w \in \Sigma^\ell\}$ and $\mathrm{tw}(A, \ell) = \max\{\mathrm{tw}(A, w) \mid w \in \Sigma^\ell\}$, as well as, $\mathrm{spw}(A) = \sup_{\ell \in \mathbb{N}}\{\mathrm{tw}(A, \ell)\}$ and $\mathrm{spw}(A) = \sup_{\ell \in \mathbb{N}}\{\mathrm{spw}(A, \ell)\}$.

An NFA's tree width will grow unboundedly with respect to the length of the input string if and only if some cycle has a nondeterministic transition [11]. Figure 1 gives a visual abstraction of this condition.

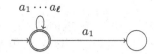

Fig. 1. NFA with infinite tree width.

Directly by the definitions, for any NFA A and $\ell \in \mathbb{N}$ we have $\mathrm{da}(A, \ell) \leq \mathrm{spw}(A, \ell) \leq \mathrm{tw}(A, \ell)$. If all states of A are final, then the ambiguity and string path width of A are equal on any string. If A has no undefined transitions, then its string path width and tree width are equal.

The *completion* of an NFA $A = (Q, \Sigma, \delta, q_0, F)$ is obtained from A by adding a sink state that is the target of all previously undefined transitions. Formally, the *completion* of A is $\widehat{A} = (Q', \Sigma, \delta', q_0, F)$, where

$$Q' = \begin{cases} Q, & \text{if } \delta(q,b) \neq \emptyset \text{ for all } q \in Q \text{ and } b \in \Sigma; \\ Q \cup \{q_{\text{sink}}\}, & \text{otherwise,} \end{cases}$$

and the transitions are defined by setting $\delta'(q_{\text{sink}}, b) = \{q_{\text{sink}}\}$ for all $b \in \Sigma$,

$$\delta'(q,b) = \begin{cases} \delta(q,b), & \text{if } \delta(q,b) \neq \emptyset; \\ \{q_{\text{sink}}\}, & \text{if } \delta(q,b) = \emptyset, \end{cases} \quad q \in Q, b \in \Sigma.$$

Directly from the definition of string path width and tree width we get:

Lemma 1. *For any NFA A and string $w \in \Sigma^*$,*

$$\text{spw}(\widehat{A}, w) = \text{tw}(A, w).$$

3 Growth of String Path Width and Tree Width

Weber and Seidl [14], based on earlier work, developed structural criteria to determine the growth rate of ambiguity of an NFA as a function of input length. We extend and modify these conditions to study the growth rate of string path width and tree width. In the following $A = (Q, \Sigma, \delta, q_0, F)$ is always an NFA.

3.1 Polynomial Growth

For an NFA A, $\text{da}(A, \ell) \in \Omega(\ell^d)$, $d \in \mathbb{N}$, if and only if A complies with a condition $(\mathbf{IDA}_d)$ [14] which means that A can be viewed to have a "subgraph" of a certain type. We refer to such subgraphs as *widgets*. The widget $(\mathbf{IDA}_d)$ is almost the same as $(\mathbf{ISPW}_d)$ defined below and represented in Fig. 2. The only difference is that $(\mathbf{IDA}_d)$ additionally requires that the state c_d must be able to reach a final state.

To characterize polynomial string path width, we use a widget, $(\mathbf{ISPW}_d)$, modified from $(\mathbf{IDA}_d)$ [14].

$(\mathbf{ISPW}_d)$: There exist states $s_1, c_1, \ldots, s_d, c_d \in Q$, strings $v_1, \ldots, v_d \in \Sigma^+$, and strings $u_2, \ldots, u_d \in \Sigma^*$ such that:

- For all $1 \leq i \leq d$: $s_i \neq c_i$, and paths (s_i, v_i, s_i), paths (s_i, v_i, c_i), and paths (c_i, v_i, c_i) are all non-empty.
- For all $2 \leq j \leq d$: paths (c_{j-1}, u_j, s_j) is non-empty.

We call the cycle on s_i a "seeding cycle" and the cycle on c_i a "catching cycle". The states s_i and c_i must be connected by the same string v_i occurring in the cycles. Note that the u_j-strings can be empty, but the v_i-strings cannot. When a string u_j is empty for some $2 \leq j \leq d$, states c_{j-1} and s_j must be the same state. That is, there exists a state which is involved in a cycle on each of the strings v_{j-1} and v_j (which may be the same string).

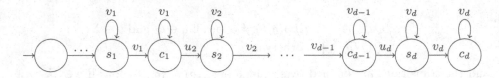

Fig. 2. Widget $(\mathbf{ISPW}_d)$.

Lemma 2. *An NFA A has string path width $\Omega(\ell^d)$ if and only if A admits a widget $(\mathbf{ISPW}_d)$, for some $d \in \mathbb{N}$.*

Proof. Let A' be obtained from A by making all of its states final. From [14] we know that A' has degree of ambiguity $\Omega(\ell^d)$ iff A' admits the widget $(\mathbf{IDA}_d)$, and the latter holds iff A admits the widget $(\mathbf{ISPW}_d)$. For any string w, $\mathrm{da}(A', w) = \mathrm{spw}(A, w)$. □

An NFA's string path width will be finite if and only if it does not admit a widget $(\mathbf{ISPW}_1)$.

Corollary 3. *For an NFA A, $\mathrm{spw}(A) \in O(1)$ iff for all $q, q' \in Q$ and $w \in \Sigma^*$ such that $q \neq q'$:*

(i) $|\mathrm{paths}(q, w, q)| \leq 1$,
(ii) $(|\mathrm{paths}(q, w, q)| = 1$ and $|\mathrm{paths}(q', w, q')| = 1)$ implies $|\mathrm{paths}(q, w, q')| = 0$.

Lemma 2 implies that an NFA A has tree width $\Theta(\ell^d)$ exactly when A admits a widget $(\mathbf{ISPW}_d)$, but does not admit a widget $(\mathbf{ISPW}_{d+1})$.

For an NFA A, the ambiguity and string path width of A on a particular string, or on strings of given length, can be very different, even assuming that A has no useless states. For example, if $\mathrm{spw}(A, \ell) \neq 0$, the string path width of A on all lengths $1, \ldots, \ell - 1$ must be positive. On the other hand, it is possible that $\mathrm{da}(A, \ell) = 0$ and $\mathrm{da}(A, \ell + 1) \neq 0$.

However, as a consequence of Lemma 2 and [14], we see that, for NFAs without useless states, the polynomial growth rates of ambiguity and string path width must coincide. Note that when A has no useless states, an $(\mathbf{ISPW}_d)$ widget is also an $(\mathbf{IDA}_d)$ widget.

Corollary 4. *If A is an NFA without useless states, then $\mathrm{spw}(A, \ell) \in \Theta(\ell^d)$ if and only if $\mathrm{da}(A, \ell) \in \Theta(\ell^d)$, for $d \in \mathbb{N}$.*

To characterize polynomial tree width, we define a new widget, $(\mathbf{ITW}_d)$, which is the same as $(\mathbf{ISPW}_d)$, except:

(i) For the "last state" c_d we remove the condition that $|\mathrm{paths}(c_d, v_d, c_d)| > 0$. That is, the final "catching loop" on state c_d does not need to be present.
(ii) For the final pair of states we modify the condition $|\mathrm{paths}(s_d, v_d, c_d)| > 0$ to be $|\delta(s_d, a)| > 0$ instead, where a is the first letter of v_d. That is, the state s_d with the final "seeding loop" only needs a nondeterministic transition on the first symbol of v_d.

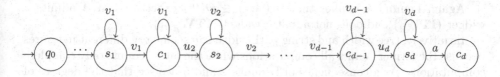

Fig. 3. Widget $(\mathbf{ITW}_d)$. The letter a must be the first symbol in v_d.

We give a visual abstraction of these alterations in Fig. 3 (cf. Fig. 2).
Next we establish the correctness result for our new criterion.

Lemma 5. *An NFA A has tree width $\Omega(\ell^d)$, $d \in \mathbb{N}$, if and only if A admits a widget $(\mathbf{ITW}_d)$.*

Proof. Suppose that A has tree width $\Omega(\ell^d)$. By Lemma 1, the completion of A, $\widehat{A}$, has string path width $\Omega(\ell^d)$ and hence by Lemma 2, $\widehat{A}$ admits the widget $(\mathbf{ISPW}_d)$. Since $s_i \neq c_i$ for $i = 1, \ldots, d$, none of the states s_i $1 \leq i \leq d$, or c_j, $1 \leq j \leq d-1$ can be the sink state of $\widehat{A}$ because the only state reachable from the sink state is itself. Thus, in the widget $(\mathbf{ISPW}_d)$ of $\widehat{A}$, only the state c_d may be the sink state and all transitions "before" entering c_d must exist also in the original NFA A. This means that A admits $(\mathbf{ITW}_d)$.

Conversely, assume that A admits a widget $(\mathbf{ITW}_d)$ and let $\widehat{A}$ be the completion of A. Using the notation of Fig. 3, denote $v_d = a \cdot v_d'$, $a \in \Sigma$, and choose $p \in \delta(c_d, v_d')$, that is, p is reached from the state s_d on string v_d and first making the transition to state c_d. If $p = s_d$, the NFA A has exponential tree width (cf. Sect. 3.2) and we are done. Thus, we can assume $p \neq s_d$. Since $\widehat{A}$ has no undefined transitions, there exist $i, k \geq 1$ and a state r of $\widehat{A}$ such that $r \in \delta'(p, v_d^i)$ and $r \in \delta'(r, v_d^k)$. Choose $0 \leq m < k$ such that

$$1 + i + m \equiv 0 \pmod{k}.$$

In the cycle from r to r on string v_d^k, let t be the state reached by v_d^m. Now the state t can be reached from s_d on string v_d^{1+i+m} and paths$(t, v_d^k, t) \neq \emptyset$. Since $1 + i + m$ is a multiple of k, the $(\mathbf{ITW}_d)$ widget can be completed to an $(\mathbf{ISPW}_d)$ widget as follows (Fig. 4):

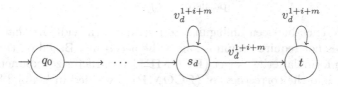

Fig. 4. Completing the $(\mathbf{ITW}_d)$ widget to a $(\mathbf{ISPW}_d)$ widget.

Thus, by Lemma 2, $\widehat{A}$ has string path width $\Omega(\ell^d)$. By Lemma 1, tw$(A, \ell) \in \Omega(\ell^d)$.   □

Again, Lemma 5 implies that $\mathrm{tw}(A, \ell) \in \Theta(\ell^d)$ exactly when A admits a widget $(\mathbf{ITW}_d)$ and does not admit a widget $(\mathbf{ITW}_{d+1})$.

Intuitively, tree width and string path width can seem very different measures because the former counts all computations while the latter counts only complete computations. As a consequence of Lemmas 2 and 5, we see that the degrees of polynomials bounding the growth rate of, respectively, the tree width and the string path width of an NFA differ by at most one.

Theorem 6. *Let A be an NFA and $d \in \mathbb{N}$.*

(i) If $\mathrm{spw}(A, \ell) \in \Theta(\ell^d)$, then $\mathrm{tw}(A, \ell)$ is in $\Theta(\ell^d)$ or in $\Theta(\ell^{d+1})$.
(ii) If $\mathrm{tw}(A, \ell) \in \Theta(\ell^d)$, then $\mathrm{spw}(A, \ell)$ is in $\Theta(\ell^d)$ or in $\Theta(\ell^{d-1})$.

From the characterization of Lemmas 2 and 5 it follows also that, for all $d \in \mathbb{N}$, there exists an NFA A such that $\mathrm{spw}(A, \ell) \in \Theta(\ell^d)$ and $\mathrm{tw}(A, \ell) \in \Theta(\ell^{d+1})$.

To conclude this section we observe that the criteria $(\mathbf{ISPW}_d)$ and $(\mathbf{ITW}_d)$ yield lower bounds for the number of states or the number of transitions of an NFA having polynomial string path (or tree) width.

Proposition 7. *Let $A = (Q, \Sigma, \delta, q_0, F)$ be an NFA and $d \in \mathbb{N}$.*

(i) If $\mathrm{tw}(A, \ell) \in \Theta(\ell^d)$, then $1 \leq d < |Q|$, and $2 \cdot d \leq |\delta|$.
(ii) If $\mathrm{tw}(A, \ell) \in \Theta(\ell^d)$, and $L(A) = w^*$, $w \in \Sigma^k$, $k \in \mathbb{N}$, then

$$1 \leq (d \cdot k) + 1 \leq |Q| \text{ and } d \cdot (k + 1) \leq |\delta|.$$

Furthermore, in case (i) (respectively, in case (ii)) there exists an NFA A such that $d = |Q| - 1$ and $2 \cdot d = |\delta|$ (respectively, $d \cdot k + 1 = Q$ and $d \cdot (k + 1) = |\delta|$).

3.2 Exponential Growth

In the following $A = (Q, \Sigma, \delta, q_0, F)$ is again always an NFA. If NFA A complies with $(\mathbf{EDA})$ (see Fig. 5), then it has exponential ambiguity [14]. This condition requires that for some state q there exist two distinct paths from q to q with the same underlying string.

$(\mathbf{EDA})$: There exists a co-reachable state $q \in Q$ and a string $w \in \Sigma^*$ such that $|\mathrm{paths}(q, w, q)| \geq 2$.

The difference between ambiguity and string path width is that the latter measure does not require computations to be accepting. Based on this observation, we can formulate the widget $(\mathbf{ECOMP})$ to characterize exponential string path width, and the correctness of $(\mathbf{ECOMP})$ is verified in Lemma 8.

In the definition of the widget $(\mathbf{EDA})$ or $(\mathbf{ECOMP})$ the string w must have a length of at least two because there can be only one path from q to q on an individual alphabet symbol. Since the cycles must have a length of at least two, it follows immediately that an NFA admitting widget $(\mathbf{ECOMP})$ has to admit $(\mathbf{ISPW}_d)$ for all $d \in \mathbb{N}$ (as should be the case).

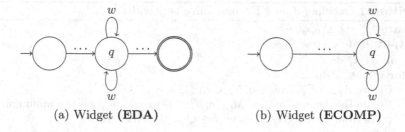

(a) Widget **(EDA)** (b) Widget **(ECOMP)**

Fig. 5. Exponential nondeterminism growth rate widgets.

(ECOMP): There exists a state $q \in Q$ and a string $w \in \Sigma^*$ such that
$$|\text{paths}(q, w, q)| \geq 2.$$

Lemma 8. *An NFA A satisfies* **(ECOMP)** *if and only if* $\text{spw}(A, \ell) \in 2^{\Theta(\ell)}$.

An NFA has exponential tree width if and only if it has exponential string path width. The "if"-direction of the following proposition is proved by applying Lemma 8 to the completion of the NFA.

Proposition 9. *Let A be an NFA. Then A has exponential tree width if and only if A has exponential string path width.*

4 Algorithms for Deciding the Growth Rate

From Theorem 6, we know that there is a relationship between the polynomial degrees of an NFA's string path width and tree width. An algorithm which decides the polynomial degree of an NFA's string path width or tree width, roughly speaking, also decides the degree of the other measure.

Palioudakis et. al [11] have shown that for an NFA A we can decide in polynomial time whether A has finite tree width, but did not give a more precise time bound for the algorithm.

Theorem 10. *Let* $A = (Q, \Sigma, \delta, q_0, F)$ *be an NFA. Then we can decide whether or not A has finite tree width in* $O(|Q|^4 \cdot |\Sigma|)$ *time.*

Proof. For $q \in Q$ and $a \in \Sigma$, we denote $A_{q,a} = (Q, \Sigma, \delta_{q,a}, q, F)$ where the transitions are defined for $p \in Q, b \in \Sigma$,

$$\delta_{q,a}(p, b) = \begin{cases} \emptyset, & \text{if } p = q \text{ and } b \neq a; \\ \delta(p, b), & \text{otherwise.} \end{cases} \tag{1}$$

In Algorithm 1, for states q and p of an NFA, the *distance* from q to p is the length of the shortest nonempty string that takes q to p. If p is not reachable

---

Algorithm 1 Deciding if an NFA has finite tree width

    Input: $A = (Q, \Sigma, \delta, q_0, F)$
    Output: finite $\in \{\text{true}, \text{false}\}$

1: **for all** $q \in Q$ **do**
2:     **for all** $a \in \Sigma$ **do**
3:         Create $A_{q,a} = (Q, \Sigma, \delta_{q,a}, q, F)$ as in (1).
4:         Create the distance matrix $M_{q,a}[p, p']$, where $M_{q,a}[p, p']$ is the minimum distance from state $p \in Q$ to state $p' \in Q$ in the NFA $A_{q,a}$.
5:     **end for**
6: **end for**
7: finite = true
8: **for all** $q \in Q$ **do**
9:     **for all** $a \in \Sigma$ **do**
10:       **if** $M_{q,a}[q, q] \neq \infty$ **then**   #q can reach itself starting with a
11:         **if** $|\delta(q, a)| \geq 2$ **then**   #q is a nondeterministic branching point
12:             finite = false
13:         **end if**
14:       **end if**
15:     **end for**
16: **end for**
17: **return** finite

---

from q, then the distance is ∞. The distance from q to itself is ∞ unless q is involved in a cycle.

Complexity analysis of Algorithm 1: Creating each NFA takes $O(|Q| + |\delta|)$ time and space, and creating each distance matrix takes $\Theta(|Q|^3)$ time and $\Theta(|Q|^2)$ space using the Floyd-Warshall reachability algorithm [1]. There are $|Q| \cdot |\Sigma|$ NFAs $A_{q,a}$ and matrices which are created. In lines 8–16, we again check each combination of state and character, but the inner work on lines 10–14 is done in constant time with the help of the reachability matrices. The algorithm then runs in $O(|Q|^4 \cdot |\Sigma|)$ time.

Correctness analysis of Algorithm 1: Recall that an NFA has infinite tree width if and only if some cycle has a nondeterministic transition. The diagonal of each distance matrix gives the self-reachability for each combination of state and character. That is, for all $q \in Q$ and $a \in \Sigma$, $M_{q,a}[q, q] \neq \infty$ means that q can reach itself in A on a string that begins with a. The algorithm returns false ("unbounded tree width") if and only if there exists a state $q \in Q$ and character $a \in \Sigma$ such that $M_{q,a}[q, q] \neq \infty$ and $|\delta(q, a)| \geq 2$. $\square$

Note that while Algorithm 1 could be modified to decide finiteness of string path width, its complexity would be worse than existing algorithms [14]. This is because the algorithm checks only for nondeterministic characters that initiate cycles, and does not check for strings across cycles.

To design efficient decision algorithms for deciding the growth rate of an NFA's tree width, we leverage existing algorithms [9,14] for deciding the growth rate of ambiguity.

Lemma 11. [modified from [14]] *Let $A = (Q, \Sigma, \delta, q_0, F)$ be an NFA. Then we can decide whether or not A's tree width is exponential in $O(|Q|^4 \cdot |\Sigma|)$ time.*

Using Algorithm 1 and Lemma 11, we can decide whether the growth rate of tree width of A is finite or exponential, and the remaining possibility is polynomial.

Corollary 12. *For an NFA $A = (Q, \Sigma, \delta, q_0, F)$, we can decide whether A's tree width is finite, polynomial, or exponential in $O(|Q|^4 \cdot |\Sigma|)$ time.*

Using another algorithm by Weber and Seidl [14], we can also determine the minimum degree of the polynomial bounding an NFA's tree width.

Proposition 13. [modified from [14]] *For an NFA $A = (Q, \Sigma, \delta, q_0, F)$ we can decide in $O(|Q|^6 \cdot |\Sigma|)$ time whether A's tree width is polynomial, and if so, the degree $d > 0$ such that $tw(A, \ell) \in \Theta(\ell^d)$.*

5   State Complexity

It is known that unambiguous NFAs may be significantly more succinct than finite tree width NFAs [11]. Since string path width lies in between the measures of ambiguity and tree width, we initiate here a descriptional complexity comparison of NFAs with finite string path width and finite tree width, respectively. We show that there exist finite string path width NFAs with m states such that an equivalent finite tree width NFA needs close to 2^m states.

Goldstine et al. [2] establishes that for certain regular languages an NFA with finite *branching* has to be as large as a DFA. Instead of the branching measure [2] the below lemma considers tree width.

Lemma 14. [modified from [2]] *Let $L \subseteq \Sigma^*$ be a regular language and $c \notin \Sigma$. If A is a finite tree width NFA for $(cLc)^*$, then A needs as many states as the minimal incomplete DFA for $(cLc)^*$.*

Let $\Sigma = \{a, b, c\}$ and for $m \in \mathbb{N}$ define

$$L_m = (a + b)^* a (a + b)^m.$$

Set $Q_m = \{0, 1, \ldots, m+2\}$ and define $A_m = (Q_m, \Sigma, \delta, 0, \{0\})$ where δ is defined by setting:

(i) $\delta(0, c) = \{1\}$, $\delta(m+2, c) = \{0\}$,
(ii) $\delta(1, a) = \{1, 2\}$, $\delta(1, b) = \{2\}$,
(iii) $\delta(i, z) = \{i+1\}$, $z \in \{a, b\}$, $2 \le i \le m+1$.

All transitions not defined above are undefined. Figure 6 depicts the NFA A_m and it is clear that $L(A_m) = (cL_mc)^*$.

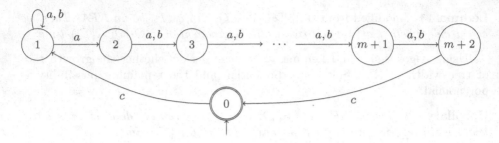

Fig. 6. NFA A_m recognizing the language $(cL_mc)^*$.

Lemma 15. $\mathrm{spw}(A_m) = m + 2$.

It is well known that the minimal DFA B_m for L_m has 2^{m+1} states—the DFA B_m just remembers the positions of symbols a among the last $m + 1$ symbols read. Based on B_m it is easy to construct an incomplete DFA C_m for $(cL_mc)^*$ by adding a new start state q_{new} that is the sole accepting state of C_m, a transition on c from q_{new} to the start state of B_m and a transition on c from each accepting state of B_m to q_{new}. The DFA C_m has $2^{m+1} + 1$ states.

Next using Lemma 14 we show that any finite tree width NFA for $(cL_mc)^*$ needs $2^{m+1} + 1$ states.

Lemma 16. *A finite tree width NFA recognizing the language $(cL_mc)^*$ needs $2^{m+1} + 1$ states, $m \geq 1$.*

Proof. We claim that all strings of $K = \{\varepsilon, b\} \cup c \cdot \{a, b\}^{m+1}$ belong to distinct congruence classes of $\equiv_{(cL_mc)^*}$. The empty string is inequivalent to all other strings of K because ε is the only string of K in $(cL_mc)^*$. The string b is inequivalent to all other string of K because it is the only string of K that is not a prefix of any string of $(cL_mc)^*$.

Consider two distinct strings $w_1, w_2 \in c \cdot \{a, b\}^{m+1}$. Since $w_1 \neq w_2$ and both strings have length $m + 2$, without loss of generality we can write

$$w_1 = cuav_1, \quad w_2 = cubv_2, \quad \text{where} \quad |v_1| = |v_2|, \quad u, v_1, v_2 \in \{a, b\}^*.$$

This means that $w_1 \cdot b^{m-|v_1|}c \in (cL_mc)^*$ and $w_2 \cdot b^{m-|v_1|}c \notin (cL_mc)^*$.

The above means that the minimal complete DFA for $(cL_mc)^*$ has (at least) $2^{m+1} + 2$ states, and hence the minimal incomplete DFA for $(cL_mc)^*$ needs $2^{m+1} + 1$ states. The claim follows from Lemma 14.   □

As a consequence of Lemmas 15 and 16 we have:

Theorem 17. *For $m \geq 1$ there exists an $(m + 3)$-state NFA with finite string path width such that any equivalent finite tree width NFA needs $2^{m+1} + 1$ states.*

Note that Lemma 14 uses the language $(cLc)^*$, while it seems that the same claim should hold also for $(Lc)^*$ and using the latter language would slightly improve the state complexity blow-up of Theorem 17. However, we have not been able to modify the original construction from [2] (that is needed for Lemma 14) to work with the simpler language. We can note that the NFA A_m is also unambiguous. The size blow-up given by Theorem 17 is slightly worse than the known blow-up of converting an unambiguous NFA to a finite tree width NFA [11].

6 Conclusion

As the main result we have shown that the tree width of an NFA A grows polynomially if and only if the string path width of A is polynomial and the degrees of the polynomials differ by at most one. Furthermore, if A has no useless states then the degree of the polynomial growth rate of string path width coincides with the degree of the polynomial bounding the ambiguity of A. We have also initiated a descriptional complexity comparison of NFAs with finite string path width and finite tree width, respectively.

A topic for further research could include the descriptional complexity comparison of NFAs with different growth rates of tree width (respectively, string path width). For example, it is known that the size of NFAs with polynomial ambiguity is exponentially separated from the size of general NFAs [5,9].

References

1. Cormen, T.H., Leiserson, C.E., Rivest, R.L., Stein, C.: Introduction to Algorithms, 3rd edn. MIT Press, Cambridge (2009)
2. Goldstine, J., Kintala, C.M.R., Wotschke, D.: On measuring nondeterminism in regular languages. Inf. Comput. **86**(2), 179–194 (1990)
3. Han, Y.S., Salomaa, A., Salomaa, K.: Ambiguity, nondeterminism and state complexity of finite automata. Acta Cybern. **23**(1), 141–157 (2017)
4. Holzer, M., Kutrib, M.: Descriptional and computational complexity of finite automata - a survey. Inf. Comput. **209**(3), 456–470 (2011). https://doi.org/10.1016/j.ic.2010.11.013
5. Hromkovič, J., Seibert, S., Karhumäki, J., Klauck, H., Schnitger, G.: Communication complexity method for measuring nondeterminism in finite automata. Inf. Comput. **172**(2), 202–217 (2002). https://doi.org/10.1006/inco.2001.3069
6. Keeler, C., Salomaa, K.: Branching measures and nearly acyclic NFAs. In: Pighizzini, G., Câmpeanu, C. (eds.) DCFS 2017. LNCS, vol. 10316, pp. 202–213. Springer, Cham (2017). https://doi.org/10.1007/978-3-319-60252-3_16
7. Keeler, C., Salomaa, K.: Cycle height of finite automata. In: Konstantinidis, S., Pighizzini, G. (eds.) DCFS 2018. LNCS, vol. 10952, pp. 200–211. Springer, Cham (2018). https://doi.org/10.1007/978-3-319-94631-3_17
8. Kutrib, M., Pighizzini, G.: Recent trends in descriptional complexity of formal languages. Bull. EATCS **111**, 70–86 (2013)
9. Leung, H.: Separating exponentially ambiguous finite automata from polynomially ambiguous finite automata. SIAM J. Comput. **27**(4), 1073–1082 (1998)
10. Leung, H.: Descriptional complexity of NFA of different ambiguity. Int. J. Found. Comput. Sci. **16**(5), 975–984 (2005)

11. Palioudakis, A., Salomaa, K., Akl, S.G.: State complexity of finite tree width NFAs. J. Autom. Lang. Comb. **17**(2–4), 245–264 (2012)
12. Ravikumar, B., Ibarra, O.H.: Relating the type of ambiguity of finite automata to the succinctness of their representation. SIAM J. Comput. **18**(6), 1263–1282 (1989). https://doi.org/10.1137/0218083
13. Shallit, J.: A Second Course in Formal Languages and Automata Theory. Cambridge University Press, Cambridge (2008)
14. Weber, A., Seidl, H.: On the degree of ambiguity of finite automata. Theor. Comput. Sci. **88**(2), 325–349 (1991). https://doi.org/10.1016/0304 3975(91)90381-B

Descriptional Complexity of Iterated Uniform Finite-State Transducers

Martin Kutrib[1], Andreas Malcher[1], Carlo Mereghetti[2]([⊠]) [iD],
and Beatrice Palano[3] [iD]

[1] Institut für Informatik, Universität Giessen, Arndtstr. 2, 35392 Giessen, Germany
{kutrib,andreas.malcher}@informatik.uni-giessen.de
[2] Dipartimento di Fisica "Aldo Pontremoli", Università degli Studi di Milano,
Via Celoria 16, 20133 Milano, Italy
carlo.mereghetti@unimi.it
[3] Dipartimento di Informatica "G. degli Antoni", Università degli Studi di Milano,
Via Celoria 18, 20133 Milano, Italy
palano@unimi.it

Abstract. We introduce the deterministic computational model of an *iterated uniform finite-state transducer* (IUFST). A IUFST performs the same length-preserving transduction on several left-to-right sweeps. The first sweep takes place on the input string, while any other sweep processes the output of the previous one. The IUFST accepts or rejects upon halting in an accepting or rejecting state along its sweeps. First, we focus on constant sweep bounded IUFSTs. We study their descriptional power vs. deterministic finite automata, and the state cost of implementing language operations. Then, we focus on non-constant sweep bounded IUFSTs, showing a nonregular language hierarchy depending on sweep complexity. The hardness of some classical decision problems on constant sweep bounded IUFSTs is also investigated.

Keywords: Iterated transducers · State complexity · Sweep complexity · Decidability

1 Introduction

Finite-state transducers are finite automata with an output and they have been studied at least since 1950s. A typical application of finite-state transducers is, for example, the lexical analysis of a computer program or an XML document. Here, the correct formatting of the input is verified, comments are removed, the correct spelling of the commands is checked, and the sequence of input symbols is translated into a list of tokens. The output produced is subsequently processed by a pushdown automaton that realizes the syntactic analysis. Another example is the use of cascading finite-state transducers. Here, one has a finite number of transducers $T_1, T_2, \ldots, T_n$, where the output of T_i is the input for the next

© IFIP International Federation for Information Processing 2019
Published by Springer Nature Switzerland AG 2019
M. Hospodár et al. (Eds.): DCFS 2019, LNCS 11612, pp. 223–234, 2019.
https://doi.org/10.1007/978-3-030-23247-4_17

transducer T_{i+1}. Such cascades of finite-state transducers have been used, for example, in [5] to extract information from natural language texts. On the other hand, the Krohn-Rhodes decomposition theorem shows that every regular language can be represented as the cascade of several finite-state transducers each of which having a "simple" algebraic structure [7,8]. Cascades of deterministic pushdown transducers are investigated in [4] and it is shown that a proper infinite hierarchy in between the deterministic context-free and deterministic context-sensitive languages exists with respect to the number of transducers applied. All the examples considered so far have in common that the subsequently applied transducers are, at least in principal, different transducers. Another point of view is taken in [3,14], where subsequently applied *identical* transducers are studied. Such *iterated* finite-state transducers are considered as language generating devices starting with some symbol in the initial state of the transducer, iteratively applying in multiple sweeps the transducer to the output produced so far, and eventually halting in an accepting state of the transducer after a last sweep. These iterated finite-state transducers are quite powerful, since in the nondeterministic case non-recursive languages can be generated where the underlying transducer comprises of three states. Even in the deterministic case, one state suffices to generate the class of D0L Lindenmayer systems and two states are sufficient to generate languages which are neither context-free nor in 0L. It is an essential feature that the underlying finite-state transducer is not length-preserving. Several restrictions on finite-state transducers are studied in [16] with respect to the question of whether the (arbitrary) iteration of the restricted transducers is still computationally universal.

In this paper, we will consider iterated finite-state transducers as language accepting devices. In addition, to have a simple device, the underlying transducer is considered to be a Mealy machine [15], that is, a deterministic length-preserving device where each input symbol is translated according to its transition function into an output symbol. To be more precise, an *iterated uniform finite-state transducer* (IUFST) works in several sweeps on a tape which is initially the input concatenated with a right endmarker. In every sweep the finite-state transducer starts in its initial state at the first tape cell, is applied to the tape, and prints its output on the tape. The input is accepted or rejected, if the transducer halts in an accepting or rejecting state.

We start our investigations of such devices having a *fixed number* $k \geq 1$ of sweeps. Since in this case the language accepted by a k-IUFST is always a regular language, it is of interest to compare such devices with deterministic finite automata (DFA) by investigating their *descriptional complexity* and the state cost of implementing language operations. General information on descriptional complexity can be found in the survey [10] and many results on the operational state complexity are surveyed in [6]. In addition, the NL-completeness of commonly considered decision problems on k-IUFSTs is pointed out.

We will also consider the case when the number of sweeps is *not bounded by a fixed finite number*. In this case, the resulting IUFSTs can be considered as restricted variants of one-tape Turing machines that iteratively sweep from left to right, starting at the first tape cell always in their initial state. It turns out that such devices can accept non-regular languages as soon as the number of sweeps is at least the logarithm of the length of the input. Moreover, there is a hierarchy depending on the number of sweeps and all commonly studied decidability questions turn out to be not even semidecidable.

The paper is organized as follows. In Sect. 2, we present the model of IUFSTs, and provide an example of a language accepted by a constant sweep bounded IUFST, with a number of states which is exponentially smaller than that of any equivalent DFA. In Sect. 3, we focus on the descriptional power of *constant* sweep bounded IUFSTs (k-IUFSTs), providing example of languages where iterated transduction either helps or does not help in reducing the number of states of equivalent DFAs. Section 4 is first devoted to study the optimal state cost of simulations between k-IUFSTs and DFAs. Next, the impact on the number of states is studied, of modifying the number of sweeps on k-IUFSTs. The optimal state cost of implementing Boolean language operations and reversal on k-IUFSTs is investigated, and finally the NL-completeness of typical decision problems on k-IUFSTs is proved. In Sect. 5, we consider *non-constant* sweep bounded IUFSTs. First, we prove that $o(\lg n)$ sweep bounded IUFSTs accept regular languages only, and show that such a logarithmic sweep lower bound is tight for nonregular acceptance. Next, we exhibit a nonregular language hierarchy with respect to sweep complexity.

2 Definitions and Preliminaries

We denote the set of positive integers and zero $\{0, 1, 2, ...\}$ by $\mathbb{N}$. The *reversal* of a word w is denoted by w^R, and for the length of w we write $|w|$. The reversal of a language $L \subseteq \Sigma^*$ is denoted by L^R, its complement by $\overline{L}$. By $\lg n$ we denote the logarithm of n to base 2. Throughout the article two devices are said to be *equivalent* if and only if they accept the same language.

An iterated uniform finite-state transducer is basically a deterministic finite-state transducer which processes the input in multiple passes (also sweeps). In the first pass it reads the input word followed by an endmarker and emits an output word. In the following passes it reads the output word of the previous pass and emits a new output word. It can be seen as a restricted variant of a one-tape Turing machine. The number of passes taken, the *sweep complexity*, is given as a function of the length of the input. Since here we are interested in weak preprocessing devices, we will consider length-preserving deterministic finite-state transducers, also known as Mealy machines.

Formally, we define an *iterated uniform finite-state transducer* (IUFST) as a system $T = \langle Q, \Sigma, \Delta, q_0, \triangleleft, \delta, F_+, F_- \rangle$, where Q is the set of *internal states*, Σ is the set of *input symbols*, Δ is the set of *output symbols*, q_0 is the initial state, $\triangleleft \in \Delta \setminus \Sigma$ is the *endmarker*, $F_+ \subseteq Q$ is the set of *accepting states*, $F_- \subseteq (Q \setminus F_+)$ is the set of *rejecting states*, and $\delta \colon Q \times (\Sigma \cup \Delta) \to Q \times \Delta$ is the *transition function*, which is total on $(Q \setminus (F_+ \cup F_-)) \times (\Sigma \cup \Delta)$ and where the endmarker is emitted only if it is read, i.e., there are no transitions $\delta(p, x) = (q, \triangleleft)$ with $x \neq \triangleleft$. The IUFST *halts* when the transition function is undefined (which may happen only for states from $F_+ \cup F_-$) or if it enters an accepting or rejecting state at the end of a sweep. Since the transducer is applied in multiple passes, i.e., in any but the initial pass it operates on the output of the previous pass, the transition function depends on input symbols from $\Sigma \cup \Delta$. Let $v \in \Delta^*$ be the output produced by T on input $w \in (\Sigma \cup \Delta)^*$ in a complete sweep. Then we denote v by $T(w)$. A word $w \in \Sigma^*$ is *accepted* by an IUFST T if there is an $r \geq 1$ such that $w_1 = T(w\triangleleft), w_{i+1} = T(w_i)$, $1 \leq i < r$, and the transducer T halts on w_r in an accepting state. That is, the initial input is a word over the input alphabet Σ followed by the endmarker, and the output computed after $r-1$ iterations drives T in a final sweep where it halts in an accepting state. Similarly, an input $w \in \Sigma^*$ is *rejected* by T if there is an $r \geq 1$ such that T halts in the final sweep on w_{r-1} in a rejecting state. Note that the output of the last sweep is not used. The language accepted by T is $L(T) = \{ w \in \Sigma^* \mid w \text{ is accepted by } T \}$.

Let $s \colon \mathbb{N} \to \mathbb{N}$ be a function. If any word of length n is accepted or rejected in at most $s(n)$ sweeps, the IUFST is said to be of *sweep complexity* $s(n)$. In this case, we use the notation $s(n)$-IUFST.

In order to clarify this notion we continue with an example.

Example 1. For $k \geq 1$, we consider the language $E_k = \{a, b\}^* b \{a, b\}^{k-1}$, whose words are characterized by having the letter b at the kth position from the right. Any deterministic finite automaton (DFA) needs at least 2^k states to accept E_k. The following k-IUFST $T = \langle Q, \Sigma, \Delta, q_a, \triangleleft_0, \delta, F_+, F_- \rangle$ accepts E_k with 3 states only. Set $Q = \{q_a, q_b, q_-\}$, $\Sigma = \{a, b\}$, $\Delta = \{a, b, \triangleleft_0, \triangleleft_1, \ldots, \triangleleft_{k-1}\}$, $F_+ = \{q_b\}$, $F_- = \{q_-\}$, and specify the transition function as:

(1) $\delta(q_a, a) = (q_a, a)$ (5) $\delta(q_b, a) = (q_a, b)$

(2) $\delta(q_a, b) = (q_b, a)$ (6) $\delta(q_b, b) = (q_b, b)$

(3) $\delta(q_a, \triangleleft_i) = (q_a, \triangleleft_{i+1})$,   (7) $\delta(q_b, \triangleleft_i) = (q_a, \triangleleft_{i+1})$,
           for $0 \leq i \leq k - 2$ for $0 \leq i \leq k - 2$

(4) $\delta(q_a, \triangleleft_{k-1}) = (q_-, \triangleleft_{k-1})$ (8) $\delta(q_b, \triangleleft_{k-1}) = (q_b, \triangleleft_{k-1})$

The basic idea of the construction is to shift symbol by symbol the input word to the right (states q_a and q_b), whereby an a is inserted at the first position and the last symbol is removed. In this way, in the first $k - 1$ sweeps the input is shifted $k - 1$ positions to the right. Now it is sufficient to check whether the last symbol is a b which is done in the last sweep. The number of the current sweep is given by the index of the endmarker.   ∎

3   Iterated Transductions vs. DFAs

As seen in Example 1, iterated transduction may lead to dramatically decrease the number of states for accepting regular languages. Here, we propose another family of languages showing the high descriptional power of k-IUFST. For any integer $k \geq 2$, we define the language

$$B_k = \{ b_1 \# b_2 \# \cdots \# b_m \mid b_i \in \{0, 1\}^k, m > 1, \exists i < m \colon b_i = b_m \}.$$

For recognizing B_k on a DFA, 2^{2^k+1} states are necessary and sufficient. Instead:

Theorem 2. *For any $k \geq 2$, the language B_k can be recognized by a 2^k-IUFST with $2^k(k+4)$ states.*

Proof. We informally explain the behaviour of a 2^k-IUFST T for B_k. At the first sweep, T stores the first block b_1 and "erase" any other occurrence of $b_1\#$ by replacing it with $b_1\#_d$. In case $b_1 = b_m$, T accepts, otherwise it rewrites $\lhd$ by $\lhd_1$ to store the sweep number, and continues. At the ith sweep, T searches a non-erased block to store, erases the occurrences of the stored block along the string, and matches it against b_m. If the stored block matches b_m, T accepts, otherwise it rewrites $\lhd_{i-1}$ with $\lhd_i$ to record the sweep number, and continues. Clearly, within 2^k sweeps, T correctly accepts or rejects the input string. The number of states of T is as follows: $2^{k+1} - 1$ to store a block not yet checked in previous sweeps, plus $2^k(k+2)$ states to perform matching with every subsequent block along the string and to fix the outcome of matching, plus 1 state to continue the computation when, by reading the endmarker, T realizes it is not the last sweep. So, the total number of states is $2^{k+1} - 1 + 2^k(k+2) + 1 = 2^k(k+4)$.   □

However, some languages are so hard that even iterated transduction cannot reduce the size for their recognition. We are going to present a family of unary languages for which using k-IUFST does not help in reducing the number of states of equivalent DFAs. Let p be any prime number. We define

$$L_p = \{\, a^{m \cdot p} \mid m \geq 0 \,\}.$$

Theorem 3. *Let $k \geq 1$. Then p states are necessary and sufficient for a k-IUFST to accept L_p.*

Proof. For the upper bound, consider the minimal DFA A for L_p, which has exactly p states. The DFA A can be turned into a p-state k-IUFST, as explained in Lemma 6 below.

For the lower bound, suppose by contradiction there exists a k-IUFST T accepting L_p with $x < p$ states. Consider an input string $a^{m \cdot p}$, for m large enough, accepted by T at the endmarker after exactly k sweeps (these acceptance requirements can be assumed without loss of generality).

Since the input is unary, in the first sweep T runs into a cycle of length, say c_1. Let β_1 be the output produced while running through one cycle. Then the input $a^{m \cdot p}$ is rewritten as $\alpha_{1,1}\beta_1^*\gamma_{1,1}$ with $|\beta_1| = c_1 = x_1 \leq x < p$, such that T enters and exits the cycle on β_1 in the same state. In the second sweep, T eventually runs into a cycle of length, say c_2, on processing β_1^*. Since $|\beta_1| = x_1$, we derive $c_2 = x_2 \cdot x_1$, for some $x_2 \leq x < p$. Let β_2 be the output produced while running through one cycle. Then T rewrites β_1^* as $\alpha_{2,1}\beta_2^*\gamma_{2,1}$ with $|\beta_2| = x_2 \cdot x_1$, and the current string after the second sweep has the form $\alpha_{1,2}\alpha_{2,1}\beta_2^*\gamma_{2,1}\gamma_{1,2}$. This process continues until the kth sweep, where T eventually runs into a cycle of length, say c_k, on processing β_{k-1}^*. Since $|\beta_{k-1}| = x_{k-1} \cdot x_{k-2} \cdots x_1$, we derive $c_k = x_k \cdot x_{k-1} \cdots x_1$, for some $x_k \leq x < p$. Let β_k be the output produced while running through one cycle. Then T rewrites β_{k-1}^* as $\alpha_{k,1}\beta_k^*\gamma_{k,1}$ with $|\beta_k| = x_k \cdot x_{k-1} \cdots x_1$ and the current string w after the kth sweep has the form

$$\alpha_{1,k}\alpha_{2,k-1} \cdots \alpha_{k,1}\beta_k^\ell \gamma_{k,1} \cdots \gamma_{2,k-1}\gamma_{1,k},$$

for some $\ell \geq 1$. Since the string w is accepted by T at the end of the kth sweep, also the string $\alpha_{1,k}\alpha_{2,k-1} \cdots \alpha_{k,1}\beta_k^{\ell-1}\gamma_{k,1} \cdots \gamma_{2,k-1}\gamma_{1,k}$ is accepted by T at the end of the kth sweep. But $|\alpha_{1,k}\alpha_{2,k-1} \cdots \alpha_{k,1}\beta_k^{\ell-1}\gamma_{k,1} \cdots \gamma_{2,k-1}\gamma_{1,k}| = m \cdot p - |\beta_k| = m \cdot p - c_k$. Since $c_k = x_k \cdot x_{k-1} \cdots x_1$ and the x_i are all less than p, and p is prime, $m \cdot p - c_k$ cannot be a multiple of p. This means that T accepts a string not in L_p, a contradiction. $\square$

4   Descriptional Complexity

In this section, we approach in a more general way the study of the descriptional power of k-IUFST vs. DFAs by providing general simulations between the two models. First, we consider the cost of turning a k-IUFST into an equivalent DFA:

Lemma 4. *Let $k > 0$ be an integer. Every n-state k-IUFST can be converted to an equivalent DFA with at most n^k states.*

The result presented in Lemma 4 turns out to be optimal.

Lemma 5. *There exists a family $\{L_{n,k}\}_{n,k>0}$ of unary languages such that each language $L_{n,k}$ is accepted by an n-state k-IUFST, whereas any equivalent DFA needs at least n^k states.*

Proof. For any $n, k > 0$, we define $L_{n,k} = \{ a^{c \cdot n^k} \mid c \geq 0 \}$.

The k-IUFST $T = \langle Q, \Sigma, \Delta, q_1, \triangleleft_0, \delta, F_+, F_- \rangle$ accepts $L_{n,k}$ with n states only. We set $Q = \{q_1, q_2, \ldots, q_n\}$, $\Sigma = \{a\}$, $\Delta = \{a, 1, 2, \ldots, n, \bar{n}, \triangleleft_0, \triangleleft_1, \ldots, \triangleleft_{k-1}\}$, $F_+ = \{q_n\}$, $F_- = \{q_2, \ldots, q_{n-1}\}$, and specify the transition function as:

(1) $\delta(q_i, \sigma) = \begin{cases} (q_{i+1}, i) & \text{if } \sigma \in \{a, n\} \\ (q_i, i) & \text{if } \sigma \in \{1, 2, \ldots, n-1, \bar{n}\} \end{cases}$ for $1 \leq i \leq n-1$

(2) $\delta(q_n, \sigma) = \begin{cases} (q_1, n) & \text{if } \sigma \in \{a, n\} \\ (q_n, \bar{n}) & \text{if } \sigma \in \{1, 2, \ldots, n-1, \bar{n}\} \\ (q_2, \sigma) & \text{if } \sigma \in \{\triangleleft_0, \triangleleft_1, \ldots, \triangleleft_{k-1}\} \end{cases}$

(3) $\delta(q_1, \triangleleft_i) = (q_1, \triangleleft_{i+1})$ for $0 \leq i \leq k-2$

(4) $\delta(q_1, \triangleleft_{k-1}) = (q_n, \triangleleft_{k-1})$

The basic idea is that, along the first sweep, T checks whether the length of the input string is a multiple of n by rewriting it as a sequence of consecutive blocks of the form "$12 \cdots n$", followed by $\triangleleft_1$. For the second sweep, T checks whether the length of the input string is a multiple of n^2 by rewriting n consecutive blocks "$12 \cdots n$" with the block "$1^n \ 2^n \ \cdots \ (n-1)^n \ \bar{n}^{n-1}n$", followed by $\triangleleft_2$. For the third sweep, T checks whether the length of the input string is a multiple of n^3 by rewriting n consecutive blocks "$1^n \ 2^n \ \cdots \ (n-1)^n \ \bar{n}^{n-1}n$" with the block "$1^{n^2} \ 2^{n^2} \ \cdots \ (n-1)^{n^2} \ \bar{n}^{n^2-1}n$", followed by $\triangleleft_3$. Clearly, by Transition (4), the input string can be accepted after the kth sweep only upon reading $\triangleleft_{k-1}$. In this case, the length of the input is easily seen to be a multiple of n^k.

The fact that n^k states are necessary for a DFA to accept $L_{n,k}$ follows from a trivial pumping argument. $\square$

Let us now focus on the opposite simulation, that is, DFAs by k-IUFST.

Lemma 6. *For* $n \geq 3$, *every* n-*state* DFA *can be converted into an equivalent* n-*state* k-IUFST, *with* $k \geq 1$.

Lemma 6 is stated for at least three states. For DFAs with less than three states, we can choose either to maintain the same number of states and perform one sweep only, or to add a new state and perform k sweeps.

One may expect that the size of a k-IUFST may always be decreased by increasing the number of sweeps. However by Theorem 3, the construction provided by Lemma 6 is optimal.

4.1 States Versus Sweeps

Here we turn to study the impact of modifying the number of sweeps on the size of iterated transducers. The possibility of trading states for input sweeps and vice versa has been investigated in the literature for several models of computations (see, e.g., [2,13]). Let us start with a simple observation on the minimal number of states necessary to establish a sweep complexity of at least two.

Lemma 7. *Let* $k \geq 2$ *be an integer and* T *be some* k-IUFST *with input alphabet* Σ. *Unless* T *accepts the trivial languages* $\emptyset$ *or* Σ^*, *it has at least three states.*

Proof. Let $L(T)$ be non-trivial. Then there are inputs that have to be accepted as well as inputs that have to be rejected. To this end, two states are necessary. On the other hand, T must not be in one of these two states at the end of the first sweep. Otherwise it would halt and could not start the second sweep. So, an additional state is necessary.   □

Concerning the relations between the necessary number of states and the number of sweeps we have the following situation: Theorem 3 shows that there are languages for which additional sweeps do not help to decrease the number of states at all. By Lemma 4, any n-state k-IUFST can be converted into an equivalent DFA with at most n^k states. Conversely, due to Lemma 7 we cannot reduce the number of states below three by increasing the number of sweeps. So, there is an upper bound for the number of sweeps that may help. In other words, for any regular language L we have a fixed sweep range from 1 to some k_L in which we can trade states for sweeps and vice versa. For example, the sweep range for language L_p of Theorem 3 is given by $k_{L_p} = 1$, that is, it is just one sweep. In general, the next theorem gives a lower bound for the number of necessary states when one sweep is omitted.

Theorem 8. *Let* $k \geq 2$ *and* $n \geq 3$ *be integers, and* T *be an* n-*state* k-IUFST *such that the minimal* DFA *for* $L(T)$ *has* n^k *states. Then any* $(k-1)$-IUFST *for* $L(T)$ *must have at least* $\lceil n^{k/k-1} \rceil$ *states.*

Proof. Assume a $(k-1)$-IUFST T' for $L(T)$ with strictly less than $\lceil n^{k/k-1} \rceil$ states. If $n^{k/k-1}$ is an integer, this means at most $n^{k/k-1} - 1$ states. So, by Lemma 4, we could construct from T' a DFA for $L(T)$ with at most $(n^{k/k-1} - 1)^{k-1} < n^k$

states, a contradiction. Similarly, if $n^{k/k-1}$ is not an integer, we have at most $\lfloor n^{k/k-1} \rfloor$ states. Again, by Lemma 4, we could construct a DFA accepting $L(T)$ with $(\lfloor n^{k/k-1} \rfloor)^{k-1} < n^k$ states, a contradiction.   □

Example 9. For $k \geq 2$ and $n \geq 3$, let us consider the language $L_{n,k}$ of Lemma 5, where an n-state k-IUFST accepting $L_{n,k}$ is constructed. Moreover, we noticed that the minimal DFA for $L_{n,k}$ has n^k states. So, any $(k-1)$-IUFST T' accepting $L_{n,k}$ has at least $\lceil n^{k/k-1} \rceil$ states.   ■

Theorem 8 shows that omitting one sweep in the sweep range may increase the number of necessary states. However, once we have this increased number of states, the next question is whether this number of states can be used to decrease the number of sweeps furthermore for free. For example, assume that we have a 3-state 16-IUFST. Then Theorem 8 says that any equivalent 15-IUFST needs at least 4 states. However, since 4^{14} is still greater than 3^{16}, four states could be enough to reduce the number of sweeps by two. The next theorem provides a gradual reduction of the number of sweeps and the necessary states exemplarily for the language $E_k = \{a,b\}^* b \{a,b\}^{k-1}$ of Example 1.

Theorem 10. *Let $\ell \geq 1$ and $k = 2^\ell$ be integers. Then the useful sweep range for language E_k is from 1 to 2^ℓ. Moreover, for any $i \in \{0, 1, \ldots, \ell - 1\}$ there is a 2^i-IUFST accepting E_k with $2^{2^{\ell-i}}$ states, and for $i = \ell$ there is a 2^i-IUFST accepting E_k with 3 states.*

Proof. For $i = 0$ the assertion follows since, in this case, we have a one-sweep IUFST which needs as many states as a DFA to accept E_k, i.e., 2^{2^ℓ} states as claimed. For $i = \ell$, the assertion follows immediately from the construction of Example 1. For the remaining cases we modify the construction of Example 1 as follows. Instead of shifting the input k times by one position to the right, now we shift it 2^i times by $2^{\ell-i}$ positions to the right. Since $2^i \cdot 2^{\ell-i} = 2^\ell = k$, altogether it is shifted again k positions to the right, so the construction does it. To shift the input by $2^{\ell-i}$ positions, $2^{2^{\ell-i}}$ states are necessary. For $i = \ell$, Lemma 7 gives the lower bound of three states, where one state is needed to start a new sweep. For $i < \ell$, there are enough states to be used to this purpose, i.e., that are neither accepting nor rejecting and can be entered upon reading the endmarker.   □

4.2   The State Cost of Language Operations on k-IUFSTs

As naturally done for many models of computation accepting regular languages (see, e.g., [1]), we now analyze the state complexity of language operations on k-IUFSTs. To this aim, we asssume that their transition functions are always defined, so that acceptance/rejection takes place on the endmarker only, at the jth sweep, for some $1 \leq j \leq k$. If not, transition functions can be easily completed by adding at most two states where we maintain the accept or reject outcome obtained in the middle of the input, while reaching the endmarker.

Let us start with Boolean operations. The first we consider is intersection:

Theorem 11. *Let $m, n, k \geq 1$ be integers, T_1 be an m-state k-IUFST and T_2 be an n-state k-IUFST. Then $m \cdot n$ states are sufficient for a k-IUFST to accept $L(T_1) \cap L(T_2)$.*

The cost of implementing intersection given in Theorem 11 is optimal, as proved in the following

Theorem 12. *Let $k \geq 1$ be an integer. There exist infinitely many integers $m, n > 1$ such that an m-state k-IUFST T_1 and an n-state k-IUFST T_2 can be built, for which $m \cdot n$ states are necessary to accept $L(T_1) \cap L(T_2)$ on a k-IUFST.*

Proof. Let m and n be co-prime, that is, $\gcd(m, n) = 1$. As explained in the proof of Lemma 5, the languages $L_{m,k}$ and $L_{n,k}$ can be accepted, respectively, by an m-state k-IUFST T_1 and n-state k-IUFST T_2. Since m and n are co-prime, we have that $L(T_1) \cap L(T_2) = L_{m \cdot n, k}$. This latter language cannot be accepted with less than $m \cdot n$ states on any k-IUFST T. Otherwise, by applying to T the construction in Lemma 4, we would obtain a DFA for $L_{m \cdot n, k}$ with less than $(m \cdot n)^k$ states, which is a contradiction. □

Complementing languages does not increase the size of k-IUFST:

Theorem 13. *Let $k, n \geq 1$ be integers and T be an n-state k-IUFST. Then n states are sufficient and necessary in the worst case for a k-IUFST to accept $\overline{L(T)}$.*

Proof. For the size upper bound, it is enough to switch accepting and rejecting states on T, thus obtaining an n-state k-IUFST for $\overline{L(T)}$. For the size lower bound, consider the language $L_{n,k}$ in the proof of Lemma 5. As pointed out, such a language has a minimal DFA with n^k states. Suppose, by contradiction, that $\overline{L_{n,k}}$ can be accepted by a k-IUFST M with $m < n$ states. By using on M the switching technique above, an m-state k-IUFST M' is obtained for $\overline{\overline{L_{n,k}}} = L_{n,k}$. Now, by Lemma 4, M' can be turned into an equivalent DFA with $m^k < n^k$ states, a contradiction. □

Finally, we focus on union of languages. We obtain a cost similar to implementing intersection.

Theorem 14. *Let $m, n, k \geq 1$ be integers, T_1 be an m-state k-IUFST and T_2 be an n-state k-IUFST. Then $m \cdot n$ states are sufficient and necessary in the worst case for a k-IUFST to accept $L(T_1) \cup L(T_2)$.*

Proof. The size upper bound follows from the upper bounds for intersection and complementation by De Morgan's laws.

For the size lower bound, assume by contradiction that less than $m \cdot n$ states are sufficient to implement union on k-IUFST. Consider the languages $L_{m,k}$ and $L_{n,k}$ with co-prime m and n, used in Theorem 12 to show the optimality of the cost $m \cdot n$ of intersection on k-IUFST. Clearly, we have $L_{m,k} \cap L_{n,k} = \overline{\overline{L_{m,k}} \cup \overline{L_{n,k}}}$. By Theorem 13, for $\overline{L_{m,k}}$ and $\overline{L_{n,k}}$, respectively, m and n states are sufficient on a k-IUFST. Yet, by our absurdum assumption, less than $m \cdot n$ states are sufficient to accept their union. In turn, again by Theorem 13, complementing the union language can be done with less than $m \cdot n$ states on a k-IUFST. This contradicts Theorem 12.   □

Let us conclude this section by discussing the cost of performing reversal on k-IUFST:

Theorem 15. *Let $k, n \geq 1$ be integers and T be an n-state k-IUFST. Then 2^{n^k} states are sufficient and at least $2^{\frac{n^k}{k2^k}}$ states are necessary in the worst case for a k-IUFST to accept $L(T)^R$.*

Proof. For the state upper bound, we transform T into an equivalent n^k-state DFA A according to Lemma 4. Next, by standard construction [17], A can be turned into a 2^{n^k}-state DFA A' for $L(A)^R = L(T)^R$. Finally, by Lemma 6, the DFA A' can be simulated by a 2^{n^k}-state k-IUFST.

For the state lower bound, let the language $C_{n,k} = \bigcup_{c>0} \{a,b\}^{c \cdot n^k - 1} b \{a,b\}^*$. The minimal DFA for $C_{n,k}{}^R$ has at least 2^{n^k} states, which means, by Lemma 4, that any k-IUFST for $C_{n,k}{}^R$ must have at least $2^{n^k}/k$ states. By suitably adapting the k-IUFST for the language $L_{n,k}$ provided in the proof of Lemma 5, we can obtain a $2n$-state k-IUFST for $C_{n,k}$. Whence, the claimed result follows.   □

4.3 Decidability Questions for k-IUFSTs

In this subsection, we obtain that all commonly studied decidability questions for k-IUFSTs are NL-complete So, for k-IUFSTs the questions of testing emptiness, universality, finiteness, infiniteness, inclusion, or equivalence have the same computational complexity as for DFAs [11,12].

Theorem 16. *Let $k \geq 1$ be an integer. Then for k-IUFSTs the problems of testing emptiness, universality, finiteness, infiniteness, inclusion, and equivalence are NL-complete.*

5   Hierarchy of Non-constant Sweep Complexities

We turn to consider $s(n)$-IUFSTs where $s(n)$ is a non-constant function. Since for any constant $k \geq 1$ any k-IUFST accepts a regular language, the first natural question is the following: "How many sweeps are necessary to cross the edge to non-regularity?" The answer is that there is no sublogarithmic sweep complexity that gives an IUFST the power to accept a non-regular language.

Proposition 17. *Let $s(n) \in o(\lg n)$. The language accepted by any $s(n)$-IUFST is regular.*

Proof. From a given $s(n)$-IUFST T, it is not hard to construct an equivalent one-tape Turing machine M with time complexity $2n \cdot s(n)$. It is shown in [9] that any one-tape Turing machine with a time complexity of order $o(n \lg n)$ accepts a regular language. Since $s(n) \in o(\lg n)$, the time complexity of M is of order $o(n \lg n)$ and, thus, $L(M) = L(T)$ is regular.   □

In fact, the gap between constant and 'useful' non-constant sweep complexities ends at a logarithmic level. The witness language given by the following lemma is even unary and non-context-free.

Lemma 18. *The non-context-free unary language* $L_{\text{uexpo}} = \{\, a^{2^k} \mid k \geq 0 \,\}$ *is accepted by a six-state* $s(n)$-IUFST *with* $s(n) \in O(\lg n)$.

Next, we turn to extend the sweep complexity hierarchy beyond the logarithm. To this end, we consider sweep complexities of order $O(\sqrt{n})$. The goal is to show that there is a language accepted by some $s(n)$-IUFST with $s(n) \in O(\sqrt{n})$ that cannot be accepted by any $s(n)$-IUFST with $s(n) \in o(\sqrt{n})$.

Lemma 19.
(1) The copy language with center markers $L_{\text{cpc}} = \{\, w\$^m w \mid w \in \{a,b\}^*, m \geq 1 \,\}$
is accepted by an $s(n)$-IUFST *with* $s(n) \in O(n)$.
(2) The copy language with single marker $\{\, w\$ w \mid w \in \{a,b\}^* \,\}$ *is accepted by an* $s(n)$-IUFST *with* $s(n) \in O(n)$.
(3) Let Σ_1 *be an alphabet not containing the symbol* $\$$ *and* Σ_2 *be an arbitrary alphabet. Then language* $L_{\text{eq}} = \{\, u\$v \mid u \in \Sigma_1^*, v \in \Sigma_2^*, \text{ and } |u| = |v| \,\}$ *is accepted by some* $s(n)$-IUFST *with* $s(n) \in O(n)$.

The second ingredient to show that there is a language accepted by some $s(n)$-IUFST with $s(n) \in O(\sqrt{n})$ that cannot be accepted by any $s(n)$-IUFST with $s \in o(\sqrt{n})$ is the acceptance of a language whose word length are quadratic.

Lemma 20. *The language* $L_{\text{sqr}} = \{\, \#a^{m-1}\#a^{m-2}\cdots\#a^1\# \mid m \geq 0 \,\}$ *is accepted by an* $s(n)$-IUFST *with* $s(n) \in O(\sqrt{n})$.

Now we are prepared to provide the witness language

$$L_{cpsq} = \{\, w\$w\#a^{m-1}\#a^{m-2}\cdots\#a^1\# \mid m \geq 0, w \in \{a,b\}^{m-1} \,\}.$$

Theorem 21. *The language* L_{cpsq} *is accepted by an* $s(n)$-IUFST *with* $s(n) \in O(\sqrt{n})$.

To show that the witness language L_{cpsq} is not accepted by any $s(n)$-IUFST with $s(n) \in o(\sqrt{n})$, we use Kolmogorov complexity and incompressibility arguments.

Theorem 22. *The language* L_{cpsq} *cannot be accepted by any* $s(n)$-IUFST *with* $s(n) \in o(\sqrt{n})$.

Finally, the sweep complexity hierarchy can be extended beyond the square root. By Lemma 19 we know already that the copy language with center markers $L_{\text{cpc}} = \{\, w\$^m w \mid w \in \{a,b\}^*, m \geq 1 \,\}$ is accepted by an $s(n)$-IUFST with $s(n) \in O(n)$. The following theorem separates this level of the sweep complexity hierarchy from the one induced by $s(n) \in O(\sqrt{n})$:

Theorem 23. *The copy language with center markers* L_{cpc} *cannot be accepted by any* $s(n)$-IUFST *with* $s(n) \in o(n)$.

Acknowledgements. The authors wish to thank the anonymous referees for useful and kind comments.

References

1. Bednárová, Z., Geffert, V., Mereghetti, C., Palano, B.: The size-cost of Boolean operations on constant height deterministic pushdown automata. Theor. Comput. Sci. **449**, 23–36 (2012). https://doi.org/10.1016/j.tcs.2012.05.009
2. Bianchi, M.P., Mereghetti, C., Palano, B.: Complexity of Promise Problems on Classical and Quantum Automata. In: Calude, C.S., Freivalds, R., Kazuo, I. (eds.) Computing with New Resources. LNCS, vol. 8808, pp. 161–175. Springer, Cham (2014). https://doi.org/10.1007/978-3-319-13350-8_12
3. Bordihn, H., Fernau, H., Holzer, M., Manca, V., Martín-Vide, C.: Iterated sequential transducers as language generating devices. Theor. Comput. Sci. **369**(1–3), 67–81 (2006). https://doi.org/10.1016/j.tcs.2006.07.059
4. Citrini, C., Crespi-Reghizzi, S., Mandrioli, D.: On deterministic multi-pass analysis. SIAM J. Comput. **15**(3), 668–693 (1986). https://doi.org/10.1137/0215049
5. Friburger, N., Maurel, D.: Finite-state transducer cascades to extract named entities in texts. Theor. Comput. Sci. **313**(1), 93–104 (2004). https://doi.org/10.1016/j.tcs.2003.10.007
6. Gao, Y., Moreira, N., Reis, R., Yu, S.: A survey on operational state complexity. J. Autom. Lang. Comb. **21**(4), 251–310 (2017)
7. Ginzburg, A.: Algebraic Theory of Automata. Academic Press (1968)
8. Hartmanis, J., Stearns, R.E.: Algebraic Structure Theory of Sequential Machines. Prentice-Hall (1966)
9. Hartmanis, J.: Computational complexity of one-tape turing machine computations. J. ACM **15**(2), 325–339 (1968). https://doi.org/10.1145/321450.321464
10. Holzer, M., Kutrib, M.: Descriptional complexity - an introductory survey. In: Martín-Vide, C. (ed.) Scientific Applications of Language Methods, pp. 1–58. Imperial College Press (2010)
11. Jones, N.D.: Space-bounded reducibility among combinatorial problems. J. Comput. System Sci. **11**(1), 68–85 (1975)
12. Jones, N.D., Laaser, W.T.: Complete problems for deterministic polynomial time. Theor. Comput. Sci. **3**(1), 105–117 (1976)
13. Malcher, A., Mereghetti, C., Palano, B.: Descriptional complexity of two-way pushdown automata with restricted head reversals. Theor. Comput. Sci. **449**, 119–133 (2012). https://doi.org/10.1016/j.tcs.2012.04.007
14. Manca, V.: On the generative power of iterated transductions. In: Ito, M., Paun, G., Yu, S. (eds.) Words, Semigroups, and Transductions - Festschrift in Honor of Gabriel Thierrin, pp. 315–327. World Scientific (2001)
15. Mealy, G.H.: A method for synthesizing sequential circuits. Bell Syst. Tech. J. **34**, 1045–1079 (1955). https://doi.org/10.1002/j.1538-7305.1955.tb03788.x
16. Pierce, A.: Decision problems on iterated length-preserving transducers. Bachelor's thesis, SCS Carnegie Mellon University, Pittsburgh (2011)
17. Salomaa, A., Wood, D., Yu, S.: On the state complexity of reversals of regular languages. Theor. Comput. Sci. **320**(2–3), 315–329 (2004)

On Classes of Regular Languages Related to Monotone WQOs

Mizuhito Ogawa[1] and Victor Selivanov[2,3(✉)]

[1] Japan Advanced Institute of Science and Technology, Nomi, Japan
`mizuhito@jaist.ac.jp`
[2] A.P. Ershov Institute of Informatics Systems SB RAS, Novosibirsk, Russia
`vseliv@iis.nsk.su`
[3] Kazan Federal University, Kazan, Russia

Abstract. We study relationships of monotone well quasiorders to regular languages and ω-languages, concentrating on decidability of the lattices of upper sets on words and infinite words. We establish rather general sufficient conditions for decidability. Applying these conditions to concrete natural monotone WQOs, we obtain new decidability results and new proofs of some known results.

Keywords: Regular language · Monotone WQO ·
Lattice of upper sets · Periodic extension · Decidability ·
Difference hierarchy

1 Introduction

In this work, we continue the study of relationships of well quasiorders (WQO) to regular languages and ω-languages initiated in [2,12] and continued by several people (see [8] and references therein for languages of finite words). In contrast with these works, we concentrate on the lattices of languages of upper sets of monotone WQOs on words and of induced WQOs on infinite words. In particular, we investigate decidability of such lattices and of levels of difference hierarchies over such lattices.

On this way, we identify natural apparently new classes of regular languages and prove decidability of them. We establish rather general sufficient conditions guaranteeing decidability. Applying these conditions to some natural monotone WQOs, we obtain new decidability results and new proofs of some known results. Our approach also suggests many interesting open questions.

M. Ogawa—This research was partially supported by Japan Society for the Promotion of Science (JSPS), Core-to-Core Program (A. Advanced Research Networks).
V. Selivanov—The research of V. Selivanov was supported by Russian Science Foundation, project 18-11-00100.

M. Hospodár et al. (Eds.): DCFS 2019, LNCS 11612, pp. 235–247, 2019.
https://doi.org/10.1007/978-3-030-23247-4_18

After recalling some preliminaries in the next section we describe in Sect. 3 some general properties of the mentioned classes of regular languages. In Sect. 4, we prove decidability of some of those classes. In Sects. 5 and 6, we study similar questions for ω-languages. We conclude in Sect. 7 with mentioning some of the remaining open questions.

2 Preliminaries

Here we recall some notation, notions and facts used throughout the paper. Some more special information is recalled in corresponding sections below.

We use standard set-theoretic notation, in particular $P(S)$ denotes the set of subsets of a set S which forms a Boolean algebra under $\cup, \cap, ^-$. For a class $\mathcal{C} \subseteq P(S)$ of subsets of S, $BC(\mathcal{C})$ is the Boolean closure of $\mathcal{C}$ (i.e., the Boolean algebra generated by $\mathcal{C}$ within $(P(S); \cup, \cap, ^-, \emptyset, S)$), and co-$\mathcal{C} = \{\bar{C} \mid C \in \mathcal{C}\}$ is the class of complements $\bar{C} = S \setminus C$ of elements of $\mathcal{C}$.

We use standard notation and terminology on partially ordered sets (posets) and quasiordered sets, which may be found in [1]. Recall that a *quasiorder* (QO) on a non-empty set S is a reflexive transitive binary relation on S. We denote QOs by symbols like $\leq, \preceq, \sqsubseteq$, possibly with indices. A *partial order* on S is an antisymmetric QO. The strict part of a QO $(S; \leq)$ is $< = \leq \setminus \geq$. Any QO $(S; \leq)$ induces the partial order $(S/\simeq; \leq)$, where the set $S/\simeq$ is the quotient set of S under the equivalence relation $\simeq = \leq \cap \geq$ on S, i.e., the set $S/\simeq$ consists of all equivalence classes $[a] = \{x \mid x \simeq a\}$, $a \in S$. The partial order $\leq$ is overloaded by $[a] \leq [b] \leftrightarrow a \leq b$.

Definition 1. *A QO $\leq$ on Σ^* is* monotone *if $u \leq v$ implies $xuy \leq xvy$, for all $x, y \in \Sigma^*$.*

A *well quasiorder* (WQO) on S is a QO that has neither infinite strictly descending chains nor infinite antichains. There are several interesting and useful characterizations of WQOs of which we will frequently use the following: a QO $\leq$ on S is a WQO iff for every non-empty upward closed set U in $(S; \leq)$ there are finitely many $x_1, \ldots, x_n \in U$ such that $U = \uparrow x_1 \cup \cdots \cup \uparrow x_n$ where $\uparrow x = \{y \mid x \leq y\}$ for $x \in S$.

It is known that if $(S; \leq)$ is a WQO then every QO on S that extends $\leq$, as well as every subset of S with the induced QO, are also WQOs. Also, the Cartesian product of two WQOs is a WQO, and if $(S; \leq)$ is QO and $P, Q \subseteq S$ are such that $(P; \leq), (Q; \leq)$ are WQOs then $(P \cup Q; \leq)$ is a WQO. There are also many other useful closure properties of WQOs including the following: If Q is a WQO, then $(Q^*; \leq^*)$ is a WQO where Q^* is the set of finite sequences in Q and $(x_1, \ldots, x_m) \leq^* (y_1, \ldots, y_n)$ means that for some strictly increasing $\varphi : \{1, \ldots, m\} \rightarrow \{1, \ldots, n\}$ we have $x_i \leq y_{\varphi(i)}$ for all i (Higman's lemma [5]). In particular, the embedding relation on words over a finite alphabet is a WQO.

A couple of our proofs use a stronger notion of the hierarchy of WQOs (e.g., ω^2-WQO) and a better quasiorder (BQO). Since they are more technical than a WQO, we just make corresponding references to the literature [7, 9–11].

We assume the reader to be familiar with the standard notions and facts of automata theory which may be found in [13,19]. Throughout the paper, we work with a fixed alphabet Σ (a finite nonempty set the elements of which are called letters). Let Σ^* and Σ^+ be the sets of finite (respectively, of finite non-empty) words over Σ. Sets of words are called languages. The empty word is denoted by ε, uv stands for the concatenation of words $u, v \in \Sigma^*$. By Σ^n, $\Sigma^{\leq n}$, and $\Sigma^{>n}$, we denote the set of words u of length n (i.e., $|u| = n$), length less-than-equal n (i.e., $|u| \leq n$), and length greater than n (i.e., $|u| > n$), respectively.

We use standard notation and terminology related to automata and regular expressions. In particular, $L(\mathcal{A})$ denote the language recognized by a finite automaton $\mathcal{A}$. Languages recognized by finite automata are called regular. The class of such languages is denoted by $\mathcal{R}_\Sigma$ or just by $\mathcal{R}$. This class is closed under union, intersection and complement, i.e. $(\mathcal{R}; \cup, \cap, \bar{\,}, \emptyset, \Sigma^*)$ is a Boolean algebra.

Let Σ^ω be the set of infinite words (also called ω-words) $\alpha = \alpha(0)\alpha(1)\cdots$, $\alpha(i) \in \Sigma$, over Σ. For factors of infinite words we sometimes use notation like $\alpha[m, n) = \alpha(m)\cdots\alpha(n-1) \in \Sigma^{n-m}$. Sets of infinite words are called ω-languages. We use standard notation and terminology related to automata on ω-words (such as Büchi automata) and ω-regular expressions. E.g., $v_1 v_2 \cdots$ is the infinite concatenation of $v_i \in \Sigma^+$ and $V_1.V_2.\cdots = \{v_1 v_2 \cdots \mid v_i \in V_i\}$ for all $V_i \subseteq \Sigma^+$. In particular, $v^\omega = vv\cdots$ is the ω-power of $v \in \Sigma^+$. Let $L^\omega(\mathcal{A})$ be the ω-language recognized by a Büchi automaton $\mathcal{A}$. Languages recognized by Büchi automata are called regular. The class of such languages is denoted by $\mathcal{R}_\Sigma^\omega$ or just by $\mathcal{R}^\omega$. This class is closed under union, intersection and complement.

A basic fact of automata theory (Myhill-Nerode theorem) states that a language $L \subseteq \Sigma^*$ is regular iff it is closed w.r.t. some congruence of finite index on Σ^* (recall that a congruence is an equivalence relation $\equiv$ such that $u \equiv v$ implies $xuy \equiv xvy$, for all $x, y \in \Sigma^*$). In [2] the following version of Myhill-Nerode theorem was established:

Theorem 2 (Theorem 3.3 in [2]). *A language $L \subseteq \Sigma^*$ is regular iff it is upward closed w.r.t. some monotone WQO on Σ^*.*

Associate with any monotone WQO $\leq$ the class $\mathcal{L}_\leq$ of upward closed sets (also known as upper sets) in $(\Sigma^*; \leq)$. By the above theorem, $\mathcal{L}_\leq$ is a class of regular languages. One of the main objectives of this paper is the study of such and some other related classes. In particular, we are interested in the standard question for automata theory on the decidability of such classes (a class of regular languages is decidable if there is an algorithm which, for a given finite automaton $\mathcal{A}$, determines whether the language $L(\mathcal{A})$ is in the class). We also study analogous questions on classes of regular ω-languages defined in a similar way based on an ω-version of Theorem 2 established in [12]. Since this requires more technicalities, we recall the details in the corresponding sections below.

Let us recall some information on the difference hierarchies. By a *base in a set* S we mean any class $\mathcal{L}$ of subsets of S which is closed under union and intersection and contains $\emptyset, S$ as elements. For any $k < \omega$, let $\mathcal{L}(k)$ be the class of sets of the form $\bigcup_i (L_{2i} \setminus L_{2i+1})$, where $L_0 \supseteq L_1 \supseteq \cdots$ is a descending sequence of sets from $\mathcal{L}$ and $L_i = \emptyset$ for $i \geq k$. The sequence $\{\mathcal{L}(k)\}_{k<\omega}$ is called the *difference hierarchy over $\mathcal{L}$*. As is well-known, $\mathcal{L}(k)\cup\text{co-}\mathcal{L}(k) \subseteq \mathcal{L}(k+1)$ for each k, and the class $\bigcup_k \mathcal{L}(k)$ coincides with the Boolean closure $BC(\mathcal{L})$ of $\mathcal{L}$.

Associate with any QO $(Q; \leq)$ the base $\mathcal{L}_\leq$ in Q consisting of all upper sets of Q, including the empty set; a set $L \subseteq Q$ is upper if $x \in L$ and $x \leq y$ imply $y \in L$. By an *alternating chain* of length k for a set $K \subseteq Q$ we mean a sequence $(x_0, \ldots, x_k)$ of elements of Q such that $x_0 \leq \cdots \leq x_k$ and $x_i \in K \leftrightarrow x_{i+1} \notin K$ for every $i < k$. Such a chain is called a 1-alternating chain if $x_0 \in K$, otherwise it is called a 0-alternating chain. Variants of the following fact from [18] frequently appear when treating the difference hierarchies.

Proposition 3. *Let $(Q; \leq)$ be a QO, $\mathcal{L}_\leq$ the base of upper sets, and $K \subseteq Q$. For every $k < \omega$, $K \in \mathcal{L}(k)$ iff K has no 1-alternating chain of length k.*

3   Classes of Languages Related to Monotone WQOs

Here we make some observations on how the classes $\mathcal{L}_\leq$ look like.

Let $\mathcal{Q}(S)$ be the class of QOs on S. Define binary operations $\sqcap, \sqcup$ on $\mathcal{Q}(S)$ as follows: let $\leq \sqcap \leq'$ be the intersection of $\leq, \leq'$, and let $\leq \sqcup \leq'$ be the transitive closure of $\leq \cup \leq'$. Then $\leq \sqcap \leq'$ and $\leq \sqcup \leq'$ are respectively the infimum and the supremum of $\leq, \leq'$ in the poset $(\mathcal{Q}(S); \subseteq)$. Clearly, the equality $=_S$ and $S \times S$ are respectively the smallest and the largest elements of this poset. Therefore, the structure $(\mathcal{Q}(S); \sqcap, \sqcup, =_S, S \times S)$ is a bounded lattice. The set $\mathcal{W}(S)$ of WQOs on S is closed under both operations, hence $(\mathcal{W}(S); \sqcap, \sqcup, S \times S)$ is the substructure of $(\mathcal{Q}(S); \sqcap, \sqcup, S \times S)$ with the largest element $S \times S$. We removed equality from the signature because if S is infinite then $=_S$ is not a WQO.

Lemma 4. *For every QO $\leq$ on S, $(\mathcal{L}_\leq; \cup, \cap, \emptyset, S)$ is a substructure of the structure $(P(S); \cup, \cap, \emptyset, S)$. The function $\leq \mapsto \mathcal{L}_\leq$ is an isomorphic embedding of $(\mathcal{Q}(S); \subseteq)$ into the poset $(Sub(P(S)); \supseteq)$ of substructures of the structure $(P(S); \cup, \cap, \emptyset, S)$.*

Below we consider variants of $(\mathcal{Q}(S); \sqcap, \sqcup, S \times S)$ and $(Sub(P(S)); \sqcup, \sqcap, \{\emptyset, S\})$ where, for each $\mathcal{L}, \mathcal{M} \in Sub(P(S))$, $\mathcal{L} \sqcup \mathcal{M}$ is the substructure generated by $\mathcal{L} \cup \mathcal{M}$, $\mathcal{L} \sqcap \mathcal{M}$ is the intersection of $\mathcal{L}, \mathcal{M}$, and $\{\emptyset, S\}$ is the smallest element of $Sub(P(S))$. Note that the restriction of $\leq \mapsto \mathcal{L}_\leq$ to $\mathcal{W}(S)$ is an isomorphic embedding of $(\mathcal{W}(S); \sqcap, \sqcup, S \times S)$ into $(Sub(P(S)); \sqcup, \sqcap, \{\emptyset, P(S)\})$. In the particular case $S = \Sigma^*$ we can restrict the function $\leq \mapsto \mathcal{L}_\leq$ to the class $\mathcal{M}(\Sigma^*)$ of monotone WQOs. We collect some properties of this restriction which show, in particular, that any class $\mathcal{L}_\leq$ is a small portion of $\mathcal{R}$.

Proposition 5. *1. $\leq \mapsto \mathcal{L}_\leq$ is an embedding of $(\mathcal{M}(\Sigma^*); \sqcap, \sqcup, \Sigma^* \times \Sigma^*)$ into the structure $(Sub(\mathcal{R}); \sqcup, \sqcap, \{\emptyset, \Sigma^*\})$ of substructures of $(\mathcal{R}; \cup, \cap, \emptyset, \Sigma^*)$.*
2. For any monotone WQO $\leq$, the bounded lattice $\mathcal{L}_\leq$ contains no infinite sequence of nonempty pairwise disjoint elements and is a proper subset of $\mathcal{R}$.
3. For any monotone WQO $\leq$, the bounded lattice $\mathcal{L}_\leq$ is Boolean iff $\leq$ is a congruence of finite index.

4. *The poset* $(\{\mathcal{L}_\leq \mid \leq \in \mathcal{M}(\Sigma^*)\}; \subseteq)$ *is directed, has no maximal elements and satisfies* $\bigcup \{\mathcal{L}_\leq \mid \leq \in \mathcal{M}(\Sigma^*)\} = \mathcal{R}.$

There are many examples of monotone WQOs of which we mention here four infinite series. The first one is formed by the congruences of finite index. In particular, this class contains the so called syntactic congruences $\equiv_L$ of regular languages L defined by: $u \equiv_L v$ iff $\forall x, y \in \Sigma^* (xuv \in L \leftrightarrow xvy \in L)$.

The second one is formed by the monotone WQOs of finite index (i.e., the associated congruence of which is of finite index). This class contains, e.g., the syntactic QOs $\leq_L$ associated with each regular language L as follows [14]: $u \leq_L v$ iff $\forall x, y \in \Sigma^* (xuv \in L \rightarrow xvy \in L)$. Note that the associated congruence of $\leq_L$ is $\equiv_L$. This class also contains QOs associated with various one-sided Ehrenfeucht-Fraisse games (several examples may be found in [18]). For every such QO $\leq$, the Boolean algebra $BC(\mathcal{L}_\leq)$, which is equal to $\mathcal{L}_\simeq$, is finite.

Although the examples of monotone WQOs above are important for the general theory, they are not very interesting for this paper because the decidability problem for them is solved in an obvious way. Decidability issues are more interesting for monotone WQOs of infinite index. A typical example is the embedding partial order on words. We will discuss two infinite series of such QOs which will be used below to illustrate our methods.

The third infinite series consists of monotone WQOs studied in [3,17]. For any $k < \omega$ the following partial order was studied: $u \leq_k v$, if either $u = v \in A^{\leq k}$ or $u, v \in A^{>k}$ such that $p_k(u) = p_k(v)$, $s_k(u) = s_k(v)$, and there is a k-embedding $f : u \rightarrow v$. Here $p_k(u)$ (resp. $s_k(u)$) is the prefix (resp. suffix) of u of length k, and the k-embedding f is a monotone injective function from $\{0 \ldots, |u|-1\}$ to $\{0 \ldots, |v|-1\}$ such that $u(i) \cdots u(i+k) = v(f(i)) \cdots v(f(i)+k)$ for all $i < |u|-k$. In [3,17], it was shown that every $\leq_k$ is a monotone WQO. Note that the relation $\leq_0$ is just the embedding of words.

The fourth infinite series of monotone WQOs was introduced in [2]. A set $I \subseteq \Sigma^*$ is *unavoidable* if almost all words contain a word from I as a factor. With any finite unavoidable set I, we associate a QO $(\Sigma^*; \leq_I)$ defined by: $u \leq_I v$ iff v is obtained from u by a finite (possibly, empty) series of subsequent insertions of words from I as a factor. As shown in [2], any such $\leq_I$ is a monotone WQO.

4   Decidability of Levels $\mathcal{L}_\leq(n)$

Here we consider decidability issues for the classes of languages discussed above. First we prove a rather general sufficient condition for decidability and next illustrate this condition for the mentioned examples of monotone WQOs. In this section letters $\mathcal{A}, \mathcal{B}$, possibly with indices, are used to denote finite automata.

Definition 6. *We call a monotone WQO $\leq$ computable if it is a computable relation on Σ^* and there is a computable family $\{\mathcal{A}_u\}_{u \in \Sigma^*}$ of finite automata such that $L(\mathcal{A}_u) = \uparrow u$ for each $u \in \Sigma^*$.*

Theorem 7. *For any computable monotone WQO $\leq$, the levels $\mathcal{L}_\leq(n)$ of the difference hierarchy over $\mathcal{L}_\leq$ are decidable uniformly on n.*

Proof. We have to show that the relation $L(\mathcal{A}) \in \mathcal{L}_{\leq}(n)$ is decidable. By the Post theorem from computability theory (see [16]), it suffices to show that the relation itself and its complement $L(\mathcal{A}) \notin \mathcal{L}_{\leq}(n)$ are semidecidable (i.e., computably enumerable). First we show semidecidability of the relation $L(\mathcal{A}) \in \mathcal{L}_{\leq}$. By the definition of $\mathcal{L}_{\leq}$, $L(\mathcal{A}) \in \mathcal{L}_{\leq}$ iff $L(\mathcal{A}) = \emptyset$ or

$$\exists m < \omega \exists u_0, \cdots, u_m \in \Sigma^* (L(\mathcal{A}) = L(\mathcal{A}_{u_0}) \cup \cdots \cup L(\mathcal{A}_{u_m})).$$

As is well known, the relations $L(\mathcal{A}) = \emptyset$ and $L(\mathcal{A}) = L(\mathcal{A}_{u_0}) \cup \cdots \cup L(\mathcal{A}_{u_m})$ are decidable, hence the relation $L(\mathcal{A}) \in \mathcal{L}_{\leq}$ is semidecidable.

Turning to the level n of the difference hierarchy, we consider for technical reasons only the case $n = 2m$ of even n (the case of odd n is treated in a similar way). By the definition of $\mathcal{L}_{\leq}(n)$, we have: $L(\mathcal{A}) \in \mathcal{L}_{\leq}(n)$ iff

$$\exists \mathcal{B}_0, \dots, \mathcal{B}_{n-1} \big(L(\mathcal{B}_0), \dots, L(\mathcal{B}_{n-1}) \in \mathcal{L}_{\leq} \wedge$$
$$L(\mathcal{B}_0) \supseteq \cdots \supseteq L(\mathcal{B}_{n-1}) \wedge$$
$$L(\mathcal{A}) = \bigcup_{i<m} L(\mathcal{B}_{2i}) \setminus L(\mathcal{B}_{2i+1}) \big).$$

Since the relations in the first conjunct are semidecidable and all other relations in big parenthesis are computable, the relation $L(\mathcal{A}) \in \mathcal{L}_{\leq}(n)$ is semidecidable. On the other hand, by Proposition 3 we have: $L(\mathcal{A}) \notin \mathcal{L}_{\leq}(n)$ iff

$$\exists u_0, \dots, u_n \in \Sigma^* \big(u_0 < \cdots < u_n \wedge u_0 \in L(\mathcal{A}) \wedge \forall i < n(u_i \in L(\mathcal{A}) \leftrightarrow u_{i+1} \notin L(\mathcal{A})) \big).$$

Since all relations in big parenthesis are computable, the relation $L(\mathcal{A}) \notin \mathcal{L}_{\leq}(n)$ is semidecidable. □

We believe that Theorem 7 applies to many monotone WQOs (maybe, even to all finitely presented ones). One only has to check the computability of a given WQO. Here we observe that this is really the case for the examples of monotone WQOs discussed in Sect. 3.

Corollary 8. *For all $k, n < \omega$, the levels $\mathcal{L}_{\leq_k}(n)$ of the difference hierarchy over $\mathcal{L}_{\leq_k}$ are decidable uniformly on k, n.*

Proof. By Theorem 7, we have to show that the monotone WQOs $\leq_k$ are computable uniformly in k. This was shown in [3, 17]. □

The above corollary is not new, earlier obtained in [3, 17]. Moreover, in those papers, the decidability of classes $BC(\mathcal{L}_{\leq_k})$ was also established. We hope that this last fact would be generalized to a wider class of monotone WQOs. In contrast, the next corollary of Theorem 7 seems not explicitly mentioned elsewhere.

Theorem 9. *For any finite unavoidable set $I \subseteq \Sigma^*$, the levels $\mathcal{L}_{\leq_I}(n)$ of the difference hierarchy over $\mathcal{L}_{\leq_I}$ are decidable uniformly on n.*

Proof. By Theorem 7, we only have to show that the monotone WQO $\leq_I$ is computable. This follows from an inspection of the proofs of Lemmas 4.6 and 4.7 in [2]. We also note that, by Theorem 4.13 in [2], it is decidable whether I is unavoidable. Therefore, we also have uniformity on I. □

5   Extending Monotone WQOs to Infinite Words

Here we discuss how to extend notions and results about monotone WQOs to infinite words, based on [12]. Fix a monotone WQO $\leq$ on Σ^*. A QO $(\Sigma^\omega, \preceq)$ is a *monotone extension* of $(\Sigma^*, \leq)$ if $\forall i(u_i \leq v_i)$ implies $u_1u_2u_3\cdots \preceq v_1v_2v_3\cdots$. We define important subclasses of monotone extensions.

Definition 10 (Definition 2.1 in [12]). *Let $(\Sigma^*; \leq)$ be a monotone WQO.*

1. *A QO $(\Sigma^\omega; \preceq)$ is a* periodic extension *of $(\Sigma^*; \leq)$ if $\preceq$ is a monotone extension of $\leq$, and for each $\alpha \in \Sigma^\omega$ there exist $u, v \in \Sigma^*$ with $\alpha \simeq uv^\omega$, where $\simeq = \preceq \cap \succeq$. The set of periodic extensions of $\leq$ is denoted by $PE(\leq)$.*
2. *A WQO $(\Sigma^\omega; \preceq)$ is a* regular extension *of $(\Sigma^*; \leq)$ if $\preceq$ is a monotone extension of $\leq$, and for each $\alpha \in \Sigma^\omega$ the upward closed set $\uparrow \alpha$ w.r.t. $\preceq$ is a regular ω-language. The set of regular extensions of $\leq$ is denoted by $RE(\leq)$.*

Definition 11 (Definition 3.1 in [12]). *A monotone extension $(\Sigma^\omega; \preceq)$ of a monotone WQO $(\Sigma^*; \leq)$, is a* continuous extension, *if $(\Sigma^\omega; \preceq)$ is a WQO, and*

- *For each $u, v \in \Sigma^*$ and $\alpha, \beta \in \Sigma^\omega$, $u \leq v$ and $\alpha \preceq \beta$ imply $u\alpha \preceq v\beta$.*
- *Let $u_j, v_j \in \Sigma^*$ for each j and let $\alpha_i = v_1 \cdots v_{i-1}u_i \cdots$ for each i and $\alpha_\infty = v_1v_2\cdots$. For $\beta \in \Sigma^\omega$, if $u_i \leq v_i$ and $\alpha_i \preceq \beta$ for each i, then $\alpha_\infty \preceq \beta$; and if $u_i \geq v_i$ and $\alpha_i \succeq \beta$ for each i, then $\alpha_\infty \succeq \beta$.*

The set of continuous extensions of $\leq$ is denoted by $CE(\leq)$.

The following ω-versions of Theorem 2 are fundamental for this paper.

Theorem 12 (Theorem 2.2 and 3.2 in [12]). *For any $L \subseteq \Sigma^\omega$ we have:*

1. *L is regular iff L is upward closed under some periodic extension of a monotone WQO.*
2. *L is regular iff L is upward closed under some continuous extension of a monotone WQO.*

We prove some relationships between introduced classes of extensions.

Theorem 13. *For a monotone WQO $\leq$, $CE(\leq) \subseteq RE(\leq) = PE(\leq) \subseteq W(\Sigma^\omega)$.*

Proof. Since Theorem 12 and its proof imply $PE(\leq) \cup CE(\leq) \subseteq RE(\leq)$ and $PE(\leq) \subseteq W(\Sigma^\omega)$, we show $RE(\leq) \subseteq PE(\leq)$. Let $\preceq$ be a regular extension of $\leq$. For every $\alpha \in \Sigma^*$, we have to find $x, y \in \Sigma^*$ such that $\alpha \simeq xy^\omega$.

The upward closed set $\uparrow \alpha = L_\preceq(\alpha)$ is a regular ω-language so there is a congruence $\approx$ of finite index on Σ^* that saturates $\uparrow \alpha$, i.e., $\uparrow \alpha = \bigcup U.V^\omega$ for $\approx$-classes U, V with $V.V \subseteq V$ such that $U.V^\omega \cap U'.V'^\omega \neq \phi$ implies $U = U'$ and $V = V'$. Since $\leq$ is a WQO, there are finitely many (modulo $\leq \cap \geq$) minimal elements $\{x_1, \cdots, x_l\}$ and $\{y_1, \cdots, y_k\}$ of U and V, respectively. Since $\alpha \in U.V^\omega$, let $\alpha = uv_1v_2\cdots$ with $u \in U$ and $v_i \in V$. Then, $x_i \leq u$ for some

i, and for all $j', s > 0$ there is j with $y_j \leq v_{j'} \cdots v_{j'+s}$ (recall that $V.V \subseteq V$). By Ramsey theorem, we have $1 \leq j_1 < j_2 < \cdots$ and $j, j' \leq k$ such that $y_j \leq v_{j_1} \cdots v_{j_2-1}, v_{j_2} \cdots v_{j_3-1}, \cdots$ and $y_{j'} \leq v_1 \cdots v_{j_1-1}$. For any $\approx$-class U' with $x_i y_{j'} \in U'$, $\alpha \in U.V^\omega \cap U'.V^\omega$ implies $U = U'$. Let $x_{i'} \leq x_i y_{j'}$. Since $\preceq$ is a monotone extension of $\leq$, $x_{i'} y_j^\omega \preceq \alpha$. Since $x_{i'} y_j^\omega \in U.V^\omega \subseteq\uparrow \alpha$, $\alpha \preceq x_{i'} y_j^\omega$. □

Although we do not know whether $CE(\leq) = PE(\leq)$ for each monotone WQO $\leq$ at the moment, we guess this holds in natural cases.

Lemma 14. *For a monotone WQO $(\Sigma^*; \leq)$, $PE(\leq)$ (resp. $CE(\leq)$) is closed under intersection.*

Proof. Let $\preceq_1, \preceq_2 \in PE(\leq)$. Since $\preceq = \preceq_1 \cap \preceq_2$ is a monotone extension of $\leq$, it remains to show that, for each $\alpha \in \Sigma^\omega$, there are $u, v \in \Sigma^*$ with $\alpha \simeq uv^\omega$. Let $\approx_1$ and $\approx_2$ be finite congruences saturating $L_{\preceq_1}(\alpha)$ and $L_{\preceq_2}(\alpha)$, respectively. Then, $\approx = \approx_1 \cap \approx_2$ is a finite congruence saturating $L_{\preceq_1}(\alpha) \cap L_{\preceq_2}(\alpha)$. By the proof of Theorem 13, there exist $\approx$-classes U, V with $\alpha \in U.V^\omega$, and minimal elements $u \in U$ and $v \in V$ with $\alpha \approx uv^\omega$, which leads $\alpha \simeq uv^\omega$.

For $CE(\leq)$, the statement is immediate from Definition 11. □

Associate with any monotone WQO $\leq$, the class $\mathcal{L}_\leq^\omega$ of ω-languages which are upper sets w.r.t. some periodic extension of $\leq$, i.e., $\mathcal{L}_\leq^\omega = \bigcup \{\mathcal{L}_\preceq \mid \preceq \in PE(\leq)\}$.

Proposition 15. *1. $\preceq \mapsto \mathcal{L}_\preceq$ is an embedding from $(PE(\leq); \sqcap, \sqcup, \Sigma^\omega \times \Sigma^\omega)$ into the structure $(Sub(\mathcal{R}^\omega); \sqcup, \sqcap, \{\emptyset, \mathcal{R}^\omega\})$ of substructures of $(\mathcal{R}^\omega; \cup, \cap, \emptyset, \Sigma^\omega)$.*
2. For any $\preceq \in PE(\leq)$, every sequence of nonempty pairwise disjoint elements of $\mathcal{L}_\preceq$ is finite.
3. $\mathcal{L}_\leq^\omega$ is closed under union and intersection.
4. $\bigcup \{\mathcal{L}_\leq^\omega \mid \leq \in \mathcal{M}(\Sigma^*)\} = \mathcal{R}^\omega$.

The study of classes $\mathcal{L}_\leq^\omega$ becomes simpler if there is the smallest periodic extension $\preceq$ of $\leq$, i.e., the smallest element of $(PE(\leq); \subseteq)$. The reason is that in this case $\mathcal{L}_\leq^\omega = \mathcal{L}_\preceq$. Note that, for a periodic (resp. continuous) extension $\preceq$, if a monotonic extension $\preceq'$ of $\leq$ holds $\preceq \subseteq \preceq'$, $\preceq'$ is also a periodic (resp. continuous) extension of $\leq$. Currently, we do not know whether every monotone WQO has the smallest periodic extension. Instead, we show the existence of the smallest continuous extension (Theorem 18), if $\leq$ is a monotone ω^2-WQO over Σ^*.

Lemma 16. *Let $\leq$ be a monotone WQO over Σ^*. Assume that a transfinite sequence $(\preceq_\lambda)_{\lambda \in \Lambda}$ with $\preceq_\lambda \in PE(\leq)$ holds $\preceq_\lambda \supseteq \preceq_{\lambda'}$ if $\lambda < \lambda'$. Let $\preceq = \bigcap_{\lambda \in \Lambda} \preceq_\lambda$. Then, for each $\alpha \in \Sigma^\omega$, there is a countable subset $\Delta \subseteq \Lambda$ such that*

1. For $\lambda \in \Lambda$, there is $\lambda' \in \Delta$ with $\lambda < \lambda'$.
2. For $\lambda \in \Delta$, there are $\approx_\lambda$-classes U_λ, V_λ saturating $L_{\preceq_\lambda}(\alpha)$ and minimal elements (w.r.t. $\preceq_\lambda$) $u_\lambda \in U_\lambda$, $v_\lambda \in V_\lambda$ such that $\alpha \in U_\lambda.V_\lambda^\omega$ and $u_\lambda v_\lambda^\omega \simeq_\lambda \alpha$.
3. For $\lambda, \lambda' \in \Delta$ with $\lambda < \lambda'$, $u_\lambda \leq u_{\lambda'}$ and $v_\lambda \leq v_{\lambda'}$.
4. α is the upper limit of $(u_\lambda v_\lambda^\omega)_{\lambda \in \Delta}$ (w.r.t. $\preceq$), i.e., $\overline{\lim}_{\lambda \in \Delta} u_\lambda v_\lambda^\omega \simeq \alpha$.

Proof. From the proof of Theorem 13, for each $\alpha \in \Sigma^\omega$ and $\lambda \in \Lambda$, there exist $\approx_\lambda$-classes U_λ, V_λ saturating $L_{\preceq_\lambda}(\alpha)$ with $\alpha \in U_\lambda.V_\lambda^\omega$ and minimal elements $u_\lambda \in U_\lambda$, $v_\lambda \in V_\lambda$ with $\alpha \approx_\lambda u_\lambda v_\lambda^\omega$. Since $\leq$ is a monotone WQO, there is a countable subset $\Delta \subseteq \Lambda$ (by Ramsey-type argument [6]) such that $u_\lambda \leq u_{\lambda'}$, $v_\lambda \leq v_{\lambda'}$ for $\lambda, \lambda' \in \Delta$ with $\lambda < \lambda'$ and

$$(*) \quad \text{for each } \lambda \in \Lambda, \text{ there is } \lambda' \in \Delta \text{ with } \lambda < \lambda'.$$

Since $\preceq_\kappa \in PE(\leq)$ for each $\kappa \in \Lambda$, $u_\lambda v_\lambda^\omega \preceq_\kappa u_{\lambda'} v_{\lambda'}^\omega$. Since $\alpha \approx_\kappa u_\kappa v_\kappa^\omega$, $u_\kappa v_\kappa^\omega \preceq_\kappa \alpha$. Thus, for each $\lambda, \lambda' \in \Delta$ with $\lambda < \lambda'$, $u_\lambda v_\lambda^\omega \preceq_{\lambda'} \alpha$ (by instantiating λ' to κ). With the condition (*), for each $\lambda \in \Delta$, we have $u_\lambda v_\lambda^\omega \preceq \alpha$.

Assume that $\overline{lim}_{\lambda \in \Delta} u_\lambda v_\lambda^\omega \simeq \alpha$ does not hold. Then, there exists β such that $\beta \prec \alpha$ with $u_\lambda v_\lambda^\omega \preceq \beta$ for each $\lambda \in \Delta$. Since $\beta \prec \alpha$, there exists $\lambda' \in \Delta$ with $\beta \prec_{\lambda'} \alpha$, which contradicts to $\alpha \simeq_{\lambda'} u_{\lambda'} v_{\lambda'}^\omega$. $\square$

Corollary 17. *Let $\leq$ be a monotone ω^2-WQO over Σ^* and let $\{\preceq_\lambda\}_{\lambda \in \Lambda}$ be a transfinite sequence of regular WQOs such that each $\preceq_\lambda$ is a monotone extension of $\leq$ with $\preceq_\lambda \supseteq \preceq_{\lambda'}$ for $\lambda < \lambda'$. Then, $\preceq = \bigcap_{\lambda \in \Lambda} \preceq_\lambda$ is a WQO.*

Proof. We borrow the notations in Lemma 16. For each $\alpha \in \Sigma^\omega$, we set $Seq(\alpha) = ((u_\lambda, v_\lambda))_{\lambda \in \Delta}$. Since $\leq \times \leq$ is an ω^2-WQO on $\Sigma^* \times \Sigma^*$, the embedding $\hookrightarrow$ on $(\Sigma^* \times \Sigma^*)^\omega$ is a WQO [9]. Then, for each infinite sequence $\alpha_1, \alpha_2, \cdots$, there are i, j with $i < j$ and $Seq(\alpha_i) \hookrightarrow Seq(\alpha_j)$, which implies $\alpha_i \preceq \alpha_j$ by Lemma 16. $\square$

Note that the assumption of ω^2-WQO frequently holds for typical WQOs, e.g., $\leq_k$ [3,17] and $\leq_I$ [2]. An exception is Rado's example [15].

Theorem 18. *Let $\leq$ be a monotone ω^2-WQO over Σ^*. Then, $CE(\leq)$ has the smallest element (w.r.t. the set inclusion).*

Proof. Note that a continuous extension of $\leq$ is a periodic extension by Theorem 13. For each descending chain $(\preceq_\lambda)_{\lambda \in \Lambda}$ in $CE(\leq)$, there is a lower bound (actually, the lower limit $\bigcap_{\lambda \in \Lambda} \preceq_\lambda$) by Lemma 16. Since $\bigcap_{\lambda \in \Lambda} \preceq_\lambda$ is a WQO by Corollary 17, $\bigcap_{\lambda \in \Lambda} \preceq_\lambda \in CE(\leq)$ from Definition 11. Therefore, there is a minimal element $\preceq$ in $CE(\leq)$ by Zorn's Lemma. This $\preceq$ is the smallest; otherwise, there exists an incomparable element $\preceq'$ in $CE(\leq)$. Since $\preceq \cap \preceq' \subset \preceq$, $\preceq'$ is a continuous extension of $\leq$ by Lemma 14, which contradicts to the minimality. $\square$

Corollary 19. *Let $\leq$ be a monotone ω^2-WQO over Σ^*. If $CE(\leq)=PE(\leq)$, $PE(\leq)$ has the smallest element (w.r.t. the set inclusion).*

Although Corollary 19 suggests that many monotone WQOs have smallest periodic extensions, the proof is nonconstructive and gives no hint how such an extension looks like. It makes sense to look for explicit descriptions of smallest periodic extensions for concrete natural monotone WQOs. Here we provide such descriptions for monotone WQOs in Sect. 3.

For any $k < \omega$, define the binary relation $\preceq_k$ on Σ^ω as follows: $\alpha \preceq_k \beta$ if $p_k(\alpha) = p_k(\beta)$ and there is a k-embedding $f : \alpha \to \beta$. Here $p_k(\alpha) = \alpha[0, k)$ is the prefix of α of length k, and the k-embedding f is a monotone injective function on ω such that $\alpha[i, i+k] = \beta[f(i), f(i)+k]$ for all $i < \omega$. Note that the relation $\leq_0$ is just the embedding of ω-words.

For any $\alpha \in \Sigma^\omega$ and $n \geq 1$, let $F_n(\alpha)$ (resp. $F_n^\infty(\alpha)$) be the set of $u \in \Sigma^n$ such that u is a factor of α (resp. u occurs in α as a factor infinitely often). Let $F_n(v)$ for $v \in \Sigma^+$ be defined similarly, $F(v) = \bigcup_n F_n(v)$, and $F^\infty(\alpha) = \bigcup_n F_n^\infty(\alpha)$. The next two lemmas are included without proof in order to help the reader to reconstruct omitted details in the proof of Theorem 22.

Lemma 20. 1. $F_n^\infty(\alpha) \neq \emptyset$.
2. If $x \in F_n^\infty(\alpha)$ and $m > n$ then x is a factor of some $y \in F_m^\infty(\alpha)$.
3. If x is a factor of $y \in F_n^\infty(\alpha)$ then $x \in F_{|x|}^\infty(\alpha)$.
4. If there is a k-embedding of α into β then $F_{k+1}^\infty(\alpha) \subseteq F_{k+1}^\infty(\beta)$.

Define the binary relation R_k on Σ^ω by: $\alpha R_k \beta$ iff there exist factorizations $\alpha = u_0 u_1 \cdots, \beta = v_0 v_1 \cdots$ such that $u_i, v_i \in \Sigma^+$ and $u_i \leq_k v_i$ for all i.

Lemma 21. 1. $R_k \subseteq \preceq_k$.
2. For any $\alpha \in \Sigma^\omega$ there exist $u, v \in \Sigma^+$ such that $\alpha R_k \beta R_k \alpha$ where $\beta = uv^\omega$.
3. $\alpha R_k \beta$ iff $\alpha \preceq_k \beta$ and $F_{2k}^\infty(\alpha) \cap F_{2k}^\infty(\beta) \neq \emptyset$.
4. If $u^\omega \preceq_k v^\omega$ then $u^\omega R_k \gamma R_k v^\omega$ for some $\gamma \in \Sigma^\omega$.

Theorem 22. For any $k < \omega$, $\preceq_k$ is the smallest periodic extension of $\leq_k$.

Proof. Obviously, $\preceq_k$ is a QO. By Lemma 21(1), $\preceq_k$ is a monotone extension of $\leq_k$. By Lemma 21(2), $\preceq_k$ is a periodic extension of $\leq_k$.

It remains to show that $\preceq_k \subseteq \preceq$ for every $\preceq \in PE(\leq_k)$. Since $\preceq$ is a monotone extension of $\leq_k$, $R_k \subseteq \preceq$. Since $\preceq$ is transitive, $TC(R_k) \subseteq \preceq_k$, where $TC(R_k)$ is the transitive closure of R_k. Hence, it suffices to show that $\preceq_k \subseteq TC(R_k)$.

Let $\alpha \preceq_k \beta$. By Lemma 21(2), $\alpha R_k uv^\omega R_k \alpha$ and $\beta R_k u_1 v_1^\omega R_k \beta$ for some u, v, u_1, v_1. By Lemma 21(4), $uv^\omega R_k \gamma R_k u_1 v_1^\omega$ for some γ. Thus, $\alpha TC(R_k)\beta$. □

Remark 23. The analogue R of the relation R_k may be defined for any monotone WQO $\leq$, and again we have $TC(R) \subseteq \preceq$ for each $\preceq \in PE(\leq)$. Thus, if $TC(R)$ is a periodic extension of $\leq$ then it is the smallest one. So in the search of the smallest periodic extension $TC(R)$ is the first candidate.

Theorem 24. For any finite unavoidable set $I \subseteq \Sigma^+$, the relation $\preceq_I = R_I$ is the smallest periodic extension of $\leq_I$.

Proof Sketch. The relation R_I is the smallest monotone extension of $\leq_I$. It is easy to check that R_I is a QO. An inspection of the proofs of Lemma 4.7 and Theorem 4.8 in [2] shows that the relation $\leq_I$ is not only a WQO but also a BQO. The standard technique of BQO-theory applies to show that $\preceq_I$ is a BQO, hence also a WQO. By Theorem 13, it suffices to show that any upper set $\uparrow \alpha$ w.r.t. $\preceq_I$ is regular.

$\uparrow \alpha$ is accepted by a pushdown Büchi automaton, which pushes when it starts to read an inserted element u of I and pops when u is read while reading α. By Lemma 4.7 in [2], the size of the stack is bounded by the smallest number k_0 such that any word in $\Sigma^{\geq k_0}$ has a factor from I. Thus, the pushdown Büchi automaton is reduced to a finite Büchi automaton. □

6 Decidability of Levels $\mathcal{L}_{\preceq}(n)$

Here we consider, in parallel to Sect. 4, decidability issues for the classes of ω-languages related to monotone WQOs. First we prove a rather general sufficient condition for decidability and next illustrate this condition for the mentioned examples of periodic extensions of monotone WQOs. Letters $\mathcal{A}, \mathcal{B}$, possibly with indices, are now used to denote Büchi automata.

Definition 25. *Let $\leq$ be a monotone WQO. By a computable periodic extension of $\leq$ we mean a periodic extension $\preceq$ of $\leq$ such that the 4-ary relation $uv^\omega \preceq u_1 v_1^\omega$ on Σ^+ is computable and there is a computable family $\{\mathcal{A}_{u,v}\}_{u,v \in \Sigma^+}$ of Büchi automata such that $L^\omega(\mathcal{A}_{u,v}) = \{\alpha \mid uv^\omega \preceq \alpha\}$ for all $u, v \in \Sigma^+$.*

The proof of next result is similar to that of Theorem 7.

Theorem 26. *For any computable periodic extension $\preceq$ of a monotone WQO $\leq$, the levels $\mathcal{L}_{\preceq}(n)$ of difference hierarchy over $\mathcal{L}_{\preceq}$ are decidable uniformly on n.*

We illustrate Theorem 26 by the monotone WQOs from Sect. 3. Note that by Theorem 22 we have $\mathcal{L}_{\preceq_k} = \mathcal{L}^\omega_{\leq_k}$ and $\mathcal{L}_{\preceq_I} = \mathcal{L}^\omega_{\leq_I}$.

Theorem 27. *The levels $\mathcal{L}_{\preceq_k}(n)$ of the difference hierarchy over $\mathcal{L}_{\preceq_k}$ are decidable uniformly on k, n.*

Proof. By Theorem 26, it suffices to show that $\preceq_k$ is a computable periodic extension of $\leq_k$ uniformly on k. Since $uv^\omega \preceq_k u_1 v_1^\omega$ iff $u \leq_k u_1 v_1^{|u|}$ and $v \leq_k v_1^{|v|}$ for all $k < \omega$ and $u, u_1, v, v_1 \in \Sigma^+$, the relation $uv^\omega \preceq_k u_1 v_1^\omega$ is computable uniformly on k.

It remains to find a computable family $\{\mathcal{A}_{k,u,v}\}_{k<\omega, u,v \in \Sigma^+}$ of Büchi automata such that $L^\omega(\mathcal{A}_{k,u,v}) = \{\alpha \mid uv^\omega \preceq_k \alpha\}$ for all $k < \omega, u, v \in \Sigma^+$. From k, u, v it is straightforward to compute a first order sentence $\varphi_{k,u,v}$ of signature $\{<, Q_a \mid a \in \Sigma\}$ such that $L^\omega_{\varphi_{k,u,v}} = \{\alpha \mid uv^\omega \preceq_k \alpha\}$ where L^ω_φ is the set of ω-words that satisfy a given sentence φ (see [19] for details of the logical approach to regular languages). By the Büchi-Trakhtenbrot theorem, there is a computable family $\{\mathcal{A}_{k,u,v}\}_{k<\omega, u,v \in \Sigma^+}$ of Büchi automata such that $L^\omega(\mathcal{A}_{k,u,v}) = L^\omega_{\varphi_{k,u,v}}$ for all $k < \omega, u, v \in \Sigma^+$. $\square$

Theorem 28. *For every finite unavoidable set of words I, the levels $\mathcal{L}_{\preceq_I}(n)$ of the difference hierarchy over $\mathcal{L}_{\preceq_I}$ are decidable uniformly on n.*

Proof. By Theorem 26, it suffices to show that $\preceq_k$ is a computable periodic extension of $\leq_k$. As above, for all $u, u_1, v, v_1 \in \Sigma^+$ we have: $uv^\omega \preceq_I u_1 v_1^\omega$ iff $u \leq_I u_1 v_1^{|u|}$ and $v \leq_I v_1^{|v|}$, hence the relation $uv^\omega \preceq_I u_1 v_1^\omega$ is computable.

If $\alpha = uv^\omega$ then the Büchi automaton $\mathcal{A}_{u,v}$ constructed in the proof of Theorem 24 verifies the second condition of the computability of $\preceq_I$. $\square$

7   Conclusion and Open Questions

We hope that the above results clearly demonstrate that the classes of upper sets induced by monotone WQOs and their extensions to infinite words are interesting and deserve further investigation. Many interesting questions remain open, we mention some of them below.

1. It is already clear that the class of monotone WQOs is rich. However, we still do not know whether this class is countable.
2. Is there a nice classification of finitely presented monotone WQOs? Are all such WQOs computable?
3. Does every finitely presented monotone WQO have the smallest periodic extension? Are all such extensions computable?
4. Our methods of proving decidability are easy and natural but they do not provide any upper complexity bounds at all. One has to develop new methods which do provide reasonable upper bounds. Such methods for a natural class of monotone WQOs were developed in [4].
5. Ideas and notions of this paper are related to those in the literature on (ordered) semigroups and ω-semigroups [13,14]. Further investigation of these relationships seems promising.

References

1. Davey, B.A., Priestley, H.A.: Introduction to Lattices and Order. Cambridge (1994)
2. Ehrenfeucht, A., Haussler, D., Rozenberg, G.: On regularity of context-free languages. Theor. Comput. Sci. **27**, 311–332 (1983)
3. Glaßer, C., Schmitz, H.: The boolean structure of dot-depth one. J. Autom. Lang. Comb. **6**(4), 437–452 (2001). https://doi.org/10.25596/jalc-2001-437
4. Glaßer, C., Schmitz, H., Selivanov, V.L.: Efficient algorithms for membership in boolean hierarchies of regular languages. Theor. Comput. Sci. **646**(C), 86–108 (2016). https://doi.org/10.1016/j.tcs.2016.07.017
5. Higman, G.: Ordering by divisibility in abstract algebras. Proc. Lond. Math. Soc. **s3–2**(1), 326–336 (1952). https://doi.org/10.1112/plms/s3-2.1.326
6. Kříž, I., Thomas, R.: Ordinal types in ramsey theory and well-partial-ordering theory. In: Neše tř il, J., Rödl, V. (eds.) Mathematics of Ramsey Theory. Algorithms and Combinatorics, vol. 5. Springer, Heidelberg (1990). https://doi.org/10.1007/978-3-642-72905-8_7
7. Laver, R.: Better-quasi-orderings and a class of trees. In: Studies in foundations and combinatorics, Advances in mathematics: Supplementary studies, vol. 1, pp. 31–48. Academic Press (1978)
8. de Luca, A., Varricchio, S.: Finiteness and Regularity in Semigroups and Formal Languages. Monographs in Theoretical Computer Science. Springer, Heidelberg (1999). https://doi.org/10.1007/978-3-642-59849-4
9. Marcone, A.: Foundations of BQO theory. Trans. AMS **345**(2), 641–660 (1994)
10. Marcone, A.: Fine analysis of the quasi-orderings on the power set. Order **18**(4), 339–347 (2001). https://doi.org/10.1023/A:1013952225669
11. Nash-Williams, C.S.J.A.: On well-quasi-ordering transfinite sequences. Math. Proc. Cambridge Philos. Soc. **61**, 33–39 (1965)

12. Ogawa, M.: Well-quasi-orders and regular omega-languages. Theor. Comput. Sci. **324**(1), 55–60 (2004). https://doi.org/10.1016/j.tcs.2004.03.052
13. Perrin, D., Pin, J.: Infinite Words, Pure and Applied Mathematics, vol. 141 (2004)
14. Pin, J.: Positive varieties and infinite words. In: Lucchesi, C.L., Moura, A.V. (eds.) LATIN 1998. LNCS, vol. 1380, pp. 76–87. Springer, Heidelberg (1998). https://doi.org/10.1007/BFb0054312
15. Rado, R.: Partial well-ordering of sets of vectors. Mathematika **1**, 89–95 (1954)
16. Rogers Jr., H.: Theory of recursive functions and effective computability. McGraw-Hill, New York (1967)
17. Selivanov, V.L.: A logical approach to decidability of hierarchies of regular star—free languages. In: Ferreira, A., Reichel, H. (eds.) STACS 2001. LNCS, vol. 2010, pp. 539–550. Springer, Heidelberg (2001). https://doi.org/10.1007/3-540-44693-1_47
18. Selivanov, V.L.: Hierarchies and reducibilities on regular languages related to modulo counting. RAIRO Theor. Inform. Appl. **43**(1), 95–132 (2009)
19. Thomas, W.: Automata on infinite objects. In: Handbook of Theoretical Computer Science, vol. B, pp. 133–192. Elsevier Science Publishers (1990)

State Complexity of GF(2)-Concatenation and GF(2)-Inverse on Unary Languages

Alexander Okhotin$^{(\boxtimes)}$ and Elizaveta Sazhneva

St. Petersburg State University, 7/9 Universitetskaya Nab.,
Saint Petersburg 199034, Russia
alexander.okhotin@spbu.ru, sazhneva.eliza@yandex.ru

Abstract. The paper investigates the state complexity of two operations on regular languages, known as GF(2)-concatenation and GF(2)-inverse (Bakinova et al., "Formal languages over GF(2)", LATA 2018), in the case of a one-symbol alphabet. The GF(2)-concatenation is a variant of the classical concatenation obtained by replacing Boolean logic in its definition with the GF(2) field; it is proved that GF(2)-concatenation of two unary languages recognized by an m-state and an n-state DFA is recognized by a DFA with $2mn$ states, and this number of states is necessary in the worst case, as long as m and n are relatively prime. This operation is known to have an inverse, and the state complexity of the GF(2)-inverse operation over a unary alphabet is proved to be exactly $2^{n-1} + 1$.

1 Introduction

Union and concatenation of formal languages are defined in terms of conjunction and disjunction: a string is in $K \cup L$ if it is in K *or* in L, and a string w is in $K \cdot L$, if, for some partition $w = uv$, $u \in K$ *and* $v \in L$—a disjunction of $|w| + 1$ conjunctions. New variants of these two operations, obtained by replacing disjunctions with *exclusive OR*, have recently been proposed by Bakinova et al. [1]. Union $(K \cup L)$ is thus replaced with symmetric difference $(K \triangle L)$, whereas for concatenation $(K \cdot L)$, once the disjunction is replaced with exclusive OR, the condition of the *existence of a partition* turns into the condition that *the number of partitions must be odd*.

$$K \cdot L = \{\, w \mid \# \text{ of partitions } w = uv, \text{ with } u \in K \text{ and } v \in L, \text{ is non-zero} \,\}$$
$$K \odot L = \{\, w \mid \# \text{ of partitions } w = uv, \text{ with } u \in K \text{ and } v \in L, \text{ is odd} \,\}$$

The latter operation is called *GF(2)-concatenation*, because it is actually a weighted concatenation with weights in the GF(2) field. For example, $\{\varepsilon, a\} \cdot \{\varepsilon, a\} = \{\varepsilon, a, aa\}$, but $\{\varepsilon, a\} \odot \{\varepsilon, a\} = \{\varepsilon, aa\}$, because two partitions of a

Supported by Russian Science Foundation, project 18-11-00100.

cancel each other. Notably, GF(2)-concatenation is *invertible*: for every language $L \subseteq \Sigma^*$ with $\varepsilon \in L$, there exists a unique language $L^{-1} \subseteq \Sigma^*$ that satisfies $L \odot L^{-1} = L^{-1} \odot L = \{\varepsilon\}$. For instance, $\{\varepsilon, a\}^{-1} = a^*$, because $\{\varepsilon, a\}^{-1} \odot a^* = \{\varepsilon\}$: indeed, every non-empty string in the latter GF(2)-concatenation has two partitions. Symmetric difference is the *GF(2)-union*.

Table 1. State complexity of unambiguous, classical and GF(2)-variants of union, concatenation and star.

	Union	Concatenation	Star
Unambiguous	(⊎) $mn - 1$ [6]	(UNAMB·) $m2^{n-1} - 2^{n-2}$ [4]	(UNAMB*) $\frac{3}{8}2^n + 1$ [6]
Classical	(∪) mn [9]	(·) $\quad m2^n - 2^{n-1}$ [9]	(*) $\quad \frac{3}{4}2^n$ [9]
GF(2)	(△) mn [2]	(⊙) $\quad m \cdot 2^n$ [1]	($^{-1}$) $\quad 2^n + 1$ [1]

Using GF(2)-operations instead of the classical operations gives rise to a new variant of formal language theory. For instance, *GF(2)-grammars*, defined by Bakinova et al. [1] and subsequently studied by Makarov and Okhotin [8], are incomparable in power to classical grammars with union and concatenation, but still have a parsing algorithm working in time $O(n^\omega)$, with $\omega < 3$, and can be parsed by circuits of depth $O((\log n)^2)$.

The family of regular languages is closed under both the GF(2)-concatenation and the GF(2)-inversion operations. For a pair of languages recognized by an m-state and an n-state DFA, their GF(2)-concatenation is recognized by a DFA with $m \cdot 2^n$ states; this number of states is necessary in the worst case, witnessed by automata over a 2-symbol alphabet [1]. Similarly, the GF(2)-inverse of a language recognized by an n-state DFA is recognized by a DFA with $2^n + 1$ states, and this bound is tight for alphabets containing at least 3 symbols [1].

To compare with the classical case, classical concatenation has state complexity $m2^n - 2^{n-1}$, and classical Kleene star, or the quasi-inverse, has state complexity $\frac{3}{4}2^n$ [9]. Another point of comparison is with *unambiguous concatenation* and *unambiguous star*, defined by restricting the arguments, so that each string has a unique representation; classical operations and GF(2)-operations are two incomparable generalizations of the unambiguous operations. Unambiguous concatenation has state complexity $m2^{n-1} - 2^{n-2}$ [4], whereas the state complexity of the unambiguous star is $\frac{3}{8}2^n + 1$ [6]. The state complexity of unambiguous, classical and GF(2)-variants of the three main operations on formal languages is compared in Table 1. All results refer to the case of DFA.

The goal of this paper is to investigate the state complexity of the GF(2)-operations in the case of a unary alphabet [1]. In general, unary state complexity is substantially different from the case of multiple-symbol alphabets. The trade-offs between different types of automata over a unary alphabet were studied by Chrobak [3], Mereghetti and Pighizzini [10], Geffert et al. [5], Kunc and Okhotin [7], Okhotin [11], and others. The state complexity of operations on unary DFA was first investigated by Yu et al. [13], who proved that concatenation is representable with mn states, and this bound is tight for relatively prime m and n; the state complexity of star on unary languages is $(n - 1)^2 + 1$.

How do the GF(2)-operations stand in comparison? For the GF(2)-concatenation of unary languages recognized by DFA with m and n states, the results generally resemble the classical case: it shall be established in Sect. 2 that $2mn$ states are sufficient, and for relatively prime m, n, this number of states is necessary. On the other hand, the case of GF(2)-inverse of a unary language is substantially different from the classical case; the state complexity turns out to be $2^{n-1} + 1$, which is established in Sects. 3–6 by determining a connection between the states of a DFA recognizing a GF(2)-inverse and the coefficients of a certain associated sequence of polynomials over GF(2).

2 GF(2)-Concatenation

As usual, a DFA is defined as a quintuple $(\Sigma, Q, q_0, \delta, F)$, where Σ is the input alphabet and Q is a finite set of states, with initial state $q_0 \in Q$, transition function $\delta \colon Q \times \Sigma \to Q$ and accepting states $F \subseteq Q$. This paper considers DFA over a unary alphabet $\Sigma = \{a\}$, where the transition function defines a sequence of states $q_0, q_1, \ldots$, with $q_{i+1} = \delta(q_i, a)$. Let j be the least number with $q_j = q_i$ for some $i < j$. This is the point where the automaton starts to behave periodically; the states $q_0, \ldots, q_{i-1}$ are called the *tail*, and the periodic part $q_i, \ldots, q_{j-1}$ is called the *cycle*. If the tail is empty, the automaton is called *cyclic*.

The known construction for GF(2)-concatenation of two given DFA, $\mathcal{A} = (\Sigma, P, p_0, \eta, E)$ and $\mathcal{B} = (\Sigma, Q, q_0, \delta, F)$, works as follows [1]. The language $L(\mathcal{A}) \odot L(\mathcal{B})$ is recognized by a DFA $\mathcal{C}$ with the set of states $P \times 2^Q$. In a state (p, S), with $p \in P$ and $S \subseteq Q$, the automaton simulates the computation of $\mathcal{A}$ in the first component p, while S is the set of all states reached *an odd number of times* in the ongoing simulated computations of $\mathcal{B}$. The initial state of $\mathcal{C}$ is $(p_0, \{q_0\})$ if $\varepsilon \in L(\mathcal{A})$ and $(p_0, \varnothing)$ otherwise. Its transition function, $\pi \colon (P \times 2^Q) \times \Sigma \to P \times 2^Q$, is defined on a pair (p, S) as follows. Each currently simulated computation of $\mathcal{B}$ is continued, represented by the following set S'.

$$S' = \{ q' \mid \text{the number of states } q \in S, \text{ with } q' = \delta(q, a), \text{ is odd} \}$$

If the simulated automaton $\mathcal{A}$ passes through an accepting state, then the transition $\pi((p, S), a)$ also adds a new computation to the set S'.

$$\pi((p, S), a) = \begin{cases} (\eta(p, a), S'), & \text{if } \eta(p, a) \notin E; \\ (\eta(p, a), S' \triangle \{q_0\}), & \text{if } \eta(p, a) \in E. \end{cases}$$

A state (p, S) is marked as accepting, if S contains an odd number of accepting states of $\mathcal{B}$.

$$F' = \{ (p, S) \mid |S \cap F| \text{ is odd} \}$$

This completes the known construction, which is valid for every alphabet.

In the case of a unary alphabet, the state complexity of GF(2)-concatenation on two unary DFA is first investigated in the special case of both automata being cyclic, each with a unique accepting state. Under these restrictions, the state complexity depends only on the number of states in the given automata.

Lemma 1. *Let A and B be two minimal cyclic DFA over a unary alphabet, one with the cycle of length m and the other with the cycle of length n, and each with a single accepting state. Then, the GF(2)-concatenation $L(A) \odot L(B)$ is recognized by a cyclic DFA with period of length $\frac{2mn}{\gcd(m,n)}$, and this is the minimal DFA for this language.*

Proof. Let $A = (\{a\}, P, 0, \eta, E)$, with $P = \{0, \ldots, m-1\}$, $\eta(i,a) = i+1 \bmod m$ for all $i \in P$, and $E = \{e\}$. Similarly, let $B = (\{a\}, Q, 0, \delta, F)$, with $Q = \{0, \ldots, n-1\}$, $\delta(i,a) = i+1 \bmod n$ for all $i \in Q$, and $F = \{f\}$.

Let $C = (\Sigma, Q', q_0, \pi, F')$ be the DFA recognizing the GF(2)-concatenation $L(A) \odot L(B)$, with the set of states $Q' = \{(p,S) \mid p \in P, S \subseteq Q\}$, and with accepting states $F' = \{(p,S) \mid p \in P, f \in S\}$.

Claim. For all $p \in P$ and $k \in \{1, \ldots, \frac{n}{\gcd(m,n)} - 1\}$, there are exactly two reachable subsets $S_1, S_2 \subseteq Q$ with $|S_1| = |S_2| = k$ and $\pi((p, S_1), a) \neq \pi((p, S_2), a)$. For $k = 0$ or $k = \frac{n}{\gcd(m,n)}$, there is a unique reachable subset (p, S) with $(p, S) \in Q'$ and $|S| = k$. Accordingly, Q' contains $\frac{2mn}{\gcd(m,n)}$ reachable states.

Assume that $e \neq 0$. After reading a^e, the automaton reaches the state $(e, \{0\})$. From this point on, consider the states reached by the automaton after reading repetitive blocks a^m. The state in the first component is rejecting until the last symbol in the block, and hence the states in both components are cyclically shifted by m, until the accepting state e reappears in the first component. At the last step, a new state 0 is added to the second component, while all pre-existent states in the second component have been shifted by $m \pmod n$. Altogether, the following states are visited.

$$\pi((0, \varnothing), a^e) = (e, \{0\})$$
$$\pi((e, \{0\}), a^m) = (e, \{0, k_1\}) \qquad \text{where } k_1 \equiv m \pmod n$$
$$\pi((e, \{0, k_1\}), a^m) = (e, \{0, k_1, k_2\}) \qquad \text{where } k_2 \equiv 2m \pmod n, \text{ etc.}$$

The subset continues to grow until some j-th step, with $\delta(k_j, a^m) = 0$. This means that $(j+1)m \equiv 0 \pmod n$. Since j is the least such number, it must be $j = \frac{n}{\gcd(m,n)} - 1$. Therefore, $\pi((e, \varnothing), a^{jm}) = (e, \{0, k_1, k_2, \ldots k_j\})$.

From this point on, consider further computations upon reading repetitive blocks a^m. The states in the second component keep cyclically shifting, and the states 0 added in the end of each block cancel out these states in the same order as they were added.

$$\pi((e, \{0, k_1, k_2, \ldots k_j\}), a^m) = (e, \{k_1, k_2, \ldots k_j\})$$
$$\pi((e, \{k_1, k_2, \ldots k_j\}), a^m) = (e, \{k_2, k_3, \ldots k_j\}), \qquad \text{etc.}$$

In the end, $\pi((e, \{0, k_1, k_2, \ldots k_j\}), a^{jm}) = (e, \varnothing)$. Finally, after reading a^{m-e}, the automaton returns to its initial state.

$$\pi((e, \varnothing), a^{m-e}) = (0, \varnothing)$$

Overall, the automaton for the GF(2)-concatenation is a cycle on $\frac{2mn}{\gcd(m,n)}$ states.

Claim. The period $\frac{2mn}{\gcd(m,n)}$ is minimal.

The idea of the argument is that $\mathcal{C}$ has a block of $m+n$ consecutive rejecting states, and that this block occurs only once in the automaton. □

Theorem 2. *Let $\mathcal{A}$ and $\mathcal{B}$ be any two DFA over a unary alphabet, with m and with n states, respectively. Then, the GF(2)-concatenation $L(\mathcal{A}) \odot L(\mathcal{B})$ is recognized by a DFA with $2mn$ states.*

For relatively prime m and n, this number of states is necessary in the worst case.

Proof (a sketch). Let $\mathcal{A}$ have the set of states $P = \{0, 1, \ldots, m-1\}$, with accepting states $E \subseteq P$. For each state $i \in P$, define a DFA $\mathcal{A}_i$ by setting i in $\mathcal{A}$ as the only accepting state. Then, $L(\mathcal{A}) = \bigcup_{i \in E} L(\mathcal{A}_i)$, and the union is disjoint. Let the language be periodic starting from k, with period $m - k$.

Similarly, let the set of states of $\mathcal{B}$ be $Q = \{0, 1, \ldots, n-1\}$, with accepting states $F \subseteq Q$. Let $\mathcal{B}_j$ be $\mathcal{B}$ with j as the only accepting state, so that $L(\mathcal{B}) = \bigcup_{i \in F} L(\mathcal{B}_i)$. Let the periodic part begin at ℓ, with period $n - \ell$.

Then, the desired GF(2)-concatenation can be represented as follows.

$$L(\mathcal{A}) \odot L(\mathcal{B}) = \left(\bigcup_{i \in E} L(\mathcal{A}_i) \right) \odot \left(\bigcup_{j \in F} L(\mathcal{B}_j) \right) = \left(\bigtriangleup_{i \in E} L(\mathcal{A}_i) \right) \odot \left(\bigtriangleup_{j \in F} L(\mathcal{B}_j) \right) =$$

$$= \bigtriangleup_{\substack{i \in E \\ j \in F}} L(\mathcal{A}_i) \odot L(\mathcal{B}_j)$$

Each of these $|E| \cdot |F|$ languages is periodic beginning from $k + \ell - 1$, with period $2(m - k)(n - \ell)$; the proof is omitted due to space constraints. These languages are then joined into a single automaton with at most $2mn$ states.

For the lower bound, Lemma 1 with relatively prime m, n provides the desired witness languages. □

3   Automaton for GF(2)-Inverse

With respect to GF(2)-concatenation, every language L containing the empty string is *invertible*, in the sense that there is a language L^{-1} satisfying $L \odot L^{-1} = L^{-1} \odot L = \{\varepsilon\}$. The *GF(2)-inverse* operation, $f(L) = L^{-1}$, preserves regularity, and its state complexity is $2^n + 1$ [1].

Theorem A (Bakinova et al. [1, Thm. 2]). *For every language L over an alphabet Σ, with $\varepsilon \in L$, a string $w \in \Sigma^*$ is in L^{-1} if and only if it has an odd number of representations of the form $w = w_1 w_2 \ldots w_k$, with $k \geqslant 0$ and $w_1, \ldots, w_k \in L \setminus \{\varepsilon\}$.*

As proved by Bakinova et al. [1], for every n-state DFA $\mathcal{A} = (\{a\}, Q, q_0, \delta, F)$, with $\varepsilon \in L(\mathcal{A})$, the language $L(\mathcal{A})^{-1}$ is recognized by a DFA $\mathcal{C} = (\{a\}, 2^Q \cup \{q_0'\}, q_0', \delta', F')$ defined as follows. The states of $\mathcal{C}$ are all subsets of Q and a new initial state q_0', Its transition function is $\delta' \colon (2^Q \cup \{q_0'\}) \times \{a\} \to 2^Q \cup \{q_0'\}$. The transition in the state q_0' produces a singleton state corresponding to a single computation of $\mathcal{A}$.

$$\delta'(q_0', a) = \{\delta(q_0, a)\}$$

In a state $S \subseteq Q$, first let $S' = \{ q \mid \# \text{ of states } p \in S \text{ with } \delta(p, a) = q \text{ is odd} \}$. Then the transition is defined as follows.

$$\delta'(S, a) = \begin{cases} S', & \text{if } |S \cap F| \text{ is even} \\ S' \triangle \delta(q_0, a), & \text{if } |S \cap F| \text{ is odd} \end{cases}$$

The set of accepting states is $F' = \{ S \mid |S \cap F| \text{ is odd} \} \cup \{q_0'\}$.

Example 3. Consider the following 5-state unary DFA.

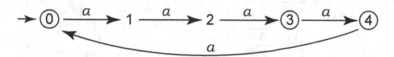

The DFA for its inverse, constructed by the above method, is shown in Fig. 1. It has a cycle of length 15 and a tail of length 2 (along with 16 unreachable states).

In the general case, the DFA for the GF(2)-inverse $L(\mathcal{A})^{-1}$ of an n-state DFA $\mathcal{A}$ has $2^n + 1$ states, and it is known that this number is necessary in the worst case, for alphabets with at least three symbols [1]. It turns out that in the unary case it is always sufficient to use $2^{n-1} + 1$ states.

This upper bound is easy to establish for non-cyclic automata.

Lemma 4. *Let $\mathcal{A} = (\{a\}, Q, 0, \delta, F)$ be an n-state non-cyclic DFA with $0 \in F$. Then, the DFA for the GF(2)-inverse $L(\mathcal{A})^{-1}$ constructed as above, has at most $2^{n-1} + 1$ reachable states.*

Proof. Indeed, no subset containing the state 0 is ever reached, since this state is not reachable by any transitions. □

For cyclic automata $\mathcal{A}$, a deeper analysis of the automaton for its inverse is needed, since the set of unreachable states is harder to specify. The first result to be established is the following dependence between the membership of individual states in the subsets.

Lemma 5. *Let $\mathcal{A} = (\{a\}, Q, 0, \delta, F)$ be a cyclic DFA with $Q = \{0, \dots, n-1\}$, $\delta(i, a) = i + 1 \bmod n$ for all i, and $0 \in F$. Let $C = (\{a\}, 2^Q \cup \{q_0'\}, q_0', \delta', F')$ be the DFA recognizing the GF(2)-inverse of $L(\mathcal{A})$, defined as above. For each $i \geqslant 1$, let $S_i \subseteq Q$ be the state of C reached upon reading the string a^i.*

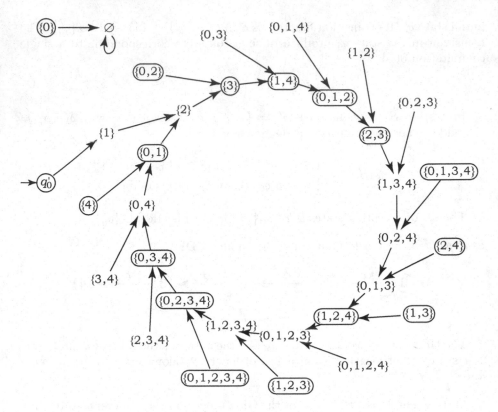

Fig. 1. DFA for the GF(2)-inverse of the language in Example 3.

Denote the membership of the j-th state in S_i by a Boolean value $S_i^j \in \{0,1\}$, with $S_i^j = 1$ if $j \in S_i$, and $S_i^j = 0$ otherwise. Then, the membership of state 1 in each set S_i is determined by the set S_{i-1} by the following formula.

$$S_i^1 = \sum_{f \in F \setminus \{0\}} S_{i-1}^f \qquad \text{(for } i \geqslant 2)$$

Furthermore, the membership of 0 in S_i depends on its membership in the previous $n-1$ states as follows.

$$S_i^0 = \sum_{f \in F \setminus \{0\}} S_{i-f}^0 \qquad \text{(for } i \geqslant n+1)$$

Proof (a sketch). The formula for S_i^1 is directly inferred from the definition of automata. The second formula is inferred from this one using the following two observations: first, 0 is in S_i if and only if 1 is in $S_{i-(n-1)}$; second, a state f is in S_{i-n} if and only if 0 is in S_{i-f}. $\qquad\square$

4 Polynomials for GF(2)-Inverse

The subsets reached by the automaton for the GF(2)-inverse of a cyclic language L have a useful characterization in terms of certain polynomials over GF(2). First, based on the automaton for L, a sequence of polynomials shall be constructed, and then the leading coefficients of these polynomials shall correspond to the membership of state 0 in the subsets of the automaton for L^{-1}.

A few definitions are due. Let $f(x) = a_{n-1}x^{n-1} + \ldots + a_1x + a_0$ be a polynomial of degree $n - 1$ over GF(2), with $a_0, \ldots, a_{n-1} \in \{0,1\}$ and with $a_{n-1} = 1$.

For every $i \geq 0$, let $p_i(x)$ be the polynomial obtained by taking x^i modulo $f(x)$; this is a polynomial of degree at most $n - 2$. The polynomials $p_i(x)$ form a sequence, in which the first term is $p_0(x) = 1$, and every succeeding term is obtained from the previous term as follows: if a polynomial $p_i(x)$ does not contain the monomial x^{n-2}, then the next term is $p_{i+1}(x) = x \cdot p_i(x)$; and if there is a monomial x^{n-2} in $p_i(x)$, then the next term is $p_{i+1}(x) = x \cdot p_i(x) + f(x)$; in other words, x^{n-1} is replaced with $a_{n-2}x^{n-2} + \ldots + a_1x + a_0$.

The first n terms in the sequence $\{x^i \bmod f(x)\}_{i=0}$ are $1, x, x^2, \ldots, x^{n-2}$, $x^{n-1} + f(x)$. The form of the subsequent terms non-trivially depends on f.

A polynomial $f(x)$ of degree $n-1$ is called *primitive*, if this sequence contains all $2^{n-1} - 1$ non-zero polynomials. For each $n \geq 2$, primitive polynomials are known to exist.

For all $i \geq 0$ and $j \in \{0, \ldots, n - 2\}$, let $b_{i,j} \in \{0,1\}$ be the coefficient at the monomial x^j in $p_i(x)$. The coefficient at the term x^{n-2} in $p_i(x)$ depends on the coefficients at the same term in the preceding $n - 1$ polynomials in the sequence.

Lemma 6. *For every $i \geq n - 1$, the coefficient $b_{i,n-2}$ depends on the earlier coefficients as follows, with all arithmetic in GF(2).*

$$b_{i,n-2} = \sum_{k=0}^{n-2} b_{i-(n-1-k),\, n-2} a_k$$

Let $\mathcal{A} = (\{a\}, Q, 0, \delta, F)$ be a cyclic unary DFA with the set of states $Q = \{0, \ldots, n - 1\}$ and with $0 \in F$. The corresponding polynomial over GF(2) is defined as $f(x) = \sum_{j \in F} x^{n-1-j}$. In the sequence of polynomials x^i modulo $f(x)$, let $b_{i,n-2}$ be the coefficient at x^{n-2} in the i-th polynomial. Then, by Lemma 6, each coefficient is expressed through the preceding $n - 1$ coefficients as follows.

$$b_{i,n-2} = \sum_{k=0}^{n-2} \left(b_{i-(n-1-k),n-2} \cdot (n - 1 - k \overset{?}{\in} F) \right) = \sum_{j \in F \setminus \{0\}} b_{i-j,n-2}$$

This is the same recurrent formula as in Lemma 5.

Example 7 (continued from Example 3). For the 5-state cyclic automaton with accepting states $F = \{0, 3, 4\}$, the corresponding polynomial is $f(x) = x^4 + x + 1$. Then, the sequence x^i modulo $f(x)$ begins with the following polynomials. $p_0(x) = 1$, $p_1(x) = x$, $p_2(x) = x^2$, $p_3(x) = x^3$, $p_4(x) = x + 1$, $p_5(x) = x^2 + x$, etc.

The following table puts the subsets reachable by the automaton alongside the polynomials in this sequence. The acceptance status of each subset is provided for reference.

i	S_{i+2}	$p_i(x)$	$a^{i+2} \overset{?}{\in} L^{-1}$
0	$\{2\}$	1	$-$
1	$\{3\}$	x	$+$
2	$\{1,4\}$	x^2	$+$
3	$\{0,1,2\}$	x^3	$+$
4	$\{2,3\}$	$x+1$	$+$
5	$\{1,3,4\}$	x^2+x	$-$
6	$\{0,2,4\}$	x^3+x^2	$-$
7	$\{0,1,3\}$	x^3+x+1	$-$
8	$\{1,2,4\}$	x^2+1	$+$
9	$\{0,1,2,3\}$	x^3+x	$-$
10	$\{1,2,3,4\}$	x^2+x+1	$-$
11	$\{0,2,3,4\}$	x^3+x^2+x	$+$
12	$\{0,3,4\}$	x^3+x^2+x+1	$+$
13	$\{0,4\}$	x^3+x^2+1	$-$
14	$\{0,1\}$	x^3+1	$+$

For every i, the state 0 is in the subset S_{i+2} if and only if the polynomial contains the term x^3. This is not a coincidence, and this correspondence shall now be established in the general case.

5   Upper Bound for the GF(2)-Inverse

The following two binary sequences turn out to be identical. First, there is the sequence $\{S_i^0\}$ representing the membership of the state 0 in the subsets reached by the automaton for the GF(2)-inverse. The other sequence is the sequence $\{b_{i,n-2}\}$ of coefficients at x^{n-2}.

Lemma 8. *Let $\mathcal{A} = (\{a\}, Q, 0, \delta, F)$ be a cyclic DFA with $Q = \{0, \ldots, n-1\}$ and $0 \in F$. For each $i \geqslant 1$, let $S_i \subseteq Q$ be the state of the automaton for the inverse given in Sect. 3, reached upon reading the string a^i. For each $i \geqslant 1$, let $p_i(x)$ be x^i taken modulo $f(x) = \sum_{j \in F} x^{n-1-j}$. Then, for every $i \geqslant 0$, the state 0 is in S_{i+2} if and only if the monomial x^{n-2} is in $p_i(x)$.*

The proof is by induction on i: the base cases are $i \in \{0, 1, \ldots, n-2\}$, on which the sequences coincide. The induction step follows by Lemmata 5 and 6, since both sequences are defined by the same formulae on the same data.

Lemma 9. *Assume that the sequence $\{S_i^0\}_{i=0}^{\infty}$ has period p beginning at ℓ, in the sense that $S_i^0 = S_{i+p}^0$ for all $i \geqslant \ell$. Then, the sequence of states $\{S_i\}_{i=0}^{\infty}$ has period p beginning at ℓ.*

Lemma 10. *Let $\mathcal{A} = (\{a\}, Q, 0, \delta, F)$ be an n-state cyclic DFA with $0 \in F$. Then, the DFA for the GF(2)-inverse $L(\mathcal{A})^{-1}$, constructed as in Sect. 3, has at most $2^{n-1} + 1$ reachable states.*

Proof (a sketch). The sequence of polynomials x^i modulo $f(x) = \sum_{j \in F} x^{n-1-j}$ contains at most $2^{n-1} - 1$ distinct polynomials. By Lemma 8, this sequence coincides with the sequence of state 0, and then, by Lemma 9, the sequence of subsets has the same total length of the tail and the period. This gives the desired upper bound on the number of states. □

6   Lower Bound for the GF(2)-Inverse

The lower bound shall be established using cyclic witness languages. The following property of GF(2)-inverses of cyclic unary languages comes useful.

Lemma 11. *Let $L \subseteq a^*$, with $\varepsilon \in L$, be a unary language recognized by an n-state cyclic DFA. Then, its GF(2)-inverse L^{-1} contains a string a^ℓ, with $\ell \geqslant n+1$, if and only if the number of representations $a^\ell = a^{\ell-j} a^j$, with $a^{\ell-j} \in L^{-1}$, $a^j \in L \setminus \{\varepsilon\}$ and $j < n$, is odd.*

The proof is by establishing the equivalence with the condition in Theorem A.

For any language $L \subseteq a^*$, with $\varepsilon \in L$, let $\alpha_i = 1$ if $a^i \in L^{-1}$, and $\alpha_i = 0$ otherwise. Then the condition in Lemma 11 can be written down as the following formula.

Lemma 12. *Let $L \subseteq a^*$ be a language, with $\varepsilon \in L$, recognized by an n-state cyclic DFA. Then, $\alpha_i = \sum_{j \in F \setminus \{0\}} \alpha_{i-j}$ for $i \geqslant n+1$.*

As in Sect. 4, let $f(x) = a_{n-1} x^{n-1} + \ldots + a_1 x + a_0$ be a primitive polynomial over GF(2), with $a_{n-1} = a_0 = 1$ (primitive polynomials of any degree over GF(2) are known to exist). For every $i \geqslant 0$, let $p_i(x) = b_{i,n-2} x^{n-2} + \ldots + b_{i,1} x + b_{i,0}$ be x^i modulo $f(x)$. Since f is primitive, by definition, all polynomials $p_0(x), \ldots, p_{2^{n-1}-2}$ are pairwise distinct, and then $p_{2^{n-1}-1} = p_0(x) = 1$.

It turns out that the sequence of coefficients at x^{n-2} has the same period as the sequence of full polynomials.

Lemma 13. *The minimal period of the sequence $\{b_{i,n-2}\}_{i=0}^{\infty}$ is $2^{n-1} - 1$.*

Lemma 14. *The sequence $\{b_{i,n-2}\}_{i=0}^{\infty}$ contains all binary substrings of length $n - 1$, except for $(0, \ldots, 0)$.*

A cyclic automaton $\mathcal{A}_f$ corresponding to this primitive polynomial $f(x) = a_{n-1} x^{n-1} + \ldots + a_1 x + a_0$ is defined as $\mathcal{A}_f = (\{a\}, Q, 0, \delta, F)$, with $Q = \{0, \ldots, n-1\}$, $\delta(i, a) = i+1 \bmod n$ for all i, and $F = \{n-1-i \mid a_i = 1\}$ (by the same principle as in Lemma 8).

Let $L = L(\mathcal{A}_f)$, and consider the sequence $\{\alpha_i\}_{i=0}^{\infty}$ defined as above. The goal is to prove that $(\alpha_2, \ldots, \alpha_n) \neq (0, \ldots, 0)$.

Table 2. State complexity of unambiguous, classical and GF(2)-variants of sum, concatenation and star: the case of a unary alphabet.

	Sum	Concatenation	Star
Unambiguous	$(\uplus) \leqslant \frac{1}{2}mn$ [6]	$(\text{UNAMB}\cdot)\ m+n-1$ [6]	$(\text{UNAMB}*)\ n-2$ [6]
Classical	$(\cup) \leqslant mn$ [12]	$(\cdot) \qquad \leqslant mn$ [13]	$(*) \qquad (n-1)^2+1$ [13]
GF(2)	$(\triangle)\ mn$	$(\odot) \qquad \leqslant 2mn$	$(^{-1}) \qquad 2^{n-1}+1$

Lemma 15. *Let L be a unary language with $\varepsilon \in L$ and $L \neq \{\varepsilon\}, a^*$, which is recognized by a DFA with n states. Then, the inverse L^{-1} contains a string of length between 2 and n.*

Since the sequence $\{\alpha_i\}_{i=2}^{\infty}$ begins with something other than $n-1$ zeroes, by Lemma 13, the binary substring $(\alpha_2, \ldots, \alpha_n)$ occurs somewhere in the sequence $\{b_{i,n-2}\}_{i=0}^{\infty}$. By Lemma 12, the rest of the terms of the sequence $\{\alpha_i\}$ are defined by the same formula as the sequence $\{b_{i,n-2}\}$, which makes the binary strings $\alpha_2, \ldots, \alpha_{2^{n-1}}$ and $b_{0,n-2}, \ldots, b_{2^{n-1}-2}$ identical up to a cyclic shift. In particular, the period of the sequence $\{\alpha_i\}_{i=2}^{\infty}$ is $2^{n-1}-1$.

It remains to determine the length of the tail. Since the construction in Sect. 3 produces $2^{n-1}+1$ states, the length of the tail is at most 2. It turns out that it cannot be shortened, because the strings a and $a^{2^{n-1}}-1$ have different membership status.

Lemma 16. $\alpha_1 \neq \alpha_{2^{n-1}+1}$, *and therefore the length of the tail is 2.*

The following theorem has thus been established.

Theorem 17. *For every $n \geqslant 2$, there exists a language L, with $\varepsilon \in L$, recognized by n-state unary cyclic DFA, for which the minimal DFA recognizing its GF(2)-inverse L^{-1} has $2^{n-1}+1$ states.*

7   Future Work

The results of this paper are summarized and compared to related results in Table 2.

A problem proposed for future research is to determine the number of states in NFA needed to represent these operations. There are two different modes of nondeterminism involved: existential nondeterminism in NFA and parity nondeterminism in both GF(2)-operations. Intuitively, one kind of nondeterminism cannot help implementing another kind, and the following straightforward construction might actually turn out to be the best possible: first, determinize the arguments, with a blow-up of the order $e^{(1+o(1))\sqrt{n \ln n}}$ [3]; and then, apply the constructions for deterministic automata presented in this paper. Could this construction be substantially improved upon?

References

1. Bakinova, E., Basharin, A., Batmanov, I., Lyubort, K., Okhotin, A., Sazhneva, E.: Formal languages over GF(2). In: Klein, S.T., Martín-Vide, C., Shapira, D. (eds.) LATA 2018. LNCS, vol. 10792, pp. 68–79. Springer, Cham (2018). https://doi.org/10.1007/978-3-319-77313-1_5

2. Brzozowski, J.A.: Quotient complexity of regular languages. J. Autom. Lang. Comb. 15(1/2), 71–89 (2010). https://doi.org/10.25596/jalc-2010-071

3. Chrobak, M.: Finite automata and unary languages. Theor. Comput. Sci. 47(3), 149–158 (1986). https://doi.org/10.1016/0304-3975(86)90142-8

4. Daley, M., Domaratzki, M., Salomaa, K.: Orthogonal concatenation: language equations and state complexity. J. UCS 16(5), 653–675 (2010). https://doi.org/10.3217/jucs-016-05-0653

5. Geffert, V., Mereghetti, C., Pighizzini, G.: Converting two-way nondeterministic unary automata into simpler automata. Theor. Comput. Sci. 295, 189–203 (2003). https://doi.org/10.1016/S0304-3975(02)00403-6

6. Jirásková, G., Okhotin, A.: State complexity of unambiguous operations on deterministic finite automata. In: Konstantinidis, S., Pighizzini, G. (eds.) DCFS 2018. LNCS, vol. 10952, pp. 188–199. Springer, Cham (2018). https://doi.org/10.1007/978-3-319-94631-3_16

7. Kunc, M., Okhotin, A.: Describing periodicity in two-way deterministic finite automata using transformation semigroups. In: Mauri, G., Leporati, A. (eds.) DLT 2011. LNCS, vol. 6795, pp. 324–336. Springer, Heidelberg (2011). https://doi.org/10.1007/978-3-642-22321-1_28

8. Makarov, V., Okhotin, A.: On the expressive power of GF(2)-grammars. In: Catania, B., Královič, R., Nawrocki, J., Pighizzini, G. (eds.) SOFSEM 2019. LNCS, vol. 11376, pp. 310–323. Springer, Cham (2019). https://doi.org/10.1007/978-3-030-10801-4_25

9. Maslov, A.N.: Estimates of the number of states of finite automata. Soviet Math. Doklady 11, 1373–1375 (1970)

10. Mereghetti, C., Pighizzini, G.: Optimal simulations between unary automata. SIAM J. Comput. 30(6), 1976–1992 (2001). https://doi.org/10.1137/S009753979935431X

11. Okhotin, A.: Unambiguous finite automata over a unary alphabet. Inf. Comput. 212, 15–36 (2012). https://doi.org/10.1016/j.ic.2012.01.003

12. Pighizzini, G., Shallit, J.: Unary language operations, state complexity and Jacobsthal's function. Int. J. Found. Comput. Sci. 13(1), 145–159 (2002). https://doi.org/10.1142/S012905410200100X

13. Yu, S., Zhuang, Q., Salomaa, K.: The state complexities of some basic operations on regular languages. Theor. Comput. Sci. 125(2), 315–328 (1994). https://doi.org/10.1016/0304-3975(92)00011-F

Pushdown Automata and Constant Height: Decidability and Bounds

Giovanni Pighizzini and Luca Prigioniero[✉]

Dipartimento di Informatica, Università degli Studi di Milano, Milan, Italy
{pighizzini,prigioniero}@di.unimi.it

Abstract. It cannot be decided whether a pushdown automaton accepts using constant pushdown height, with respect to the input length, or not. Furthermore, in the case of acceptance in constant height, the height cannot be bounded by any recursive function in the size of the description of the machine. In contrast, in the restricted case of pushdown automata over a one-letter input alphabet, i.e., unary pushdown automata, the above property becomes decidable. Moreover, if the height is bounded by a constant in the input length, then it is at most exponential with respect to the size of the description of the pushdown automaton. This bound cannot be reduced. Finally, if a unary pushdown automaton uses nonconstant height to accept, then the height should grow at least as the logarithm of the input length. This bound is optimal.

1 Introduction

The investigation of computational devices working with a limited amount of resources is a classical topic in automata theory. It is well known that by limiting the memory size of a device by some constant, the computational power of the resulting model cannot exceed that of finite automata. For instance, if we consider pushdown automata in which the maximum height of the pushdown is limited by some constant, the resulting devices, called *constant-height pushdown automata*, can recognize only regular languages. Despite their limited computational power, constant-height pushdown automata are interesting since they allow more succinct representations of regular languages than finite automata [5]. A natural generative counterpart of these devices are *non-self-embedding context-free grammars*, roughly context-free grammars without "true" recursion [4], which have been recently showed to be polynomially related in size to constant-height pushdown automata [7].

In this paper, we focus on standard pushdown automata, namely with an unrestricted pushdown store, that, however, are able to accept their inputs by making use only of a constant amount of the pushdown store. More precisely, we say that a pushdown automaton M *accepts in constant height* h, for some given h, if for each word in the language accepted by M there exists one accepting computation in which the maximum height reached by the store is bounded

© IFIP International Federation for Information Processing 2019
Published by Springer Nature Switzerland AG 2019
M. Hospodár et al. (Eds.): DCFS 2019, LNCS 11612, pp. 260–271, 2019.
https://doi.org/10.1007/978-3-030-23247-4_20

by h. Notice that this does not prevent the existence of accepting or rejecting computations using an unbounded pushdown height.

It is a simple observation that a pushdown automaton $\mathcal{M}$ accepting in constant height h can be converted into an equivalent constant-height pushdown automaton: in any configuration it is enough to keep track of the current height in order to stop and reject when a computation tries to exceed the height limit. The description of the resulting constant-height pushdown automaton has size polynomial in h and in the size of the description of $\mathcal{M}$.

While studying these size relationships, we tried to understand *how large can h be with respect to the size of the description of $\mathcal{M}$*. We discovered that h can be arbitrarily large. Indeed, in the first part of the paper we prove that there is no recursive function bounding the maximal height reached by the pushdown store in a pushdown automaton accepting in constant height, with respect to the size of its description. We also prove that it cannot be decided if a pushdown automaton accepts in constant height.

In the second part of the paper we restrict the attention to the case of pushdown automata with a one-letter input alphabet, namely *unary pushdown automata*. By studying the structure of the computations of these devices, we are able to prove that, in contrast to the general case, it can be decided whether or not they accept in constant height. Furthermore, we also prove that if a unary pushdown automaton $\mathcal{M}$ accepts in height h, constant with respect to the input length, then h can be bounded by an exponential function in the size of $\mathcal{M}$. By presenting a suitable family of pushdown automata, we show that this bound cannot be reduced.

In the final part of the paper, we consider pushdown automata that accept using height which is not constant in the input length. Our aim is to investigate how the pushdown height grows. In particular, we want to know if there exists a minimum growth of the pushdown height, with respect to the length of the input, when it is not constant. The answer to this question is already known and it derives from results on Turing machines: the height of the store should grow at least as a double logarithmic function [1]. This lower bound cannot be increased, because a matching upper bound recently obtained in [3]. As a consequence of the constructions presented in the second part of the paper, we are able to prove that in the unary case this lower bound is logarithmic. We also show that it cannot be further increased.

For brevity reasons, many of the proofs are only outlined in this version of the paper.

2   Preliminaries

We assume the reader familiar with the standard notions from formal language and automata theory as presented in classical textbooks, e.g., [9]. As usual, the cardinality of a set S is denoted by $\#S$, the length of a string x is denoted by $|x|$, the empty string is denoted by ε.

We first recall the notion of *pushdown automata* and present the form for these devices that will be used in the paper. A *pushdown automaton* (PDA, for short) is a tuple $\mathcal{M} = \langle Q, \Sigma, \Gamma, \delta, q_0, Z_0, F \rangle$ where Q is the finite *set of states*, Σ is the *input alphabet*, Γ is the *pushdown alphabet*, $q_0 \in Q$ is the *initial state*, $Z_0 \in \Gamma$ is the *start symbol*, $F \subseteq Q$ is the set of *final states*. Without loss of generality, we make the following assumptions about PDAs:

1. at the start of the computation the pushdown store contains only the start symbol Z_0, being at height 0; this symbol is never pushed on or popped off the stack;
2. the input is accepted if and only if the automaton reaches a final state, the pushdown store contains only Z_0 and all the input has been scanned;
3. if the automaton moves the input head, then no operations are performed on the stack;
4. every **push** adds exactly one symbol on the stack.

Note that the transition function δ of a PDA $\mathcal{M}$ can be written as

$$\delta : Q \times (\Sigma \cup \{\varepsilon\}) \times \Gamma \to 2^{Q \times (\{-, \mathtt{pop}\} \cup \{\mathtt{push}(A) | A \in \Gamma\})}.$$

In particular, for $q, p \in Q$, $A, B \in \Gamma$, $\sigma \in \Sigma$, $(p, -) \in \delta(q, \sigma, A)$ means that the PDA $\mathcal{M}$, in the state q, with A at the top of the stack, by consuming the input σ, can reach the state p without changing the stack contents; $(p, \mathtt{pop}) \in \delta(q, \varepsilon, A)$ $((p, \mathtt{push}(B)) \in \delta(q, \varepsilon, A)$, $(p, -) \in \delta(q, \varepsilon, A)$, respectively) means that $\mathcal{M}$, in the state q, with A at the top of the stack, without reading any input symbol, can reach the state p by popping off the stack the symbol A on the top (by pushing the symbol B on the top of the stack, without changing the stack, respectively).

Now we present the main measure we consider in the paper, namely the *pushdown height*. The height of a PDA $\mathcal{M}$ in a given configuration is the number of symbols in the pushdown store *besides* the start symbol Z_0. Hence, in the initial and in the accepting configurations the height is 0. The height in a computation $\mathcal{C}$ is the maximum height reached in the configurations occurring in $\mathcal{C}$.

We say that $\mathcal{M}$ uses height $h(x)$ on an accepted input $x \in \Sigma^*$ if and only if $h(x)$ is the minimum pushdown height necessary to accept x, namely, there exists a computation accepting x using pushdown height $h(x)$, and no computations accepting x using height less than $h(x)$. Moreover, if x is rejected then $h(x) = 0$. To study pushdown height with respect to input lengths, we consider the worst case among all possible inputs of the same length. Hence, we define $h(n) = \max \{h(x) \mid x \in \Sigma^*, |x| = n\}$. When there is a constant H such that, for each n, $h(n)$ is bounded by H, we say that $\mathcal{M}$ *accepts in constant height*. Each PDA accepting in constant height can be easily transformed into an equivalent finite automaton. So the language accepted by it is regular.

In the following, by the *size of a* PDA we mean the length of its description. Notice that for each PDA in the above-defined form, over a fixed input alphabet Σ, the size is polynomial in the cardinalities of the set of states and of the pushdown alphabet.[1]

---

[1] In some papers PDAs are presented in different forms. As pointed out in [2], it is possible to turn the definition of PDAs into these equivalent forms, with a polynomial increase in size and by preserving the property of being constant height.

We now present some technical notions that will be useful in order to state our results. Let $\mathcal{M} = \langle Q, \Sigma, \Gamma, \delta, q_0, Z_0, F \rangle$ be a fixed PDA.

A *surface pair* is defined by a state $q \in Q$ and a symbol $A \in \Gamma$, and it is denoted by $[qA]$. The surface pair in a given configuration is defined by the current state and the topmost stack symbol, namely the only part of the stack which is relevant in order to decide the next move.

A *surface triple* is defined by two states $q, p \in Q$ and a symbol $A \in \Gamma$, and it is denoted by $[qAp]$. Surface triples are used to study parts of computations starting and ending at the same pushdown height and that do not go below that height in between. More precisely, a $[qAp]$-*computation* on an input string $x \in \Sigma^*$ is a computation $\mathcal{C}$ which starts from the state q with A on the top of the pushdown at some height h and the input head on the tape cell containing the leftmost symbol of x, and ends in the state p with A on the top of the pushdown at the same height h and the input head on the cell to the right of the cell containing the rightmost symbol of x, without reaching pushdown height less than h in between. We also say that $\mathcal{C}$ *consumes* the input x. We point out that, during $\mathcal{C}$, the symbol A at height h is never replaced and $\mathcal{C}$ does not depend on h and on the symbols in the pushdown store at height less than h. The *stack increment* during $\mathcal{C}$ is the difference between the maximum stack height in $\mathcal{C}$ and the stack height at the beginning and at the end of $\mathcal{C}$. Notice that the surface pairs at the beginning and at the end of $\mathcal{C}$ are $[qA]$ and $[pA]$.

We denote by $L_{[qAp]}$ the set of input strings consumed in all possible $[qAp]$-computations. By suitably modifying $\mathcal{M}$, we can obtain a PDA accepting $L_{[qAp]}$ which, hence, is context free.

An *horizontal loop* on a surface pair $[qA]$ is any $[qAq]$-computation consuming *at least one input symbol*. By considering a computation of 0 moves, we always have $\varepsilon \in L_{[qAq]}$. Hence $[qA]$ *has a horizontal loop* when $L_{[qAq]}$ contains at least one more string.

If a $[qAp]$-computation $\mathcal{C}$ contains a proper $[qAp]$-subcomputation $\mathcal{C}'$, for the *same* triple $[qAp]$, which starts with stack higher than at the beginning of $\mathcal{C}$, then the pair $(\mathcal{X}, \mathcal{Y})$ where $\mathcal{X}$ is the prefix of $\mathcal{C}$ ending in the first configuration of $\mathcal{C}'$, and $\mathcal{Y}$ is the suffix of $\mathcal{C}$ starting from the last configuration of $\mathcal{C}'$, is called *vertical loop*. Notice that at the end of $\mathcal{X}$ a nonempty string $A\alpha$ is on the pushdown above the occurrence of A which was on the top at the beginning of $\mathcal{C}$, and such a string is popped off during $\mathcal{Y}$.

It is well known that context-free languages defined over a one-letter alphabet are regular [6]. The size costs of the conversions of unary PDAs and context-free grammars into equivalent finite automata have been studied in [13].

3   Undecidability and Non-Recursive Bounds

In this section we prove that it cannot be decided whether a PDA accepts in constant height or not. Furthermore, the trade-off between the sizes of PDAs accepting in constant height and the maximal heights that are reached by their pushdown stores is not recursive.

These results are proved by using a technique introduced in [8], based on suitable encodings of single-tape Turing machine computations. Roughly, configurations of a such machine $\mathcal{T}$ with state set Q and alphabet Γ are denoted in a standard way as strings from $\Gamma^* Q \Gamma^*$. A computation consisting of m configurations $\alpha_1, \alpha_2, \ldots, \alpha_m$ is encoded as a string of blocks, separated by a delimiter $\$ \notin Q \cup \Gamma$, where the ith block is α_i when i is odd, α_i^R when i is even (in the following, we use $\alpha_i^{(R)}$ to denote either α_i^R or α_i according to the parity of the index i). Hence, the (encoding of a) *valid computation* of $\mathcal{T}$ on input w is a string $\mathcal{C} = \alpha_1 \$ \alpha_2^R \$ \alpha_3 \$ \alpha_4^R \$ \cdots \$ \alpha_m^{(R)}$, for some integer $m \geq 1$ such that:

1. $\alpha_i \in \Gamma^* Q \Gamma^*$, i.e., α_i encodes a configuration of $\mathcal{T}$, $i = 1, \ldots, m$;
2. α_1 encodes the initial configuration on input w;
3. α_{i+1} is reachable in one step from α_i, $i = 1, \ldots, m-1$;
4. α_m is a halting configuration of $\mathcal{T}$.

A *partial valid computation* is defined in a similar way, by dropping Condition 4.

As proved in [8], the complement of the set of all valid computations of $\mathcal{T}$ is a context-free language.

Theorem 1. *It is undecidable whether a* PDA *accepts in constant height.*[2]

Proof. (outline) We give a reduction from the halting problem. Let $\mathcal{T}$ be a deterministic Turing machine. With an easy modification, we suppose that arbitrarily long computations use arbitrarily large amounts of tape.

Given an input w, let $\alpha_1, \alpha_2, \ldots$ be the (possibly infinite) sequence of configurations in the computation of $\mathcal{T}$ on w. By adapting the techniques used in [8] to prove the above mentioned result, we describe a PDA $\mathcal{M}_{\mathcal{T},w}$ accepting the complement of the language $partial(\mathcal{T}, w)$ of partial computations of $\mathcal{T}$ on w.

Given an input $\mathcal{D} = \beta_1 \$ \beta_2^R \$ \cdots \$ \beta_r^{(R)}$, with $\beta_i \in (Q \cup \Gamma)^*$, $i = 1, \ldots, r$, $\mathcal{M}_{\mathcal{T},w}$ guesses which one among Conditions 1, 2 and 3 is not satisfied. For the first two conditions, the finite control is sufficient. For the third condition, $\mathcal{M}_{\mathcal{T},w}$ nondeterministically selects one block $\beta_i^{(R)}$, $1 \leq i \leq r$, copies it on the pushdown store and checks the condition by scanning the $(i+1)$th block, if any, while suitably comparing it with the block just saved on the store. (If $i = r$ then the verification fails.) Suppose that $\mathcal{D}$ satisfies Conditions 1 and 2, but not Condition 3. Then, there is a computation which accepts $\mathcal{D}$ using pushdown height equal to the length of the first block $\beta_i^{(R)}$ for which the condition is not satisfied, i.e., the block corresponding to the largest i such that $\beta_j = \alpha_j$ for $j = 1, \ldots, i$. Since the pushdown height used to accept a string x is defined as the *minimum* pushdown height in accepting computations on x, we conclude that the pushdown height used to accept $\mathcal{D}$ is bounded by $|\alpha_i|$. So, if $\mathcal{T}$ halts on w, then the maximum amount of the pushdown store used to accept a string in $(partial(\mathcal{T}, w))^c$ is bounded by the length of the largest configuration reached by $\mathcal{T}$ on w. Otherwise, for each integer h, any string $\alpha_1 \$ \alpha_2^R \$ \cdots \alpha_i \$ \beta^R$, where i is odd, $|\alpha_i| \geq h$, $\beta \in \Gamma^* Q \Gamma^*$, and $\beta \neq \alpha_{i+1}$, requires height at least h to be accepted.

---

[2] We point out that for *unambiguous* PDAs, the property is decidable [10].

Hence, $\mathcal{T}$ halts on w if and only if $\mathcal{M}_{\mathcal{T},w}$ accepts in constant height. $\qquad\square$

As already observed in the introduction, any PDA $\mathcal{M}$ accepting in constant height h can be converted into an equivalent constant-height PDA. From such a machine, equivalent NFAs and DFAs with a number of states exponential and double exponential in h, respectively, are easily obtained. In the worst case these bounds cannot be reduced [5]. We now show that, however, h cannot be bounded by any recursive function in the size of $\mathcal{M}$.

Theorem 2. *For any recursive function $f : \mathbb{N} \to \mathbb{N}$ and for infinitely many integers n there exists a PDA of size n accepting in constant height $H(n)$, where $H(n)$ cannot be bounded by $f(n)$.*[3]

Proof (outline). The argument is derived from [12, Prop. 7]. For $n > 0$, let $\mathcal{BB}_n$ be a *busy beaver* with a set of n states Q_n and tape alphabet $\Gamma = \{1, \flat\}$, namely a single-tape deterministic Turing machine that, starting with an empty tape, ends the computation with a string on the tape in which the number of $1's$, denoted as $\Sigma(n)$, is maximum. It is known that $\Sigma(n)$ cannot be bounded by any recursive function [14]. Hence, also the maximal length of configurations occurring in such a computation cannot be bounded by any recursive function.

Let $\mathcal{C}_n$ be the encoding of the valid computation of $\mathcal{BB}_n$ on ε. By adapting the arguments used to prove Theorem 1, we can define a PDA $\mathcal{M}_n$, whose description has a size polynomial in n, which accepts all the strings over $(Q_n \cup \Gamma \cup \{\$\})^*$ different from $\mathcal{C}_n$, and such that each string different from $\mathcal{C}_n$ is accepted using height bounded by the length of the longest configuration occurring in $\mathcal{C}_n$. Since n is fixed, $\mathcal{M}_n$ accepts in constant height. Furthermore, by suitably modifying $\mathcal{C}_n$, we can obtain a string that requires height equal to the maximal length of configurations occurring in $\mathcal{C}_n$ to be accepted by $\mathcal{M}_n$.

This allows to conclude that the pushdown height used by $\mathcal{M}_n$ cannot be bounded by any recursive function in the size of $\mathcal{M}_n$. $\qquad\square$

Corollary 3. *There is no recursive function bounding the size blowup from PDAs accepting in constant height to finite automata.*

4   Constant Height Decidability in the Unary Case

In Sect. 3 we proved that it cannot be decided if a PDA accepts in constant height. This section is devoted to showing that this property turns out to be decidable in the restricted case of PDAs with a one-letter input alphabet. We first give an informal outline of the argument.

Any accepting computation on a sufficiently long input should contain horizontal or vertical loops. The use of vertical loops can lead to computations using unbounded height. However, we prove that if an accepting computation on an input a^ℓ visits a surface pair on which there exists a horizontal loop, then there is another accepting computation for the same input in which almost all

---

[3] Notice that here $H(n)$ is a function of the size of the PDA and *not* of the input.

occurrences of the vertical loops are replaced by occurrences of such horizontal loop. The number of vertical loops which remain in the resulting computation is bounded by a constant. As a consequence, the amount of pushdown store sufficient to accept a^ℓ is also bounded by a constant. In contrast, when all accepting computations on a long string a^ℓ do not visit any surface pair having a horizontal loop, vertical loops and an increasing of the stack cannot be avoided. Hence, the given PDA works in constant height if and only if the cardinality of $L_v \setminus L_h$ is finite, where L_h (L_v, resp.) is the set of strings which are accepted by a computation visiting a (not visiting any, resp.) surface pair having a horizontal loop. Since we are considering a unary alphabet, languages L_v and L_h are regular. So the finiteness of their difference is decidable. To obtain these results, we refine some of the arguments given in [13] to study the size costs of the transformations of unary context-free grammars and pushdown automata into equivalent finite automata.

4.1   Loops and Grammars

Let $G = \langle V, \Sigma, P, S \rangle$ be a context-free grammar in *binary normal form*, an extension of Chomsky normal form where, besides productions $A \to BC$ and $A \to a$, also *unit productions* $A \to B$ and ε-*productions* are allowed. Let $v = \#V$ be the number of variables of G.

If T is a parse tree whose root is labeled with a variable $A \in V$ and such that the labels of the leaves, from left to right, form a string $\alpha \in (V \cup \Sigma)^*$, then we write $T : A \stackrel{*}{\Rightarrow} \alpha$. Furthermore, we indicate by $\nu(T)$ the set of variables occurring as labels of the nodes in T. As usual, the *height of a derivation tree T* is the maximum number of edges from the root to a leaf of T. A *gap tree* from a variable $A \in V$, also called A-*gap tree*, is a tree corresponding to a nonempty derivation of the form $A \stackrel{*}{\Rightarrow} xAy$, with $x, y \in \Sigma^*$.

Let us suppose that G is unary, i.e., $\Sigma = \{a\}$. The following lemma will be crucial to obtain the main result of this section. It states that each long enough string a^ℓ in the language generated by G can be derived by pumping a derivation tree of some short string by many occurrences of a *same* gap tree. Furthermore, such a gap tree can be arbitrarily chosen among the A-gap trees generating "short" nonempty strings, with A occurring in the derivation of a^ℓ.

Lemma 4. *For any derivation tree $T : S \stackrel{*}{\Rightarrow} a^\ell$ and for any A-gap tree $T_A :$ $A \stackrel{*}{\Rightarrow} a^i A a^j$, with $0 < i + j \leq 2^{v^2} - 2^{v^2 - v}$ and $A \in \nu(T)$, there exists a derivation tree $T' : S \stackrel{*}{\Rightarrow} a^\ell$ which is obtained by pumping a tree $T_0 : S \stackrel{*}{\Rightarrow} a^{\ell_0}$ such that $\nu(T_0) = \nu(T)$, $0 \leq \ell_0 \leq 2^{v^2 - 1} + (2^{v^2} - 2^{v^2 - v})^2$, with $k \geq 0$ occurrences of T_A.*

Proof (outline). First, the tree T is "un-pumped" by removing several gap trees, up to find a tree $T_r : S \stackrel{*}{\Rightarrow} a^{\ell_r}$, with $\ell_r \leq 2^{v^2 - 1}$ and $\nu(T_r) = \nu(T)$. The tree T_r is then "re-pumped" to get T_0, by using a number bounded by a constant of occurrences of the removed gap trees. The tree T', which generates the same string as the original T, can be obtained by pumping T_0 with a suitable number of occurrences of T_A. The possibility of doing these transformations, which finally produce a different tree for the same string, derives from a result related to Diophantine equations [11, Lemma 2.6] and from the fact that in the unary case terminal symbols commute.   □

4.2   Simulating Vertical Loops by a Horizontal Loop

Let us consider a fixed (not necessarily unary) PDA $M = \langle Q, \Sigma, \Gamma, \delta, q_0, Z_0, F \rangle$. We define the grammar $G = \langle V, \Sigma, P, S \rangle$, where the elements of V are triples $[qAp]$, with $q, p \in Q$, $A \in \Gamma$, plus the start symbol S (hence $v = \#V = 1 + (\#Q)^2 \cdot \#\Gamma$), and P contains the following productions:

1. $[qAp] \rightarrow [qAr][rAp]$, for $q, p, r \in Q$, $A \in \Gamma$;
2. $[qAp] \rightarrow [q'Bp']$, for $q, q', p, p' \in Q$, $A, B \in \Gamma$ such that $(q', push(B)) \in \delta(q, \varepsilon, A)$ and $(p, pop) \in \delta(p', \varepsilon, B)$;
3. $[qAp] \rightarrow \sigma$, for $q, p \in Q$, $\sigma \in \Sigma \cup \{\varepsilon\}$, $A \in \Gamma$ such that $(p, -) \in \delta(q, \sigma, A)$;
4. $[qAq] \rightarrow \varepsilon$, for $q \in Q$, $A \in \Gamma$;
5. $S \rightarrow [q_0 Z_0 q]$, for $q \in F$.

Applying standard techniques, we can prove that G generates the language accepted by M. Since we are interested in the amount of stack used by M, we state such equivalence in a stronger form, which also considers the use of the stack in the computations. In particular, we relate the stack increment to the *unit production height* which, for a derivation tree T of the above grammar G, is defined as the maximum number of edges corresponding to unit productions in a path from the root to a leaf in T. As a consequence of a technical lemma, which is omitted, we obtain:

Corollary 5. *For any integer $h \geq 0$, a string x is accepted by M using pushdown height h if and only if there is a derivation tree T of x in G with unit production height h.*

Let us restrict to the unary case. Using Corollary 5, we can reformulate Lemma 4 in terms of pushdown automata. Roughly, we can say that for each computation $\mathcal{C}$ accepting a "long" input, there is another computation accepting the same input, which is obtained by pumping a suitable computation $\mathcal{C}_0$, chosen from a finite set, with a repeated pattern which is arbitrarily selected from another finite set that depends on $\mathcal{C}_0$. We will use this property to replace in an accepting computation $\mathcal{C}$ almost all the vertical loops with many occurrences of a horizontal loop, in the case a surface pair $[rB]$ having a horizontal loop occurs in $\mathcal{C}$. In this way, we will be able to obtain an accepting computation on the same input using a bounded amount of pushdown storage.

Theorem 6. *Let $\mathcal{C}$ be an accepting computation on input a^ℓ which visits a surface pair $[rB]$ having a horizontal loop. Then there exists another accepting computation on a^ℓ which uses pushdown height at most $2^{O(v^2)}$.*

Proof (outline). First, we observe that if $\mathcal{C}$ visits the surface pair $[rB]$ then there exists a derivation tree $T : S \overset{*}{\Rightarrow} a^\ell$ with $[rBr] \in \nu(G)$. In fact, one of the triples $[rBs]$ or $[sBr]$ for some $s \in Q$ should appear in the derivation tree corresponding to $\mathcal{C}$. Since G contains the productions $[rBs] \to [rBr][rBs]$, $[sBr] \to [sBr][rBr]$ and $[rBr] \to \varepsilon$, we can suitably modify the tree in order to introduce one occurrence of $[rBr]$, without changing the derived string.

Now we select a $[rBr]$-gap tree $T_{[rBr]}$ deriving a "short" non empty string, i.e., $T_{[rBr]} : [rBr] \overset{*}{\Rightarrow} a^i[rBr]a^j$, with $0 < i + j \leq 2^{v^2} - 2^{v^2-v}$. According to Lemma 4, we can obtain another tree $T' : S \overset{*}{\Rightarrow} a^\ell$ by pumping a tree $T_0 : S \overset{*}{\Rightarrow} a^{\ell_0}$, such that $\nu(T_0) = \nu(T)$, $0 \leq \ell_0 \leq 2^{v^2-1} + (2^{v^2} - 2^{v^2-v})^2$, with $k \geq 0$ occurrences of $T_{[rBr]}$.

We observe that in the tree T' the k occurrences of $T_{[rBr]}$ could be nested, possibly giving a stack height in the corresponding computation which linearly increases with k. To fix this problem, we modify T' as we now describe.

Let u be a node of T_0 labeled by $[rBr]$ and T_u be the subtree of T_0 rooted at u, such that T_0 is pumped starting from u with $t > 1$ nested occurrences of $T_{[rBr]}$. We rearrange these t occurrences of $T_{[rBr]}$ in a sequence by inserting, starting from node u, a subtree corresponding to a derivation $[rBr] \overset{*}{\Rightarrow} [rBr]^t$ obtained by using $t - 1$ times the production $[rBr] \to [rBr][rBr]$. To each leaf of this subtree we append one occurrence of the $[rBr]$-gap tree $T_{[rBr]}$. Finally, to the leaf labeled $[rBr]$ of the first occurrence of $T_{[rBr]}$ we append the tree T_u, and to each of the remaining $t - 1$ leaves labeled $[rBr]$ we append one leaf labeled with the empty word.

Let T'' be the tree obtained after this modification, which still generates a^ℓ. Using Corollary 5 we now estimate the amount of pushdown store used in the computation $\mathcal{C}''$ corresponding to T''. The unit production height of T'' is bounded by the maximum number h_0 of such edges in a path in T_0 plus the maximum number h_1 of such edges in a path in $T_{[rBr]}$ which, in turn, are bounded by the height of T_0 and $T_{[rBr]}$, respectively. We can prove that $h_0 + h_1$ is $2^{O(v^2)}$. According to Corollary 5, this allows us to conclude that a^ℓ is accepted by a computation which uses pushdown height $2^{O(v^2)}$. $\square$

4.3   Decidability

We are now able to prove the main result of this section:

Theorem 7. *Let $\mathcal{M}$ be a unary PDA with n states and m pushdown symbols. Then $\mathcal{M}$ accepts in constant height if and only if it accepts in height bounded by $2^{O(v^2)}$, where $v = n^2m + 1$.*

Proof (outline). Let L be the language accepted by $\mathcal{M}$. We also consider the following two languages L_h and L_v, whose union gives L:

- L_h is the set of strings accepted by the computations of $\mathcal{M}$ which visit at least one surface pair having a horizontal loop.

– L_v is the set of strings accepted by the computations of $\mathcal{M}$ which visit only
surface pairs that do not have horizontal loops.

According to Theorem 6, all strings in L_h are accepted in constant height $2^{O(v^2)}$.

If the set $L_v \setminus L_h$ is infinite, then it should contain arbitrarily long strings.
It can be verified that an arbitrarily high stack is required to accept them.

Otherwise, $\mathcal{M}$ accepts in constant height. In this case, we evaluate the height
of the stack used to accept the strings in $L_v \setminus L_h$. We can modify $\mathcal{M}$ to obtain
PDAs $\mathcal{M}_v$ and $\mathcal{M}_h$ accepting languages L_v and L_h, respectively. According
to Corollary 2 in [13], these automata can be converted into equivalent DFAs
with $2^{O(v^2)}$ states. Hence $L_v \setminus L_h$, which is finite, is accepted by a DFA with less
than $2^{O(v^2)}$ states. So, the longest string in $L_v \setminus L_h$ has length at most $2^{O(v^2)}$.
This implies that each string in $L_v \setminus L_h$ is accepted by $\mathcal{M}$ using height $2^{O(v^2)}$. $\square$

Corollary 8. *It is decidable whether a unary PDA accepts in constant height.*

5 Size Versus Height in the Unary Case

The arguments used in Sect. 4 to prove that it is decidable whether a unary PDA
$\mathcal{A}$ accepts in constant height, give an exponential upper bound for the maximum
stack height, with respect to the size of $\mathcal{A}$. We can prove that such an exponential
bound cannot be reduced:

Theorem 9. *For each integer $k > 0$ there exists a PDA $\mathcal{M}_k$ having a size polynomial in k and accepting in height which is constant with respect to the input
length but exponential in k.*

Proof (outline). For each integer $k > 0$, let us consider the language $H_k = \{a^t \mid t = \alpha 2^k + \beta(2^k + 1), \alpha, \beta \geq 0\}$. We can define a PDA $\mathcal{M}_k$ of size $O(k)$ which
accepts each string in H_k by computations consisting of two parts. In the first
part, a horizontal loop which consumes 2^k input symbols is repeated an arbitrary
number $\alpha \geq 0$ of times. This uses constant height $O(k)$. In the second part, a
vertical loop consuming $2^k + 1$ input symbols occurs $\beta \geq 0$ times, using height $\beta + k - 1$. According to Theorem 6, each accepting computation can be replaced by
an equivalent accepting computation in which the number of occurrences of the
vertical loop is bounded by a constant. Hence $\mathcal{M}_k$ accepts in constant height.

However, an height exponential in k is necessary. In fact, let $a^t \in H_k$ be the
string obtained by choosing $\alpha = 0$ and $\beta = 2^k - 1$, namely, $t = (2^k - 1)(2^k + 1)$.
We can prove that the only solution of the equation $t = \alpha' 2^k + \beta'(2^k + 1)$,
with integers $\alpha', \beta' \geq 0$ is $\alpha' = \alpha = 0$ and $\beta' = \beta = 2^k - 1$. This allows
to conclude that the only accepting computation on a^t is the one which uses
height $\beta + k - 1 \geq 2^k$. Hence, to accept a^t an exponential height, with respect
the size of $\mathcal{M}_k$, is necessary. $\square$

6   An Optimal Lower Bound for Non-Constant Height

In this section we turn our attention to PDAs accepting in non-constant height. It is known that in this case the height of the pushdown store should grow at least as the function $\log \log n$, with respect to the input length n [1]. Furthermore, this lower bound is optimal [3]. We show that in the unary case the optimal bound increases to a logarithmic function.

Let us start by proving the lower bound:

Theorem 10. *Let $\mathcal{M}$ be a unary PDA using height $h(n)$. Then either $h(n)$ is bounded by a constant or there exists $c > 0$ such that $h(n) \geq c \log n$ infinitely often.*

Proof (outline). According to the proof of Theorem 7, if $h(n)$ is not constant, then there exist infinitely many strings in $L_v \setminus L_h$ that are accepted only by computations that use vertical loops and do not visit surface pairs having horizontal loops. Let $\mathcal{M}_v$ be the PDA accepting L_v and, for $a^n \in L_v \setminus L_h$, $\mathcal{M}_{h(n)}$ be the PDA obtained by bounding the height of the pushdown of $\mathcal{M}_v$ to $h(n)$.

Using Corollary 2 in [13], we can prove that there exists an NFA $\mathcal{N}_{h(n)}$ equivalent to $\mathcal{M}_{h(n)}$ whose number of states is bounded by $2^{d \cdot h(n)+1} + 1$, where $d = 2 \cdot (\#Q)^2 \cdot \#\Gamma$.

Since $\mathcal{M}_{h(n)}$ has stack height bounded by $h(n)$, it cannot have vertical loops. Furthermore, accepting computations of $\mathcal{M}_v$ do not use surface pairs with horizontal loops. Hence, the language accepted by $\mathcal{M}_{h(n)}$ is finite. Thus, in $\mathcal{N}_{h(n)}$ the string a^n is accepted by a path without any repeated state. This implies that $\mathcal{N}_{h(n)}$ must have more than n states.

Given any constant c, if $h(n) < c \log n$, then the number of states of $\mathcal{N}_{h(n)}$ would be $2^{d \cdot h(n)+1} + 1 < 2^{d \cdot c \log n + 1} + 1 = 2n^{d \cdot c} + 1$. For c sufficiently small, e.g., $c < 1/(2d)$, we get that the number of states of $\mathcal{N}_{h(n)}$ is less than n, provided that n is not too small. This gives a contradiction. Hence, it must exist a constant c such that $h(n) \geq c \log n$ infinitely often.   □

We now prove a matching upper bound:

Theorem 11. *There exists a unary PDA accepting every word a^ℓ, $\ell > 0$, using pushdown height exactly $\lfloor \log_2 \ell \rfloor + 1$ and the empty word using height 0.*

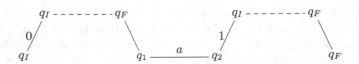

Fig. 1. The evolution of the pushdown store of $\mathcal{A}$ during the recursive subroutine leading from q_I to q_F, when recursive calls are made. The dashed lines should be replaced either by an ε-move or, recursively, by the same pattern.

Proof (outline). Consider the PDA $\mathcal{A} = \langle Q, \{a\}, \Gamma, \delta, q_I, Z_0, \{q_F\}\rangle$, where $Q = \{q_I, q_1, q_2, q_F\}$, $\Gamma = \{Z_0, 0, 1\}$, and δ defined as follows, for $X \in \Gamma$:

1. $\delta(q_I, \varepsilon, X) = (q_F, -)$;
2. $\delta(q_I, \varepsilon, X) = (q_I, \text{push}(0))$;
3. $\delta(q_F, \varepsilon, 0) = (q_1, \text{pop})$;

4. $\delta(q_1, a, X) = (q_2, -)$;
5. $\delta(q_2, \varepsilon, X) = (q_I, \text{push}(1))$;
6. $\delta(q_F, \varepsilon, 1) = (q_F, \text{pop})$.

From the initial state q_I, the PDA $\mathcal{A}$ can reach the final state q_F with the same pushdown height either with an ε-move (Transition 1) or by using a computation path making two recursive calls and consuming one input symbol as depicted in Fig. 1. Each string in a^* is accepted by $\mathcal{A}$. Furthermore, pushdown height h is necessary and sufficient to accept all strings of length ℓ, with $2^{h-1} \le \ell < 2^h$. □

References

1. Alberts, M.: Space complexity of alternating Turing machines. In: Budach, L. (ed.) FCT 1985. LNCS, vol. 199, pp. 1–7. Springer, Heidelberg (1985). https://doi.org/10.1007/BFb0028785
2. Bednárová, Z., Geffert, V., Mereghetti, C., Palano, B.: Removing nondeterminism in constant height pushdown automata. Inform. Comput. **237**, 257–267 (2014)
3. Bednárová, Z., Geffert, V., Reinhardt, K., Yakaryilmaz, A.: New results on the minimum amount of useful space. Internat. J. Found. Comput. Sci. **27**(2), 259–282 (2016). https://doi.org/10.1142/S0129054116400098
4. Chomsky, N.: A note on phrase structure grammars. Inform. Control **2**(4), 393–395 (1959). https://doi.org/10.1016/S0019-9958(59)80017-6
5. Geffert, V., Mereghetti, C., Palano, B.: More concise representation of regular languages by automata and regular expressions. Inform. Comput. **208**(4), 385–394 (2010). https://doi.org/10.1016/j.ic.2010.01.002
6. Ginsburg, S., Rice, H.G.: Two families of languages related to ALGOL. J. ACM **9**(3), 350–371 (1962). https://doi.org/10.1145/321127.321132
7. Guillon, B., Pighizzini, G., Prigioniero, L.: Non-self-embedding grammars, constant-height pushdown automata, and limited automata. In: Câmpeanu, C. (ed.) CIAA 2018. LNCS, vol. 10977, pp. 186–197. Springer, Cham (2018). https://doi.org/10.1007/978-3-319-94812-6_16
8. Hartmanis, J.: Context-free languages and Turing machine computations. In: Mathematical Aspects of Computer Science. Proceedings of Symposia in Applied Mathematics, vol. 19, pp. 42–51. American Mathematical Society (1967)
9. Hopcroft, J.E., Ullman, J.D.: Introduction to Automata Theory, Languages and Computation. Addison-Wesley, Boston (1979)
10. Malcher, A., Meckel, K., Mereghetti, C., Palano, B.: Descriptional complexity of pushdown store languages. J. Autom. Lang. Comb. **17**(2–4), 225–244 (2012)
11. Mereghetti, C., Pighizzini, G.: Optimal simulations between unary automata. SIAM J. Comput. **30**(6), 1976–1992 (2001)
12. Meyer, A.R., Fischer, M.J.: Economy of description by automata, grammars, and formal systems. In: Proceedings of 12th Annual Symposium on Switching and Automata Theory, pp. 188–191. IEEE Computer Society (1971)
13. Pighizzini, G., Shallit, J., Wang, M.: Unary context-free grammars and pushdown automata, descriptional complexity and auxiliary space lower bounds. J. Comput. Syst. Sci. **65**(2), 393–414 (2002). https://doi.org/10.1006/jcss.2002.1855
14. Rado, T.: On non-computable functions. Bell Syst. Tech. J. **41**(3), 877–884 (1962). https://doi.org/10.1002/j.1538-7305.1962.tb00480.x

On the Decidability of Finding a Positive ILP-Instance in a Regular Set of ILP-Instances

Petra Wolf[✉]

FB 4 - Abteilung Informatikwissenschaften, Universität Trier, Trier, Germany
wolfp@uni-trier.de

Abstract. The regular intersection emptiness problem for a decision problem P ($int_{\text{Reg}}(P)$) is to decide whether a potentially infinite regular set of encoded P-instances contains a positive one. Since $int_{\text{Reg}}(P)$ is decidable for some NP-complete problems and undecidable for others, its investigation provides insights in the nature of NP-complete problems. Moreover, the decidability of the int_{Reg}-problem is usually achieved by exploiting the regularity of the set of instances; thus, it also establishes a connection to formal language and automata theory. We consider the int_{Reg}-problem for the well-known NP-complete problem INTEGER LINEAR PROGRAMMING (ILP). It is shown that any DFA that describes a set of ILP-instances (in a natural encoding) can be reduced to a finite core of instances that contains a positive one if and only if the original set of instances did. This result yields the decidability of $int_{\text{Reg}}(\text{ILP})$.

Keywords: Deterministic finite automaton · Regular languages · Regular intersection emptiness problem · Decidability · Integer linear programming

1 Introduction

The problem INTEGER LINEAR PROGRAMMING (ILP for short) asks whether a given set of inequalities with integer coefficients has an integer solution. ILP is among the first problems for which NP-hardness was shown (it is on Karp's original list of 21 NP-complete problems) and it is of great practical relevance in mathematical optimisation. There is a large number of academic prototypes as well as commercial implementations of ILP-solvers that are applied in various contexts; therefore ILP is arguably of similar importance as the well-known Boolean satisfiability problem. For recent theoretical papers on ILP see, e. g., [5, 7].

Linear and Integer Linear Programs are often used to model observations of the real world under the assumption that some properties are present. Important fields of applications are for example image segmentation [12] and motion

M. Hospodár et al. (Eds.): DCFS 2019, LNCS 11612, pp. 272–284, 2019.
https://doi.org/10.1007/978-3-030-23247-4_21

segmentation [13]. These models often face uncertainties due to lack of information or measurement errors [10]. One possibility to handle this problem is to take every possible instance into account, in which the uncertainty is replaced by an actual value and ask whether one of them is solvable. In doing so, we get a potentially *infinite* set of instances under which we seek a solvable one. For example, suppose we have a system of two inequalities $a_{11}x_1 + a_{12}x_2 \le b_1$ and $a_{21}x_1a_{22}x_2 \le b_2$ with two integer variables x_1 and x_2 and only partial knowledge of the coefficients $a_{11}, a_{12}, b_1, a_{21}, a_{22}, b_2$. Due to measurement inaccuracies all we know is that a_{11} is a power of 2; a_{12} is even and negative; b_1 is positive and less than 100; a_{21} is congruent to 3 modulo 29; a_{22} is 1 less than an odd power of 2; and b_2 is negative. The described inequalities form an infinite family of inequalities and the described system represents an infinite family S of instances of ILP. Since each coefficient fits a regular pattern, a DFA can describe the encodings of exactly the instances in S.

Compact representations of finite sets of instances have already been considered for other problems. In graph modification,[1] the task is to transform a given graph using a given set of edit operations into a graph of a certain graph-family using as few operations as possible [2,14]. The possible edit operations give rise to an edit distance [8] with respect to the set of graphs; thus, the above described task can be seen as checking whether the set of all graphs within a certain distance from the given graph contains a member of the specified graph-family. The same can be done for string-problems where a given string is to be transformed (by using certain operations) into a target string [4].

Searching for a positive instance among infinitely many instances of a problem P seems to be a natural generalization of this setting. If we consider regular sets of instances, this task can be formalised as checking whether a given regular language of P-instances (represented by a deterministic finite automaton) and the fixed language of positive P-instances have a non-empty intersection. This was the original viewpoint of the line of research introduced by Güler et al. [9,23], where this problem is called the int_{Reg}-*problem of* P (or $int_{\text{Reg}}(P)$ for short).[2]

The int_{Reg}-problem has independently been studied under the name *regular realizability problem* $RR(L)$, where the *filter language* L plays the role of problem P as defined above, i.e., $RR(L) = int_{\text{Reg}}(L)$ (see [1,15–17,19–21]). The RR problem appeared when considering *models of generalized nondeterminism* (GNA) where an auxiliary memory is used as a source of nondeterminism [18]. For each GNA class there are complete $RR(L)$ problems where the filter language L consists of prefixes of GNA-certificates (or guess words) [19]. That fact already gives RR-problems which are complete under log space reductions for LOG, NLOG, P, NP, PSPACE, EXP, and Σ_1. This observation motivated the attempt to present with the RR-problem 'a specific class of algorithmic problems that represents complexities of all known complexity classes [...] in a unified way' [20]. It turned out that RR-problems are universal in the sense that for any prob-

---

[1] A Dagstuhl seminar on 'Graph Modification Problems' was held in 2014 [2].

[2] Note that this problem is only well-defined if it is clear how P is represented as a language, i.e., we have to define how P-instances are encoded as strings.

lem P, there exists an RR-problem $RR(L)$ with the same complexity (note that P and L are different languages). In [21], instead of focusing on which complexity classes can be covered by an RR-problem, the authors concentrate on context-free filter languages and present examples for which $RR(L)$ is either P-complete, NLOG-complete or has an intermediate complexity. In [17] the decidability of the RR-problem with languages of permutations of binary words as filters have been considered. In this line of research, the filter languages are closely related to computations of specific machine models. As a consequence the regularity of the input language is not exploited at all and the hard part of a problem is coded into regular languages consisting of single words only. In [20] the author notes that the presented reductions 'cut off almost all properties of regular languages'.

In [1], $int_{\mathrm{Reg}}(L)$ has been studied for L with low computational complexity, but which describe structural properties of words that have high relevance for combinatorics on words and formal language theory (e.g., set of primitive words, palindromes, etc.). In this regards, (efficient) decision procedures are obtained.

In contrast to these research questions, the line of work initiated in [9,23] focuses on classical (hard) computational problems as filter languages and respective decision procedures heavily take advantage of the regularity of the set of input instances. Investigating the int_{Reg}-problem for NP-complete problems shows that the decidability of their int_{Reg}-problem is not trivial, e. g., $int_{\mathrm{Reg}}(\text{SAT})$ is decidable [9], whereas $int_{\mathrm{Reg}}(\text{BOUNDED TILING})$ is not [23].[3] This is particularly interesting because the original hardness proofs of SAT and BOUNDED TILING are both given by directly encoding Turing-machine computations into a problem instance [3,6]. Finding a generic characterization of NP-complete problems with a decidable int_{Reg}-problem is still an open problem. This work continues this line of research and we will focus on the NP-complete integer linear programming problem as the filter language, i. e., we investigate the problem $int_{\mathrm{Reg}}(\text{ILP})$.

Our main result is that $int_{\mathrm{Reg}}(\text{ILP})$ is decidable. The idea is to transform the given DFA that represents the regular set of instances into a condensed one that accepts a finite set of instances, such that the condensed set contains a positive instance if and only if this is the case for the original set.[4] This is done by first identifying for all pairs of states the set of coefficients that can be read between these two states, and then choosing a finite number of representatives for each such set of coefficients (in a sense, these are the coefficients that are 'most promising' regarding possible solutions). Then, again for all pairs of states, we identify a set of whole inequalities that can be read between these two states and that only have coefficients from the set of 'promising' coefficients constructed before. Finally, we will again choose suitable representatives for those sets of inequalities, from which we will construct the desired condensed automaton. We will also give bounds on the number and length of words accepted by the

---

[3] LOGSPACE and P also contain problems with undecidable int_{Reg}-problem [23].

[4] Our construction uses similar ideas as given in [11].

condensed automaton and, in the conclusions, discuss the chosen encoding and present an alternative encoding. The presented arguments can easily be adapted to proof the decidability of the int_{Reg}-problem for Linear Programming (with integer coefficients). Due to space restrictions some proofs are omitted.

2 Preliminaries

We assume the reader to be familiar with the basics of formal language theory and the complexity class NP. For a language descriptor A (e.g., regular expressions or automata), $L(A)$ denotes the language described by A. With $[n]$, $n \in \mathbb{N}$ we denote the set $\{1, \ldots, n\}$. A deterministic finite automaton (DFA) A is a tuple $(Q, \Sigma, \delta, q_0, F)$ where Q is a finite set of states, Σ a finite alphabet, $\delta \colon Q \times \Sigma \to Q$ the (partial) transition function, q_0 the start state, and F is the set of final states. The transition function δ extends to the function $\delta^* \colon Q \times \Sigma^* \to Q$ in the usual way. We will only consider partial automata where every state is *coaccessible*, i.e., from every state, some final state is reachable.

We first give a formal definition of the problem INTEGER LINEAR PROGRAMMING. While the standard-form of ILP varies in different areas, we refer to the definition in [22] where this problem is called LIQ. We will refer to the described problem as ILP. The problem is NP-complete if we ask for solutions in $\mathbb{Z}$ [22].

Definition 1 (ILP).
Given: Finite set $\mathcal{A}$ of pairs (α, β) where $\alpha \in \mathbb{Z}^m$ and $\beta \in \mathbb{Z}$.
Question: Is there an m-tuple $x \in \mathbb{Z}^m$ such that $\alpha^\mathsf{T} \cdot x \leq \beta$ for all $(\alpha, \beta) \in \mathcal{A}$?

The problem will be encoded in the following way. The whole set $\mathcal{A}$ will be encoded in one word. For each pair (α, β) the elements of α and the β-value are encoded in binary over $\{0,1\}$. Each positive integer will be preceded with a $+$ while each negative integer will be preceded with a $-$. The integers of α will be separated from β by a $\leq$ symbol. The inequalities themselves are terminated by \$-symbols. Since we want to talk about *regular* languages of ILP-instances, we aim to have an encoding which is verifiable by a finite automaton. Therefore, we allow the inequalities of an ILP-instance to have different numbers of variables. The assignment of the coefficients to the variables is implicitly made by the order in which the coefficients occur. So, the i-th encoded coefficient in an inequality refers to variable x_i and is referenced as the coefficient with index i. As the inequalities of an ILP-instance may have different numbers of coefficients, they are interpreted as filled up with coefficients zero until all inequalities have the same number of coefficients and hence the same number of variables. Alternative encodings are discussed in Sect. 5. More formally,

$$L_{\text{enc}} := L\left(\left(([+|-][0|1(0|1)^*])^* \leq [+|-][0|1(0|1)^*]\$\right)^* \right)$$

is the *set of all encoded* ILP-*instances* and with ILP$_{\text{enc}}$ we denote the set of all *solvable* encoded ILP-instances. As an example, consider the following integer linear program and its encoding:

$$\{((5,1,0,-7),15),((0,-8,1,0),-4),((1,0,0,0),-1)\},$$
$$+101+1+0-111 \leq +1111\,\$\,-0-1000+1 \leq -100\,\$\,+1 \leq -1\,\$.$$

Note that coefficients zero can either occur with a $+$ or a $-$ sign.

The question we want to investigate is whether the set of solvable ILP-instances, encoded in the above described way, and a regular language, given by an automaton, have a non-empty intersection.

Definition 2 ($int_{\mathrm{Reg}}(\mathrm{ILP})$).
Given: Deterministic finite automaton A.
Question: Is $L(A) \cap \mathrm{ILP}_{enc} \neq \emptyset$?

3 Construction of the Condensed Automaton

We will follow the ideas presented in [9] of investigating what kinds of loops can occur in the automaton without violating the encoding format, namely loops inside a coefficient, loops over whole coefficients, and loops over whole inequalities.

Definition 3. *Let $A = (Q, \Sigma, \delta, q_0, F)$ be a DFA. We define for all $q, q' \in Q$ and $s \in \{+, -\}$ the coefficient transition set $\Lambda_{q,q'}^s$ and β-transition sets $B_{q,q'}^s$ as*

$$\Lambda_{q,q'}^s = \{si \mid i \in \{0,1\}^* \wedge \exists \sigma \in \Sigma \backslash \{0,1,\$\} : \delta^*(q,si) = q' \wedge \delta(q',\sigma) \neq \emptyset\}.$$

$$B_{q,q'}^s = \{si \mid i \in \{0,1\}^* \wedge \delta^*(q,si) = q' \wedge \delta(q',\$) \neq \emptyset\}.$$

Intuitively speaking, these transition sets contain all coefficients and β-values which can be *completely* read between q and q'. Note that automata recognizing the transition sets are easily obtained from the original automata. When q, q' and s is clear from the context, then we will simply write Λ and B.

We now want to find a set of representatives $\mathrm{reps}(\Lambda)$ for each coefficient transition set Λ. The set $\mathrm{reps}(\Lambda)$ will contain only the smallest and largest coefficient, which in the following we will denote *extreme* coefficients, from the set Λ. Since all inequalities are of the form $\alpha_1 x_1 + \cdots + \alpha_n x_n \leq \beta$, increasing the absolute value of a positive summand $\alpha_i x_i$ makes the inequality system harder to be solved, while decreasing it may only enlarge the set of solutions (correspondingly for negative summands). So, we only have to consider the largest and smallest coefficient α_i contained in the coefficient transition set. The largest and smallest coefficient will correspond, in combination with a negative and positive x_i value, respectively, to the smallest negative and positive summand, respectively. If a coefficient transition set is infinite, it contains coefficients with an arbitrarily large magnitude, which we will represent by the meta-characters $+\infty$ and $-\infty$ in order to indicate that we can replace them with large enough values. Similarly, if a β-transition set $B_{q,q'}^+$ is infinite, we will use $+\infty$-symbol as a representative (indicating that we can find arbitrary large β-values and therefore such inequalities can be ignored), and for β-transition sets $B_{q,q'}^-$ we choose the element with the smallest magnitude as representative.

Definition 4. *For transition sets* $\Lambda^s_{q,q'}$ *and* $B^s_{q,q'}$, *we define:*

$$\operatorname{reps}(\Lambda^+_{q,q'}) := \begin{cases} \{\min(\Lambda^+_{q,q'}), +\infty\}, & \text{if } |\Lambda^+_{q,q'}| = \infty; \\ \{\min(\Lambda^+_{q,q'}), \max(\Lambda^+_{q,q'})\}, & \text{otherwise,} \end{cases}$$

$$\operatorname{reps}(\Lambda^-_{q,q'}) := \begin{cases} \{-\infty, \max(\Lambda^-_{q,q'})\}, & \text{if } |\Lambda^-_{q,q'}| = \infty; \\ \{\min(\Lambda^-_{q,q'}), \max(\Lambda^-_{q,q'})\}, & \text{otherwise,} \end{cases}$$

$$\operatorname{reps}(B^+_{q,q'}) := \begin{cases} \{+\infty\}, & \text{if } |B^+_{q,q'}| = \infty; \\ \{\max(B^+_{q,q'})\}, & \text{otherwise,} \end{cases}$$

$$\operatorname{reps}(B^-_{q,q'}) := \{\max(B^-_{q,q'})\}.$$

Since the transition sets are given by finite automata, it can be checked whether they are finite or infinite. The next step is to identify all inequalities which can be completely read in between two states and that only contain extreme coefficients, i.e., members from $\operatorname{reps}(\Lambda)$ and $\operatorname{reps}(B)$ as coefficients and β-values.

Definition 5. *Let* $A = (Q, \Sigma, \delta, q_0, F)$ *be a DFA with* $L(A) \subseteq L_{enc}$. *For every pair of states* $q, q' \in Q$ *we define the* inequality transition set $\Xi_{q,q'}$ *as:*

$$\Xi_{q,q'} = \{s_1 i_1 s_2 i_2 \ldots s_k i_k \le s_b j\$ \mid k \in \mathbb{N}, \exists p_0, \ldots, p_{k+2} : \bigwedge_{\ell=1}^{k} s_\ell i_\ell \in \operatorname{reps}(\Lambda^{s_\ell}_{p_{\ell-1}, p_\ell})$$

$$\wedge p_0 = q \wedge \delta(p_k, \le) = p_{k+1} \wedge s_b j \in \operatorname{reps}(B^{s_b}_{p_{k+1}, p_{k+2}}) \wedge \delta(p_{k+2}, \$) = q'\}.$$

Now we want to pick finitely many representatives for every inequality transition set $\Xi_{q,q'}$. Some sets Ξ contain for every partial solution x an inequality which can be satisfied by an extension of x.[5] For those inequality transition sets, we simply choose \$ as the representative to indicate that this transition set does not participate in the problem as we can always find a satisfiable inequality in it. Two types of inequality transition sets have this property. If $\Xi_{q,q'}$ contains an inequality with an $+\infty$-symbol as β-value, then an inequality with an arbitrary high actual β-value can be read in between q and q'. So, for every value of the left side of the inequality we can read an even larger right side. The other type of Ξ sets are those which contain inequalities with an unbounded number of non-zero coefficients. Recall that the Ξ sets only contain coefficients which are representatives of Λ sets and hence the number of different coefficients in all Ξ sets is finite. Hence, the only reason an Ξ set is infinite is because the number of coefficients in the inequalities can be arbitrarily large. Therefore, those inequality transition sets are exactly the sets which are infinite after we removed all inequalities ending with *more* than $|Q| = n$ consecutive coefficients zero. By removing more than n consecutive coefficients zero from the end of the sum, we ensure that there is a non-zero coefficient under the last n coefficient. If the set is still infinite we can find inequalities with non-zero coefficients with an arbitrary

---

[5] An extension $v' \in \mathbb{Z}^n$ of $v \in \mathbb{Z}^m$ with $n > m$ coincides with v in all positions $i \le m$.

high index. If the modified inequality transition sets are finite, we simply pick the whole set as the set of representatives. Inequalities with more than n consecutive coefficients zero after the last non-zero coefficient can also be ignored, because there is an equivalent inequality with less than n coefficients zero in the inequality transition set. With this considerations in mind, we define for all states $q, q' \in Q$ a set of representatives $\mathrm{reps}(\Xi_{q,q'})$ for the inequality transition set $\Xi_{q,q'}$.

Definition 6. *Let* $L_{Val} := L([+|-]([0|1(0|1)^*]\|\infty))$ *and let* $L_{Trash} := L((L_{Val})^*$ $([+|-]0)^{>n} \le L_{Val}\$)$. *For every inequality transition set* $\Xi_{q,q'}$ *we define*

$$\mathrm{reps}(\Xi_{q,q'}) := \begin{cases} \{\$\}, & \text{if } \exists w \in \Xi_{q,q'} \text{ which ends with } +\infty\$; \\ & \text{or } |\Xi_{q,q'} \backslash L_{Trash}| = \infty; \\ \Xi_{q,q'} \backslash L_{Trash}, & \text{otherwise.} \end{cases}$$

Note that there are only finitely many sets $\mathrm{reps}(\Xi_{q,q'})$ which are by construction all of a finite size.

We will now construct a condensed automaton which will have the finitely many inequalities, chosen as a representative, as its alphabet.

Definition 7. *Let* $A = (Q, \Sigma, \delta, q_0, F)$ *be a deterministic finite automaton with* $L(A) \subseteq L_{enc}$. *We define* $\mathrm{cond}(A) := (Q, \Sigma', \delta', q_0, F)$ *with the alphabet* $\Sigma' = \bigcup_{q,q' \in Q} \mathrm{reps}(\Xi_{q,q'})$ *and* $\delta' = \{(q, \xi, q') \mid \xi \in \mathrm{reps}(\Xi_{q,q'})\}$.

Lemma 12 will show that we only have to consider simple paths in $\mathrm{cond}(A)$.

4   Correctness of the Condensed Automaton

We will now present several lemmas which in the end will prove that $L(A) \cap \mathrm{ILP}_{enc} \neq \emptyset$ if and only if $L'(\mathrm{cond}(A)) \cap \mathrm{ILP}_{enc} \neq \emptyset$. With $L'(\mathrm{cond}(A))$ we refer to the language $L(\mathrm{cond}(A))$ where the wild-cards ∞ are replaced by actual coefficients. First, we will show that it is sufficient to consider only the largest and smallest coefficient which can be read in between two states.

Lemma 8. *Let* $A = (Q, \Sigma, \delta, q_0, F)$ *be a DFA, let* $w \in L(A) \cap \mathrm{ILP}_{enc}$ *with solution* $\boldsymbol{x}$ *and let* α_{ij} *be the j-th coefficient of the i-th inequality of w. Let* $w = w'\alpha_{ij}w''$. *If* $\alpha_{ij} = a_{ij}b_{ij}c_{ij}$, $b_{ij} \neq \varepsilon$, *and* $\delta^*(q_0, w'a_{ij}) = \delta^*(q_0, w'a_{ij}b_{ij})$, *then the following holds:*

1. *Assume* $x_j \ge 0$ *and* α_{ij} *has a $+$ sign. Let w' result from w by replacing α_{ij} with $a_{ij}c_{ij}$. Then* $w' \in L(A) \cap \mathrm{ILP}_{enc}$ *and* $\boldsymbol{x}$ *is a solution for w'.*

2. *Assume* $x_j \ge 0$ *and* α_{ij} *has a $-$ sign. Let w' result from w by replacing α_{ij} with $a_{ij}(b_{ij})^2c_{ij}$. Then* $w' \in L(A) \cap \mathrm{ILP}_{enc}$ *and* $\boldsymbol{x}$ *is a solution for w'.*

3. *Assume* $x_j \le 0$ *and* α_{ij} *has a $+$ sign. Let w' result from w by replacing α_{ij} with $a_{ij}(b_{ij})^2c_{ij}$. Then* $w' \in L(A) \cap \mathrm{ILP}_{enc}$ *and* $\boldsymbol{x}$ *is a solution for w'.*

4. *Assume* $x_j \le 0$ *and* α_{ij} *has a $-$ sign. Let w' result from w by replacing α_{ij} with $a_{ij}c_{ij}$. Then* $w' \in L(A) \cap \mathrm{ILP}_{enc}$ *and* $\boldsymbol{x}$ *is a solution for w'.*

Next, we will focus on whole inequalities and show that restricting the inequalities in words from $L(A)$ to the above defined representatives does not affect the existence of a solvable ILP-instance in $L(A)$. We already explained before Definition 6 that for every solution vector x we can replace the inequalities with an $+\infty$-symbol as β-value by inequalities with actual β-values, which are satisfied by x. With respect to inequality transition sets containing inequalities with arbitrarily large non-zero coefficients, we will show next how to simultaneously replace such inequalities in a way that the replacements are satisfied by an extension of x. So, if the ILP-instance is solvable without inequalities from sets Ξ which are represented by \$-symbols, then we can enlarge the instance and the solution to include those inequalities.

For the next lemma, we want to distinguish the infinite inequality transition sets without an unbounded β-value from the finite ones.

Definition 9.

$$Inf_\Xi := \{\Xi_{q,q'} \mid \mathrm{reps}(\Xi_{q,q'}) = \{\$\} \wedge \Xi_{q,q'} \cap (L(L_{Val}{}^* \leq +\infty\$)) = \emptyset)\}$$
$$Fin_\Xi := \{\Xi_{q,q'} \mid \mathrm{reps}(\Xi_{q,q'}) \neq \{\$\}\}$$

We will now find alternative representatives for the sets in Inf_Ξ such that if an ILP-instance consisting only of inequalities from the sets in Fin_Ξ has a solution x, then we can extend the ILP-instance with any combination of alternative representatives of the sets in Inf_Ξ, such that x can be extended to a solution of the extended ILP-instance (we shall prove this in Lemma 11). This shows that we can ignore inequalities from the sets in Inf_Ξ, i. e., the ones with representative \$.

Definition 10. *Let* $\sigma\colon [|Inf_\Xi|] \to Inf_\Xi$ *be an arbitrary but fixed ordering of the sets in* Inf_Ξ. *Let* $n := |Q|$ *and* $\#_\pm(w)$ *denote the number of signs in an inequality* w. *The function* $\min_{\mathrm{lex}}$ *returns the lexicographical minimal element of a set[6]. For every* $1 \leq i \leq |Inf_\Xi|$ *we define for the inequality transition set* $\sigma(i)$ *in* Inf_Ξ *a set of* alternative representatives arep *as*

$$arep(\sigma(i)) \leftarrow \min_{\mathrm{lex}}(\{w \in \sigma(i) \mid (i+1) \cdot n < \#_\pm(w) \leq (i+2) \cdot n\}).$$

For each fixed i the assignment of $arep(\sigma(i))$ in the above definition can be determined by computing the intersection of two regular sets given by DFAs, yielding a finite language. This finite language can be enumerated in order to find the lexicographical minimal element. The idea is to pick inequalities as alternative representatives which together form a matrix in row echelon form. For every inequality we assign the variable x_k with the highest indexed non-zero coefficient α_k with a value of which magnitude is large enough, such that the summand $\alpha_k x_k$ dominates the inequality. An inequality in the sets of Fin_Ξ can only consist of up to $n = |Q|$ different coefficients. The definition of $arep(\Xi)$

---

[6] The function $\min_{\mathrm{lex}}$ is used to make the definition clear. Any other element of the set could be used as well.

ensures that the representatives of $\Xi \in \mathrm{Inf}_{\Xi}$ contain more coefficients than any representative of the finite inequality transition sets. It also ensures that the number of coefficients contained in the representing inequality is strictly monotonously rising with the order σ. Especially, the index of the highest non-zero coefficient of $arep(\sigma(i+1))$ is higher than the index of the highest non-zero coefficient of $arep(\sigma(i))$.

Lemma 11. *Let w be a solvable ILP-instance consisting only of inequalities from sets in Fin_{Ξ}. Let $\boldsymbol{x}$ be a valid solution of w. Then, for every ILP-instance w' consisting of w and additional inequalities from $\{arep(\Xi) \mid \Xi \in \mathrm{Inf}_{\Xi}\}$ the vector $\boldsymbol{x}$ can be extended to a solution $\boldsymbol{x}'$ of w'.*

Proof. Let $\boldsymbol{x} = (x_1, x_2, \ldots, x_i)$, let m be the number of variables in w', and let $var\text{-}set(\xi)$ be a function returning the variables appearing in the inequality ξ with a non-zero coefficient. Let $coeff(\xi, y_j)$ denote the coefficient of variable y_j in the inequality ξ, let $value(y_j)$ denote the assigned value x_j of the variable y_j, and let $\beta(\xi)$ refer to the right side β of the inequality ξ. Algorithm 1 assigns values to the new variables $y_{i+1}, y_{i+2}, \ldots, y_m$ appearing in w' such that $\boldsymbol{x}' = (x_1, \ldots, x_i, x_{i+1}, \ldots, x_m)$ is a solution of the instance w' and works as follows. We go through the inequalities appearing in w' which have been chosen

---

Algorithm 1. Extending solution $\boldsymbol{x}$ of ILP-instance w to solution $\boldsymbol{x}'$ of w'.

AssignedVars $\leftarrow \{y_1, \ldots, y_i\}$
for $j \leftarrow 1$ to $|\mathrm{Inf}_{\Xi}|$ **do**
    CurIneq $\leftarrow arep(\sigma(j))$,   ToAssign $\leftarrow \emptyset$
    if CurIneq appears in w' **then**
        ToAssign $\leftarrow var\text{-}set(\text{CurIneq}) \backslash$ AssignedVars
        MaxVar $\leftarrow y_k \in$ ToAssign with highest index k
        for all $y \in$ ToAssign$\backslash\{$MaxVar$\}$ **do**
            $value(y) \leftarrow 0$
        end for
        SumOthCoeff $\leftarrow \displaystyle\sum_{y_l \in \{var\text{-}set(\text{CurIneq})\backslash\{\text{MaxVar}\}\}} coeff(\text{CurIneq}, y_l) \cdot value(y_l)$
        CoeffMaxVar $\leftarrow coeff(\text{CurIneq}, \text{MaxVar})$, $b \leftarrow \beta(\text{CurIneq})$
        $value(\text{MaxVar}) \leftarrow |b - \text{SumOthCoeff}| \cdot (-1)\frac{\text{CoeffMaxVar}}{|\text{CoeffMaxVar}|}$
        AssignedVars $\leftarrow$ AssignedVars $\cup$ ToAssign
    end if
end for

---

as alternative representatives for the sets in Inf_{Ξ} in the same order as when we assigned the representatives. Thus, the number of appearing variables per inequality is rising. In every considered inequality, there is at least one variable which has not appeared in the previously considered inequalities. We assign the new variables with a zero value, except for the variable with the highest index. This variable (MaxVar) gets a value which compensates all the other summands in the inequality. The sign of MaxVar is converse to the sign of its coefficient

resulting in a negative summand. We can choose the value of MaxVar freely, since the variable has not appeared in any other inequality we considered earlier. If it appears in any later considered inequality, there will always be at least one new variable in the inequality which has not appeared earlier, and which can again compensate every other summand. It is easy to see that the considered inequality CurIneq is satisfied by the chosen variable assignment. Hence, $x' = (x_1, \ldots, x_i, value(y_{i+1}), \ldots, value(y_m))$ is a solution of the ILP-instance w'.
$\square$

Only simple paths in $\mathrm{cond}(A)$ have to be considered in order to find a solvable ILP-instance in $L'(\mathrm{cond}(A))$.

Lemma 12. *Let* $w, w' \in L_{enc}$ *and* w' *be* w *without an arbitrary inequality* ξ *from* w. *(So,* w' *is* w *with one inequality less.) If* $w \in \mathrm{ILP}_{enc}$ *then* $w' \in \mathrm{ILP}_{enc}$.

We will now show that if there is a solvable ILP-instance in $L'(\mathrm{cond}(A))$, then we can replace any \$-symbols in this instance by actual inequalities, resulting in a solvable ILP-instance in $L(A)$. On the other hand, if there is a solvable ILP-instance in $L(A)$ the modifications we made on A while constructing $\mathrm{cond}(A)$ preserve the existence of a solvable ILP-instance in the obtained language $L'(\mathrm{cond}(A))$.

Theorem 13. *Let* $A = (Q, \Sigma, \delta, q_0, F)$ *be a deterministic finite automaton with* $L(A) \subseteq L_{enc}$. *Then,* $L(A) \cap \mathrm{ILP}_{enc} \neq \emptyset$ *if and only if* $L'(\mathrm{cond}(A)) \cap \mathrm{ILP}_{enc} \neq \emptyset$.

Proof Sketch. Let $w \in L(A) \cap \mathrm{ILP}_{enc}$. We only keep those inequalities in w which are read between some states q and q' on the path labeled with w in A and for which $\Xi_{q,q'} \in \mathrm{Fin}_\Xi$. All other inequalities in w are replaced by \$-symbols. Then, wherever possible we pump the coefficients in w up or down, corresponding to the sign of the associated variable in x until we obtain an ILP-instance w' in $L'(\mathrm{cond}(A))$. It holds that w' is also solvable.

Let $w \in L'(\mathrm{cond}(A)) \cap \mathrm{ILP}_{enc}$. The corresponding ILP-instance in $L(\mathrm{cond}(A))$ only consists of inequalities from Ξ sets in Fin_Ξ or \$-symbols. We first replace all \$-symbols which are representatives of Ξ sets in Inf_Ξ by alternative representatives from Definition 10. According to Lemma 11 the obtained ILP-instance is still solvable. Then, we replace the leftover \$-symbols which are representatives of Ξ sets which contain inequalities with an unbounded β-value. Since we know a solution for the considered ILP-instance, we can pick inequalities with large enough β-value such that the obtained ILP-instance w' is satisfied by an extension of the considered solution. In w' all \$-symbols are replaced by actual inequalities and hence $w' \in L(A)$. As w' is also solvable $L(A) \cap \mathrm{ILP}_{enc} \neq \emptyset$ follows.
$\square$

Now, we are ready to put the pieces together and present our main result. In the following, we give a decision procedure for the int_{Reg}-problem of ILP.

Theorem 14. *The problem* $int_{\mathrm{Reg}}(\mathrm{ILP})$ *is decidable.*

282   P. Wolf

Proof. Since L_{enc} is regular, we can restrict $L(A)$ to the regular language $L(A) \cap L_{\text{enc}}$. Let $A' = (Q, \Sigma, \delta, q_0, F)$ be a deterministic finite automaton with $L(A') = L(A) \cap L_{\text{enc}}$. For the automaton A', the Definitions 3 and 4 describe the construction of coefficient transition sets and assigning their representatives. In Definition 5 inequality transition sets are constructed based on those representatives. These inequality transition sets get representatives themselves in Definition 6. In Definition 7 a new automaton $\text{cond}(A')$ is defined, based on the representatives for the inequality transition sets. All those constructions can be computed by an algorithm. Theorem 13 states that $L(A') \cap \text{ILP}_{\text{enc}} \neq \emptyset \Leftrightarrow L'(\text{cond}(A')) \cap \text{ILP}_{\text{enc}} \neq \emptyset$. Finally, Lemma 12 tells us that if there is a solvable ILP-instance in $L'(\text{cond}(A'))$ at all, then there is a solvable ILP-instance w' in $L'(\text{cond}(A'))$ with a corresponding ILP-instance $w \in L(\text{cond}(A'))$ which can be read on a simple path in $\text{cond}(A')$. The instance w is obtained from w' by replacing coefficients with an absolute value above $3|Q| \cdot (|Q|2^{|Q|})^{2|Q|+4}(1 + 2^{|Q|})$ by ∞-symbols. Since there are only finitely many simple paths in an automaton, and testing a given ILP-instance for solvability can be done in finite time, we can test all words in $L'(\text{cond}(A'))$ which correspond to labels of simple paths in $\text{cond}(A')$ for membership in ILP_{enc} in finite time. Hence, $L(A) \cap \text{ILP}_{\text{enc}} \neq \emptyset$ is decidable. $\square$

5   Conclusion

The number of considered words in $L'(\text{cond}(A))$ is bounded by $2^{\mathcal{O}(|Q|^2 \log(|Q|))}$. The length of considered words in $L(\text{cond}(A))$ regarding the alphabet Σ' of $\text{cond}(A)$ is bounded by $\mathcal{O}(|Q|)$. Finally, the length of considered words regarding the alphabet Σ of A, meaning that we replace \$- and ∞-symbols by actual substrings over Σ, is bounded by $\mathcal{O}(|Q|^7)$. Therefore, we can guess some word in $L'(\text{cond}(A))$ and check its membership in ILP_{enc} by solving the represented ILP-instance. Since ILP is NP-complete $int_{\text{Reg}}(\text{ILP}) \in \text{NP}$ follows. For a given ILP-instance, we can construct a DFA accepting only this instance in polynomial time. Hence $int_{\text{Reg}}(\text{ILP})$ is NP-complete.

According to [19], the presented results are stable under applying a length-preserving morphism to the encoding scheme. The results are also stable under changing the binary encoding to any base-k encoding. Recall that in order to talk about regular sets of problem-instances, we want to have a problem encoding which can be verified by a deterministic finite automaton. In particular, we can not verify with a DFA that all variables appear in a certain inequality or that the inequalities have the same length. Therefore, we have implicitly filled the inequalities with coefficients zero to ensure the same number of variables per inequality. Note that this forbids an explicit matrix representation of an ILP-instance. Instead of referencing the variables of an inequality implicitly by the number and order of the coefficients we could also use another encoding, where we explicitly name the variable and the coefficient. In this setting multiple occurrences of the same variable would be possible and would be interpreted as a summation of terms. Here, we would define transition sets for coefficients and for variables. We would not pump the number of variables in an inequality but instead pump the label of a variable to make it independent of other variables and inequalities. We would still treat the coefficients in the same way and we would also consider only simple paths. In terms of the 'int_{Reg}-techniques' of [23] we would switch from the replacing technique to the separating technique and the int_{Reg}-problem of ILP in this variable-explicit encoding would still be decidable.

Although we considered partial DFAs, the construction also works for partial NFAs. It might be worthwhile to investigate further extensions of $int_{Reg}(\mathrm{ILP})$ such as Boolean combinations of inequalities or quadratic programming.

Acknowledgment. The author thanks Markus L. Schmid for proofreading and helpful discussions and is grateful to the anonymous reviewers for their suggestions. The author was partially supported by DFG (FE 560/9-1).

References

1. Anderson, T., Loftus, J., Rampersad, N., Santean, N., Shallit, J.: Detecting palindromes, patterns and borders in regular languages. Inf. Comput. **207**(11), 1096–1118 (2009). https://doi.org/10.1016/j.ic.2008.06.007
2. Bodlaender, H.L., Heggernes, P., Lokshtanov, D.: Graph modification problems (Dagstuhl seminar 14071). Dagstuhl Rep. **4**(2), 38–59 (2014)
3. Cook, S.A.: The complexity of theorem-proving procedures. In: Harrison, M.A., Banerji, R.B., Ullman, J.D. (eds.) Proceedings of 3rd Annual ACM Symposium on Theory of Computing, STOC 1971, pp. 151–158. ACM, New York (1971)
4. Cormode, G., Muthukrishnan, S.: The string edit distance matching problem with moves. ACM Trans. Algorithms **3**(1), 2:1–2:19 (2007)
5. Eiben, E., Ganian, R., Knop, D., Ordyniak, S.: Unary integer linear programming with structural restrictions. In: Lang, J. (ed.) Proceedings of 27th International Joint Conference on Artificial Intelligence, IJCAI 2018, pp. 1284–1290 (2018)
6. Emde Boas van, P.: The Convenience of Tilings. Lecture Notes in Pure and Applied Mathematics, pp. 331–363. Marcel Dekker Inc., New York (1997)
7. Ganian, R., Ordyniak, S.: The complexity landscape of decompositional parameters for ILP. Artif. Intell. **257**, 61–71 (2018)
8. Gao, X., Xiao, B., Tao, D., Li, X.: A survey of graph edit distance. PAA Pattern Anal. Appl. **13**(1), 113–129 (2010). https://doi.org/10.1007/s10044-008-0141-y
9. Güler, D., Krebs, A., Lange, K.-J., Wolf, P.: Deciding regular intersection emptiness of complete problems for PSPACE and the polynomial hierarchy. In: Klein, S.T., Martín-Vide, C., Shapira, D. (eds.) LATA 2018. LNCS, vol. 10792, pp. 156–168. Springer, Cham (2018). https://doi.org/10.1007/978-3-319-77313-1_12
10. Hladík, M.: Interval linear programming: a survey. In: Mann, Z.A. (ed.) Linear Programming – New Frontiers in Theory and Applications, Chap. 2, pp. 85–120. Nova Science Publishers, New York (2012)
11. Lange, K., Reinhardt, K.: Set automata. In: Combinatorics, Complexity and Logic; Proceeding, DMTCS 1996, pp. 321–329 (1996)
12. Lempitsky, V.S., Kohli, P., Rother, C., Sharp, T.: Image segmentation with a bounding box prior. In: ICCV 2009, pp. 277–284. IEEE Computer Society (2009)
13. Li, H.: Two-view motion segmentation from linear programming relaxation. In: Proceedings of IEEE Computer Society Conference on Computer Vision and Pattern Recognition (CVPR 2007), pp. 1–8. IEEE Computer Society (2007)

14. Liu, Y., Wang, J., Guo, J.: An overview of kernelization algorithms for graph modification problems. Tsinghua Sci. Technol. **19**(4), 346–357 (2014)
15. Rubtsov, A.A.: Regular realizability problems and regular languages. CoRR abs/1503.05879 (2015). http://arxiv.org/abs/1503.05879
16. Rubtsov, A.A., Vyalyi, M.N.: Regular realizability problems and models of a generalized nondeterminism. CoRR abs/1105.5894 (2011). http://arxiv.org/abs/1105.5894
17. Tarasov, S., Vyalyi, M.: Orbits of linear maps and regular languages. In: Kulikov, A., Vereshchagin, N. (eds.) CSR 2011. LNCS, vol. 6651, pp. 305–316. Springer, Heidelberg (2011). https://doi.org/10.1007/978-3-642-20712-9_24
18. Vyalyi, M.N.: On models of a nondeterministic computation. In: Frid, A., Morozov, A., Rybalchenko, A., Wagner, K.W. (eds.) CSR 2009. LNCS, vol. 5675, pp. 334–345. Springer, Heidelberg (2009). https://doi.org/10.1007/978-3-642-03351-3_31
19. Vyalyi, M.N.: On regular realizability problems. Probl. Inf. Transm. **47**(4), 342–352 (2011)
20. Vyalyi, M.N.: On expressive power of regular realizability problems. Probl. Inf. Transm. **49**(3), 276–291 (2013). https://doi.org/10.1134/S0032946013030058
21. Vyalyi, M.N., Rubtsov, A.A.: On regular realizability problems for context-free languages. Probl. Inf. Transm. **51**(4), 349–360 (2015). https://doi.org/10.1134/S0032946015040043
22. Wagner, K., Wechsung, G.: Computational Complexity. Springer, Netherlands (1986)
23. Wolf, P.: Decidability of the regular intersection emptiness problem. Master's thesis, Wilhelm Schickhard Institut für Informatik, Universität Tübingen (2018)

How Does Adiabatic Quantum Computation Fit into Quantum Automata Theory?

Tomoyuki Yamakami[✉]

Faculty of Engineering, University of Fukui, 3-9-1 Bunkyo, Fukui 910-8507, Japan
TomoyukiYamakami@gmail.com

Abstract. Quantum computation has emerged as a powerful computational medium of our time, having demonstrated the efficiency in solving the integer factoring and searching a database faster than any currently known classical computer algorithm. Adiabatic evolution of quantum systems have been studied as a potential means that physically realizes such quantum computation. Up to now, all the research on adiabatic quantum systems has dealt with polynomial time-bounded computation and little attention has been paid to, for example, adiabatic quantum systems consuming only constant memory space. Such quantum systems can be modeled in a form similar to quantum finite automata. This exposition dares to ask a bold question of how to make adiabatic quantum computation fit into the rapidly progressing framework of quantum automata theory. As our answer to this eminent but profound question, we first lay out a basic framework of adiabatic evolutionary quantum systems (AEQSs) with limited computational resources and then establish their close connection to quantum finite automata. We also explore fundamental structural properties of languages solved quickly by such adiabatic evolutionary quantum systems.

Keywords: Adiabatic quantum computation ·
Quantum finite automata · Hamiltonian · Schrödinger equation

1 Motivations and a Quick Overview

1.1 Adiabatic Quantum Computation

Quantum computation has gained large popularity over the past few decades. There are several important milestones to remember in our time. Shor proposed polynomial-time quantum algorithms of factoring a positive integer and computing discrete logarithms whereas Grover presented a quantum way to locate a key in a unstructured database quadratically faster than traditional search algorithms. Basis of such quantum computation has been modeled typically by quantum Turing machines and quantum circuits. See, e.g., [8,10,14].

© IFIP International Federation for Information Processing 2019
Published by Springer Nature Switzerland AG 2019
M. Hospodár et al. (Eds.): DCFS 2019, LNCS 11612, pp. 285–297, 2019.
https://doi.org/10.1007/978-3-030-23247-4_22

In a given quantum system, its quantum state $|\psi(t)\rangle$ evolves according to the Schrödinger equation $i\hbar\frac{d}{dt}|\psi(t)\rangle = H(t)|\psi(t)\rangle$ using a specified time-dependent *Hamiltonian* $H(t)$ (which is simply a Hermitian matrix), where $\hbar$ is the reduced *Planck constant*. In early 2000's, Farhi, Goldstone, Gutmann, and Sipser [6] and Farhi, Goldstone, Gutmann, Lapan, Lundgren, and Preda [5] developed quantum algorithms based on a variant of quantum annealing, called *adiabatic quantum computation*, in which an initial quantum system whose ground state is easily prepared gradually evolves to find a solution represented by a ground state (i.e., an eigenvector of the smallest eigenvalue) of a final quantum system. A crucial point is how fast this evolution takes place. Unfortunately, it turns out that the algorithm of Farhi et al. [5] requires exponential time to execute [4].

Adiabatic quantum computation is dictated by a quadruple $(n, \varepsilon, H_{ini}, H_{fin})$ of two Hamiltonians H_{ini} and H_{fin} of dimension 2^n and a closeness bound ε such that H_{ini}'s ground state is easily prepared and the outcome of the system becomes the ground state of H_{fin} and this ground state is ε-close to the desired solution. Such a quantum system starts with the ground state $|\psi_g(0)\rangle$ of $H(0) = H_{ini}$ at time $t = 0$. If $H(t)$ changes sufficiently slowly, the evolving quantum state $|\psi(t)\rangle$ stays close to the ground state $|\psi_g(t)\rangle$ of $H(t)$. For the efficiency of adiabatic quantum computation, we have concerned with the *evolution time* of the underlying quantum system and the *structural complexity* of two Hamiltonians used in the system. The running time of the system is determined roughly by the evolution time of the system and is basically proportional to the reciprocal of the *spectral gap* of H_{ini} and H_{fin} according to the well-known *adiabatic theorem* [9,11]. See Sect. 2.3.

Later, van Dam, Mosca, and Vazirani [4] gave a detailed analysis of adiabatic quantum computation and presented how to simulate adiabatic quantum computation on quantum circuits. In addition, Aharonov, van Dam, Kemp, Landau, Lloyd, and Regev [1] demonstrated how to simulate quantum circuit computation by adiabatic quantum computation and thus established the (polynomial) equivalence between adiabatic quantum computation and standard quantum computation.

Although adiabatic quantum computation is no more powerful than standard quantum computation, it seems to remain as significant potentials to realize restricted variants of quantum computation. With the current technology, it is still difficult to build a large-scale adiabatic quantum computing device since making local evolution in a large system is quite sensitive to *decoherence*. It is rather better to make global evolution in a small system. It thus remains more realistic to prepare Hamiltonians of adiabatic quantum computation using a memory-restricted quantum device. We may wonder what would happen if we restrict our attention onto a constant-memory model of quantum Turing machine, which is conceptually realized by appropriately modified *quantum finite automata families*. To seek for yet-unearthed potentials of adiabatic quantum computation in such a realistic setting, this exposition intends to make a new, bold step by taking an automata-theoretic approach toward adiabatic quantum computability. Since adiabatic quantum computation follows the gradual evolution between ground states of two Hamiltonians H_{ini} and H_{fin}, the key to the realization of such computation relies on how easily we can build these Hamiltonians. This fact motivates us to consider the circumstances where the matrices are "generated" by memory-restricted device, namely, quantum finite automata. This exposition reports an initial result of our bold attempt to deal with adiabatic quantum computation from a viewpoint of quantum finite automata.

At first glance, since our desired quantum algorithm to solve a given decision problem requires outcomes for one-bit solutions, it seems sufficient for us to prepare either $|1\rangle$ or $|0\rangle$ as a unique ground state of a final Hamiltonian H_{fin}. For such a preparation, however, we should know the solution well ahead of quantum computation. Without knowing any solution of the problem, we might not in general prepare H_{fin} prior to the start of the computation. Farhi et al. [5]'s idea of designing a final Hamiltonian H_{fin} to solve Search-2SAT (i.e., a search version of the satisfiability problem for 2CNF formulas) is to encode a solution of the problem directly into H_{fin} without knowing the solution. In a similar fashion, we want to find a way to prepare H_{fin} without apparently computing any solution to the target problem. This exposition proposes the use of quantum finite automata as a mechanical tool to directly generate Hamiltonians as the automata read input symbols one by one. In this way, we can prepare Hamiltonians even without knowing a solution to a given decision problem.

1.2   Quantum Automata Theory

A quantum finite automaton takes an input string given onto its read-only input tape and, as reading the input symbol one by one, it changes inner states in a quantum manner until it finally terminates. This process can be described by quantum transitions of inner states chosen according to input symbols. The theory of quantum finite automata has been developed significantly since the first installment of quantum finite automata in the 1990s (see, e.g., a survey [3]).

Since a paradigm of adiabatic quantum computation looks quite different from a standard framework of quantum finite automata, we certainly face the following challenging question. Is it possible for us to make adiabatic quantum computation fit into the framework of quantum automata theory?

1.3   An Overview of Main Contributions

This exposition attempts to answer the aforementioned question of how adiabatic quantum computation fits into quantum automata theory.

We need to define a scaled-down model for adiabatic quantum computation, aiming at capturing an essence of such computation in terms of quantum finite automata. For this purpose, we introduce an *adiabatic evolutionary quantum system* (AEQS, pronounced as "eeh-ks") consisting of an input alphabet, a size parameter, a closeness bound, two Hamiltonians for each input, and acceptance/rejection criteria for each input size (whose precise definition will be given in Sect. 2.4).

Lemma 1. *For any language L over an alphabet Σ, there is a series of AEQSs $\{S_x\}_{x \in \tilde{\Sigma}}$ of finite size such that, for any x, S_x computes L(x).*

Although this lemma demonstrates the power of AEQSs, it does not provide us with a constructive mechanism of generating AEQSs.

In this exposition, we are focused on how to prepare two Hamiltonians of AEQSs using variants of quantum finite automata. The way of algorithmic construction of Hamiltonians also adds practicality to our adiabatic quantum computation. After giving the basic notions and notation in Sect. 2, we will demonstrate how to design (or program) AEQSs for several languages (in Proposition 2) in Sect. 3.

Concerning the computational complexity of AEQSs, we wish to further limit the behaviors of AEQSs. To describe the families of decision problems (or equivalently, languages) associated with AEQSs under a set $\mathcal{F}$ of certain "natural" conditions on key ingredients, two Hamiltonians, we use the notation AEQS($\mathcal{F}$). In general, the complexity class AEQS($\mathcal{F}$) is composed of all decision problems (or languages), each of which is solved (or recognized) with "high-accuracy" by a certain AEQS whose Hamiltonians satisfy the conditions specified by $\mathcal{F}$. This helps us discuss various types of conditions, which play essential roles in determining the computational complexity of AEQSs. Of all possible types of conditions, we are focused on the following 4 condition types.

Firstly, we are interested in how to "generate" two Hamiltonians of AEQSs. In particular, we consider the case where those Hamiltonians are generated by certain *one-way quantum quasi-automata families* (abbreviated as 1qqaf's), each 1qqa of which acts as a means to produce a series of *Kraus operators* according to each input symbol so that the product of its adjoint and itself matches the target Hamiltonians (whose precise definition will be given in Sect. 2.2). We use the notation $\mathcal{F} = $ "1qqaf" to denote the use of 1qqaf's to generate Hamiltonians of AEQSs. We also define another condition set $\mathcal{F} = $ "2cqqaf" using *two-way classical-head quantum quasi-automata families* (or 2cqqaf's) in place of 1qqa's. In a similar manner, we define $\mathcal{F} = $ "1qpdqa" to mean the use of *one-way quantum pushdown quasi-automata families* (abbreviated as 1qpdqaf's) induced from a quantum version of pushdown automata.

Secondly, we are concerned with the *(system) size* of AEQSs, where the (system) size of an AEQS is the logarithm of the dimension of its Hamiltonians. We write $\mathcal{F} = $ "constsize" (constant size), $\mathcal{F} = $ "logsize" (logarithmic size), and $\mathcal{F} = $ "linsize" (linear size) to express the sizes of target AEQSs.

Thirdly, we pay attention to the value of the *spectral gap* of a final Hamiltonian of an AEQS, where the spectral gap is the difference between the first and the second smallest eigenvalues. This value provides an upper bound of the runtime of the AEQS. For instance, if the final Hamiltonian of an AEQS have their spectral gap inverse-polynomially large, then the adiabatic evolution of the AEQS takes only polynomially many steps. Notice that, even if Hamiltonians are generated by 1qqa's, there seems a chance that the spectral gap is exponentially small. From this fact, we introduce the notation $\mathcal{F} = $ "polygap" to mean that the spectral gap is at least $1/n^{O(1)}$ (i.e., inverse-polynomially large).

Similarly, $\mathcal{F}$ = "constgap" indicates that the spectral gap is at least $1/O(1)$ (i.e., constantly large).

Fourthly, we look into the *ground energy level* of a final Hamiltonian of an AEQS. In certain cases [5,6], it is possible to set the ground energy of a final Hamiltonian to be 0. This motivates us to define $\mathcal{F}$ = "0-energy" for the situation where the ground energy of a final Hamiltonian is 0 for every input x.

Proposition 2. *Let $\mathbb{N}$ denote the set of all natural numbers. The following statements hold.*

1. *For each fixed string $a \in \{0,1\}^*$, the regular language $L_a = \{ax \mid x \in \{0,1\}^*\}$ is in* AEQS(1qqaf, constsize, constgap).
2. *The reversible unary language L_{even} defined as $L_{even} = \{a^{2n} \mid n \in \mathbb{N}\}$ is in* AEQS(1qqaf, constsize, constgap, 0-energy).
3. *The deterministic context-free language $L_{eq} = \{0^n 1^n \mid n \in \mathbb{N}\}$ is in* AEQS(2cqqaf, logsize, polygap).
4. *The language TRI consists of all strings of the form $w_1 \# w_2 \# w_3$ such that $w_1, w_2, w_3 \in \{0,1\}^*$, $|w_1| = |w_2| = |w_3|$, $(w_1 = w_2^R)$ XOR $(w_1 = w_3^R)$. This language is in* AEQS(1qpdqaf, linsize, polygap).

We show a more general theorem below. 1MOQFA is a language family characterized by bounded-error 1-way measure-once quantum finite automata [12].

Theorem 3. 1MOQFA $\subseteq$ AEQS(1qqa, constsize, constgap, 0-energy).

Next, we target the class REG of all regular languages. If we use 1qqaf's to generate Hamiltonians, then we obtain the following relations.

Theorem 4. REG $\subseteq$ AEQS(1qqaf, linsize, constgap, 0-energy).

We further explore structural properties of AEQS($\mathcal{F}$). A language family $\mathcal{L}$ is said to be *closed under* a binary operation $\circ$ if, for any two languages $L_1, L_2 \in \mathcal{L}$, $L_1 \circ L_2$ also belongs to $\mathcal{L}$. We say that $\mathcal{F}$ *allows a swap of acceptance/rejection criteria* if the new AEQS obtained from any given AEQS satisfying $\mathcal{F}$ by exchanging its $S_{acc}^{(n)}$ and $S_{rej}^{(n)}$ also satisfies $\mathcal{F}$, where $S_{acc}^{(n)}$ and $S_{rej}^{(n)}$ respectively denote sets of indices providing criteria for acceptance and rejection of ground states. Additionally, we say that $\mathcal{F}$ *allows the amplification of accuracy* if, for any AEQS satisfying $\mathcal{F}$ and any constant $c > 0$, there always exists another computationally-equivalent AEQS with $\mathcal{F}$ whose accuracy is at least c times as high as the original AEQS's.

Proposition 5. *Let $\mathcal{F}$ be any nonempty set of conditions. Each of the following statements holds.*

1. AEQS($\mathcal{F}$) *is closed under complementation if $\mathcal{F}$ allows a swap of acceptance/rejection criteria.*
2. AEQS($\mathcal{F}$) *is closed under XOR if $\mathcal{F}$ allows the amplification of accuracy.*

This exposition is merely the initial attempt to expand the scope of adiabatic quantum computability and to relate it to quantum finite automata using the new notion of AEQSs. We expect that this exposition marks the beginning of a series of exciting research works, aiming at the deeper understanding of adiabatic quantum computation.

2 Preparations: Notions and Notation

2.1 Numbers, Vectors, and Matrices

The notation $\mathbb{N}$ expresses the set of all *natural numbers* (that is, nonnegative integers) and we set $\mathbb{N}^+ = \mathbb{N} - \{0\}$. Given two integers m, n with $m \leq n$, the *integer interval* $[m, n]_{\mathbb{Z}}$ is the set $\{m, m+1, m+2, \ldots, n\}$, which is compared to a real interval $[a, b]$. Let $\mathbb{C}$ denote the set of all *complex numbers*; in particular, we set $\imath = \sqrt{-1}$. All *polynomials* are assumed to have nonnegative integer coefficients and all *logarithms* are taken to the base 2.

We deal with finite-dimensional Hilbert spaces. To express (column) vectors of such a space, we use Dirac's notation $|\cdot\rangle$. A *density operator* (or a density matrix) expresses a mixed quantum state. Given a complex matrix A, $A^\dagger$ indicates the complex conjugate transpose of A. For any matrix A and its index pair (q, r), the notation $A[q, r]$ indicates the (q, r)-entry of A. Similarly, for a vector v, $v[i]$ denotes the ith entry of v. Given any square complex matrix A, the notation e^A expresses a *matrix exponential* defined by $e^A = \sum_{k=0}^{\infty} \frac{1}{k!} A^k$ (where $0! = 1$ and $A^0 = I$) and the *spectral norm* $\|A\|$ is defined by $\|A\| = \max_{|\phi\rangle \neq 0}\{\frac{\||A|\phi\rangle\|_2}{\||\phi\rangle\|_2}\}$, where $\|\cdot\|_2$ indicates the ℓ_2-norm. For a number $\varepsilon \in [0, 1]$ and for two vectors v_1 and v_2 in the same Hilbert space, we say that v_1 is ε-*close to* v_2 if $\|v_1 - v_2\|_2 \leq \varepsilon$. The *commutator* $[A, B]$ of square matrices A and B is defined as $AB - BA$.

We use the notation W for the *Walsh-Hadamard transform*. For convenience, we write $|\hat{a}\rangle = W|a\rangle$ for any $a \in \{0, 1\}$. The *Hadamard basis* is $\{|\hat{0}\rangle, |\hat{1}\rangle\}$ and the *computational basis* is $\{|0\rangle, |1\rangle\}$.

A *Hamiltonian* is a complex Hermitian matrix. For any Hamiltonian H, we set $\Delta(H)$ to be the *spectral gap* of H, which is the difference between the lowest eigenvalue and the second lowest eigenvalue of H. The lowest eigenvalue is called the *ground energy* of H and its eigenvector is called the *ground state* of H.

2.2 Languages and Quantum Quasi-Automata

An *alphabet* is a finite nonempty set of "symbols" or "letters." A *string* over an alphabet Σ is a finite sequence of symbols in Σ. The *length* of a string x is the total number of symbols in x and is denoted by $|x|$. In particular, the *empty string* has length 0 and is denoted by λ. The notation Σ^* stands for the set of all strings over Σ. A *language* over Σ is a subset of Σ^*. Hereafter, we freely identify a decision problem with its associated language.

A *one-way quantum finite automaton*[1] (abbreviated as a 1qfa) *with mixed states and quantum operations* M is a septuple $(Q, \Sigma, \{\cent, \$\}, \{A_\sigma\}_{\sigma \in \check{\Sigma}},$

---

[1] This model is called general quantum finite automata in a survey [3].

q_0, Q_{acc}, Q_{rej}), where Q is a finite set of inner states, Σ is an (input) alphabet, $\xcent$ and $\$$ are respectively the *left endmarker* and the *right endmarker*, $\check{\Sigma} = \Sigma \cup \{\xcent, \$\}$, and each A_σ is a *quantum operation*[2] acting on the Hilbert space of linear operators on the *configuration space* spanned by the basis vectors $\{|q\rangle \mid q \in Q\}$ [2,7,15]. Such a quantum operation A_σ has a Kraus representation with *Kraus operators* (or operation elements) $\{A_{\sigma,j}\}_{j \in [k]}$ for a certain constant $k \in \mathbb{N}^+$. More precisely, A_σ takes the form $A_\sigma(H) = \sum_{j=1}^{k} A_{\sigma,j} H A_{\sigma,j}^\dagger$ for any linear operator H and satisfies the completeness relation $\sum_{j=1}^{k} A_{\sigma,j}^\dagger A_{\sigma,j} = I$. In particular, when $k = 1$, we identify $A_{\sigma,1}$ with A_σ and then obtain $A_\sigma(H) = A_\sigma H A_\sigma^\dagger$. Given strings $y_1, y_2, \cdots, y_k$ in $\check{\Sigma}$, we abbreviate a matrix multiplication $A_{y_k} \cdot A_{y_{k-1}} \cdots A_{y_2} \cdot A_{y_1}$ as $A_{y_1 y_2 \cdots y_{k-1} y_k}$. Given a language L, M *recognizes* with error probability at most ε if, for any $x \in L$, $\mathrm{tr}(P_{acc} A_{\xcent x \$}(\rho_0)) \geq 1 - \varepsilon$ and, for any $x \notin L$, $\mathrm{tr}(P_{rej} A_{\xcent x \$}(\rho_0)) \geq 1 - \varepsilon$, where $\rho_0 = |q_0\rangle\langle q_0|$ and P_{acc} and P_{rej} are projections onto the spaces spanned by $\{|q\rangle \mid q \in Q_{acc}\}$ and by $\{|q\rangle \mid q \in Q_{rej}\}$, respectively. This model is in essence equivalent to a *garbage-tape model* used in [16]. In contrast, a *one-way measure-once quantum finite automaton* (or a 1moqfa) applies only unitary operators until it reads $\$$. The *state complexity* of a finite automaton is the total number of inner states of the automaton. We write 1MOQFA and $1QFA_{mix}$ to denote the collections of all languages recognized respectively by bounded-error 1moqfa's and bounded-error 1qfa's with mixed states and quantum operators.

We attempt to run quantum finite automata to produce Hamiltonians, which are necessary to carry out adiabatic quantum computation. For this purpose, we need to modify the aforementioned model of 1qfa's so that they can produce "matrices." A *one-way quantum quasi-automata family* (or a 1qqaf, for short) is a family of 1qqa's equipped with mixed states and quantum operations with no use of initial state and final state. More formally, a 1qqaf $\mathcal{M} = \{M_n\}_{n \in \mathbb{N}}$ is a family $\{(Q^{(n)}, \Sigma, \{\xcent, \$\}, \{A_\sigma^{(n)}\}_{\sigma \in \check{\Sigma}}, \Lambda_0^{(n)})\}_{n \in \mathbb{N}}$, where each $A_\sigma^{(n)}$ is a quantum operation on the Hilbert space of linear operators on the configuration space and $\Lambda_0^{(n)}$ is a Hermitian operator acting on the same space. The nth machine M_n can produce a matrix $A_{\xcent x \$}^{(n)}$ for any given input $x \in \Sigma^n$. Notice that $A_{\xcent x \$}^{(n)}(B)$ is a Hermitian matrix for any Hermitian B. From this fact, we say that a family $\{H^{(n)}\}_{n \in \mathbb{N}}$ of Hamiltonians is *generated by a 1qqaf* $\mathcal{M}$ if $H^{(n)}$ coincides with $A_{\xcent x \$}^{(n)}(\Lambda_0)$ for every index $n \in \mathbb{N}$.

As a natural extension of 1qqa's, in a model of *2-way classical-head quantum quasi-automata family* (or 2cqqaf), when a two-way tape head reads an input symbol σ, firstly we use a deterministic procedure to apply either a quantum operation A_σ to or a projection measurement on a finite quantum register and, secondly we deterministically move the tape head; in the case of a measurement, we utilize a result of the measurement as well.

Similarly to [13], a *1-way quantum pushdown quasi-automata family* (or a 1qpdqaf) is a family of 1-way quantum quasi-automata equipped with a stack in which we can push and pop stack symbols as an input tape head reads input symbols.

---

[2] This is a completely positive, trace preserving map and is also called a *superoperator*.

2.3   Adiabatic Evolution of a Quantum System

Loosely following [6], we briefly discuss how a quantum system evolves according to the Schrödinger equation of the following general form: $i\hbar\frac{d}{dt}|\psi(t)\rangle = H(t)|\psi(t)\rangle$ for a time-dependent Hamiltonian $H(t)$ and a time-dependent quantum state $|\psi(t)\rangle$. To carry out adiabatic quantum computation, we prepare two Hamiltonians H_{ini} and H_{fin} acting on the same Hilbert space and, for a sufficiently large constant $T > 0$, we define $H(t) = \left(1 - \frac{t}{T}\right)H_{ini} + \frac{t}{T}H_{fin}$ for a time parameter $t \in [0, T]$, provided that $[H_{ini}, H_{fin}] \neq 0$. To ensure $[H_{ini}, H_{fin}] \neq 0$, we often use the *Hadamard basis* for H_{ini} and the *computational basis* for H_{fin} [5].

At time $t = 0$, we assume that the quantum system is initialized to be the ground state $|\psi_g(0)\rangle$ of H_{ini}. We allow the system to gradually evolve by applying $H(t)$ *discretely* from time $t = 0$ to $t = T$. Let $|\psi(t)\rangle$ denote the quantum state at time $t \in [0, T]$. This evolutionary process is referred to as an *adiabatic evolution according to H for T steps*. We take the smallest value T for which $|\psi(T)\rangle$ is ε-close to the ground state of H_{fin}. For convenience, we call this T the *minimum evolution time* of the system. The *runtime* of the system is then defined to be $T \cdot \max_{t \in [0,T]} \|H(t)\|$ and the *outcome* of the system is the quantum state $|\psi(T)\rangle$. The *adiabatic theorem* [9,11] gives a lower bound on T. The following assertion is taken from [1]. For any constant $\delta > 0$, if $T \geq \Omega\left(\frac{\|H_{fin} - H_{ini}\|^{1+\delta}}{\varepsilon^\delta \min_{t \in [0,T]}\{\Delta(H(t))^2 + \delta\}}\right)$, then $|\psi(T)\rangle$ (with an appropriately chosen *global phase*) is ε-close to the ground state of H_{fin}, provided that $H(t)$ has a unique ground state for each value $t \in [0, T]$.

For a practical simulation of the system, it is useful to consider a refinement of the time intervals. Let R be a fixed number satisfying $T \ll R$ and consider a refined time interval of $[\frac{jT}{R}, \frac{(j+1)T}{R}]$ for each index $j \in [0, R-1]_{\mathbb{Z}}$.

Lemma 6. *Given a quantum system* $(n, \varepsilon, H_{ini}, H_{fin})$ *of adiabatic evolution, let T be the minimum evolution time. Let U_T denote a unitary matrix satisfying $|\psi(T)\rangle = U_T|\psi(0)\rangle$. Let R be a number with $T \ll R$. Let $\alpha_j = \frac{1}{\hbar}\frac{T}{R}\left(1 - \frac{2j+1}{2R}\right)$ and $\beta_j = \frac{1}{\hbar}\frac{T}{R}\frac{2j+1}{2R}$ for each index $j \in [0, R-1]_{\mathbb{Z}}$. It then follows that U_T can be approximated by the matrix $V_R = \left(e^{-i\alpha_R H_{ini}} \cdot e^{-i\beta_R H_{fin}}\right) \cdots \left(e^{-i\alpha_1 H_{ini}} \cdot e^{-i\beta_1 H_{fin}}\right)$.*

2.4   Adiabatic Evolutionary Quantum Systems

Our major target of this exposition is decision problems (or equivalently, languages). Instead of searching solutions as in [5], we are asked to determine "acceptance" (yes) or "rejection" (no) of any given input string. Let us define our quantum systems that evolve adiabatically. Since adiabatic quantum computation is dictated by the ground states of an initial Hamiltonian and a final Hamiltonian, we thus need to specify these Hamiltonians for each given input.

We loosely adapt the definition of Aharonov et al. [1] but modify it significantly to match our purpose. First of all, we wish to realize adiabatic quantum computation by a new notion of an *adiabatic evolutionary quantum system* (or an AEQS, pronounced as "eeh-ks"). An AEQS S is a septuple $(m, \Sigma, \{H_{ini}^{(x)}\}_{x \in \Sigma^*}, \{H_{fin}^{(x)}\}_{x \in \Sigma^*}, \{S_{acc}^{(n)}\}_{n \in \mathbb{N}}, \{S_{rej}^{(n)}\}_{n \in \mathbb{N}})$, where $m : \Sigma^* \to \mathbb{N}$ is a size function, Σ is an (input) alphabet, both $H_{ini}^{(x)}$ and $H_{fin}^{(x)}$ are Hamiltonians acting on the same Hilbert space of $2^{m(x)}$ dimension (where this space is referred to as the system's *evolution space*), and $S_{acc}^{(n)}$ and $S_{rej}^{(n)}$ are sets of indices representing acceptance and rejection (where each pair $(S_{acc}^{(n)}, S_{rej}^{(n)})$ is called an *(acceptance/rejection) criteria pair*). The function $m(x)$ is particularly called the *(system) size* of $\mathcal{S}$, expressing how large the evolution space is.

An evolution process of an AEQS can be described as in Sect. 2.3. Letting T_x indicate the minimum evolution time of this system, we define $H^{(x)}(t)$ to be $\left(1 - \frac{t}{T_x}\right) H_{ini}^{(x)} + \frac{t}{T_x} H_{fin}^{(x)}$ for any real number $t \in [0, T_x]$. At time $t = 0$, the AEQS is initialized to be the ground state $|\psi_g(0)\rangle$ of $H^{(x)}(0)$ $(= H_{ini}^{(x)})$. The system slowly evolves by applying $H^{(x)}(t)$ discretely from time $t = 0$ to $t = T_x$. The AEQS is considered to take the runtime of $T_x \cdot \max_{t \in [0, T_x]} \|H^{(x)}(t)\|$.

To solve a mathematical problem using the adiabatic evolution of a quantum system, following [5], we may assume that $H_{ini}^{(x)} = \sum_{u \in S_0^{(x)}} h(u)|u\rangle\langle u|$, where $S_0^{(x)}$ is the set of all indices for which $|u\rangle$ are eigenvectors of $H_{ini}^{(x)}$ and $h(u)$ is a real value associated with $|u\rangle$. The ground state $|\psi_g(0)\rangle$ of $H_{ini}^{(x)}$ is $|u_0\rangle$ if u_0 satisfies that $u_0 \in S_0^{(x)}$ and $h(u_0) = \min\{h(u) \mid u \in S_0^{(x)}\}$.

To work on decision problems, in particular, we need to specify *accepting and rejecting quantum states* in the evolution space on which $H^{(x)}(t)$ acts. This can be done by incorporating the two sets $S_{acc}^{(n)}$ and $S_{rej}^{(n)}$. We define $QS_{acc}^{(n)}$ and $QS_{rej}^{(n)}$ respectively to be the Hilbert spaces spanned by $\{|u\rangle \mid u \in S_{acc}^{(n)}\}$ and $\{|u\rangle \mid u \in S_{rej}^{(n)}\}$. We call $QS_{acc}^{(n)}$ and $QS_{rej}^{(n)}$ the *accepting space* and the *rejecting space*, respectively.

To determine the outcome of an AEQS, we want to design the AEQS to make the ground state of $H_{fin}^{(x)}$ sufficiently "close" to a certain accepting or rejecting quantum state, which belongs to $QS_{acc}^{(m(x))} \cup QS_{rej}^{(m(x))}$. The closeness of the ground state of $H_{fin}^{(x)}$ to such a quantum state corresponds to the *accuracy* of the AEQS to the desired solution of a decision problem on each input x.

Definition 7. *Given a decision problem L and any constant $\varepsilon \in [0, 1]$, we say that an AEQS $\mathcal{S} = (m, \Sigma, \{H_{ini}^{(x)}\}_{x \in \Sigma^*}, \{H_{fin}^{(x)}\}_{x \in \Sigma^*}, \{S_{acc}^{(n)}\}_{n \in \mathbb{N}}, \{S_{rej}^{(n)}\}_{n \in \mathbb{N}})$ solves (or recognizes) L with accuracy at least ε if (i) for each input $x \in \Sigma^*$, there exists a unique ground state $|\psi_g(0)\rangle$ of $H_{ini}^{(x)}$, (ii) for any string $x \in L$, the ground state of $H_{fin}^{(x)}$ is $\sqrt{2}(1 - \varepsilon)$-close to a certain quantum state in $QS_{acc}^{(m(x))}$, and (iii) for any string $x \in \Sigma^* - L$, the ground state of $H_{fin}^{(x)}$ is $\sqrt{2}(1 - \varepsilon)$-close to a certain quantum state in $QS_{rej}^{(m(x))}$. The adiabatic quantum size complexity of L is $m(x)$, where "x" expresses a "symbolic" input.*

Proof Sketch of Lemma 1. Let Σ be any alphabet and let L be any language over Σ. For each fixed string $x \in \Sigma^*$, we define an AEQS $\mathcal{S}_x$ as follows: $H_{ini}^{(x)} = |-\rangle\langle-|$ and $H_{fin}^{(x)} = |\overline{L}(x)\rangle\langle\overline{L}(x)|$, where $|-\rangle = \frac{1}{\sqrt{2}}(|0\rangle - |1\rangle)$ and $\overline{L}(x) = 1 - L(x)$

for every input $x \in \Sigma^*$ and $L(x)$ is the characteristic function of L. Note that the ground state of $H_{ini}^{(x)}$ is $|+\rangle = \frac{1}{\sqrt{2}}(|0\rangle + |1\rangle)$ and that of $H_{fin}^{(x)}$ is $|L(x)\rangle$. It then follows that $x \in L$ iff $\mathcal{S}_x$ outputs $L(x)$. The accuracy of $\mathcal{S}_x$ thus turns out to be 1. □

We consider a complexity class of decision problems solved by certain AEQSs.

Definition 8. *Let $\mathcal{F}$ indicate a set of conditions imposed on Hamiltonians. The complexity class,* highly-accurate AEQS($\mathcal{F}$), *is the collection of all languages, each of which is recognized by a certain AEQS on each input with accuracy at least an absolute constant $\varepsilon \in (\hat{\alpha}, 1]$ and Hamiltonians of the AEQS satisfy the conditions specified by $\mathcal{F}$, where $\hat{\alpha} = 1 - \sqrt{1 - 1/\sqrt{2}}$. Since we discuss only highly-accurate AEQS's in the subsequent sections, we often drop the prefix "highly-accurate" and simply call them AEQS's.*

As an example, we may use $\mathcal{F}$ to specify a type of quantum quasi-automata, such as 1qqa's. We may also use $\mathcal{F}$ to refer to the condition that the spectral gaps of Hamiltonians are at most the reciprocal of a certain polynomial. By the adiabatic theorem, this condition ensures that the corresponding AEQSs run for polynomially many steps.

One of the difficulties that we face in constructing an AEQS is how to prepare its Hamiltonians, in particular, $H_{fin}^{(x)}$ and to define (acceptance/rejection) criteria pairs $(S_{acc}^{(n)}, S_{rej}^{(n)})$. In this exposition, we relate AEQSs to 1qqaf's. Since AEQSs are dictated by Hamiltonians, we say that an AEQS $\mathcal{S}$ is *generated by 1qqaf's* if (1) there exist two 1qqaf's $\mathcal{M}_0$ and $\mathcal{M}_1$ such that $H_{ini}^{(x)}$ and $H_{fin}^{(x)}$ are generated respectively by $\mathcal{M}_0$ and $\mathcal{M}_1$ for each input $x \in \Sigma^*$, and (2) $S_{acc}^{(i)} = S_{acc}^{(j)}$ and $S_{rej}^{(i)} = S_{rej}^{(j)}$ for any pair $i, j \in \mathbb{N}$. We can expand this definition to 2cqqaf's and 1qpdqaf's. Possibly, we can relax Condition (2) by requiring a certain one-way reversible finite automaton (or 1rfa) to determine whether or not "q is in $S_{acc}^{(n)}$" (as well as "q is in $S_{rej}^{(n)}$") from inputs of the form $(1^n, q)$.

In the subsequent section, we will demonstrate how to design (or program) AEQSs for the simple languages given in Proposition 2.

3   How to Program AEQSs: Proof of Proposition 2

In what follows, we will demonstrate only (1)–(2) of Proposition 2.

(1) We want to construct the desired AEQS for the language $L_a = \{ax \mid x \in \{0,1\}^*\}$ for each fixed string $a \in \{0,1\}^*$. Here, we consider only the simplest case where $a = 0$. Write Σ for $\{0,1\}$ for simplicity.

Our goal is to construct $H_{ini}^{(x)} = W_3 \mathrm{diag}(0, 1, 1) W_3^{\dagger}$, $H_{fin}^{(0y)} = \mathrm{diag}(1, 3/4, 1/4)$, and $H_{fin}^{(1y)} = \mathrm{diag}(1, 1/4, 3/4)$ using 1qqa's, where W_3 is an appropriate 3×3 unitary matrix forcing the condition $[H_{ini}^{(x)}, H_{fin}^{(x)}] \neq 0$. Since the ground energy of $H_{fin}^{(x)}$ is $1/4$, it follows that the spectral gap is $\frac{3}{4} - \frac{1}{4} = \frac{1}{2}$.

To generate the Hamiltonian $H_{fin}^{(x)}$, we need to define an appropriate 1qqa. Let $m(x) = |x|$, $Q = \{q_\phi, q_0, q_1\}$, $S_{acc}^{(|x|)} = \{q_1\}$ and $S_{rej}^{(|x|)} = \{q_0\}$. We choose $\Lambda_0 = |q_0\rangle\langle q_0| + |q_1\rangle\langle q_1|$. We further define Kraus operators $\{A_{\sigma,i}\}_{\sigma\in\check{\Sigma}, i\in[5]}$ as follows. Let $A_{\phi,1}|q_\phi\rangle = |q_\phi\rangle$, $A_{\phi,2}|q_0\rangle = \frac{1}{\sqrt{2}}|q_\phi\rangle$, $A_{\phi,3}|q_0\rangle = \frac{1}{\sqrt{2}}|q_0\rangle$, $A_{\phi,4}|q_1\rangle = \frac{1}{\sqrt{2}}|q_\phi\rangle$, $A_{\phi,5}|q_1\rangle = \frac{1}{\sqrt{2}}|q_1\rangle$, and $A_{\$,i} = A_{\phi,i}$. Moreover, let $A_{0,1}|q_\phi\rangle = |q_0\rangle$, $A_{0,2}|q_0\rangle = |q_0\rangle$, $A_{0,3}|q_1\rangle = |q_1\rangle$, $A_{1,1}|q_\phi\rangle = |q_1\rangle$, $A_{1,2} = A_{0,2}$, and $A_{1,3} = A_{0,3}$. For all other pairs $(\sigma, i) \in \check{\Sigma} \times [5]$, let $A_{\sigma,i}|q\rangle = 0$. It then follows that $\sum_{i=1}^{5} A_{\sigma,i}^{\dagger} A_{\sigma,i} = I$ for any $\sigma \in \check{\Sigma}$. It is not difficult to show that $A_{\phi 0y\$}(\Lambda_0) = H_{fin}^{(0y)}$ and $A_{\phi 1y\$}(\Lambda_0) = H_{fin}^{(1y)}$.

(2) Next, we are focused on the reversible unary language $L_{even} = \{a^{2n} \mid n \in \mathbb{N}\}$. Let $m(x) = |x|$, $Q = \{q_0, q_1, q_2\}$, $S_{acc}^{(|x|)} = \{q_1\}$, and $S_{rej}^{(|x|)} = \{q_2\}$. Let $U_\phi|q_0\rangle = |q_1\rangle$, $U_\phi|q_1\rangle = |q_0\rangle$, $U_\phi|q_2\rangle = |q_2\rangle$, and $U_\$ = I$. Moreover, let $U_a|q_0\rangle = |q_0\rangle$, $U_a|q_1\rangle = |q_2\rangle$, and $U_a|q_2\rangle = |q_1\rangle$. It then follows that, for any input $x \in \{a\}^*$, $U_{\phi x\$}|q_0\rangle = |q_1\rangle$ if $x \in L_{even}$ and $U_{\phi x\$}|q_0\rangle = |q_2\rangle$ if $x \notin L_{even}$. Let us define $H_{fin}^{(x)} = U_{\phi x\$}\Lambda_0 U_{\phi x\$}^{\dagger}$, where $\Lambda_0 = \sum_{q\in Q-\{q_0\}} |q\rangle\langle q|$. Since $U_{\phi x\$}|q_1\rangle = |q_0\rangle$ and $U_{\phi x\$}|q_2\rangle = |q_2\rangle$ if $x \in L_{even}$, and $|q_1\rangle$ otherwise, it follows that $H_{fin}^{(x)} = |q_0\rangle\langle q_0| + \overline{L}_{even}(x)|q_1\rangle\langle q_1| + L_{even}(x)|q_2\rangle\langle q_2|$, where $L_{even}(x)$ is the characteristic function of L_{even} and $\overline{L}_{even}(x) = 1 - L_{even}(x)$. The ground state of $H_{fin}^{(x)}$ thus becomes $|q_1\rangle$ if $x \in L_{even}$, and $|q_2\rangle$ otherwise. Therefore, we obtain $\Delta(H_{fin}^{(x)}) = 1$. Note that the ground energy is 0.

4   Basic Simulations Between QFAs and AEQSs

4.1   Proof of Theorem 3

Aharonov et al. [1] demonstrated how to simulate quantum circuits by adiabatic quantum computation with polynomial overhead. Our concern here is the AEQSs of constant size, and thus our situation significantly differs from their's.

Proof Sketch of Theorem 3. We intend to show that 1MOQFA $\subseteq$ AEQS(1qqaf, constsize, constgap, 0-energy). Let $L \in$ 1MOQFA and choose a 1moqfa $M = (Q, \Sigma, \{\phi, \$\}, \{U_\sigma\}_{\sigma\in\check{\Sigma}}, q_0, Q_{acc}, Q_{rej})$ for L with error probability at most ε for a certain constant $\varepsilon \in [0, 1/2)$. For simplicity, we assume that $|Q|$ is of the form 2^{k_0} for a certain constant $k_0 \in \mathbb{N}^+$ and that all elements in Q are expressed as k_0-bit strings. Let $\rho_0 = |q_0\rangle\langle q_0|$ and $\rho_{i+1} = U_{x_i}\rho_i U_{x_i}^{\dagger}$ for each $i \in [0, n+1]_{\mathbb{Z}}$, where x_i denotes the $(i + 1)$th symbol of $\phi x\$$. Let P_{acc} and P_{rej} be two projections onto the Hilbert spaces H_{acc} and H_{rej} spanned by $\{|q\rangle \mid q \in Q_{acc}\}$ and $\{|q\rangle \mid q \in Q_{rej}\}$, respectively. Note that, for any $x \in L$, $\text{tr}(P_{acc}\rho_{n+2}) \geq 1 - \varepsilon$ and, for any $x \notin L$, $\text{tr}(P_{rej}\rho_{n+2}) \geq 1 - \varepsilon$.

Our goal is to show how to simulate M by a suitable AEQS. We define $H_{ini}^{(x)}$ and $H_{fin}^{(x)}$ of the desired AEQS as $H_{ini}^{(x)} = W^{\otimes k_0}\Lambda_0 W^{\otimes k_0}$ and $H_{fin}^{(x)} = U_{\phi x\$}\Lambda_0 U_{\phi x\$}^{\dagger}$, where $\Lambda_0 = \sum_{q\in Q-\{q_0\}} |q\rangle\langle q|$.

For each $x \in \Sigma^*$, let $|\phi_x\rangle = U_{\xi x \$}|q_0\rangle$. By the definition of $H_{fin}^{(x)}$, $|\phi_x\rangle$ is its ground state because $H_{fin}^{(x)}|\phi_x\rangle = U_{\xi x \$}\Lambda U_{\xi x \$}^{\dagger}U_{\xi x \$}|q_0\rangle = U_{\xi x \$}\Lambda|q_0\rangle = 0$. Note that, if $x \in L$, then $\|P_{acc}|\phi_x\rangle\|^2 \geq 1 - \varepsilon$. This implies that there is a vector $|\phi_{acc}\rangle \in H_{acc}$ such that $|\langle\phi_{acc}|\phi_x\rangle|^2 \geq 1 - \varepsilon$. We then obtain $\||\phi_x\rangle - |\phi_{acc}\rangle\|^2 \leq 1 - |\langle\phi_{acc}|\phi_x\rangle|^2 \leq \varepsilon$. Hence, $|\phi_x\rangle$ is $\sqrt{\varepsilon}$-close to $|\phi_{acc}\rangle$. Thus, the accuracy is more than $\hat{\alpha}$ (defined earlier). A similar argument handles the case of $x \notin L$.

Next, we consider nonzero eigenvalues of $H_{fin}^{(x)}$. Let $|\psi_q\rangle = U_{\xi x \$}|q\rangle$ for each $q \in Q$. It then follows that $U_{\xi x \$}\Lambda_0 U_{\xi x \$}^{\dagger} = \sum_{q \in Q-\{q_0\}}(U_{\xi x \$}|q\rangle\langle q|U_{\xi x \$}^{\dagger}) = \sum_{q \in Q-\{q_0\}}|\psi_q\rangle\langle\psi_q|$. Since $U_{\xi x \$}$ is unitary, $\{|\psi_q\rangle\}_{q \in Q-\{q_0\}}$ consists of all nonzero eigenvectors and they must be 1. Therefore, the spectral gap of $H_{fin}^{(x)}$ is 1.   □

4.2   Proof of Theorem 4

Finally, we are ready to describe the proof of Theorem 4. This proof is composed of two critical simulations between AEQSs and 1qfa's with mixed states and quantum operators. Since REG = 1QFA$_{mix}$, it suffices to simulate such a 1qfa by an appropriately chosen AEQS.

Lemma 9. *Any 1qfa M with mixed states and quantum operations can be exactly simulated by a certain AEQS whose Hamiltonians are generated by certain linear-size 1qqaf's with the spectral gap of 1 and the ground energy of 0.*

Proof of Theorem 4. Let L be any regular language. Take a 1qfa M with mixed states and quantum operators that recognizes L with bounded-error probability. By Lemma 9, there exists an AEQS S that simulates M.   □

References

1. Aharonov, D., van Dam, W., Kemp, J., Landau, Z., Lloyd, S., Regev, O.: Adiabatic quantum computation is equivalent to standard quantum computation. SIAM J. Comput. **37**(1), 166–194 (2007). https://doi.org/10.1137/S0097539705447323
2. Ambainis, A., Beaudry, M., Golovkins, M., Çikusts, A., Mercer, M., Thérien, D.: Algebraic results on quantum automata. Theory Comput. Syst. **39**, 165–188 (2006). https://doi.org/10.1007/s00224-005-1263-x
3. Ambainis, A., Yakaryilmaz, A.S.: Automata and quantum computing. CoRR abs/1507.01988 (2015). https://arxiv.org/abs/1507.01988
4. Dam van, W., Mosca, M., Vazirani, U.: How powerful is adiabatic quantum computation? In: Proceedings of 42nd Annual Symposium on Foundations of Computer Science, FOCS 2001, pp. 279–287. IEEE Computer Society (2001). https://doi.org/10.1109/SFCS.2001.959902
5. Farhi, E., Goldstone, J., Gutmann, S., Lapan, J., Lundgren, A., Preda, D.: A quantum evolution algorithm applied to random instances of an NP-complete problem. Science **292**, 472–476 (2001). https://doi.org/10.1126/science.1057726
6. Farhi, E., Goldstone, J., Gutmann, S., Sipser., M.: Quantum computation by adiabatic evolution. CoRR abs/quant-ph/0001106 (2000). https://arxiv.org/abs/quant-ph/0001106

7. Freivalds, R., Ozols, M., Mančinska, L.: Improved constructions of mixed state quantum automata. Theor. Comput. Sci. **410**, 1923–1931 (2009). https://doi.org/10.1016/j.tcs.2009.01.028
8. Gruska, J.: Quantum Computing. McGraw-Hill (2000)
9. Kato, T.: On the adiabatic theorem of quantum mechanics. J. Phys. Soc. Jap. **5**, 435–439 (1951)
10. Kitaev, A., Shen, A., Vyalyi, M.: Classical and Quantum Computation. AMS, Providence (2002)
11. Messiah, A.: Quantum Mechanics. Wiley, New York (1958)
12. Moore, C., Crutchfield, J.P.: Quantum automata and quantum grammars. Theor. Comp. Sci. **237**(1–2), 275–306 (2000). https://doi.org/10.1016/S0304-3975(98)00191-1
13. Nakanishi, M.: Quantum pushdown automata with garbage tape. Int. J. Found. Comput. Sci. **29**(3), 425–446 (2018). https://doi.org/10.1142/S0129054118500132
14. Nielsen, M.A., Chuang, I.L.: Quantum Computation and Quantum Information. Cambridge University Press (2000)
15. Yakaryilmaz, A., Say, A.C.C.: Unbounded-error quantum computation with small space bounds. Inf. Comput. **209**(6), 873–892 (2011). https://doi.org/10.1016/j.ic.2011.01.008
16. Yamakami, T.: Nonuniform families of polynomial-size quantum finite automata and quantum logarithmic-space computation with polynomial-size advice. In: Martín-Vide, C., Okhotin, A., Shapira, D. (eds.) LATA 2019. LNCS, vol. 11417, pp. 134–145. Springer, Cham (2019). https://doi.org/10.1007/978-3-030-13435-8_10

Author Index

Beier, Simon   74
Brzozowski, Janusz A.   86

Davies, Sylvie   86, 98

Fernau, Henning   111, 124
Freund, Rudolf   1

Gabric, Daniel   137
Gelle, Kitti   147

Han, Yo-Sub   158
Holub, Štěpán   137
Holzer, Markus   74
Hospodár, Michal   98
Hoyrup, Mathieu   171

Iván, Szabolcs   147

Jirásková, Galina   184

Kari, Jarkko   35
Kari, Lila   197
Keeler, Chris   210
Ko, Sang-Ki   158
Krajňáková, Ivana   184
Kuppusamy, Lakshmanan   111
Kutrib, Martin   223

Madan, Abhishek   86
Malcher, Andreas   223
Mereghetti, Carlo   223

Nagy, Benedek   46
Ng, Timothy   197

Ogawa, Mizuhito   235
Okhotin, Alexander   248

Palano, Beatrice   223
Pighizzini, Giovanni   57, 260
Prigioniero, Luca   260

Raman, Indhumathi   111
Rojas, Cristóbal   171

Salomaa, Kai   158, 210
Sazhneva, Elizaveta   248
Selivanov, Victor   171, 235
Shallit, Jeffrey   137
Stull, Donald M.   171

Vu, Martin   124

Wolf, Petra   272

Yamakami, Tomoyuki   285

Printed in the United States
By Bookmasters